Learning 3ds max

A Tutorial Approach
Release 4

Sham Tickoo
Professor
Department of Manufacturing Engineering Technologies and Supervision
Purdue University Calumet
Hammond, Indiana

Publisher
The Goodheart-Willcox Company, Inc.
Tinley Park, Illinois

Library of Congress Catalog Card Number 2001033399
International Standard Book Number 1-56637-855-9

1 2 3 4 5 6 7 8 9 10   02   05 04 03 02 01

Library of Congress Cataloging-in-Publication Data

Tickoo, Sham
   Learning 3ds Max : a tutorial approach, release 4 / Sham Tickoo.
      p. cm.
   ISBN 1-56637-855-9
   1. Computer animation. 2. Computer graphics. 3. 3ds Max 4
(Computer file). I. Title
TR897.7 .T57 2001
006.6'96--dc21   2001033399

Introduction

3D Studio is one of the best PC-based 3D design and animation software packages in the world. 3D Studio MAX, now called **3ds max**, is designed specifically for the entertainment industry. Its sister software 3D Studio VIZ is designed for the AEC field. 3D Studio is used to create 3D models of any complexity. You can create both characters and objects, assign materials to them, place them in environments of your choice, render them, and add animation to the scene. Characters created and placed in environments can be animated as real life characters. You can create scenes from predefined 3D objects or loft 2D shapes along paths.

You can also add cameras and lights to the scene. To bring the scene to life, you can render the scene creating realistic effects by casting shadows, controlling background and atmosphere, and defining the material and surface characteristics. To add motion, **3ds max** has complete keyframe animation capabilities. You can animate movement of the objects in the scene, a change in the material and shape of the objects, and animate lights and cameras to create movie effects.

This book is written to get you started with **3ds max** in the shortest possible time. The first chapter of the book gives you an overview of **3ds max** to provide a good idea of what the software can do for you. The book has several chapters, each a tutorial, that cover different aspects of **3ds max**. The tutorials use a step-by-step approach supported by illustrations. At the end of each chapter are a Self-Evaluation Test, Exercises, and Answers to the Self-Evaluation Test. The Self-Evaluation Test can be used to evaluate progress and the knowledge of commands. The Exercises can be used as assignments.

Supplemental Information on the World Wide Web

Additional tutorials, projects, and exercises to complement this text can be found on the author's web site. To access this material, use your web browser and Internet connection to log onto the site:

http://www.calumet.purdue.edu/public/mets/tickoo/max/MAX.htm

This web site is maintained independent of Goodheart-Willcox Publisher. Goodheart-Willcox is unable to provide technical support for this site.

About the Author

Sham Tickoo is a professor of Manufacturing Engineering Technologies at Purdue University Calumet. He has been in the education and training profession since 1981, teaching drafting and design, CAD/CAM, AutoCAD, AutoLISP, and 3D Studio. In addition to his academic career, Professor Tickoo has been employed as a design and quality control engineer, consultant, and software developer.

Contents

Chapter 1

Overview

Learning Objectives

After completing this chapter, you will be able to:
- Launch the program 3ds max.
- Identify the different components of 3ds max screen.
- Explain various tools available on the status bar and the prompt line.
- Use various navigation controls.
- Create a basic animation.
- Use various tools on the **Main** toolbar.
- Create a rendering.
- Play an animation.

Tutorial Description

In this tutorial, you will load a predefined scene by using the pull-down menus in the menu bar. You will also create some new objects and use the different navigation controls to see their effect. You will then modify the scene using the different tools in the **Main** toolbar. You will render the scene and add a simple animation to it.

Starting 3ds max

During the 3ds max installation process, a folder is added to the Windows **Start** menu. This folder contains the 3ds max program and utility shortcuts. To launch 3ds max, access this folder.

1. Pick the **Start** button on the Windows task bar to display the menu.

2. Select **Programs** to display the program folders. Select the **discreet** folder to display the **3ds max 4** folder.

3. Select the **3ds max 4** shortcut to launch 3ds max, Figure 1-1. If a **3ds max 4** shortcut icon appears on your desktop, you can also launch 3ds max by double-clicking on that icon.
    The 3ds max screen is displayed with its different components and the default four-viewport configuration.

3ds max Screen Components

The 3ds max screen consists of the pull-down menus, **Main** toolbar, **Command Panel**, animation controls, time controls, viewport navigation tools, the status bar, and the prompt line, Figure 1-2.

Figure 1-1. Using the Windows **Start** menu to launch 3ds max.

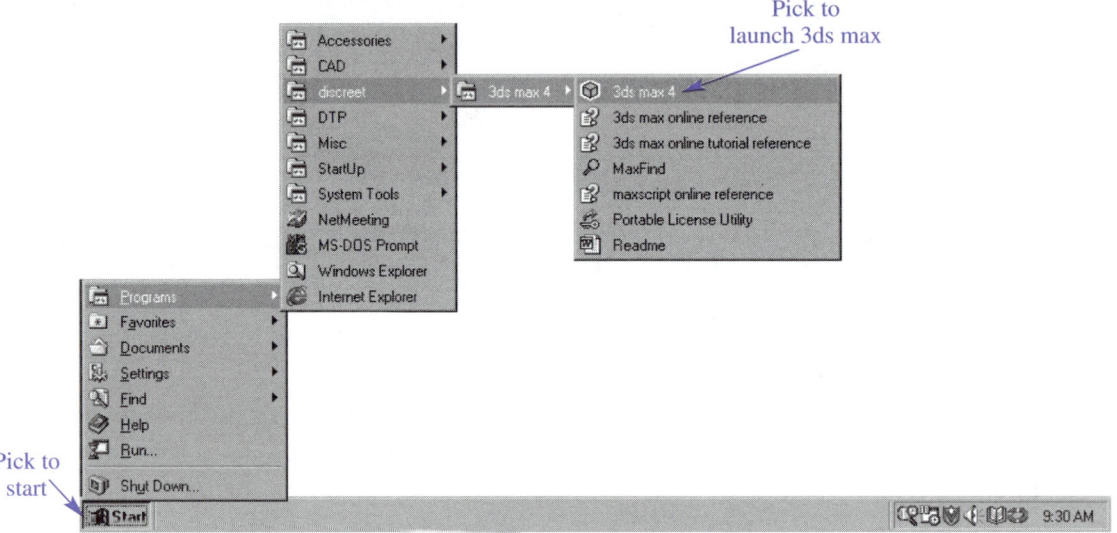

Figure 1-2. The default appearance of 3ds max at a screen resolution of 800 × 600.

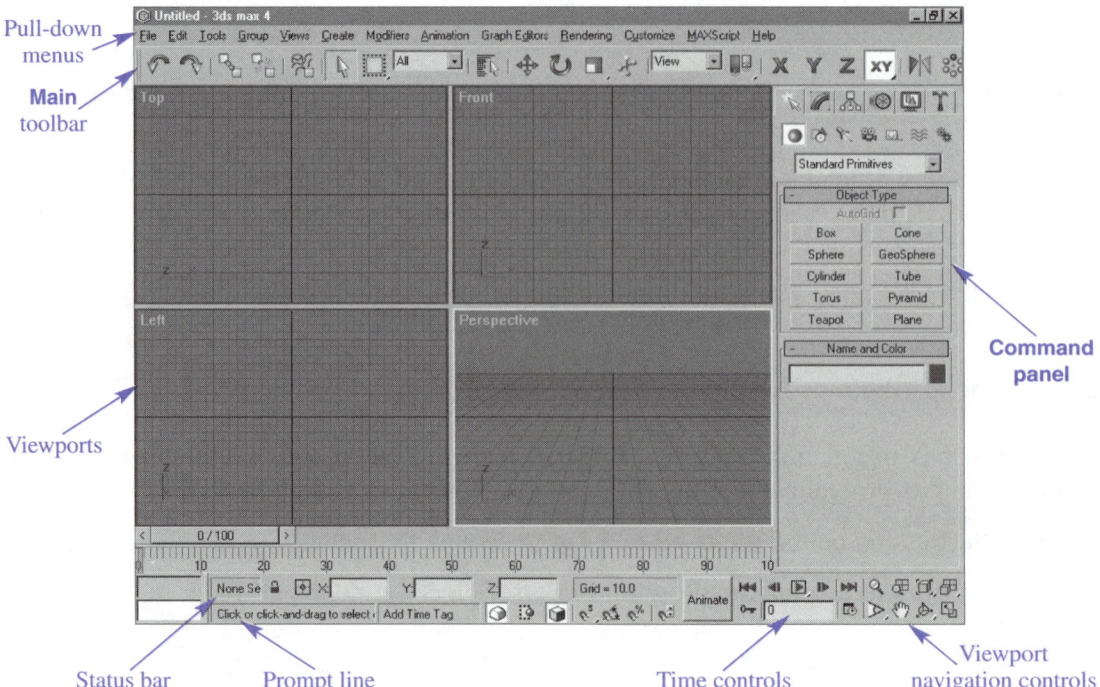

Menu bar

The menu bar is displayed at the top of the screen and contains the pull-down menus. Some of the pull-down menus are standard Windows menus, such as **File**, **Edit**, and **Help**. Other pull-down menus, such as **Create**, **Modifiers**, and **Animation**, are 3ds max pull-down menus. When you select a title in the menu bar, 3ds max displays a corresponding pull-down menu listing commands and their keyboard alternatives.

1. Move the cursor to the menu bar at the top of the screen. Select **File** to display the pull-down menu, Figure 1-3.

2. Move the cursor down and select **Open...** from the pull-down menu.
   The **Open File** dialog box is displayed, Figure 1-4.

3. Navigate to the 3ds max \Scenes\FeaturesScenes\Maxscript folder. Select the file MSDEMO1.max from the folder. Pick the **Open** button.
   A biped (two legged) character is displayed in the four viewports of 3ds max, Figure 1-5.

Figure 1-3. The **File** pull-down menu.

File pull-down menu

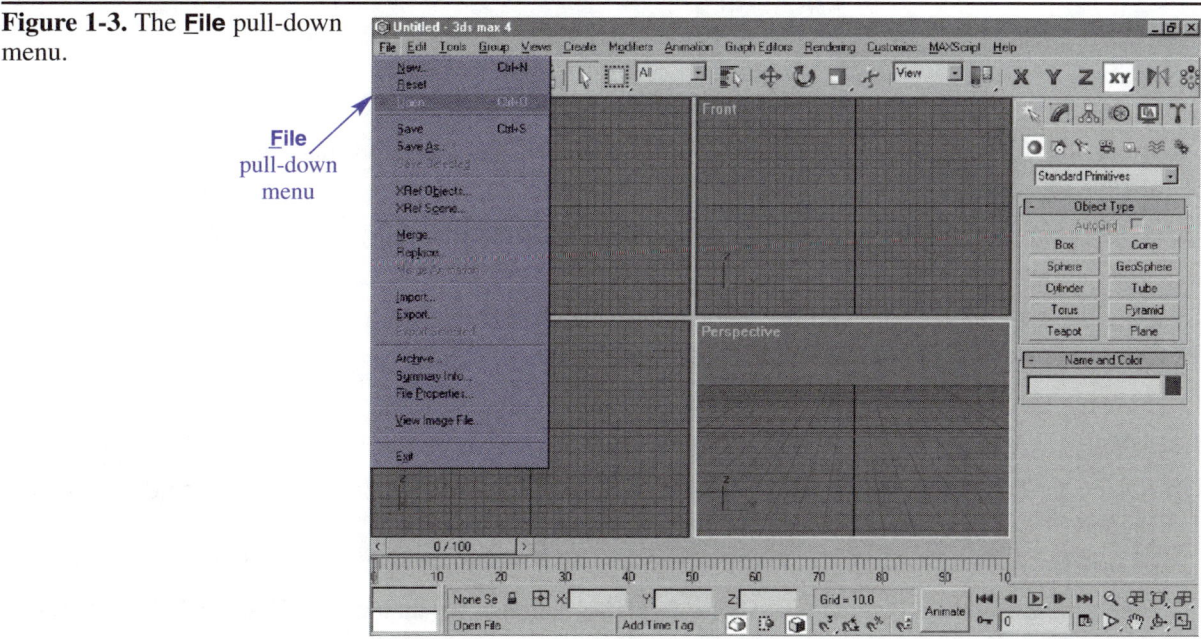

Figure 1-4. Opening a 3ds max scene.

Current folder   Select a file to open   Preview

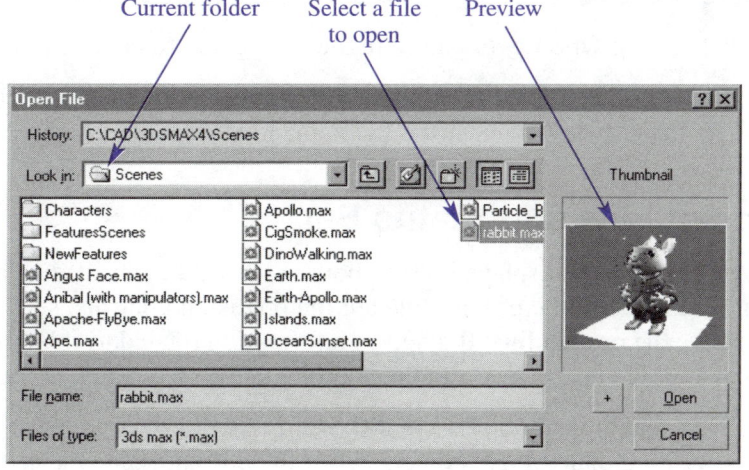

Figure 1-5. The msdemo1.max scene is opened.

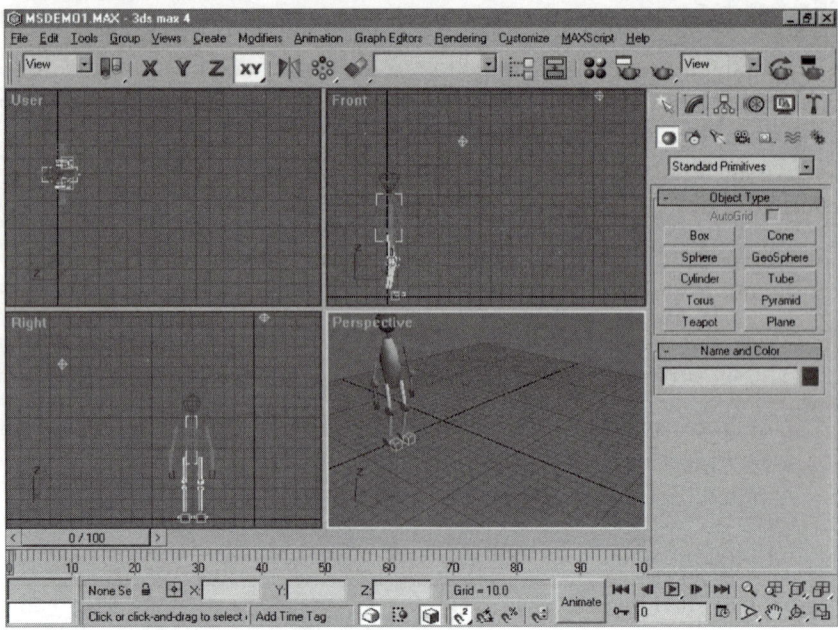

4. Select the **Edit** pull-down menu and then pick **Select By** from the menu to display a cascading menu.

5. Select **Name** in the cascading menu. The **Select Objects** dialog box is displayed.
   You can also open this dialog box by pressing [H] on the keyboard.

6. Pick the **All** button at the bottom of the object list.
   All object names are highlighted in the object list.

7. Pick the **Select** button in the dialog box.
   The dialog box is closed and all objects in the scene turn white to indicate they are selected.

Mirror Selected Objects

8. Select the **Tools** pull-down menu and then select the **Mirror...** option. The **Mirror** dialog box is displayed.
   You can also open this dialog box by picking the **Mirror Selected Objects** button on the **Main** toolbar.

9. Select the **Copy** radio button in the **Clone Selection:** area of the dialog box. Then, pick the **OK** button.
   A copy of the character is mirrored, Figure 1-6. The copy remains selected.

10. Select **Save As...** from the **File** pull-down menu.
    The **Save File As** dialog box is displayed, Figure 1-7.

11. Pick the **Up One Level** button in the dialog box to change to the \Scenes\FeaturesScenes folder.

12. Type My_MS_Demo1.max in the **File name:** text box and select the **Save** button.
    The model is saved under the file name My_MS_Demo1. 3ds max saves with the extension .max.

Prompt Line and Status Bar

The prompt line is displayed at the bottom of the screen. It displays information about the selected command. Next to the prompt line are the precision controls, such as **Snap**. The status bar is located just above the prompt line. It displays information related to selected objects. The coordinate points of the cursor location are given in the coordinate display, which is located next to the status bar.

1. Select **Reset** from the **File** pull-down menu.
   A warning dialog box is displayed. If the current scene has not been saved, a warning dialog box also appears indicating this and asking if you want to save.

Figure 1-6. The bipedal character is mirrored.

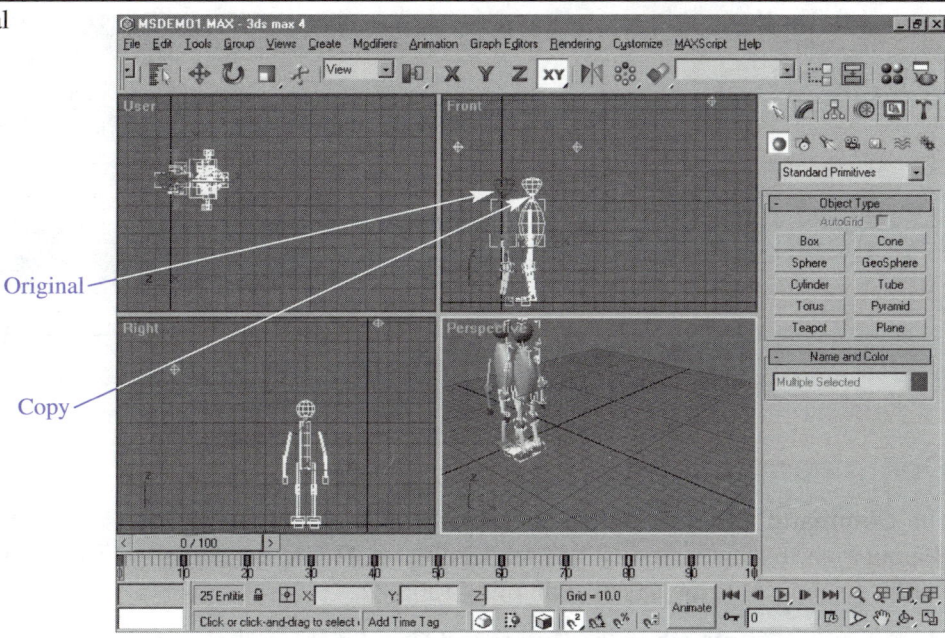

Figure 1-7. Saving a scene.

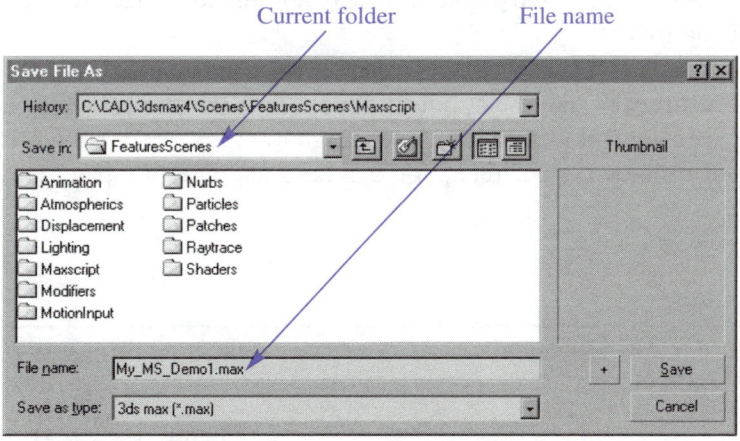

2. Answer **Yes** in the dialog box to indicate you really want to reset.

3. Select the **2D Snap Toggle** button from the **Snap** flyout at the bottom of the screen.
   This restricts the movement of the cursor to the default **Snap** setting, which is grid points.

2D Snap Toggle

4. Right-click anywhere in the Top viewport to make it activate.
   The Top viewport in enclosed by a yellow box indicating it is active.

5. Move the cursor in the Top viewport and observe the coordinate display.
   The display shows the X, Y, Z coordinates of the cursor as it is moved.

6. Right-click on the **2D Snap Toggle** button. The **Grid and Snap Settings** dialog box is displayed.
   You can also access the **Grid and Snap Settings** dialog box by selecting **Grid and Snap Settings...** in the **Customize** pull-down menu.

7. Select the **Home Grid** tab in the dialog box.

8. Select the **All Viewports** radio button. Type 5 in the **Grid Spacing** spinner text box and press [Enter], Figure 1-8.
   The grid spacing is changed and is visible in all the viewports. Close the dialog box.

Figure 1-8. The **Home Grid** tab of the **Grid and Snap Settings** dialog box.

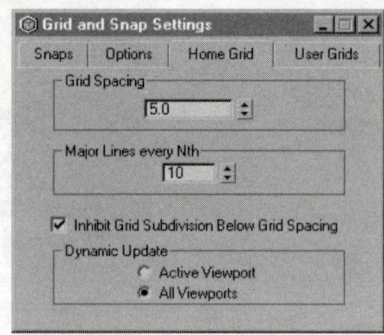

Command Panel

The **Command Panel** is, by default, placed on the right side of the screen. There are six tabs that contain tools to create, modify, and model objects, Figure 1-9. When you select a tab in the **Command Panel**, a subpanel is displayed containing rollouts.

Create

Geometry

1. Select the **Create** tab in the **Command Panel** if it is not already selected.

   A subpanel is displayed containing tools to create geometry, shapes, lights, etc.

2. Select the **Geometry** button, if it is not already selected. Pick the **Cylinder** button in the **Object Type** rollout.

   A subpanel is displayed containing rollouts for the cylinder. It contains the **Name and Color**, **Creation Method**, **Keyboard Entry**, and **Parameters** rollouts. A minus (–) sign indicates the particular rollout is open. A plus sign (+) indicates a rollout is closed. If some of the rollouts are not visible on the screen, you can hold and drag the pan icon (hand) up to display the rest of the rollouts.

Figure 1-9. The **Command Panel**.

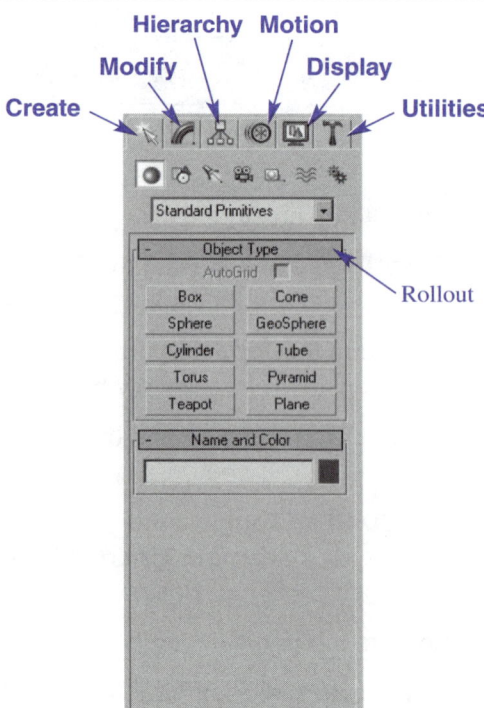

3. Open the **Keyboard Entry** rollout. Type 20 in the **Radius** spinner and 50 in the **Height** spinner. With the Top viewport active, pick the **Create** button.
   A cylinder is created and displayed in all viewports. 3ds max automatically names it Cylinder01, which is displayed in the **Name and Color** rollout in the **Command Panel**, Figure 1-10. You can also pick and drag the mouse to create the cylinder.

Viewport Navigation Controls

The viewport navigation controls are located at the lower-right corner of the 3ds max window, Figure 1-11. These tools are used to navigate around the different viewports individually or together.

1. Select the **Zoom Extents All** button.
   The cylinder fills all the viewports.

2. Right-click anywhere in the Front viewport to make it active.

3. Select the **Region Zoom** button from the navigation controls.
   The cursor appears as a small magnifying glass surrounded by a dashed line.

4. Drag a window around the top of the cylinder. Do this by picking a point near the upper-left corner of the cylinder, holding, moving the cursor to the opposite corner of the window, and releasing.
   The top of the cylinder fills the Front viewport.

Zoom Extents All

Region Zoom

Figure 1-10. A cylinder is created using the **Keyboard Entry** rollout.

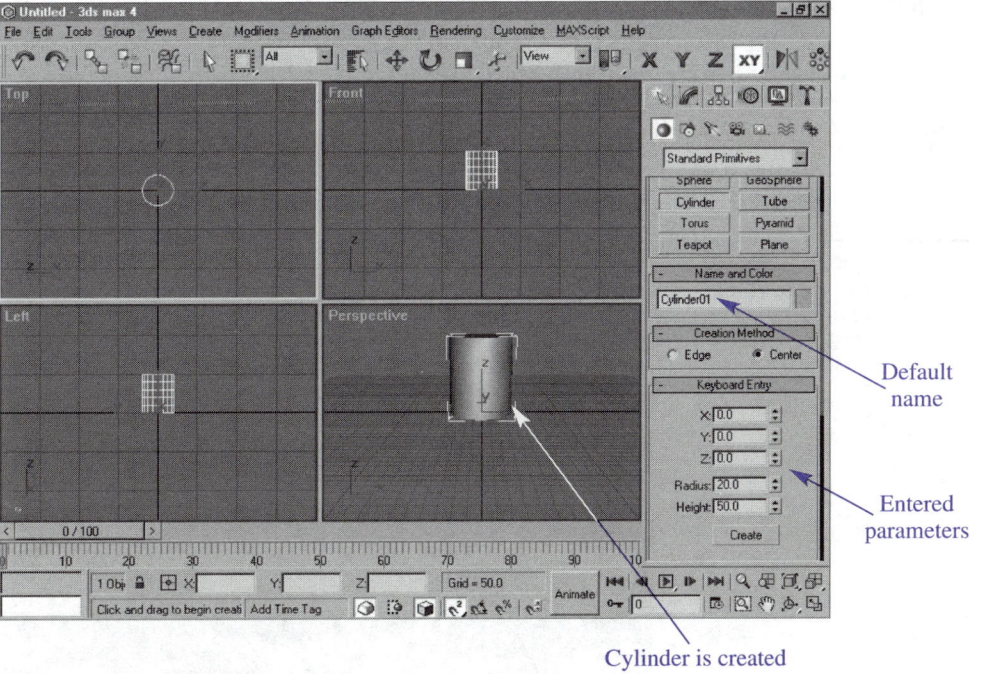

Default name

Entered parameters

Cylinder is created

Figure 1-11. The various tools in the viewport navigation controls.

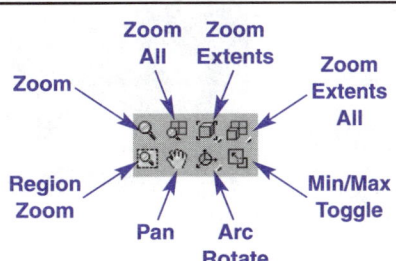

Zoom All
Zoom Extents
Zoom
Zoom Extents All
Region Zoom
Pan
Arc Rotate
Min/Max Toggle

Zoom

5. Make the Top viewport active.

6. Select the **Zoom** button from the navigation controls.
   The cursor appears as a small magnifying glass.

7. Move the cursor to the center of the viewport. Pick and drag down vertically until the object is displayed around half of its original size.

Pan

8. Select the **Pan** button from the navigation controls.
   The cursor appears as a hand.

9. Pick and drag the cursor to place the cylinder near the lower-left corner of the Top viewport.

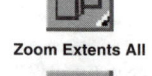

Zoom Extents All

10. Select the **Zoom Extents All** button.
    The cylinder is zoomed to its extents in all the viewports.

Arc Rotate

11. Make the Front viewport active. Then, select the **Arc Rotate** button.
    The cursor similar to two ellipses and a yellow circle trackball is placed in the center of the current viewport.

12. Pick and drag the cursor inside the trackball to display an angled view of the cylinder, Figure 1-12. Right-click to end the command. The name of the viewport changes from Front to User.
    For the **Arc Rotate** tool, if you drag the cursor outside the trackball, the view rotates around its Z axis.

Min/Max Toggle

13. Select the **Min/Max Toggle**. You can also press [W] on the keyboard.
    The viewport is maximized, Figure 1-13.

14. With the User viewport active, press the [F] key on the keyboard to change to the Front viewport. Also, press the [W] key to return to the previous viewport configuration.
    The previous viewport configuration is displayed.

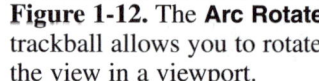

Zoom Extents All

15. Use the **Zoom Extents All** button to zoom the cylinder to its extents in all viewports.

Figure 1-12. The **Arc Rotate** trackball allows you to rotate the view in a viewport.

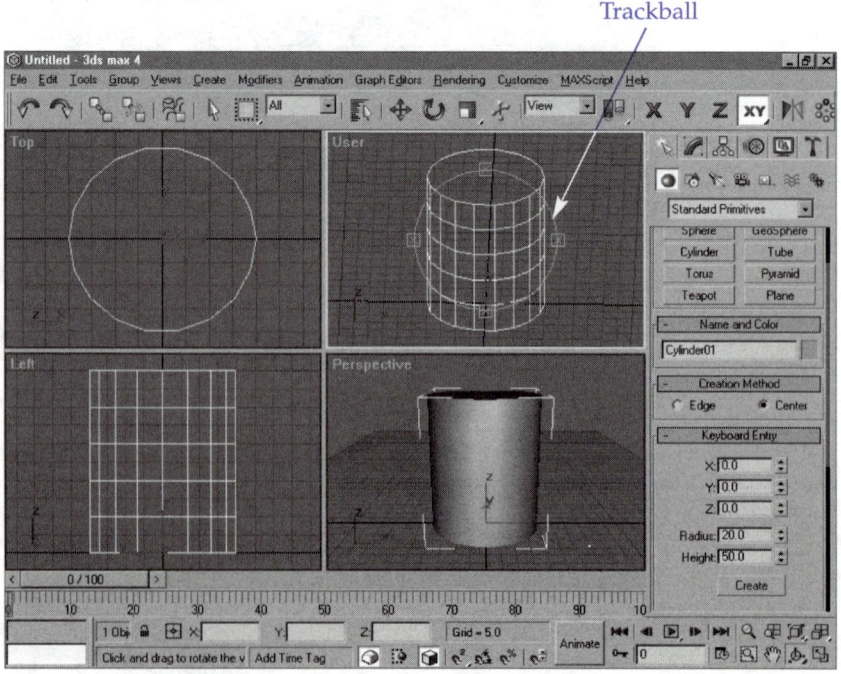

Figure 1-13. A maximized viewport.

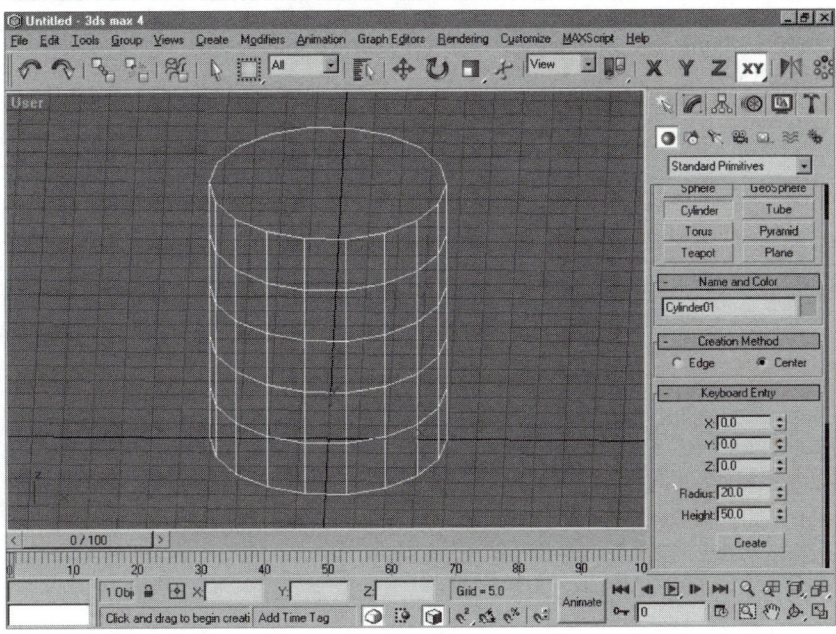

Selecting and Moving Objects

The **Main** toolbar is displayed below the pull-down menus. It contains various tools used for modifying scenes, Figure 1-14. Some of the buttons on a toolbar may not be visible on the screen display. You can move the cursor onto an "empty" area of the toolbar to display the pan cursor. Then, drag this cursor to the left or right to display the hidden buttons. Also, you can place the cursor over a button to display the tooltip, giving you the name of the tool.

1. In the **Create** panel, pick the **Box** button in the **Object Type** rollout. Draw a box in the Top viewport using the **Keyboard Entry** rollout. Make the box 40 × 150 × 40.

2. Pick the **Select object** button on the **Main** toolbar.

3. Pick on the cylinder to select it.
   The cylinder turns white to indicate it is selected.

4. Pick the **Select by Name** button on the **Main** toolbar.
   The **Select Objects** dialog box is displayed with Box01 highlighted, Figure 1-15.

5. Select Cylinder01 from the list. You can use the [Ctrl] key to select more than one object. Then, pick the **Select** button in the dialog box.
   The cylinder is deselected and the box is selected.

Select object

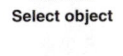

Select by Name

Figure 1-14. The **Main** toolbar contains various tools for modifying a scene.

Pull-down menus

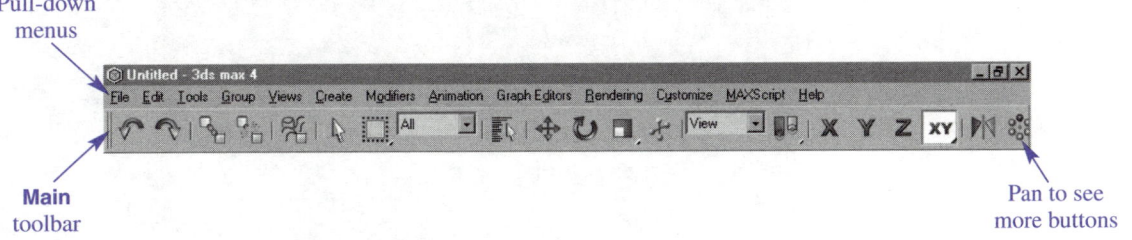

Main toolbar

Pan to see more buttons

Figure 1-15. The **Select Objects** dialog box allows you to select objects by their name.

Currently selected object

Objects in the scene

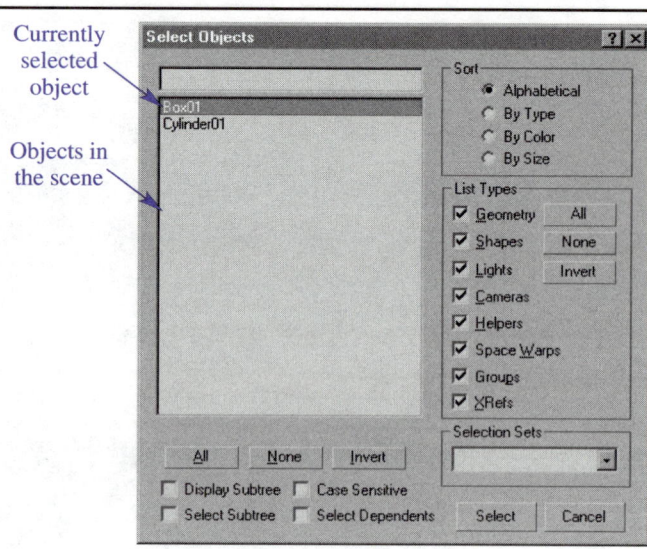

Select and Move

Restrict to Y

Restrict to X

6. Pick the **Select and Move** button on the **Main** toolbar. Also, pick the **Restrict to Y** button.

7. Activate the Front viewport. Turn off the **2D Snap Toggle** by picking on it.
   The X, Y, Z transform restrictions do not work when the **Snap** toggle is on.

8. Pick and hold on the cylinder. Move it up until its bottom edge touches the top edge of the box.
   The movement of the cylinder is restricted along the Y direction of the viewport.

9. Pick the **Restrict to X** button on the **Main** toolbar to restrict the movement along X direction.

10. Pick the **Select and Move** button, if not already selected. Move the cylinder right in the Front viewport until it is on the right end of the box. Then, move it back to the center of the box.
    When moving objects, use viewport navigation controls to place the objects accurately.

11. Activate the Left viewport. Then, move the cylinder left until it is not over the box. See Figure 1-16.

12. Pick the **Zoom Extents All** button.

Figure 1-16. The cylinder is moved.

Copying and Rotating Objects

When moving an object, you can choose to create a copy of the original in the new location. The original object remains in its original location. In addition to moving an object, you can rotate an object.

1. Pick the **Select and Move** and **Restrict to Y** buttons on the **Main** toolbar.

2. Hold the [Shift] key on the keyboard. In the Left viewport, pick the box and drag it up until its bottom edge touches the top edge of the cylinder. Then, release the mouse button.
   The **Clone Options** dialog box is displayed, Figure 1-17.

3. Make sure the **Copy** radio button is selected and the name is displayed as Box02 in the **Name:** text box. Select the **OK** button.
   The copy of the original box is created on top of the cylinder, Figure 1-18.

Select and Rotate

4. Pick the **Select and Rotate** button on the **Main** toolbar. Make sure the **Restrict to Y** button is also selected.

5. In the Left viewport, pick on the upper box (Box02) and drag the cursor down until the Y value in the coordinate display is 45.
   The box is rotated 45 degrees about its Y axis.

Figure 1-17. The **Clone Options** dialog box allows you to make a copy of an existing object.

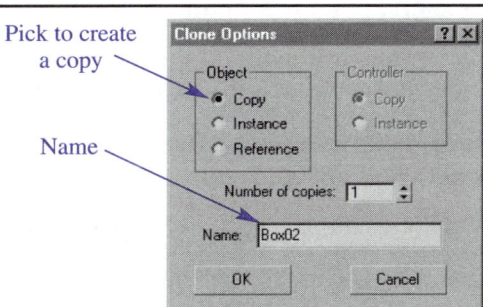

Pick to create a copy

Name

Figure 1-18. A copy of the box is created

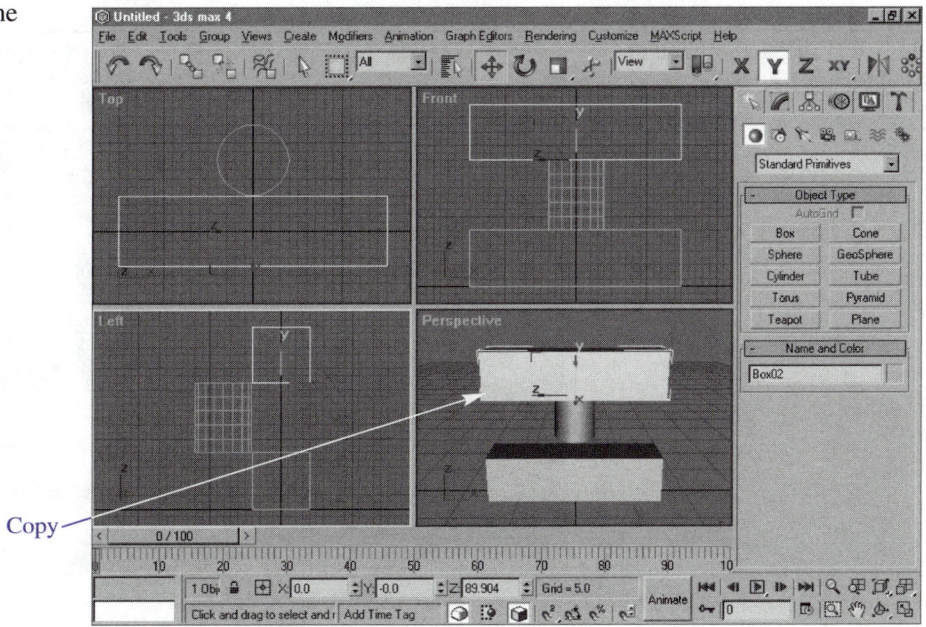

Copy

Scaling Objects

Select and Uniform Scale

You can scale an object up or down. In addition, you can uniformly scale an object on all its local axes, or nonuniformly scale the object.

1. Pick the **Select and Uniform Scale** button on the **Main** toolbar.

2. In the Left viewport, pick the upper box (Box02) and drag the cursor down until the X, Y, Z values in the coordinate display are 60.
   The box is uniformly scaled to 60 percent of its original size, Figure 1-19.

Arraying Objects

An array is a regular pattern of objects created from an original. You can create a rectangular or polar (radial) array of objects.

Create

1. Activate the Top viewport and select **2D Snap Toggle** to turn it on.

2. Select **Create** in the **Command Panel**. Then, select the **Geometry** button, if not already selected.

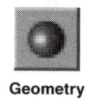

Geometry

3. Pick **Sphere** in the **Object Type** rollout.
   The rollouts for a sphere are displayed.

4. Place the cursor at the grid point nearest the bottom-left corner of the large box.

5. Pick and drag the cursor one grid point to the left. Release the mouse button.
   A sphere with a radius of five units is created inside the bottom left corner of the large box.

6. Pick **Select and Move** and make sure the **Restrict to Y** button is selected on the **Main** toolbar. Turn off the **2D Snap Toggle** button.

7. In the Front viewport, move the sphere to the top edge of the large box, Figure 1-20.

Array

8. With the Front viewport active and the sphere selected, pick the **Array** button on the **Main** toolbar.
   The **Array** dialog box is displayed, Figure 1-21.

9. In the **Incremental** area of the dialog box, enter 150 in the **X** spinner of the **Move** row (first row).

Figure 1-19. The top box is rotated and scaled.

Object is rotated and scaled

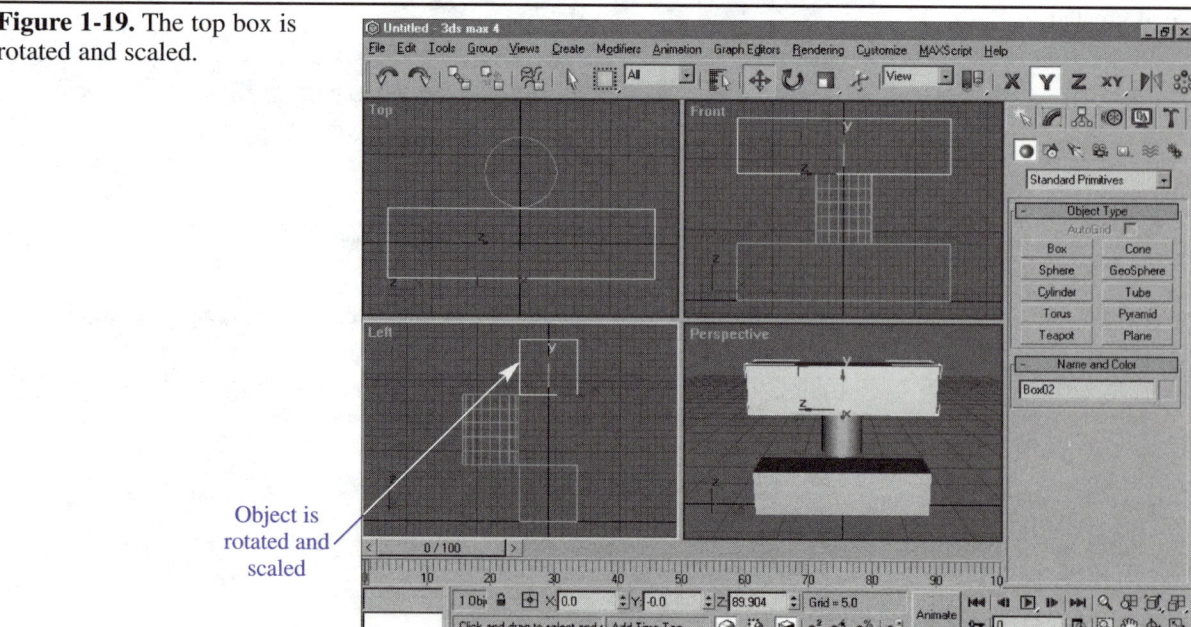

Figure 1-20. A sphere is added to the scene.

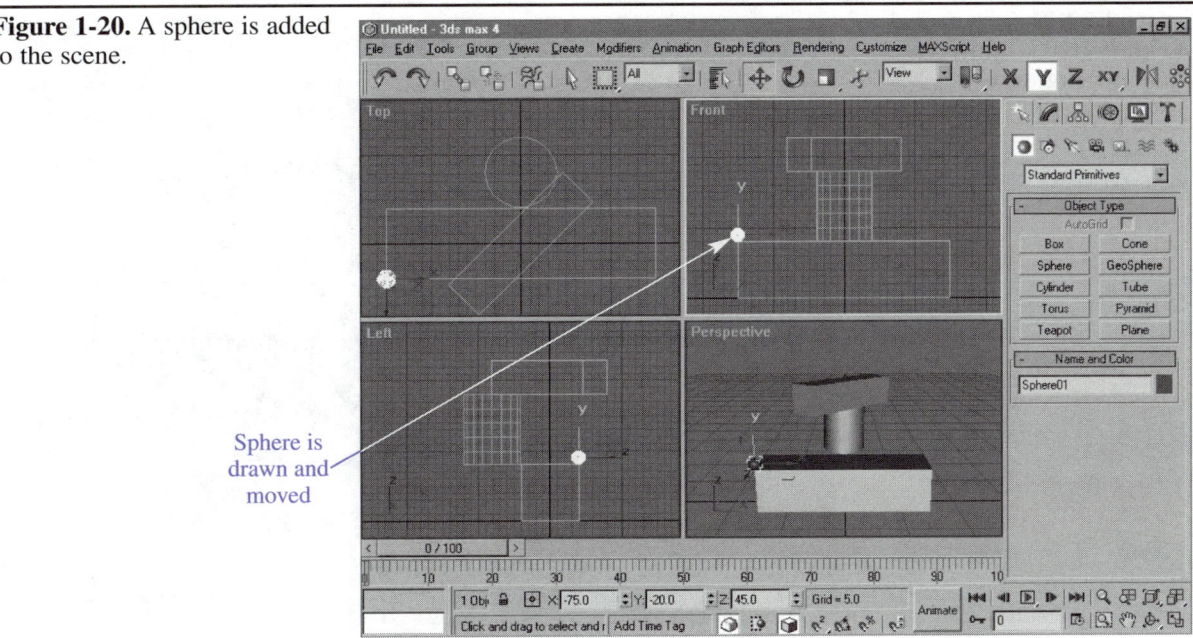

Sphere is drawn and moved

Figure 1-21. The **Array** dialog box allows you to create rectangular or polar (radial) arrays.

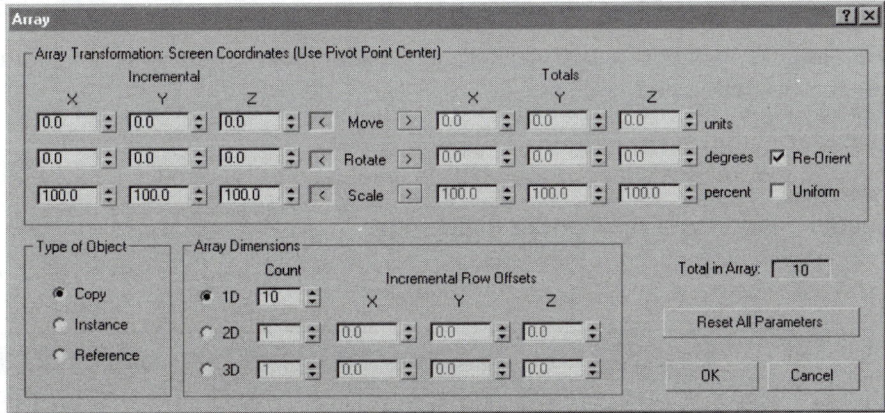

10. In the **Array Dimensions** area of the dialog box, enter 2 in the **1D Count** spinner. Then, select the **2D** radio button and enter 2 in the **2D Count** spinner. Also enter 40 in the **Y** spinner in the **2D** row.

11. Select the **OK** button in the dialog box. A 2D linear array of the sphere is created on top of the large box, Figure 1-22.

    1D produces a simple, straight-line array using the incremental values. When you set 2D count to more than one, it produces the given number of 1D arrays using the row offsets. In other words, it creates a "plane" of objects. In the above steps, you created an array of the sphere by moving it along the X axis at a distance of 150 (incremental), and then created two rows (2D) of this linear array along the Y axis at a distance of 40 (row offset).

Figure 1-22. The sphere added
in Figure 1-20 is arrayed on
top of the large box.

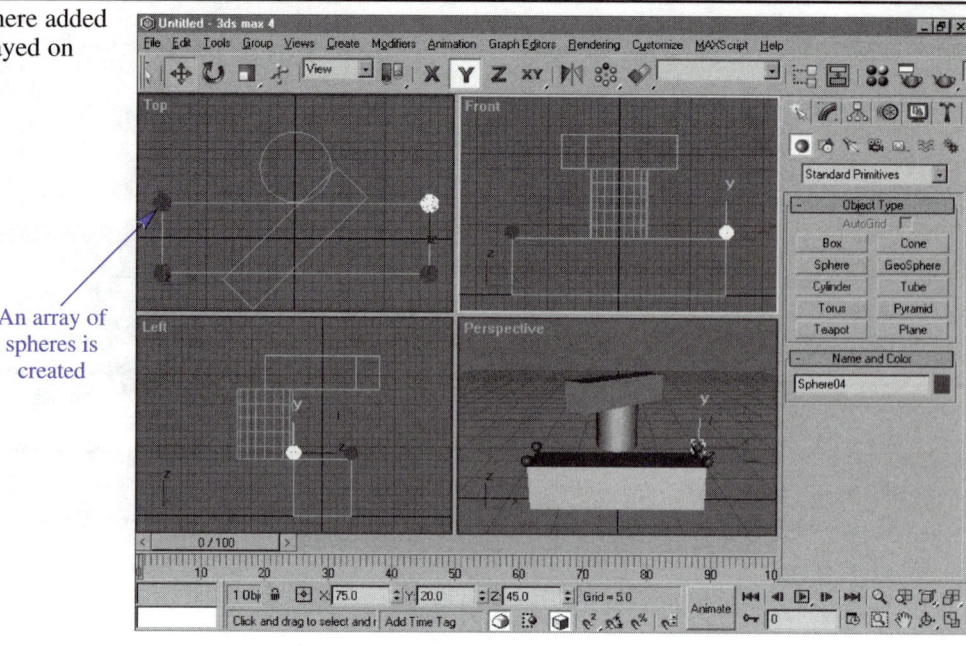

An array of
spheres is
created

Rendering a Scene

Render Scene

1. Make the Perspective viewport active. Select the **Render Scene** button on the **Main** toolbar.
   The **Render Scene** dialog box is displayed.

2. Select the **Render** button at the bottom of the dialog box.
   The rendered view of the Perspective viewport is displayed in the render window, Figure 1-23.

3. Close the render window and the **Render** dialog box.

Figure 1-23. A rendered
scene is shown in the render
window.

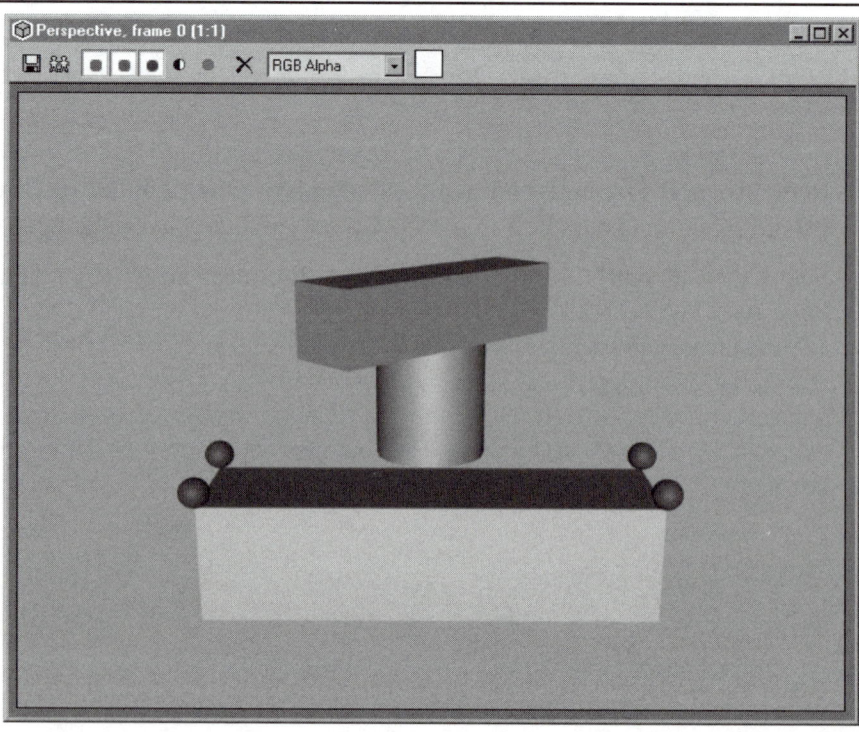

Animation Tools

The animation controls are located at the lower-right side of the 3ds max screen, next to the viewport navigation tools, Figure 1-24. These controls are used to navigate through an animation. They can also be used to control the various features while playing the animation. Below the viewports is the **Time** slider. This slider displays the frame number of the current animation frame, and the total number of frames in the animation. By dragging the **Time** slider left or right, you can also navigate through the animation.

1. Make the Top viewport active and make sure the **2D Snap Toggle** is unselected.

2. Select the **Toggle Animation Mode** button from the animation controls.
   The **Toggle Animation Mode** button is depressed and turns red. A red box surrounds the Top viewport to indicate you are in animation mode.

Toggle Animation
Mode

3. Type 25 in the current frame text box and press [Enter]. You can also drag the **Time** slider to frame 25, or pick the > arrow on the **Time** slider to advance one frame at a time.
   The **Time** slider moves to frame 25.

4. Pick the **Select and Move** and **Restrict to Y** buttons on the **Main** toolbar.

5. Pick and move the lower-left sphere up until its upper edge is at the center of the large box, Figure 1-25.
   This sets an animation key, which is a definition of the animated movement.

Figure 1-24. The animation controls are used to navigate through an animation.

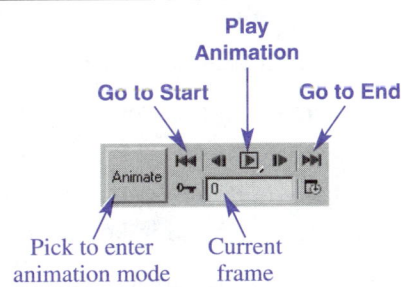

Figure 1-25. The first sphere is moved while in animation mode. A movement animation key is automatically set for the sphere.

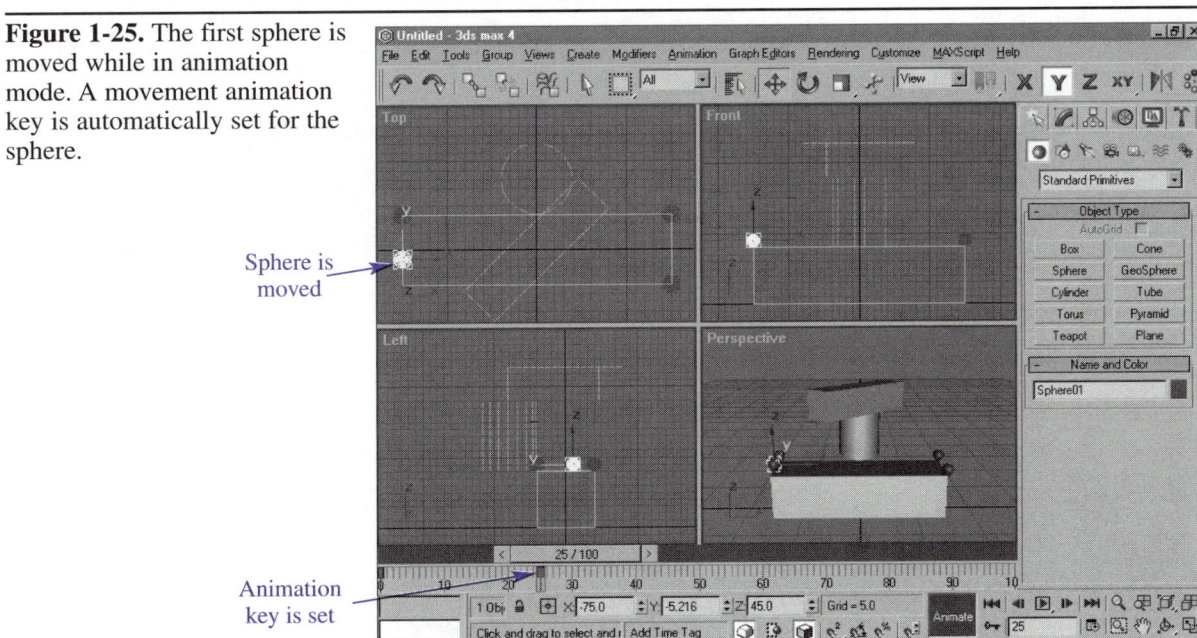

6. Pick and move the upper-left sphere down until its lower edge is at the center of the large box.
   The two spheres on the left side touch each other at the center of the large box.

7. Pick and move the lower-right sphere up until its upper edge is at the center of the large box.

8. Pick and move the upper-right sphere down until its lower edge is at the center of the large box.

9. Pick the **Select and Rotate** and **Restrict to Z** buttons in the **Main** toolbar.

10. Pick and rotate the small box until the Z value in the coordinate display is 45.
    This sets a rotation animation key for the small box.

11. Type 50 in the current frame text box and press [Enter].
    The **Time** slider moves to frame 50.

12. With the **Select and Rotate** button and the **Restrict to Z** buttons selected, rotate the small box again until the Z value in the coordinate display is 45.
    This sets another rotation animation key for the small box.

13. Type 75 in the current frame text box and press [Enter].
    The **Time** slider moves to frame 75.

14. Rotate the small box again until the Z value in the coordinate display is 45.
    This sets a third rotation animation key for the small box.

Go to End

15. Pick the **Go to End** button in the animation controls.
    The **Time** slider moves to the last frame of the animation, which is frame 100.

16. Pick and rotate the smaller box again until the Z value in the coordinate display is 45.
    This sets a fourth rotation animation key for the small box.

17. Pick the **Select and Move** and **Restrict to Y** buttons in the **Main** toolbar.

18. Move the lower-left sphere down to its original position.
    This sets a second movement animation key for the sphere.

19. Move the upper-left sphere up to its original position.
    This sets a second movement animation key for the sphere.

20. Move the lower-right sphere down to its original position, and the upper-right sphere up to its original position.
    This sets second movement animation keys for these two spheres.

21. Select the **Toggle Animation Mode** button to exit animation mode.
    The button is no longer red and depressed.

Play Animation

22. Make the Perspective viewport active. Then, pick the **Play Animation** button.
    The animation is previewed in the Perspective viewport, Figure 1-26.

Stop

23. To stop the animation, pick the **Stop** button.

24. Select the **Go to Start** button to move to frame 0.

Go to Start

25. Save the scene as Ch01.max in the folder of your choice.

Figure 1-26. The completed animation is previewed in the Perspective viewport.

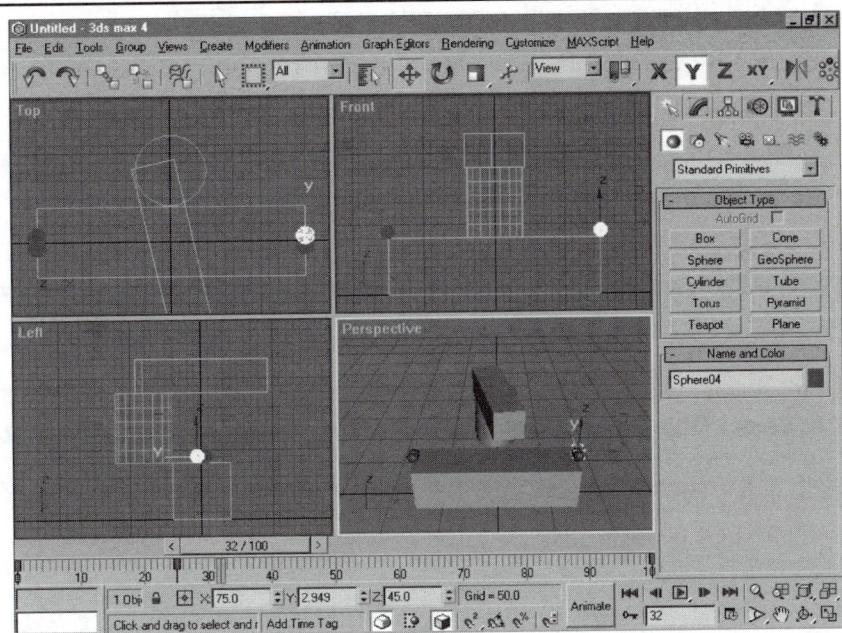

Self-Evaluation Test

Answer the following questions. Then compare your answers with the correct answers given at the end of this chapter.

1. The menu bar is displayed at the top of the screen and contains the _____.

2. If you right-click on a **Snap Toggle** button, the _____ dialog box is displayed where you can change various snap settings.

3. The _____ shows the X, Y, Z coordinates of the cursor location.

4. The _____, located on the right side of the 3ds max screen, contains commands to create, modify, and model objects.

5. A selected object is displayed _____ in the viewports to indicate it is selected.

6. When you pick the **Select by Name** button, the _____ dialog box is displayed.

7. You can use the _____ key on the keyboard along with the **Select and Move** button to make a copy of the selected object.

8. When you select the _____ button, a trackball (yellow circle) appears in the current viewport and the name of the viewport changes to User.

9. The _____ button is used to add motion to the scene.

10. You can play a preview of the animation by picking the _____ button.

Exercises

Open any of the scenes supplied with 3ds max in the \scenes directory. Then, perform the following operations.

1. If the scene has one viewport displayed, pick the **Min/Max Toggle** button to switch to the scene's previous viewport configuration.

2. Add any object to the scene using the **Create** tab in the **Command Panel**.

3. Use the different navigation controls to see their effect.

4. Use the different tools on the **Main** toolbar to modify the scene by moving, rotating, and scaling objects.

5. Create a simple animation. Then, play the animation.

6. Reset 3ds max without saving the scene.

Answers

The following are the correct answers to the questions in the Self-Evaluation Test.

1. pull-down menus; 2. **Grid and Snap Settings**; 3. coordinate display; 4.**Command Panel**; 5. white; 6. **Select Objects**; 7. [Shift]; 8. **Arc Rotate**; 9. **Toggle Animation Mode**; 10. **Play Animation**

Chapter 2

Creating a Scene

Learning Objectives

After completing this chapter, you will be able to:

- ⭘ Create and edit standard primitives.
- ⭘ Assign materials to objects.
- ⭘ Position and adjust lights and a camera.
- ⭘ Animate a scene.
- ⭘ Render an animated scene to an AVI file.
- ⭘ Play an animation rendered to an AVI file.

Tutorial Description

In this tutorial, you will create some of the 3ds max standard primitive objects, and then edit them using the **Parameters** rollout. You will then assign basic materials to the objects, and add lights, a camera, and motion to the scene. You will finally render the animated scene to a file.

Resetting the System

It is recommended that you reset the system before starting a new tutorial. This sets the system to 3ds max default values and erases all existing data. If you want to save the existing scene, make sure you do so before resetting 3ds max.

1. Select **Reset** from the **File** menu.

    A warning dialog box is displayed on the screen asking you if you really want to reset.

2. Select the **Yes** button in the dialog box or press the [Y] key on the keyboard.

    The system is reset.

Creating a Box

You will first create a box that will be used as a base for other objects. A box is a standard 3ds max primitive.

Create

Geometry

1. Select the **Create** tab in the **Command Panel**, if not already selected.
   Different buttons and rollouts pertaining to the **Create** tab are displayed.

2. Select the **Geometry** button, if it is not already selected.

3. Select **Standard Primitives** in the drop-down list.

4. Activate the Top viewport and then select the **Box** button in the **Object Type** rollout.
   All the rollouts for the creation of a box are displayed. These include the **Name and Color**, **Creation Method**, **Keyboard Entry**, and **Parameters** rollouts. A plus (+) sign indicates the rollout is closed and a minus (–) sign indicates the rollout is open.

5. Open the **Keyboard Entry** rollout, if it is not already open.

6. Enter 530 in the **Length:** spinner, 300 in the **Width:** spinner, and 20 in the **Height:** spinner. Then, pick the **Create** button in the **Keyboard Entry** rollout.
   A box is created in the center of the Top viewport.

7. Open the **Name and Color** rollout, if it is not already open.

8. Type Base in place of Box01 in the text box and press the [Enter] key.
   The box you just created is named Base.

9. Pick on the **Color** swatch.
   The **Object Color** dialog box is displayed.

Zoom Extents All

10. Pick a light red color swatch and then select the **OK** button to exit the dialog box.
    Base is assigned a light red color.

11. Pick the **Zoom Extents All** button.
    The box is zoomed to its extents in all the viewports, Figure 2-1.

12. Right-click to end the command.

Figure 2-1. The box is zoomed to its extents in all the viewports.

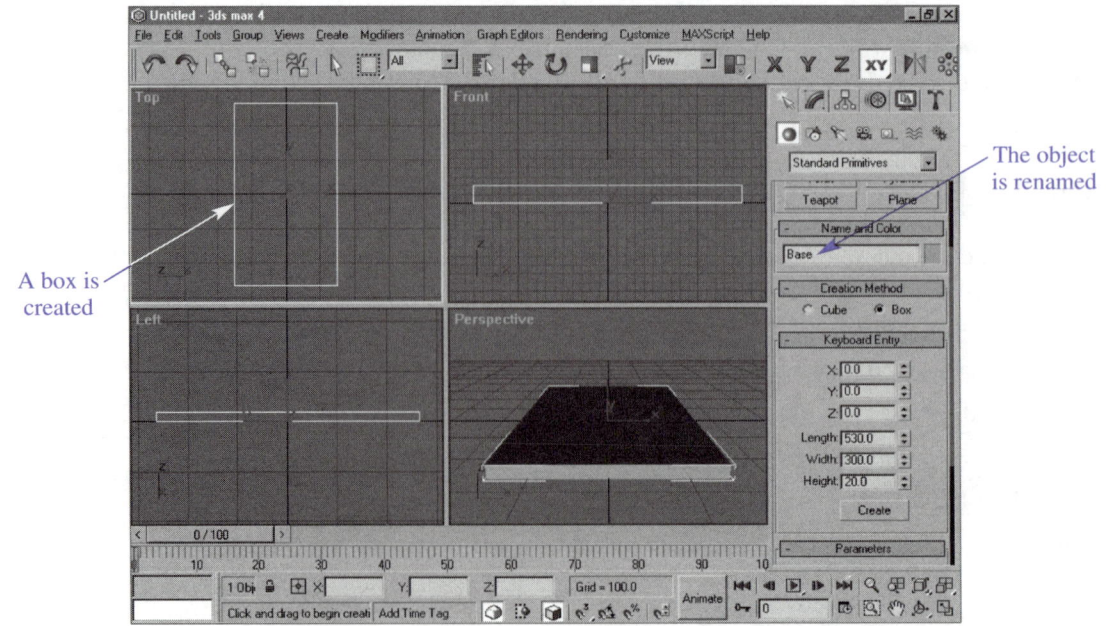

Creating a Tube

1. Make the Front viewport active.

2. Pick the **Create** tab in the **Command Panel**. Pick the **Geometry** button. In the **Object Type** rollout, select the **Tube** button.
   Rollouts pertaining to the creation of a tube are displayed. These include the **Name and Color**, **Creation Method**, **Keyboard Entry**, and **Parameters** rollouts.

Create

Geometry

3. Open the **Keyboard Entry** rollout, if it not already open.

4. Enter 25 in the **Inner Radius:** spinner, 30 in the **Outer Radius:** spinner, and 300 in the **Height:** spinner. Then, pick the **Create** button in the rollout.
   A tube is created.

5. With the tube still selected, open the **Parameters** rollout, if it is not already open.

6. Check the **Slice On** check box and enter 270 in the **Slice From:** spinner and 90 in the **Slice To:** spinner.
   The tube is sliced in half along its length.

7. Open the **Name and Color** rollout, if it is not already open. Pick the color swatch.
   The **Object Color** dialog box is displayed.

8. Pick a light green color, and then select the **OK** button.
   The sliced tube is displayed in green.

9. Name the object Sliced Tube.

10. Select the **Zoom Extents All** button, Figure 2-2.

11. Right-click to end the command.

Zoom Extents All

Figure 2-2. A sliced tube is created.

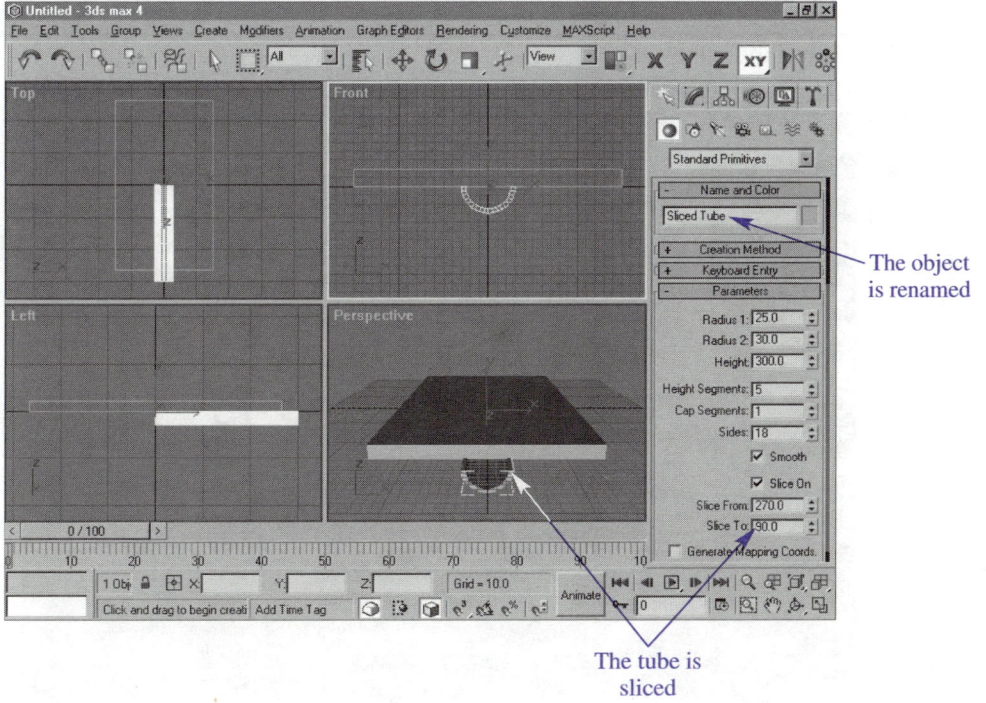

The object is renamed

The tube is sliced

Moving the Tube

Select and Move

Restrict to Y

1. Activate the Top viewport.

2. Pick the **Select and Move** button on the **Main** toolbar.

3. Select the **Restrict to Y** button on the **Main** toolbar.
   The movement of the tube will be restricted along the Y axis.

4. Select the tube in the Top viewport.
   The tube turns white, indicating it is selected.

5. Pick and hold on the tube, then drag the mouse up until the Y value in the coordinate display is about 150.
   The tube is placed approximately in the middle of the Base.

6. Activate the Front viewport.

Zoom

7. Select the **Zoom** button. Pick in the center of the Front viewport and drag the mouse down until the objects are displayed about half of their previous size.

Pan

8. Select the **Pan** button and pan the view so both objects are located at the bottom of the Front viewport.

9. Pick the **Select and Move** button and select the tube.
   The tube turns white, indicating it is selected.

10. Make sure the **Restrict to Y** button is selected in the **Main** toolbar.
    The movement of the tube is restricted to the Y axis.

11. Move the tube up until the Y value in the coordinate display is about 350.
    The tube is now above the Base.

12. Select the **Zoom Extents All** button to zoom to the extents of the objects in all viewports, Figure 2-3.

Figure 2-3. The sliced tube is moved.

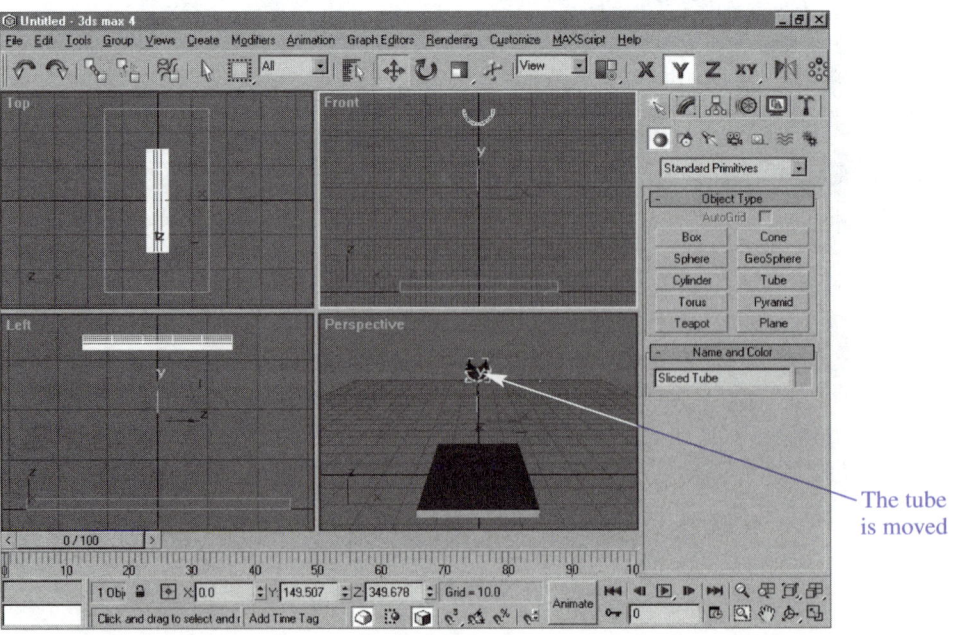

The tube is moved

Rotating the Tube

1. Activate the Left viewport.
2. Pick the **Select and Rotate** button on the **Main** toolbar. Also, pick the **Restrict to Z** button, if not already selected.

   The rotation will be restricted around the viewport's Z axis.

Restrict to Z

3. Pick and hold the tube. Drag the cursor up until the Z value coordinate display is –5 degrees.

   The tube is rotated clockwise around the Z axis by 5 degrees, Figure 2-4.

Figure 2-4. The tube is rotated clockwise around the Z axis by 5 degrees.

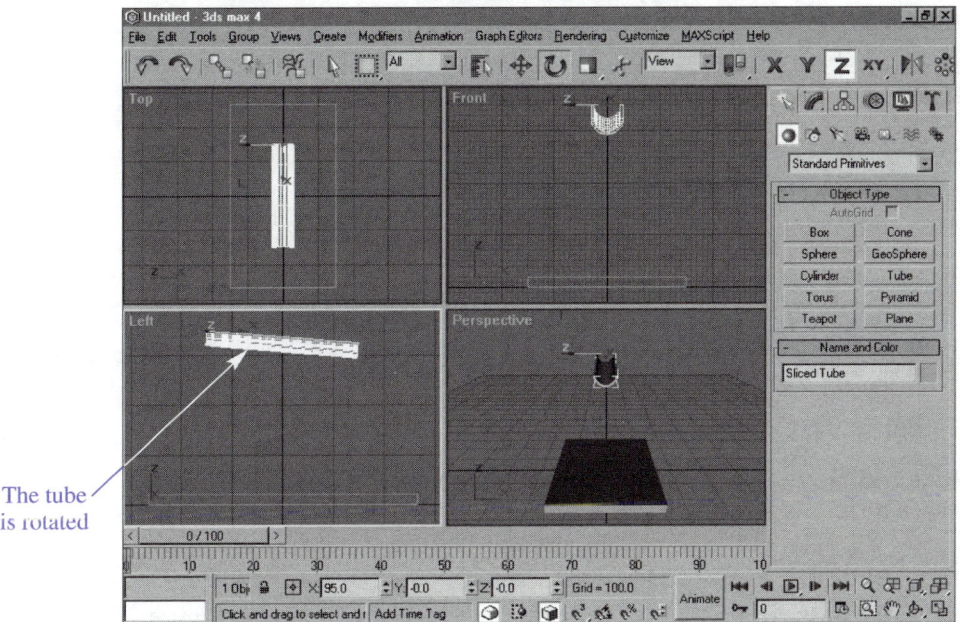

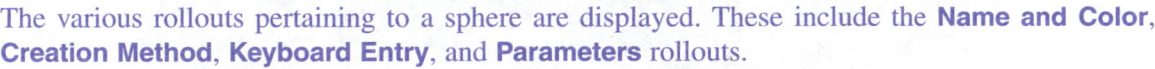

The tube is rotated

Creating a Sphere

1. Select **Create** in the **Command Panel**, then pick the **Geometry** button. In the **Object Type** rollout, select the **Sphere** button.

   The various rollouts pertaining to a sphere are displayed. These include the **Name and Color**, **Creation Method**, **Keyboard Entry**, and **Parameters** rollouts.

Create

Geometry

2. Activate the Left viewport.

3. Open the **Parameters** rollout, if it is not already open. Set the value in the **Segments:** spinner to 32, and make sure the **Smooth** check box is checked.

4. Open the **Keyboard Entry** rollout, and enter 22 in the **Radius:** spinner. Pick the **Create** button in the rollout.

   A sphere is created at the bottom of the Base, Figure 2-5.

5. Using the **Name and Color** rollout, assign a light blue color to the sphere. Also, name the sphere Ball.

   The sphere you created is named Ball and is displayed in light blue.

6. Right-click to end the command.

Figure 2-5. A sphere is created at the bottom of the Base.

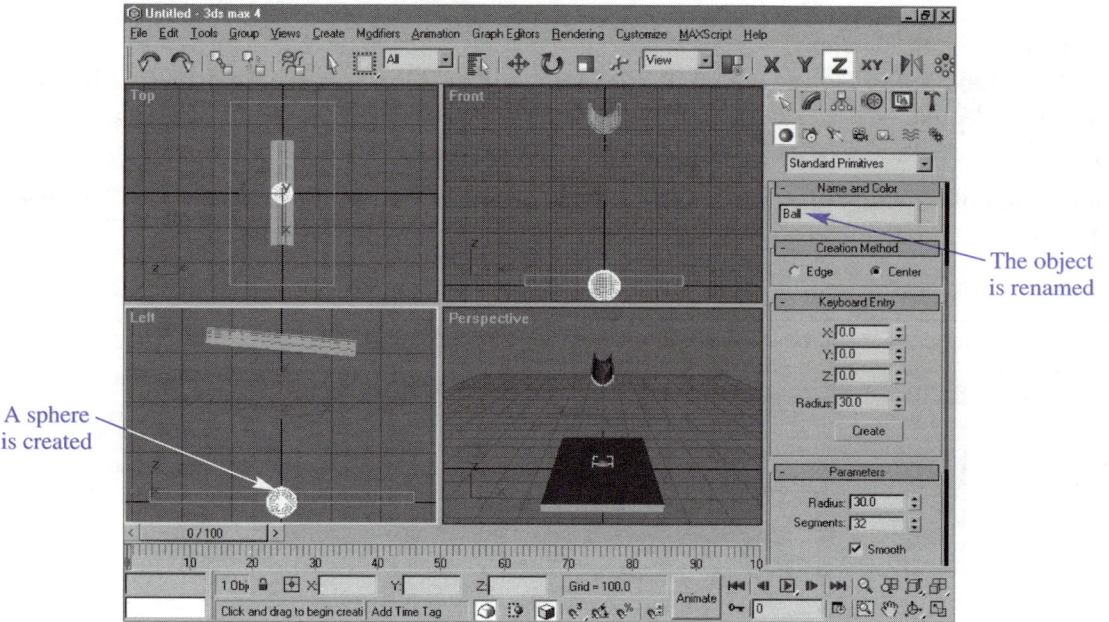

The object is renamed

A sphere is created

Moving the Ball

1. Activate the Front viewport.

2. Pick the **Select and Move** and the **Restrict to Y** buttons in the **Main** toolbar.
   The movement will be restricted to the viewport's Y axis.

3. Select the sphere and move it up until the Y value in the coordinate display is about 350.

4. Select the **Zoom Extents All** button to zoom the objects to their extents, Figure 2-6.

Figure 2-6. The sphere is moved up.

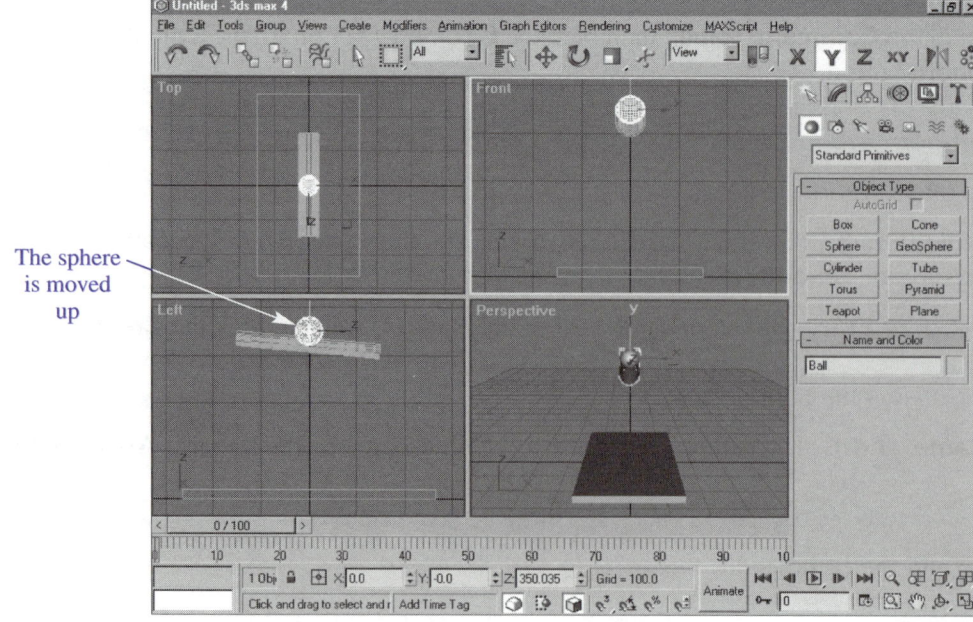

The sphere is moved up

5. Activate the Top viewport.

6. Pick the **Select and Move** and **Restrict to Y** buttons on the **Main** toolbar, if not already selected.

7. Move the sphere up until the Y value in the coordinate display is about 135.
   The Ball is placed at the left end of the tube.

8. Select the **Zoom Extents All** button to zoom the objects to their extents.

Creating a Torus

Create

Geometry

1. Pick the **Create** tab in the **Command Panel**, then pick the **Geometry** button. In the **Object Type** rollout, select the **Torus** button.

2. Activate the Top viewport, if it is not already activated.

3. Open the **Keyboard Entry** rollout. Enter 75 in the **Major Radius:** spinner and 15 in the **Minor Radius:** spinner. Then, pick the **Create** button in the rollout.
   A torus is created at the bottom of the Base.

4. In the **Name and Color** rollout, change the object color to a light yellow.
   The torus is displayed in yellow.

5. Name the torus Ring.

6. Select the **Zoom Extents All** button to zoom to the extents of the objects, Figure 2-7.

7. Right-click to end the command.

Figure 2-7. The sphere is moved to the end of the sliced tube.

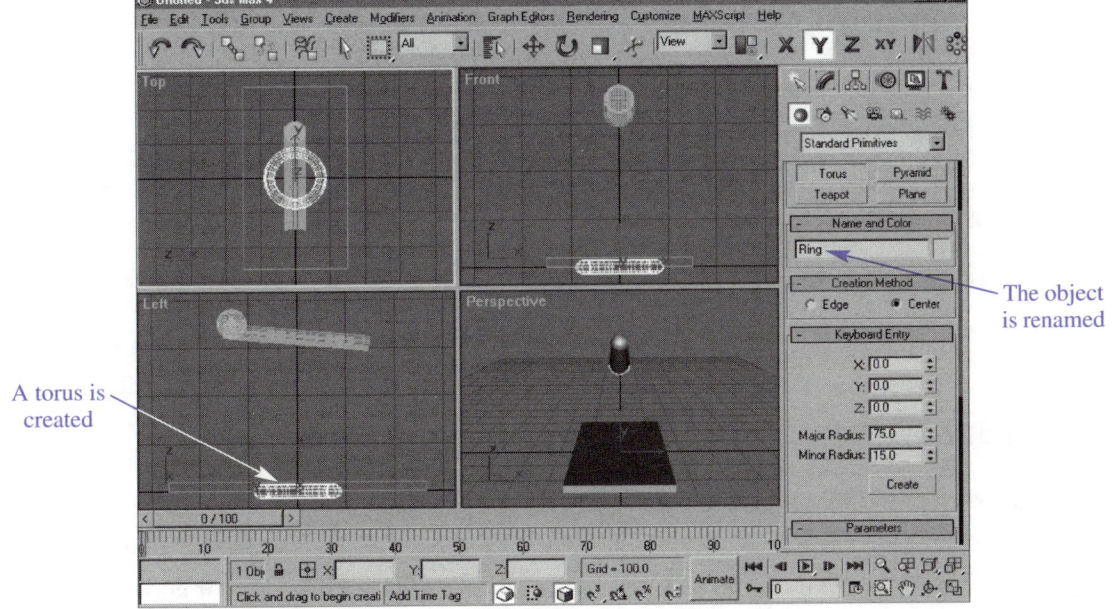

A torus is created

The object is renamed

Moving Ring

1. Activate the Front viewport.

2. Pick the **Select and Move** and **Restrict to Y** buttons in the **Main** toolbar, if not already selected.

3. Move the torus up until the Y value in the coordinate display is about 160.
   The Ring is placed about halfway between the Sliced Tube and the Base.

4. Select the **Zoom Extents All** button to zoom the objects to their extents.

5. Activate the Top viewport.

6. Pick the **Select and Move** and **Restrict to Y** buttons in the **Main** toolbar, if not already selected.

7. Move the torus up until the Y value in the coordinate display is about 130.
   The Ring is approximately centered on the Ball.

8. Select the **Zoom Extents All** button to zoom the objects to their extents, Figure 2-8.

Figure 2-8. A torus is added to the scene.

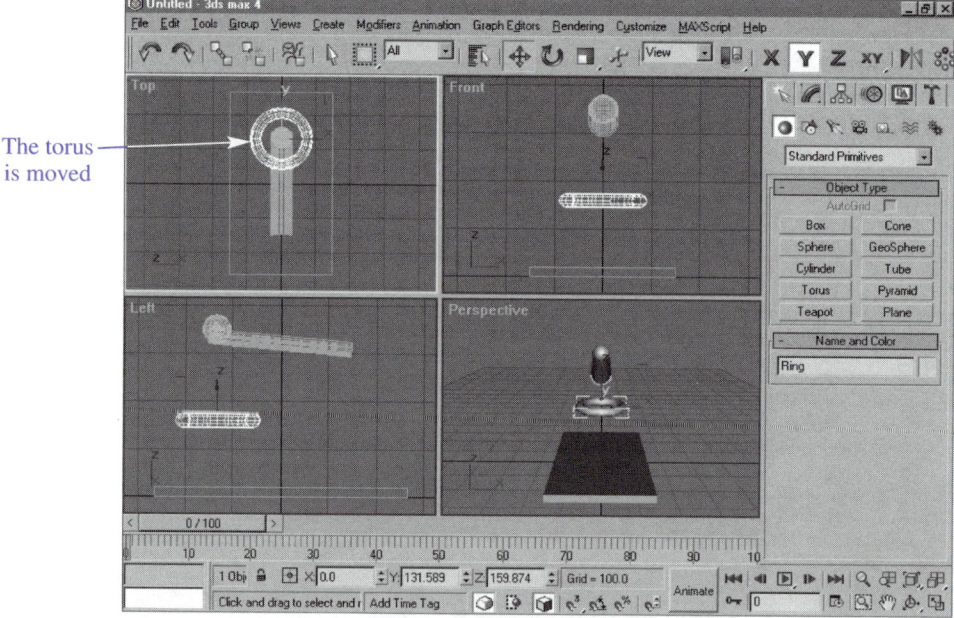

Saving Your Work

1. Select **Save** from the **File** pull-down menu.
   Since the scene has not yet been saved, the **Save File As** dialog box is displayed, Figure 2-9.

2. Type Ch02.max in the **File name:** text box. Also, change to the folder of your choice. Then, select the **Save** button in the dialog box.
   The scene is saved in the folder you specified.

Figure 2-9. The scene is saved using the **Save File As** dialog box.

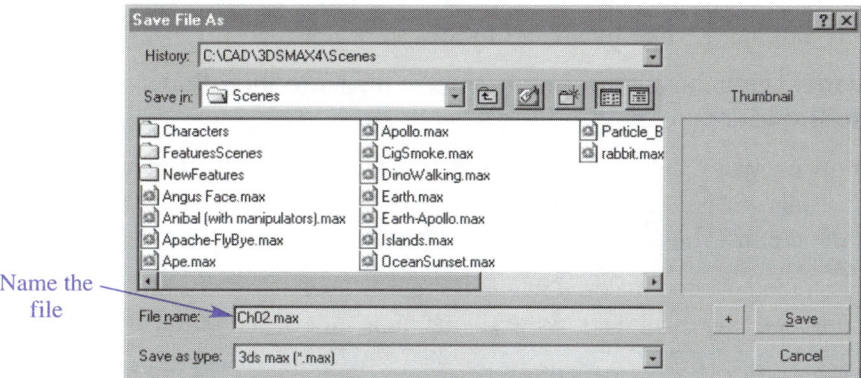

Name the file

Assigning Materials

In this part of the tutorial, you will first select the material from the library of materials. Then, you will assign the selected material to objects.

Assigning a Material to the Base

1. Select the Base in any viewport by picking on it with the **Select object** button on the **Main** toolbar active.
   The Base turns white to indicate it is selected.

Select object

2. Select the **Material Editor** button on the **Main** toolbar. If the **Material Editor** button is not visible in the **Main** toolbar, pan the toolbar to the left.
   The **Material Editor** is opened, Figure 2-10.

Material Editor

Figure 2-10. The **Material Editor**.

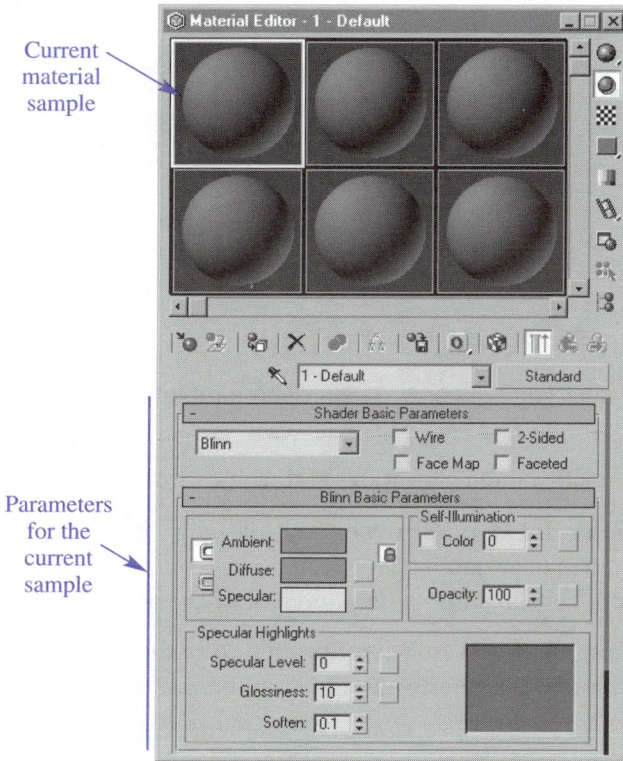

Current material sample

Parameters for the current sample

Get Material

3. The **Material Editor** has slots containing sample spheres. Pick on the first material sample slot to select it.
   The current sample slot has a white boundary around it.

4. Pick the **Get Material** button below the sample slots in the **Material Editor**.
   The **Material/Map Browser** is displayed, Figure 2-11.

5. In the **Material/Map Browser**, select the **Mtl Library** radio button in the **Browse From** area.
   The different materials present in the 3dsmax.mat library are displayed. If no materials are displayed, select the **Open...** button and open the 3dsmax.mat file.

Assign Material to Selection

6. Double-click on the Wood_Ashen material name in the list. Then, close the **Material/Map Browser**.
   The Wood_Ashen material is displayed in the first sample slot of the **Material Editor**.

7. Pick the **Assign Material to Selection** button below the sample slots in the **Material Editor**.
   Since the Base is selected, the Wooden_Ashen material is assigned to it.

8. Close the **Material Editor**.
   Notice the material in Perspective viewport.

Figure 2-11. The
Material/Map Browser.

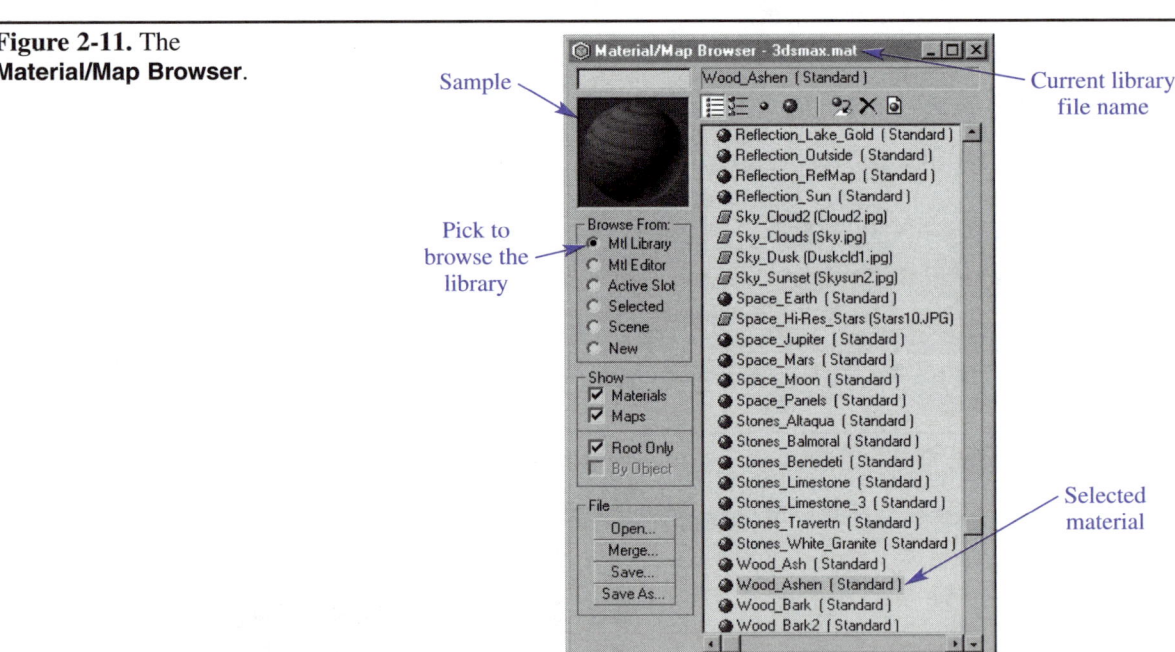

Sample

Current library
file name

Pick to
browse the
library

Selected
material

Assigning a Material to the Ball

1. Select the Ball in any viewport. Then, open the **Material Editor**.
   The Ball turns white indicating it is selected.

2. Select the second sample slot in the **Material Editor**.

Get Material

3. Open the **Material/Map Browser** by picking the **Get Material** button. Double-click on Metal_Brushed in the list to load the material. You can minimize or close the **Material/Map Browser**.
   The material is displayed in the second slot of the **Material Editor**.

Assign Material to Selection

4. Pick the **Assign Material to Selection** button in the **Material Editor**.
   The material Metal_Brushed is assigned to the Ball.

Assigning a Material to the Ring

1. Select the Ring in any viewport.
   The Ring turns white indicating it is selected.

2. Select the third sample slot in the **Material Editor**.

3. In the **Material/Map Browser**, double-click on Bricks_Yellow in the list to load the material.
   The material is displayed in the third slot of the Material Editor.

4. Pick the **Assign Material to Selection** button in the **Material Editor**.
   The material Bricks_Yellow is assigned to the Ring.

Assign Material
to Selection

Assigning a Material to the Sliced Tube

1. Select the Sliced Tube in any viewport.
   The object turns white indicating it is selected.

2. Select the fourth sample slot in the **Material Editor**.

3. In the **Material/Map Browser**, double-click on Metal_Dark_Gold in the list to load the material.
   The material is displayed in the fourth slot of the **Material Editor**.

4. Pick the **Assign Material to Selection** button in the **Material Editor**.
   The material Metal_Dark_Gold is assigned to the Sliced Tube.

Assign Material
to Selection

5. Close the **Material Editor** and the **Material/Map Browser**.

Adding Lights

In this part of the tutorial, you will create and position two lights in the scene. The lights should be positioned away from the object to prevent bright, or "hot," spots. For this reason, you may need to zoom out to create more space around the objects.

1. Activate the Top viewport.

2. Select the **Zoom All** button in the viewport navigation controls.
   The cursor appears as a small magnifying glass with a small grid attached to it.

Zoom All

3. Pick near the center of the objects in the Top viewport, and drag the cursor down until the objects are displayed about one-fourth their original size.

4. Pick **Create** in the **Command Panel**. Pick the **Lights** button and select **Standard** in the drop-down list.

Create

Lights

5. Pick the **Omni** button in the **Object Type** rollout.
   The different rollouts pertaining to the creation of omni lights are displayed. These include the **Name and Color**, **General Parameters**, **Projector Parameters**, **Attenuation Parameters**, **Shadow Parameters**, and **Shadow Map Params** rollouts.

6. You will use the default settings in all rollouts. Next, pick a point in the upper-right corner of the Top viewport to place the light.
   An omni light named Omni01 is placed at the selected point.

7. Select another point in the lower-left corner of the viewport.
   A second omni light, named Omni02, is placed at the selected point.

8. Pick the **Select and Move** and **Restrict to XY Plane** buttons in the **Main** toolbar and select Omni01 in the Left viewport. Zoom as needed to see the light.
   The movement of the light is restricted in the XY plane.

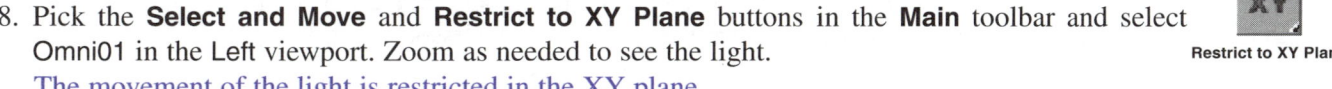

Restrict to XY Plane

9. Move Omni01 to the upper-left hand corner of the viewport.

Field-of-View

10. Similarly, select Omni02 and move it near the upper-right corner of the viewport.

11. Select the **Zoom Extents All** button to zoom to the extents of the objects. Then, use the **Field-of-View** button and zoom in on the Perspective viewport.
    The two omni lights you created are displayed and illuminate the scene, Figure 2-12.

Figure 2-12. Two omni lights are added to the scene.

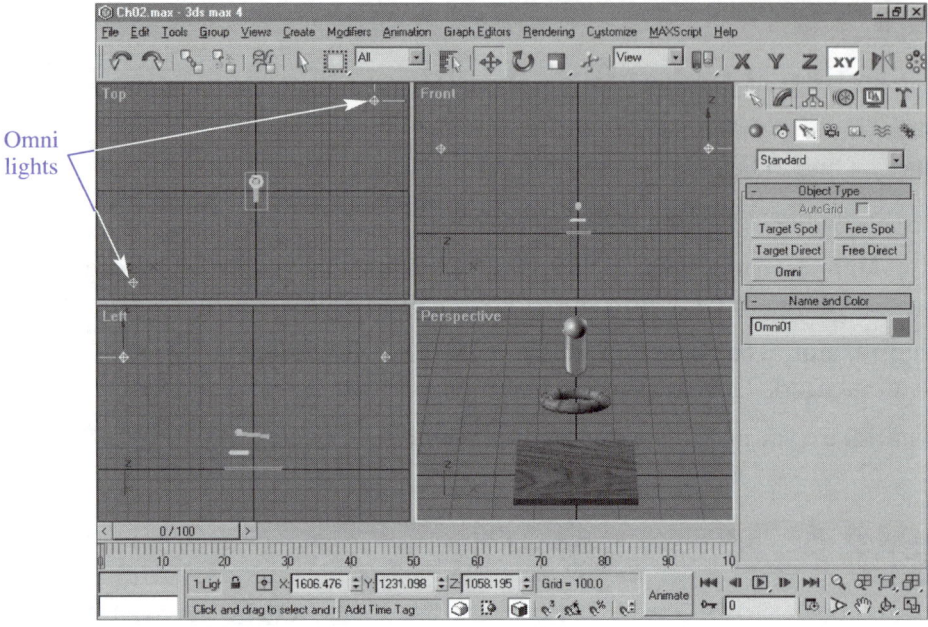

Adding Cameras

At this stage, you have four different views of the object, one displayed in each of the four viewports. The Perspective viewport displays a 3D view of the objects. By adding a camera to the scene, you can look at the object from any direction and from any distance.

Create

Cameras

1. Activate the Top viewport. Pick **Create** in the **Command Panel**. Then, pick the **Cameras** button and select **Standard** in the drop-down list.

2. In the **Object Type** rollout, select the **Target** button.
   The **Name and Color**, **Parameters**, and **Depth of Field Parameters** rollouts for target cameras are displayed.

3. Pick in the lower-left corner of the Top viewport to position the camera, and then drag the crosshairs to approximately the center of the objects and release the mouse button.
   The first point you pick is the location of the camera. The point where you release the mouse button defines location of the target for the camera. The camera is given the default name of Camera01.

4. Right-click to end the command.

5. Activate the Perspective viewport. Then, press the [C] key on the keyboard.
   The Perspective viewport is changed to the Camera01 viewport.

Figure 2-13. A 3D view is displayed in the Camera01 viewport.

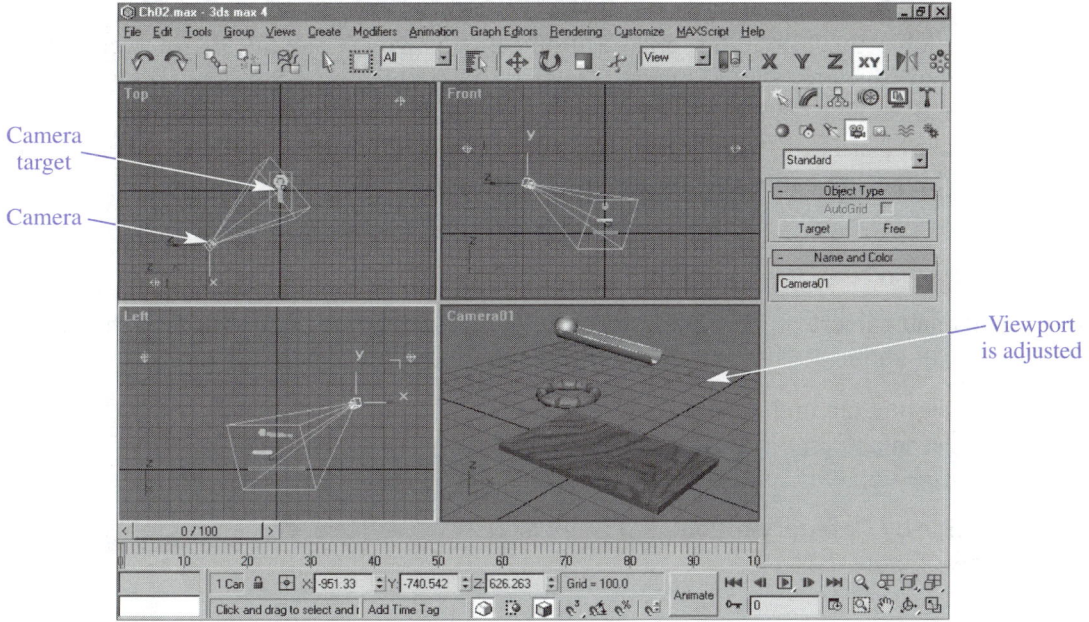

6. Activate the Left viewport. Pick the **Select and Move** and **Restrict to XY Plane** buttons on the **Main** toolbar, if not already selected.

7. Select Camera01 and move it until a good 3D view of the objects is displayed in the Camera01 viewport. See Figure 2-13.
   As you move the camera, the Camera01 viewport is dynamically updated to reflect the change.

8. Activate the Camera01 viewport and select the **Truck Camera** button in the viewport navigation controls.
   When a camera viewport is active, the **Truck Camera** button replaces the **Pan** button.

Truck Camera

9. Move the **Truck Camera** cursor in the Camera01 viewport to place the objects in the center of the viewport.

10. Select the **Field-of-View** button and zoom on the objects.

Field-of-View

11. Continue using the **Truck Camera** and **Field-of-View** buttons until you are satisfied with the view in the Camera01 viewport.

12. Save the scene.
    The scene is saved in the same folder under the same name as when it was first saved.

Rendering a Still Image

1. Activate the Camera01 viewport.

2. Select the **Render Scene** button on the **Main** toolbar.
   The **Render Scene** dialog box is displayed.

Render Scene

3. Accept the default settings, and pick the **Render** button in the dialog box.
   The **Rendering** dialog box is displayed indicating the progress, and the rendered image is displayed in the render window. The **Rendering** dialog box is automatically closed when the rendering is complete.

4. Close both the render window and the **Render Scene** dialog box.

Adding Animation to the Scene

When you create objects, place lights, and position cameras, you create the "base" scene without any motion. In 3ds max, this base scene is called frame 0. As you add motion to the scene by rearranging objects, lights, and cameras on a frame other than frame 0, you create animation keys. The frames on which keys are placed are called keyframes. The frames between frame 0 and the keyframes, and from keyframe to keyframe, are automatically created by 3ds max.

Hiding the Lights and Camera

Since the lights and camera are not going to be animated, it may be helpful to hide them. The effect of the lights is still applied to the scene, and the camera viewport remains displayed.

Display

1. Select the **Display** tab in the **Command Panel**.
   The rollouts available in the **Display** tab are the **Display Color**, **Hide by Category**, **Hide**, **Freeze**, **Display Properties**, and **Link Display** rollouts.

2. Open the **Hide by Category** rollout, if it is not already open. Then, check the **Lights** and **Cameras** check boxes, Figure 2-14.
   Both lights and the camera are hidden in all the viewports.

3. Select the **Zoom Extents All** button to zoom to the extents of the objects.

Figure 2-14. Hiding all lights and cameras.

Check to hide

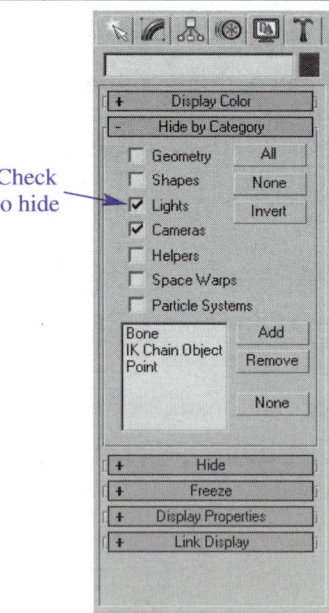

Creating Animation Keys for the Sliced Tube

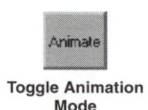
Toggle Animation Mode

1. Make the Left viewport active.

2. Pick the **Toggle Animation Mode** button.
   The button turns red and is depressed to indicate you are in animation mode. The Left viewport also has a red box around it.

3. Type 40 in the current frame text box in the animation controls.
   The **Time** slider moves to frame 40.

4. Pick the **Select and Rotate** and **Restrict to Z** buttons on the **Main** toolbar.
   The rotation is restricted to the Z axis of the viewport.

Figure 2-15. A rotation animation key is added for the Sliced Tube object.

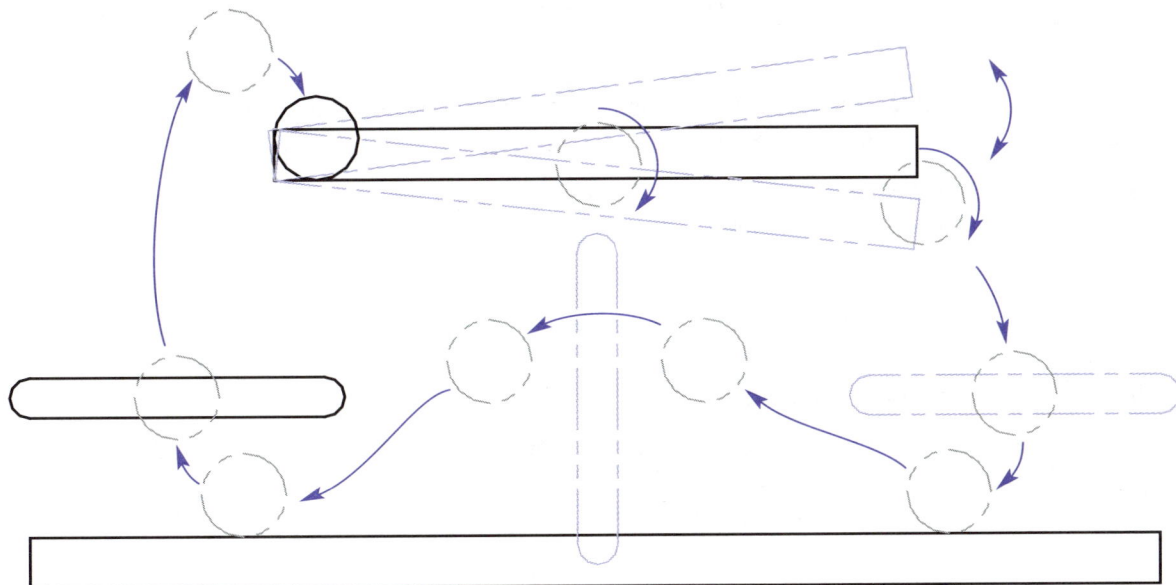

5. Select the Sliced Tube and rotate it until the Z value in the coordinate display is 5 degrees. Refer to Figure 2-15.
   The tube is parallel to the Base.

6. Move to frame 70.

7. Make sure that the **Select and Rotate** and **Restrict to Z** buttons are selected. Rotate the tube again until the Z value in the coordinate display is 5 degrees.
   The tube is tilted upward at an angle of 5 degrees from horizontal.

8. Move to frame 100.

9. Make sure that the **Select and Rotate** and **Restrict to Z** buttons are selected. Rotate the tube down until the Z value in the coordinate display shows –10 degrees.
   The tube is rotated to its original position.

10. Exit animation mode. Make the camera viewport active and select the **Play Animation** button.
    The animation is played in the camera viewport. You can play the animation in any other viewport you wish.

11. Select the **Stop Animation** button to stop the playback.

12. Select the **Go to Start** button to go to the beginning of the animation.

Creating Animation Keys for the Ring

1. Pick the **Toggle Animation Mode** button to enter animation mode. Activate the Left viewport.

Toggle Animation Mode

2. Move to frame 10.

3. Pick the **Select and Move** and the **Restrict to X** buttons on the **Main** toolbar.
   Movement is restricted to the X axis of the viewport.

4. Select the Ring and move it to the right. Place it below the tube, almost at its center.

5. Now, pick the **Select and Rotate** button and make sure that the **Restrict to Z** button is selected on the **Main** toolbar.
   Rotation is restricted around the Z axis of the viewport.

6. Select the Ring and rotate it until the Z value in the coordinate display is –90 degrees.
The ring is perpendicular to the Base.

7. Move to frame 20.

8. Pick the **Select and Move** button. Make sure that the **Restrict to X** button is selected in the **Main** toolbar. Move the Ring to the right so it is at the right-hand edge of the Sliced Tube.

9. Pick the **Select and Rotate** button. Rotate the Ring until the Z value in the coordinate display is –90 degrees. Make sure that the rotation is restricted around the Z axis.
The Ring is again parallel to the Base.

10. Move to frame 50.

11. Pick the **Select and Move** button. Move the **Ring** back to the center of the Sliced Tube. Make sure the movement is restricted along the X axis.

12. Pick the **Select and Rotate** button in the **Main** toolbar. Rotate the Ring until the Z value in the coordinate display is 90 degrees. Make sure the **Restrict to Z** button is selected.
The Ring is rotated perpendicular to the Base.

13. Move to frame 70.

14. Pick the **Select and Move** button. Move the Ring left to its original position. Make sure that the movement of **Ring** is restricted along the X axis.

15. Pick the **Select and Rotate** button. Rotate the Ring until the Z value in the coordinate display is 90 degrees. Make sure the **Restrict to Z** button is selected.
The Ring is in its original position and orientation.

16. Exit animation mode. Activate the camera viewport. Then, pick the **Play Animation** button to view and check the motion of the Ring.

17. Select the **Stop Animation** button to stop the playback. Pick the **Go to Start** button to go to the beginning of the animation.

Creating Animation Keys for the Ball

1. Activate the Left viewport and enter animation mode.

2. Move to frame 10.

3. Pick the **Select and Move** and **Restrict to XY Plane** buttons in the **Main** toolbar.
The movement is restricted to the XY plane of the viewport.

4. Select the Ball and move it to the right. Place it almost at the middle of the Sliced Tube.

5. Pick the **Select and Rotate** and the **Restrict to Z** buttons in the **Main** toolbar.
Rotation is restricted around the Z axis.

6. Rotate the Ball until the Z value in the coordinate display is –90 degrees.

7. Move to frame 20.

8. Pick the **Select and Move** button. Make sure the **Restrict to XY Plane** button is selected in the **Main** toolbar. Move the Ball to the right so it is at the edge of the Sliced Tube.

9. Pick the **Select and Rotate** button. Rotate the Ball until the Z value in the coordinate display is –90 degrees. Make sure that the rotation of the Ball is restricted around the Z axis.

10. Move to frame 30.

11. Pick the **Select and Move** button and move the Ball a little down so it just passes through the Ring, almost at the center. Make sure that the movement is restricted to the XY plane.

12. Advance to frame 40.

13. Move the Ball down to touch the Base.

14. Advance to frame 50.

15. Move the Ball up and to the left so it is in the center of the Ring.

16. Advance to frame 60.

17. Move the Ball down and to the left so it passes through the Ring.

18. Advance to frame 70.

19. Move the Ball down and to the left so it is on the Base under the center of the Ring.

20. Advance to frame 80.

21. Move the Ball up so it is in the center of the Ring.

22. Advance to frame 90.

23. Move the Ball up and place it a little above the Sliced Tube at its left end.

24. Advance to frame 100.

25. Move the Ball down to its original position. Exit animation mode.

26. Make the camera viewport current. Pick the **Play Animation** button to check the motion of the Ball. Select the **Stop Animation** button when you want to stop the playback.
    If all the objects are not displayed in the camera viewport during the animation, use the **Field-of-View** button to "zoom out."

27. Pick the **Go to Start** button to move to frame 0, or you can simply drag the **Time** slider to frame 0.

Rendering the Animation

In this part of the tutorial, you will render the animation to a file. The rendered animation is then ready for viewing.

Render Scene

1. With the camera viewport current, select the **Render Scene** button on the **Main** toolbar.
   The **Render Scene** dialog box is displayed on the screen.

2. In the **Time Output** area of the dialog box, select the **Active Time Segment** radio button.

3. In the **Render Output** area, pick the **Files...** button.
   The **Render Output File** dialog box is displayed.

4. Select **AVI File (*.avi)** from the **Save as type:** drop-down list.

5. In the **File name:** text box, type Ch02.avi. Then, select the **Save** button.
   The **Video Compression** dialog box is displayed, Figure 2-16.

6. Select the **OK** button in the **Video Compression** dialog box to accept the defaults.
   The file name and its path are displayed in the **Files...** field of the **Render Scene** dialog box.

Figure 2-16. The **Video Compression** dialog box contains settings for the animation file.

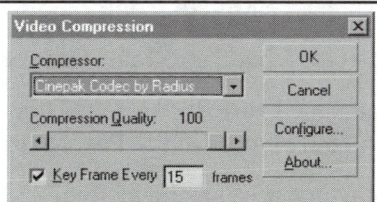

7. Make sure the **Save File** check box in the **Render Output** area of the **Render Scene** dialog box is checked.

8. Pick the **Render** button in the dialog box.
   It takes several minutes to render the animation frame by frame.

9. After the rendering is complete close the rendered window and the **Render Scene** dialog box to return to the original screen.

Viewing the Animation

1. Select **View Image File...** from the **File** pull-down menu.
   The **View File** dialog box is displayed on the screen.

2. Select the Ch02.avi file from the list in the dialog box, and then pick the **Open** button.
   Windows Media Player plays the animation, Figure 2-17.

3. Close Media Player and return to 3ds max.

Figure 2-17. Windows Media Player is used for animation playback.

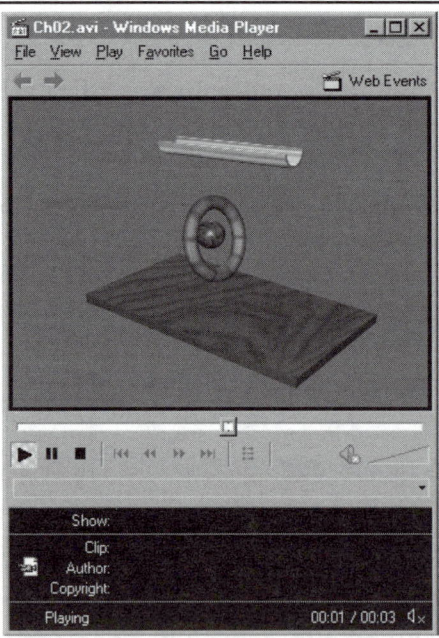

Self-Evaluation Test

Answer the following questions. Then compare your answers with the correct answers given at the end of this chapter.

1. When you reset 3ds max, all existing data is _____.

2. The _____ rollout can be used to modify the size of a standard primitive that you have just created.

3. A _____ sign indicates that the rollout is closed and a _____ sign indicates that the rollout is open.

4. You can create a sliced tube by selecting the _____check box and entering values in the **Slice From:** and **Slice To:** spinners in the **Parameters** rollout.

5. To restrict the movement of an object along its Y axis, select the _____ button on the **Main** toolbar.

6. Select the _____ button to zoom to the extents of the objects in all viewports.

7. Lights should be positioned _____ objects to avoid hotspots.

8. When a camera is created in the scene, you can change the active viewport to the camera viewport by pressing the _____ key on the keyboard.

9. The _____ button allows you to zoom in a camera viewport.

10. To play a rendered animation, the animation must be rendered to _____.

Exercises

Create the objects shown on frame 0 using your own dimensions. Then, perform the following operations.

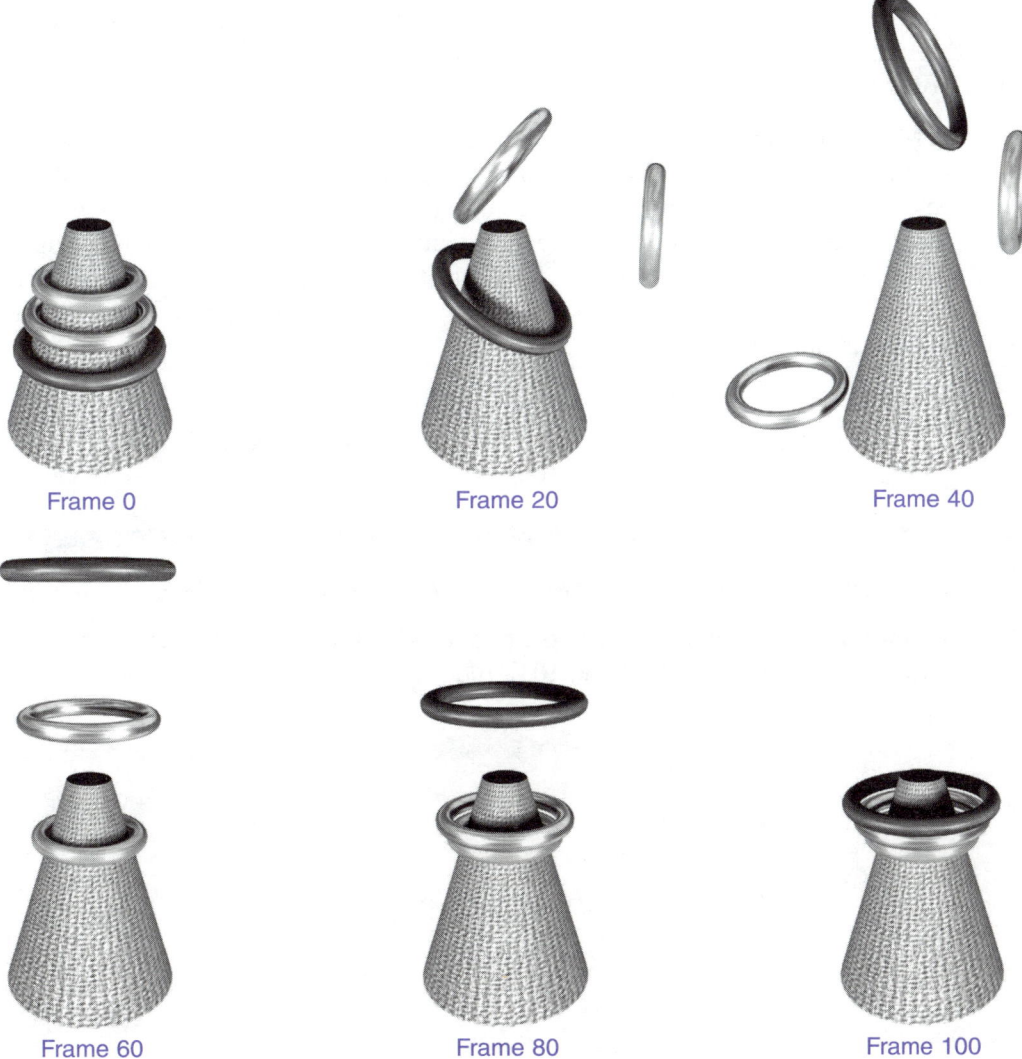

Frame 0   Frame 20   Frame 40

Frame 60   Frame 80   Frame 100

1. Assign the standard material Fabric_Tan_Carpet to the cone, Metal_Galvanized to the largest torus, Metal_Chrome to the middle torus, and Metal_Dark_Gold to the smallest torus.

2. Add two omni lights to the scene.

3. Add a camera to the scene. Also, adjust the location and field of view (FOV) of the camera to get a good view of the objects in the camera viewport.

4. Render the still image of the camera viewport.

5. Use animation and move the rings (tori). The three rings fly off the cone and return in reverse order.

Small torus: Moves straight up from frame 0 to frame 10. Then, from frame 10 to frame 20, it rotates through an angle of –90 degrees around its Z axis, and moves to the right and down. From frame 20 to 30, it rotates through an angle of –90 degrees about its Z axis, and moves down to lie on the "ground." Between frames 30 and 40, it rotates around its Z axis through an angle of 90 degrees, and moves up and to the left. Between frames 40 and 50, it rotates around its Z axis again through an angle of 90 degrees, and moves to the left so it is above the cone. Between the frames 50 and 60, it moves down onto the cone and remains in this position for the rest of the animation.

Middle torus: On keyframes 20, 30, and 40, moves straight up, rotates, and moves to the left and down in a similar fashion to the small torus. It also rotates around its Z axis through an angle of 90 degrees twice on the way and is finally aligned with the "ground." Then, on keyframes 50, 60, and 70, the middle torus moves up again to the right, retraces its path and rotation, and finally is placed on the truncated cone above the smallest torus. It rotates around its Z axis twice through –90 degrees over these frames.

Large torus: Moves straight up between frames 0 and 30 to above the cone. Then, from frame 30 to 40, it moves further up, and between frames 40 and 50 it rotates around its Z axis through an angle of –90 degrees. From frame 50 to 60, the torus rotates again around its Z axis through an angle of –90 degrees. From frame 60 to 70, it rotates one more time around its Z axis through an angle of –90 degrees. Between frame 70 and 80, it rotates a final time through an angle of –90 degrees around its Z axis. From frame 80 to 90, it moves down to just above the cone. From frame 90 to 100, it moves down on top of the middle torus.

6. Render the animation to a file named ex02.avi in the folder of your choice.

7. Play the rendered animation file. Save the scene as ex02.max in the folder of your choice.

Answers

The following are the correct answers to the questions in the Self-Evaluation Test.

1. erased; 2. **Parameters**; 3. plus/minus; 4. **Slice On**; 5. **Restrict to Y**; 6. **Zoom Extents All**; 7. away from (or far from); 8. [C]; 9. **Field-of-View**; 10. a file.

Chapter 3

Creating Shapes

Learning Objectives

After completing this chapter, you will be able to:
○ Create various standard primitives.
○ Create objects by revolving a shape.
○ Create objects by lofting a shape along a path.
○ Assign materials to the objects.
○ Position and adjust lights and a camera.
○ Animate a scene.
○ Render an animated scene.

Tutorial Description

In this tutorial, you will create a dresser consisting of a cabinet, two drawers, and a mirror. You will also create a bowl with a couple of rubber bands inside, and place this on the dresser. Finally, you will assign materials to the objects, create lights and a camera, and render the scene.

Resetting the System

It is recommended that you reset the system before starting a new tutorial. This sets the system to 3ds max default values and erases all existing data. If you want to save the existing scene, make sure you do so before resetting 3ds max.

Grid Setting

Before creating the components, change the grid setting. This will help accurately locate objects.

1. Right-click on the **3D Snap Toggle** button.
   The **Grid and Snap Settings** dialog box is displayed.

3D Snap Toggle

2. Select the **Home Grid** tab in the dialog box. Enter 5.0 in the **Grid Spacing** spinner. Make sure the **Inhibit Grid Subdivision Below Grid Spacing** check box is *not* checked. Exit the dialog box.
The grid spacing is set to 5.

Saving Your Work

1. Select **Save** from the **File** pull-down menu. You can also press [Ctrl][S] on the keyboard.
The **Save File As** dialog box is displayed.

2. In the dialog box, type Ch03.max in the **File name:** text box and pick the **Save** button.

Creating the Outer Frame

Create

Geometry

You will start creating the dresser by drawing the outer frame of the dresser. Standard primitives are used to create the frame.

1. Activate the Top viewport. Pick **Create** in the **Command Panel**. Then, pick the **Geometry** button. Select **Standard Primitives** from the drop-down list.

2. Select the **Box** button in the **Object Type** rollout.
The rollouts corresponding to a box primitive are displayed.

3. Open the **Keyboard Entry** rollout and enter 150 in the **Length:** spinner, 200 in the **Width** spinner, and 130 in the **Height** spinner. Select the **Create** button.
A box is created.

4. In the **Name and Color** rollout, name the box Frame, Outer.

Zoom Extents All

Select and Squash

5. Select the **Zoom Extents All** button.
The box is zoomed to its extents in all the viewports.

6. Pick the **Select and Squash** button from the **Scale** flyout. Select the **Yes** button in the 3ds max warning dialog box that is displayed, confirming that you want to continue.
The cursor changes to the **Select and Squash** cursor.

7. In the Front viewport, hold down the [Shift] key. Then select the box and scale it down until the coordinate display reads 94%, 94%, 106%. Release both the pick button of the mouse and the [Shift] key.
The **Clone Options** dialog box is displayed.

8. Select **OK** in the **Clone Options** dialog box to accept the name Frame, Outer01.
A scaled down copy of the box is created inside the original.

9. Pick the **Select and Move** and **Restrict to Y** buttons in the **Main** toolbar. In the Front viewport, move the Frame, Outer01 object up so it is centered on the Frame, Outer object. The Y value in the coordinate display should be about 3.5.

10. Pick the **Restrict to X** button. In the Left viewport, move the Frame, Outer01 object about nine units to the right.
The right edge of Frame, Outer01 is placed inside Frame, Outer, Figure 3-1.

11. Select Frame, Outer in any viewport.
The object turns white, indicating it is selected.

12. Pick **Create** in the **Command Panel**. Select the **Geometry** button.

13. Select **Compound Objects** from the drop-down list.

Figure 3-1. Two boxes are drawn to create the frame of the dresser.

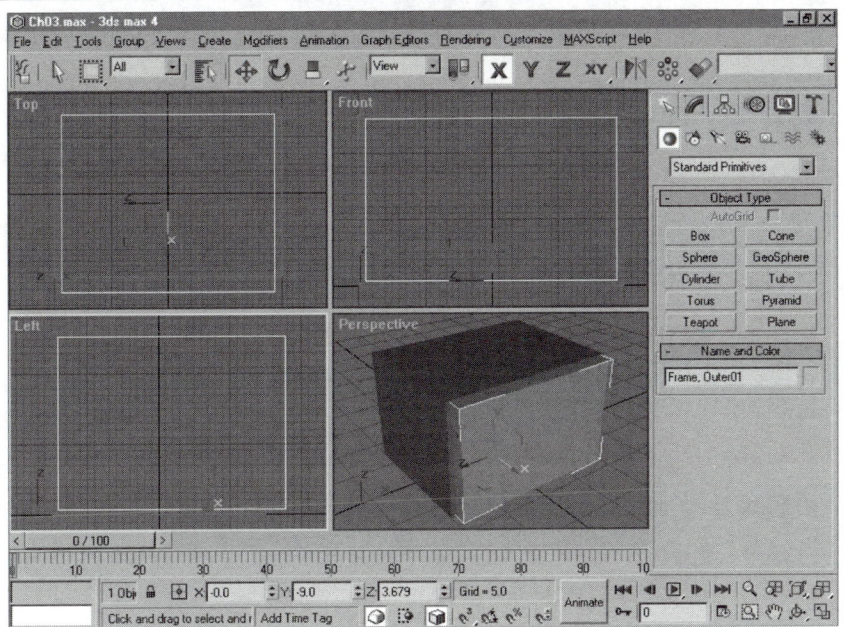

14. Select the **Boolean** button in the **Object Type** rollout.
    The rollouts for a Boolean object are displayed.

15. In the **Operations** area of the **Parameters** rollout, make sure the **Subtraction (A-B)** radio button is on.

16. In the **Pick Boolean** rollout, select the **Pick Operand B** button. Make sure the **Move** radio button is on.

17. Pick the Frame, Outer01 object in any viewport.
    The inner box is removed from the outer box, creating the outer frame of the dresser, Figure 3-2.

18. Save the scene.

Figure 3-2. The outer frame of the dresser is created.

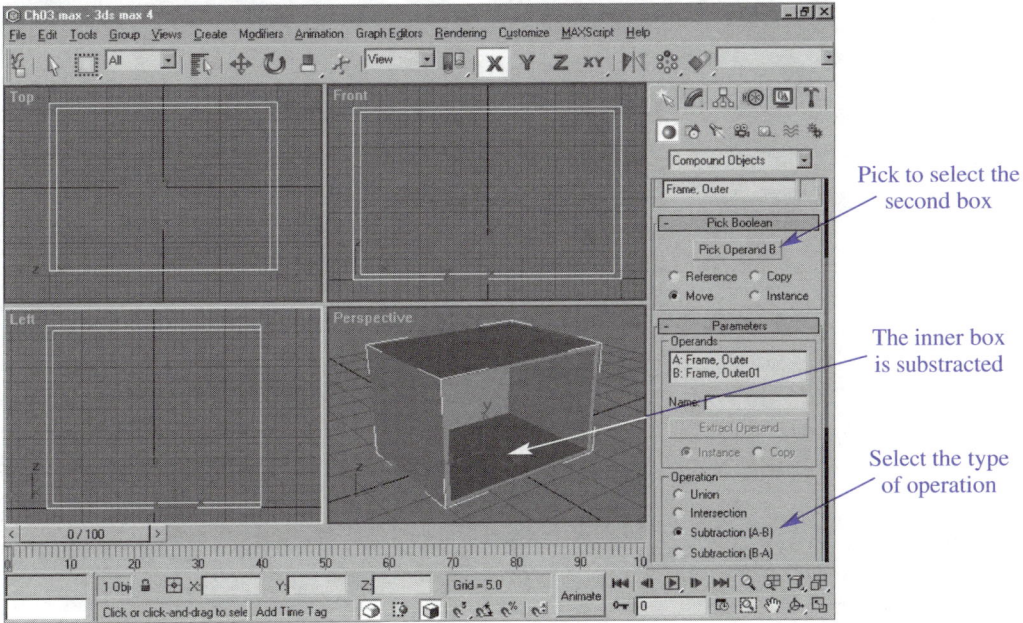

Pick to select the second box

The inner box is substracted

Select the type of operation

Creating the Inner Partition

Create

Geometry

You will now create the inner partition walls inside the outer frame. The partition is created from standard primitives.

1. Activate the Top viewport. Pick **Create** in the **Command Panel**. Pick the **Geometry** button. Select **Standard Primitives** from the drop-down list.

2. Select the **Box** button in the **Object Type** rollout.
   The rollouts corresponding to a box primitive are displayed.

3. In the **Keyboard Entry** rollout, enter 145 in the **Length:** spinner, 190 in the **Width:** spinner, and 5 in the **Height:** spinner. Then, pick the **Create** button.
   A box is created.

4. In the **Name and Color** rollout, name the box Partition.

5. Pick the **Select and Move** and **Restrict to X** buttons on the **Main** toolbar.

6. In the Left viewport, move the Partition so its right-hand edge aligns with the right-hand edge of the Frame, Outer object.

7. Select the **2D Snap toggle** button from the **Snap Toggle** flyout. Then, move the Partition up until the Y value in the coordinate display is 90, Figure 3-3.

8. Activate the Top viewport and prepare to draw another box.

9. In the **Keyboard Entry** rollout for a box, enter 145 in the **Length:** spinner, 5 in the **Width:** spinner, and 31 in the **Height:** spinner. Select the **Create** button.
   A box is created.

10. In the **Name and Color** rollout, name the box Partition01.

11. Turn on 2D snap. In the Left viewport, move Partition01 up until the Y value in the coordinate display is 95.

Figure 3-3. The horizontal portion of the partition is moved into its correct location.

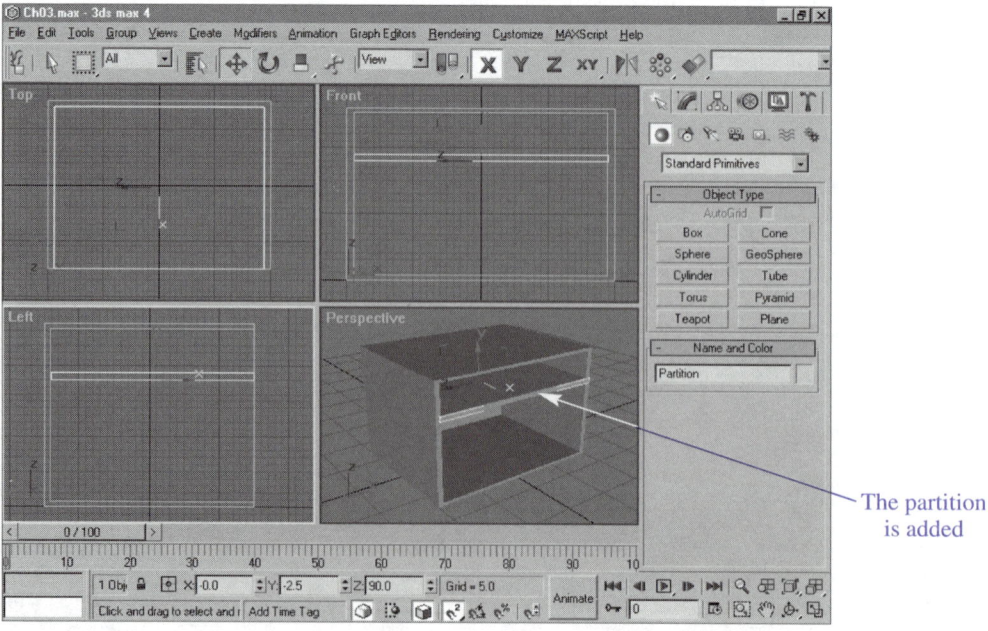

The partition is added

12. Turn off 2D snap. Pick the **Restrict to Y** button on the **Main** toolbar. Move Partition01 so its right-hand edge aligns with the right-hand edge of Frame, Outer.

13. Pick the **Select object** button and select Partition.

Select object

14. Pick **Create** in the **Command Panel** and pick the **Geometry** button. Select **Compound Objects** from the drop-down list.

15. Select the **Boolean** button in the **Object Type** rollout. In the **Parameters** rollout, select the **Union** radio button.

16. In the **Pick Boolean** rollout, select the **Pick Operand B** button. Then, select Partition01 in any viewport.
    Partition01 is joined with Partition, Figure 3-4.

17. Save the scene.

Creating a Drawer

Create

Geometry

1. Select **Create** in the **Command Panel**. Then, pick the **Geometry** button. Select **Standard Primitives** from the drop-down list.

2. Activate the Top viewport. Pick the **Box** button in the **Object Type** rollout.

3. In the **Keyboard Entry** rollout, enter 145 in the **Length:** spinner, 92.5 in the **Width:** spinner, and 31 in the **Height:** spinner. Then, pick the **Create** button.
   A box is created.

4. In the **Name and Color** rollout, name the box Drawer01.

5. Draw another box with the Top viewport active. In the **Keyboard Entry** rollout, enter 135 in the **Length:** spinner, 82.5 in the **Width:** spinner, and 31 in the **Height:** spinner. Then, pick the **Create** button.
   A smaller box is created inside Drawer01.

Figure 3-4. The two parts of the partition are joined.

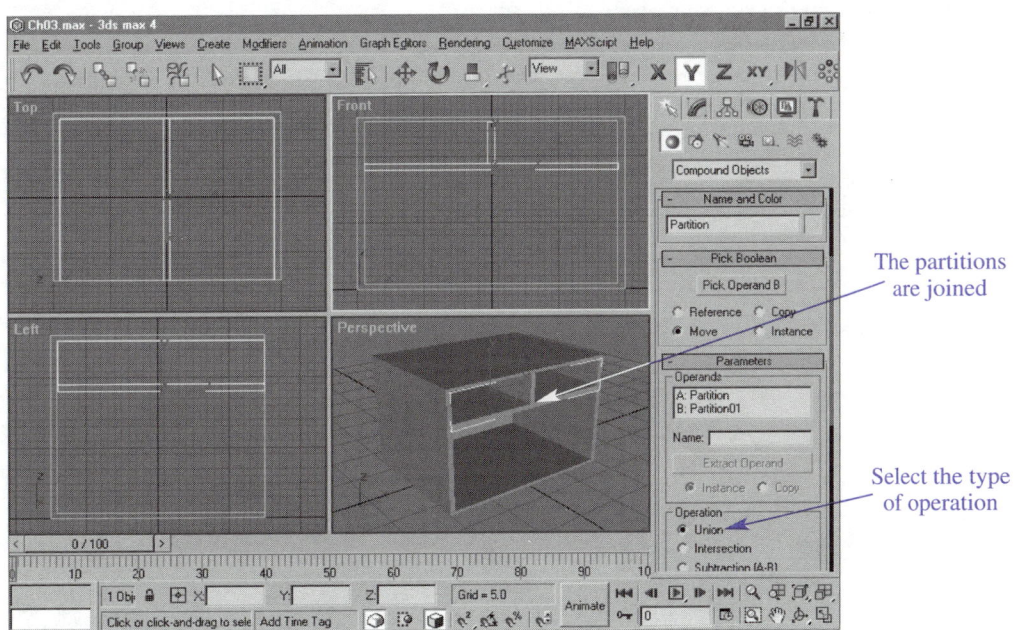

The partitions are joined

Select the type of operation

Select object

6. In the Left viewport, move the smaller box up 5 units on the Y axis.

7. Pick the **Select object** button and select Drawer01.

8. Pick **Create** in the **Command Panel** and select the **Geometry** button. Select **Compound Objects** from the drop-down list. Then, pick the **Boolean** button in the **Object Type** rollout.

9. In the **Parameters** rollout, make sure the **Subtraction (A-B)** radio button is selected.

10. In the **Pick Boolean** rollout, select the **Pick Operand B** button. Then, select the smaller box inside Drawer01.
    A drawer is created, Figure 3-5.

11. Save the scene.

Creating the Knob for the Drawer

You will now create a knob handle for the drawer. This is created as a line with a lathe modifier applied to it.

Region Zoom

1. Select the **Region Zoom** button in the viewport navigation controls. In the Top viewport, zoom in on the front area of Drawer01, Figure 3-6. Right-click to end the command.

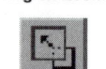
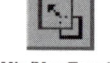
Min/Max Toggle

2. Press the [W] key on the keyboard to maximize the Top viewport. You can also use the **Min/Max Toggle** button in the viewport navigation controls.

3. Right-click on the **Snap Toggle** button to display the **Grid and Snap Settings** dialog box. Select the **Home Grid** tab and enter 2.5 in the **Grid Spacing** spinner. Close the dialog box.

Create

4. Select **Create** in the **Command Panel**. Then, pick the **Shapes** button and select **Splines** from the drop-down list.

5. In the **Object Type** rollout, select the **Line** button.

Shapes

6. Turn on 2D snap. Pick on the front edge of the drawer as shown in Figure 3-7.

7. Move the mouse straight down 5 units (2 grid boxes) and pick to set the second vertex.

Figure 3-5. The first drawer is created.

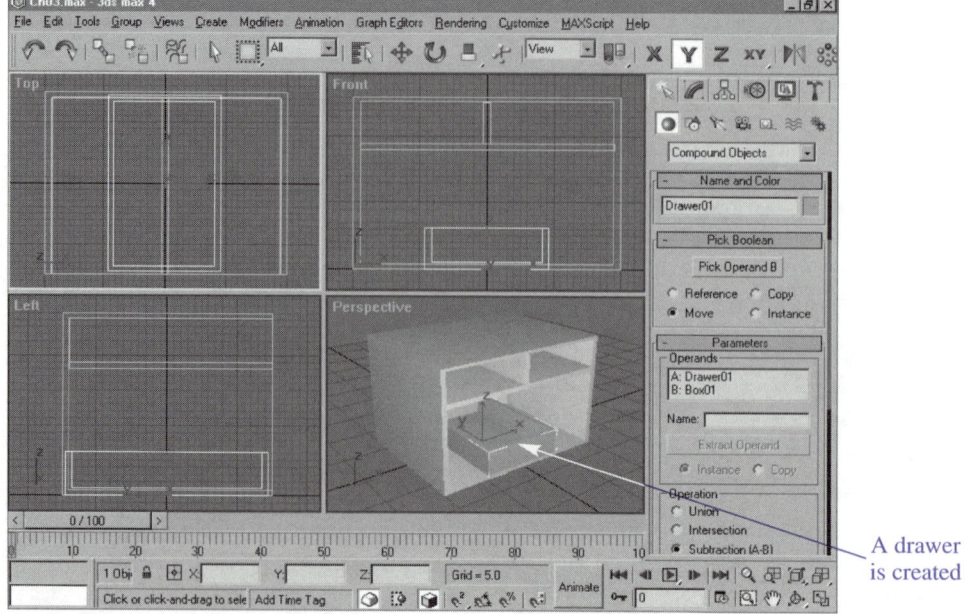

A drawer
is created

Figure 3-6. Preparing to draw the spline profile of the knob.

Figure 3-7. The spline profile of the knob is roughed out.

First point

Rough profile

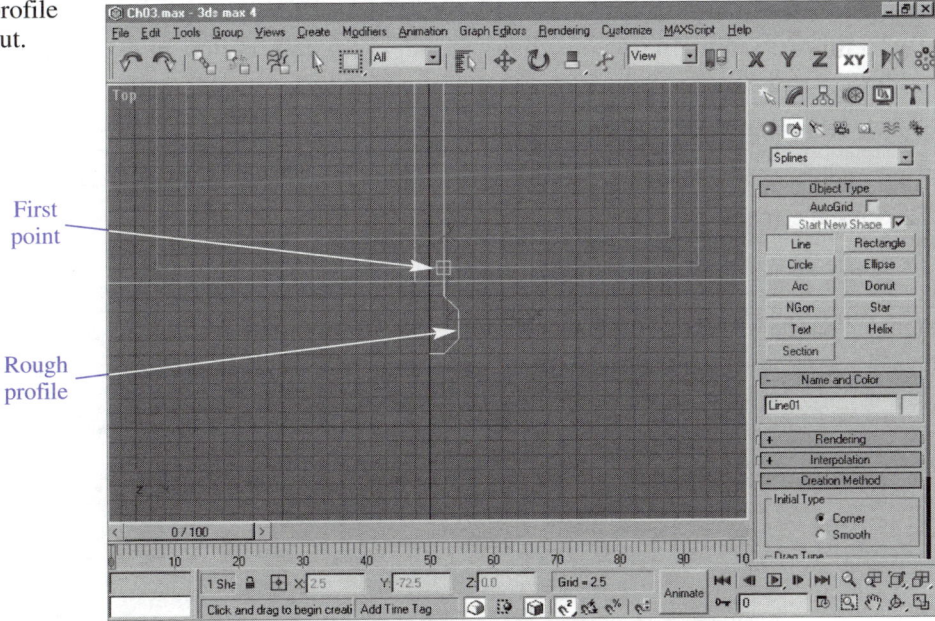

8. Similarly, set the rest of the vertices. From the second vertex, move the cursor to the right 2.5 units, and down 2.5 units. Pick to set the third vertex. From the third vertex, move the cursor down 5 units and pick. From the fourth vertex, move the cursor to the left 2.5 units, and down 2.5 units. Pick to set the fifth vertex. From the fifth vertex, move the cursor to the left 2.5 units and pick.

9. Right-click to exit the **Line** command. Use the **Region Zoom** button to zoom in on the spline, then right-click to exit the command. Name the spline Knob01.
   A rough profile of the knob is created.

10. With the spline (line) selected, pick **Modify** in the **Command Panel**.

11. In the **Selection** rollout, pick the **Vertex** button.
    This selects the vertex sub-object editing level for the spline.

Modify

Vertex

12. Right-click on the second vertex you created. The quad menu is displayed. In the top-left quadrant of the quad menu, select **Bezier**.
    The vertex is converted to a Bézier vertex. The Bézier handles are displayed and the spline is curved through this vertex.

13. Right-click on the third vertex, and select **Bezier** from the quad menu.
    The third vertex is converted to a Bézier vertex.

14. Turn off snap, if it is on.

15. Pick the **Select and Move** button.

16. With the third vertex selected, move the lower Bézier handle (green square) down and to the left until a smooth curve is created, Figure 3-8.
    If you make a mistake when moving the Bézier handles, select the **Undo** button on the **Main** toolbar to undo the previous change.

Undo

17. Change the fourth and fifth vertices to Bézier. Then, adjust the handles to change the curvature of the spline. Move the last vertex (sixth vertex) down to produce a good shape for the knob.

18. Pick the **Vertex** button in the **Selection** rollout to exit sub-object mode.

19. In the **Modifiers** pull-down menu, select **Patch/Spline Editing** to display a cascading menu. Select **Lathe** from the cascading menu.
    The lathe modifier is applied to the spline, and the spline is revolved around its middle.

20. To properly align the revolved spline, select the **Min** button in the **Align** area of the **Parameters** rollout. See Figure 3-9.

21. Press the [W] key on the keyboard.
    The previous viewport configuration is displayed.

22. Save the scene.

Figure 3-8. The vertices of the knob profile are adjusted to produce a curved shape.

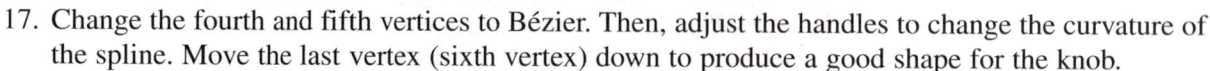

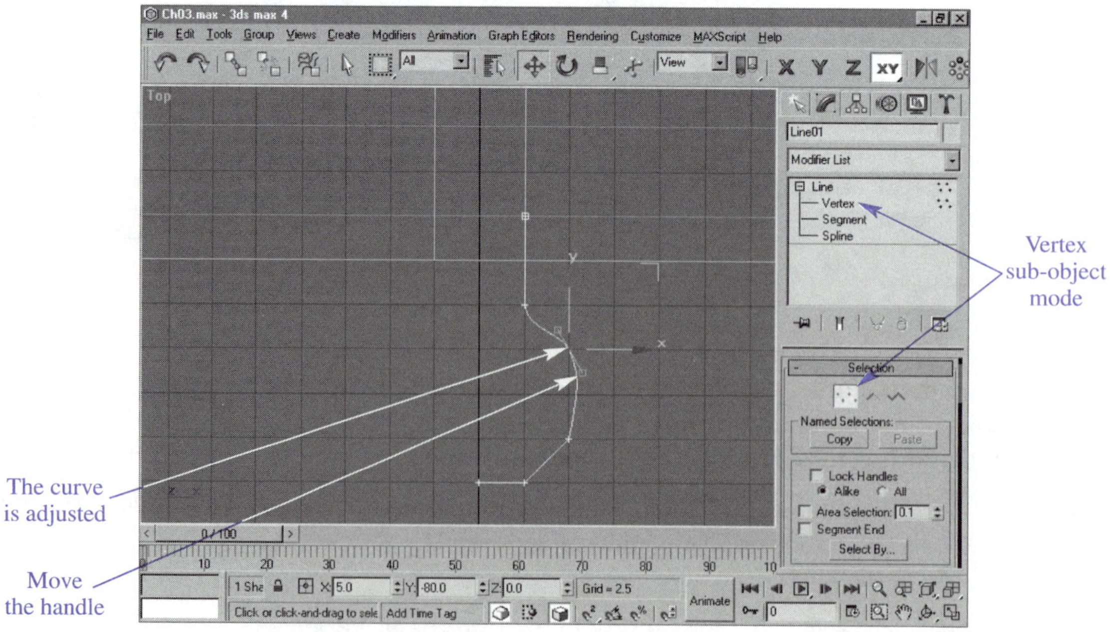

Figure 3-9. A lathe modifier is applied to the knob profile to create the final object.

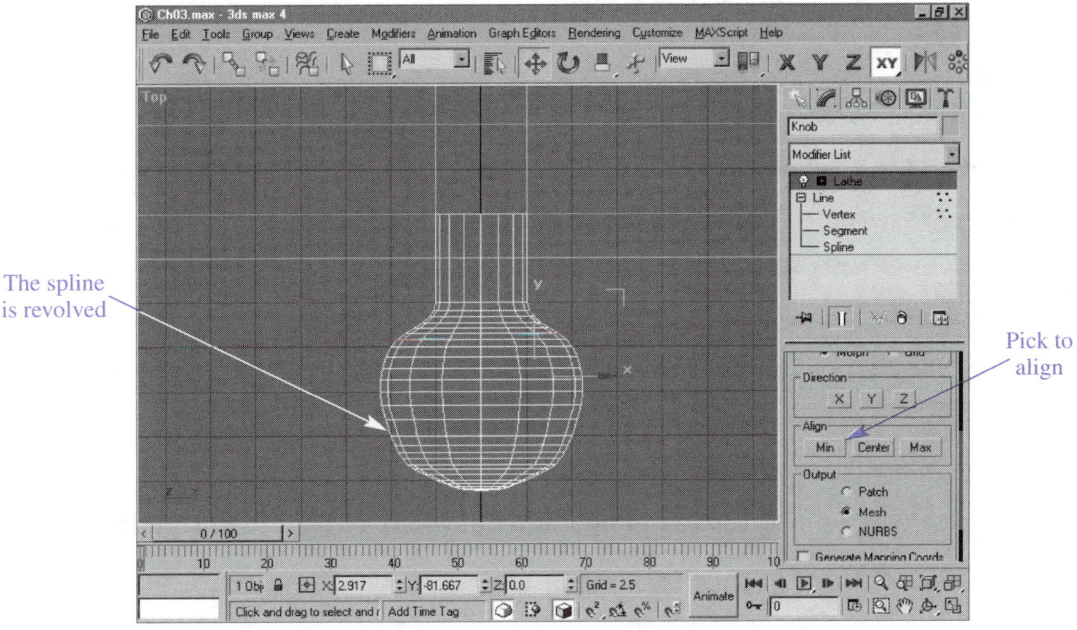

The spline is revolved

Pick to align

Positioning and Copying the Objects

The handle knob and the drawer now need to be moved into their correct positions. You also need to make a copy of the drawer and knob, and position the copies.

1. Activate the Left viewport. Make sure the **Select and Move** and **Restrict to Y** buttons are selected.

2. Move the Knob01 up so it is vertically centered on the drawer.

3. Pick the **Select by Name** button.
   The **Select Objects** dialog box is displayed.

Select by Name

4. As Knob01 is already selected, it is highlighted in the list. Hold down the [Ctrl] key on the keyboard and pick Drawer01 in the list, Figure 3-10. Pick the **Select** button in the dialog box to select both objects.
   The Knob01 and Drawer01 objects turn white indicating they are selected.

Figure 3-10. Selecting multiple objects in the **Select Objects** dialog box.

These objects will be selected

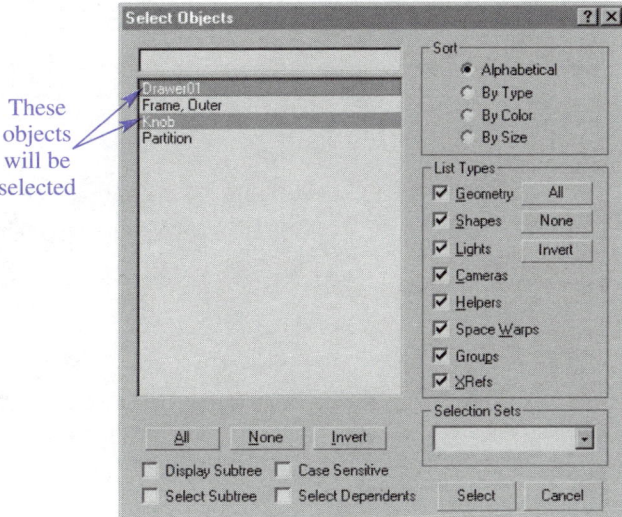

5. Pick the **Restrict to X** button. Move the objects to the right so the front edge of Drawer01 is aligned with the front edge of the Frame, Outer object.
   You may want to maximize the viewport when aligning the objects.

6. In the Front viewport, move both objects to the left so the left edge of Drawer01 touches the inner edge of the Frame, Outer object.

7. Pick the **Restrict to Y** button.

8. Move the objects up and place them in between the Partition and the Frame, Outer objects.

9. Select the **Zoom Extents All** button to zoom to the extents of all objects, Figure 3-11.

Zoom Extents All

10. Pick the **Restrict to X** button. Activate the Front viewport, if it is not already active.

11. Holding the [Shift] key down, move both the drawer and knob to the right so they fit between the right-hand side of the Partition and the Frame, Outer objects. Release the mouse button when in position.
    The **Clone Options** dialog box is displayed.

12. Accept the default name that appears in the **Name:** text box of the **Clone Options** dialog box. Then, pick the **OK** button.
    Copies of the drawer and knob are placed in their correct positions. The names of the copies are numbered "one higher" than the originals. The cloned drawer is named Drawer02 and the cloned knob is named Knob02.

13. Save the scene.

Creating the Cabinet Doors

Create

Geometry

You will now create doors for the cabinet below the drawers using standard primitives. These doors overlap at the edges where they meet. A small groove is visible where the doors meet.

1. Activate the Top viewport. Pick **Create** in the **Command Panel**. Then, pick the **Geometry** button. Select **Standard Primitives** in the drop-down list.

Figure 3-11. The first drawer and knob are in their correct locations.

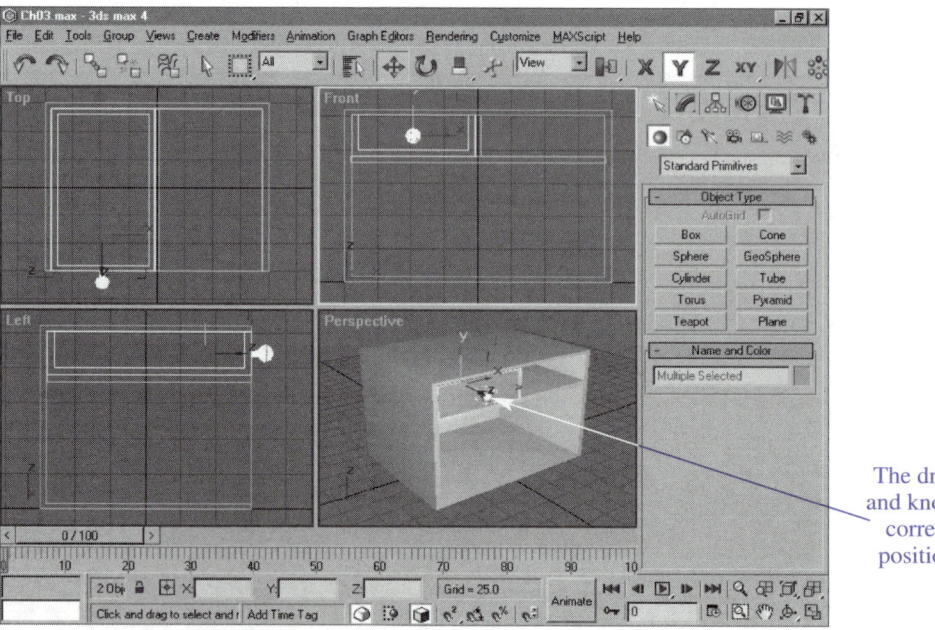

The drawer and knob are correctly positioned

2. Pick the **Box** button in the **Object Type** rollout.

3. In the **Keyboard Entry** rollout, enter 5 in the **Length:** spinner, 93 in the **Width:** spinner, and 85 in the **Height:** spinner. Then, pick the **Create** button.
   A box is created.

4. In the **Name and Color** rollout, name the box Door01.

5. Pick **Select and Move** and **Restrict to X** in the **Main** toolbar.

6. Move Door01 left until it is aligned with the inner edge of Frame, Outer. Maximize the viewport, then zoom in on the inner edge of Frame, Outer. Precisely align Door01 with the inner edge of Frame, Outer.

7. Return to the previous viewport configuration. Then, pick the **Zoom Extents All** button.

8. Holding the [Shift] key down, move Door01 right and align its right edge exactly with the inner edge of the Frame, Outer object on the right-hand side.
   The **Clone Options** dialog box is displayed.

9. Type Door02 in the **Name:** text box and select **OK**.
   A copy of Door01 is created, Figure 3-12.

10. With the Top viewport active, pick **Create** in the **Command Panel**. Pick the **Geometry** button and select **Standard Primitives** in the drop-down list. Then, select the **Box** button in the **Object Type** rollout.

11. In the **Keyboard Entry** rollout, enter 2.5 in the **Length:** spinner, 6 in the **Width:** spinner, and 85 in the **Height:** spinner. Then, pick the **Create** button.
    A small box is created. This box will be used to make the overlapping "flap" on the door.

12. Zoom in on the area containing the small box.

13. Pick the **Select and Move** and **Restrict to XY Plane** buttons on the **Main** toolbar. Align the left edge of the small box with the right-hand edge of Door01 (the left-hand door), Figure 3-13. Also align the top (back) edges of the two objects.

Figure 3-12. Two doors are drawn. They need to be moved to their correct locations.

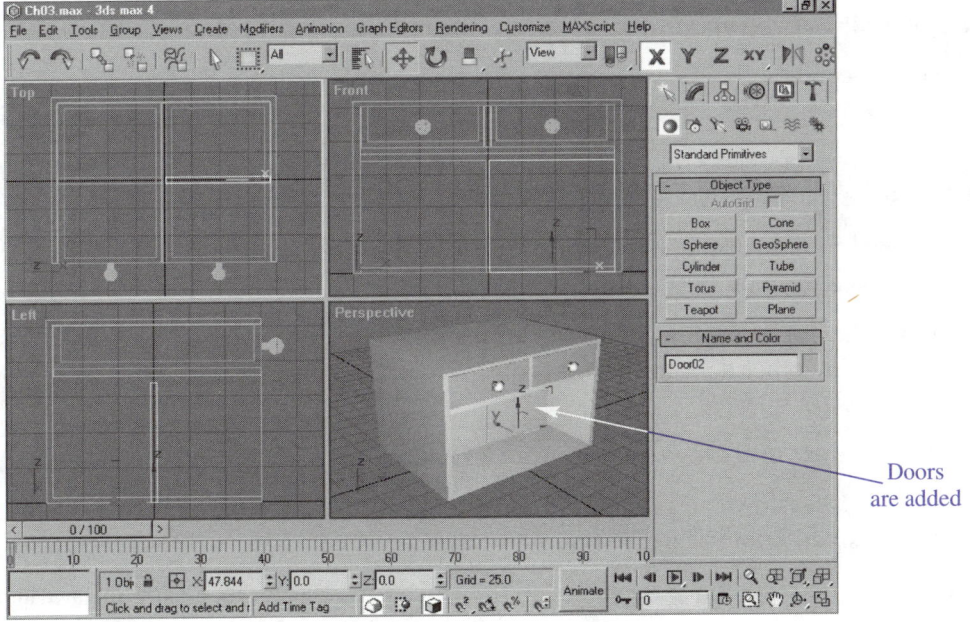

Doors are added

Figure 3-13. Drawing a box that will be used to modify the doors.

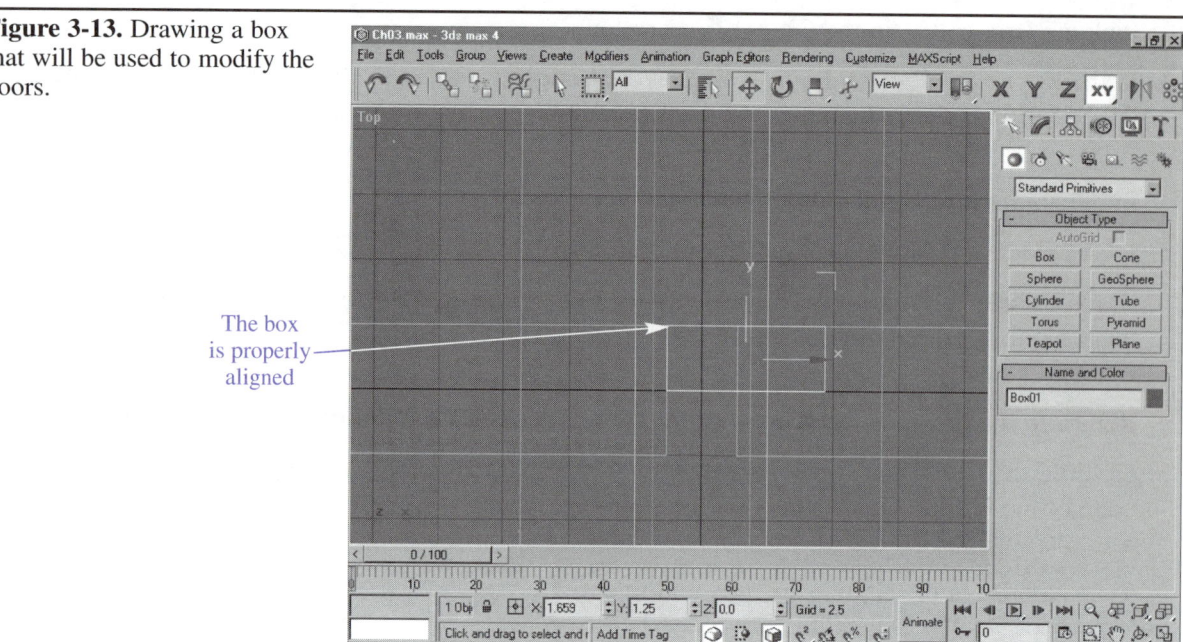

The box is properly aligned

14. Select Door01. Pick **Create** in the **Command Panel**. Then, pick the **Geometry** button and select **Compound Objects** from the drop-down list. Select **Boolean** in the **Object Type** rollout.

15. Pick the **Union** radio button in the **Parameters** rollout. Then, pick the **Copy** radio button in the **Pick Boolean** rollout. Select the **Pick Operand B** button and then select the small box in the viewport.
    A copy of the small box is joined to Door01.

16. Right-click in the viewport to exit the command. Then, select Door02. Pick the **Boolean** button in the **Object Type** rollout.

17. In the **Parameters** rollout, pick the **Subtraction (A-B)** radio button. Then, pick the **Move** radio button in the **Pick Boolean** rollout. Select the **Pick Operand B** button and then select the small box in the viewport. Use the [H] key and the **Pick Object** dialog box to select the small box. Right-click to exit the command.
    The small box is subtracted from Door02, Figure 3-14.

18. Display all four viewports and select the **Zoom Extents All** button.

19. Save the scene.

Moving the Doors and Copying Knobs

You now need to move the doors into their correct positions. After that, you need to copy the drawer knobs and place them on the doors.

1. Activate the Top viewport. Select one of the doors in the viewport. Then, hold down the [Ctrl] key and select the other door in the viewport.
   Both doors are selected.

2. Pick the **Select and Move** and **Restrict to Y** buttons.

3. Move the doors down and so they align with the bottom edge of the Frame, Outer (this is the front of the dresser). Zoom as needed.

4. In the Left viewport move the doors so they are between Frame, Outer and Partition.

Figure 3-14. The doors have been modified.

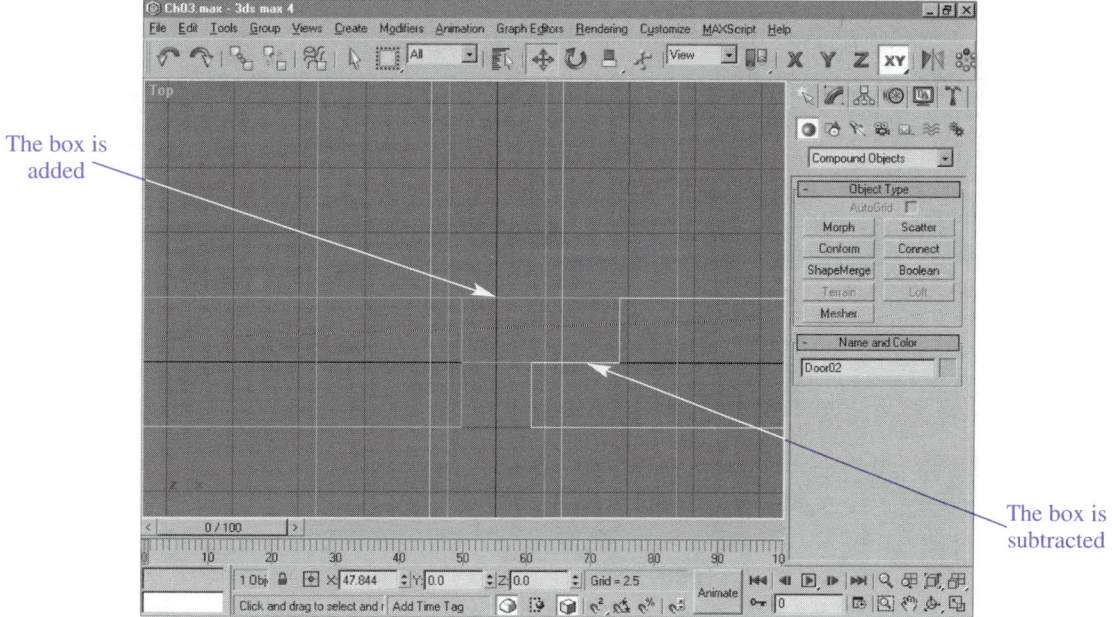

The box is added

The box is subtracted

5. Activate the Front viewport. Hold down the [Shift] key and select Knob01. Move the knob down to the middle of the door.
   The **Clone Options** dialog box is displayed.

6. Enter Knob03 in the **Name:** text box of the **Clone Options** dialog box and then select the **OK** button.
   A copy of the original knob is created.

7. Select the **Restrict to X** button. In the Front viewport, move the knob right so it is close to the overlapping edge of the door.

8. Hold the [Shift] key and select Knob03. Move it onto Door02 close to the overlapping edge.
   The **Clone Options** dialog box is displayed.

9. Enter Knob04 in the **Name:** text box and then select the **OK** button.
   The knobs for the doors are correctly placed, Figure 3-15.

Creating the Legs

You will now create the legs for the dresser cabinet. These are drawn as a line, and then a lathe modifier is applied to the line.

1. Make the Front viewport current. Press the [W] key to maximize the viewport.

2. Select the **Pan** button to pan the view up so some "empty space" is displayed at the bottom of the viewport.

Pan

3. Select the **2D Snap Toggle** button to turn on snap.

4. Pick **Create** in the **Command Panel**. Then, pick the **Shapes** button and select **Splines** from the drop-down list.

Create

5. In the **Object Type** rollout, select the **Line** button.

Shapes

6. Pick on the lower edge of the Outer, Frame at X = –72.5, as shown in the coordinate display.

Figure 3-15. The doors and knobs have been moved to their correct locations.

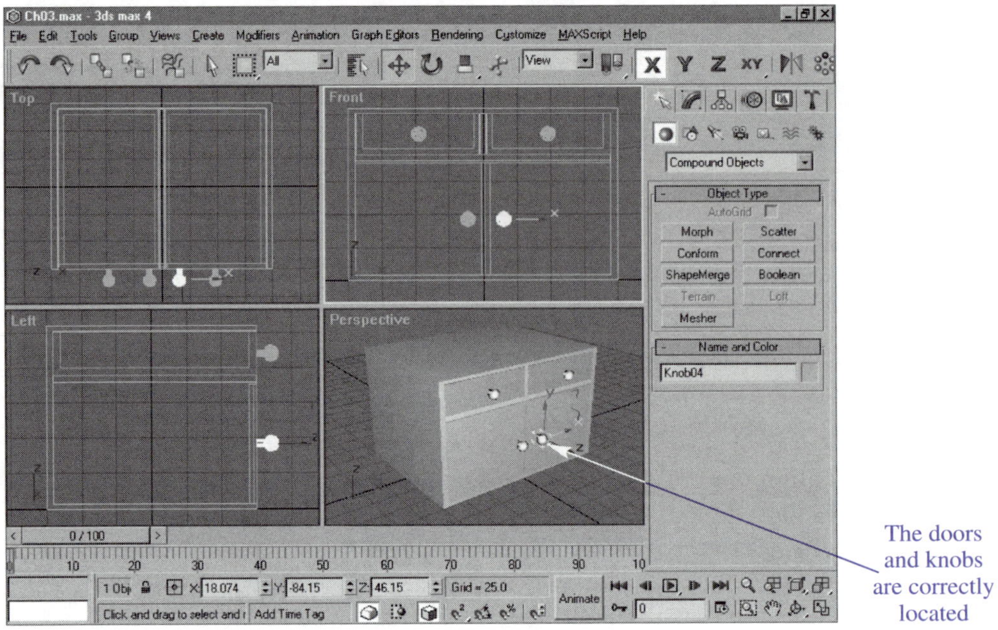

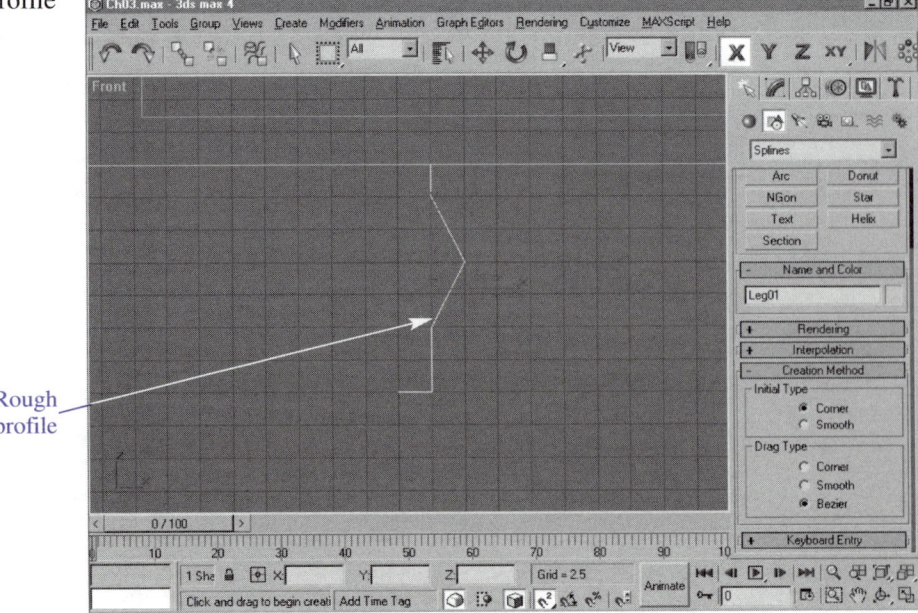

The doors
and knobs
are correctly
located

7. Place additional vertices at the following world coordinates.

–72.5	0.0	– 2.5
–70.0	0.0	– 7.5
–72.5	0.0	–12.5
–72.5	0.0	–17.5
–75.0	0.0	–17.5

8. Right-click to exit the command. Zoom in on the spline. Name the spline Leg01.
   A rough profile of the leg is created, Figure 3-16.

Modify

Figure 3-16. The spline profile
of the legs is roughed out.

Rough
profile

9. With the spline selected, pick **Modify** in the **Command Panel**.

10. In the **Selection** rollout, pick the **Vertex** button to enter sub-object mode.
    The vertices appear on the spline profile.

Vertex

11. Turn off snap.

12. Right-click on the third vertex from the top of the profile, to display the quad menu. In the quad menu, select **Bezier** in the upper-left quadrant.
    The vertex is converted to a Bézier vertex, and the spline is curved at this vertex.

13. Move the handles slightly to get a rounded shape in the middle. Pick the **Vertex** button in the **Selection** rollout to exit sub-object mode.

14. Pick **Patch/Spline Editing** in the **Modifiers** pull-down menu. Then, select **Lathe** in the cascading menu.
    The profile is revolved around its middle.

15. To properly align the profile, select the **Min** button in the **Align** area of the **Parameters** rollout. See Figure 3-17.

16. Press the [W] key on the keyboard to return to the previous viewport configuration.

17. Pick the **Select and Move** and **Restrict to Y** buttons.

18. In the Top viewport, move Leg01 down so it is equidistant from each side at the lower-left corner.

19. While holding the [Shift] key down move Leg01 up so it is equidistant from each side at the upper-left corner. In the **Clone Options** dialog box, enter Leg02 in the **Name** edit box and then select the **OK** button.

20. Select both legs. Copy them to the right-hand side of the dresser.

21. Save the scene.

Figure 3-17. A lathe modifier is applied to the leg profile to create the final object.

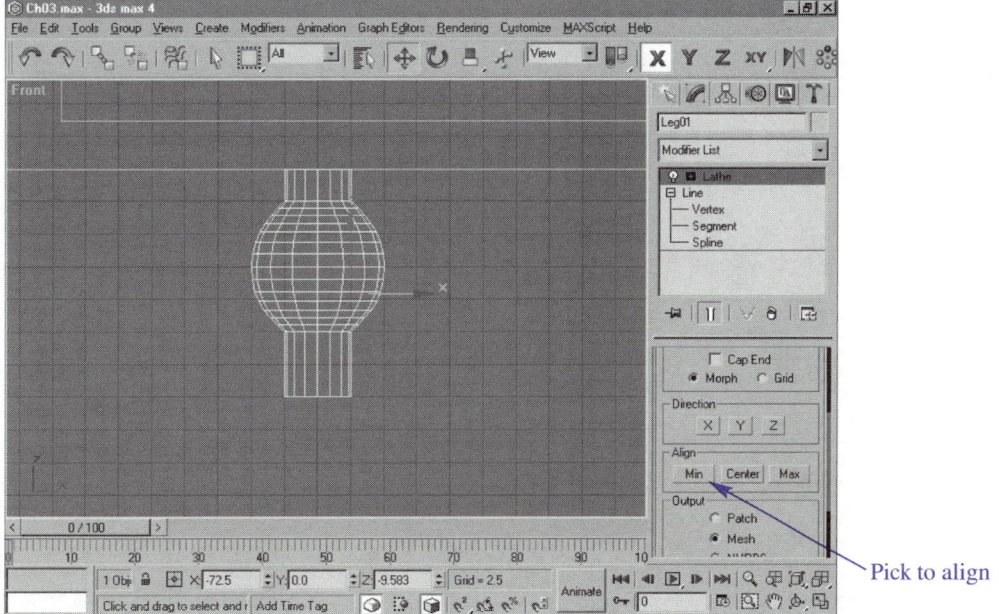

Pick to align

Creating the Mirror Frame

You will now create a frame for the mirror. This can be done by drawing an ellipse to be used as a path. Another shape will be lofted along the path.

Zoom

Create

Shapes

1. Activate the Front viewport and maximize it.

2. Select the **Zoom** button. Pick near the center of the cabinet and drag the cursor down until the objects are displayed about one-third their original size.

3. Select the **Pan** button. Pan the view so the top of the dresser is toward the bottom of the viewport.

4. Pick **Create** in the **Command Panel**. Then, pick the **Shapes** button and select **Splines** from the drop-down list. Select the **Ellipse** button in the **Object Type** rollout.

5. In the **Keyboard Entry** rollout, enter 230 in the **Length:** spinner and 130 in the **Width:** spinner. Then, pick the **Create** button.
   An ellipse is created near the center of the dresser.

6. Pick the **Select and Move** and **Restrict to Y** buttons. Move the ellipse up so its lower vertex is on the dresser top. In the **Name and Color** rollout, name the ellipse Mirror Frame.

7. Return to the previous viewport configuration. Then, in the Top viewport, move the ellipse so it aligns with the back edge of the dresser. Zoom as needed, Figure 3-18.

8. With the ellipse selected, pick **Clone** in the **Edit** pull-down menu. The **Clone Options** dialog box is displayed. Name the copy Mirror Back and pick the **OK** button.
   A copy of the ellipse is created. This copy will be used later to create a back for the mirror.

Create

Shapes

9. Pick **Create** in the **Command Panel**. Then, pick the **Shapes** button and select **Splines** in the drop-down list.

10. With the Top viewport active, pick the **Star** button in the **Object Type** rollout.

11. In the **Parameters** rollout, enter 4 in the **Points:** spinner. In the **Keyboard Entry** rollout, enter 3 in the **Radius 1:** spinner and 6 in the **Radius 2:** spinner. Then, pick the **Create** button.
    A four-pointed star is created. This shape will be lofted along the ellipse path to create the mirror frame.

Figure 3-18. An ellipse is created and moved to its correct location.

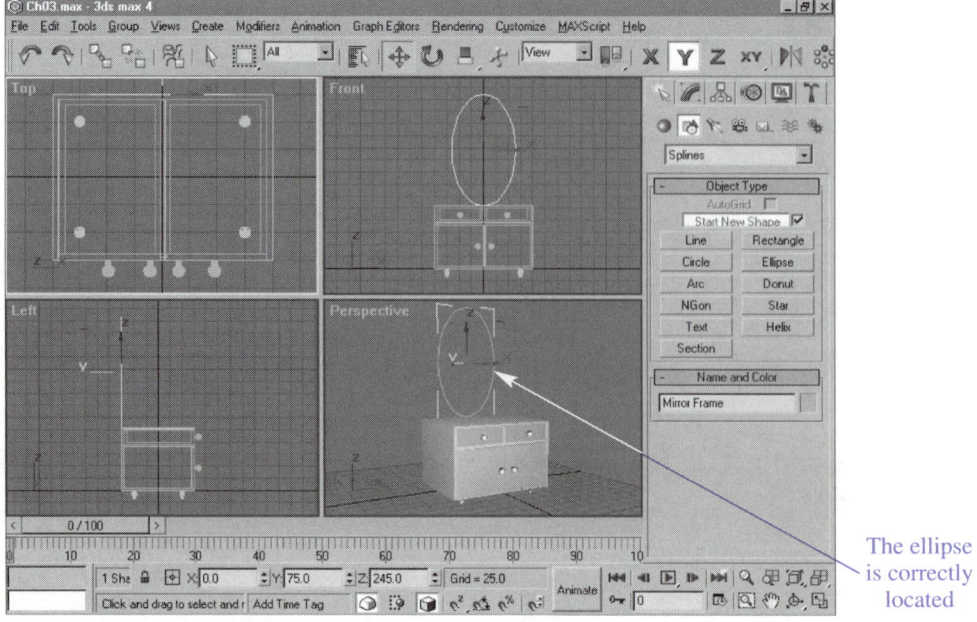

The ellipse is correctly located

12. Maximize the Top viewport. Select the **Region Zoom** button and drag a window around the star in the viewport. Right-click to end the command.

13. With the star selected, pick **Patch/Spline Editing** from the **Modifiers** pull-down menu. Then, pick **Edit Spline** from the cascading menu.
    An edit spline modifier is applied to the star. Since the star is a parametric shape, this modifier is used to edit the shape without collapsing it into an editable spline.

14. With the star selected, pick **Modify** in the **Command Panel**. Make sure **Edit Spline** is selected in the modifier stack.
    *The rollouts for the edit spline modifier are displayed in the **Modify** tab.*

Modify

15. In the **Selection** rollout, pick the **Spline** button.
    Picking this button enters spline sub-object editing mode.

Spline

16. Pick anywhere on the star. The current spline selection (the star) turns red. Right-click to display the quad menu. Select **Curve** from the upper-left quadrant of the quad menu.
    *The pointed vertices become curved. Note: **Curve** is already checked when the quad menu is opened, but select it again to "round" the vertices.*

17. Right-click anywhere in the viewport to display the quad menu. Select **Sub-objects** in the upper-left quadrant. Then, select **Vertex** in the cascading menu.
    The sub-object mode is changed from spline to vertex.

18. Select the lower vertex on the star and press the [Delete] key on the keyboard.
    The vertex of the star is deleted.

19. Using the quad menu, change the sub-object mode from vertex to segment. Pick the lower segment of the star (where the deleted vertex was). Right-click on the selected segment and pick **Line** in the upper-left quadrant of the quad menu. Pick the **Segment** button in the **Selection** rollout to exit sub-object mode.
    The bottom curved segment becomes a straight line, Figure 3-19.

Segment

20. Return to the four-viewport configuration. Pick **Create** in the **Command Panel**. Select the **Geometry** button and pick **Compound Objects** in the drop-down list.

Create

Geometry

Figure 3-19. A star is modified to use as a loft shape.

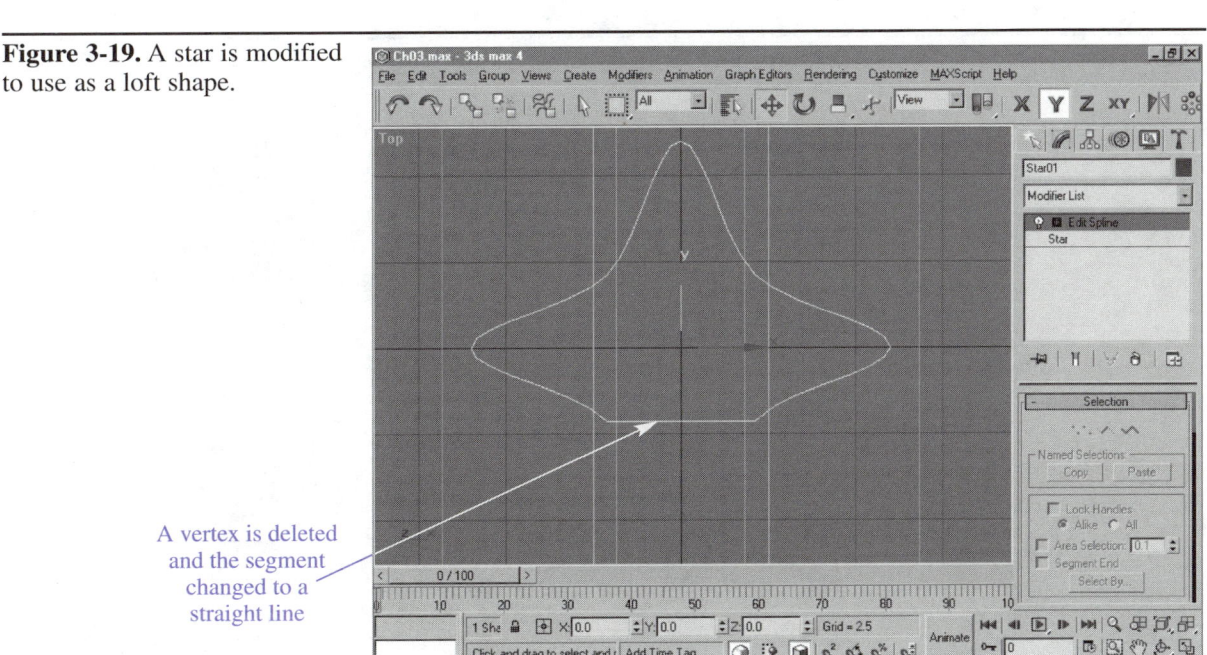

A vertex is deleted and the segment changed to a straight line

Select by Name

21. Activate the Front viewport. Pick the **Select by Name** button to display the **Select Objects** dialog box. Select the Mirror Frame ellipse.

22. Select the **Loft** button in the **Object Type** rollout. In the **Creation Method** rollout, pick the **Get Shape** button. Make sure the **Move** radio button is on. Then, pick the modified star. Name the loft object Mirror Frame Loft in the **Name and Color** rollout.
    The star is lofted along the ellipse. The "flat edge" of the star is at the back of the dresser.

23. Make sure the **Skin** check box is checked in the **Display** area of the **Skin Parameters** rollout.

24. Right-click to end the last command. Pick the **Zoom Extents All** button, Figure 3-20.

25. Save the scene.

Creating the Back Ply and the Frame Post

You will now create a back for the mirror. This is easily created using the extrude modifier. You will also create the frame post to hold the mirror frame to the dresser.

Select by Name

1. Pick **Select by Name** button to display the **Select Objects** dialog box. Select the Mirror Back ellipse, which was copied from the Mirror Frame ellipse.

2. Select **Mesh Editing** in the **Modifiers** pull-down menu. Then, select **Extrude** in the cascading menu.
   An extrude modifier is applied to the ellipse.

3. Pick **Modify** in the **Command Panel**. Make sure **Extrude** is selected in the modifier stack.
   *The rollouts for the extrude modifier are displayed in the **Modify** tab.*

4. In the **Parameters** rollout, enter 2 in the **Amount:** spinner.

Region Zoom

5. Make the Top viewport active and maximize it. Select the **Region Zoom** button. Drag a window around a small portion of the extruded ellipse and the mirror frame.

6. Pick the **Select and Move** and **Restrict to Y** buttons.

Figure 3-20. The mirror frame is created.

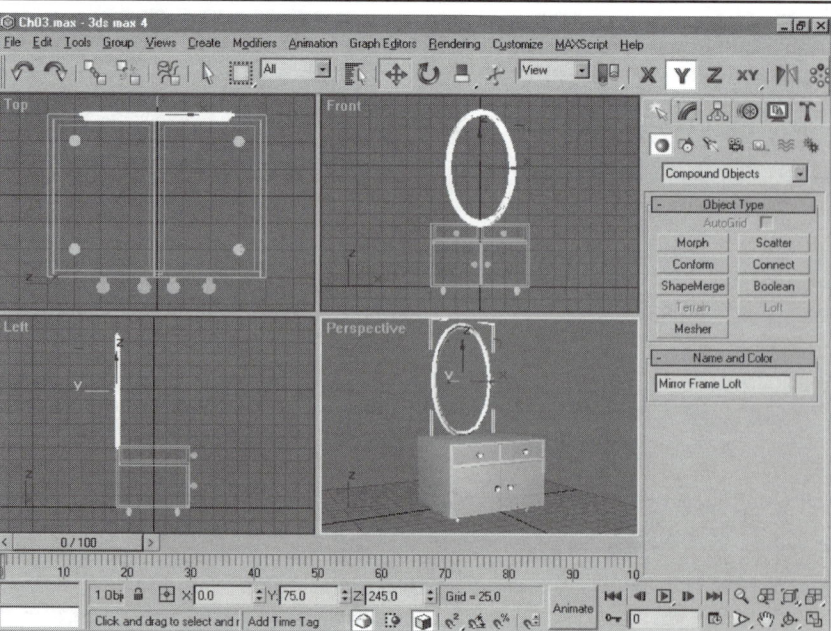

7. Move the Mirror Back object up so its lower edge aligns with the upper edge of the Mirror Frame object.

8. Select both the Mirror Back and Mirror Frame objects.

9. Move both objects so the top edge of the back aligns with the top edge of the dresser. Return to the four-viewport configuration and pick the **Zoom Extents All** button.

Create

10. With the Top viewport active, pick **Create** in the **Command Panel**. Pick the **Geometry** button and select **Standard Primitives** from the drop-down list. Pick the **Box** button in the **Object Type** rollout.

Geometry

11. In the **Keyboard Entry** rollout, enter 8 in the **Length:** spinner, 20 in the **Width:** spinner, and 150 in the **Height:** spinner. Then, pick the **Create** button. In the **Name and Color** rollout, name the box Mirror Post.

A box is created.

12. Pick the **Select and Move** button and move the post up in the Top viewport so its lower edge aligns with the top edge of the mirror back.

13. Return to the four-viewport configuration.

14. In the Front viewport, move the post up so it is centered on the dresser top.

The upper half of the post aligns with the mirror back; the lower half aligns with the dresser back.

15. Select the post, mirror frame, and mirror back.

16. Move the objects up in the Front viewport so there is a small gap between the top of the dresser and the bottom of the mirror frame, Figure 3-21.

17. Save the scene.

Creating a Bowl and Rubber Bands

You will now create a bowl placed on top of the dresser. You will also create a pair of rubber bands inside the bowl.

Figure 3-21. The mirror, mirror frame, and post are moved to their correct locations.

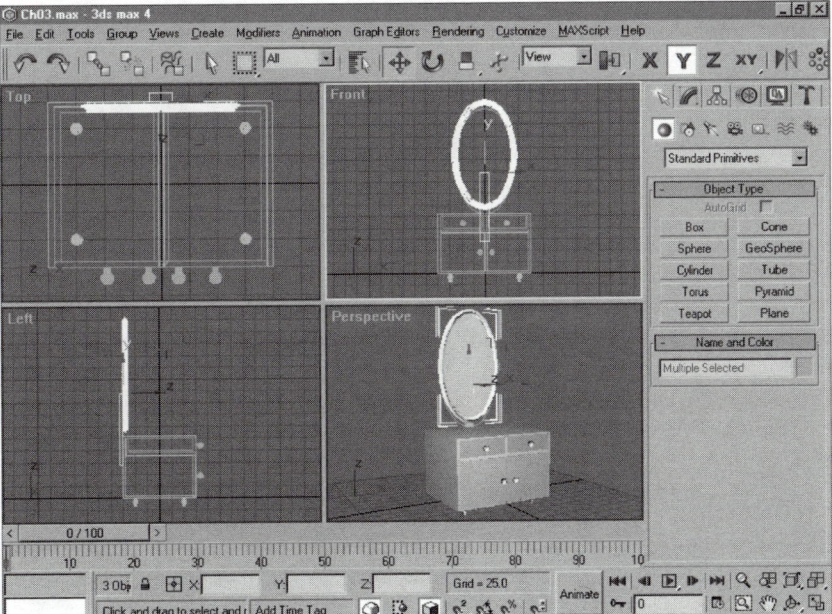

Create

Geometry

1. Activate the Top viewport.

2. Pick **Create** in the **Command Panel**. Pick the **Geometry** button and select **Standard Primitives** in the drop-down list. Pick the **Sphere** button in the **Object Type** rollout.

3. In the **Keyboard Entry** rollout, enter 20 in the **Radius:** spinner and then select the **Create** button. In the **Name and Color** rollout, name the sphere Bowl.
   A sphere is created near the bottom of the dresser.

4. With the sphere still selected, pick the **Chop** radio button in the **Parameters** rollout to turn it on. Then, enter 0.5 in the **Hemisphere:** spinner.
   The sphere is "chopped" in half.

5. Pick the **Select and Move** and **Restrict to Y** buttons. In the Left viewport move the bowl to the top of the dresser.

6. Pick the **Restrict to X** button. In the Top viewport, move the bowl to the left so it is to one side of the mirror.

Select and Rotate

Use Selection Center

7. Pick the **Select and Rotate** and **Restrict to X** buttons. Also, pick the **Use Selection Center** button from the **Use Center** flyout on the **Main** toolbar. Then, rotate the bowl 180°, Figure 3-22.

8. Activate the Front viewport. Using the **Region Zoom** button, zoom in on the bowl. Right-click to end the command. Then, maximize the viewport.

9. With the bowl selected, pick **Mesh Editing** in the **Modifiers** pull-down menu. Then, select **Edit Mesh** in the cascading menu.
   An edit mesh modifier is applied to the parametric sphere.

Modify

Vertex

10. With the bowl selected, pick **Modify** in the **Command Panel**. Make sure **Edit Mesh** is selected in the modifier stack. Then, in the **Selection** rollout, pick the **Vertex** button.
    Picking the button enters vertex sub-object editing mode, and all the vertices on the bowl are displayed as blue dots.

11. Pick the **Select and Move** and **Restrict to Y** buttons. Select the lowest vertex on the bowl, which turns red when selected. Move this vertex up so it vertically aligns with the next layer of vertices. Zoom as needed.
    The base of the bowl is flattened.

Figure 3-22. A sphere is created to use as a bowl.

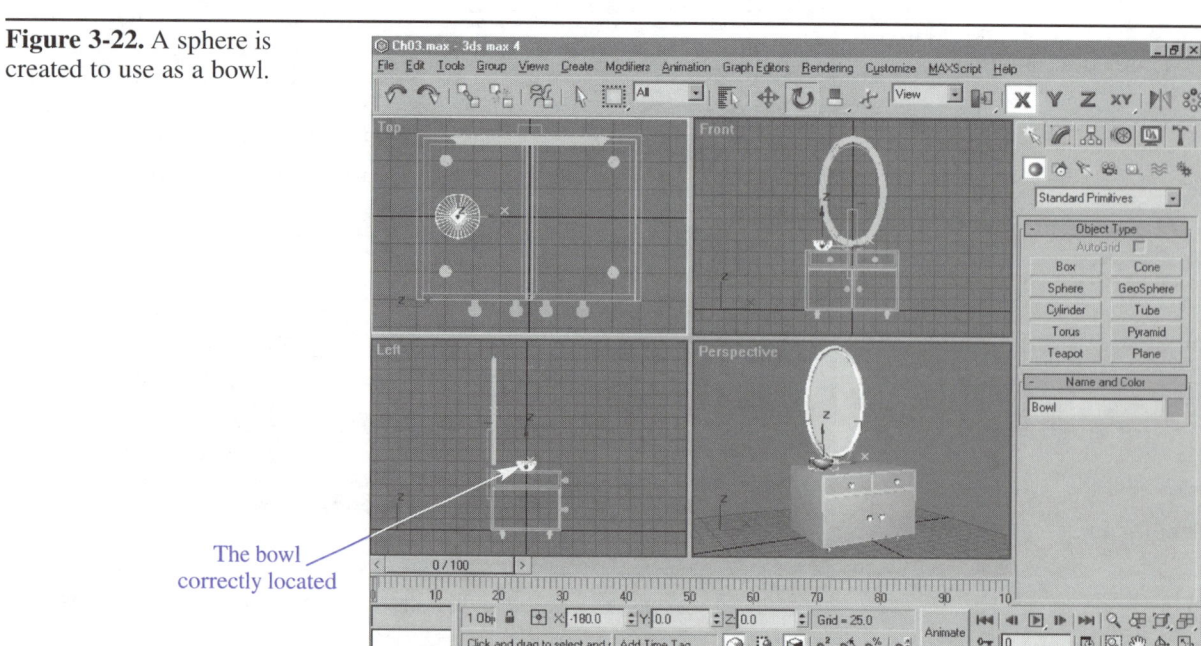

The bowl correctly located

12. Drag a window around the bottom layer of vertices to select all of them. Move these vertices up so they align with the next layer of vertices.
   The base of the bowl is flattened more.

13. Drag a window around the top layer of vertices of the bowl to select all of them. Move them down so they align with the next lower layer of vertices.

14. Select the top layer of vertices again by dragging a window around all of them. Move them down about half the distance to the next lower layer.
   A lip is formed on the bowl.

15. Now, select the top *two* layers of vertices. Move these vertices down about the same distance as the last layer.
   The bowl becomes more parabolic in shape, rather than spherical.

16. Select the top *three* layers of vertices. Move these down about the same distance as the last two layers. Pick the **Vertex** button in the **Selection** rollout to exit sub-object mode.
   The bowl is further flattened, Figure 3-23.

17. Pick the **Restrict to Y** button and then move the bowl down so it aligns with the top of the dresser.

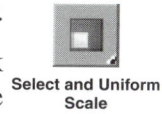
Select and Uniform Scale

18. Pick the **Select and Uniform Scale** button on the **Main** toolbar. Hold the [Shift] key down, pick on the bowl, and scale the bowl down to 96%, as indicated in the coordinate display. In the **Clone Options** dialog box, name the copy Bowl Drill and select the **OK** button.
   A small copy of the bowl is created.

Create

19. With the copy of the bowl selected, pick **Create** in the **Command Panel**. Then, pick the **Geometry** button. Select **Compound Objects** from the drop-down list. Pick the **Boolean** button in the **Object Type** rollout.

Geometry

20. In the **Parameters** rollout, pick the **Subtraction (B-A)** radio button. In the **Pick Boolean** rollout, select the **Pick Operand B** button and pick the original bowl.
   The bowl is hollowed out.

21. Return to the four-viewport configuration and select the **Zoom Extents All** button.

Figure 3-23. The sphere is modified to create a less curved bowl.

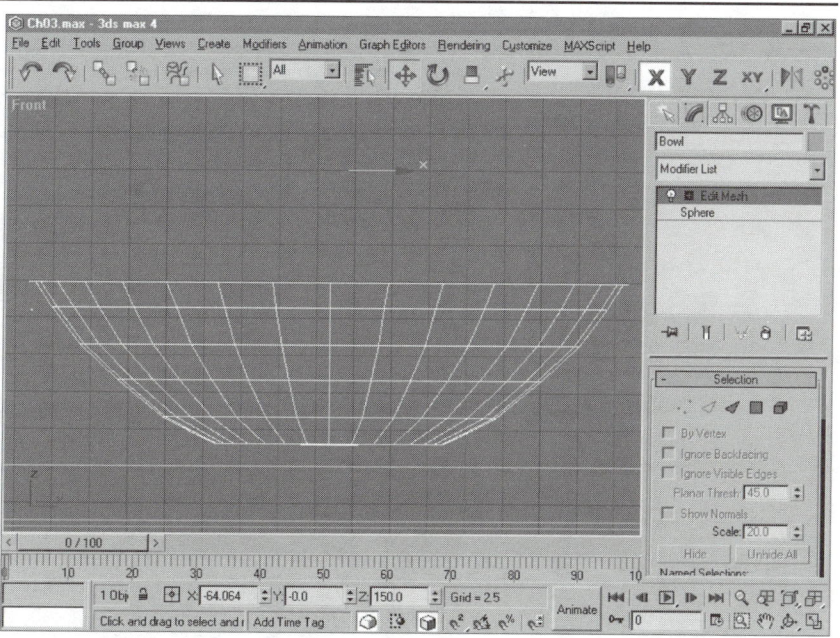

Create

Geometry

22. With the Front viewport active, pick **Create** in the **Command Panel**. Pick the **Geometry** button. Then, select **Extended Primitives** from the drop-down list.

23. Pick the **Torus Knot** button in the **Object Type** rollout. In the **Keyboard Entry** rollout, enter 3.0 in the **Major Radius:** spinner and 0.6 in the **Minor Radius:** spinner. Then, pick the **Create** button. In the **Name and Color** rollout, name the torus knot Band01.
A torus knot rubber band is created.

24. Maximize the Front viewport.

25. Pick the **Select and Move** and **Restrict to XY Plane** buttons. Move the rubber band so it is inside the bowl, Figure 3-24.

26. Pick the **Select and Rotate** and **Restrict to XY Plane** buttons. Holding the [Shift] key down, move the cursor a little down and to the left. In the **Clone Options** dialog box, enter Band02 and select the **OK** button.

27. Move Band02 to the right and place it on the base of the bowl.

28. Return to the four-viewport configuration and then select the **Zoom Extents All** button.

29. Save the scene.

Assigning Materials

In this part of the tutorial, you will select materials from the material library. Then, you will assign the materials to the objects.

Select by Name

Material Editor

Get Material

1. Use the **Select by Name** button to select the Frame, Outer, Mirror Post, and Partition objects.

2. Pick the **Material Editor** button on the **Main** toolbar to open the **Material Editor**.

3. Pick the first sample slot, if it is not already selected.

4. Pick on the **Diffuse:** color swatch. In the **Color Selector** that appears, choose a dark brown color. Then, close the **Color Selector**.

Figure 3-24. Rubber bands are added to the scene as torus knots.

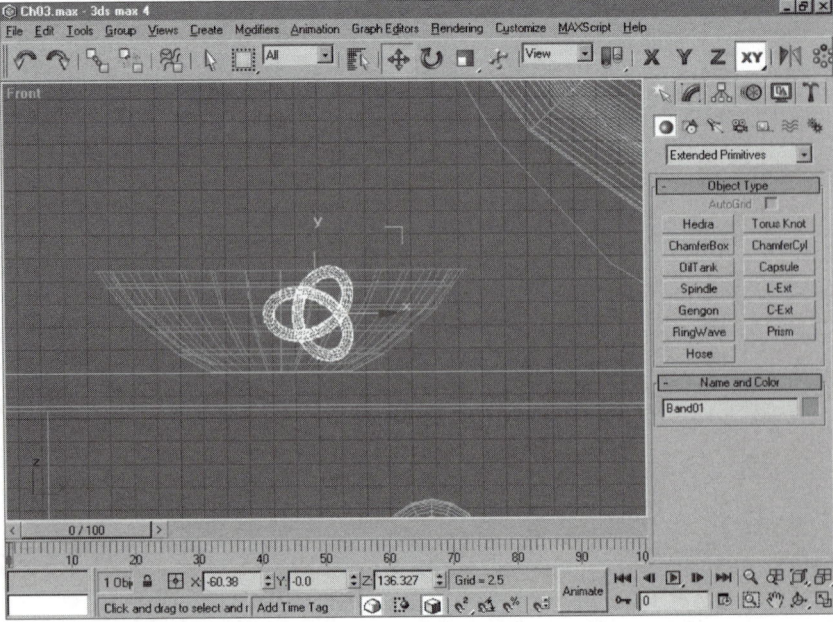

5. Pick the **Assign Material to Selection** button below the slots in the **Material Editor**.
   The material is assigned to the selected objects.

Assign Material
to Selection

6. In a similar manner, define a light tan material in an unused material sample slot. Assign it to both drawers and both doors.

7. Pick an unused material sample in the **Material Editor**. Then, pick the **Get Material** button to open the **Material/Map Browser**.

8. In the **Material/Map Browser**, pick the **Mtl Library** radio button in the **Browse From:** area.
   The materials in the 3dsmax.mat material library are displayed.

9. Double-click on the material Metal_Dark_Gold in the list. Then, select the four knobs and the four legs in the viewports. Finally, pick the **Assign Material to Selection** button.

10. In a similar manner, assign the material Metal_Galvanized to the mirror frame, Wood_Ash to the mirror back, Reflection_Sun to the bowl, and Fabric_Blue_Carpet to the two rubber bands.

11. Close the **Material/Map Browser** and the **Material Editor**.

Creating Lights and a Camera

1. Select the **Zoom All** button.

Zoom All

2. In the Top viewport, pick near the center of the objects and, holding the mouse button down, drag the cursor down until the objects are displayed about one-fourth their original size.

3. Pick **Create** in the **Command Panel**. Pick the **Cameras** button and select **Standard** in the drop-down list. Then, pick the **Target** button in the **Object Type** rollout.

Create

4. Pick in the lower-right corner of the Top viewport to position the camera. Holding the mouse button down, drag the crosshairs to the center of the objects and release to define the target point.

Cameras

5. Make the Perspective viewport active. Press the [C] key on the keyboard.
   The Perspective viewport becomes the Camera01 viewport.

6. Activate the Left viewport and pick the **Select and Move** button. Make sure **Restrict to XY Plane** is also selected.

7. Move the target up and place it in the middle of the objects. Similarly move the camera up and place it at the same level as the target.
   As you move the camera and the target, the camera viewport is dynamically updated.

8. Move the camera in the Front viewport until you get a desired view of the objects in the camera viewport, Figure 3-25.

9. Activate the Camera01 viewport. Use the **Truck Camera** button to place the objects in the center. Right-click to end the command.

Truck Camera

10. Pick **Create** in the **Command Panel**. Pick the **Lights** button and select **Standard** in the drop-down list. Then, pick the **Omni** button in the **Object Type** rollout.

Create

11. Accept the default settings and pick a point in the lower-left corner of the Top viewport.
    An omni light is placed at the point selected.

Lights

12. Pick a point near the upper-right corner of the Top viewport.
    Another omni light is placed.

13. Use the **Select and Move** button in the Front and Left viewports and move the lights to produce a desirable effect on the scene.

14. Pick the **Zoom Extents All** button.

15. Save the scene.

Figure 3-25. The camera view is adjusted.

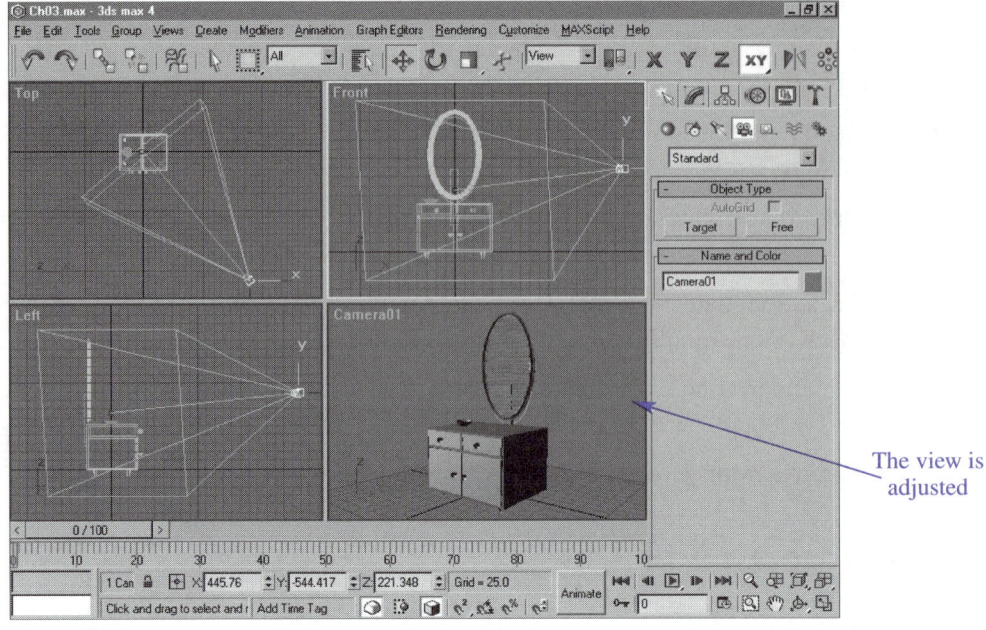

The view is
adjusted

Rendering the View

Render Scene

1. Activate the Camera01 viewport and select the **Render Scene** button on the **Main** toolbar. The **Render Scene** dialog box is opened.

2. Accept the default settings and pick the **Render** button near the bottom of the dialog box. When the rendering is complete, the image is displayed in the render window, Figure 3-26.

3. Close the render window and **Render Scene** dialog box. Save the scene.

Figure 3-26. The finished
scene is rendered.

Self-Evaluation Test

Answer the following questions. Then compare your answers with the correct answers given at the end of this chapter.

1. To use the different Boolean functions, pick **Create** in the **Command Panel**. Then, pick the **Geometry** button and select _____ from the drop-down list.

2. You can use the _____ key on the keyboard to maximize or minimize a viewport.

3. You can press _____ on the keyboard to save your work.

4. The _____ modifier is used to revolve a spline profile around an axis.

5. The _____ type of vertex has handles, and the spline into and out of the vertex is curved.

6. When you pick the **Material Editor** button on the **Main** toolbar, the _____ is displayed.

7. To change the Perspective view into a camera viewport, press the _____ key on the keyboard.

8. The _____ modifier is used to give "height" or "thickness" to a spline.

Exercises

Create the following objects using your own dimensions. Create the top, frame, and legs of the table using box standard primitives. For the frame, copy and rotate the box and then use Boolean operations as needed. Use profiles to create the jar and the lid. Add a sphere on the lid. Apply materials to the objects. Create lights and a camera. Then, render the scene.

Answers

The following are the correct answers to the questions in the Self-Evaluation Test.

1. **Compound Objects**; 2. [W]; 3. [Ctrl][S]; 4. lathe ; 5. Bézier; 6. **Material Editor**; 7. [C]; 8. extrude.

Chapter 4

Modifying Splines

Learning Objectives

After completing this chapter, you will be able to:

○ Create 2D shapes.
○ Modify vertices and segments.
○ Modify the spline.
○ Change Bézier splines.
○ Lock Bézier handles.
○ Create and adjust splines.
○ Work with coordinate centers.

Tutorial Description

In this tutorial, you will create a display sign for a company that includes a name and logo. The logo is created from 2D shapes, such as lines, circles, rectangles, and arcs. You will need to modify the vertices and segments of the spline shapes. You will also modify the shapes with respect to coordinate centers.

Resetting the System

First reset the 3ds max. This sets the system to default values and erases all existing data. If you want to save the existing file, make sure you do so before resetting 3ds max.

1. Select **Reset** from the **File** pull-down menu.
   A dialog box is displayed on the screen asking you whether you really want to reset.

2. Select the **Yes** button in the dialog box or press the [Y] key.
   The system is reset.

Creating 2D Shapes

Min/Max Toggle

2D Snap Toggle

Create

Shapes

Zoom Extents

You will first create 2D shapes. These shapes are created as splines in the form of polygons.

1. Activate the Top viewport and select the **Min/Max Toggle** button.
   The Top viewport is maximized. You can also use the [W] key to maximize the viewport.

2. Select the **2D Snap Toggle** button in the snap flyout.
   The cursor will snap to the default snap setting, which is grid points.

3. Pick **Create** tab in the **Command Panel**, then select the **Shapes** button. Select **Splines** from the drop-down list.

4. Pick the **Rectangle** button in the **Object Type** rollout.
   All the rollouts for a rectangle are displayed. These include the **Name and Color**, **Rendering**, **Interpolation**, **Creation Method**, **Keyboard Entry**, and **Parameters** rollouts.

5. Select a point on the lower-left corner of the screen at coordinates –100, –100, 0, as shown in the coordinated display. Then, drag the cursor upwards and to the right to coordinates 80, 0, 0. Release the mouse button.
   A rectangle named Rectangle01 is created in the Top viewport.

6. Select the **Zoom Extents** button.
   The rectangle is zoomed to its extents.

7. With the **Rectangle** button selected in **Object Type** rollout, pick a point at coordinates –90, –10, 0. Then, drag the cursor down and to the right to coordinates –30, –40, 0.
   A rectangle named Rectangle02 is created in the top left corner of Rectangle01, Figure 4-1.

8. Save the scene as Ch04.max in the folder of your choice.

Figure 4-1. Two rectangles are created.

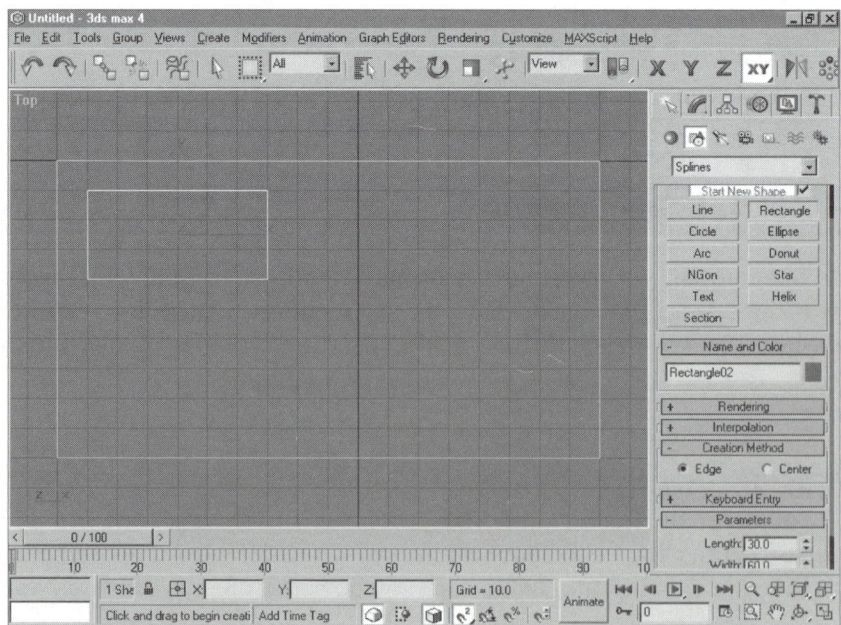

Modifying Vertices

1. With Rectangle02 selected, pick <u>P</u>atch/Spline Editing in the M<u>o</u>difiers pull-down menu. Then, pick **Edit Spline** in the cascading menu.
    An edit spline modifier is applied to the parametric rectangle shape.

Modify

2. Pick **Modify** in the **Command Panel**. With **Edit Spline** selected in the modifier stack, pick the **Vertex** button in the **Selection** rollout.
    Picking the button enters vertex sub-object mode.

Vertex

3. Right-click on lower-right vertex of Rectangle02 to display the quad menu.

4. In the upper-left quadrant of the quad menu, select **Smooth**.
    The vertex is changed to a smooth type vertex, and the shape is curved into and out of the vertex.

5. Similarly, change the upper-left corner of Rectangle02 to a smooth type vertex.
    The shape is curved into and out of the upper-left vertex, Figure 4-2.

6. Pick the **Vertex** button in the **Selection** rollout to exit sub-object mode.

7. Save the scene.

Modifying Bézier Vertices

There are two types of Bézier vertices—Bézier and Bézier corner. You can use the Bézier handles on either of these two types to change the shape of the spline leading into and out of the vertex.

Modify

1. With Rectangle02 selected, pick **Modify** in the **Command Panel**. With **Edit Spline** selected in the modifier stack, pick the **Vertex** button on the **Selection** rollout.
    Picking the button enters vertex sub-object mode.

Vertex

2. Pick the **Select and Move** and **Restrict to XY Plane** buttons on the **Main** toolbar.

Select and Move

Figure 4-2. Two of the vertices on the small rectangle have been edited.

Restrict to XY Plane

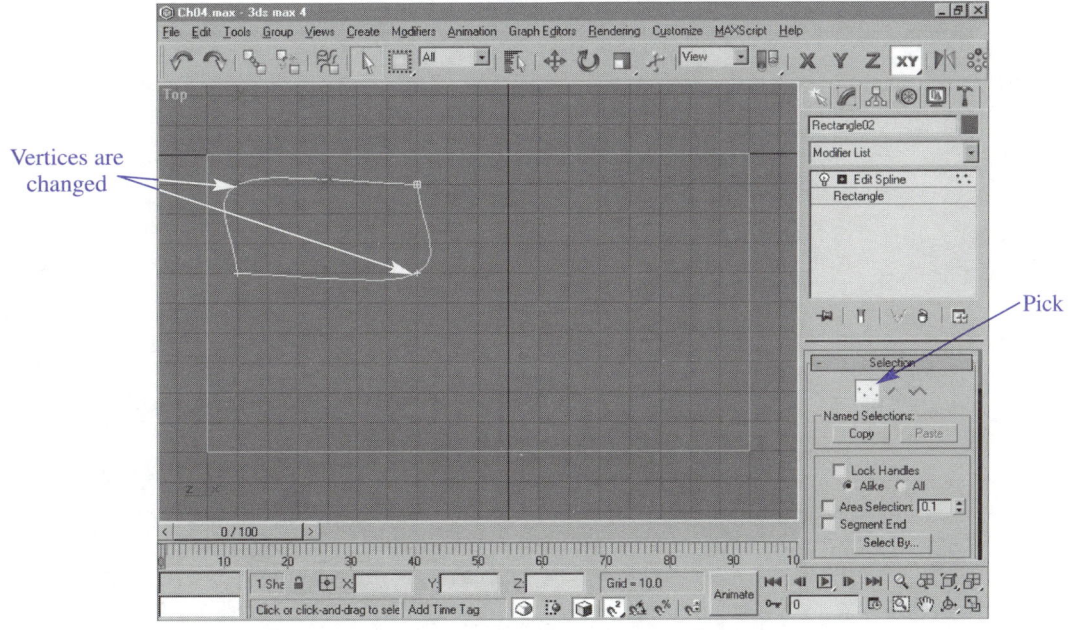

Vertices are changed

Pick

3. Pick the upper-right vertex of Rectangle02 to select it.
   The two Bézier handles (green squares) are displayed at the vertex. They are perpendicular to each other. Since they are not in the same line, this indicates the vertex is Bézier corner. The handles work independent of each other.

4. Select the Bézier handle (green square) on the top and, while holding the mouse button down, drag the cursor down until the coordinate display shows 0, –10, 0.
   The curve shape is modified.

5. Select the Bézier handle on the right. Move it down and to the left until the coordinate display shows –10, –10, 0.
   The curve is further modified.

6. Select the lower left vertex of Rectangle02.
   The two Bézier handles are displayed at the vertex.

7. Select the Bézier handle at the bottom and move it until the coordinate display shows –10, 10, 0. You will need to zoom in so you are not picking on the transform gizmo, but rather picking the handle itself.
   The curve is modified.

8. Select the Bézier handle on the left and move it until the coordinate display shows 10, 10, 0. If you are zoomed in on the vertex, pick the **Zoom Extents** button.
   The curve is further modified, Figure 4-3.

9. Now, right-click on the upper right vertex to display the quad menu. Select **Bezier** in the upper-left quadrant.
   The two Bézier handles are displayed. They are in a straight line, indicating the vertex is a Bézier vertex. Moving one handle affects the other handle.

10. Select the lower handle (green square). Move it up and to the right until the coordinate display shows 10, 30, 0.
    The curve is modified. If you press the [Shift] key while moving a Bézier handle, the Bézier vertex is converted into a Bézier corner vertex.

11. Similarly, convert the lower left vertex into a Bézier vertex.
    The two vector handles are displayed in a straight line.

Figure 4-3. Using Bézier handles to adjust the vertex.

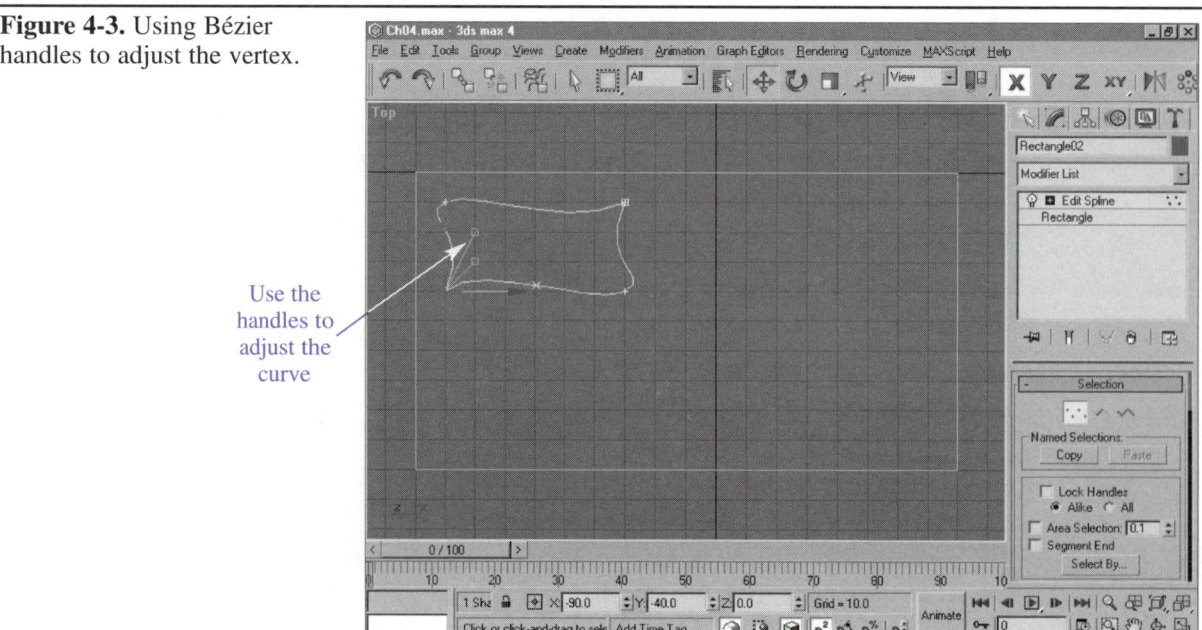

Use the handles to adjust the curve

Figure 4-4. Editing a vertex.

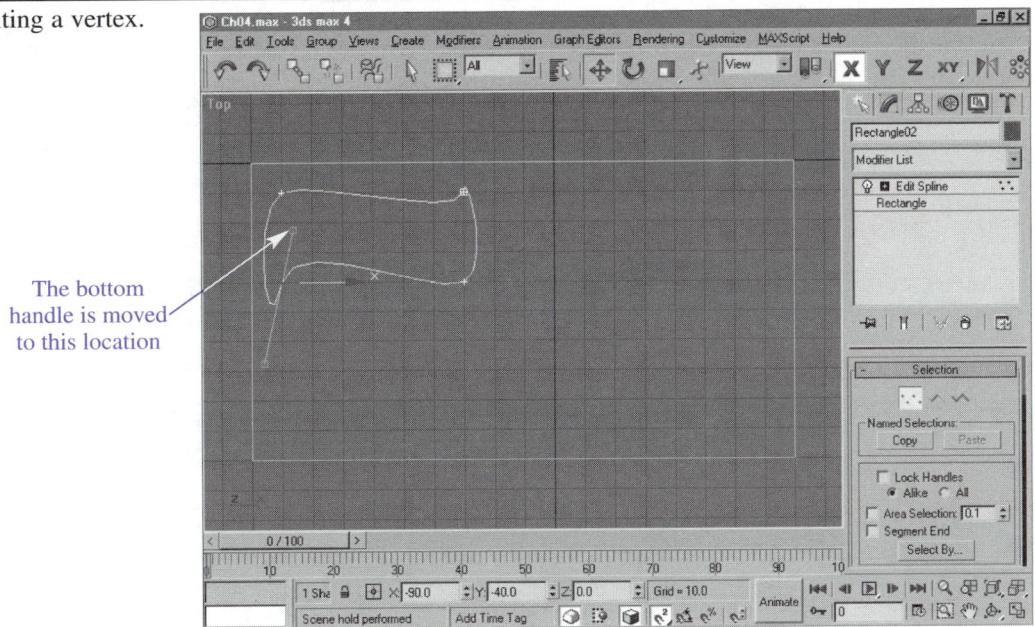

The bottom handle is moved to this location

12. Select the handle at the bottom. Move it up and to the right until the coordinate display shows approximately 10, 30, 0. You do not need to get the exact coordinates.
    The curve is further modified, Figure 4-4.

13. Pick the **Vertex** button in the **Selection** rollout to exit sub-object mode.

14. Save the scene.

Creating an Ellipse

1. Select the **Region Zoom** button and drag a window around Rectangle02 to zoom in on it.

2. Pick **Create** in the **Command Panel**. Then, pick the **Shapes** button and select **Splines** from the drop-down list.

3. Select the **Ellipse** button in the **Object Type** rollout.
   The rollouts for an ellipse are displayed.

4. Select any point within Rectangle02, drag the cursor to any other point, and release the mouse button.
   An ellipse is created within Rectangle02.

5. With the ellipse still selected, enter a value of 12 in the **Length:** spinner and a value of 35 in the **Width:** spinner in the **Parameters** rollout.
   The parameters of the ellipse are changed.

6. Turn off snap.

7. Pick the **Select and Move** and the **Restrict to XY Plane** buttons on the **Main** toolbar. Move the ellipse (Ellipse01) and place it in the center of Rectangle02, Figure 4-5.

8. Save the scene.

Region Zoom

Create

Shapes

Figure 4-5. An ellipse is created inside the small rectangle.

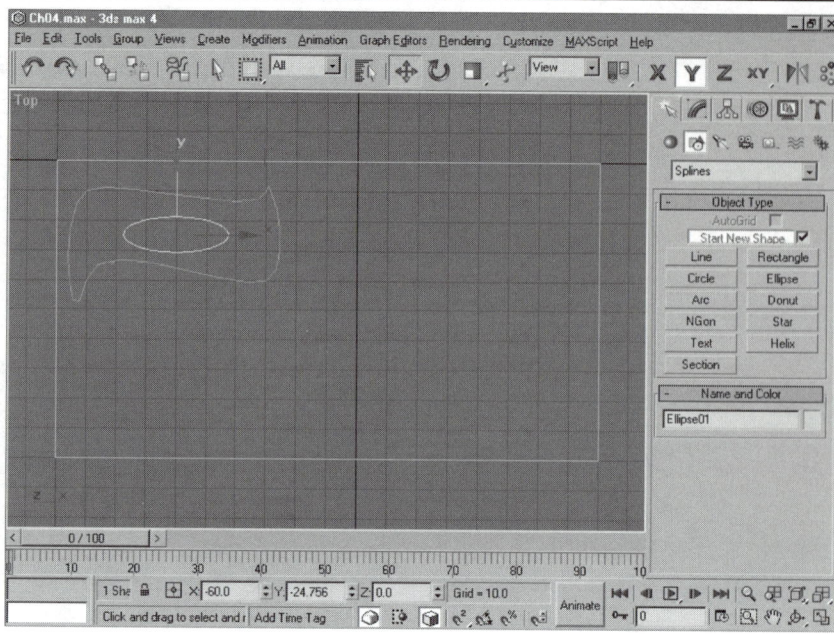

Locking Handles

The two handles at a Bézier or Bézier corner vertex lead into and out of the vertex. You can modify the handles of vertices separately, as discussed earlier. It is also possible to lock the handles of all selected vertices, and then affect the segments associated with them in the same manner.

When the **Alike** option is active, moving a single Bézier handle moves all Bézier handles that are similar to the one selected. When the **All** option is active, all Bézier handles move in a similar manner.

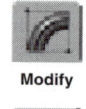

Modify

Vertex

1. With Ellipse01 selected, pick **Patch/Spline Editing** in the **Modifiers** pull-down menu. Then, select **Edit Spline** in the cascading menu.
   An edit spline modifier is applied to the parametric ellipse.

2. Pick **Modify** in the **Command Panel**. Make sure **Edit Spline** is selected in the modifier stack. Then, pick the **Vertex** button in the **Selection** rollout.
   Picking the button enters vertex sub-object mode.

3. Select all the vertices of Ellipse01 by dragging a window around the entire shape.
   Bézier handles are displayed at all the vertices.

4. In the **Selection** rollout, check the **Lock Handles** check box. Also, pick the **All** radio button.

5. Make sure the **Select and Move** button is selected on the **Main** toolbar. Also, select the **Restrict to Y** button.

6. Select the upper handle of the vertex on the right and drag it up until the Y value in the coordinate display is about 9.
   All the vertices in the ellipse are modified at the same time, Figure 4-6.

7. Pick the **Vertex** button in the **Selection** rollout to exit sub-object mode.

8. Save the scene.

Figure 4-6. All vertices of the ellipse are transformed in the same way at the same time.

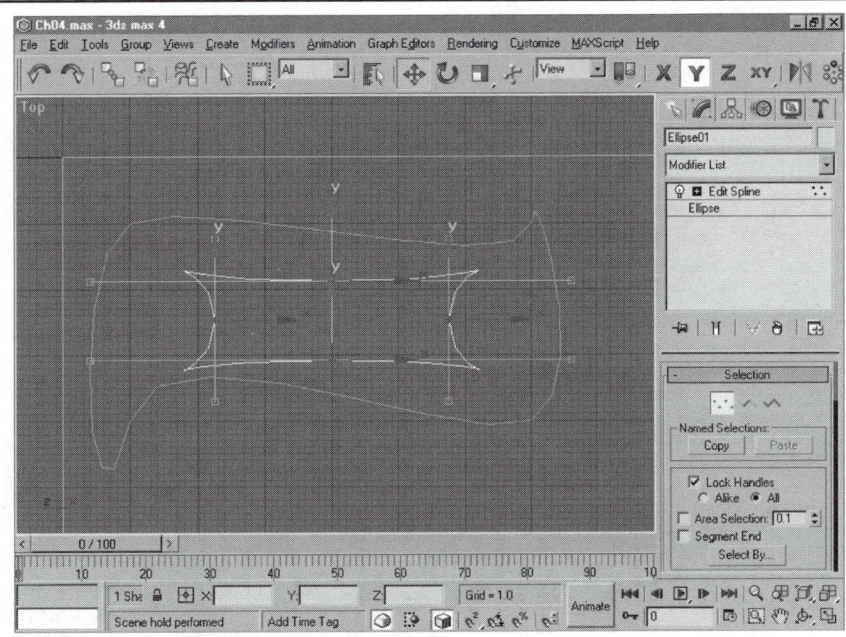

Creating and Adjusting Splines

1. Maximize the Top viewport, if not already. Use the **Zoom** button and zoom in on the modified ellipse until the next "set" of grid lines is displayed. Right-click to end the command.

2. Pick **Create** in the **Command Panel**. Pick the **Shapes** button and select **Splines** in the drop-down list. Also, select the **2D Snap Toggle** button to turn snap on.

3. Pick the **Star** button in the **Object Type** rollout. In the **Parameters** rollout, set the **Points:** spinner to 6.

4. Pick a point at coordinates –82, –18, 0 and then drag the cursor up to coordinates –82, –12, 0. Release the mouse button and move the cursor down until the coordinate display shows –82, –15, 0. Pick to set the inner radius. Pan if needed before picking the first point.
   A star named Star01 is created near the upper-left corner of Ellipse01, Figure 4-7.

5. Pick the **Select and Move** button on the **Main** toolbar. Also, select the **Restrict to XY Plane** button.

6. With Star01 selected, pick **Patch/Spline Editing** in the **Modifiers** pull-down menu. Then, pick **Edit Spline** from the cascading menu.
   An edit spline modifier is applied to the parametric star shape.

7. With the star selected, pick **Modify** in the **Command Panel**. Make sure **Edit Spline** is selected in the modifier stack. Then, pick the **Segment** button in the **Selection** rollout.

8. Select one of the two segments of Star01 that lie within the modified ellipse. Hold the [Ctrl] key and select the other segment of Star01 that lies within the ellipse. Refer to Figure 4-7.
   These segments turn red indicating they are selected.

9. Pick the **Delete** button in the **Geometry** rollout. You can also press the [Delete] key on the keyboard.
   The two selected segments are removed from the spline.

10. Pick the **Segment** button to exit sub-object mode. Also, turn off snap.

Zoom

Create

Shapes

Modify

Segment

Figure 4-7. A star is created. Take note of the two segments which will be deleted.

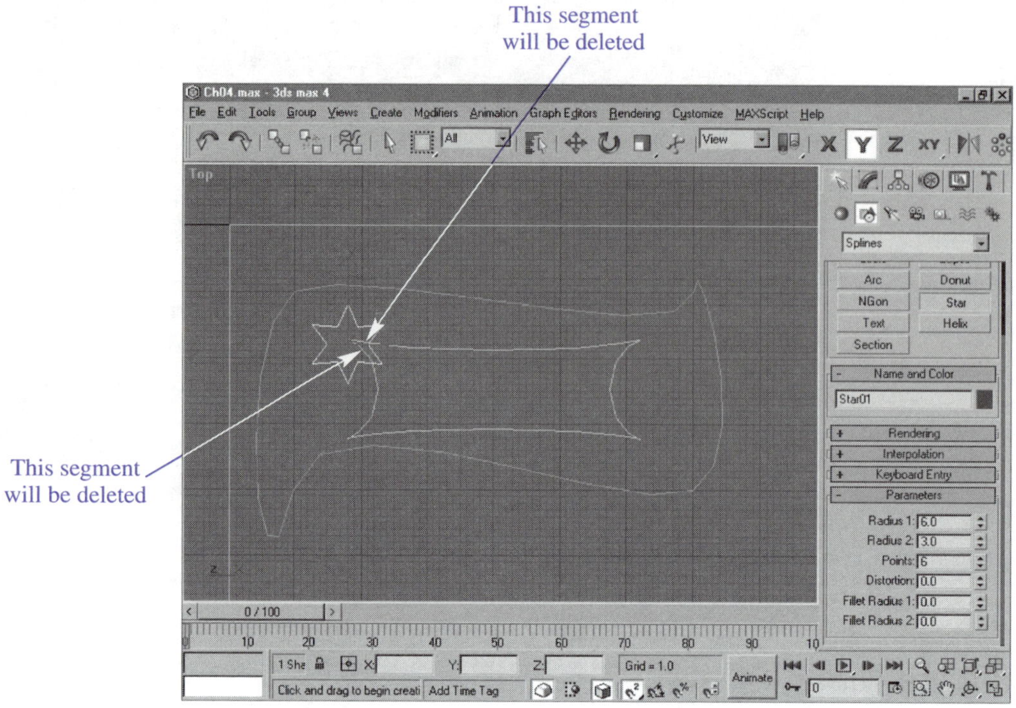

11. Pick the **Select and Move** and **Restrict to XY Plane** buttons on the **Main** toolbar. Move Star01 right so its open ends meet the sides of Ellipse01 exactly. Zoom as needed.

12. Pick **Create** in the **Command Panel**. Pick the **Shapes** button and select **Splines** from the drop-down list.

13. Select the **Text** button in the **Object Type** rollout.
    The rollouts for a text object are displayed.

14. In the **Parameters** rollout, enter 8 in the **Size:** spinner. The text MAX Text appears in the **Text:** edit box, which is used for this activity. Also, make sure **Arial** is displayed in the font drop-down list at the top of the **Parameters** rollout.

15. Pick any point inside Ellipse01.
    The text is placed, and the object is named Text01.

16. Pick the **Select and Move** button and move the text to place it almost in the center of Ellipse01, Figure 4-8.

17. Save the scene.

Using the [Shift] Key

You can use the [Shift] key with the transform commands to make a copy of the original object. The copy is transformed, while the original object remains in its same location and orientation.

1. Activate the Top viewport and maximize it, if it is not already. Then, pick the **Zoom Extents** button.

2. Pick the **Region Zoom** button and zoom in on about 1/4 of Rectangle01 at the upper-right corner of the rectangle. Make sure a portion of the top and right sides of Rectangle01 are displayed.

Figure 4-8. Text is placed in the center of the edited ellipse.

3. Pick **Create** in the **Command Panel**. Then, pick the **Shapes** button and select **Spline** from the drop-down list. Pick the **Rectangle** button in the **Object Type** rollout.
   Rollouts for a rectangle are displayed.

Create

4. Pick the **2D Snap Toggle** button to turn snap on.

Shapes

5. Pick a point inside Rectangle01 at coordinates 70, –10, 0 as shown in the coordinate display. Drag the cursor down to coordinates 40, –40, 0 and release the mouse button.
   A rectangle named Rectangle03 is created in the upper-right corner of Rectangle01. The rectangle is a 30 unit by 30 unit square.

6. Name the rectangle Square in the **Name and Color** rollout.

7. Turn snap off.

8. Pick the **Select and Rotate** button in the **Main Toolbar**. Make sure that the **Restrict to Z** button is also selected.

Select and Rotate

9. Pick the **Use Pivot Point Center** button in the transform center flyout on the **Main** toolbar.
   This flyout is located to the right of the **Restrict to X** button on the **Main** toolbar. When the **Use Pivot Point Center** button is selected, the selected objects are transformed about their individual pivot points. If you pick the **Use Selection Center** button in the flyout, the selected objects are transformed about the center of the selection set.

Restrict to Z

Use Pivot Point Center

10. Hold the [Shift] key down and rotate the square 45º, as shown in the coordinate display. Release the mouse button and the [Shift] key.
    The **Clone Options** dialog box is displayed.

11. In the **Clone Options** dialog box, name the copy Square 45 deg and pick the **OK** button.
    A copy of the square is created at 45º to the original, Figure 4-9.

12. Pick the **Select and Uniform Scale** button and the **Restrict to XY Plane** button on the **Main** toolbar.

Select and Uniform Scale

13. Drag a window around both the squares to select them.

14. Hold down the [Shift] key on the keyboard, pick on the selection, and drag the cursor down until the coordinate display shows 50%, 50%, 50%.
    The **Clone Options** dialog box is displayed.

15. Select **OK** in the **Clone Options** dialog box to accept the default names.

    A copy of Square and Square 45 deg are scaled to half the original size, Figure 4-10.

16. Display the four-viewport configuration and pick the **Zoom Extents All** button.

17. Save the scene.

Figure 4-9. A copy of the square is rotated 45°.

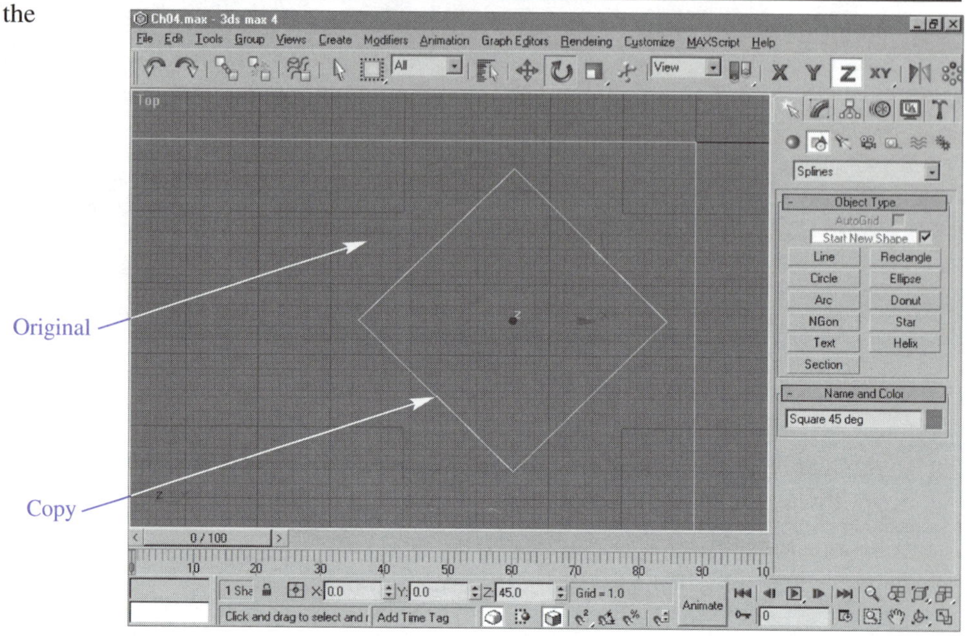

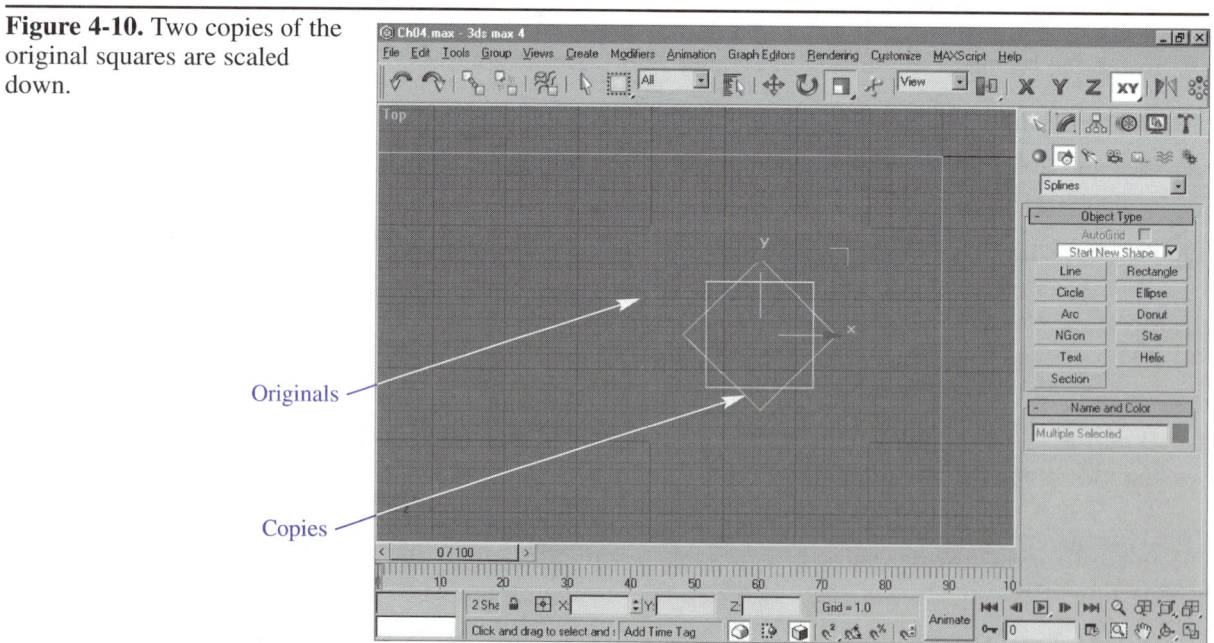

Figure 4-10. Two copies of the original squares are scaled down.

Creating and Adjusting Splines

1. Maximize the Top viewport. Then, use the **Region Zoom** button to zoom in on the squares. Select the **2D Snap Toggle** button to turn snap on.

2. Pick **Create** in the **Command Panel**, then select the **Shapes** button. Pick **Splines** from the drop-down list.

Create

Shapes

3. Pick the **NGon** button in the **Object Type** rollout.
   Rollouts for an ngon are displayed. An ngon is a regular polygon with the number of sides you set.

4. In the **Parameters** rollout, enter 8 in the **Sides:** spinner.

5. Select a point at coordinates 55, –25, 0. This is the center of the squares. Drag the cursor up to coordinates 55, –18, 0.
   An eight-sided ngon (octagon) is created at the center of the squares, Figure 4-11. The default name is NGon01.

6. With NGon01 selected, select **Patch/Spline Editing** in the **Modifiers** pull-down menu. Then, pick **Edit Spline** in the cascading menu.
   An edit spline modifier is applied to the parametric ngon.

7. With NGon01 selected, pick **Modify** in the **Command Panel**. Make sure **Edit Spline** is selected in the modifier stack.

Modify

8. Pick the **Segment** button in the **Selection** rollout to enter segment sub-object editing mode.

Segment

9. Select the first three segments clockwise from the top vertex. You may want to turn snap off. You can drag a window to select all three segments, or use the [Ctrl] key to pick them one at a time.
   The selected segments turn red, indicating they are selected.

10. Pick the **Delete** button in the **Geometry** rollout or press the [Delete] key on the keyboard.
    The selected segments are removed from the ngon. It is now an "open" spline.

11. Pick the **Spline** button in the **Selection** rollout to enter spline sub-object editing mode.

Spline

12. Pick anywhere on NGon01.
    The entire ngon turns red, indicating it is selected.

Figure 4-11. An ngon is created..

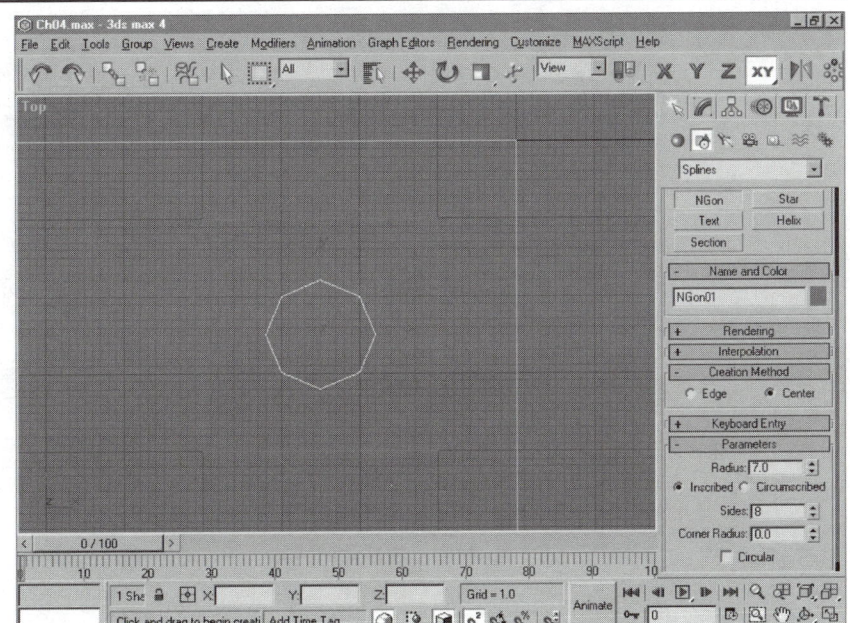

13. Pick the **Close** button in the **Geometry** rollout.
The open end of the spline is closed by adding a curved segment between the vertices, Figure 4-12.

14. Pick the **Spline** button in the **Selection** rollout to exit sub-object mode.

15. Pick the **Select and Rotate** button on the **Main** toolbar Also pick the **Restrict to Z** button.

16. Rotate the ngon until the Z value in the coordinate display is –112.5.
The spline is rotated –112.5 degrees around its Z axis. The top "flat" of the ngon is parallel to the world X axis.

17. Display the four-viewport configuration and pick the **Zoom Extents All** button.

18. Save the scene.

Creating and Adjusting Splines

1. With the ngon selected, enter vertex sub-object editing mode. Also, turn snap on.

2. Pick the **Insert** button in the **Geometry** rollout.

3. Move the cursor and place it on the middle of the angled segment on the left.
The cursor changes to the "insert" cursor.

4. Pick and release the mouse button. Move the cursor to the coordinates 55, –25, 0 and pick. Right-click to end the command.
After the first pick, the new vertex is "attached" to the cursor and the segment bends as you move the cursor. The new vertex is placed when you pick again, as you did in the center of the ngon.

5. Move the cursor again and place it on the middle of the angled segment on the right. Pick and release the mouse button. Move the cursor to coordinates 55, –25, 0 and pick. Right-click to end the command.
The ngon is reshaped and begins to appear similar to a three-leaf clover.

Figure 4-12. The ngon is edited.

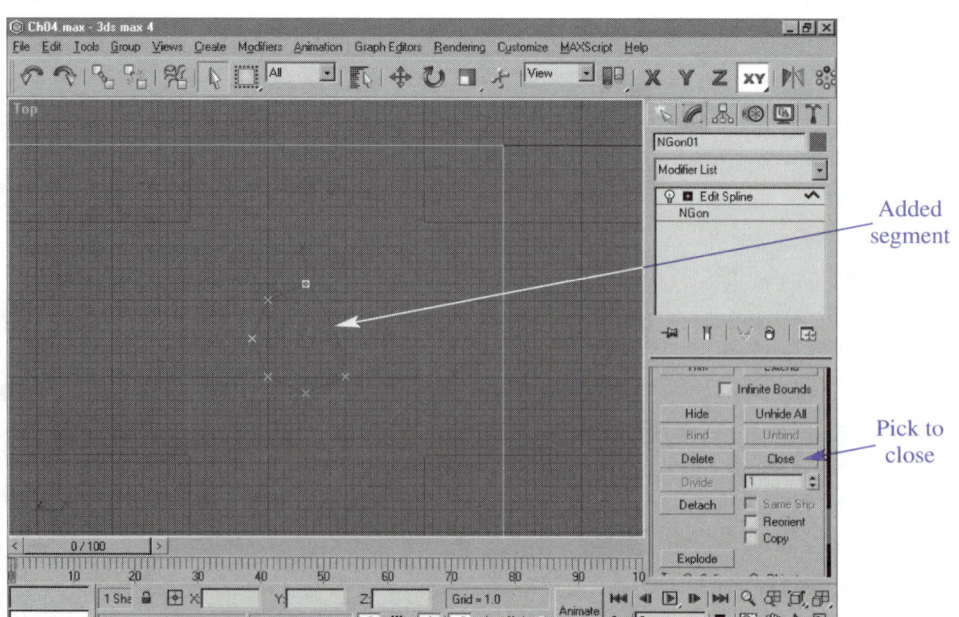

Added segment

Pick to close

6. Move the cursor again and place it on the middle of the curved segment at the bottom. Pick and release the mouse button. Move the cursor to coordinates 55, –25, 0 and pick. Right-click to end the command.
   The ngon is reshaped and more closely resembles a three-leaf cover, Figure 4-13.

7. Pick the **Vertex** button in the **Selection** rollout to exit sub-object mode. Leave the display zoomed in on the ngon and save the scene.

Creating and Modifying a Spline

Create

Shapes

1. Pick **Create** in the **Command Panel**. Pick the **Shapes** button and select **Splines** in the drop-down list. Turn snap on, if it is not already.

2. Pick the **Rectangle** button in the **Object Type** rollout.

3. Pick near the center of Ngon01 at coordinates 54, –26, 0. Drag the cursor down to coordinates 55, –32, 0. In the **Name and Color** rollout, name the rectangle Stem.
   A rectangle is created to be used as the stem of the clover.

4. Pick the **Select and Move** button on the **Main** toolbar. Also pick the **Restrict to XY Plane** button.

5. With Stem selected, pick **Patch/Spline Editing** in the **Modifiers** pull-down menu. Then, pick **Edit Spline** in the cascading menu.
   An edit spline modifier is applied to the parametric rectangle.

6. With Stem selected, pick **Modify** in the **Command Panel**. Make sure **Edit Spline** is selected in the modifier stack. Then, pick the **Vertex** button in the **Selection** rollout.
   Picking the button enters vertex sub-object editing mode.

7. Select the vertex on the lower-right corner of Stem and move it to the right until the coordinate display shows 1, 0, 0.

8. Similarly, move the lower-left vertex to the left until the coordinate display shows –1, 0, 0.
   The base of the stem is made thicker.

Figure 4-13. The ngon is edited and transformed to resemble clover leaves.

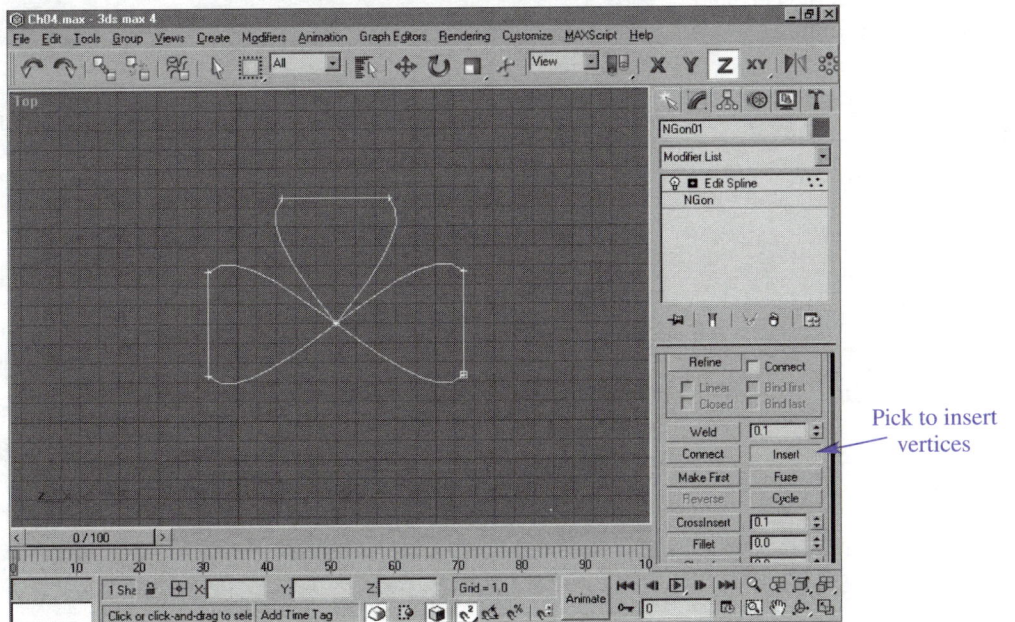

Pick to insert vertices

9. Select the upper-right vertex of Stem.

   The two Bézier handles are displayed at a right angle, indicating the vertex is a Bézier corner vertex.

10. Move the lower handle slightly to the left. You may want to turn snap off.

    The right side of the stem is curved.

11. Select the upper-left vertex of Stem.

    The two Bézier handles are displayed at a right angle, indicating the vertex is a Bézier corner vertex.

12. Move the lower handle slightly to the right.

    The left side of the stem is curved.

13. Pick the **Vertex** button in the **Selection** rollout to exit sub-object mode.

14. Pick the **Select and Move** and **Restrict to X** buttons on the **Main** toolbar. Move Stem to the right so it is in the center of the ngon "leaves," Figure 4-14.

15. Display the four-viewport configuration and pick the **Zoom Extents All** button. Save the scene.

Creating More Text

Create

Shapes

1. Pick **Create** in the **Command Panel**. Pick the **Shapes** button and select Splines from the drop-down list.

2. Pick the **Text** button in the **Object Type** rollout.

3. In the **Parameters** rollout, type My Own Company in the **Text:** edit box.

4. Enter 25 in the **Size:** spinner.

5. In the fonts drop-down list, select a script-style font. If one is not installed on your machine, select Arial as the font.

6. Turn snap on. Maximize the Top viewport, and pick at coordinates –10, –80, 0.

   The text is placed, Figure 4-15.

7. Leave the Top viewport maximized and save the scene.

Figure 4-14. A stem is created by editing a rectangle.

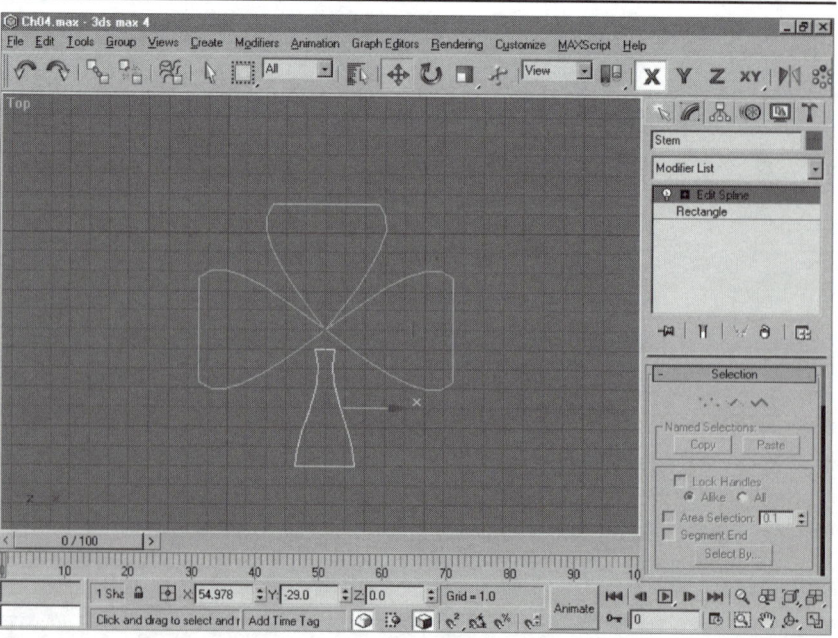

Figure 4-15. More text is added to the scene.

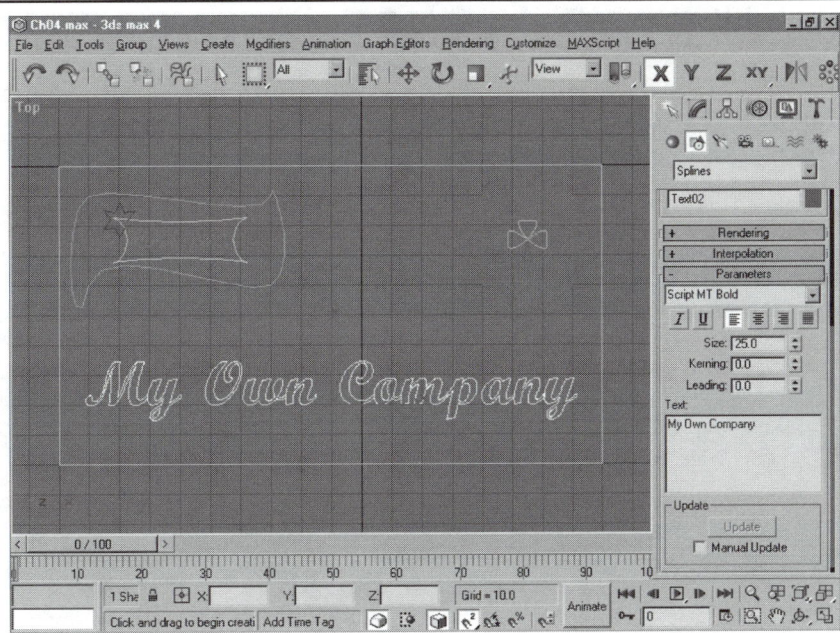

Creating and Copying an Arc

Create

1. Pick **Create** in the **Command Panel**. Pick the **Shapes** button and select **Splines** from the drop-down list.

Shapes

2. Pick the **Arc** button in the **Object Type** rollout. Turn snap on.
   The rollouts for an arc are displayed.

3. With the Top viewport maximized, pick a point at coordinates –50, –70, 0 as shown in the coordinate display. Drag the cursor to coordinates 0, –70, 0.

4. Release the pick button of the mouse and move the cursor up and to the left to coordinates –20, –50, 0 and pick.
   An arc is created above the text. The default name is Arc01.

Select and Uniform Scale

5. Pick the **Select and Uniform Scale** button in the **Main** toolbar. Make sure the **Restrict to XY Plane** button is also selected. Turn snap off.

6. Hold down the [Shift] key and scale down the arc to 90%, as shown in the coordinate display.
   The **Clone Options** dialog box is displayed.

7. Pick the **OK** button in the **Clone Options** dialog box to accept the default name for the copy.
   A smaller copy of Arc01 is created. It is assigned the default name Arc02, Figure 4-16.

8. Leave the Top viewport maximized and save the scene.

Creating and Modifying a Circle

1. Pick the **Region Zoom** button and drag a window around the arcs.

2. Turn snap on.

Create

3. Pick **Create** in the **Command Panel**. Pick the **Shapes** button and select **Splines** from the drop-down list. Pick the **Circle** button in the **Object Type** rollout.
   The rollouts for a circle are displayed.

Shapes

Figure 4-16. An arc and a scaled down copy are added to the scene.

4. Select a point at coordinates –25, –61, 0 and drag the cursor up to coordinates –25, –55, 0. Release the mouse button.
   A circle is created.

5. With the circle selected, pick **Patch/Spline Editing** in the **Modifiers** pull-down menu. Then, pick **Edit Spline** in the cascading menu.

Modify

6. With the circle selected, pick **Modify** in the **Command Panel**. Make sure **Edit Spline** is selected in the modifier stack. Then, pick the **Vertex** button in the **Selection** rollout to enter sub-object mode.

7. Right-click on the left-hand vertex to display the quad menu. Select **Corner** from the upper-left quadrant.
   The spline is no longer curved as in enters and leaves the vertex.

8. Similarly, convert the right-hand vertex to a corner vertex.

9. Pick the **Select and Move** and **Restrict to XY Plane** buttons on the **Main** toolbar. Select the left-hand vertex and move it left until the coordinate display shows –1, 0, 0.

10. Similarly, move the right-hand vertex to the right until the coordinate display shows 1, 0, 0.
    The circle is pointed on the left and right sides, Figure 4-17.

11. Pick the **Vertex** button in the **Selection** rollout to exit sub-object mode.

12. Leave the Top viewport maximized and save the scene.

Creating a Donut

Create

Shapes

1. Pick **Create** in the **Command Panel**. Pick the **Shapes** button and select **Splines** from the drop-down list.

2. Turn snap on. Pick the **Donut** button in the **Object Type** rollout.
   The rollouts for a donut are displayed.

3. Pick a point at coordinates –25, –61, 0. Drag the cursor up to coordinates –25, –57, 0 and release the mouse button.

Figure 4-17. The circle is pointed on the sides.

Figure 4-18. A donut is created in the middle of the edited circle.

4. Next, move the cursor down and pick at coordinates –25, –59, 0.
   A donut is created in the center of the circle, Figure 4-18.

5. Leave the Top viewport maximized and save the scene.

Creating Lines

Create

Shapes

1. Pick the **Zoom All** button. Turn snap on.

2. Pick **Create** in the **Command Panel**. Pick the **Shapes** button and select **Splines** from the drop-down list. Then, pick the **Line** button in the **Object Type** rollout.

3. Pick a point at coordinates –90, –90, 0.

4. Select the next point at coordinates 70, –80, 0.

5. Select the next point at coordinates –10, –90, 0.

6. Pick on the first endpoint.
   A dialog box is displayed asking if you want to close the spline..

7. Pick the **Yes** button in the **Spline** dialog box to close the spline.
   A closed spline is created, Figure 4-19.

8. Leave the Top viewport maximized and save the scene.

Modifying Splines

Modify

1. With the line selected, pick **Modify** in the **Command Panel**.
   Since a line is not a parametric shape, but rather created as an editable spline, an edit spline modifier does not need to be applied in order to edit the spline at the sub-object level.

2. Pick the **Spline** button in the **Selection** rollout.

3. Right-click anywhere on the spline to display the quad menu. Select **Line** from the upper-left quadrant.
   You will notice that **Curve** is checked by default, and when you select **Line**, there is no visible change in the spline. This is because a curve-type segment can be curve or straight.

4. Display the quad menu again and select **Curve** in the upper-left quadrant.
   The segments of the spline are converted to curve-type segments. The spline is slightly curved when converted.

Figure 4-19. A triangle is created from three lines.

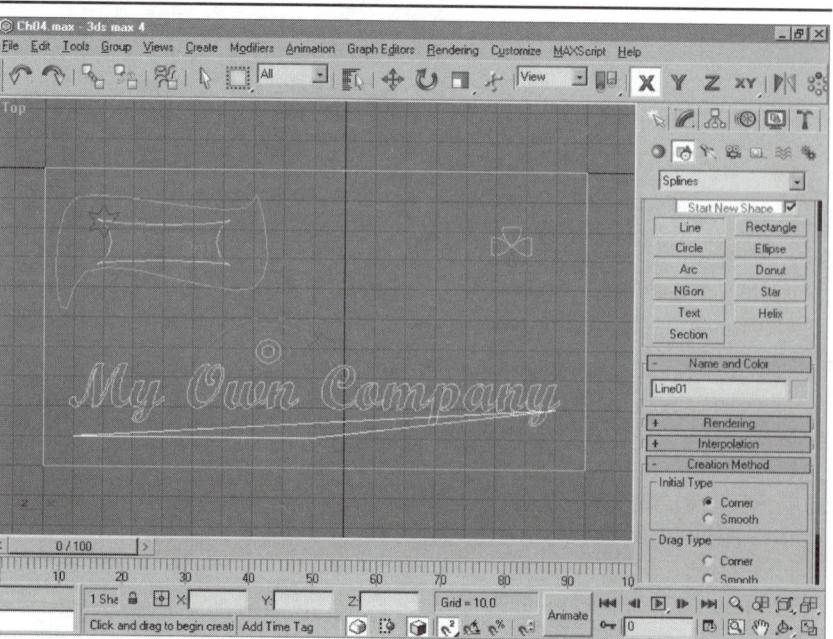

Figure 4-20. The completed scene.

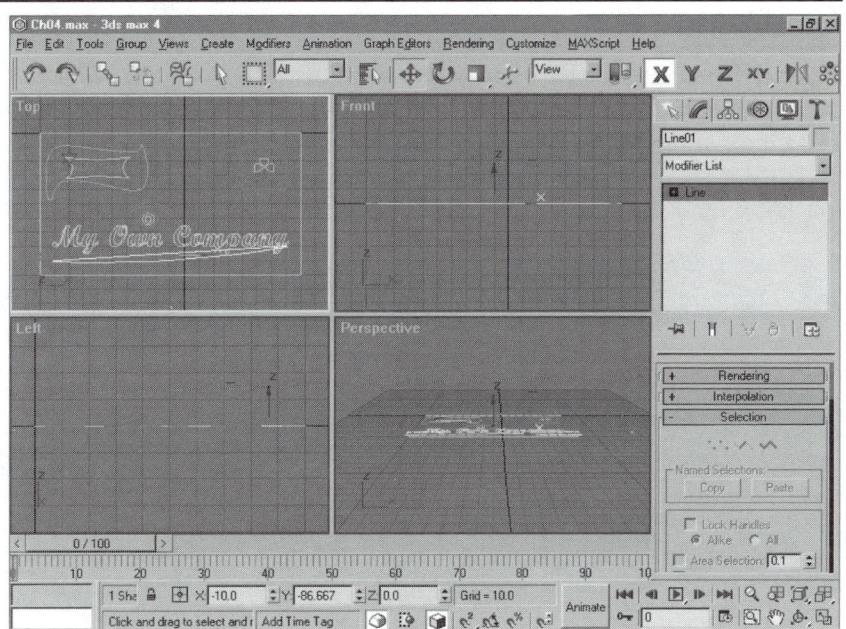

5. Pick the **Vertex** button in the **Selection** rollout to exit sub-object mode.

6. Display the four-viewport configuration and pick the **Zoom Extents All** button, Figure 4-20.

7. Save the scene.

Self-Evaluation Test

Answer the following questions. Then compare your answers with the correct answers given at the end of this chapter.

1. When you pick the _____ in the **Selection** rollout, you enter vertex sub-object editing mode.

2. You can convert between vertex types using the _____ menu.

3. You can change the curvature of a spline leading into and out of a Bézier vertex using the _____.

4. The two types of Bézier vertices are _____ and _____.

5. The handles on a _____ vertex can be adjusted independent of each other.

6. The _____ vertex has two handles in a straight line, forcing the selected segment into a curve.

7. Using the [Shift] key while transforming the handle of a Bézier vertex converts the vertex into a _____ vertex.

8. By checking the _____ check box and picking the _____ radio button, all Bézier handles on the selected vertices that are similar are affected in the same manner when only one handle is transformed.

9. You can delete a selected segment from an object by picking the _____ button in the **Geometry** rollout or by pressing the [Delete] key.

10. While using the **Use Pivot Point Center** button with the **Select and Rotate** command, multiple selected objects are rotated about _____.

Exercises

Using 3ds max *create the shapes shown below. Use your own dimensions. Make copies and transform them as needed. Edit shapes at the sub-object level as needed. When complete, save the scene as* ex04.max *in the folder of your choice.*

Answers

The following are the correct answers to the questions in the Self-Evaluation Test.

1. **Vertex**; 2. quad; 3. Bézier handles; 4. Bézier, Bézier corner; 5. Bézier corner; 6. Bézier; 7. Bézier corner; 8. **Lock Handles**, **Alike**; 9. **Delete**; 10. their individual pivot points.

Chapter 5

Lofting Objects

Learning Objectives

After completing this chapter, you will be able to:

- ○ Create an object by revolving a shape around an axis.
- ○ Loft spline objects along a path.
- ○ Change the shape steps and path steps.
- ○ Change levels.
- ○ Remove the twist from multiple loft objects.
- ○ Move and copy different shapes to different path levels.
- ○ Use the **Scale** deformation tool on a loft object.

Tutorial Description

In this tutorial, you will create a lamp on a table. The table consists of a base and a glass top. The lamp consists of a base, shade and frame, socket, and lightbulb. You will then apply materials to the objects, add a spotlight and omni lights, create a camera, and finally render the scene.

Creating the Table Base

First, create the base of the table. The shape begins as a shape that will be revolved around an axis. Use the **Line** command to create the shape.

1. Reset 3ds max by selecting **Reset** from the **File** pull-down menu. Then, select **Yes** in the dialog box that is displayed or press the [Y] key on the keyboard.
   The system is reset.

2. Activate the Front viewport and select the **Min/Max Toggle** button to maximize the viewport.
   You can also press the [W] key on the keyboard to maximize the current viewport.

Min/Max Toggle

3. Right-click on the **Snap Toggle** flyout.
   The **Grid and Snap Settings** dialog box is displayed.

2D Snap Toggle

Create

Shapes

4. In the **Grid and Snap Settings** dialog box, select the **Home Grid** tab and type 1.0 in the **Grid Spacing** spinner. Make sure the **Inhibit Grid Subdivision Below Grid Spacing** check box is not checked. Close the dialog box

5. Select the **2D Snap Toggle** button from the **Snap Toggle** flyout to turn snap on.

6. Pick **Create** in the **Command Panel**. Then, pick the **Shapes** button and select **Splines** from the drop-down list.

7. Select the **Line** button in the **Object Type** rollout.
   The rollouts for a line are displayed. These include the **Name and Color**, **Rendering**, **Interpolation**, **Creation Method**, and **Keyboard Entry** rollouts.

8. Move the cursor to coordinates 0, 0, 70 as shown in the coordinate display. Zoom out as needed. Pick to set the first vertex of the shape.

9. Next, sequentially pick points at the following coordinates, as shown in the coordinate display. Refer to Figure 5-1. (−50, 0, 70), (−50, 0, 60), (−40, 0, 60), (−40, 0, 50), (−30, 0, 50), (−30, 0, 40), (−20, 0, 40), (−20, 0, −40), (−30, 0, −40), (−30, 0, −50), (−40, 0, −50), (−40, 0, −60), (−50, 0, −60), (−50, 0, −70), (0, 0, −70). Right-click to end the command.
   A single line profile of the table base is created.

10. In the **Name and Color** rollout, name the spline Table Base. Also, change the object display color to light yellow.

11. Save the scene as Ch05.max in the folder of your choice.

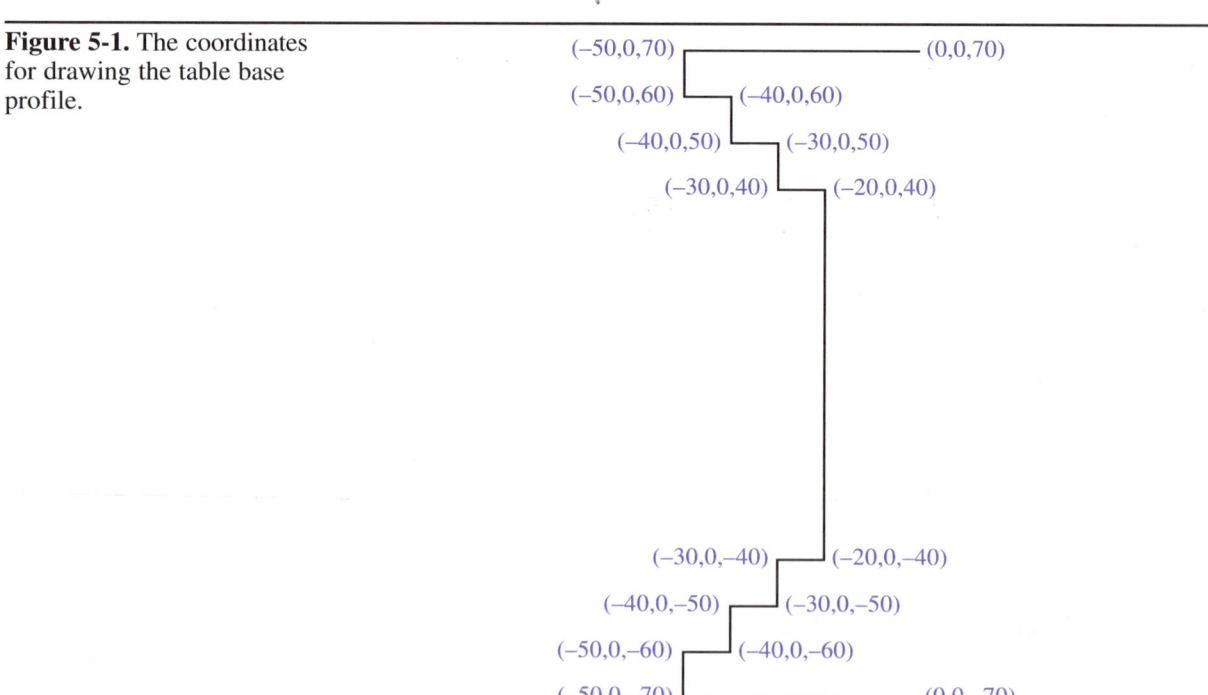

Figure 5-1. The coordinates for drawing the table base profile.

Making the Table Base

The profile of the table base is now created as a single line. To create the base, the spline needs to be revolved around its axis. The lathe modifier is used to revolve the spline.

1. Display the four-viewport configuration.

2. Select the profile of the table base, if not already selected.

3. Pick **Patch/Spline Editing** in the **Modifiers** pull-down menu. Then, select **Lathe** in the cascading menu.

The profile spins around its axis at the middle. The **Modify** tab is also automatically opened.

4. To correctly align the revolved surface, select the **Max** button in the **Align** area of the **Parameters** rollout. See Figure 5-2.

5. Pick the **Select and Move** button on the **Main** toolbar.

Select and Move

6. Move Table Base straight up until the Y value in the coordinate display is 70. The X and Z values should be 0.

The base now sits on the world XY plane.

7. Select the **Zoom Extents All** button.

The object is zoomed to its extents in all the viewports.

Zoom Extents All

8. Save the scene.

Figure 5-2. A lathe modifier is used to create the table base.

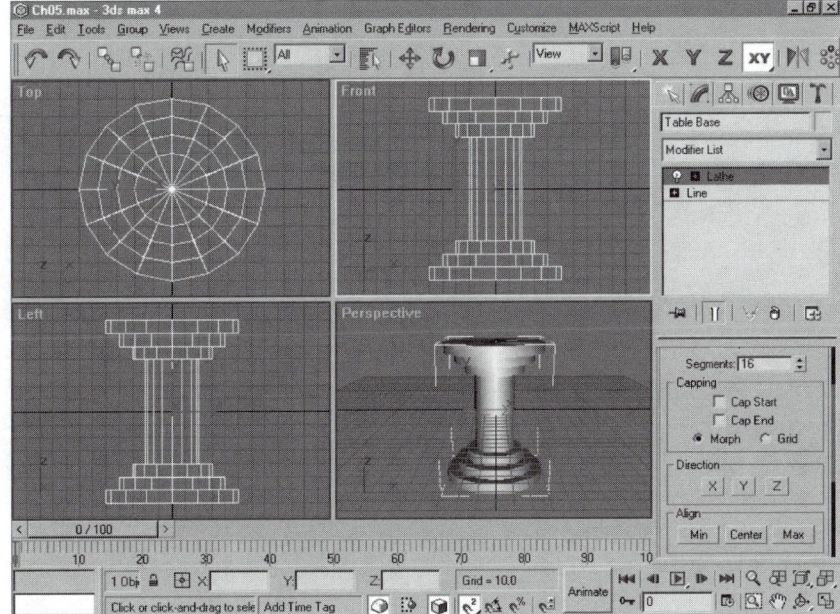

Creating the Table Top

1. Activate the Top viewport. Select the **Zoom All** button. Pick in the middle of the Top viewport and drag the cursor down until the object is displayed about half of its original size. Right-click to end the command.

Zoom All

2. Turn snap on, if it is not already.

3. Pick **Create** in the **Command Panel**. Then, select the **Shapes** button and pick **Splines** from the drop-down menu.

Create

Shapes

4. Pick the **Circle** button in the **Object Type** rollout.

The rollouts for a circle are displayed.

5. Pick at the center of Table Base at coordinates 0, 0, 0. Drag the cursor up until the coordinate display shows 0, 100, 0.

A circle is created.

6. In the **Name and Color** rollout, name the circle Table Top and change the object display color to light blue.

7. With the circle selected, pick **Mesh Editing** in the **Modifiers** pull-down menu. Then, pick **Extrude** in the cascading menu.

   An extrude modifier is applied to the spline, and the **Modify** tab is automatically opened.

8. In the **Parameters** rollout in the **Modify** tab, type 4.0 in the **Amount:** spinner.

   The circle is extruded four units in the positive direction.

9. Activate the Front viewport. Pick the **Select and Move** button on the **Main** toolbar.

10. Move Table Top up until it is exactly on top of Table Base, Figure 5-3. The Y value in the coordinate display should be 140. The X and Z values should be 0.

11. Save the scene.

Figure 5-3. The table top is placed on top of the base.

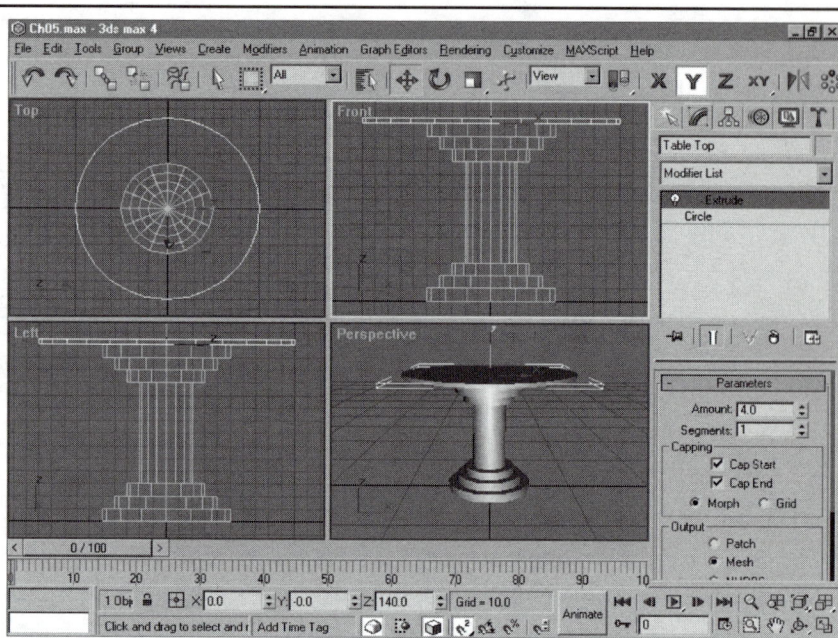

Lofting

Spline shapes are converted into mesh objects when lofted. The shapes are placed along a path to give the object three dimensions. This whole process of conversion is called *lofting*. There can be a number of shapes lofted along a single path.

Creating the Lamp Base Shapes

1. Make the Front viewport current and maximize it.

2. Zoom in until the next subgrid is displayed.

Pan

3. Select the **Pan** button. Pan the viewport down so only Table Top is visible at the bottom of the viewport.

Create

4. Pick **Create** in the **Command Panel**. Pick the **Shapes** button and select **Splines** from the drop-down list.

Shapes

5. Pick the **Line** button in the **Object Type** rollout. Turn snap on, if it is not already.

6. Select a point near the left edge of the table at coordinates –40, 0, 150. Pick the next point at coordinates –40, 0, 300 and right-click to end the command.
   A vertical line is created.

7. Display the four-viewport configuration, activate the Top viewport, and maximize it.

8. Pick **Display** in the **Command Panel**. In the **Hide** rollout, pick the **Hide by Hit** button. Then, pick Table Base in the viewport and right-click to end the command.
   Table Base is no longer visible.

Display

9. Pick **Create** in the **Command Panel**. Pick the **Shapes** button and select **Splines** from the drop-down list.

Create

10. Pick the **Rectangle** button in the **Object Type** rollout. Select the first point at coordinates –70, 30, 0. Pick the other corner of the rectangle at coordinates –20, –20, 0. Name the rectangle Square in the **Name and Color** rollout.
    A square is created in the viewport, Figure 5-4.

Shapes

11. Select the **Region Zoom** button and drag a window around Square to zoom in on it.

Region Zoom

12. Pick **Create** in the **Command Panel**. Pick the **Shapes** button and select **Splines** from the drop-down list. Pick the **Circle** button in the **Object Type** rollout. Pick the center of the circle at coordinates –45, 5, 0. Pick the second point at coordinates –45, 12, 0.

13. With the circle still selected, type 21.5 in the **Radius:** spinner in the **Parameters** rollout.
    The circle is assigned a new radius.

14. Pick the **Circle** button again in the **Object Type** rollout, if it is not already selected. Pick the center of the circle at coordinates –45, 5, 0. Pick the second point anywhere to create a smaller circle within the circle you just created. Change the radius to 16.0 using the **Parameters** rollout.

15. Draw another circle centered on –45, 5, 0 with a radius of 13.0.

16. Draw another circle centered on –45, 5, 0 with a radius of 10.0.

17. Draw another circle centered on –45, 5, 0 with a radius of 5.0.
    Five concentric circles within Square are created, Figure 5-5.

18. Save the scene.

Figure 5-4. A square is drawn, which will be lofted to create the lamp base.

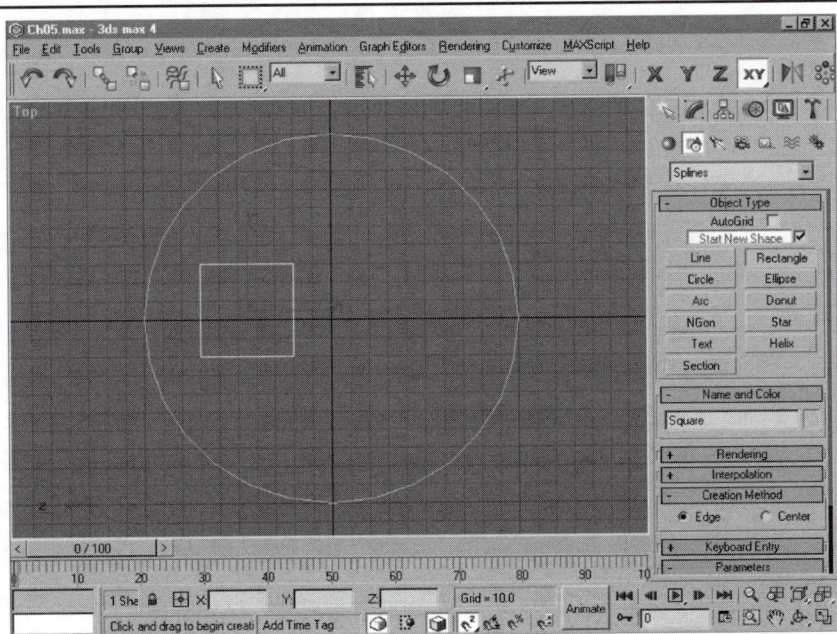

Figure 5-5. Circles are drawn to be used as additional shapes on the loft object.

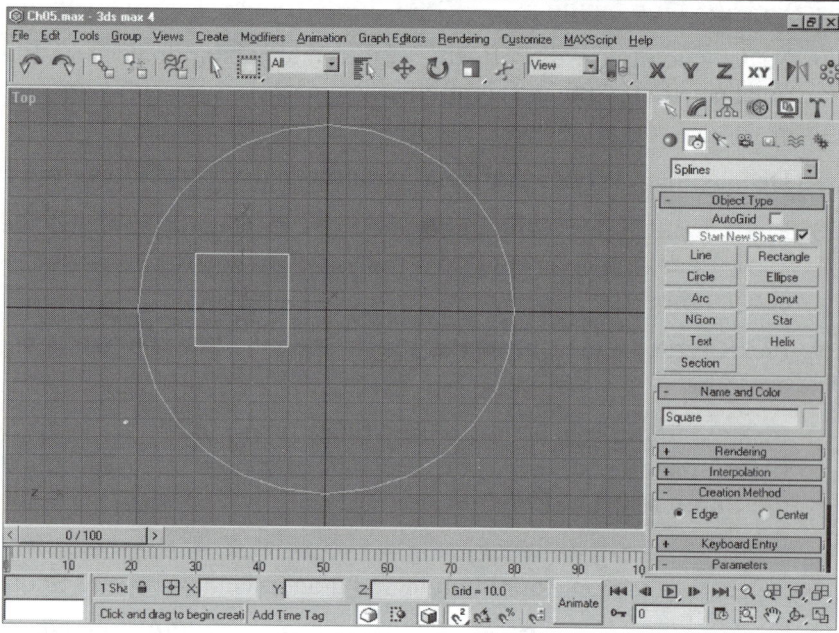

Lofting Spline Objects

Create

Geometry

1. Display the four-viewport configuration.

2. Select Line01 (the straight vertical line) in the Front viewport. Then, pick **Create** in the **Command Panel**. Pick the **Geometry** button and select **Compound Objects** in the drop-down list.
   The **Object Type** rollout for compound objects is displayed.

3. Pick the **Loft** button in the **Object Type** rollout.
   The **Creation Method**, **Surface Parameters**, **Path Parameters**, and **Skin Parameters** rollouts are displayed.

4. Select the **Get Shape** button in the **Creation Method** rollout. Pick the **Instance** radio button to select it.

5. Move the cursor over Square in the Top viewport. The cursor changes to a "get shape" cursor. Pick Square.
   An instance of Square is placed on the line (path) at its first vertex, and lofted along the path. A small yellow cross indicates the current vertex of the path, which in this case is the first vertex.

6. With the loft object (Loft01) selected, pick the **Zoom Extents All Selected** button.
   The loft object is zoomed to its extents in all viewports.

Changing Levels

You can add different shapes at different levels of the path. In this way, you can create a loft object with different cross sections.

1. In the **Path Parameters** rollout, check the **On** check box next to the **Snap:** spinner.
   The **Snap:** spinner is enabled.

2. Make sure that the **Percentage** radio button is selected. Then, type 5.0 in the **Snap:** spinner and press [Enter].
   Now, the yellow cross will snap to multiples of 5 percent as you move along the selected path.

3. Pick the up arrow of the **Path:** spinner until 10.0 is displayed. You can also type 10.0 in the spinner and press [Enter].
   The small yellow cross mark moves up to 10 percent of the path length.

4. Pick the **Get Shape** button in the **Creation Method** rollout so it is depressed. Then, pick Square again.

An instance of Square is placed at the 10 percent location on the path.

5. Pick the up arrow of the **Path:** spinner until 20.0 is displayed.

The small yellow cross moves up to the 20 percent location.

6. Pick the **Get Shape** button in the **Creation Method** rollout so it is depressed. Then, select Circle03.

Circle03 is placed at the 20 percent location. The loft object is blended from the square to the circle, Figure 15-6.

7. Move to the 25% level of the path. Pick the **Get Shape** button in the **Creation Method** rollout so it is depressed. Then, select Circle02.

Circle02 is placed at the 25 percent location of the path.

8. Move to the 30% level of the path. Pick the **Get Shape** button in the **Creation Method** rollout so it is depressed. Then, select Circle03 again.

Circle03 is placed at the 30 percent location of the path.

9. Move to the 50% level of the path. Pick the **Get Shape** button in the **Creation Method** rollout so it is depressed. Then, select Circle01.

Circle01 is placed at the 50 percent location of the path.

10. Move to the 70% level of the path. Pick the **Get Shape** button in the **Creation Method** rollout so it is depressed. Then, select Circle05.

Circle05 is placed at the 70 percent level of the path.

11. Move to the 75% level of the path. Pick the **Get Shape** button in the **Creation Method** rollout so it is depressed. Then, select Circle04.

Circle04 is placed at the 75 percent level of the path.

12. Move to the 80% level of the path. Pick the **Get Shape** button in the **Creation Method** rollout so it is depressed. Then, select Circle05.

Circle05 is placed at the 80 percent level of the path.

Figure 5-6. A circle is added above the squares in the loft object.

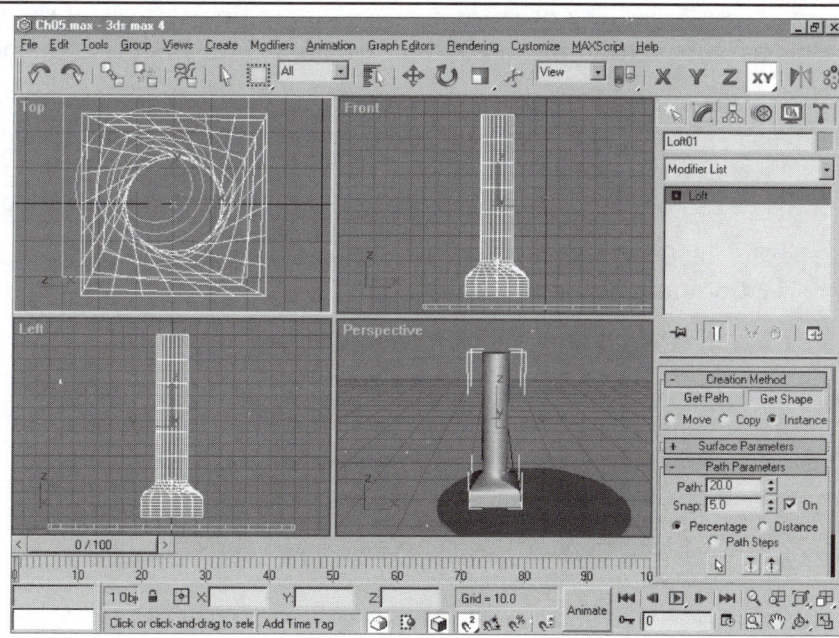

Figure 5-7. All additional shapes are added to the loft object.

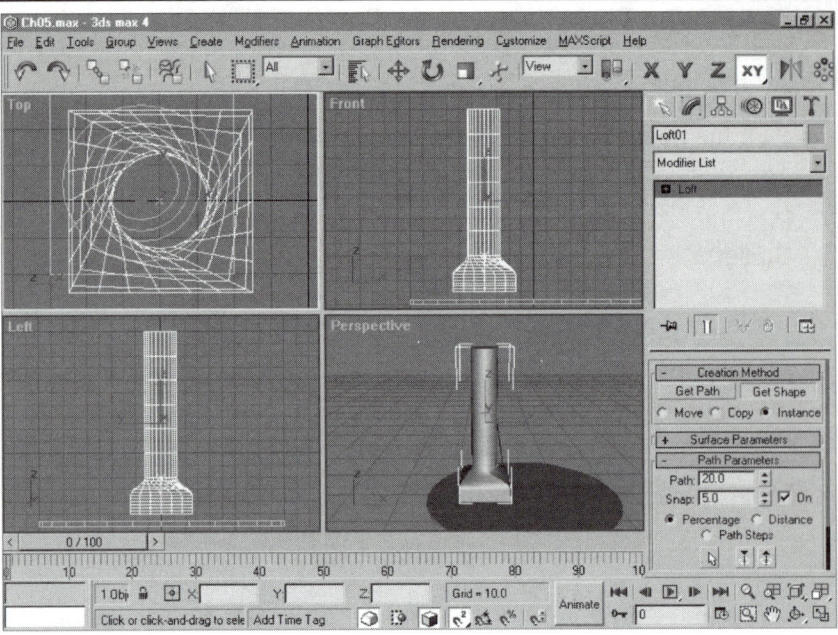

13. Finally, move to the 100% level of the path. Pick the **Get Shape** button in the **Creation Method** rollout so it is depressed. Then, select Circle05.
    Circle05 is placed at the end of the path. See Figure 5-7.

14. In the **Name and Color** rollout, name the loft object Lamp Base.

15. Save the scene.

Removing the Twist

If you look close at the bottom of Lamp Base, there is a slight "twist" in the skin between the square and the first circle. The twist results because the first vertices of the two shapes do not align. This problem can be fixed using the **Compare** button in the **Shape Commands** rollout, as follows.

Modify

1. With the loft object selected, pick **Modify** in the **Command Panel**. In the modifier stack, pick the plus (+) next to the entry **Loft** to expand the sub-object tree. Then, highlight **Shape** in the sub-object tree to navigate to that sub-object editing level. See Figure 5-8.
   Shape sub-object mode is entered and the **Shape Commands** rollout is displayed.

2. Select the **Compare** button in the **Shape Commands** rollout.
   The **Compare** dialog box is displayed.

Pick Shape

3. Select the **Pick Shape** button in the **Compare** dialog box.

4. Move the cursor over the loft object (Lamp Base) in the Perspective viewport and pick on the square at the 10 percent path location.
   The square is displayed in the **Compare** dialog box. The first vertex of the square is displayed with a small box around it.

5. With the **Pick Shape** button active, move the cursor in the viewport and place it over the circle at the 20 percent path location. Pick the circle.
   The circle is displayed in the **Compare** dialog box. You can see how the first vertices do not align, Figure 5-9.

Figure 5-8. Selecting the shape sub-object level.

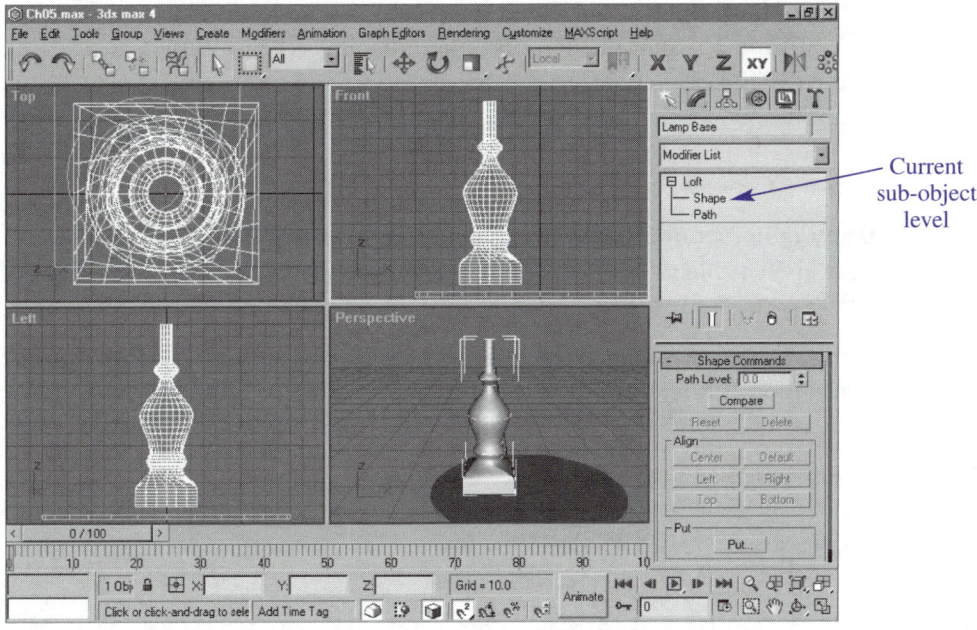

Figure 5-9. The first vertices must align to remove the twist on the loft object.

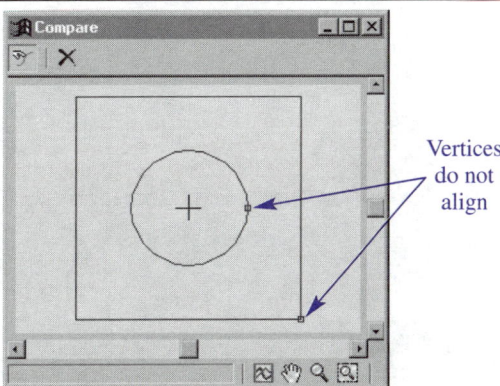

6. Pick the **Select and Rotate** button on the **Main** toolbar. Also, pick the **Restrict to Z** button.

7. In the Front viewport, select the circle *in the loft object* and rotate it 45 degrees.
The first vertices are aligned, as shown in the **Compare** dialog box.

8. Close the **Compare** dialog box.
The twist is removed from Lamp Base.

9. In the modifier stack, pick **Loft** to exit sub-object mode. The entry is highlighted grey when sub-object mode has been exited. Save the scene.

Copying and Moving Shapes

You have seen how multiple shapes can be placed along a path to create a complex loft object. In addition, the shapes within a loft object can be moved and copied to different levels of the path.

1. Select Lamp Base. Pick **Modify** in the **Command Panel**. In the modifier stack, expand the sub-object tree and pick **Shape** to navigate to that sub-object level.

2. Turn off snap, if it is on.

3. Pick the **Select and Move** and **Restrict to Z** buttons in the **Main** toolbar.

4. In the Front or Left viewport, hold down the [Shift] key and drag the circle at the 75 percent path location up until the Y value in the coordinate display is approximately 15. Release the mouse button and the [Shift] key.

   While moving the shape, it is not possible to move it beyond another shape on the path. However, while using the [Shift] key, it is possible to copy the shape anywhere on the path. The **Copy Shape** dialog box is displayed when the mouse button is released.

5. Pick the **Copy** radio button in the dialog box. Then, pick the **OK** button.

   A copy of the circle is placed on the path at approximately the 85 percent path location, Figure 5-10. The new circle is selected at the shape sub-object level.

6. With the new shape selected at the sub-object level, enter 85 in the **Path Level:** spinner in the **Shape Commands** rollout.

   The circle moves to exactly the 85 percent path location.

7. Exit sub-object mode and save the scene.

Figure 5-10. One of the circle shapes is copied along the path.

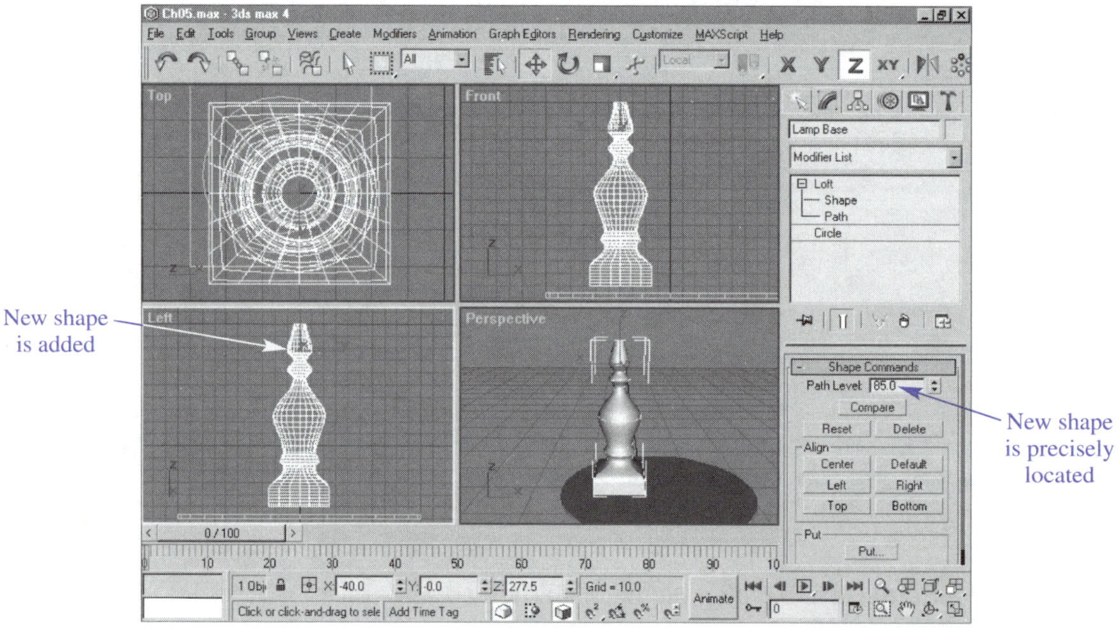

Creating Shapes for the Shade

The shade is created by lofting a shape along a path, and then modifying the lofted object. Begin by creating the shape to be lofted.

1. Display the four-viewport configuration, if it is not already displayed. Pick the **Zoom Extents All** button to zoom to the extents of all the objects in all viewports. Activate the Top viewport.

2. Turn snap on.

3. Pick **Create** in the **Command Panel**. Then, pick the **Shapes** button and select **Splines** from the drop-down list.

4. Pick the **Star** button in the **Object Type** rollout.

   Rollouts for a star are displayed.

5. Enter 15 in the **Points:** spinner in the **Parameters** rollout.

6. Pick a point at coordinates –40, 0, 0. Pick the second point at coordinates –40, 60, 0. Pick the third point at coordinates –40, 40, 0. In the **Name and Color** rollout, name the star Shade Shape.
   A star with 15 points is created.

7. Activate the Front viewport. Pan the viewport so the Table Top and Lamp Base objects are at the bottom of the viewport.

8. Pick **Create** in the **Command Panel**. Then, pick the **Shapes** button and select **Splines** from the drop-down list. Then, pick the **Line** button in the **Object Type** rollout.

9. Pick a point at coordinates 30, 0, 290. Pick the second point at coordinates 30, 0, 400. Right-click to end the command. In the **Name and Color** rollout, name the line Shade Path.
   A line is created, which will be the path for the lamp shade loft object.

10. Save the scene.

Creating Shade

1. Select Shade Path. Then, pick **Create** in the **Command Panel**. Pick the **Geometry** button in the **Command Panel**. Select **Compound Objects** in the drop-down list.

2. Pick the **Loft** button in the **Object Type** rollout.

3. Pick the **Get Shape** button in the **Creation Method** rollout. Make sure the **Instance** radio button is selected.

4. Pick Shade Shape in the Top viewport. In the **Name and Color** rollout, name the loft Shade.
   The star is lofted along the line.

5. Pick the **Zoom Extents All Selected** button to zoom to the extents of the loft object, Figure 5-11.

6. Save the scene.

Figure 5-11. The initial form of the shade is created.

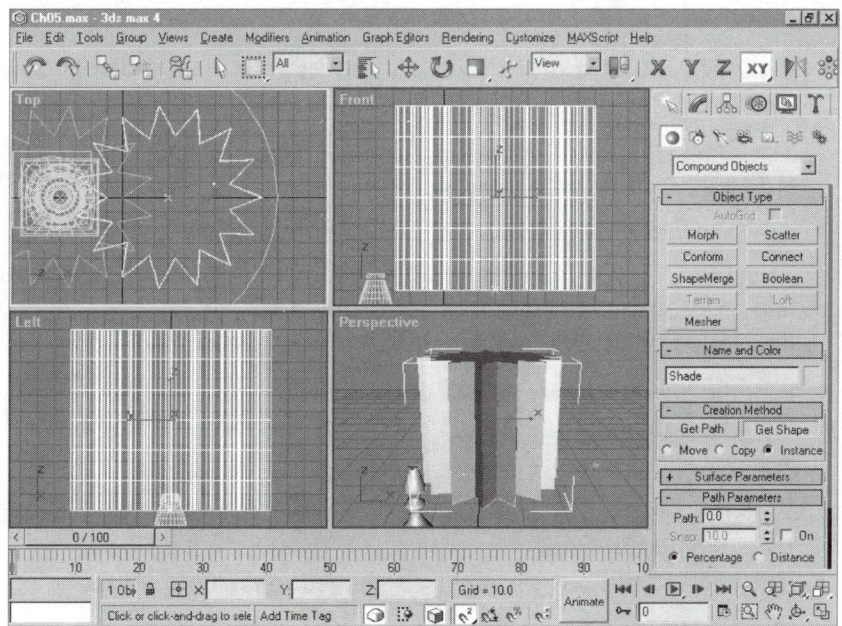

Using Scale Deformation

1. With the loft object Shade selected, pick **Modify** in the **Command Panel**.

2. Open the **Deformations** rollout.
   Buttons corresponding to the five types of deformations are available in this rollout.

3. Select the **Scale** button in the **Deformations** rollout. The **Scale Deformation** dialog box is displayed, Figure 5-12.
   The horizontal red line represents profile of the loft object. The left point of the line represents the first vertex of the path. The number in the ruler at the top represents the length of the path in a percentage. The location of the line on either side represents the scale in a percentage. The left and right vertices currently at the same vertical point (100), which means the loft object is not scaled.

Figure 5-12. The **Scale Deformation** dialog box is used to scale the profile of a loft object.

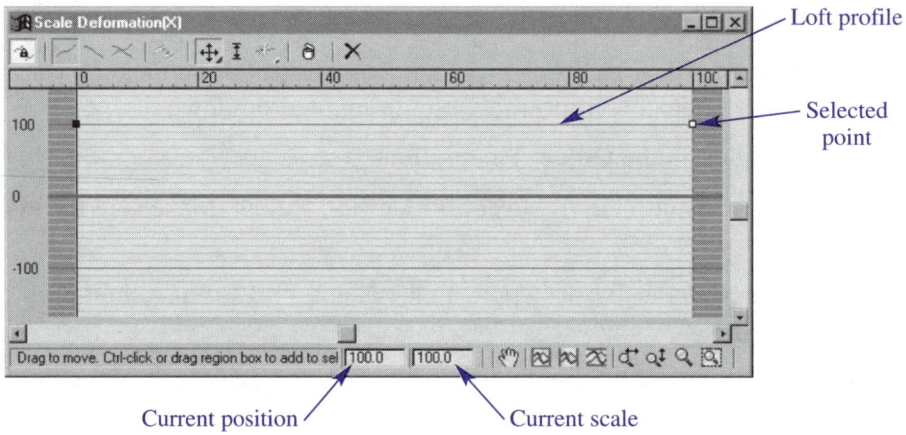

4. Make sure the **2D Snap Toggle** button in the main 3ds max screen is on.

2D Snap Toggle

5. Pick the **Move Control Point** button in the **Scale Deformation** dialog box, if it is not already selected.

Move Control Point

6. Move the right-hand control point down five "lines" until 50 is displayed in the right-hand text box at the bottom of the dialog box.
   The lofted object is scaled to 50 percent of its original size at the last vertex.

7. Select the left hand control point and move it up four "lines" until 140 is displayed in the right-hand text box at the bottom of the dialog box.
   The lofted object is scaled to 140 percent of its original size at the first vertex.

Insert Corner Point

8. Pick the **Insert Corner Point** button in the deformation dialog box. Then, pick on the red line near the 90% location. Refer to the ruler at the top of the dialog box.
   A new control point is added.

9. With the new point selected, type 90 in the left-hand text box at the bottom of the dialog box and press the [Enter] key.
   The new control point is precisely moved to the 90% position.

10. Pick the **Move Control Point** button in the deformation dialog box. Move the new control point down until 50 is displayed in the right-hand text box at the bottom of the dialog box, Figure 5-13.
    The basic shape of the shade is complete.

11. Close the **Scale Deformation (X)** dialog box and save the scene.

Figure 5-13. The basic form of the shade is complete.

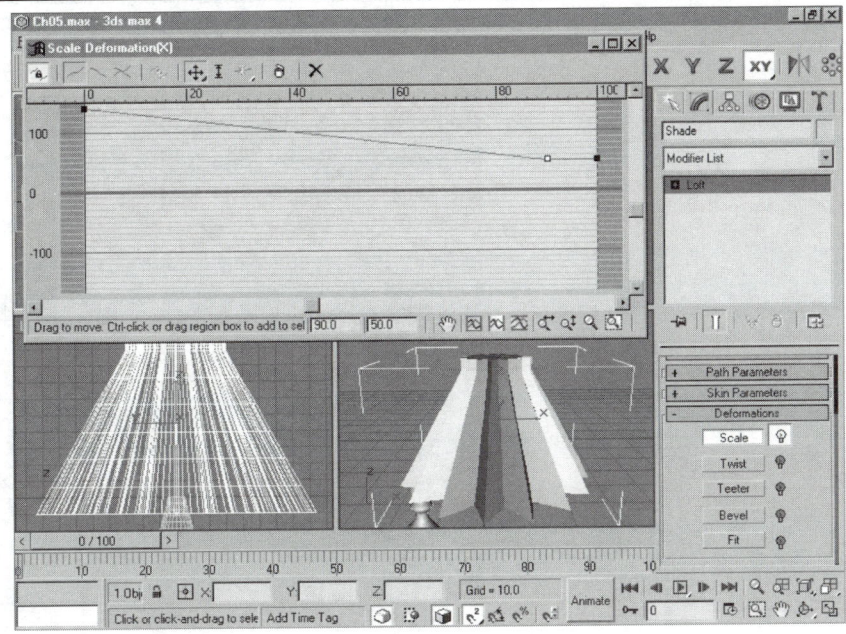

Modifying the Shade

1. Pick the **Select and Non-uniform Scale** button from the **Scale** flyout on the **Main** toolbar.
   A 3ds max warning dialog box is displayed. Pick the **Yes** button to continue.

Select and
Non-uniform Scale

2. Make sure the **Restrict to XY Plane** button is selected on the **Main** toolbar.

3. Hold the [Shift] key down, pick Shade the Top viewport, and scale the object down until the coordinate display shows 95%, 95%, 100%.
   The **Clone Options** dialog box is displayed.

4. Name the copy Shade Drill and pick the **OK** button in the dialog box. Make sure the **Copy** radio button is selected in the **Object** area of the **Clone Options** dialog box.
   A scaled down copy of the shade is created.

5. Using the **Select by Name** button, select Shade.
   Shade turns white indicating it is selected.

Select by Name

6. Pick **Create** in the **Command Panel**. Select the **Geometry** button and pick **Compound Objects** from the drop-down list.

7. Pick the **Boolean** button in the **Object Type** rollout.
   Rollouts for Boolean objects are displayed.

8. In the **Operation** area of the **Parameters** rollout, make sure the **Subtraction (A-B)** radio button is selected. Select the **Pick Operand B** button in the **Pick Boolean** rollout.

9. Use the **Select by Name** button to select Shade Drill.
   Shade is hollowed out, Figure 5-14.

10. Right-click to end the command, and then save the scene.

Creating the Framework

1. Display the four-viewport configuration. Pick the **Zoom Extents All** button to zoom to the extents of all the objects in all viewports.

2. Make the Top viewport current and maximize the viewport.

Figure 5-14. The shade is complete.

3. Pick **Create** in the **Command Panel**. Pick the **Shapes** button and select **Splines** from the drop-down list. Pick the **Circle** button in the **Object Type** rollout.

4. Pick a point at coordinates 30, 0, 0 and drag the cursor to coordinates 30, 20, 0. In the **Name and Color** rollout, name the circle Frame Path01.
   A circle is created centered on Shade.

5. Draw another circle centered at coordinates 30, 0, 0 with a radius of 60. Name the circle Frame Path02.

6. Draw a small circle anywhere in the viewport with a radius of 1.0. Name the circle Frame Shape.

7. Select Frame Path02. Then, pick **Create** in the **Command Panel**. Pick the **Geometry** button and select **Compound Objects** from the drop-down list.

8. Pick the **Loft** button in the **Object Type** rollout.

9. In the **Creation Method** rollout, pick the **Get Shape** button and select Frame Shape in the viewport. Then, name the loft object Frame Ring01 in the **Name and Color** rollout.
   The small circle is lofted along the larger circle path.

10. Pick the **Select object** button on the **Main** toolbar. Select Frame Path01.

11. Pick the **Loft** button in the **Object Type** rollout. Then select the **Get Shape** button in the **Creation Method** rollout and pick Frame Shape. Then, name the loft object Frame Ring02 in the **Name and Color** rollout.
    The small circle is lofted along the other circle path, Figure 5-15.

12. Display the four-viewport configuration. Activate the Front viewport and maximize it.

13. Pick the **Select and Move** button on the **Main** toolbar.

14. Select Frame Ring01. Move it up until its bottom edge is flush with the bottom of Shade. The Y value in the coordinate display should be 290.

15. Select Frame Ring02. Move it up until its top edge is flush with the top of Shade.
    You may need to move it part of the way, then zoom in and move it the rest of the way.

Select and Uniform Scale

16. Pick the **Select and Uniform Scale** button from the **Scale** flyout in the **Main** toolbar. Make sure the **Restrict to XY Plane** button is also selected.

Figure 5-15. Two "rings" of the frame are created.

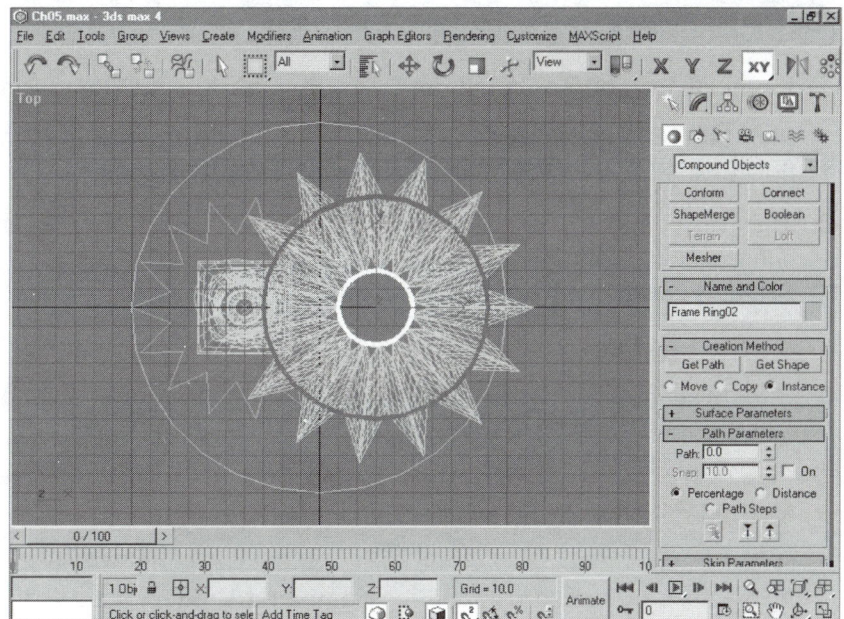

17. Hold the [Shift] key down, select Frame Ring02, and scale it down until the coordinate display shows 65%, 65%, 65%. Release the [Shift] key and the mouse button. The **Clone Options** dialog box is displayed.

18. Make sure the **Copy** radio button is selected, name the copy Frame Ring03, and pick the **OK** button in the dialog box. A scaled down copy of Frame Ring01 is created.

19. Pick the **Select and Move** button. Move Frame Ring03 down 50 units on the local Y axis so it is in the middle of Shade, Figure 5-16.

20. Display the four-viewport configuration. Activate the Left viewport and maximize it.

21. Save the scene.

Figure 5-16. A third ring is created for the frame and located in the middle of the shade.

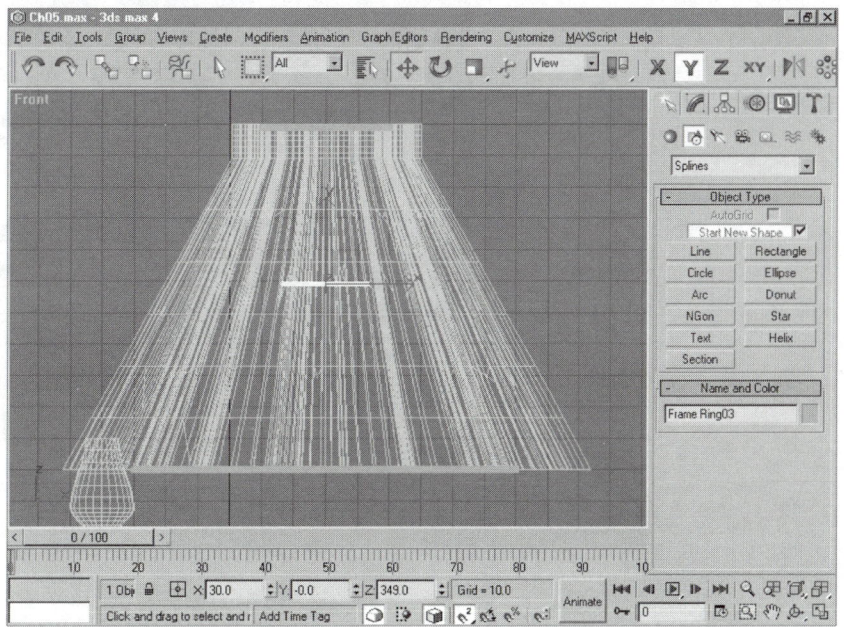

Adding Struts to the Framework

1. Using the **Region Zoom** button, drag a window around Frame Ring02 and Frame Ring03.

2. Pick **Create** in the **Command Panel**. Select the **Shapes** button and pick **Splines** from the drop-down list. Pick the **Line** button in the **Object Type** rollout.

3. Turn snap on, if it is not already. Pick a point at coordinates 0, –13, 349. Pick a second point at coordinates 0, –20, 399. Right-click to end the command.
   A line is created between the two rings.

4. If necessary, move Frame Ring02 and Frame Ring03 up or down so they touch the line.

5. With the line selected, pick **Create** in the **Command Panel**. Pick the **Geometry** button and select **Compound Objects** from the drop-down list.

6. Pick the **Loft** button in the **Object Type** rollout. Then, pick the **Get Shape** button in the **Creation Method** rollout. Pick the **Instance** radio button.

7. Pick the small circle used as the shape for the frame rings. You may need to select it by its name. Name the loft Frame Post01 in the **Name and Color** rollout.
   The circle is lofted along the line.

8. Display the four-viewport configuration.

9. In the Front viewport, use the **Region Zoom** button to zoom in on Frame Ring02, Frame Ring02, and Frame Post01.

10. Pick the **Select and Move** and **Restrict to X** buttons on the **Main** toolbar and move the loft 30 units to the right, Figure 5-17.

11. Save the scene.

Figure 5-17. A vertical post is created for the frame.

Figure 5-18. The **Mirror** dialog box is used to mirror the vertical post of the frame.

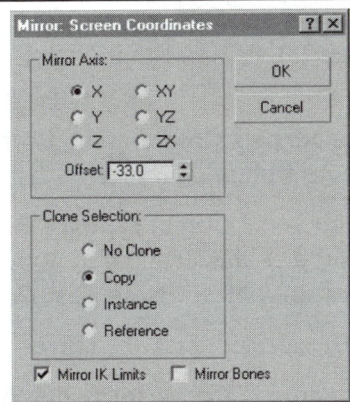

Mirroring the Strut

1. Select Frame Post01 in the Left viewport. Then, pick the **Mirror Selected Objects** button on the **Main** toolbar.
The **Mirror** dialog box is displayed, Figure 5-18.

2. In the **Mirror Axis** area of the dialog box, select the **X** radio button. Also select the **Copy** radio button in the **Clone Selection** dialog box. Finally, type −33.0 in the **Offset:** spinner and pick the **OK** button.
A copy of Frame Post01 is mirrored about the X axis and offset 33 units in the negative X direction. The copy is assigned the name Frame Post02.

3. With Frame Post02 selected, pick **Create** in the **Command Panel**. Pick the **Geometry** button and select **Compound Objects** in the drop-down list.

4. Pick the **Boolean** button in the **Object Type** rollout. Then, select the **Union** radio button in the **Operations** area of the **Parameters** rollout.

5. Select the **Pick Operand B** button in the **Pick Boolean** rollout. Make sure the **Move** radio button is on, and then select Frame Ring02.
The two objects are unioned.

6. Pick the **Boolean** button in the **Object Type** rollout again to start a new Boolean operation. Make sure the **Union** radio button is selected in the **Operation** area of the **Parameters** rollout. Then, select the **Pick Operand B** button in the **Pick Boolean** rollout and select Frame Post01.

7. Pick the **Boolean** button in the **Object Type** rollout again to start a new Boolean operation. Make sure the **Union** radio button is selected in the **Operation** area of the **Parameters** rollout. Then, select the **Pick Operand B** button in the **Pick Boolean** rollout and select Frame Ring03. Right-click to end the command.
The top and middle rings and the two posts are combined.

8. In the **Name and Color** rollout, rename the object Frame.

9. Select the **Zoom Extents All** button to zoom to the extents of all viewports. Then, activate the Front viewport and maximize it.

10. Using the **Region Zoom** button, drag a window around the bottom ring of Frame and Frame Ring01.

11. Pick **Create** in the **Command Panel**. Pick the **Shapes** button and select **Splines** from the drop-down list. Turn snap on.

12. Pick the **Line** button in the **Object Type** rollout. Pick a point at coordinates 50, 0, 400 and a second point at coordinates 90, 0, 290. Right-click to end the command.
    A line is drawn between Frame and Frame Ring01.

13. With the line selected, pick **Create** in the **Command Panel**. Pick the **Geometry** button and select **Compound Objects** from the drop-down list.

14. Pick the **Loft** button in the **Object Type** rollout. Also select the **Get Shape** button in the **Creation Method** rollout and pick the small circle lofted to create the frame. You may need to select it by its name. Name the loft object Frame Post03.

15. With Frame Post03 selected, pick the **Mirror Selected Objects** button on the **Main** toolbar.

16. In the **Mirror Axis** area of the **Mirror** dialog box, select the **X** radio button. Also select the **Copy** radio button in the **Clone Selection** dialog box. Finally, type –80.0 in the **Offset:** spinner and pick the **OK** button.

17. Select Frame in any viewport. Using Boolean operations, union Frame Post03 to Frame; Frame Post04 to Frame; and Frame Ring01 to Frame.
    The frame is complete, Figure 5-19.

18. Save the scene.

Figure 5-19. The frame is complete.

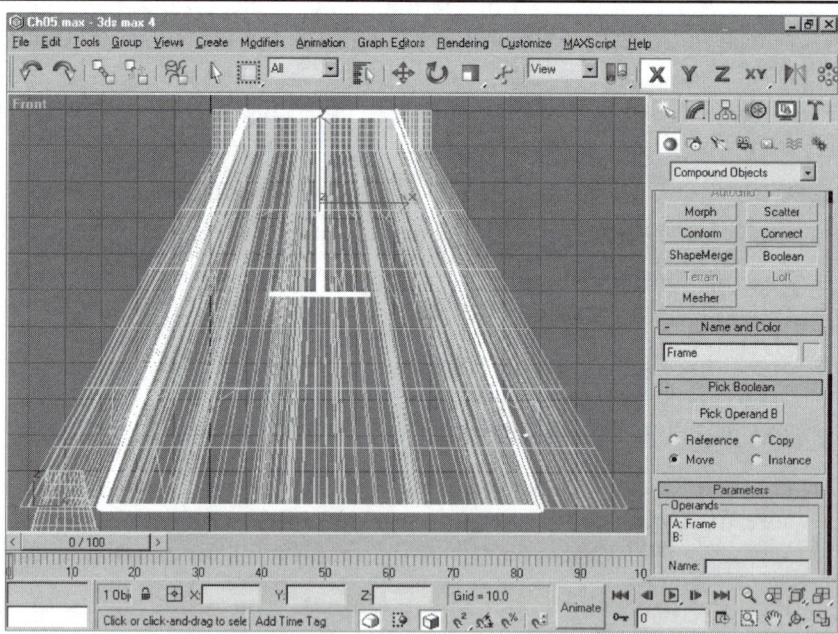

Creating the Socket

Now, you will create a socket, which holds the lightbulb as supports the shade/frame on the lamp base. The socket is created by lofting a circle along a path, and then modify it using the scale deformation tool.

1. Display the four-viewport configuration, if it is not already displayed.

2. In the Left viewport, zoom in on Shade.

3. Maximize the Left viewport. Turn snap on.

4. Pick **Create** in the **Command Panel**. Pick the **Shapes** button and select **Splines** from the drop-down list. Pick the **Line** button in the **Object Type** rollout.

5. Select a point at coordinates 0, 0, 300 and the second point at coordinates 0, 0, 350. Right-click to end the command. Name the line Socket Path.

6. With the line selected, pick **Create** in the **Command Panel**. Pick the **Geometry** button and select **Compound Objects** from the drop-down list. Pick the **Loft** button in the **Object Type** rollout.

7. Select the **Get Shape** button in the **Creation Method** rollout. Select the second smallest circle used to create Lamp Base. This is named Circle04.

8. Name the loft Socket. With Socket selected, pick **Modify** in the **Command Panel**.

9. Open the **Deformations** rollout. Then, pick the **Scale** button.
   The **Scale Deformation** dialog box is displayed.

Insert Corner Point

10. Pick the **Insert Corner Point** button in the dialog box and pick on the red line near 20 percent. Refer to the ruler at the top of the dialog box.
    A vertex is added at this point.

11. Type 20 in the left-hand text box at the bottom of the dialog box and press the [Enter] key.
    The new vertex is moved to exactly the 20 percent path location.

12. Type 30 in the right-hand text box at the bottom of the dialog box and press [Enter] to scale the profile to 30%.

13. Select the **Insert Corner Point** button and pick on the red line near 70 percent to insert another vertex. Enter 70 in the left-hand text box at the bottom of the dialog box.
    A new vertex is added and moved to exactly the 70 percent path location.

14. Type 30 in the right-hand text box at the bottom of the dialog box and press [Enter] to scale the profile to 30%.

15. Insert another vertex at the 90% path location and scale the profile to 100%.

16. Insert another vertex at the 95% path location and scale the profile to 70%.

17. Scale the profile at the 100% path location to 70% and close the **Scale Deformation** dialog box, Figure 5-20.

18. Save the scene.

Figure 5-20. The socket is complete.

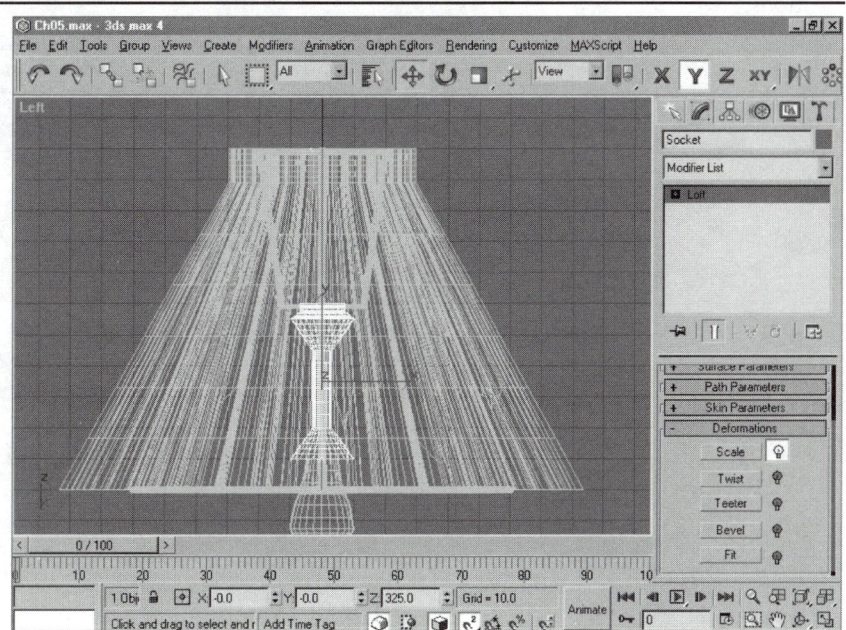

Assembling the Lamp

You have probably noticed that many of the objects in the scene are not in their correct locations. You will now assemble the objects to create the final scene.

1. Display the four-viewport configuration.

2. Activate the Front viewport and maximize it.

3. Select the **Zoom Extents All** button to zoom to the extents of the objects in the viewport.

4. Select the **Region Zoom** button and drag a window around Table Top, Lamp Base, Frame, Socket, and Shade to zoom in on them.

5. Pick the **Select and Move** and **Restrict to Y** buttons on the **Main** toolbar. Select Lamp Base and move it down so it is exactly on top of Table Top.

6. Pick the **Restrict to XY Plane** button. Move Socket and place it exactly on top of, and centered on, Lamp Base.

7. Select Frame and Shade.

8. Move both Shade and Frame to the left and down so they are centered on Lamp Base, as shown in Figure 5-21.

9. Display the four-viewport configuration.

Display

10. Pick **Display** in the **Command Panel**. Pick the **Unhide All** button in the **Hide** rollout. Table Base is displayed in all the viewports.

11. In the **Hide by Category** rollout, check the **Shapes** check box. All shapes are hidden in all viewports.

12. Pick the **Zoom Extents All** button to zoom to the extents of the objects in the viewports.

13. Save the scene.

Figure 5-21. All objects in the scene are in their correct locations.

Assigning Materials

In this part of the tutorial, you will first load materials into the **Material Editor**. Then, you will assign the materials to objects.

1. Select Table Base.

2. Pick the **Material Editor** button in the **Main Toolbar**.
   The **Material Editor** is opened.

Material Editor

3. Activate the first sample slot, then pick the **Get Material** button.
   The **Material/Map Browser** dialog box is opened.

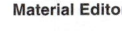

Get Material

4. Select the **Mtl Library** radio button in the **Browse From:** area of the dialog box.
   The materials in the 3dsmax.mat library file are displayed.

5. Double-click on the material Stones_Benedeti in the dialog box.
   The material is displayed in the first slot of the **Material Editor**.

6. Pick the **Assign Material to Selection** button in the **Material Editor**.
   The material is assigned to Table Base.

Assign Material to Selection

7. Select Table Top in any viewport. Assign the material Stones_Travertn to it using the same method.

8. Similarly, assign the material Wood_Oak to Lamp Base.

9. Assign the material Metal_Chrome to Frame.

10. Assign the material Metal_Dark_Gold to Socket.

11. Assign the material Metal_Galvanized to Shade. Close the **Material/Map Browser** and the **Material Editor**.

12. With Shade selected, pick **UV Coordinates** in the **Modifiers** pull-down menu. Then, select **UVW Map** in the cascading menu.
    A UVW map modifier is applied to the shade, which applies mapping coordinates. The **Modify** tab is automatically opened.

13. In the **Parameters** rollout, pick the **Shrink Wrap** radio button.

14. Save the scene.

Creating Lights and Cameras

1. Activate the Top viewport and pick the **Zoom All** button.

Zoom All

2. Pick near the center of the objects and drag the cursor down until the objects are displayed about one quarter of their original size.

3. Pick **Create** in the **Command Panel**. Pick the **Cameras** button and select **Standard** from the drop-down list.

Create

4. Pick the **Target** button in the **Object Type** rollout.

Lights

5. Pick a point in the lower-left corner of the Top viewport to position the camera. Then, drag the cursor up and pick a point in the center of the objects to set the target. Right-click to end the command.

6. Make the Perspective viewport active and then press the [C] key.
   The Perspective viewport becomes the Camera01 viewport.

7. Activate the Left viewport. Pick the **Select and Move** button and the **Restrict to XY Plane** button.

Figure 5-22. A camera is created, and the camera viewport is displayed.

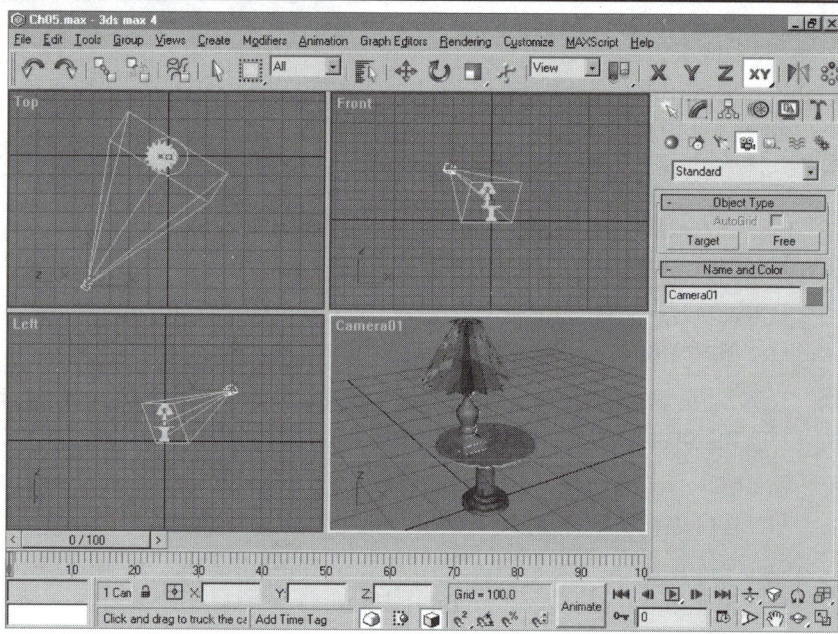

8. Move the camera and the target until you get a desired view of the objects in the Camera01 viewport.

9. Similarly, move the camera in the Front viewport adjust the camera view.
   As you move the camera, the camera viewport is dynamically updated.

Truck Camera

10. Activate the Camera01 viewport. Pick the **Truck Camera** button and "pan" the viewport so the objects are placed in the center, Figure 5-22.

Lights

11. Pick **Create** in the **Command Panel**. Pick the **Lights** button and select **Standard** from the drop-down list. Pick the **Omni** button in the **Object Type** rollout.
    The rollouts for an omni light are displayed.

12. Accept the default settings, and then pick in the lower-left corner of the Top viewport.
    An omni light (Omni01) is placed at the specified position.

13. Select another point at the upper-right corner of the viewport.
    Another omni light (Omni02) is placed at the specified position with the default settings.

14. Pick the **Select and Move** button and the **Restrict to XY Plane** button.

15. Activate the Front viewport. Move Omni01 up and place it at the upper-left corner of the viewport. Move Omni02 up and place it at the upper-right corner of the viewport.

16. Activate the Left viewport. Move Omni01 to the upper-right corner of the viewport and Omni02 to the upper-left corner of the viewport.

17. Pick the **Zoom Extents All** button, Figure 5-23.

18. Save the scene.

Figure 5-23. Two omni lights are added to the scene.

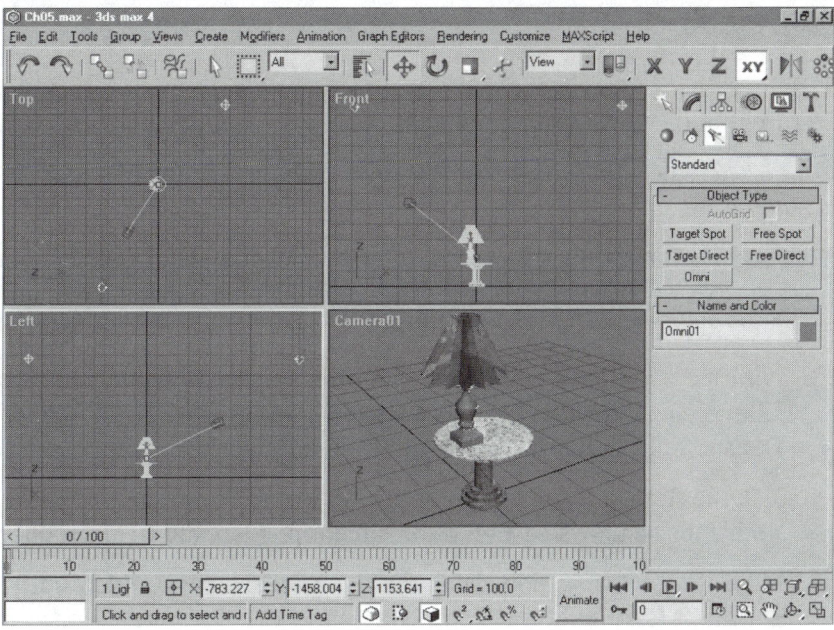

Rendering the View

1. Activate the Camera01 viewport. Pick the **Render Scene** button on the **Main** toolbar. The **Render Scene** dialog box is displayed.

Render Scene

2. Accept the default settings and pick the **Render** button at the bottom of the dialog box. The rendered image is displayed in the render window, Figure 5-24.

3. Close both the render window and the **Render Scene** dialog box to return to the drawing screen.

Figure 5-24. The scene is rendered with two omni lights providing illumination.

Using Spotlights

Create

Lights

The omni lights you have added to the scene cast light in all directions. Spotlights, on the other hand, cast light in one direction. A spotlight will be used to simulate the light cast by the lamp.

1. Pick **Create** in the **Command Panel**. Pick the **Lights** button and select **Standard** from the drop-down list.

2. Pick the **Target Spot** button in the **Object Type** rollout. Select a point at the top of Socket in the Front viewport, where the lightbulb would be, and drag the cursor down to place the target on Table Top. Make sure the spotlight is centered on Socket in the Left viewport.

3. With the spotlight selected, pick **Modify** in the **Command Panel**. In the **General Parameters** rollout, check the **Cast Shadows** check box near the top of the rollout.
   The spotlight will now cast shadows in a rendering.

Render Last

4. Pick the **Render Last** button on the **Main** toolbar to render the Camera01 viewport again.
   Notice the shadows cast onto the table top. Also, the light produces a sharp "ring" of light.

5. Close the render window. With the spotlight selected, pick **Modify** in the **Command Panel**. In the **Spotlight Parameters** rollout, enter 15 in the **Hotspot:** spinner and 55 in the **Falloff:** spinner.

6. Pick the **Render Last** button to render the Camera01 viewport again.
   Notice how the edge of the light cone cast by the spotlight is softened, while shadows are still cast, Figure 5-25.

7. Close the render window. Save the scene.

Figure 5-25. A spotlight is added inside the shade to simulate the light from a lightbulb. Notice the shadows on the table top.

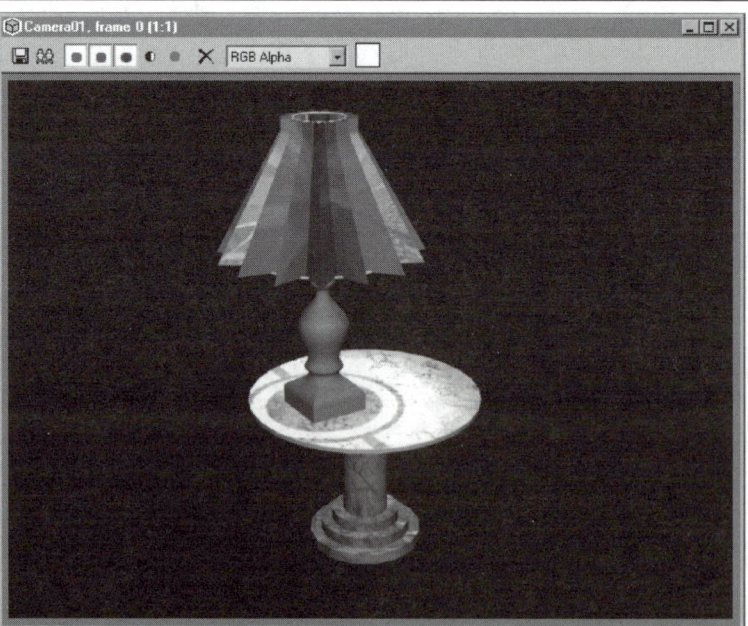

Self-Evaluation Test

Answer the following questions. Then compare your answers with the correct answers given at the end of this chapter.

1. You can use the _____ modifier to revolve a profile around one of its axes.

2. When you apply an extrude modifier to a shape, the shape is extruded by the value entered in the _____ spinner in the **Parameters** rollout.

3. Different shapes can be placed along a spline path at different levels by moving along the path using the _____ spinner and "getting" a new shape.

4. Spline polygons created as shapes are converted into _____ objects when lofted.

5. The _____ vertex of the path is indicated by a small yellow cross mark.

6. To avoid twisting while lofting multiple shapes, the _____ of the shapes should align.

7. When using the _____ key, it is possible to copy a shape anywhere along a path.

8. After creating a loft object, you can modify it further by using the buttons in the _____ rollout.

9. Which button allows you to scale an object unequally on its axes?

10. You can create and offset a mirrored copy of an object using the _____ dialog box.

Exercises

In this exercise, you will loft a hexagon along a path. You will then add different shapes at different levels of the path to create the final model of a decorative column. Then, you will add lights and materials, and render the final scene.

1. Draw the shapes as shown below. Use your own dimensions.

2. Loft the second largest hexagon along a straight line path. The path should be long enough to approximate the final object shown below.

3. Place the different shapes along different path levels.

4. Move, copy, rotate, and scale shapes along the path as needed to create the final object.

5. Add materials and lights as needed. Then, render the scene.

6. Save the scene as Ex05.max in the folder of your choice.

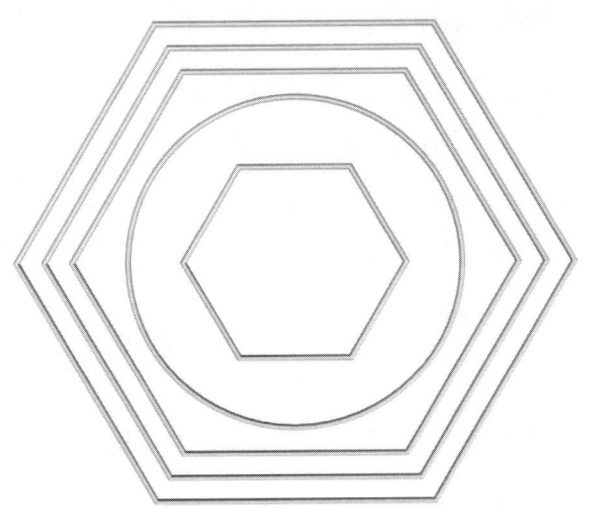

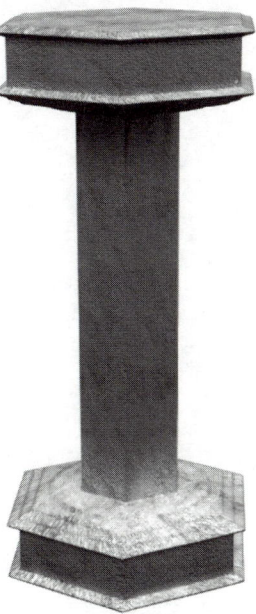

Answers

The following are the correct answers to the questions in the Self-Evaluation Test.

1. lathe; 2. **Amount:**; 3. **Path:**; 4. mesh; 5. current; 6. first vertices; 7. [Shift]; 8. **Deformations**; 9. **Select and Non-uniform Scale**; 10. **Mirror**

Chapter 6

Deformation Tools

Learning Objectives

After completing this chapter, you will be able to:

○ Create shapes and loft them.

○ Identify the loft object deformation tools.

○ Use the deformation tools on a loft object.

Tutorial Description

In this tutorial, you will create a ceiling fan consisting of a hub, three blades, and the blade connectors. You will also create lampshades below the hub. You will create these objects by lofting shapes and then modify them using the deformation tools. You will also assign materials to the objects and add lights and a camera to the scene. You will then render the scene.

Start by resetting 3ds max. This sets the system to default values and erases all existing data. If you want to save the existing file, make sure you do so before resetting 3ds max. Then, pick **Reset** in the **File** pull-down menu. Pick the **Yes** button in the dialog box that is displayed.

Creating the Hub

You will create the hub by first lofting a shape. Then, deformation tools are used to modify the loft object and produce the final shape.

2D Snap Toggle

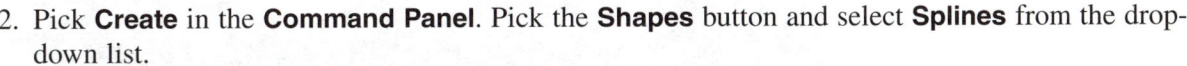
Create

1. Make the Top viewport active. Select the **2D Snap Toggle** button from the **Snap** flyout.
   The default snap, which is grid points, is turned on.

2. Pick **Create** in the **Command Panel**. Pick the **Shapes** button and select **Splines** from the drop-down list.

Shapes

3. Pick the **Circle** button in the **Object Type** rollout. Open the **Keyboard Entry** rollout. Type 40 in the **Radius:** spinner. Then, pick the **Create** button.
   A circle is created at the center of the viewport.

4. Right-click in the Front viewport to activate it. Pick the **Line** button in the **Object Type** rollout.
   The rollouts for a line are displayed.

5. Pick the first point of the line at coordinates 0, 0, 0 as shown in the coordinate display. Pick the second point at coordinates 0, 0, 20. Right-click to exit the command.

Geometry

6. Pick **Create** in the **Command Panel**. Pick the **Geometry** button and select **Compound Objects** from the drop-down list.

7. With the line selected, pick the **Loft** button in the **Object Type** rollout. Pick the **Move** radio button in the **Creation Method** rollout. Then, pick the **Get Shape** button.

8. Pick the circle in the Front viewport. In the **Name and Color** rollout, name the loft object Hub.
   The circle is lofted along the line.

9. Pick the **Zoom Extents All** button, Figure 6-1. Save the scene as Ch06.max in the folder of your choice.

Modifying the Hub

Modify

1. With the loft object selected, pick **Modify** in the **Command Panel**. Then, open the **Deformations** rollout.
   The buttons corresponding to the five deformations appear in this rollout.

2. Pick the **Bevel** button in the rollout.
   The **Bevel Deformation** dialog box is displayed. The horizontal red line represents the path steps of the loft object, with the left point of the line representing the first vertex of the path. The number in the ruler at the top represents the length of the path in a percentage. The location of the line on either side represents the bevel in a percentage.

Insert Corner Point

3. Pick the **Insert Corner Point** button at the top of the dialog box. Pick on the red line at 25%. Refer to the ruler at the top. Then, type 25 in the left-hand text box at the bottom of the dialog box and press [Enter].
   A control point is added at this location.

4. Pick on the red line at 75%. Then, type 75 in the left-hand box and press [Enter].
   A control point is added at this location.

Figure 6-1. A cylinder is created for the hub.

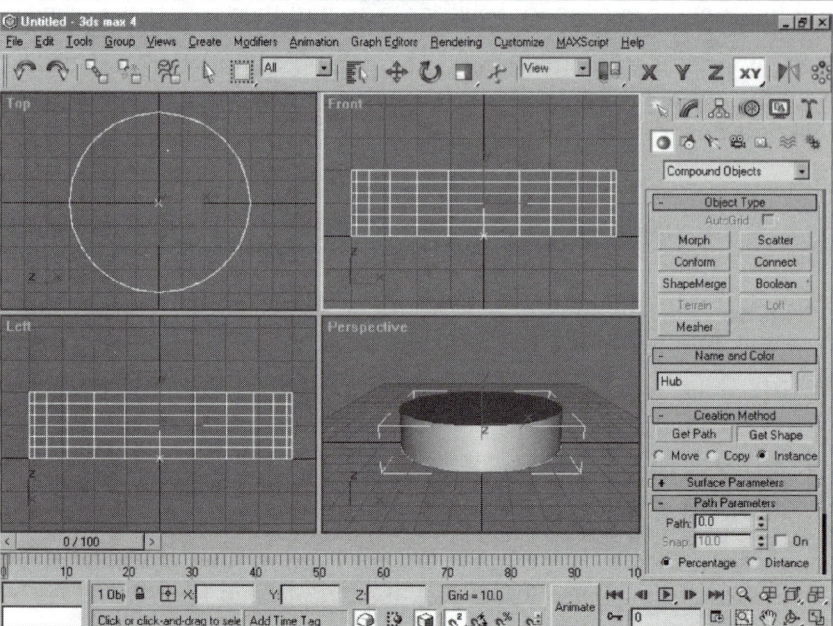

5. Pick the **Move Control Point** button. Select the first vertex at the left and move it up by one "line" so 10 is displayed in the right-hand text box at the bottom of the dialog box.
   The lower portion of the hub is beveled.

Move Control Point

6. Now move the last vertex on the right up one line. Close the **Bevel Deformation** dialog box.
   The upper portion of the hub is beveled.

7. Right-click on control point second from the left to display a shortcut menu. Select **Bezier-Smooth** from the menu.
   The lower bevel is slightly curved, Figure 6-2. Using the **Move Control Point** button, you can adjust the handles of the Bézier-type control point.

8. Close the **Bevel Deformation** dialog box.

9. Save the scene.

Creating Connectors

Create

1. Activate the Top viewport. Pick **Create** in the **Command Panel**. Pick the **Geometry** button and select **Standard Primitives** from the drop-down list.

Geometry

2. Pick the **Box** button in the **Object Type** rollout. Open the **Keyboard Entry** rollout and enter 10 in the **Length:** spinner, 30 in the **Width:** spinner, and 5 in the **Height:** spinner. Then, pick the **Create** button. In the **Name and Color** rollout, name the box Connect01.
   A small box is created and named Connect01.

3. Select the **Zoom Extents All** button.
   All objects are zoomed to their extents in all viewports.

Zoom Extents All

4. Pick the **Select and Move** and **Restrict to Y** buttons on the **Main** toolbar. Also, turn snap off.

Select and Move

5. Move Connect01 up in the Top viewport until its upper edge is placed a little above the circumference of Hub. The upper-right and upper-left corners should be outside the circumference of Hub. Zoom as needed.

Restrict to Y

Figure 6-2. The bottom bevel on the hub is curved.

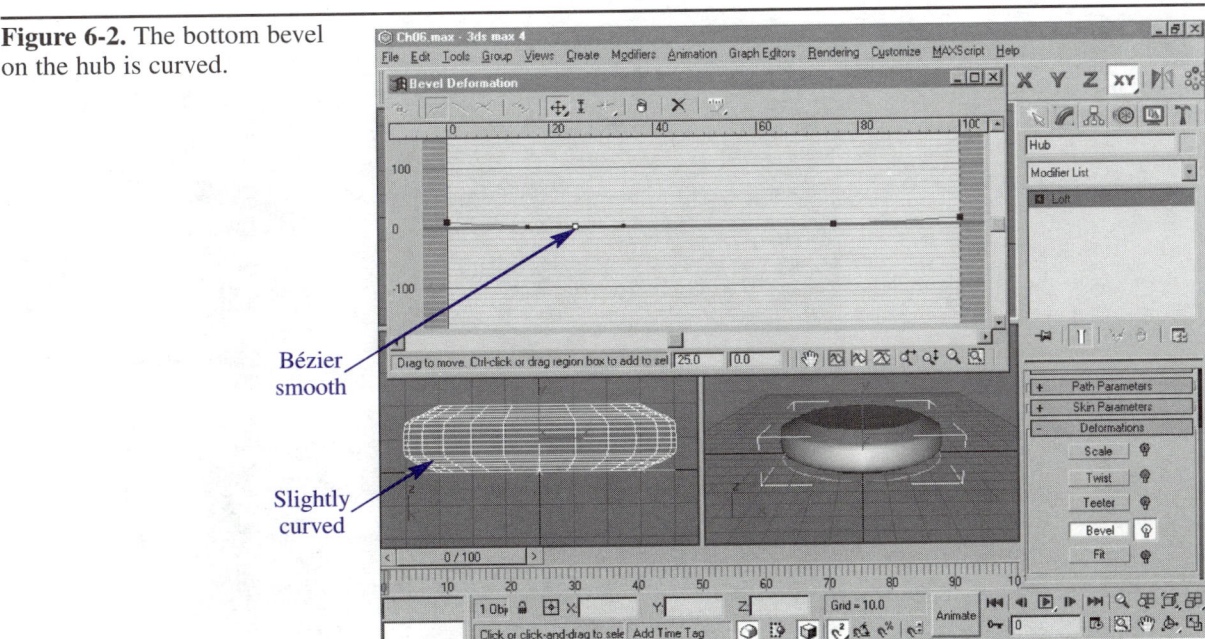

6. Activate the Left viewport and move Connect01 up until it is centered vertically on Hub, Figure 6-3.

7. Pick **Create** in the **Command Panel**. Pick the **Geometry** button and select **Compound Objects** from the drop-down list. Pick the **Boolean** from the **Object Type** rollout.

8. Select the **Intersection** radio button in the **Parameters** rollout. Also, select the **Copy** radio button in the **Pick Boolean** rollout. Then, select the **Pick Operand B** button. Select Hub in any viewport.

   The intersection Boolean operation saves only the common portion between the two objects. The rest of the individual portions are lost. Connect01 matches the outer surface of Hub. Since the **Copy** radio button was on, the original Hub remains.

9. Activate the Top viewport. Pick **Create** in the **Command Panel**. Pick the **Geometry** button and select **Standard Primitives** from the drop-down list. Pick the **Box** button in the **Object Type** rollout.

10. Open the **Keyboard Entry** rollout. Enter 30 in the **Length:** spinner, 10 in the **Width:** spinner, and 3 in the **Height:** spinner. Pick the **Create** button. In the **Name and Color** rollout, name the box Connect Tab01.

    A small box is created in the center of the viewport.

11. Pick the **Select and Move** button. Move Connect Tab01 up until both corners of its lower edge are just inside the circular (top) edge of Connect01.

12. Activate the Left viewport. Move Connect Tab01 up so its upper edge aligns with the upper edge of Connect01.

13. Select Connect01. Then, pick **Create** in the **Command Panel**. Pick the **Geometry** button and select **Compound Objects** from the drop-down list. Pick the **Boolean** button in the **Object Type** rollout.

14. In the **Parameters** rollout, select the **Union** radio button in the **Operations** area. In the **Pick Boolean** rollout, select the **Move** radio button. Then, select the **Pick Operand B** button. In any viewport, pick Connect Tab01. Right-click to end the Boolean operation.

    It may be easiest to select Connect Tab01 by its name.

15. Select Hub. Then, pick the **Boolean** button in the **Object Type** rollout.

Figure 6-3. The first part of the connector is drawn.

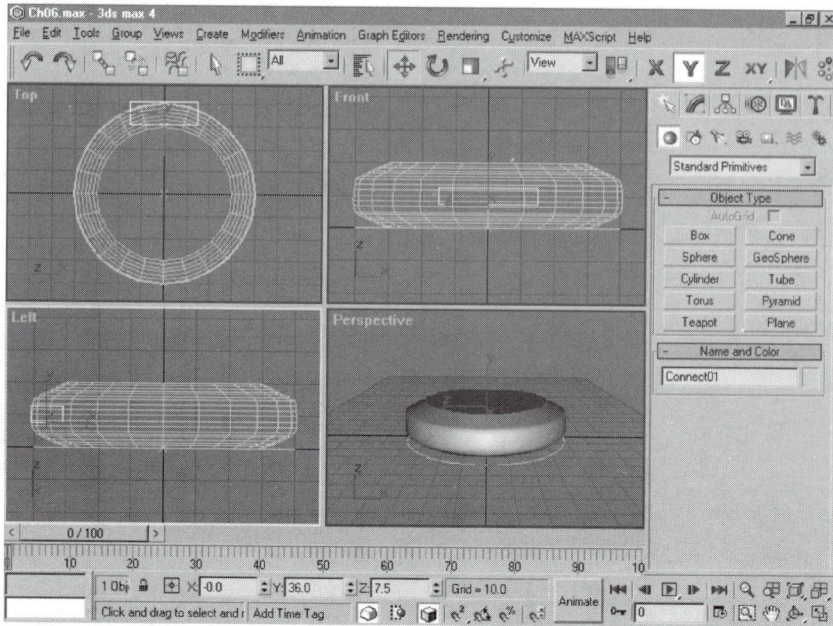

16. In the **Parameters** rollout, pick the **Subtraction (A-B)** radio button. In the **Pick Boolean** rollout, select the **Copy** radio button. Then, select the **Pick Operand B** button and select Connect01 in any viewport. Right-click to end the Boolean operation.
    A slot is created in Hub in which Connect01 fits, Figure 6-4.

17. Save the scene.

Creating More Connectors

1. Select Connect01. Then, pick **Clone** in the **Edit** pull-down menu.
   The **Clone Options** dialog box is displayed.

2. Enter **Connect02** in the **Name:** text box and pick the **OK** button.
   A copy of Connect01 is created directly on top of the original, and the copy is selected.

Selection Lock Toggle

3. Pick the **Selection Lock Toggle** button at the bottom of the 3ds max screen to lock the current selection, which is Connect02.
   The Connect02 is locked in the selection set; no other objects can be picked and selected.

Select and Rotate

4. Pick the **2D Snap Toggle** button to turn snap on. Then, pick the **Select and Rotate** button on the **Main** toolbar. Make sure the **Restrict to Z** button is selected. Also, pick the **Use Transform Coordinate Center** button from the flyout next to the **Restrict to X** button.

5. In the Top viewport, rotate the object 120°, as indicated in the coordinate display.
   Since snap is on, the point about which the object is rotated is the point picked. The selection is locked, so you can pick anywhere in the viewport and rotate the object about that point. With snap off, the point of rotation is determined by the **Transform Coordinate Center** buttons. However, even if snap is on, when **Use Pivot Point Center** is selected, the object rotates about its pivot point.

6. With Connect02 selected, pick **Clone** in the **Edit** pull-down menu to display the **Clone Options** dialog box. Name the copy Connect03 and pick the **OK** button.
   A copy of Connect02 is created and placed directly on top of the original. The copy is selected.

7. As Connect03 is selected, pick the **Selection Lock Toggle** button to lock the selection. In the Top viewport, rotate Connect03 120°, just as you did Connect02.

Figure 6-4. The connector fits inside a slot created in the hub.

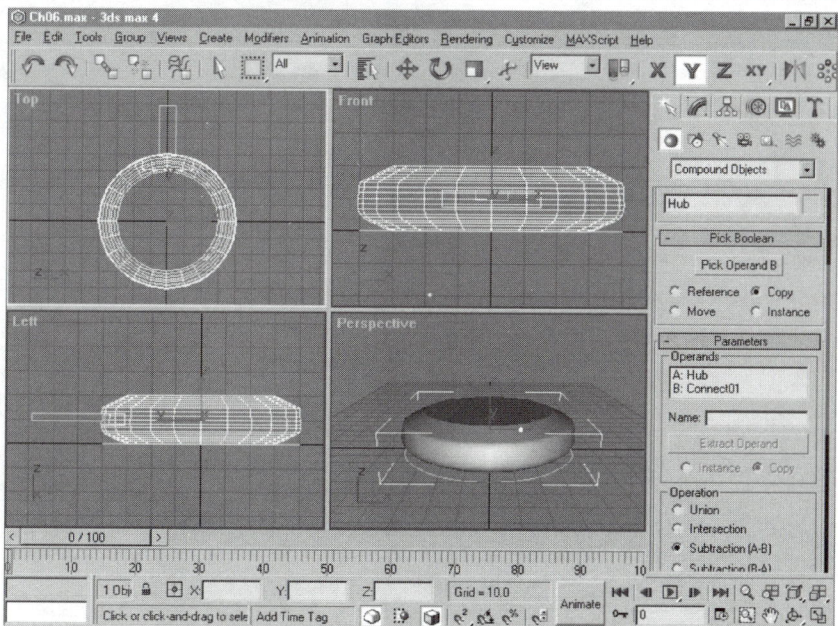

8. Pick the **Selection Lock Toggle** button to unlock the selection. Then, select Hub.

9. Pick **Create** in the **Command Panel**. Pick the **Geometry** button and select **Compound Objects** from the drop-down list. Pick the **Boolean** button in the **Object Type** rollout.

10. In the **Parameters** rollout, pick the **Subtraction (A-B)** radio button. In the **Pick Boolean** rollout, select the **Copy** radio button. Then, select the **Pick Operand B** button and select Connect02. Right-click to end the Boolean operation.
    A slot is created in Hub in which Connect02 fits.

11. Similarly, create a slot for Connect03, Figure 6-5.

12. Save the scene.

Creating the Shaft Hole

1. Pick **Create** in the **Command Panel**. Pick the **Geometry** button and select **Standard Primitives** from the drop-down list. Pick the **Cylinder** button in the **Object Type** rollout.

2. Activate the Top viewport. Open the **Keyboard Entry** rollout. Enter 2 in the **Radius:** spinner and 20 in the **Height:** spinner. Pick the **Create** button.
   A small cylinder is created in the center Hub.

3. Select Hub.

4. Pick **Create** in the **Command Panel**. Pick the **Geometry** button and select **Compound Objects** from the drop-down list. Pick the **Boolean** button in the **Object Type** rollout.

5. In the **Parameters** rollout, pick the **Subtraction (A-B)** radio button. In the **Pick Boolean** rollout, select the **Move** radio button. Then, select the **Pick Operand B** button and select the small cylinder.
   A small hole is created in Hub.

6. Save the scene.

Figure 6-5. The three connectors are finished.

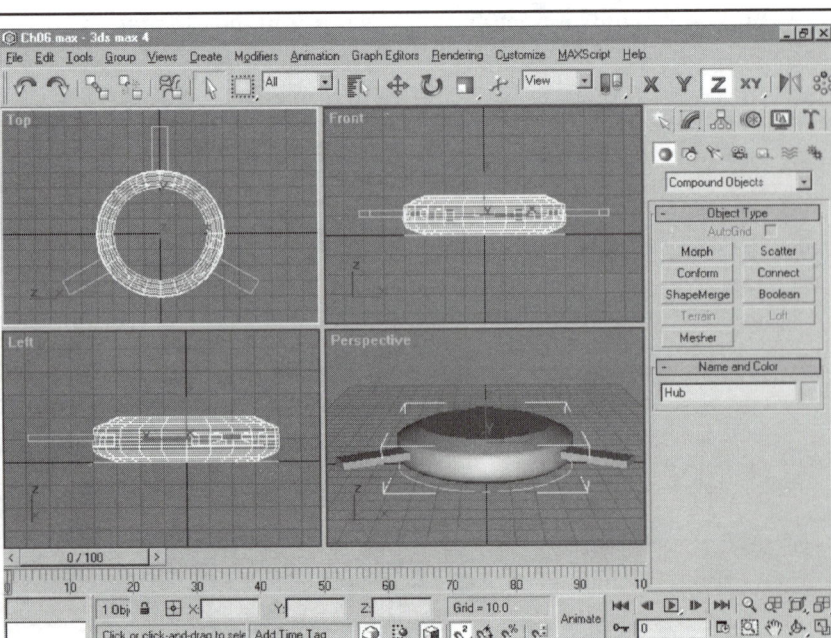

Creating the Blades

You will now create a single blade by lofting a shape and using deformation tools to modify it. You will then make two copies of the blade.

1. Zoom out in the Top viewport until the objects are displayed about half of their original size. Turn snap on, if it is not already.

2. Pick **Create** in the **Command Panel**. Pick the **Shapes** button and select **Splines** from the drop-down list. Pick the **Line** button in the **Object Type** rollout.
   The rollouts for a line are displayed.

3. Pick the first point at coordinates 0, 0, 0. Select the next point at coordinates 0, 140, 0. In the Name and Color rollout, name the line Blade Path. Right-click to exit the command.

4. Activate the Front viewport. Pick the **Rectangle** button in the **Object Type** rollout. Expand the **Keyboard Entry** rollout. Enter 2 in the **Length:** spinner and 30 in the **Width:** spinner. Then, pick the **Create** button. In the **Name and Color** rollout, name the rectangle Blade Shape.
   A small rectangle is created.

5. Maximize the Front viewport. Then, zoom in on the small rectangle.

6. With the rectangle selected, pick <u>P</u>atch/Spline Editing in the **M<u>o</u>difiers** pull-down menu. Then, select **Edit Spline** in the cascading menu.
   An edit spline modifier is applied to the parametric rectangle, and the **Modify** tab is automatically opened.

7. Expand the sub-object tree in the modifier stack. Then, select **Vertex** to enter vertex sub-object mode.
   The vertices at the four corners are available for editing.

8. Pick the **Select and Move** button and select the upper-left vertex.
   Bézier handles are displayed at a right angle to each other, indicating this is a Bézier corner vertex.

9. Move the handle on the horizontal edge up until the segment is slightly curved.

10. Move the handles at each vertex as necessary to get the shape shown in Figure 6-6. Then, pick **Edit Spline** in the modifier stack to exit sub-object mode.
    The modifier name is highlighted grey, indicating sub-object mode has been exited.

11. Display the four-viewport configuration. Pick the **Zoom Extents All** button.

Lofting the Blade

1. Activate the Top viewport. Then, select Blade Path.

2. Pick **Create** in the **Command Panel**. Pick the **Geometry** button and select **Compound Objects** from the drop-down list. Pick the **Loft** button in the **Object Type** rollout.

3. In the **Creation Method** rollout, pick the **Move** radio button. Then, pick the **Get Shape** button. Select Blade Shape. In the **Name and Color** rollout, name the loft object Blade01.
   The modified rectangle is lofted along the line, Figure 6-7.

4. Activate the Left viewport and maximize it. Turn snap of if it is on.

5. Pick the **Select and Move** and **Restrict to X** buttons on the **Main** toolbar. Move Blade01 left 47 units, as indicated in the coordinate display. Then, pick the **Restrict to Y** button and move Blade01 up so its upper edge aligns with the lower edge of Connect01.

6. Display the four-viewport configuration and pick the **Zoom Extents All Selected**. Also, turn snap on.

7. Save the scene.

Figure 6-6. The shape for lofting a fan blade is adjusted.

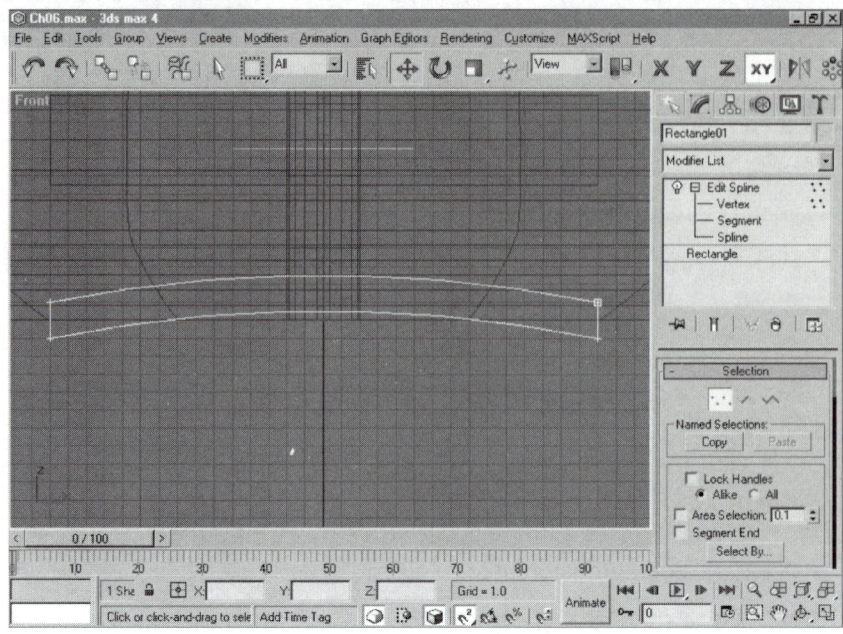

Figure 6-7. The fan blade shape is lofted along the path.

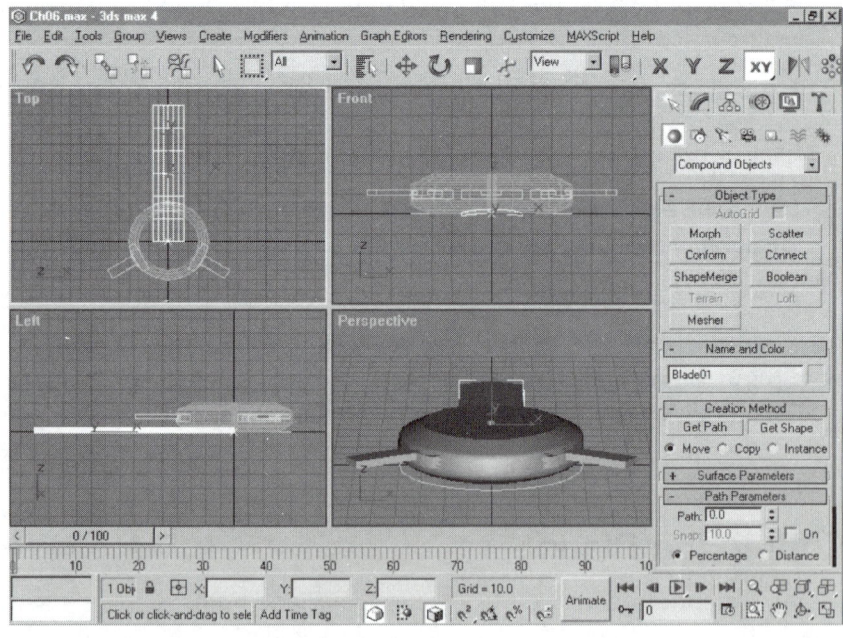

Modifying the Blade Appearance

1. With Blade01 selected, pick **Modify** in the **Command Panel**. Then, open the **Deformations** rollout. Turn snap on.

   Buttons corresponding to the five deformations appear in this rollout.

2. Pick the **Scale** button from the rollout.

   The **Scale Deformation** dialog box is displayed. The horizontal red line represents the path steps of the loft object with the first vertex of the path on the left. The number in the ruler at the top represents the length of the path in a percentage. The location of the line on either side represents the scale in a percentage. The left and right vertices at the same vertical point (100%) show the loft object is not scaled.

3. Pick the **Move Control Point** button and move the right-hand vertex down two lines so 80 is displayed in the right-hand text box at the bottom of the dialog box. Then move the left-hand vertex up by one line until 110 is displayed in the right-hand text box.

Move Control Point

   The profile of the loft object is tapered.

4. Close the **Scale Deformation** dialog box. Then, pick the **Twist** button in the **Deformations** rollout.
   The **Twist Deformation** dialog box is displayed. This dialog box is similar to the **Scale Deformation** dialog box. The horizontal red line is at the 0 position and represents the degree of twist along the path axis.

5. Move the right-hand vertex up by one line until 10 is displayed in the right-hand text box at the bottom of the dialog box.
   A slight twist is applied to Blade01 toward its tapered end, Figure 6-8.

6. Close the **Twist Deformation** dialog box and pick the **Zoom Extents All** button.

7. Save the scene.

Completing the Blade

1. Pick **Create** in the **Command Panel**. Pick the **Geometry** button and select **Standard Primitives** from the drop-down list. Pick the **Cylinder** button in the **Object Type** rollout.

2. Activate the Top viewport. In the **Keyboard Entry** rollout, enter 50 in the **Radius:** spinner and 20 in the **Height:** spinner. Select the **Create** button. In the **Name and Color** rollout, name the cylinder Blade Drill.
   A cylinder is created that overlaps a small portion of Blade01.

3. Select Blade01.

4. Pick **Create** in the **Command Panel**. Pick the **Geometry** button and select **Compound Objects** from the drop-down list. Pick the **Boolean** button in the **Object Type** rollout.

5. In the **Parameters** rollout, pick the **Subtraction (A-B)** radio button. In the **Pick Boolean** rollout, pick the **Move** radio button. Then, select the **Pick Operand B** button. Select Blade Drill.
   The inner edge of Blade01 is curved, Figure 6-9.

Figure 6-8. The fan blade is twisted.

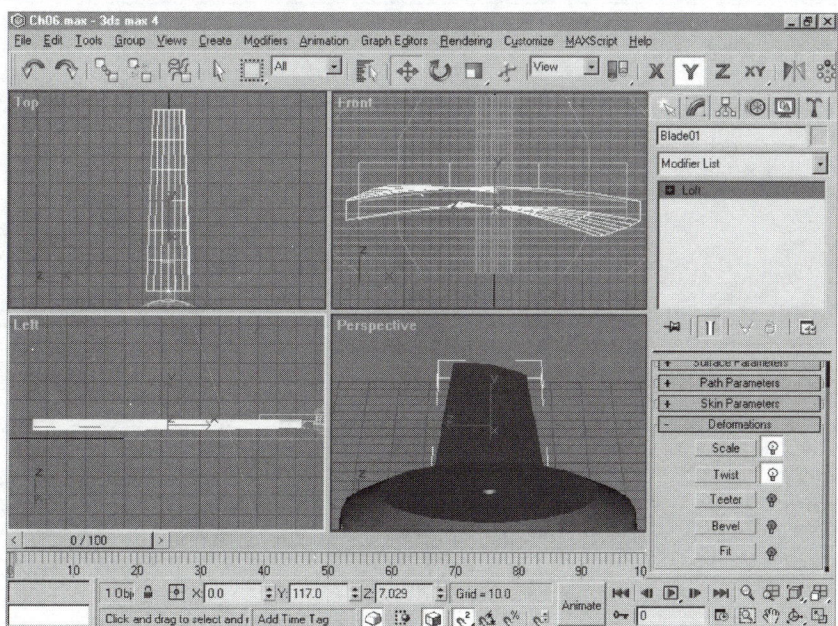

Figure 6-9. The inner edge of the fan blade is curved.

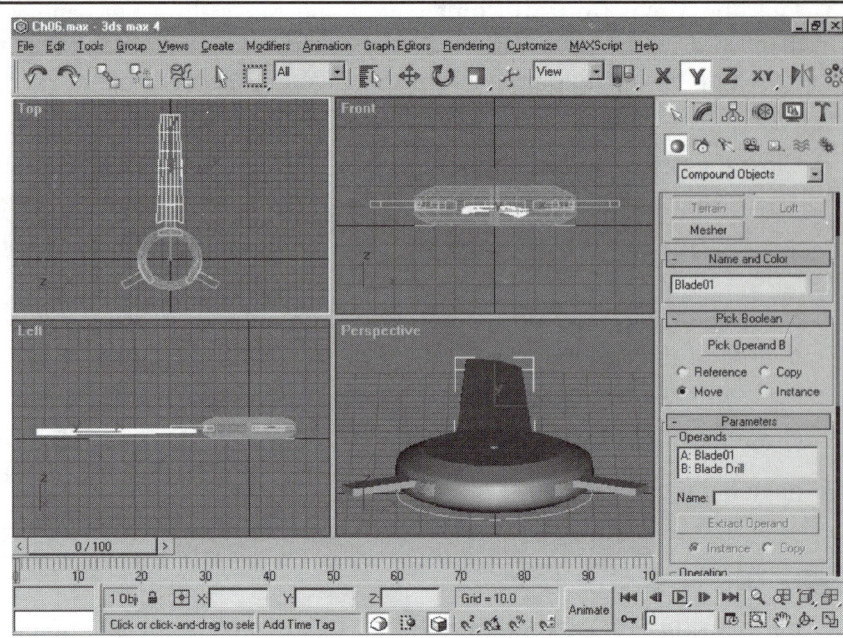

6. With Blade01 selected, pick **Clone** in the **Edit** pull-down menu. The **Clone Options** dialog box is displayed. Type Blade02 in the **Name:** text box and pick the **OK** button.
   A copy of Blade01 is created on top of the original object, and the copy is selected.

7. With Blade02 selected, pick the **Selection Lock Toggle** button. Also, pick the **Select and Rotate** button and **Use Transform Coordinate Center** button on the **Main** toolbar. Turn snap on.

8. In the Top viewport, pick at 0, 0, 0 and rotate Blade02 120°.

9. Similarly, make a clone of Blade02 and name it Blade03. Then, rotate Blade03 120° about the center of Hub, Figure 6-10.

10. Unlock the selection and pick the **Zoom Extents All** button.

11. Save the scene.

Figure 6-10. The three fan blades are created.

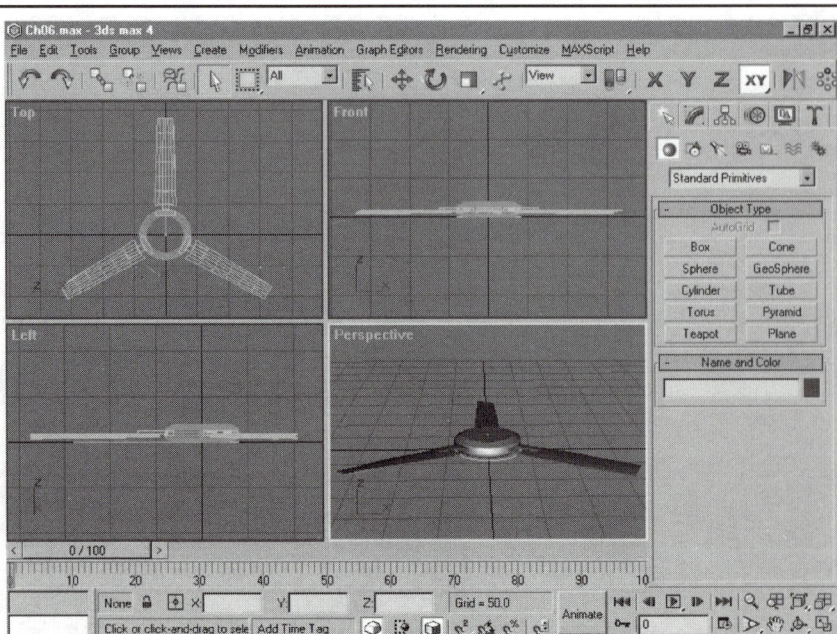

Creating the Rod

You will now create the rod which holds the fan to the ceiling. This is created from standard primitive objects.

1. Activate the Top viewport. Pick **Create** in the **Command Panel**. Pick the **Geometry** button and select **Standard Primitives** from the drop-down list. Pick the **Tube** button in the **Object Type** rollout.
   The rollouts for a tube are displayed.

2. In the **Keyboard Entry** rollout, enter 1 in the **Inner Radius:** spinner, 2 in the **Outer Radius:** spinner, and 150 in the **Height:** spinner. Select the **Create** button. In the **Name and Color** rollout, name the tube Rod.
   A rod is created passing through the hole in Hub.

3. Pick the **Cylinder** button in the **Object Type** rollout. In the **Keyboard Entry** rollout, enter 10 in the **Radius:** spinner, and 3 in the **Height:** spinner. Pick the **Create** button. In the **Name and Color** rollout, name the cylinder Rod Bottom.
   A small cylinder is created at the bottom of Hub.

4. Activate the Left viewport and maximize it.

5. Pick **Select and Move** and **Restrict to Y** buttons on the **Main** toolbar. Turn snap off. Move the cylinder down so its top edge aligns with the bottom edge of Hub.

6. Select Rod. Pick **Create** in the **Command Panel**. Pick the **Geometry** button and select **Compound Objects** from the drop-down list. Pick the **Boolean** button in the **Object Type** rollout.

7. In the **Parameters** rollout, pick the **Union** radio button. In the **Pick Boolean** rollout, select the **Move** radio button. Then, select the **Pick Operand B** button and select Rod Bottom. Again enter **Rod** in the **Name and Color** rollout. Right-click to end the Boolean operation.

8. Display the four-viewport configuration and select the **Zoom Extents All** button, Figure 6-11.

9. Save the scene.

Figure 6-11. The rod is created.

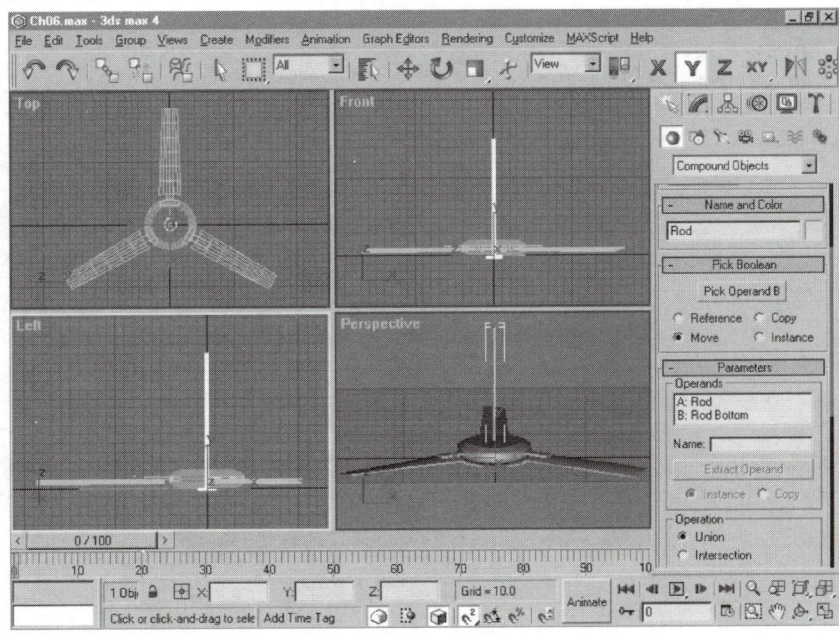

Creating the Lamp Shade Bracket

You will now create a lamp shade and attach it to the rod with the help of a bracket. These are created by lofting shapes and then applying deformation to the loft objects. First, create the bracket.

1. Activate the Front viewport and maximize it.

2. Pan the viewport up so the rod just begins to move off screen.

3. Turn on the **2D Snap Toggle** button, and right-click on it to display the **Grid and Snap Settings** dialog box. Select the **Home Grid** tab and enter 5 in the **Grid Spacing:** spinner. Close the dialog box.

4. Pick **Create** in the **Command Panel**. Pick the **Shapes** button and select **Splines** from the drop-down list. Pick the **Line** button in the **Object Type** rollout.

5. Pick the first vertex at coordinates 0.0, 0.0, 0.0 as shown in the coordinate display.

6. Continue picking to place vertices at the following coordinates, as shown in the coordinate display.

10.0	0.0	−10.0
25.0	0.0	− 5.0
35.0	0.0	−15.0
30.0	0.0	−20.0

    Right-click to exit the command. In the **Name and Color** rollout, name the line Bracket.
    A rough path for the bracket is created, Figure 6-12.

Modify

7. With Bracket selected, pick **Modify** in the **Command Panel**. Expand the sub-object tree in the modifier stack and select **Vertex** to enter vertex sub-object editing mode.

8. Turn snap off. Pick the **Select and Move** button. Right-click on the second vertex you placed to display the quad menu. Select **Bezier** from the upper-left quadrant.
    The vertex is converted and Bézier handles are displayed.

9. Move the right-hand handle up so both handles are in a horizontal line and a smooth curve is created.

Figure 6-12. A spline is created to use as a loft path for the bracket. The spline needs to be altered.

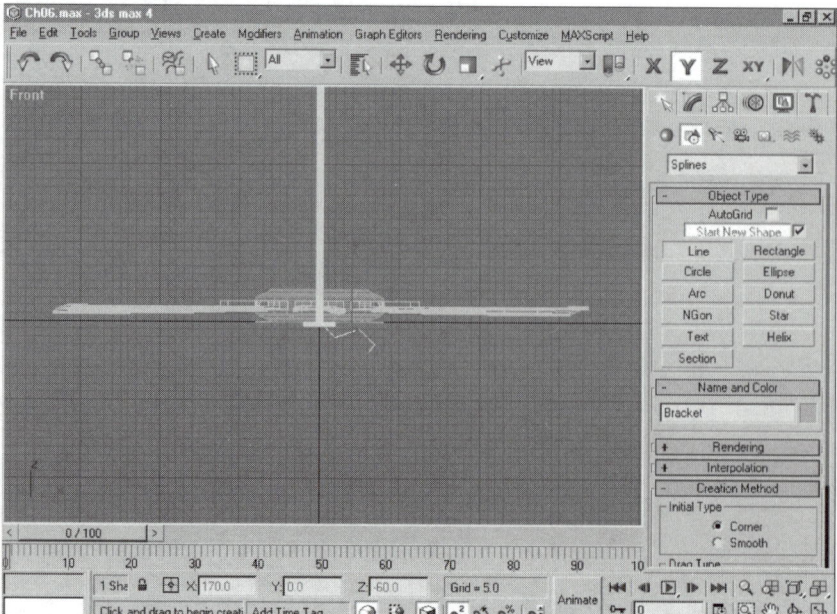

10. Similarly, convert the next two vertices (three and four) to Bézier and adjust the handles to produce a completely smooth curve. The handles of the fourth vertex should be in a vertical line. Also move the last vertex a little to the right, Figure 6-13.

11. Pick **Create** in the **Command Panel**. Pick the **Shapes** button and select **Splines** from the drop-down list. Pick the **Donut** button in the **Object Type** rollout.
    The rollouts for a donut are displayed.

12. In the **Keyboard Entry** rollout, enter 1 in the **Radius 1:** spinner and 1.5 in the **Radius 2:** spinner. Pick the **Create** button. In the **Name and Color** rollout, name the donut Bracket Shape.
    A small donut is created.

13. Select Bracket.

14. Pick **Create** in the **Command Panel**. Pick the **Geometry** button and select **Compound Objects** from the drop-down list. Pick the **Loft** button in the **Object Type** rollout.

15. In the **Creation Method** rollout, pick the **Move** radio button. Then, select the **Get Shape** button and pick Bracket Shape. Name the loft object Bracket.
    The donut is lofted along the path.

16. Save the scene.

Creating the Lamp Shade

1. Zoom into the area around Bracket and Hub leaving a small "blank" area below them, if you are not already at a similar zoom level. Also, turn snap on.

2. Pick **Create** in the **Command Panel**. Pick the **Shapes** button and select **Splines** from the drop-down list. Then, pick the **Line** button in the **Object Type** rollout.

3. Pick the first vertex at the center of the lower end of the **Bracket**. Pick the second vertex at coordinates 10, 0, –45. Right-click to end the command. In the **Name and Color** rollout, name the line Shade Path.

Figure 6-13. The bracket path is altered.

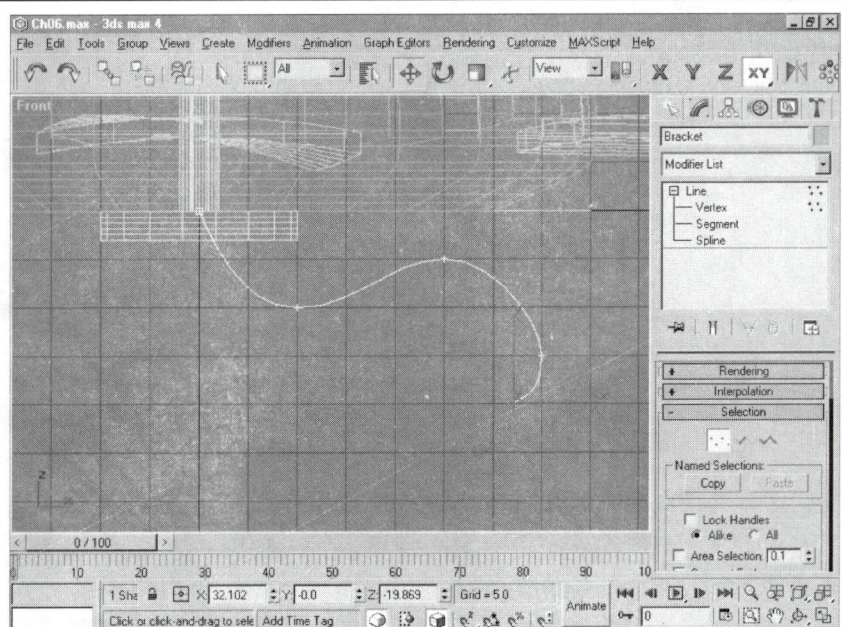

4. Pick the **Circle** button in the **Object Type** rollout. In the **Keyboard Entry** rollout, enter 15 in the **Radius:** spinner. Pick the **Create** button. In the **Name and Color** rollout, name the circle Shade Shape.

5. Select Shade Path. Pick **Create** in the **Command Panel**. Pick the **Geometry** button and select **Compound Objects** from the drop-down list. Pick the **Loft** button in the **Object Type** rollout.

6. In the **Creation Method** rollout, pick the **Get Shape** button. Select Shade Shape. In the **Name and Color** rollout, name the loft object Shade01, Figure 6-14.

7. Save the scene.

Altering the Shape of the Lamp Shade

1. With Shade01 selected, pick **Modify** in the **Command Panel**. Then, open the **Deformations** rollout and pick the **Scale** button.
   The **Scale Deformation** dialog box is displayed.

2. Pick the **Insert Corner Point** button. Then, pick on the red line at 20 percent. Refer to the ruler at the top. Then, type 20 in the left-hand text box to precisely move the control point.

3. Similarly, add a control point at 80%.

4. Pick the **Move Control Point** button. Move the control point at 0% down four lines until 60 is displayed in the right-hand text box at the bottom of the dialog box. Then, move the control point at 100% up by three lines until 130 is displayed in the right-hand text box.
   The shape of Shade01 is modified, Figure 6-15.

5. Close the **Scale Deformation** dialog box and select the **Teeter** button in the **Deformation** rollout.
   The **Teeter Deformation** dialog box is displayed.

Make Symmetrical

Display Y Axis

6. Pick the **Make Symmetrical** button in the dialog box to deselect it. Then, pick the **Display Y Axis** button.

   The red line turns green. This allows the loft object to be teetered along only the Y axis. The title bar of the dialog box indicates which axis is displayed. With **Scale**, **Teeter**, and **Fit** deformation tools, you can make changes to X and Y axes separately by making the **Make Symmetrical** button inactive and selecting the required axis button.

Figure 6-14. The shade loft object before deformations are applied.

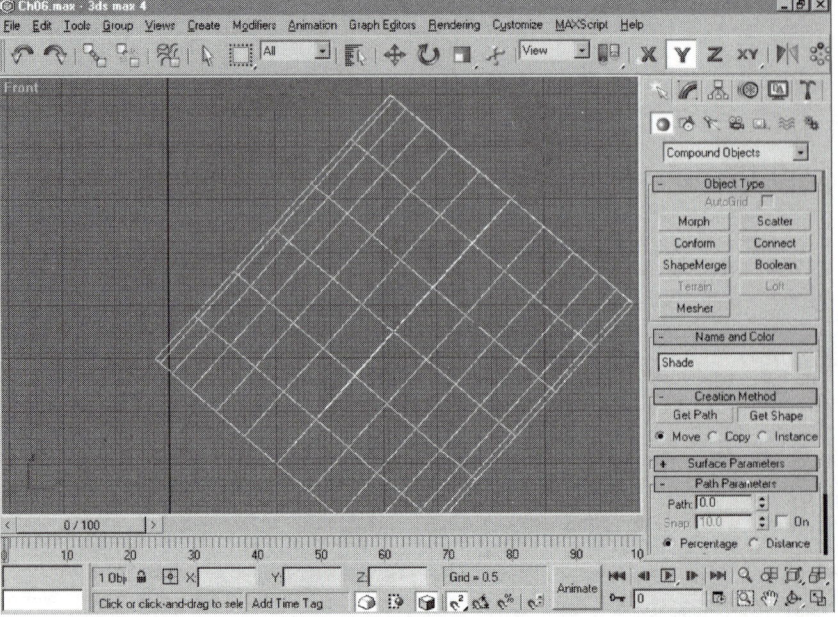

Figure 6-15. Scale deformation is applied to the shade loft object.

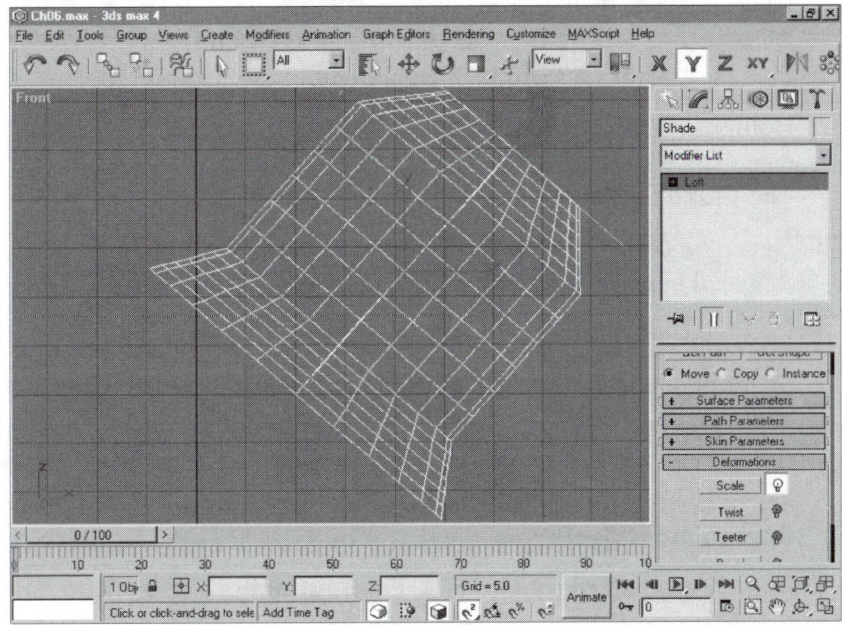

7. Pick the **Insert Corner Point** button. Then, pick on the green line near 80 percent, and type 80 in the left-hand text box at the bottom of the dialog box to move the control point to the precise position.

8. Pick the **Move Control Point** button. Move the right-hand control point up two lines until 20 is displayed in the right-hand text box.
   The base of Shade01 is teetered along Y axis, Figure 6-16.

9. Close the **Teeter Deformation** dialog box.

10. Save the scene.

Figure 6-16. The base of the shade has a teeter deformation applied.

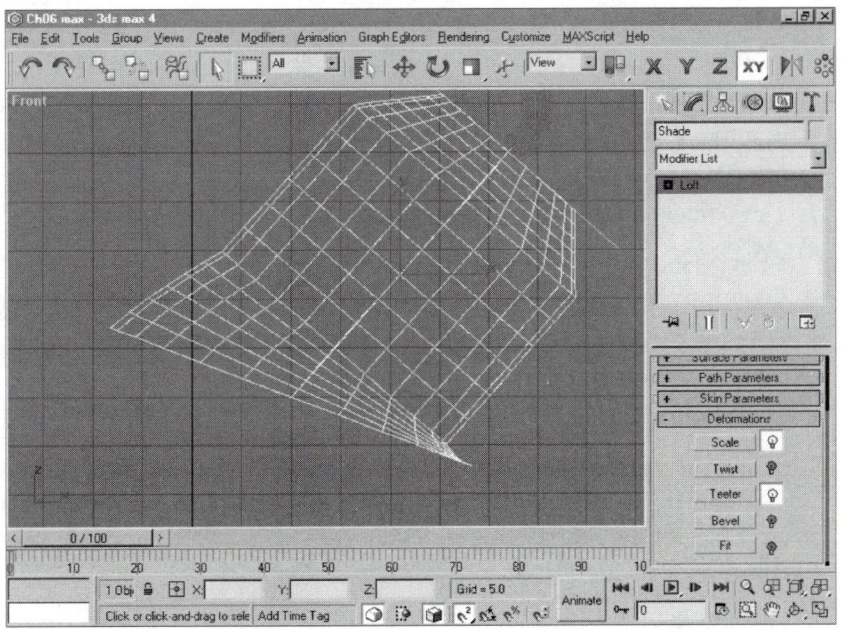

Completing the Lamp Shade

1. Pick the **Select and Uniform Scale** button on the **Main** toolbar. Also, turn snap off.

2. Hold the [Shift] key down and scale Shade01 down to 96% on all axes, as indicated in the coordinate display.
   The **Clone Options** dialog box is displayed.

3. Name the copy name Shade Drill and pick the **OK** button in the dialog box.
   A scaled copy of Shade01 is created.

4. Pick the **Select and Move** and **Restrict to XY Plane** buttons on the **Main** toolbar.

5. Move Shade Drill down so its lower edge is just outside the lower edge of Shade01. Make sure all other edges of Shade Drill are inside Shade01.
   If the entire lamp is not visible in the viewport, pan and zoom as needed.

6. Select Shade01 and pick **Create** in the **Command Panel**. Pick the **Geometry** button and select **Compound Objects** from the drop-down list. Pick the **Boolean** button in the **Object Type** rollout

7. In the **Parameters** rollout, pick the **Subtraction (A-B)** radio button. Make sure the **Move** radio button is selected in the **Pick Boolean** rollout, and then select the **Pick Operand B** button. Select Shade Drill.
   The lamp shade is hollowed out.

8. Save the scene.

Mirroring and Moving the Lamp Shade

You will now mirror the lamp shade and bracket. You will also move and place them at the required location.

1. Select both Shade01 and Bracket. Move both the objects so the top of Bracket is placed on the right edge of the lower cylinder of Rod. Make sure the slanting top edge of Bracket is placed inside the cylinder and its right edge aligns with the right edge of the cylinder.

Mirror Selected Objects

2. With both Bracket and Shade01 selected, pick the **Mirror Selected Objects** button on the **Main** toolbar.
   The **Mirror** dialog box is displayed.

3. Pick the **Copy** radio button in the **Clone Selection:** area of the dialog box. Also, enter –50.0 in the **Offset:** spinner. Pick the **OK** button.
   The objects are mirrored about the center axis of the cylinder.

4. Select Rod. Pick **Create** in the **Command Panel**. Pick the **Geometry** button and select **Compound Objects** from the drop-down list. Pick the **Boolean** button in the **Object Type** rollout.

5. In the **Parameters** rollout, pick the **Union** radio button. In the **Pick Boolean** rollout, select the **Pick Operand B** button. Then, select one of the brackets.
   The bracket is joined to Rod.

6. Select the **Boolean** button again in the **Object Type** rollout to complete the first Boolean operation and begin a second. Then, select the **Pick Operand B** button in the **Pick Boolean** rollout. Now, select the other bracket. Right-click to complete the Boolean operation.
   Both brackets are joined to Rod, Figure 6-17.

7. Display the four-viewport configuration and pick the **Zoom Extents All** button.

8. Save the scene.

Figure 6-17. The bracket and shade are mirrored, then the two brackets are unioned to the rod.

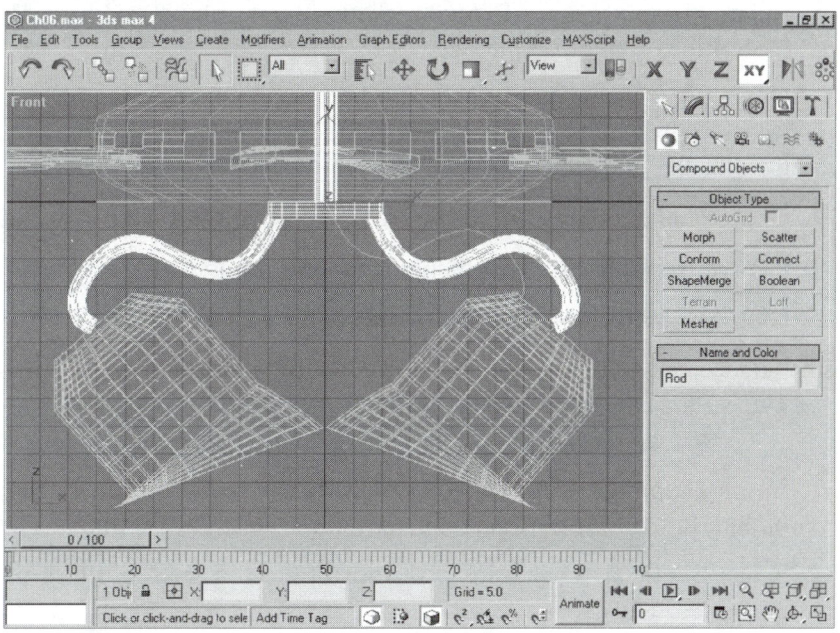

Creating the Ceiling

1. Activate the Top viewport. Pick **Create** in the **Command Panel**. Pick the **Geometry** button and select **Patch Grids** from the drop-down list. Pick the **Quad Patch** button in the **Object Type** rollout.

2. In the **Keyboard Entry** rollout, enter 1000 in the **Length:** spinner and 1000 in the **Width:** spinner. Pick the **Create** button.
   A quad patch, which is a 2D plane, is created.

3. In the Front viewport, move the quad patch up 150 units on the local Y axis. Also, rotate the quad patch 180° on the local Z axis.

4. In the **Name and Color** rollout, name the quad patch Ceiling.

5. Pick the **Zoom Extents All** button.

6. Save the scene.

Assigning Materials

In this part of the tutorial, you will select materials from the material library. Then, you will assign the selected material to the objects.

1. Pick the **Material Editor** button on the **Main** toolbar.
   The **Material Editor** is opened.

Material Editor

2. Pick the first sample slot, if it is not already selected. Then, pick the **Get Material** button below the sample slots.
   The **Material/Map Browser** is opened.

Get Material

3. In the **Material/Map Browser**, pick the **Mtl Library** radio button in the **Browse From:** area.
   The materials in the 3dsmax.mat library are displayed.

4. Double-click on the material Metal_Chrome in the dialog box.
   The material is displayed in the first slot of the **Material Editor**.

**Assign Material
to Selection**

5. In any viewport, select Blade01, Blade02, and Blade03. In the **Material Editor**, pick the **Assign Material to Selection** button.
   The material is assigned to the three blades.

6. In a similar manner, get the material Metal_Black_Plain and assign it to Rod, Connect01, Connect02, and Connect03.

7. Get the material Material_Dark_Gold and assign it to Hub, Shade01, and Shade02.

8. Get the material Wood_Cedfence and assign it to Ceiling.

9. Close the **Material Editor** and **Material/Map Browser**.

10. Select Ceiling in any viewport. Pick **UV Coordinates** in the **Modifiers** pull-down menu. Pick **UVW Map** in the cascading menu.
    A UVW map modifier is applied to the quad patch, and the **Modify** tab is automatically opened.

11. In the **Parameters** rollout, pick the **Planar** radio button. In the **Alignment:** area, pick the **Fit** button. In the **Mapping:** area, enter 5.0 in the **U Tile:** spinner.

12. Select Shade01. Then, pick **UV Coordinates** in the **Modifiers** pull-down menu. Pick **UVW Map** in the cascading menu.
    A UVW map modifier is applied to Shade01, and the **Modify** tab is automatically opened.

13. In the **Parameters** rollout, pick the **Shrink Wrap** radio button. Then, pick the **Fit** button in the **Alignment:** area.

14. Select Shade02. Then, pick **UV Coordinates** in the **Modifiers** pull-down menu. Pick **UVW Map** in the cascading menu.
    A UVW map modifier is applied to Shade02, and the **Modify** tab is automatically opened.

15. In the **Parameters** rollout, pick the **Shrink Wrap** radio button. Then, pick the **Fit** button in the **Alignment** area.

16. Save the scene.

Create

Lights

Creating Lights

1. Pick **Create** in the **Command Panel**. Pick the **Lights** button and select **Standard** in the drop-down list. Then, pick the **Omni** button in the **Object Type** rollout.

2. Accept the default settings, except check the **Cast Shadows** check box in the **General Parameters** rollout. In the Front viewport, pick a point in the middle of Shade01. Zoom as needed. Pick another point in the middle of Shade02. Make sure the **Cast Shadows** check box in the **General Parameters** rollout is checked for the second light.
   An omni light is placed inside each lamp shade.

3. Pick the **Zoom Extents All** button. In the Front viewport, pick a point slightly below the ceiling on the left edge of the viewport. Pick another point slightly below the ceiling on the right edge of the viewport. Turn shadow casting off for these two lights.
   Two more omni lights are placed, Figure 6-18.

4. Save the scene.

Figure 6-18. Lights are added to the scene.

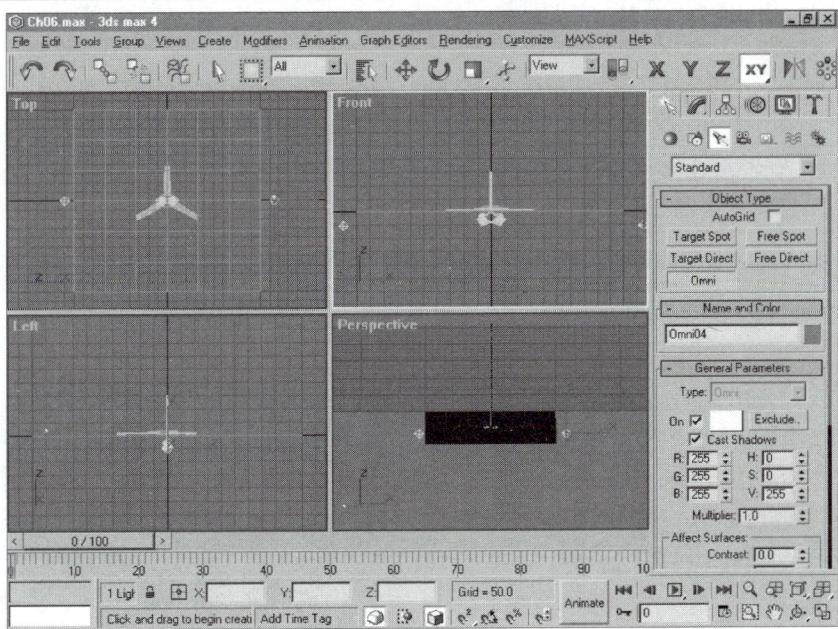

Creating a Camera

1. Pick **Create** in the **Command Panel**. Pick the **Cameras** button and select **Standard** from the drop-down list. Then, pick the **Target** button in the **Object Type** rollout.

2. In the Left viewport, pick a point at the lower-right corner of the viewport. Then, holding the mouse button down, drag the cursor to the lamp shades and release to define the target.

3. Make the Perspective viewport current. Press the [C] key on the keyboard.
   The Perspective viewport becomes the Camera01 viewport, Figure 6-18.

4. Use the **Select and Move** button to move the camera and target in the viewports until you get a desired view of the objects in the Camera01 viewport.

5. Activate the Camera01 viewport and pick the **Field-of-View** button. Zoom in the viewport until the fan fills the viewport.

6. Use **Truck Camera** button to place the objects in the center. Right-click to end the command.

7. With the Camera01 viewport active, press [G].
   The grid is turned off in the Camera01 viewport.

8. Save the scene.

Create

Cameras

Field-of-View

Truck Camera

Render Scene

Rendering the View

1. Activate the Camera01 viewport. Pick the **Render Scene** button on the **Main** toolbar. The **Render Scene** dialog box is displayed on the screen.

2. Accept the default settings and pick the **Render** button near the bottom of the dialog box. The rendered image is displayed in the render window, Figure 6-19.

3. Close the render window and save the scene.

Figure 6-19. The finished rendered scene is displayed in the render window.

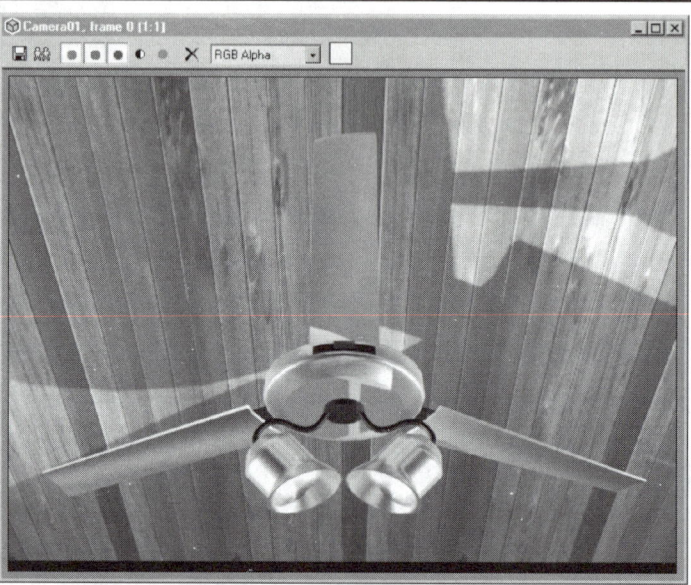

Self-Evaluation Test

Answer the following questions. Then compare your answers with the correct answers given at the end of this chapter.

1. In the **Bevel Deformation** dialog box the location of the line on either side represents the bevel in the form of a _____.

2. The _____ button at the top of the **Deformation** dialog box allows you to add a control point at the selected point.

3. In the **Scale Deformation** dialog box, the horizontal red line represents the _____ of the loft object.

4. While inserting a vertex using the **Insert Corner Point** button, you can enter a value in the _____ text box and then press the [Enter] key to place the vertex at the precise position.

5. You can right-click on the control point in any **Deformation** dialog box to display a _____ from which you can select **Bezier-Smooth** or **Bezier-Corner**.

6. You can use the _____ button to adjust the Bézier handles in a **Deformation** dialog box to get a curve.

7. In the **Twist Deformation** dialog box, the horizontal line represents the degree of twist about the _____.

8. With **Scale**, **Teeter**, and **Fit** deformation tools, you can make changes to X and Y axes separately by making the _____ button inactive and selecting the required axis button.

Exercises

In this exercise, you will create the receiver of a telephone. It is created by lofting a rectangle along a smooth line and then using deformation tools.

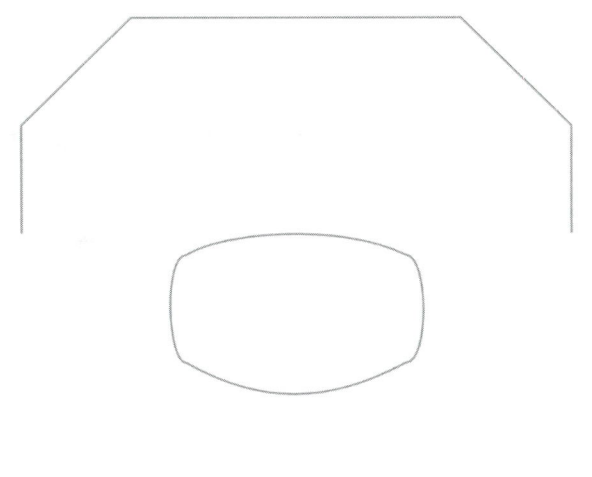
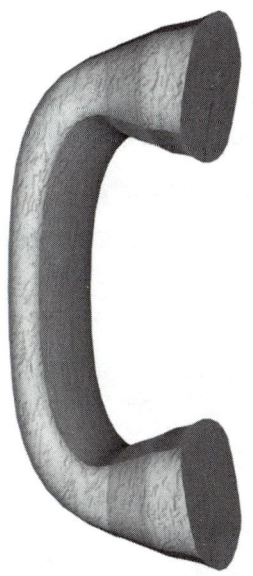

1. Draw the shapes shown. Use the **Line** command to draw the line path. Use the **Rectangle** command to draw the shape for lofting. Apply an edit spline modifier to the rectangle and modify the vertices.

2. Loft the rectangle along the line.

3. In the **Scale Deformation** dialog box, add a control point at the first dotted line and the last dotted lines. These dotted lines represent the vertices on the spline. Deselect the **Make Symmetrical** button and select the **Display X Axis** button. Move the two new control points down by two grid points to 80%. Right-click on one of the new control points and select **Bezier Smooth** from the shortcut menu. Repeat this with the other new control point. Next, convert the new control points to the Bézier corner type and curve the center portion of the profile. Close the dialog box.

4. In the **Bevel Deformation** dialog box, add a control point at the left dotted line. Add another control point between the new point and the left edge point. Add two similar control points on the opposite end. Move the two left control points and the right two control points down two lines. This creates a bevel for the mouthpiece and earpiece.

5. In the **Teeter Deformation** dialog box, add control points at 10% and 90%. Deselect the **Make Symmetrical** button and pick the **Display Y Axis** button. Move the left-hand control point up until 10 is displayed in the right-hand text box. Move the right-hand control point down by 10 units.

6. In the Top viewport, create a cylinder with a radius of 1 and a height of 10. Make these values higher if needed. Move this cylinder in the Top and Front viewports so it is in the center of the right-hand cup, and also intersects the base edge of the cup. Zoom into the right-hand cup in the Top viewport. Move the cylinder exactly to the center of the cup.

7. Pick the **Use Transform Coordinate Center** button on the **Main** toolbar. With the Top viewport active, make a circular array by entering 360 in the **Z degrees** spinner in **Rotate Totals** area in the **Array** dialog box. Uncheck **Re-orient**. Enter 10 in **1D Count** spinner and 4 in **2D Count** spinner. Then, enter a value of 10 in X and Y **Incremental Row Offsets**. Depending on your dimensions, this value may be more or less. This creates four rows in a circular array, with 10 copies in each circular row. Arrange the array centrally in the cup and make sure all the cylinders intersect the base of the cup.

8. Similarly, make holes in the other cup also.

9. Subtract the cylinders from each cup to make holes.

10. Finally, assign a material of your choice to the receiver. Also, add lights and a camera. Then, render the scene.

11. Save the scene as Ex06.max in the folder of your choice.

Answers

The following are the correct answers to the questions in the Self-Evaluation Test.

1. percentage; 2. **Insert Corner Point**; 3. profile; 4. left hand; 5. shortcut menu; 6. **Move Control Point**; 7. path; 8. **Make Symmetrical**.

Chapter 7

Primitive Objects

Learning Objectives

After completing this chapter, you will be able to:
○ Create primitive objects.
○ Modify primitive objects.
○ Apply mapping coordinates to primitive objects.
○ Apply mapped materials to primitive objects.
○ Add a background to the scene.
○ Create lights and a camera.
○ Render a camera viewport.

Tutorial Description

In this tutorial, you will create a model of a cottage using several primitive objects. You will apply mapped materials and mapping coordinates to these objects. You will also add a background to the scene. You will then create lights and a camera, and finally render the scene.

Creating the Cottage Base and a Room

You will begin creating the cottage by drawing a base structure and a room using standard primitives and Boolean operations.

1. First reset the system by selecting **Reset** from the **File** pull-down menu.

2. Activate the Top viewport.

3. Pick **Create** in the **Command Panel**. Pick the **Geometry** button and select **Standard Primitives** in the drop-down list. Then, pick the **Box** button in the **Object Type** rollout.
   The rollouts for a box are displayed.

Create

Geometry

4. Expand the **Keyboard Entry** rollout. Type 1550 in the **Length:** spinner, 2150 in the **Width:** spinner, and 85 in the **Height:** spinner. Then, pick the **Create** button. In the **Name and Color** rollout, name the box Cottage Base.
The base structure is created as a box.

Zoom Extents All

5. Pick the **Zoom Extents All** button to zoom to the extents of the object in the viewport.

6. Draw another box with the Top viewport active. Set the length to 950, the width to 1450, and the height to 800. In the **Name and Color** rollout, name the box Room.
A box is created at the center of Cottage Base, Figure 7-1.

Select and Uniform Scale

7. Pick the **Select and Uniform Scale** button on the **Main** toolbar. Hold down the [Shift] key and scale down Room in the Front viewport to 90% on all axes, as shown in the coordinate display.
The **Clone Options** dialog box is displayed.

8. Make sure the **Copy** radio button is selected in the dialog box. Name the copy Room Drill and pick the **OK** button.
A scaled-down copy of Room is created.

9. Select Room. Then, pick **Create** in the **Command Panel**. Pick the **Geometry** button and select **Compound Objects** from the drop-down list. Pick the **Boolean** button in the **Object Type** rollout.

Select and Rotate

10. In the **Operations** area of the **Parameters** rollout, pick the **Subtraction (A-B)** radio button. In the **Pick Boolean** rollout, select the **Move** radio button. Then, select the **Pick Operand B** button and pick Room Drill in the viewport.
Room is hollowed out.

Restrict to Z

11. Pick the **Select and Rotate** button on the **Main** toolbar. Make sure the **Restrict to Z** button is selected. In the Front viewport, rotate Room 180° about the local Z axis, as indicated in the coordinate display.
Room is rotated and now appears below the base.

Select and Move

12. Pick the **Select and Move** and **Restrict to Y** buttons on the **Main** toolbar. Move Room up so its bottom edge is on top of Cottage Base.

Restrict to Y

Figure 7-1. The base is created, and a box is created in the center of the base that will be the room.

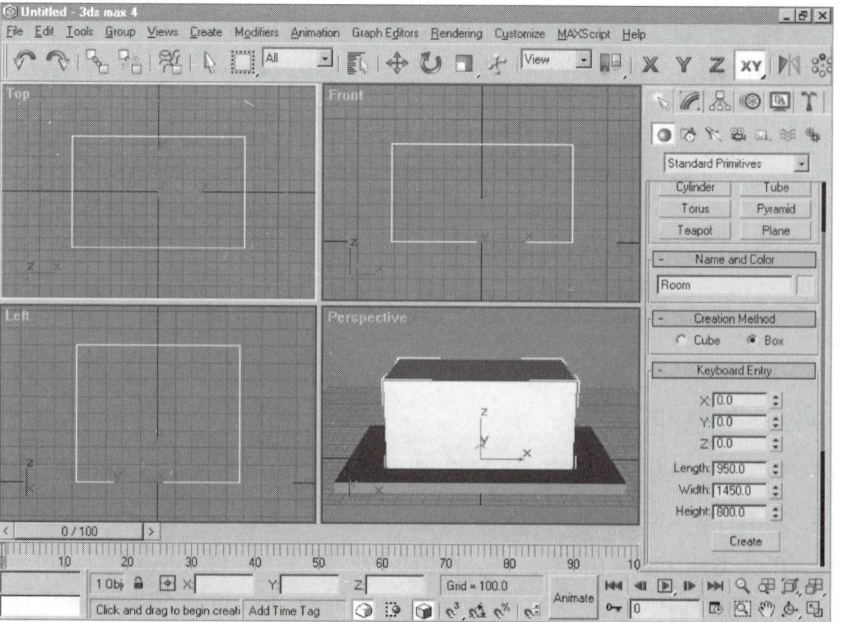

13. Activate the Top viewport. Pick the **Select and Move** button and the **Restrict to XY Plane** button on the **Main** toolbar. Move Room up and to the left so the upper-left corners of both objects align, Figure 7-2.

Restrict to XY Plane

14. Save the scene as Ch07.max in the folder of your choice.

Creating a Door and Doorway

Now, you will create a doorway into the room. You will also create a door by drawing a standard primitive and applying modifiers to it.

Zoom Extents All

2D Snap Toggle

1. Pick the **Zoom Extents All** button. Also, pick the **2D Snap Toggle** button from the **Snap** flyout. The default snap, which is grid points, is turned on.

2. Pick **Create** in the **Command Panel**. Pick the **Geometry** button and select **Standard Primitives** from the drop-down list. Pick the **Box** button in the **Object Type** rollout.

3. In the Top viewport, pick a point at coordinates –500, –200, 0. Drag the cursor up to coordinates –200, –100, 0 and release. Now, move the cursor up five grid points and pick. The value in the **Height:** spinner in the **Parameters** rollout will be 500. In the **Name and Color** rollout, name the box Door.
   A box is created at the center of the front wall of Room.

4. Turn snap off. Pick the **Select and Move** button on the **Main** toolbar. Also, pick the **Restrict to Y** button. In the Left viewport, move Door up so its bottom edge aligns with the bottom of Room.

5. Select Room. Then, pick **Create** in the **Command Panel**. Pick the **Geometry** button and select **Compound Objects** from the drop-down list. Pick the **Boolean** button in the **Object Type** rollout.

6. In the **Parameters** rollout, pick the **Subtraction (A-B)** radio button. In the **Pick Boolean** rollout, select the **Copy** radio button. Then, select the **Pick Operand B** button and select Door. Right-click to complete the operation.
   A copy of Door is used to create the doorway in the front wall of Room.

Figure 7-2. The room is hollowed out and aligned with the base.

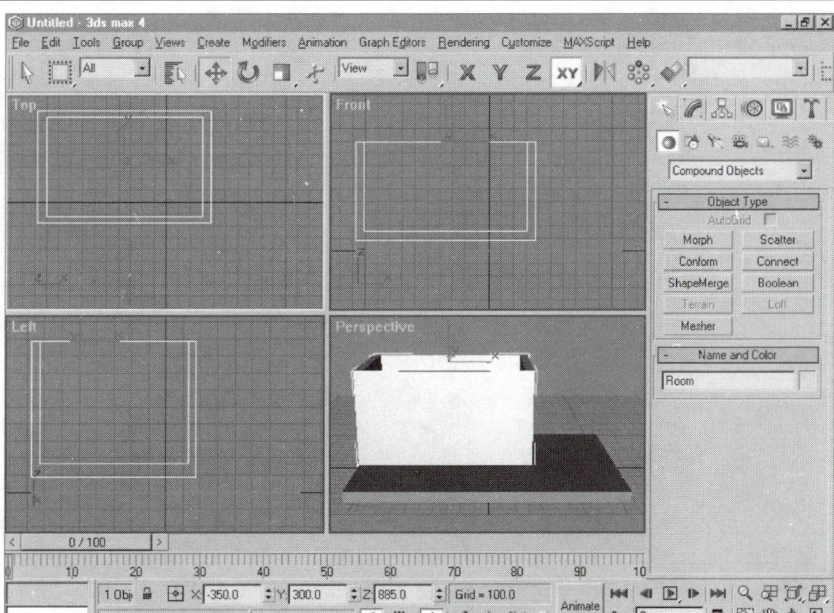

Modify

7. Select Door and then pick **Modify** in the **Command Panel**. In the **Parameters** rollout, change the value in the **Length:** spinner to 25.
   The thickness of Door is changed to its final value.

8. Also in the **Parameters** rollout, type 2 in the **Length Segs:** spinner, 3 in the **Width Segs:** spinner, and 4 in the **Height Segs:** spinner.
   The number of segments is increased on Door, which is important when modifiers are applied.

9. With Door selected, pick **Parametric Deformers** in the **Modifiers** pull-down menu. Then, pick **Lattice** in the cascading menu.
   A lattice modifier is applied to the box, and the segments of the box are displayed as a wireframe lattice.

10. In the **Struts** area of the **Parameters** rollout, type 4 in the **Radius:** spinner. Also, check the **Smooth** check boxes in the **Struts** and the **Joints** areas of the **Parameters** rollout, Figure 7-3.

11. Save the scene.

Creating a Window

1. Activate the Top viewport. Pick **Create** in the **Command Panel**. Pick the **Geometry** button and select **Standard Primitives** from the drop-down list. Then, pick the **Box** button in the **Object Type** rollout.

2. Turn snap on. Pick a point at coordinates 300, 100, 0, drag the cursor to coordinates 400, 500, 0, and release. Move the cursor up three grid points and pick. The value in the **Height:** spinner in the **Parameters** rollout is 300. In the **Name and Color** rollout, name the box Window.

3. Pick the **Select and Move** and **Restrict to Y** buttons on the **Main** toolbar. Turn snap off and move Window up in the Front viewport so its top edge aligns with the top edge of Door.

4. Select Room and then pick **Create** in the **Command Panel**. Pick the **Geometry** button and select **Compound Objects** from the drop-down list. Pick the **Boolean** button in the **Object Type** rollout.

Figure 7-3. A lattice modifier is applied to the door to simulate many small windows.

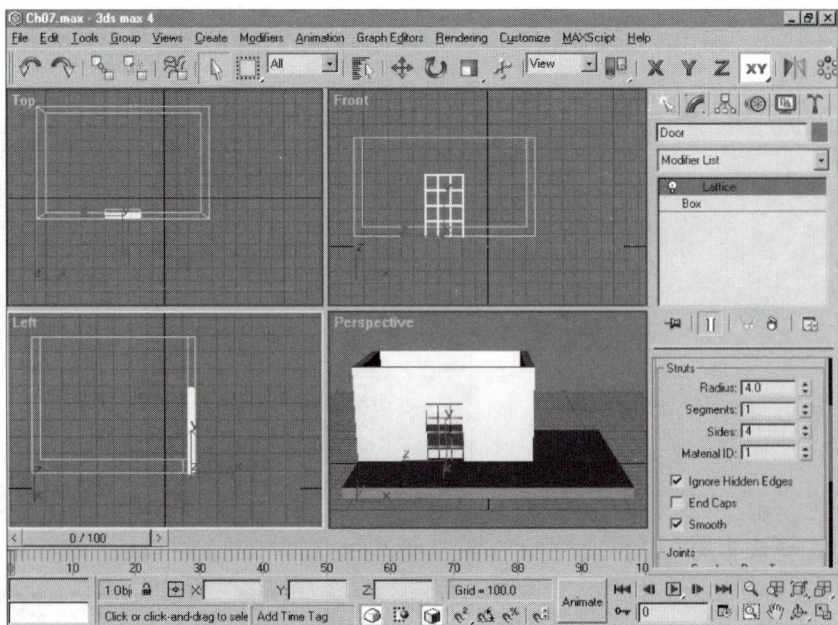

5. In the **Parameters** rollout, pick the **Subtraction (A-B)** radio button. In the **Pick Boolean** rollout, pick the **Copy** radio button. Then, select the **Pick Operand B** button and select Window. Right-click to complete the operation.
   An opening for the window is created in the right-hand wall of Room.

6. Select Window and then pick **Modify** in the **Command Panel**. In the **Parameters** rollout, change the value in the **Width:** spinner to 25.

Modify

7. Also in the **Parameters** rollout, type 4 in the **Length Segs:** spinner, 2 in the **Width Segs:** spinner, and 3 in the **Height Segs:** spinner.
   The number of segments on the box is increased.

8. With Window selected, pick **Parametric Deformers** in the **Modifiers** pull-down menu. Then, pick **Lattice** in the cascading menu. Select the **OK** button to close the list box and apply the modifier.
   A lattice modifier is applied to Window.

9. In the **Struts** area of the **Parameters** rollout, type 4 in the **Radius:** spinner. Also, check the **Smooth** check boxes in the **Struts** and the **Joints** area of the **Parameters** rollout.

10. Activate the Perspective viewport and select the **Arc Rotate** button. Pick in the center of the track-ball (yellow circle) and drag the cursor so both the front and the right walls of Room can be seen, Figure 7-4.

Arc Rotate

11. Save the scene.

Creating Pillars

You will now create pillars at the corners of the base structure using standard primitives and modifiers.

1. Activate the Top viewport. Then, pick **Create** in the **Command Panel**. Pick the **Geometry** button and select **Extended Primitives** from the drop-down list. Pick the **Gengon** button in the **Object Type** rollout.
   The rollouts for a gengon are displayed.

Figure 7-4. The Perspective viewport is rotated to get a better view.

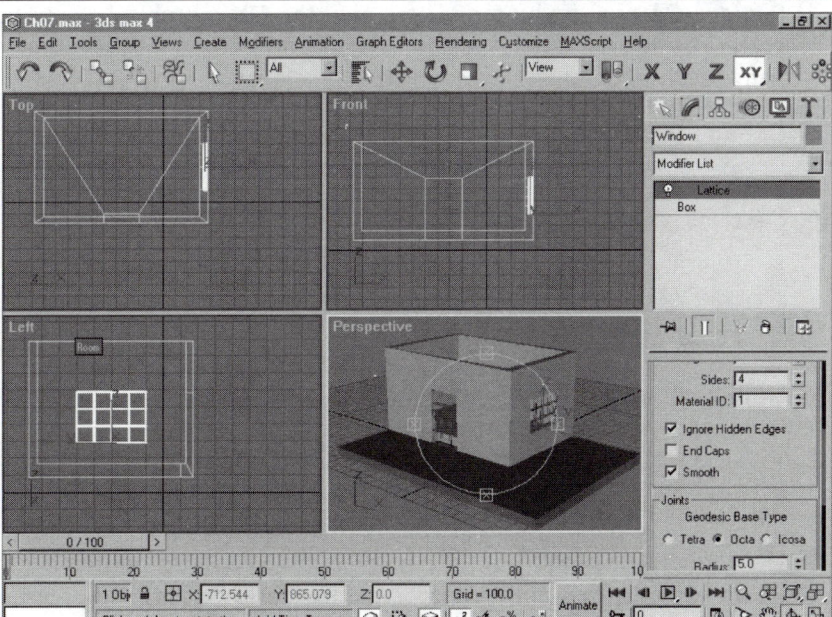

2. Turn snap on. Pick a point at coordinates –1000, –700, 0, drag the cursor to coordinates –1000, –600, 0, and release. Move the cursor up one grid point and pick. The **Height:** spinner in the **Parameters** rollout is 100. With the value in the **Fillet:** spinner 0, pick again to set a zero fillet.
   A five-sided polygon is created near the bottom left corner of Cottage Base.

3. In the **Name and Color** rollout, name the gengon Column Base01. In the **Parameters** rollout, type 6 in the **Sides:** spinner.
   The number of sides is increased from the default of five to six.

4. Turn snap off. Pick the **Select and Move** button and the **Restrict to Y** button. Activate the Front viewport and move the Column Base01 up so it is on top of Cottage Base.

5. Activate the Top viewport and pick the **Restrict to XY Plane** button. Move Column Base01 up and right so its edges align with Cottage Base.

6. Pick **Create** in the **Command Panel**. Pick the **Geometry** button and select **Standard Primitives** from the drop-down list. Then, pick the **Cylinder** button in the **Object Type** rollout.

7. Expand the **Keyboard Entry** rollout. Type 75 in the **Radius:** spinner and 700 in the **Height:** spinner. Then, pick the **Create** button. In the **Name and Color** rollout, name the cylinder Pillar01.
   A cylinder is created at the center of Cottage Base.

8. Pick the **Select and Move** button and the **Restrict to XY Plane** button. Select **Pillar** and move it to the center of Column Base01.

9. Activate the Front viewport. Pick the **Select and Move** button and the **Restrict to Y** button. Move Pillar01 up so it is on the top of Column Base01.

10. With Pillar01 selected, pick **Parametric D̲eformers** in the **M̲odifiers** pull-down menu. Then, pick **Taper** in the cascading menu.
    A taper modifier is applied to the cylinder.

11. In the **Taper** area of the **Parameters** rollout, type –0.3 in the **Amount:** spinner.
    Pillar01 narrows at the top end.

12. Activate the Top viewport. Select Column Base01 and Pillar01. Holding down the [Shift] key, move both objects to the lower-right corner of Cottage Base.
    The **Clone Options** dialog is displayed.

14. Pick the **Copy** radio button. Then, pick the **OK** button to accept the default name.
    Copies of the base and pillar are created at the lower-right corner of Cottage Base.

15. With the copies selected, hold down the [Shift] key and move them to the upper-right corner of Cottage Base. Pick the **OK** button in the **Clone Options** dialog box.
    Copies are created at the upper-right corner of Cottage Base, Figure 7-5.

16. Save the scene.

Creating the Beams

You will now create beams above the pillars. These are created as standard primitives and then Boolean operations are performed on them.

1. Activate the Front viewport and select Cottage Base. Pick the **Select and Move** and **Restrict to Y** buttons on the **Main** toolbar.

2. Hold down the [Shift] key and drag Cottage Base up until it is on top of the pillars and walls. In the **Clone Options** dialog box, name the copy Ceiling and pick the **OK** button.

Figure 7-5. Three columns with bases are created and aligned.

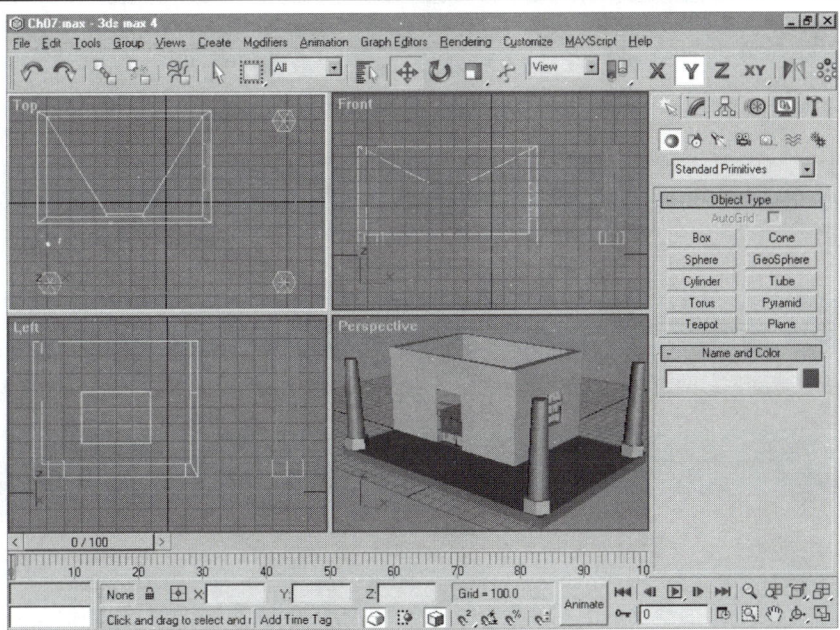

3. Activate the Top viewport. Pick the **Restrict to XY Plane** button on the **Main** toolbar and pick the **Select and Non-uniform Scale** button from the **Scale** flyout. Select **Yes** in the warning box that is displayed to confirm that you want to continue.

4. With Ceiling selected, hold down the [Shift] key and scale the object to 80% on the X and Y axes, and 100% on the Z axis. In the **Clone Options** dialog box that is displayed, name the copy Ceiling Drill and pick the **OK** button.
   A scaled-down copy of Ceiling is created.

5. Select Ceiling. Then, pick **Create** in the **Command Panel**. Pick the **Geometry** button and select **Compound Objects** from the drop-down list. Pick the **Boolean** button in the **Object Type** rollout.

6. In the **Parameters** rollout, pick the **Subtraction (A-B)** radio button. In the **Pick Boolean** rollout, pick the **Move** radio button. Then, select the **Pick Operand B** button and select Ceiling Drill. Right-click to complete the operation.
   Ceiling is hollowed out creating a ring, which is the beam structure, Figure 7-6.

8. In the **Name and Color** rollout, rename Ceiling to Beam.

9. Save the scene.

Creating the Roof

1. Pick the **Zoom All** button. In the Top viewport, pick in the center and drag the cursor down until the objects are displayed about half of their original size.

Zoom All

2. Pick **Create** in the **Command Panel**. Pick the **Geometry** button and select **Standard Primitives** from the drop-down list. Select the **Pyramid** button in the **Object Type** rollout.
   The rollouts for a pyramid are displayed.

3. Expand the **Keyboard Entry** rollout. Type 2600 in the **Width:** spinner, 2000 in the **Depth:** spinner, and 600 in the **Height:** spinner. Then, pick the **Create** button. In the **Name and Color** rollout, name the pyramid Roof.
   A pyramid is created at the center of Cottage Base.

Figure 7-6. A beam structure is created on top of the columns.

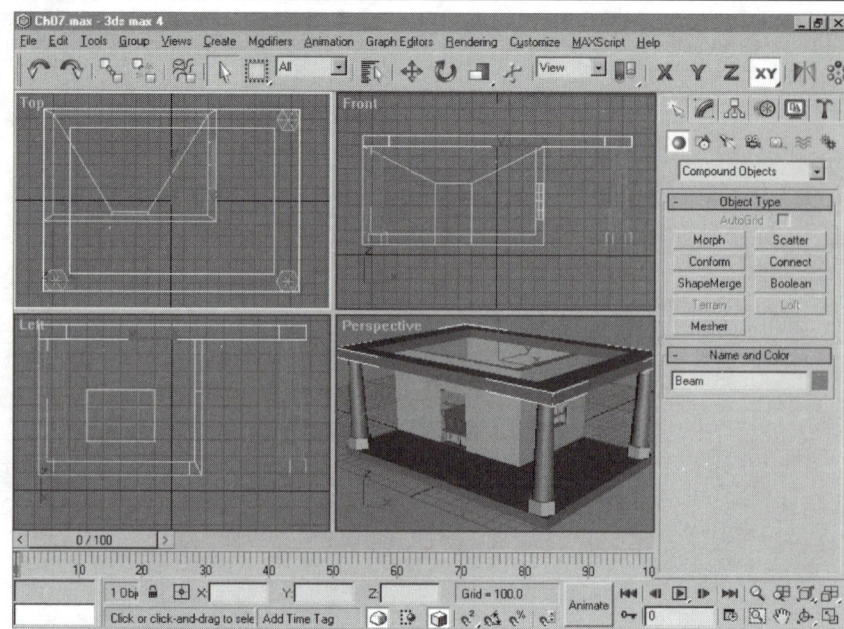

4. Activate the Front viewport. Pick the **Select and Move** and **Restrict to Y** buttons on the **Main** toolbar. Move Roof up so it is on top of the pillars.
   If parts of the objects "disappear" in the viewports, press [1] to refresh the display.

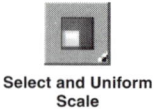

Select and Uniform Scale

5. Pick the **Select and Uniform Scale** button from the **Scale** flyout on the **Main** toolbar. With Roof selected, hold down the [Shift] key and scale the object to 80%, as indicated in the coordinate display. In the **Clone Options** dialog box, name the copy Roof Drill and pick the **OK** button.
   A scaled-down copy of Roof is created inside the original.

6. Select Roof. Then, pick **Create** in the **Command Panel**. Pick the **Geometry** button and select **Compound Objects** from the drop-down list. Pick the **Boolean** button in the **Object Type** rollout.

7. In the **Operation** area of the **Parameters** rollout, pick the **Subtraction (A-B)** radio button. In the **Pick Boolean** rollout, select the **Pick Operand B** button. Then, select Roof Drill. Right-click to complete the operation. Pick the **Zoom Extents All** button.
   Roof is hollowed out, Figure 7-7.

8. Save the scene.

Creating the Gable Structure

Create

Geometry

You will create a gable using standard primitives and Boolean operations. You will also create an opening in the gable and modify it to create a framework in it

1. Pick **Create** in the **Command Panel**. Pick the **Geometry** button and select **Extended Primitives** from the drop-down list. Then, pick the **Prism** button in the **Object Type** rollout.

2. Pick the **Isosceles** radio button in the **Creation Method** rollout. Also, pick the **2D Snap Toggle** button to turn snap on. In the Front viewport, pick a point at coordinates –300, 0, 1000, drag the cursor to coordinates 300, 0, 1500, and release. Now, move the cursor down until the value in the **Height:** spinner in the **Parameters** rollout is –700 and pick again. In the **Name and Color** rollout, name the prism Gable.
   A prism is created, which will be the gable.

Figure 7-7. The roof is created and hollowed out.

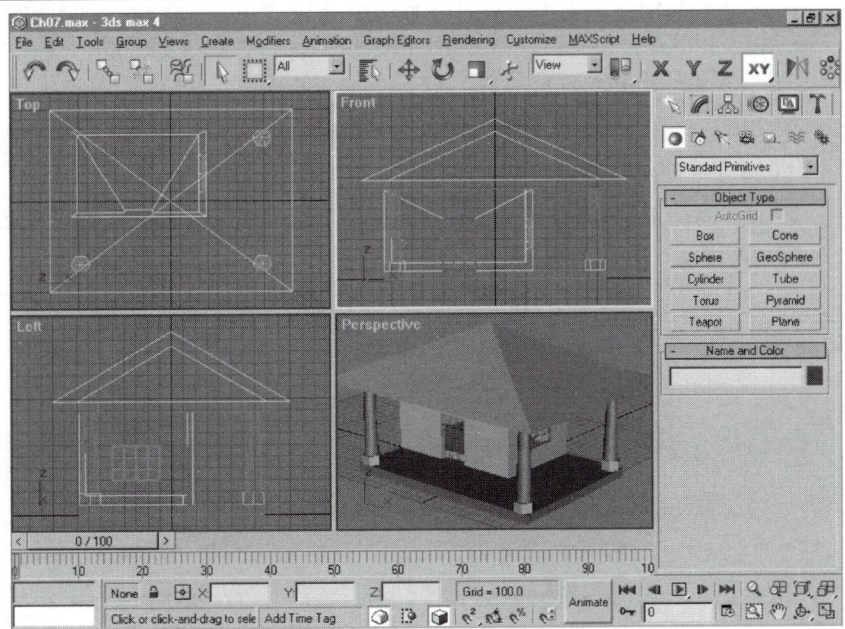

3. Turn snap off. Pick the **Select and Move** and **Restrict to XY Plane** buttons on the **Main** toolbar. In the Front viewport, move Gable down so its lower edge aligns with the lower edge of Roof.

4. Activate the Left viewport and pick the **Zoom Extents All** button.

5. Pick the **Select and Move** and **Restrict to X** buttons on the **Main** toolbar. Move Gable to the right so its upper-left corner lies just inside the right edge of Roof.

6. Pick the **Select and Squash** button from the **Scale** flyout on the **Main** toolbar. Pick **Yes** in the warning dialog box that is displayed confirming you want to continue. Also, pick the **Restrict to XY Plane** button.

Select and Squash

7. Pick the **Use Selection Center** button on the **Main** toolbar. Then, in the Front viewport, hold down the [Shift] key and squash Gable until the coordinate display is 85%, 85%, 117%. In the **Clone Options** dialog box, name the copy Gable Drill and pick the **OK** button.
   A squashed copy of Gable is created.

Use Selection Center

8. Select Gable. Then, pick **Create** in the **Command Panel**. Pick the **Geometry** button and select **Compound Objects** from the drop-down list. Pick the **Boolean** button in the **Object Type** rollout.

9. In the **Operation** area of the **Parameters** rollout, pick the **Subtraction (A-B)** radio button. In the **Pick Boolean** rollout, select the **Copy** radio button. Then, select the **Pick Operand B** button and select Gable Drill. Right-click to complete the operation.
   Gable is hollowed out.

10. Select Roof. Then, pick **Create** in the **Command Panel**. Pick the **Geometry** button and select the **Boolean** button in the **Object Type** rollout.

11. In the **Parameters** rollout, pick the **Union** radio button. In the **Pick Boolean** rollout, pick the **Move** radio button. Then, select the **Pick Operand B** button and select Gable. Right-click to complete the operation.
    Gable is combined with Roof.

12. Select Gable Drill. Then, pick **Modify** in the **Command Panel**.

Modify

13. In the **Parameters** rollout, type –50 in the **Height:** spinner. Also, type 4 in the **Side 1 Segs:**, **Side 2 Segs:**, and **Side 3 Segs:** spinners. Finally, type 2 in the **Height Segs:** spinner. Also, rename the object Gable Mullions.

14. Pick the **Select and Move** and **Restrict to X** buttons on the **Main** toolbar. Move Gable Mullions to the left so it lies within the gable of Roof. Gable Mullions should be set back about the thickness of the object.

15. With Gable Mullions selected, pick **Parametric Deformers** in the **Modifiers** pull-down menu. Then, pick **Lattice** from the cascading menu.

16. In the **Struts** area of the **Parameters** rollout, type 20 in the **Radius:** spinner. Also, check the **Smooth** check box.
    A lattice framework is created in the gable opening, Figure 7-8.

17. Save the scene.

Creating the Chimney

You will now create a chimney from standard primitives and add it to the roof using Boolean operations. You will finish the chimney by creating a border on the top.

Create

Geometry

1. Pick **Create** in the **Command Panel**. Pick the **Geometry** button and select **Standard Primitives** from the drop-down list. Pick the **Box** button in the **Object Type** rollout.

2. Activate the Top viewport. Expand the **Keyboard Entry** rollout. Type 430 in the **Length:** spinner, 430 in the **Width:** spinner, and 850 in the **Height:** spinner. Select the **Create** button. In the **Name and Color** rollout, name the box Chimney.
   A box is created in the center of the Top viewport.

3. Pick the **Select and Move** and **Restrict to XY Plane** buttons on the **Main** toolbar. In the Top viewport, move Chimney so its upper-left corner aligns with the upper-left corner of Room.

4. Activate the Front viewport. Move Chimney straight up so its bottom edge aligns with the top edge of Room.

5. Pick the **Select and Squash** button from the **Scale** flyout on the **Main** toolbar. Pick **Yes** in the warning dialog box that is displayed. Then, pick the **Restrict to XY Plane** button on the **Main** toolbar.

Figure 7-8. A window is created in the gable opening.

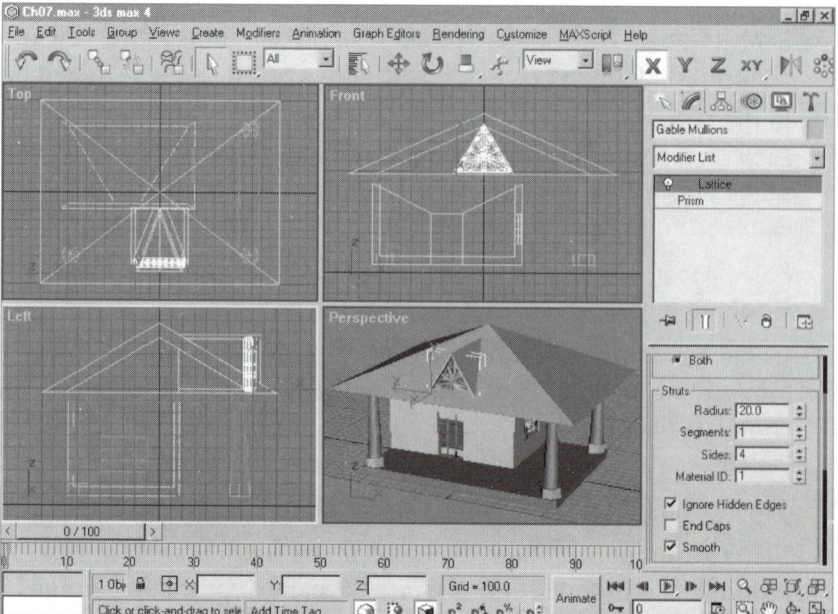

6. Activate the Top viewport. Make sure the **Use Selection Center** button on the **Main** toolbar is active. Then, hold down the [Shift] key and squash Chimney until the coordinate display reads 75%, 75%, 134%. In the **Clone Options** dialog box that is displayed, name the copy Chimney Drill and pick the **OK** button.
   A squashed copy of Chimney is created.

7. Select **Clone** from the **Edit** pull-down menu to create a copy of Chimney Drill. In the **Clone Options** dialog box that is displayed, name the copy Chimney Roof Drill and pick the **OK** button.
   A copy of Chimney Drill is created on top of the original.

8. Select Chimney. Then, pick **Create** in the **Command Panel**. Pick the **Geometry** button and select **Compound Objects** from the drop-down list. Pick the **Boolean** button in the **Object Type** rollout.

9. In the **Parameters** rollout, pick the **Subtraction (A-B)** radio button. In the **Pick Boolean** rollout, pick the **Move** radio button. Then, select the **Pick Operand B** button and select Chimney. Right-click to complete the operation.
   Chimney is hollowed out.

10. Select Roof. Pick **Create** in the **Command Panel**. Pick the **Geometry** button and select **Compound Objects** from the drop-down list. Then, pick the **Boolean** button in the **Object Type** rollout.

11. In the **Parameters** rollout, pick the **Subtraction (A-B)** radio button. In the **Pick Boolean** rollout, pick the **Move** radio button. Then, select the **Pick Operand B** button and select Chimney Roof Drill. You may need to select the object by its name. Right-click to complete the operation.
    A hole is created in Roof through which Chimney passes.

12. Activate the Top viewport and pick the **Zoom Extents All** button, Figure 7-9.

13. Pick **Create** in the **Command Panel**. Pick the **Geometry** button and select **Standard Primitives** from the drop-down list. Then, pick the **Tube** button in the **Object Type** rollout.
    The rollouts for a tube are displayed.

14. In the **Parameters** rollout, type 4 in the **Sides:** spinner and 1 in the **Height Segments:** spinner.

Figure 7-9. A chimney is created.

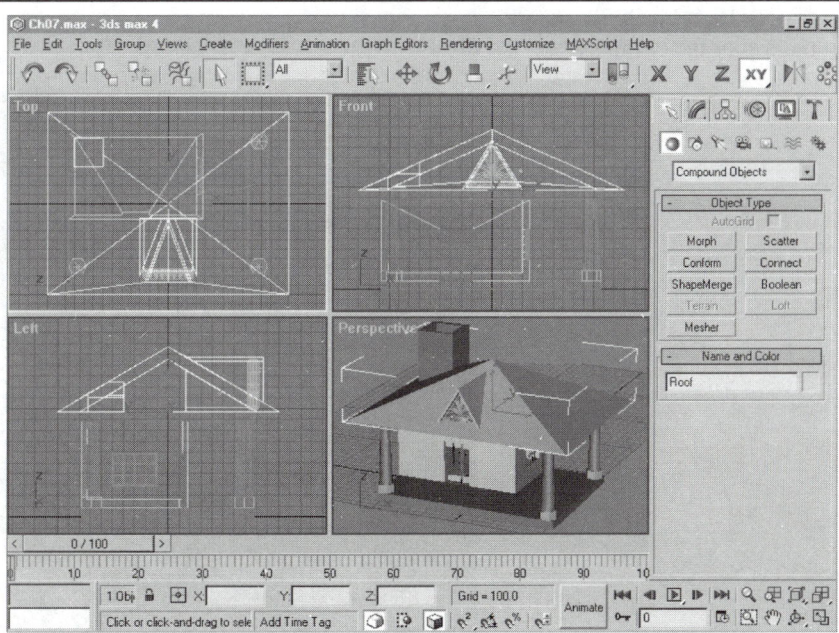

15. Expand the **Keyboard Entry** rollout. Type 305 in the **Inner Radius:** spinner, 375 in the **Outer Radius:** spinner, and 75 in the **Height:** spinner. Then, pick the **Create** button. In the **Name and Color** rollout, name the tube Border.
    A square tube is created in the center of the Top viewport.

16. Pick the **Select and Rotate** and **Restrict to Z** buttons on the **Main** toolbar. Rotate Border 45° in the Top viewport.

17. Pick the **Select and Move** and **Restrict to XY Plane** buttons on the **Main** toolbar. Move Border so it is centered on Chimney.

18. In the Front viewport, move Border up so its upper edge aligns with the upper edge of Chimney, Figure 7-10.

19. Save the scene.

Creating the Top Rail

Create

Geometry

You will now create a handrail using standard primitives. The handrail will be between the columns.

1. Pick **Create** in the **Command Panel**. Pick the **Geometry** button and select **Standard Primitives** from the drop-down list. Then, pick the **Box** button in the **Object Type** rollout.

2. Activate the Front viewport. Expand the **Keyboard Entry** rollout. Type 30 in the **Length:** spinner, 60 in the **Width:** spinner, and 1375 in the **Height:** spinner. Then, pick the **Create** button. In the **Name and Color** rollout, name the box Rail01.
   A box is created at the bottom of Cottage Base.

3. Pick the **Select and Move** and **Restrict to XY Plane** buttons on the **Main** toolbar. Move Rail01 up and to the right so it is centered on Pillar02.

4. Activate the Top viewport and pick the **Restrict to Y** button on the **Main** toolbar. Move Rail01 so one end is centered inside Pillar02 and the other end is centered inside Pillar03, Figure 7-11.

Figure 7-10. A border is added to the top of the chimney.

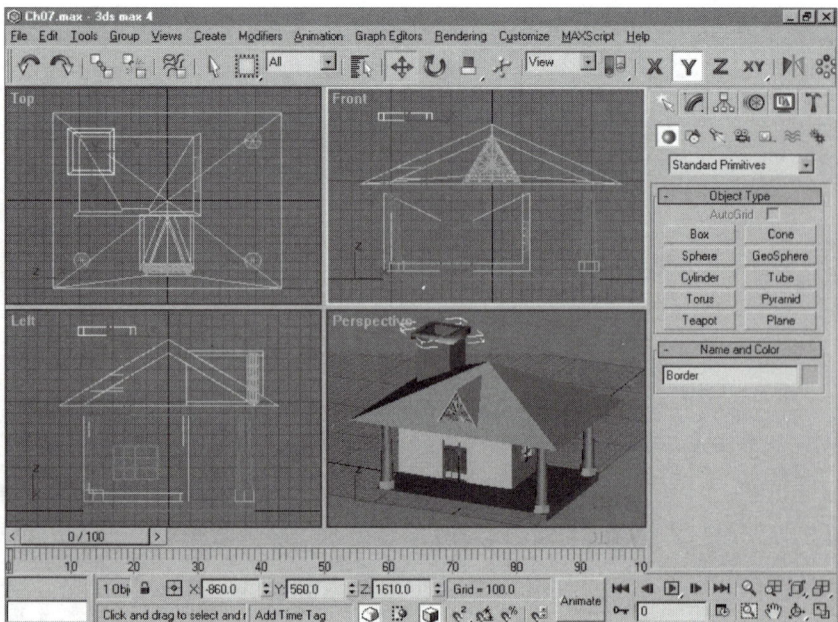

Figure 7-11. The first rail is added to the scene on the right side of the cottage.

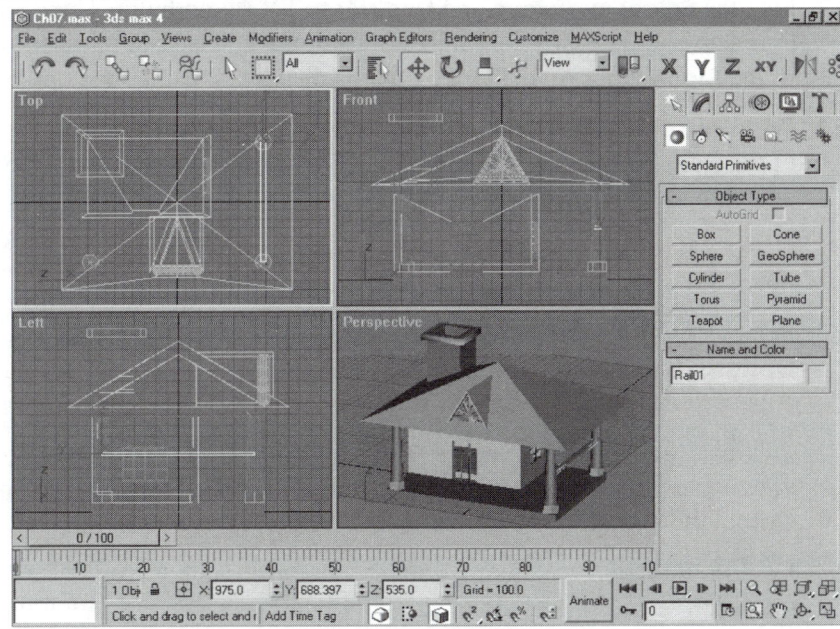

5. Select Pillar02. Then, pick **Create** in the **Command Panel**. Pick the **Geometry** button and select **Compound Objects** from the drop-down list. Then, pick the **Boolean** button in the **Object Type** rollout.

6. In the **Parameters** rollout, pick the **Subtraction (A-B)** radio button. In the **Pick Boolean** rollout, pick the **Copy** radio button. Then, select the **Pick Operand B** button and select Rail01. Right-click to complete the operation.
   A hole is created in Pillar02 in which Rail01 fits.

7. Similarly, select Pillar03 and create a hole for Rail01 using a Boolean operation. Right-click to complete the operation.

8. Pick the **Select and Rotate** button. With the Top viewport active, hold down the [Shift] key and rotate Rail01 –90°. In the **Clone Options** dialog box that is displayed, name the copy Rail02 and pick the **OK** button.
   A rotated copy of Rail01 is created centered on Pillar03.

9. With Rail02 selected, pick **Modify** in the **Command Panel**. In the **Parameters** rollout, type 600 in the **Height:** spinner.
   The span of Rail02 is reduced.

10. Pick the **Select and Move** and **Restrict to X** buttons on the **Main** toolbar. Move Rail02 so its right-hand end is in the center of Pillar03. The left-hand end of Rail02 should be flush with the wall of Room.

11. Select Pillar03. Then, pick **Create** in the **Command Panel**. Pick the **Geometry** button and select **Compound Objects** from the drop-down list. Finally, pick the **Boolean** button in the **Object Type** rollout.

12. In the **Parameters** rollout, pick the **Subtraction (A-B)** radio button. In the **Pick Boolean** rollout, pick the **Copy** radio button. Then, select the **Pick Operand B** button and select Rail02. Right-click to complete the operation.
    A hole is created in Pillar03 in which Rail02 fits.

13. Pick the **Select and Move** and **Restrict to XY Plane** buttons, and select Rail02. With the Top viewport active, hold down the [Shift] key and move Rail01 left so its lower end is centered on Pillar01. In the **Clone Options** dialog box that is displayed, name the copy Rail03 and pick the **OK** button.

14. With Rail03 selected, pick **Modify** in the **Command Panel**. In the **Parameters** rollout, type 513 in the **Height:** spinner. The top end of Rail03 should be flush with the wall of Room.
    The span of Rail03 is reduced.

15. Using a Boolean operation, subtract a copy of Rail03 from Pillar01. Right-click to complete the operation.

16. Select Rail03. Holding down the [Shift] key, rotate Rail03 90° in the Top viewport. In the **Clone Options** dialog box that is displayed, name the copy Rail04 and pick the **OK** button.
    A rotated copy of Rail03 is created.

17. Pick the **Select and Move** and **Restrict to Y** buttons on the **Main** toolbar. Move Rail04 in the Top viewport so its left-hand end is centered in Pillar01. With Rail04 selected, pick **Modify** in the **Command Panel**. In the **Parameters** rollout, type 400 in the **Height:** spinner.

18. Using a Boolean operation, subtract a copy of Rail04 from Pillar01. Right-click to complete the operation.

19. Select Rail02. Pick the **Select and Move** and **Restrict to Y** buttons on the **Main** toolbar. Then, hold down the [Shift] key and move Rail02 down so its right-hand end is centered on Pillar02. In the **Clone Options** dialog box that is displayed, name the copy Rail05 and pick the **OK** button.
    A copy of Rail02 is created.

20. With Rail05 selected, pick **Modify** in the **Command Panel**. In the **Parameters** rollout, type 1100 in the **Height:** spinner.
    The span of Rail05 is increased.

21. Move Rail05 to the left in the Top viewport so its right-hand end is centered on Pillar02.

22. Using a Boolean operation, subtract a copy of Rail05 from Pillar02. Right-click to complete the operation, Figure 7-12.

23. Save the scene.

Figure 7-12. All rails are added to the scene.

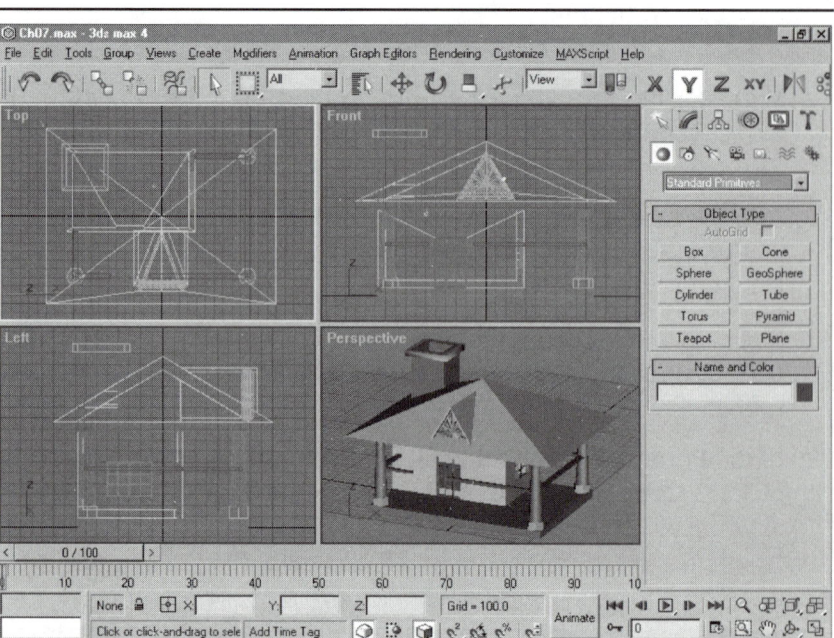

Creating the Vertical Posts

Now you will create the vertical endposts using standard primitives and add them to the handrail with Boolean operations.

1. Activate the Top viewport. Pick **Create** in the **Command Panel**. Pick the **Geometry** button and select **Standard Primitives** from the drop-down list. Then, pick the **Box** button in the **Object Type** rollout.

2. Expand the **Keyboard Entry** rollout. Type 100 in the **Length:** spinner, 100 in the **Width:** spinner, and 435 in the **Height:** spinner. Then, pick the **Create** button. In the **Name and Color** rollout, name the box Post01.
   A box is created in the center of the viewport.

3. Pick the **Select and Move** and **Restrict to XY Plane** buttons on the **Main** toolbar. Move Post01 so its right-hand edge aligns with the right-hand edge of Rail04, and it is centered top-to-bottom in the viewport with Rail04.

4. In the Front viewport, move Post01 so it sits on top of Cottage Base.

5. Pick the **Restrict to X** button on the **Main** toolbar. Select Post01, hold down the [Shift] key, and move the object so its left-hand edge aligns with the left-hand edge of Rail05. In the **Clone Options** dialog box that is displayed, name the copy Post02 and pick the **OK** button.
   A copy of Post01 is created, Figure 7-13.

6. Pick **Create** in the **Command Panel**. Pick the **Geometry** button and select **Standard Primitives** from the drop-down list. Then, pick the **Sphere** button in the **Object Type** rollout.

7. Expand the **Keyboard Entry** rollout. With the Front viewport active, type 60 in the **Radius:** spinner and pick the **Create** button. In the **Name and Color** rollout, name the sphere Globe01.
   A sphere is created at the bottom of Cottage Base.

8. Pick the **Select and Move** and **Restrict to XY Plane** buttons on the **Main** toolbar. Move Globe01 up and to the left so it is on top of and centered on Post01.

Figure 7-13. Two posts are added to the scene at the front of the cottage.

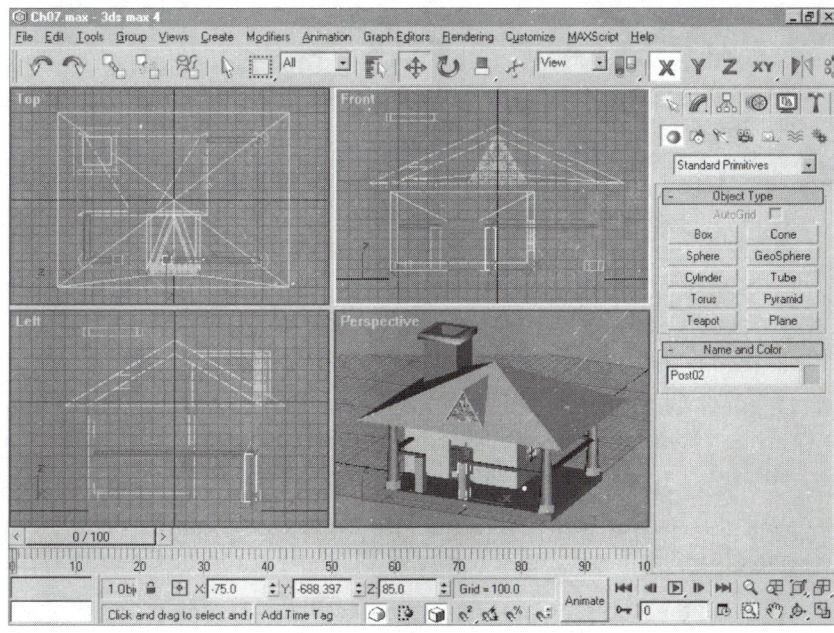

9. Activate the Top viewport and pick the **Restrict to Y** button. Move Globe01 down so it is centered on Post01.

10. Pick the **Restrict to X** button. While holding down the [Shift] key, move Globe01 to the right so it is centered on Post02. In the **Clone Options** dialog box that is displayed, name the copy Globe02 and pick the **OK** button.
    A copy of Globe01 is created on top of the second post.

11. Select Post01. Then, pick **Create** in the **Command Panel**. Pick the **Geometry** button and select **Compound Objects** from the drop-down list. Then, pick the **Boolean** button in the **Object Type** rollout.

12. In the **Parameters** rollout, pick the **Union** radio button. In the **Pick Boolean** rollout, pick the **Move** radio button. Then, select the **Pick Operand B** button and select Globe01 in the viewport. Right-click to complete the operation.
    Globe01 and Post01 are combined to form a single object.

13. Similarly, union Globe02 to Post02.

14. Save the scene.

Creating the Balusters

You will now create vertical balusters under the railing using standard primitives. Then, you will create and place copies using the **Spacing Tool**.

1. Activate the Top viewport. Then, pick **Create** in the **Command Panel**. Pick the **Geometry** button and select **Standard Primitives** from the drop-down list. Pick the **Cylinder** button in the **Object Type** rollout.

2. In the **Keyboard Entry** rollout, type 35 in the **Radius:** spinner and 435 in the **Height:** spinner. Then, pick the **Create** button. In the **Name and Color** rollout, name the cylinder Baluster01.
    A cylinder is created at the center of Cottage Base.

Spacing Tool

3. With Baluster01 selected, maximize the Top viewport and zoom in on Rail05. Then, pick the **Spacing Tool** button from the **Array** flyout.
    The **Spacing Tool** dialog box is displayed, Figure 7-14.

4. In the **Parameters** area of the **Spacing Tool** dialog box, enter a value of 5 in the **Count:** spinner. Also, select **Divide Evenly, No Objects at Ends** from the drop-down list at the bottom of the **Parameters** area.

5. Next, select the **Pick Points** button in the dialog box. Pick the first point in the center of the left-hand end of Rail05. Move the dialog box around the screen as needed. Pick the second point at the center of the right-hand end of Rail05. Make sure the two points lie on the centerline of the railing. Finally, pick the **Apply** button in the dialog box, and then the **Close** button.
    Five copies of Baluster01 are placed between Post02 and Pillar02. These are assigned the default names of Baluster02 through Baluster06.

6. Display the four-viewport configuration and activate the Front viewport. Select Baluster02 through Baluster06 using the **Select Objects** dialog box.
    The five cylinders turn white indicating they are selected.

7. Pick the **Select and Move** and **Restrict to Y** buttons on the **Main** toolbar. Move the selected objects up in the Front viewport so they sit on top of Cottage Base, Figure 7-15.

8. Activate the Top viewport and select Baluster01. Then, maximize the viewport.

Figure 7-14. The **Spacing Tool** dialog box is used to evenly space a number of copies along a path.

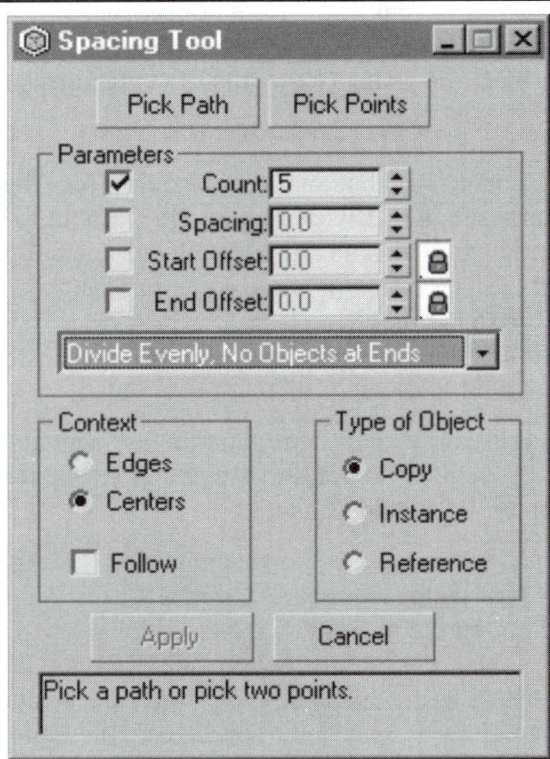

Figure 7-15. The first set of balusters is added to the scene.

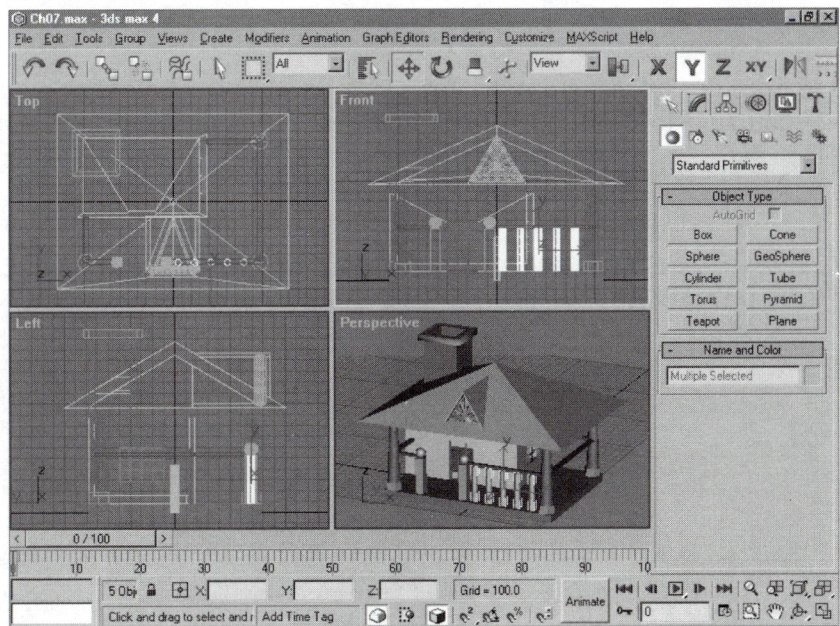

Spacing Tool

9. Pick the **Spacing Tool** button. In the **Spacing Tool** dialog box, type 7 in the **Count:** spinner in the **Parameters** area. Select **Divide Evenly, No Objects at Ends** from the drop-down list. Then, select the **Pick Points** button. Pick the first point in the center of the top end of Rail01. Pick the second point in the center of the bottom end of Rail02. In the dialog box, pick the **Apply** button, and then the **Close** button.

    Seven more balusters are added to the scene. These are assigned the default names Baluster07 through Baluster13.

10. Display the four-viewport configuration and activate the Left viewport. Pick the **Select and Move** and **Restrict to Y** buttons on the **Main** toolbar. Select Baluster07 through Baluster13. Move the selected objects up so they sit on top of Cottage Base.

11. Activate the Top viewport and select Baluster01. Maximize the viewport.

Spacing Tool

12. Pick the **Spacing Tool** button. In the **Spacing Tool** dialog box, type 2 in the **Count:** spinner in the **Parameters** area. Pick **Divide Evenly, No Objects at Ends** in the drop-down list. Then, select the **Pick Points** button. Pick the first point in the center of the left-hand end of Rail02. Pick the second point in the center of the right-hand end of Rail02. In the dialog box, pick the **Apply** button, and then the **Close** button.
Two more balusters are added to the scene. These two are assigned the default names Baluster14 and Baluster15.

13. Display the four-viewport configuration and activate the Front viewport. Select Baluster14 and Baluster15. Pick the **Select and Move** and **Restrict to Y** buttons. Then, move the objects up so they sit on top of Cottage Base.

14. Activate and maximize the Top viewport. Select Baluster01. Pick the **Spacing Tool** button. In the **Spacing Tool** dialog box, type 2 in the **Count:** spinner in the **Parameters** area. Pick **Divide Evenly, No Objects at Ends** in the drop-down list. Then, select the **Pick Points** button. Pick the first point in the center of the bottom end of Rail03. Pick the second point in the center of the top edge of Rail03. In the dialog box, pick the **Apply** button, and then the **Close** button.
Two more balusters are added to the scene. These are assigned the default names Baluster16 and Baluster17, and located between Room and Pillar01.

15. Display the four-viewport configuration and activate the Left viewport. Select Baluster16 and Baluster17. Move the two objects up so they sit on top of Cottage Base.

16. Select Baluster01. Move it up so it sits on top of Cottage Base.

17. Activate and maximize the Top viewport. Pick the **Select and Move** and **Restrict to XY Plane** buttons. Move Baluster01 so it is centered left-to-right and top-to-bottom on Rail04, Figure 7-16.

18. Save the scene.

Figure 7-16. All balusters are added to the scene.

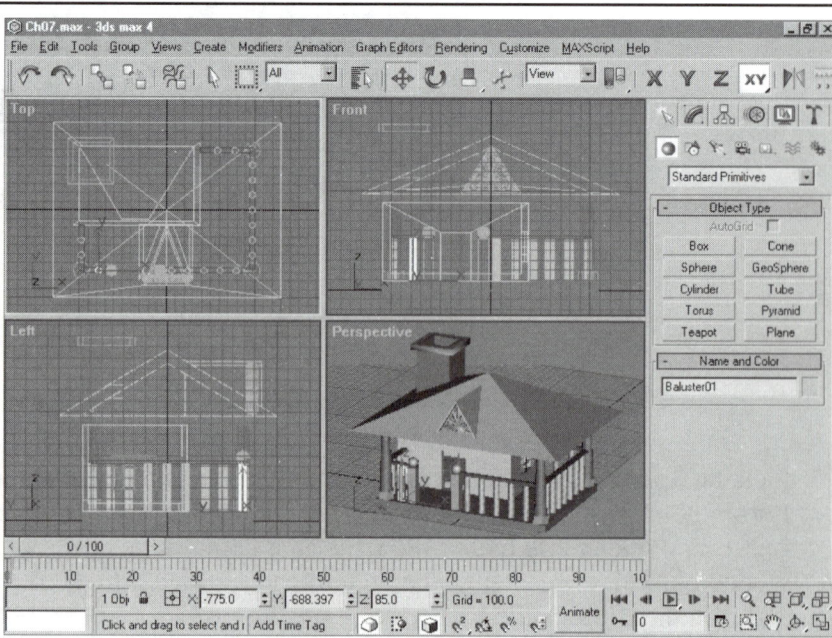

Adding a Ground Plane

You will now create a ground object on which the cottage sits. You will apply a modifier to the object to create a natural "rolling" effect. You will also add stepping-stones to the scene.

Zoom

1. Pick the **Zoom** button. Pick in the center of the Top viewport and zoom out until the objects are displayed about one-fourth of their size.

2. Pick **Create** in the **Command Panel**. Pick the **Geometry** button and select **Standard Primitives** from the drop-down list. Pick the **Plane** button in the **Object Type** rollout.

3. Turn snap on. In the **Creation Method** rollout, pick the **Square** radio button. Then, select a point in the Top viewport at coordinates 0, 0, 0 and drag the cursor to coordinates 2000, 0, 0. In the **Name and Color** rollout, name the plane Ground.
   A plane is created. A plane is designed to be drawn small and scaled up when rendered.

4. In the **Render Multipliers** area of the **Parameters** rollout, type 3.5 in the **Scale:** spinner. Also, type 3 in the **Density:** spinner. In addition, increase the value in the **Length Segs:** and **Width Segs:** spinners to 25.
   When the scene is rendered, the dimensions of the plane are increased by 3.5 times, and the density of the mesh is increased by 3 times.

5. With Ground selected, pick **Parametric Deformers** in the **Modifiers** pull-down menu. Then, pick **Noise** in the cascading menu.
   A noise modifier is applied to the plane.

6. In the **Noise:** area of the **Parameters** rollout, check the **Fractal** check box. Also, type 200 in the **Scale:** spinner. In the **Strength:** area of the rollout, type 100 in the **Z:** spinner.

7. Zoom in on an area of the Top viewport that includes Post01, Post02, and a portion of the ground in front of them.

8. Pick **Create** in the **Command Panel**. Pick the **Geometry** button and select **Standard Primitives** from the drop-down list. Then, pick the **Box** button in the **Object Type** rollout.

9. With snap on, pick a point at coordinates –500, –800, 0 in the Top viewport, drag the cursor to coordinates –200, –1000, 0, and release. Now, move the cursor up until the value in the **Height:** spinner in the **Parameters** rollout is 100 and pick in the viewport. In the **Name and Color** rollout, name the box Step01.

10. Turn snap off. Pick the **Select and Move** and **Restrict to Y** buttons on the **Main** toolbar. Holding down the [Shift] key, move Step01 down so there is a small distance between the original and the copy. In the **Clone Options** dialog box that is displayed, name the copy Step02 and pick the **OK** button.
    A copy of Step01 is created.

11. Create another copy below the first copy. Name the copy Step03.

12. Activate the Left viewport. Zoom in on the steps.

13. Select all three steps. Then, move them down so about one-fourth of the objects is visible above the ground.

14. Pick the **Zoom Extents All** button, Figure 7-17.

15. Save the scene.

Figure 7-17. The ground is created. A noise modifier is used to create the rolling effect.

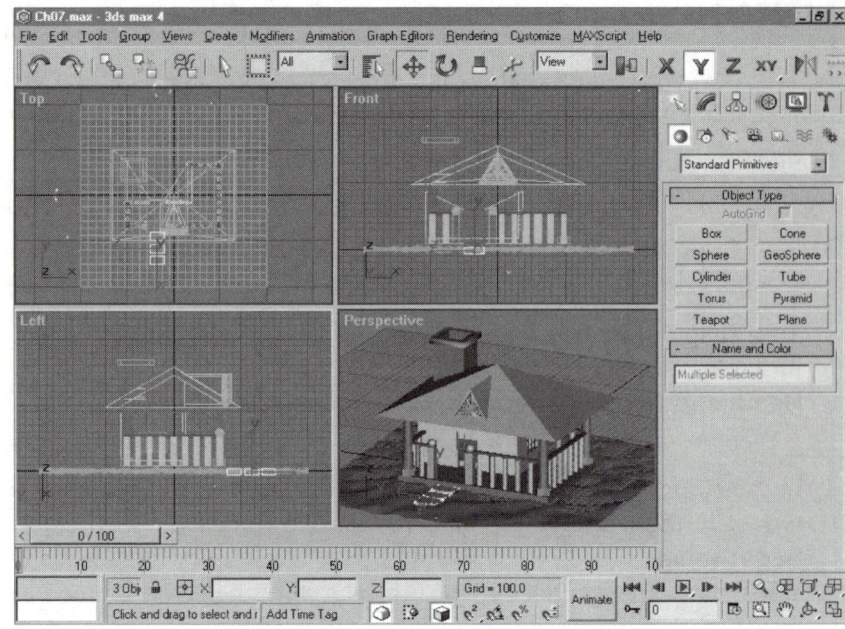

Adding Lights and a Camera

Create

Lights

1. Activate the Top viewport and zoom out so objects are displayed about half of their original size. Pick **Create** in the **Command Panel**. Pick the **Lights** button and select **Standard** from the drop-down list. Then, pick the **Omni** button in the **Object Type** rollout.

2. Pick a point at the bottom of the viewport near the centerline of the cottage. Pick again at the upper-right corner of the viewport to place another omni light.

3. Activate the Front viewport and pick the **Zoom Extents** button. Pick the **Select and Move** and **Restrict to Y** buttons on the **Main** toolbar. Move Omni02 up and place it at the upper-right corner of the viewport. Also, move Omni01 up so it is at the top of the viewport.

Create

Cameras

4. With Omni01 selected, pick **Modify** in the **Command Panel**. In the **General Parameters** rollout, check the **Cast Shadows** check box. Do the same for Omni02.

5. Pick **Create** in the **Command Panel**. Pick the **Cameras** button and select **Standard** from the drop-down list. Pick the **Target** button in the **Object Type** rollout.

6. Pick a point at the lower-right corner of the Top viewport to place the camera. Drag the cursor to the center of the cottage and release to place the target.

7. Make the Perspective viewport current and then press the [C] key to make it the Camera01 viewport. Press the [G] key to turn off the grid in the viewport.
   The grid is no longer visible in the camera viewport.

8. Pick the **Select and Move** and **Restrict to XY Plane** buttons on the **Main** toolbar. Move the camera in all viewports as needed to create a desired view in the Camera01 viewport.
   You can also use the **Truck Camera**, **Field-of-View**, and **Orbit Camera** buttons in the Camera01 viewport to adjust the view.

9. Activate the Top viewport. Pick **Create** in the **Command Panel**. Pick the **Lights** button and select **Standard** from the drop-down list. Then, pick the **Omni** button in the **Object Type** rollout. Pick at the center of Room to place another omni light. In the **General Parameters** rollout, check the **Cast Shadows** check box. Then, in the Front viewport, move the light up so it is in the center of Room.
   An interior light is added to the scene, Figure 7-18.

10. Save the scene.

Figure 7-18. Lights and a camera are added to the scene.

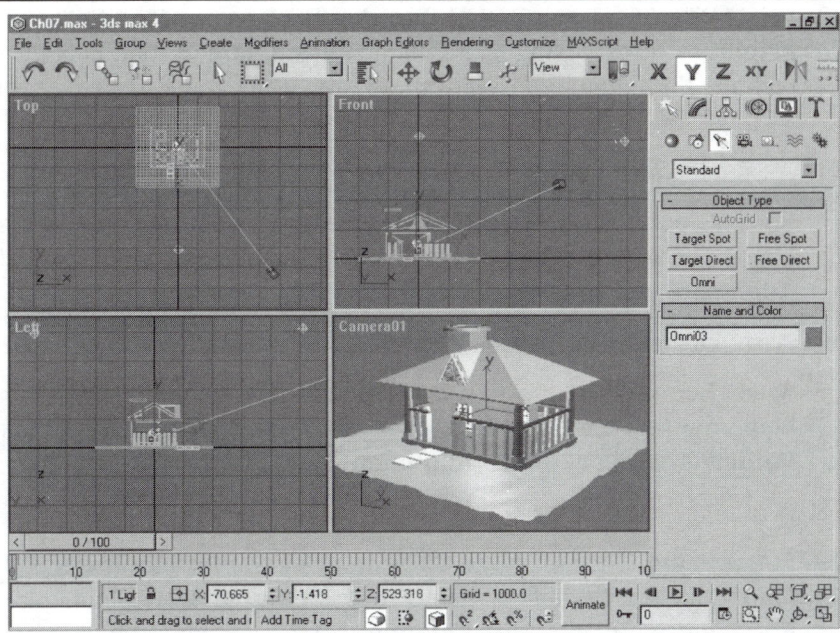

Applying Materials

In this part of the tutorial, you will select materials from the material library. You will then assign the materials to objects. First, hide the lights and camera.

1. Pick **Display** in the **Command Panel**. In the **Hide by Category** rollout, check the **Lights** and **Cameras** check boxes.
   The lights and camera are no longer visible in the viewports, but their effects are retained.

Display

2. Select the **Zoom Extents All** button to zoom to the extents of the objects in the viewport.

3. Select the object Cottage Base. Then, pick the **Material Editor** button on the **Main** toolbar.
   The **Material Editor** is displayed.

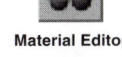
Material Editor

4. Select the first sample slot. Then, pick the **Get Material** button to display the **Material/Map Browser**. Pick the **Mtl Library** radio button in the **Browse From:** area.
   The materials in the 3dsmax.mat library file are displayed.

Get Material

5. Double-click on the material Wood_Cedfence to display it in the first sample slot of the **Material Editor**. Pick the **Assign Material to Selection** button in the **Material Editor**.
   The material Wood_Cedfence is assigned to Cottage Base.

6. Similarly, choose the material Stones_Travertn and assign it to Step01, Step02, and Step03.
   You can minimize the **Material Editor** and the **Material/Map Browser** when selecting objects.

7. Assign the material Stones_Balmoral to Column Base01, Column Base02, and Column Base03.

8. Assign the material Wood_Bubing to Rail01, Rail02, Rail03, Rail04, and Rail05.

9. Assign the material Wood_Oakgrtrt to Baluster01 through Baluster17.

10. Assign the material Wood_Walnut to Door, Window, and Gable Mullions.

11. Assign the material Stones_Altaqua to Border.

12. Select Post01. Then, pick **UV Coordinates** from the **Modifiers** pull-down menu. Then, pick **UVW Map** from the cascading menu. In the **Parameters** rollout, pick the **Box** radio button. Finally, using the **Material Editor**, assign the material Wood_Bubing to Post01. Repeat the procedure for Post02.

13. Select Pillar01. Then, pick **UV Coordinates** from the **Modifiers** pull-down menu. Then, pick **UVW Map** from the cascading menu. In the **Parameters** rollout, pick the **Cylindrical** radio button. Also, pick the **Fit** button in the **Alignment** area. Repeat the procedure for Pillar02, then Pillar03. The cylindrical mapping coordinates are applied to each of the pillars.

14. Assign the material Stones_Benedeti to the pillars.

15. Select Ground. Then, pick **UV Coordinates** from the **Modifiers** pull-down menu. Then, pick **UVW Map** from the cascading menu. In the **Parameters** rollout, pick the **Planar** radio button. In the **Alignment** area of the rollout, pick the **Fit** button.

16. Assign the material Ground_Grass to the plane.

17. Select Room. Then, pick **UV Coordinates** from the **Modifiers** pull-down menu. Then, pick **UVW Map** from the cascading menu. In the **Parameters** rollout, pick the **Box** radio button in the **Parameters** rollout. In the **Alignment** area, pick the **Fit** button.

18. Assign the material Bricks_Bricks_1 to Room.

19. Select Beam. Then, pick **UV Coordinates** from the **Modifiers** pull-down menu. Then, pick **UVW Map** from the cascading menu. In the **Parameters** rollout, pick the **Box** radio button in the **Parameters** rollout. In the **Alignment** area, pick the **Fit** button.

20. Assign the material Wood_Burloak to Beam.

21. Select Roof. Then, pick **UV Coordinates** from the **Modifiers** pull-down menu. Then, pick **UVW Map** from the cascading menu. In the **Parameters** rollout, pick the **Planar** radio button in the **Parameters** rollout.

22. Assign the material Wood_Shingle to Roof.

23. Select Chimney. Then, pick **UV Coordinates** from the **Modifiers** pull-down menu. Then, pick **UVW Map** from the cascading menu. In the **Parameters** rollout, pick the **Box** radio button in the **Parameters** rollout and then the **Fit** button in the **Alignment** area of the rollout.

24. Assign the material Bricks_Yellow to Chimney.

25. Close the **Material/Map Browser** and the **Material Editor**.

26. Save the scene.

Setting a Background

You will now add a background to the scene. The background is an environmental setting. It is an image that is displayed behind all rendered objects, much like a movie backdrop.

1. Open the **Material Editor** and select an unused sample slot.

2. Pick the **Get Material** button to display the **Material/Map Browser** dialog box. Pick the **Mtl Library** radio button in the **Browse From:** area of the dialog box.

3. Double-click on Sky_Cloud2 to load the image into the **Material Editor**. The bitmap is displayed in the selected sample slot.

4. In the **Coordinates** rollout, pick the **Environ** radio button and then select **Screen** from the **Mapping:** drop-down list. Also make sure that the **Blur offset:** spinner is set to 0. Close the **Material Editor** and the **Material/Map Browser**.

5. Pick **Environment...** in the **Rendering** pull-down menu. The **Environment** dialog box is displayed, Figure 7-19.

Figure 7-19. The **Environment** dialog box is used to specify a background image.

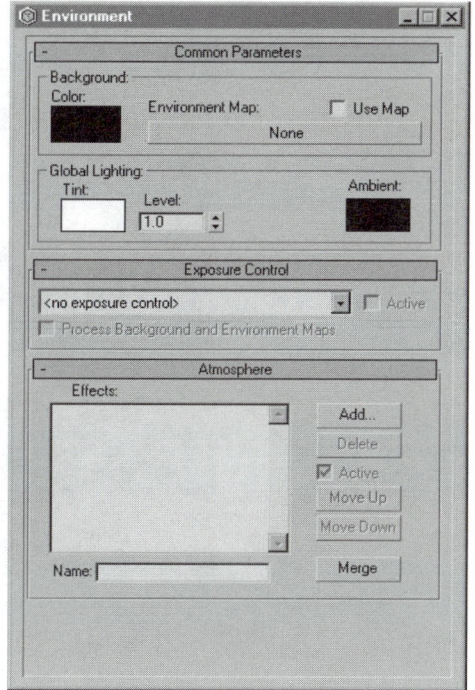

6. Pick the **Environment Map** button that is currently labeled **None**.
   The **Material/Map Browser** is displayed.

7. Pick the **Mtl Editor** radio button in the **Browse From:** area of the dialog box and then double-click on Sky_Cloud2 in the list. In the **Instance or Copy?** dialog box that appears, pick the **Instance** radio button and pick the **OK** button.
   Sky_Cloud2 replaces the **None** label in the **Environment** dialog box

8. Close the **Environment** dialog box.

9. Save the scene.

Rendering the Scene

1. Adjust the Camera01 viewport so a portion of the background will be visible above the Ground object.

2. Pick the **Render Scene** button on the **Main** toolbar. Then, pick the **Render** button in the **Render Scene** dialog box.
   The rendered view is displayed in the render window, Figure 7-20.

3. Save the scene.

Figure 7-20. The final
rendered scene.

Self-Evaluation Test

Answer the following questions. Then compare your answers with the correct answers given at the end of this chapter.

1. After you have created a standard primitives, you can change its original dimensions using the _____ rollout.

2. You can retain a copy of "operand B" used for a Boolean operation by picking the _____ radio button in the **Pick Boolean** rollout.

3. When you apply a _____ modifier, the effect is a wireframe object consisting of struts and joints.

4. The number of sides in a gengon can be set using the _____ spinner in the **Parameters** rollout.

5. The _____ modifier can be used to scale down or scale up an object toward either of its ends.

6. You can use the _____ button in the **Scale** flyout to scale an object with the same scale factor along two of its axes and a different scale factor along the third axis.

7. It is possible to create a square tube primitive by entering _____ in the **Sides:** spinner.

8. The _____ dialog box is used to place objects at equal distances along a selected path or between two selected points.

9. You can use the _____ modifier to quickly use a flat object to simulate rolling ground.

10. You can add a background to your scene by using the _____ dialog box.

Exercises

In this exercise, you will create a kitchen scene. You will create the different objects using standard primitives. You will apply modifiers to some of the primitives. Then, materials will be assigned to the objects, lights and a camera added to the scene, and the scene rendered. Refer to the illustration and use your own dimensions.

1. Create the floor as a plane. Set the rendering multipliers as needed.

2. Create the walls, shelves, the tabletop, and the cereal box from box primitives. Use Boolean operations as needed.

3. The teapot is a standard primitive.

4. Create the glasses from cylinder standard primitives. Use a taper modifier to create the form. Use a scaled down copy of the tapered cylinder to hollow out the glass.

5. Create the bowl from a sphere standard primitive. Apply an edit mesh modifier and edit the object at the sub-object level to flatten the bottom. Subtract a scaled-down copy of the modified primitive to hollow out the bowl.

6. Create the table post, seat, and legs from cylinder standard primitives.

7. Apply a bend modifier to the legs. Create a thin ring passing through the legs from a torus standard primitive. Union the ring to the legs.

8. Apply an edit mesh modifier to the seat. At the sub-object level, modify the seat so it has a curved profile.

9. Apply a UVW map modifier to the walls, floor, and shelves. Set each to an appropriate "type" of mapping.

10. Using the **Material Editor**, get appropriate materials from the default 3ds max material library file. Then, assign the materials to the objects in the scene.

11. Add a camera and lights to the scene. Then, render the scene. Save the scene as Ex07.max in the folder of your choice.

Answers

The following are the correct answers to the questions in the Self-Evaluation Test.

1. **Parameters**; 2. **Copy**; 3. lattice; 4. **Sides:**; 5. taper; 6. **Select and Squash**; 7. four; 8. **Spacing Tool**; 9. noise; 10. **Environment**

Chapter 8

Creating and Modifying Primitive Objects

Learning Objectives

- Create primitive objects.
- Modify primitive objects.
- Apply materials to different areas of a single object.
- Position and adjust lights and a camera.
- Add a background to the scene.

Tutorial Description

In this tutorial, you will create a character model of an octopus using standard primitives and various modifiers. The octopus has eight tentacles, eyes, eyebrows, and a nose. You will then assign materials to the character. Finally, you will add lights, a camera, and a background to the scene, and render the scene.

Creating and Shaping the Octopus Body

Reset 3ds max before starting the tutorial. This sets the system to default values and erases all existing data. If you want to save the existing scene, do so before resetting 3ds max.

1. Select **Reset** from the **File** pull-down menu. Then, pick the **Yes** button in the dialog box that appears.

2. Activate the Top viewport.

3. Pick **Create** in the **Command Panel**. Pick the **Geometry** button and select **Standard Primitives** from the drop-down list. Then, pick the **Sphere** button in the **Object Type** rollout.
   Rollouts for a sphere are displayed.

Create

Geometry

4. Expand the **Keyboard Entry** rollout. Then, type 150 in the **Radius:** spinner and pick the **Create** button. In the **Name and Color** rollout, name the sphere Body.
   A sphere is created in the center of the Top viewport.

5. With the sphere still selected, in the **Parameters** rollout, type 16 in the **Segments:** spinner. Also, check the **Base to Pivot** check box.
   The sphere is placed on the grid plane.

Figure 8-1. A sphere is drawn, which will form the basis of the body.

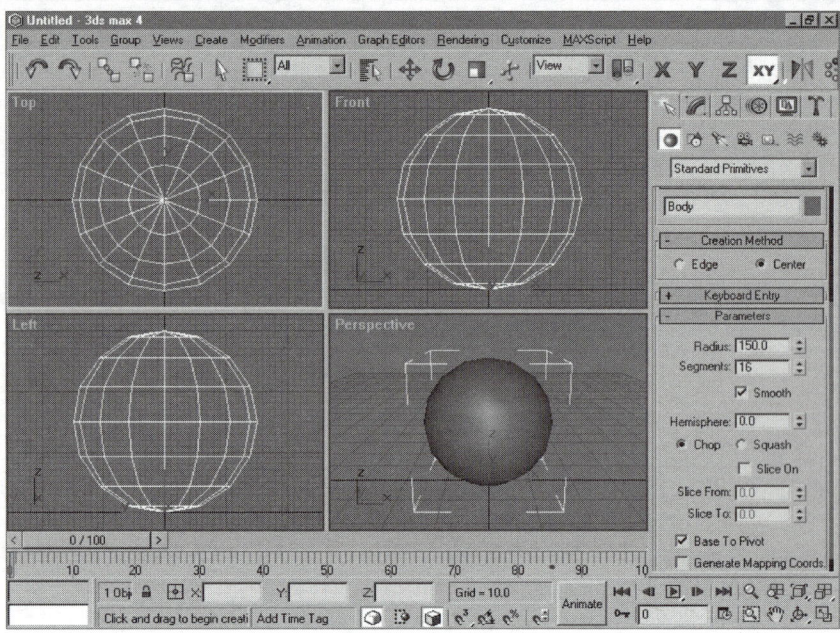

Zoom Extents All

6. Select the **Zoom Extents All** button, Figure 8-1.
   The sphere is zoomed to its extents in all the viewports.

7. With Body selected, pick **Parametric Deformers** in the **Modifiers** pull-down menu. Then, pick **Taper** in the cascading menu.
   A taper modifier is applied to the sphere, and the **Modify** tab in the **Command Panel** is automatically opened.

8. In the **Parameters** rollout, type 0.5 in the **Amount:** spinner.
   The sphere is now approximately the shape of the octopus head.

9. With Body still selected, pick **Parametric Deformers** in the **Modifiers** pull-down menu. Then, pick **Stretch** in the cascading menu.
   A stretch modifier is applied to the sphere "on top of" the taper modifier, and the **Modify** tab in the **Command Panel** is automatically opened.

10. In the **Stretch:** area of the **Parameters** rollout, type 0.1 in the **Stretch:** spinner. In the **Stretch Axis:** area of the rollout, pick the Z radio button.
    The body is slightly stretched along its Z axis to better form the head, Figure 8-2.

11. Save the scene as Ch08.max in the folder of your choice.

Creating the Tentacles

You will now create eight tentacles of the octopus. This is done by first converting the body into an editable mesh, and then extruding and transforming eight of the faces on the editable mesh.

Zoom Extents All

1. Pick the **Zoom Extents All** button to zoom to the extents of the octopus head. Activate the Front viewport and maximize it.

2. With Body selected, right-click anywhere in the viewport to display the quad menu. Select **Convert To:** in the lower-right quadrant. Then, select **Convert to Editable Mesh** in the cascading menu.
   The parametric sphere with two modifiers applied is converted to an editable mesh with no modifiers applied. The effect of the modifiers are reflected in the editable mesh, but can no longer be adjusted. The **Modify** tab in the **Command Panel** is also automatically displayed.

Figure 8-2. The basic shape of the head is created.

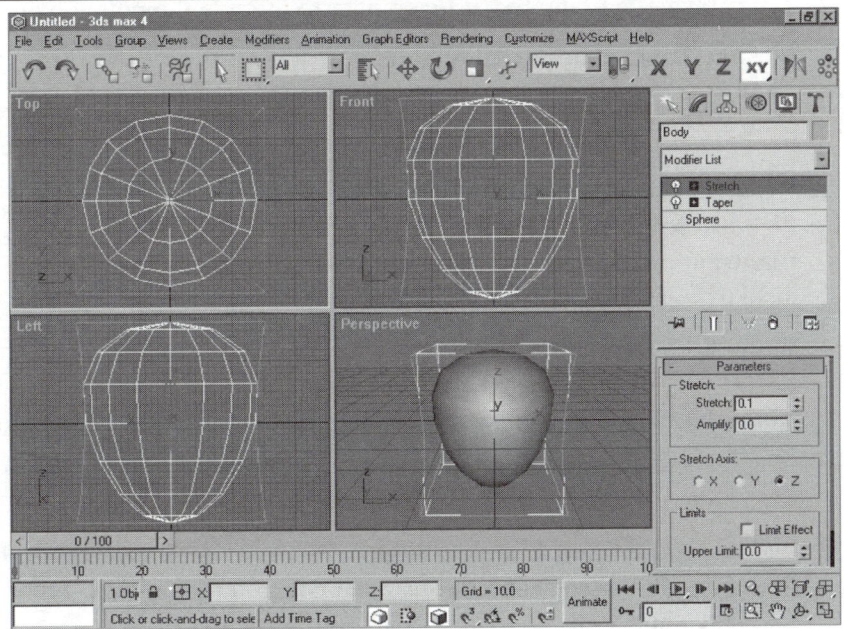

3. With **Body** selected, right-click to display the quad menu again.
   Notice that the upper-left and lower-left quadrants are now displayed. These quadrants contain tools, commands, and options specific to the selected object.

4. Pick **Extrude Polygons** in the lower-left quadrant. Then, select the polygon in the second row from the bottom and immediately to the right of the vertical centerline.
   The selected face turns red indicating it is selected, and the cursor changes to the "extrude cursor." Picking the command in the quad menu is the same as picking the **Extrude** button in the **Edit Geometry** rollout in the **Command Panel**.

5. In the **Edit Geometry** rollout in the **Command Panel**, type 100 in the **Extrude:** spinner.
   The polygon is extruded 100 units.

6. Display the four-viewport configuration and pick the **Zoom Extents All** button, Figure 8-3.

Figure 8-3. One tentacle is started.

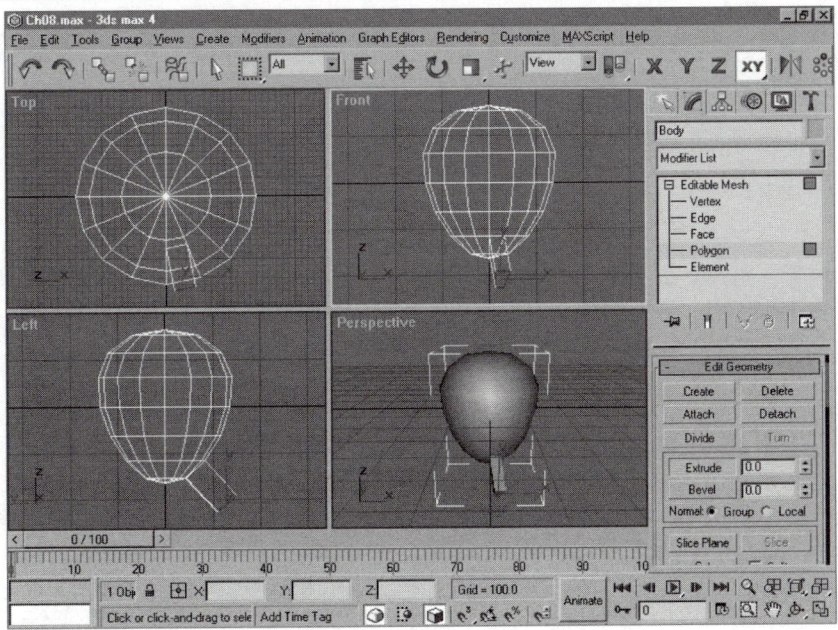

Select and Move

Restrict to Y

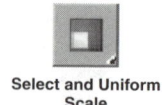

Select and Uniform Scale

7. Type 100 again in the **Extrude:** spinner to extrude the polygon an additional 100 units.

8. Pick the **Zoom Extents All** button.

9. Pick the **Select and Move** button on the **Main** toolbar. Also, pick the **Restrict to Y** button. Move the last extruded polygon up in the Left viewport so the lower edge of the "arm" is parallel to the grid lines.

10. Pick the **Select and Uniform Scale** button from the **Scale** flyout. Also, pick the **Restrict to XY Plane** button. Scale the polygon down in the Front viewport to 75%, as indicated in the coordinate display.

11. In the **Edit Geometry** rollout, pick the **Extrude** button so it is on (depressed). Type 100 in the **Extrude:** spinner to extrude the polygon another 100 units.
    Notice how the polygon is extruded along the normal of the polygon.

12. Pick the **Select and Move** and **Restrict to Y** buttons. Move the polygon up in the Left viewport so the lower edge of the "arm" is parallel to the grid lines.

13. Pick the **Select and Uniform Scale** button on the **Main** toolbar. Make sure the **Restrict to XY Plane** button is also selected. Scale the polygon down in the Front viewport to 30%.
    The polygon is reduced to almost a point, Figure 8-4.

14. Save the scene.

Creating a Second Tentacle

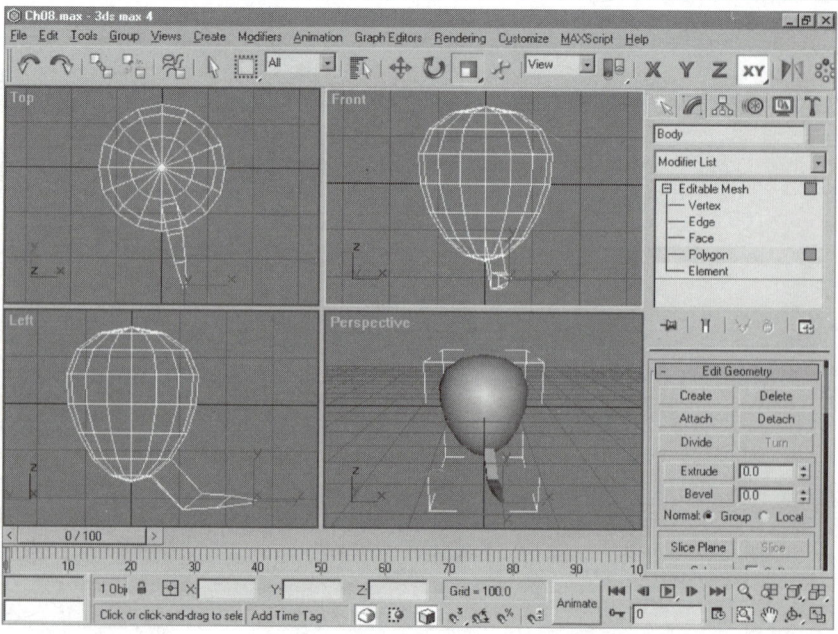

Select object

1. Pick the **Select object** button on the **Main** toolbar. In the Front viewport, select the polygon in the same row as the extruded polygon and two to the left (in other words, "skip" a polygon).

2. Pick the **Extrude** button in the **Edit Geometry** rollout. Type 100 in the **Extrude:** spinner.
   The second polygon is extruded 100 units to begin the second tentacle.

3. Type 100 in the **Extrude:** spinner again to extrude the selected polygon an additional 100 units.

4. Pick the **Select and Move** and **Restrict to Y** buttons on the **Main** toolbar. Move the last extruded polygon up in the Left viewport so the lower edge of the "arm" is parallel to the grid lines.

Figure 8-4. The basic form of the first tentacle is complete.

5. Pick the **Select and Uniform Scale** button. Make sure the **Restrict to XY Plane** button is also selected. Scale the polygon down in the Front viewport to 75%.

6. Pick the **Extrude** button in the **Edit Geometry** rollout. Type 100 in the **Extrude:** spinner. The tentacle is extended by an additional 100 units.

7. Pick the **Select and Move** and **Restrict to Y** buttons on the **Main** toolbar. Move the extruded polygon up in the Left viewport so the lower edge of the "arm" is parallel to the grid lines.

8. Pick the **Select and Uniform Scale** and **Restrict to XY Plane** buttons on the **Main** toolbar. Scale the polygon down in the Front viewport to 30%. The polygon is reduced to almost a point, Figure 8-5.

9. Save the scene.

Figure 8-5. The basic form of the second tentacle is complete.

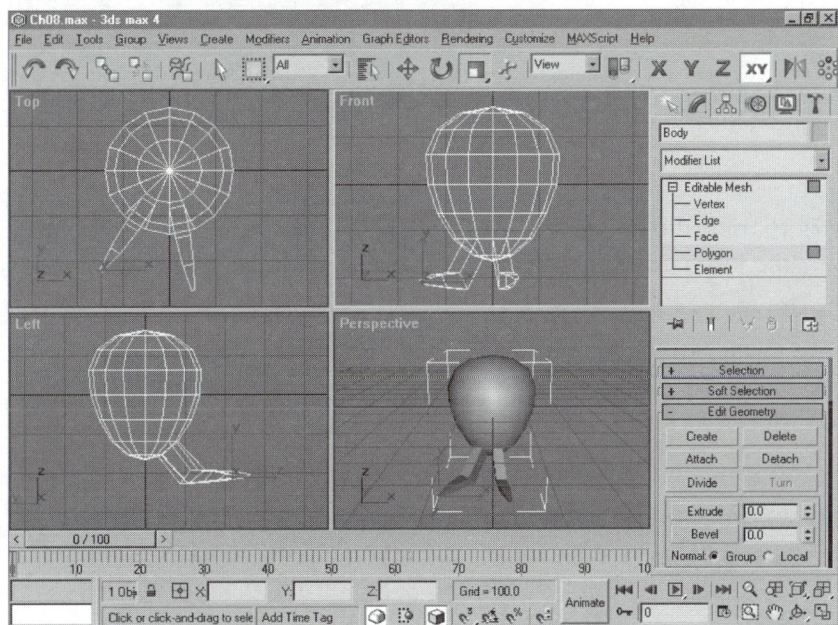

Creating Three More Tentacles

1. Pick the **Select object** button. In the Left viewport, select the polygon two to the left of the previous one. You can verify in the Top and Front viewports that the correct polygon is selected.

2. In the **Edit Geometry** rollout, type 100 in the **Extrude:** spinner. Notice how by typing a value in the spinner, the **Extrude** button does not need to be on.

3. Extrude the polygon another 100 units. Then, move the extruded polygon in the Front viewport so the lower edge of the "arm" is parallel to the grid lines.

4. Scale the selected polygon down to 75% in the Front viewport using the **Select and Uniform Scale** button. Then, extrude the polygon another 100 units.

5. Move the extruded polygon up in the Front viewport so the lower edge of the "arm" is parallel with the grid lines. Then, scale the polygon down to 30%. A third tentacle is added to the octopus, Figure 8-6.

6. Pick the **Select object** button. In the Left viewport, select the polygon two to the left of the previous one. Then, extrude it 100 units.

Figure 8-6. The basic form of
the third tentacle is complete.

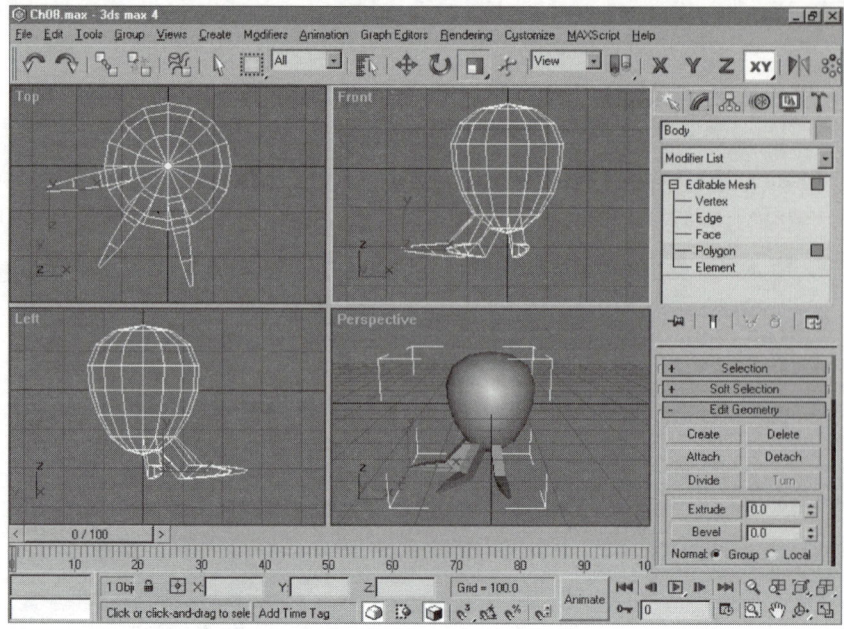

7. Extrude the polygon an additional 100 units. Then, move the polygon up in the Front viewport so the lower edge of the "arm" is parallel with the grid lines.

8. In the Left viewport, scale the polygon down to 75% using the **Select and Uniform Scale** button. Then, extrude the polygon an additional 100 units.

9. In the Front viewport, move the polygon up so the lower edge of the "arm" is parallel to the grid lines. Then, in the Left viewport, scale down the polygon to 30%.
A fourth tentacle is added to the octopus, Figure 8-7.

10. Pick the **Select object** button. In the Front viewport, select the polygon two to the right of the very first polygon you extruded. Extrude the polygon 100 units.

Figure 8-7. The basic form of
the fourth tentacle is complete.

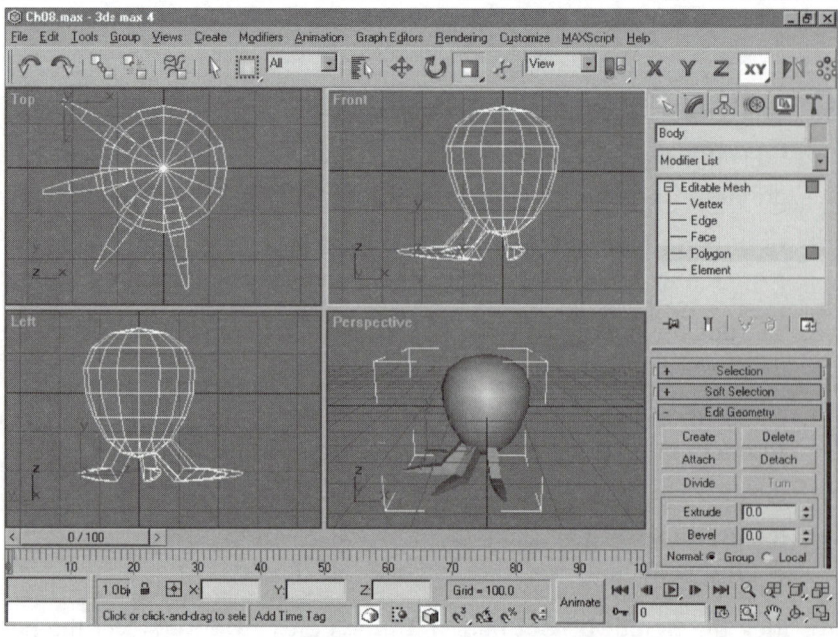

11. Extrude the polygon another 100 units. Then, move the polygon up in the Front viewport so the lower edge of the "arm" is parallel to the grid lines. Next, scale the polygon down to 75%. Finally, extrude the polygon another 100 units.

12. Move the polygon up so the lower edge of the "arm" is parallel to the grid lines. Scale the polygon down to 30%, Figure 8-8.

13. Save the scene.

Figure 8-8. The basic form of the fifth tentacle is complete.

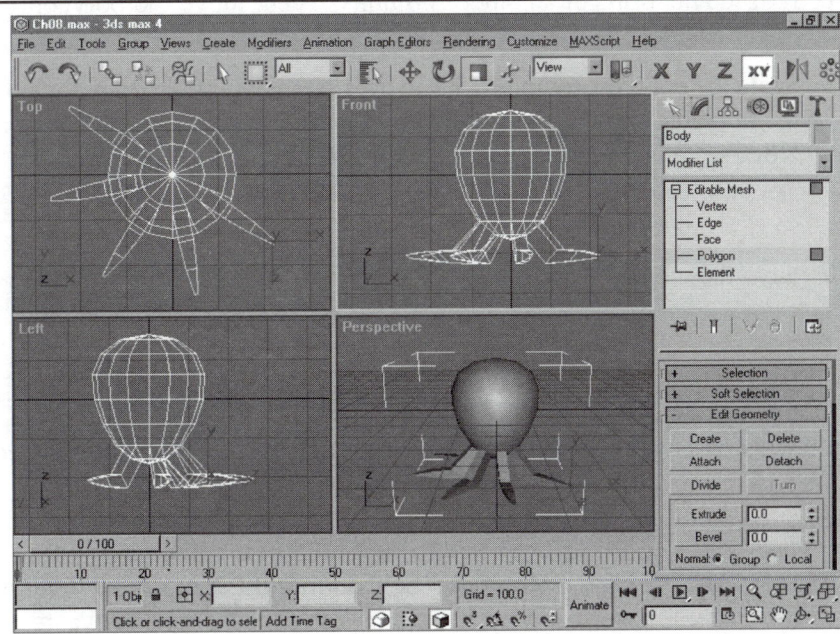

Creating the Remaining Tentacles

You will now rotate the octopus so you can see more of its faces. Then, the remaining three tentacles will be created. In order to rotate the octopus, you need to exit sub-object mode.

1. To exit sub-object mode, pick the **Editable Mesh** level in the modifier stack. The level is highlighted grey. If highlighted yellow, you are still in sub-object mode.

Select and Rotate

2. Activate the Top viewport. Pick the **Select and Rotate** button on the **Main** toolbar. Also, make sure the **Restrict to Z** is selected. Select Body and rotate it 180°, as indicated in the coordinate display.

Restrict to Z

3. With Body selected, pick **Modify** in the **Command Panel**. Then, pick the **Polygon** button in the **Selection** rollout. In the Front viewport, select the polygon immediately to the right of the vertical centerline, and in the same row as the others. Extrude the polygon 100 units.

4. Extrude the polygon another 100 units. Then, move the polygon up in the Left viewport so the lower edge of the "arm" is parallel to the grid lines. Scale the polygon down to 75% in the Front viewport.

5. Extrude the polygon another 100 units. Then, move the polygon up in the Left viewport so the lower edge of the "arm" is parallel to the grid lines. Then, scale the polygon down to 30% in the Front viewport.
Another tentacle is created.

6. Pick the **Select object** button. In the Front viewport, select the polygon two to the left of polygon you just extruded. In the **Edit Geometry** rollout, type 100 in the **Extrude:** spinner.
The polygon is extruded 100 units.

7. Extrude the polygon another 100 units. Then, move the polygon up in the Left viewport so the lower edge of the "arm" is parallel to the grid lines.

8. Scale the polygon down to 75% in the Front viewport. Then, extrude it another 100 units. Move the polygon up in the Left viewport so the lower edge of the "arm" is parallel to the grid lines. Scale the polygon down to 30%, Figure 8-9.

9. Pick the **Select object** button. In the Left viewport, select the polygon immediate to the right of the vertical centerline, and in the same row as the others. Extrude the polygon 100 units.

10. Extrude the polygon another 100 units. Then, move the polygon up in the Front viewport so the lower edge of the "arm" is parallel to the grid lines.

11. Scale the polygon down to 75% in the Left viewport. Extrude the polygon another 100 units. Move the polygon up in the Front viewport so the lower edge of the "arm" is parallel to the grid lines. Now, scale down the polygon to 30% in the Left viewport.
    The last tentacle is added to the octopus, Figure 8-10. There should now be eight tentacles evenly spaced around Body when viewed in the Top viewport.

12. Save the scene.

Creating the Eyebrows

You will now create eyebrows for the octopus. These are created using various sub-object editing methods. You will move vertices, create new ones using a cut operation, and finally extrude the new polygons.

Modify

1. Activate the Front viewport and maximize it.

2. Select Body and pick **Modify** in the **Command Panel**. In the modifier stack, expand the sub-object tree and select **Vertex** in the hierarchy. You can also pick the **Vertex** button in the **Selection** rollout.
   All vertices in the mesh are displayed, and the vertex level in the modifier stack is highlighted yellow.

3. In the fourth row from the top, select the two vertices immediately to the right of the vertical center-line. Pick the **Select and Move** and **Restrict to Y** buttons on the **Main** toolbar. Move the selected vertices up to about halfway between their original position and the next row of vertices, Figure 8-11.
   Both vertices can be selected by dragging a window around them or using the [Ctrl] key.

Figure 8-9. The basic forms of the sixth and seventh tentacles are complete.

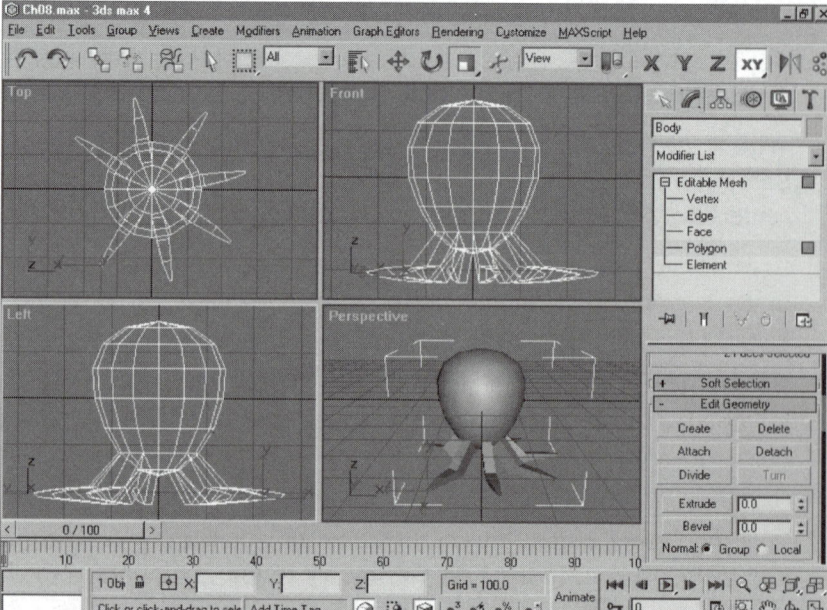

Figure 8-10. The basic form of the eighth tentacle is complete.

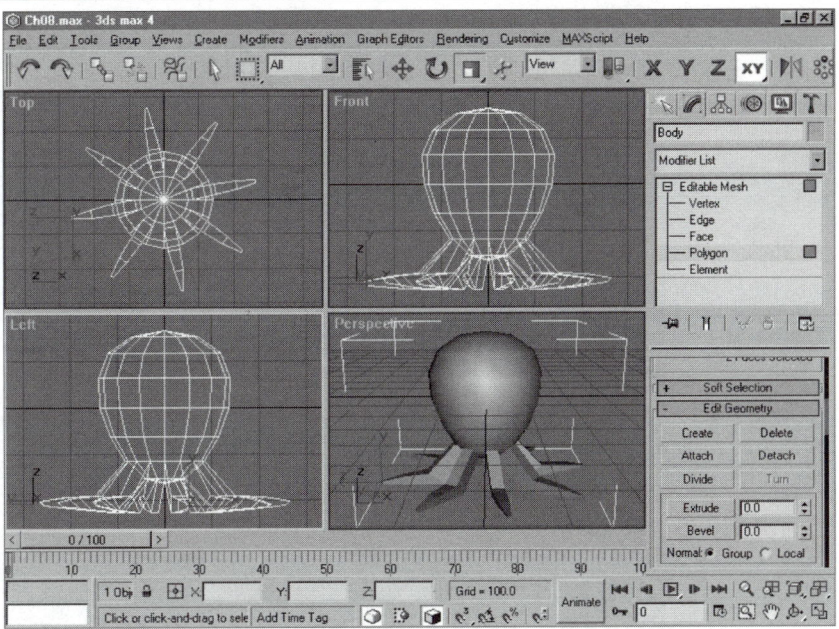

Figure 8-11. Selected vertices are moved to create the top of the first eyebrow.

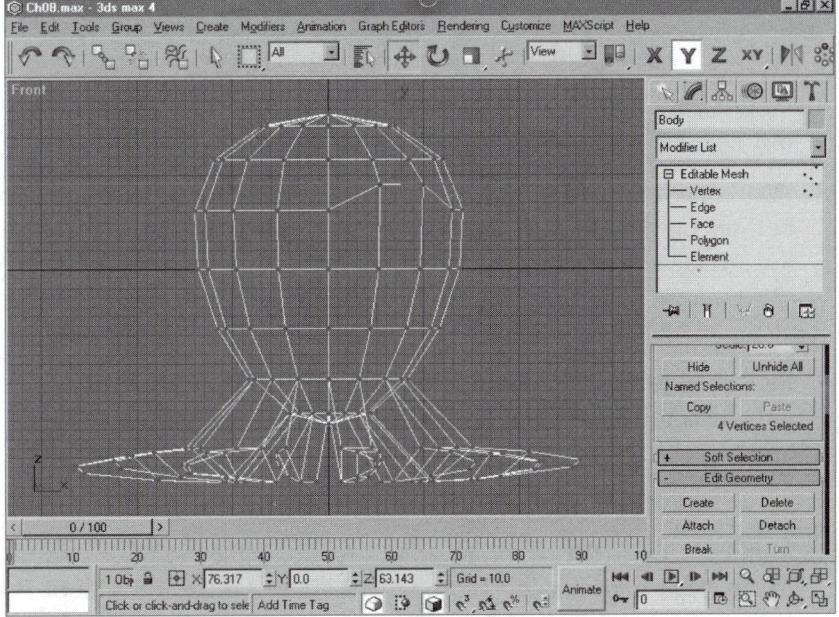

4. Now, select **Polygon** in the modifier stack to enter polygon sub-object editing mode. Then, pick the **Cut** button in the **Edit Geometry** rollout. Also, check the **Ignore Backfacing** check box at the top of the **Selection** rollout.

   This command allows you to "cut into" an existing mesh to create additional vertices, faces, and polygons.

5. Select the first point of the cut on the vertical centerline slightly below the fourth row of vertices from the top. Pick the next point slightly below the moved vertex on the vertical iso line to the right of the centerline. Pick a third point slightly below the moved vertex on the second iso line to the right of the centerline, Figure 8-12. Right-click to end the command.

   Three vertices are added to the mesh object, and the faces/polygons are subdivided to form a rough eyebrow shape.

Figure 8-12. The bottom of the eyebrow is created, and additional vertices are added for the eye socket.

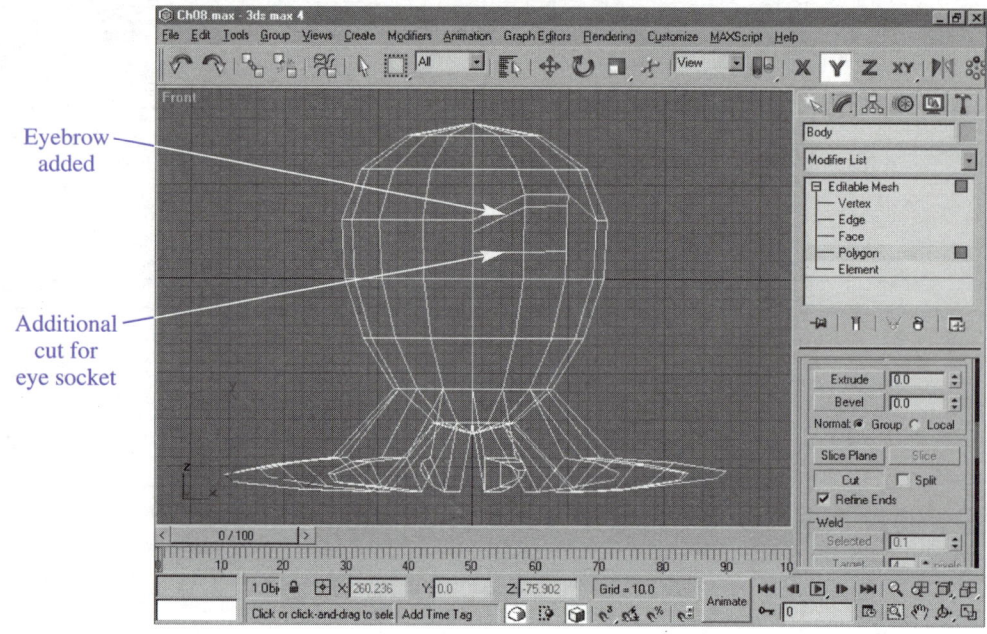

Eyebrow
added

Additional
cut for
eye socket

6. Create a horizontal cut across the two polygons below the eyebrow, Figure 8-12.
   The added vertices will be moved back into the head to create eye sockets.

7. Pick **Vertex** in the modifier stack to enter vertex sub-object editing mode. Select the two vertices just added below the eyebrows.

8. Display the four-viewport configuration. Pick the **Select and Move** and **Restrict to XY Plane** buttons on the **Main** toolbar. In the Top viewport, move the vertices slightly into the head and toward the center to create an eye socket.
   If you press the spacebar to lock the selection, moving the vertices is easier. Press the spacebar again to unlock the selection.

9. Pick **Polygon** in the modifier stack to enter polygon sub-object editing mode. In the Front viewport, select the two polygons in the eyebrow.

10. In the **Edit Geometry** rollout, type 0.2 in the **Extrude:** spinner.
    The eyebrow is extruded out from the head slightly.

11. Maximize the Front viewport. Select **Vertex** in the modifier stack to enter vertex sub-object editing mode. Next, repeat steps 3 through 10 above on the left side of Body to create the other eyebrow and eye socket, Figure 8-13.

12. Exit sub-object editing mode by picking **Editable Mesh** in the modifier stack. The label is highlighted grey. Save the scene.

Making the Eyeballs

Create

Geometry

You will now create the eyeballs in the eye sockets using standard primitives and editing them.

1. Pick **Create** in the **Command Panel**. Pick the **Geometry** button and select **Standard Primitives** from the drop-down list. Pick the **Sphere** button in the **Object Type** rollout. Also, check the **AutoGrid** check box in the **Object Type** rollout.
   AutoGrid creates a temporary drawing grid on a selected object, or face of an object.

Figure 8-13. The basic forms of two eyebrows and two eye sockets are created.

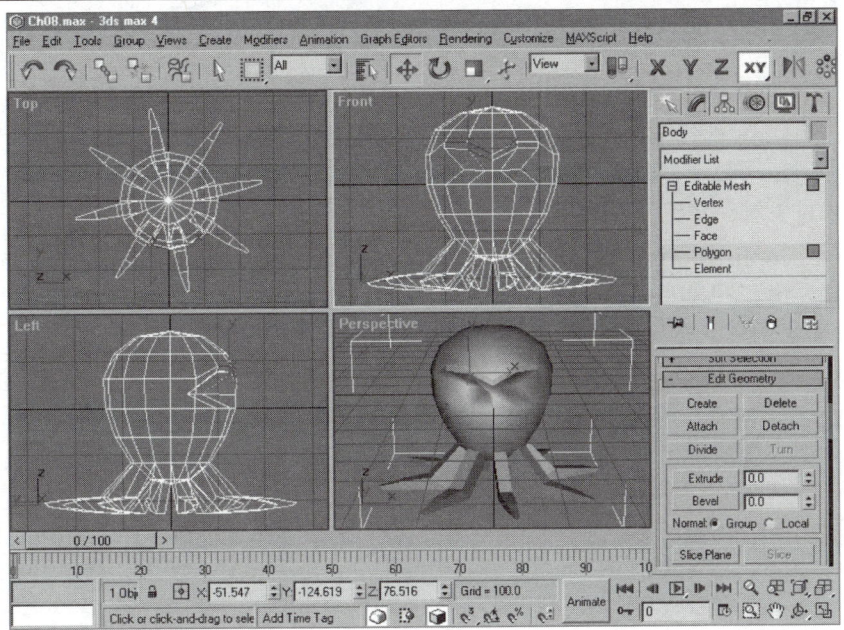

2. In the Front viewport, move the cursor to the center of the eye socket on the right side of the viewport. Pick and drag the cursor to create a sphere of any size. Then, type 30 in the **Radius:** spinner in the **Parameters** rollout. Also, make sure the **Base to Pivot** check box in the **Parameters** rollout is *not* checked. In the **Name and Color** rollout, name the sphere Eye, Left.
   A sphere of the specified radius is created normal to the selected surface.

3. Display the four-viewport configuration. In the Top viewport, move the eye as needed so it sits properly in the eye socket.

4. Similarly, create another sphere of the same radius in the other eye socket. Name the second sphere Eye, Right, Figure 8-14.

5. Save the scene.

Figure 8-14. Two eyes are added to the octopus.

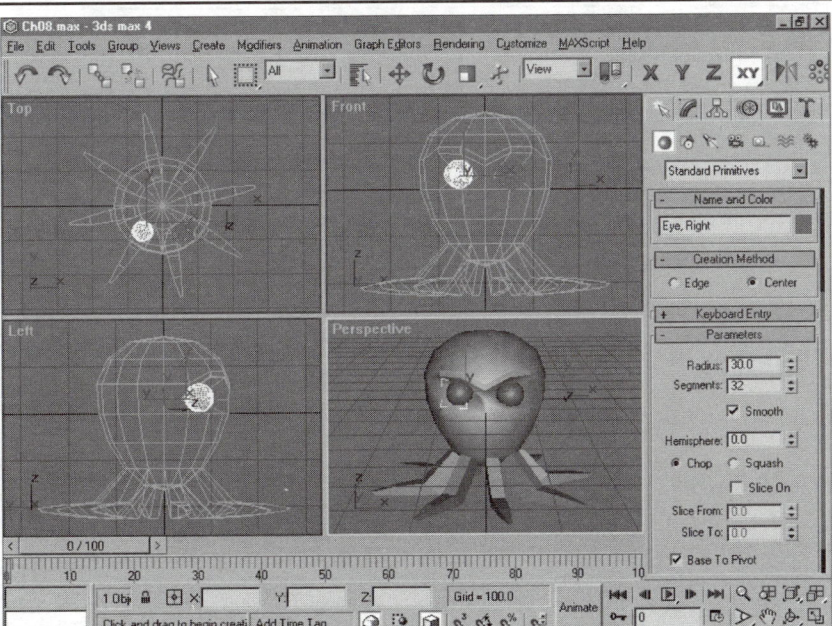

Creating the Eyelids

You will now create eyelids. These are created by first cloning the eyes, then editing the copy.

1. Pick the **Select object** button and select Eye, Left. Then, pick **Clone** from the **Edit** pull-down menu.
   The **Clone Options** dialog box is displayed.

2. In the **Clone Options** dialog box, pick the **Copy** radio button. Name the copy Eyelid, Left and pick the **OK** button.
   A copy of Eye, Left is created on top of the original.

3. With Eyelid, Left selected, pick **Modify** in the **Command Panel**. In the **Parameters** rollout, type 32 in the **Radius:** spinner. Also, type 0.6 in the **Hemisphere:** spinner.
   A hemisphere is created, which is the eyelid.

4. Pick the **Select and Rotate** and **Restrict to X** buttons in the **Main** toolbar. Also, pick **Local** from the **Reference Coordinate System** drop-down list on the **Main** toolbar. Rotate the eyelid –80º in any viewport, as indicated in the **X** text box in the coordinate display.
   You may want to change the display color of the eye or eyelid so you can better see the object rotate.

5. Similarly, clone Eye, Right to create a hemisphere for the other eyelid, Figure 8-15.

6. Save the scene.

Creating the Pupils in the Eyes

You will now create pupils in the eyes. These are created in a manner similar to how the eyelids were created.

1. Display the four-viewport configuration.

2. Select Eye, Left. Then, pick **Clone** in the **Edit** pull-down menu. In the **Clone Options** dialog box, name the copy Pupil, Left and then pick the **OK** button.

Figure 8-15. Two eyelids are added to the octopus.

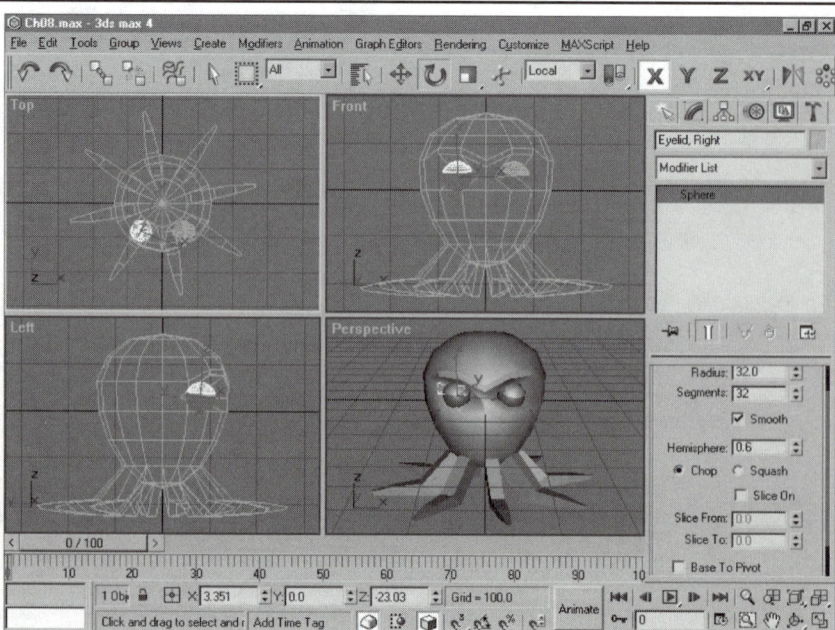

3. Change the display color of Pupil, Left to black by picking the color swatch in the **Name and Color** rollout. In the dialog box that appears, pick the black color swatch and then the **OK** button.

4. With Pupil, Left selected, pick **Modify** in the **Command Panel**. In the **Parameters** rollout, type 31 in the **Radius:** spinner and 0.85 in the **Hemisphere:** spinner.
   A pupil is created for the left eye.

5. Pick the **Select and Rotate** and **Restrict to Y** buttons on the **Main** toolbar. Make sure **Local** is selected in the **Reference Coordinate System** drop-down list on the **Main** toolbar. Then, in the Top viewport, rotate the pupil as needed so it is on the front of the eye.

6. Repeat steps 2 through 5 for Eye, Right to create a pupil for that eye as well.

7. Next, select Eye, Left and change its display color to white. Then, select Eye, Right and change its display color to white, Figure 8-16.

8. Save the scene.

Figure 8-16. Pupils are added to the eyes.

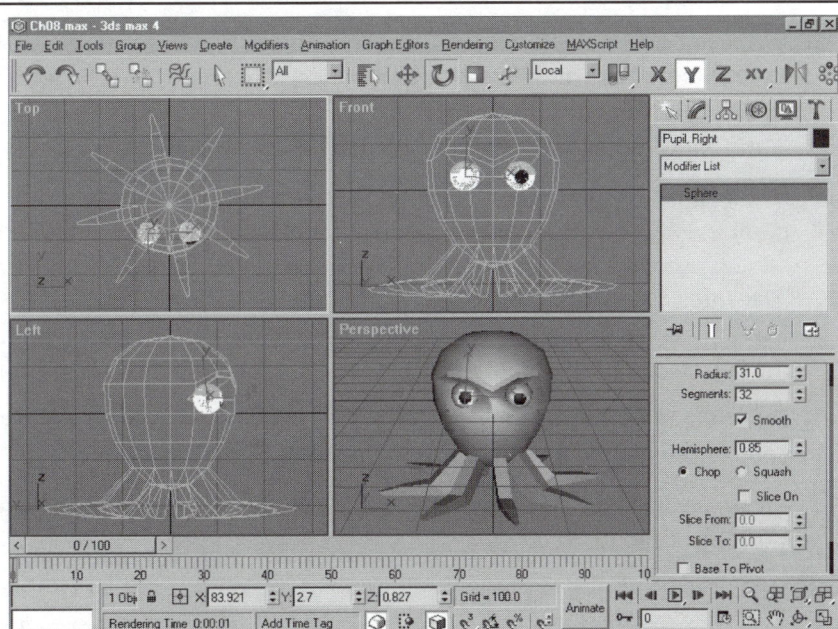

Making Adjustments

Now, the basic form of the octopus is complete. However, the shape is still very segmented and not realistic. You will now apply modifiers to create a more realistic model.

1. Select Body. Then, pick **Modify** in the **Command Panel**.

2. In the modifier stack, expand the sub-object hierarchy tree under **Editable Mesh**. Then, pick **Vertex** to enter that sub-object editing mode.

3. Pick the **Select and Move** and **Restrict to XY Plane** buttons on the **Main** toolbar. In the Top viewport, drag a window around the vertices on the end of one tentacle. Then, move the vertices out from the body about 200 units.

4. One by one, drag a window around the vertices on the end of each tentacle and move the vertices out from the body about 200 units.
   The tentacles are stretched out.

5. Now, pick **Editable Mesh** in the modifier stack to exit sub-object mode. The name should be highlighted in grey. Next, pick **Subdivision Surfaces** in the **Modifiers** pull-down menu. Next, pick **MeshSmooth** in the cascading menu.

   A mesh smooth modifier is applied to the model, and the **Modify** tab is automatically opened. Notice how the mesh on the object is now smooth.

6. In the **Subdivision Amount** rollout, type 2 in the **Iterations:** spinner.

   Notice how the mesh density is increased, Figure 8-17.

7. With Body selected, pick **Free Form Deformers** in the **Modifiers** pull-down menu. Then, pick **FFD Box** in the cascading menu.

   An FFD modifier is applied to the object, and the **Modify** tab is automatically opened. An orange lattice with control points is attached to the object. Deforming the lattice deforms the object.

8. In the **Dimensions:** area of the **FFD Parameters** rollout, pick the **Set Number of Points** button. In the dialog box that appears, type 5 in the **Length:**, **Width:**, and **Height:** spinners.

   The number of control points on each object axis is increased to 5, resulting in 125 total control points.

9. In the modifier stack, expand the sub-object hierarchy tree and pick **Control Points**. Pick the **Select and Move** and **Restrict to Y** buttons. In the Front viewport, drag a window around the very center control point.

   The control point and the four "behind" it are selected.

10. In the Top viewport, press the [Alt] key and drag a window around the top three selected control points. The selected control points, highlighted yellow, may not be visible because they are "under" the top level of control points. However, they are in the center column.

    The three control points around which the window is drawn are removed from the selection set, leaving two control points in the selection set. Since the control points "on top of" and "underneath" the selected control points are not selected, including them in the window is OK and has no effect.

11. Press the spacebar to lock the selection set of two control points. Then, move the two selected control points down until a nose is formed, Figure 8-18.

12. Press the spacebar to unlock the selection set. Then, pick **FFD (box)** in the modifier stack to exit sub-object mode.

13. Save the scene.

Figure 8-17. The mesh is smoothed and the density increased.

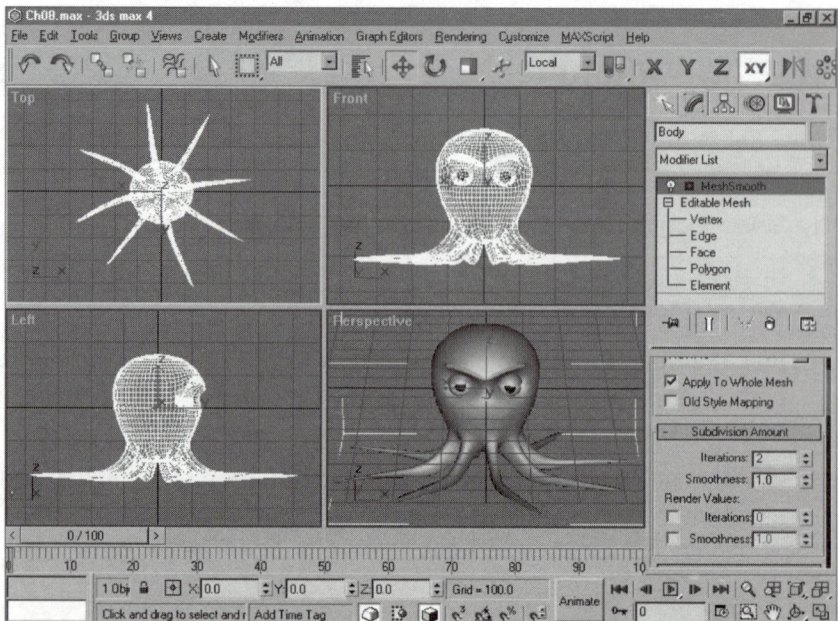

Figure 8-18. A nose is created using an FFD box modifier. Notice which control points are moved.

Creating and Applying the Octopus Material

Now you will assign different materials to different portions of **Octopus**. The multi/sub-object material type is used for this. Then, the material IDs on the octopus are set so the material is correctly applied.

1. Pick the **Material Editor** button on the **Main** toolbar.
   The **Material Editor** is displayed.

Material Editor

2. Select the first material sample slot, if it is not already selected. Then, pick the button below the material samples that is currently labeled **Standard**.
   This button is used to set the material type. When the button is picked, the **Material/Map Browser** is displayed.

3. In the **Browse From:** area of the **Material/Map Browser**, pick the **New** radio button.
   The available material types are displayed.

4. Double-click on **Multi/Sub-Object** in the list on the right side of the **Material/Map Browser**. The material type is selected and the **Material/Map Browser** is closed.
   The **Replace Material** dialog box is displayed.

5. Pick the **Discard old material?** radio button in the **Replace Material** dialog box. Then, pick the **OK** button.
   The current material definition is discarded, and the "type" button is labeled **Multi/Sub-Object**. Ten default materials are listed in the **Multi/Sub-Object Basic Parameters** rollout at the bottom of the **Material Editor**.

6. Pick in the drop-down list below the material samples. Backspace over the default name 1 - Default. Then, type Octopus Material and press [Enter].
   The material is renamed to Octopus Material. Notice in the title bar of the **Material Editor** that the new name is reflected there as well. The name of the current material sample always appears in the title bar of the **Material Editor**.

7. Pick the **Set Number** button in **Multi/Sub-Object Basic Parameters** rollout.
   The **Set Number of Materials** dialog box is displayed.

8. Type 2 in the **Number of Materials:** spinner and pick the **OK** button.
   The number of submaterials in the material is changed from ten to two.

9. Save the scene.

Defining the Submaterials

1. In the **Multi/Sub-Object Basic Parameters** rollout, pick the button currently labeled **Material #2 (Standard)**.
   You are moved down a level in the material hierarchy tree. The rollouts and settings displayed are only for the default material currently named Material #2, which is of the standard type.

2. Pick in the drop-down list below the material samples. Backspace over the default name Material #2, type the new name Octopus Green, and press [Enter].
   The name of the first submaterial is changed. Notice how the material name in the **Material Editor** title bar is still Octopus Material. This is because the "top level" material in the current hierarchy is Octopus Material.

3. The default shading type for the standard material type is Blinn. This shading will be used for this material. In the **Blinn Basic Parameters** rollout, pick the lock button next to the **Ambient:** and **Diffuse:** color swatches so it is off (not depressed). Then, pick the **Diffuse:** color swatch to open the color selector. Pick a medium-dark green of your choice, such as R140, G180, and B100, and pick the **Close** button.
   The material sample changes to an overall dark green color.

4. Pick on the **Diffuse:** color swatch, drag it, and drop it on top of the **Ambient:** color swatch. In the dialog box that appears, pick the **Copy** button.
   The diffuse color settings are copied to the ambient color.

5. Pick the **Ambient:** color swatch. In the color selector, change the **Value:** setting to produce a near black green. Then, close the color selector.

6. Pick the **Specular:** color swatch. In the color selector, define a light orange color, such as R255, G215, and B155. Then, close the color selector.

7. In the **Specular Highlights** area of the **Blinn Basic Parameters** rollout, type 35 in the **Specular Level:** spinner.
   A light orange highlight now appears on the material sample.

8. Now, pick the **Go to Parent** button below the material sample slots.
   You are returned to the parent material level of the material tree. The material name Octopus Material is displayed in the drop-down list.

9. Notice the material sample displays a "checkerboard" of the default grey color and the Octopus Green material. Now, pick the submaterial button currently labeled Material #3 (Standard).
   You are moved down the material tree to the second submaterial level.

10. Rename the material from Material #3 to Octopus Yellow. Similar to how you defined the green material, define an orange-yellow material. Define a medium orange-yellow color for the diffuse color, such as R245, G220, and B95. Use a darker color for the ambient color, and a lighter color for the specular color.

11. Return to the parent level of the material tree.
    Notice how the material sample now displays a "checkerboard" of the green and yellow materials, Figure 8-19.

12. Pick on the parent material sample, drag it into any viewport, and drop it on the octopus.
    The multi/sub-object material you just created is applied to the octopus.

13. Close the **Material Editor** and save the scene.

Figure 8-19. A multi/sub-object material is defined for the model.

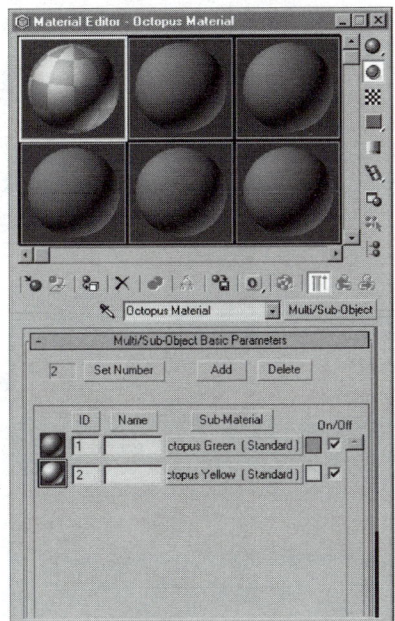

Setting the Material IDs

1. With Body selected, pick **Selection Modifiers** in the **Modifiers** pull-down menu. Then, pick **Mesh Select** in the cascading menu.

   A mesh select modifier is applied to the octopus, and the **Modify** tab is automatically opened.

2. In the modifier stack, expand the sub-object tree and pick **Face**.

   Face sub-object editing mode is entered.

3. In the Front viewport, drag a window around the main body. The upper portion of the tentacles will also be selected.

   The selected faces turn red.

4. Holding down the [Alt] key, pick the upper portions of the tentacles that are currently selected to deselect them. Zoom, pan, and switch viewports as needed. When done, only the main body portion should be selected.

5. With only the main body in the selection set, pick **Surface** in the **Modifiers** pull-down menu. Then, pick **Material** in the cascading menu.

   A material modifier is applied to the selection set only, and the **Modify** tab is automatically displayed.

6. In the **Parameters** rollout for the material modifier, type 1 in the **Material ID:** spinner.

   The selected faces are assigned the submaterial that corresponds to material ID 1, which is Octopus Green, Figure 8-20.

7. At this point, the tentacles should be displayed with the Octopus Yellow material applied. This is because in the modeling process, the entire model was assigned the material ID 2. However, if the tentacles are displayed with the Octopus Green material applied, select the faces on all tentacles using a mesh select modifier. Then, apply a material modifier to the selection and change the material ID to 2.

8. Make the Perspective viewport active. Then, pick the **Quick Render (Production)** button on the **Main** toolbar

   A still image of the octopus is rendered and displayed in the render window.

9. If needed, return to the mesh select face sub-object mode and add or remove faces from the main body selection set. Then, return to the material level in the modifier stack and rerender the scene. Continue until you have the main body selection set as you want it.

10. Save the scene.

Figure 8-20. A material modifier is applied to selected faces.

Assigning Materials to the Eyes, Eyelids, and Pupils

1. Open the **Material Editor**. Select the Octopus Material sample slot. Then, pick the button labeled **Octopus Green** in the **Multi/Sub-Object Basic Parameters** rollout and drag it onto an unused material sample slot. In the dialog box that appears, pick the **Instance** radio button and then the **OK** button.
   An instance (copy) of the Octopus Green submaterial is placed at the parent level of a new material definition.

2. Assign the instanced Octopus Green material to Eyelid, Right and Eyelid, Left.
   The material on the eyelids now matches that on the main body.

3. In the **Material Editor**, select an unused sample slot. Then, pick the **Get Material** button and get the material Reflection_Chromic from material library using the **Material/Map Browser**. Apply this material to Eye, Right and Eye, Left.

4. In the **Material Editor**, select an unused sample slot. Pick in the drop-down list below the material samples and rename the material to Pupil Black.

5. In the **Shader Basic Parameters** rollout, pick the drop-down list and select **Phong**.
   The shading type is changed to Phong.

6. In the **Phong Basic Parameters** rollout, pick the **Diffuse:** color swatch to display the color selector. Leave the diffuse and ambient colors locked, which is the default. In the color selector, change the color to black or near black. Then, close the color selector.
   The material sample is displayed black.

7. Pick the **Specular:** color swatch. In the color selector, change the color to pure white, then close the color selector.

8. In the **Specular Highlights** area of the **Shader Basic Parameters** rollout, type 100 in the **Specular Level:** spinner and 50 in the **Glossiness:** spinner.
   The material sample now has a small, bright white highlight.

9. Assign the Pupil Black material to Pupil, Left and Pupil, Right. Close the **Material Editor** and **Material/Map Browser**, if open.

10. Save the scene.

Adding Lights and a Camera

1. Display the four-viewport configuration and pick the **Zoom Extents All** button. Then, activate the Top viewport. Pick **Create** in the **Command Panel**. Pick the **Lights** button and select **Standard** from the drop-down list. Then, pick the **Omni** button in the **Object Type** rollout.
   The rollouts for an omni light are displayed.

Create

Lights

2. Pick a point at the bottom-left corner of the viewport to place an omni light. Pick a point at the bottom-right corner of the viewport to place another omni light, Figure 8-21.

Figure 8-21. Lights are added to the scene.

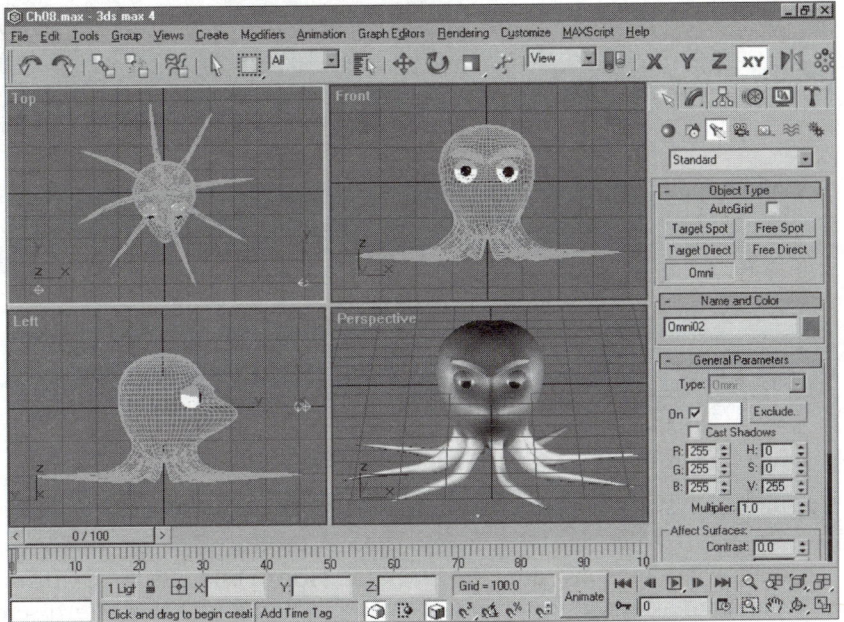

3. Activate the Left viewport. Pick the **Select and Move** and **Restrict to XY Plane** buttons on the **Main** toolbar. Move the second omni light up so it is in the upper-right corner of the viewport. Move the first omni light down so it is on the same level as the tentacles. Pick the **Zoom Extents All** button.

4. Activate the Top viewport. Then, pick **Create** in the **Command Panel**. Pick the **Cameras** button and select **Standard** from the drop-down list. Then, pick the **Target** button in the **Object Type** rollout.
   The rollouts for a target camera are displayed.

Create

Cameras

5. Select a point at the lower-right corner of the viewport to place the camera. Drag the cursor to the center of the octopus and release to place the target.

6. Make the Perspective viewport active. Then, press the [C] key to make the viewport the Camera01 viewport. Right-click on the viewport label and pick **Show Grid** in the shortcut menu to turn the grid display off.
   The grid is no longer visible in the camera viewport.

7. Pick the **Select and Move** and **Restrict to XY Plane** buttons. Move the camera in the Front, Left, and Top viewports until a desired view is displayed in the Camera01 viewport, Figure 8-22.
   *You can also adjust the Camera01 viewport by using the **Truck Camera**, **Field-of-View**, and **Orbit Camera** buttons with the camera viewport active.*

8. Save the scene.

Figure 8-22. A camera is added to the scene, and adjusted to get a desired view.

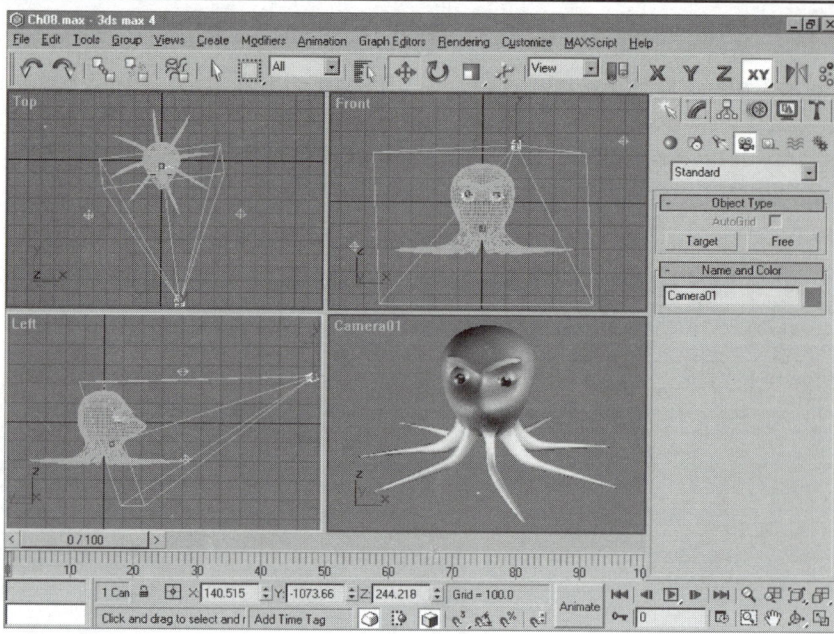

Setting a Background

1. Open the **Material Editor**. Select an unused material sample slot.

2. Pick the small square button next to the **Diffuse:** color swatch to display the **Material/Map Browser** dialog box. In the **Browse From:** area of the dialog box, pick the **Mtl Library** radio button. In the **Show** area, uncheck the **Root Only** check box if it is checked.
   The map assigned to the small square button is used as a diffuse color map for the material, and also appears in the **Maps** rollout for the material. In this application, the material is not used, but an instance of the diffuse color map is used as the environment background.

3. Scroll down to the middle of the list and locate the entry **Reflection: Map #19 (Chromblu.jpg)**. Double-click on the entry to load it as a diffuse color map. Then, close the **Material/Map Browser**. You are moved to the diffuse color map level of the material tree, and the selected image is displayed in the material sample slot.

4. Pick in the drop-down list below the material samples and rename the map Background Image Map. In the **Coordinates** rollout, pick the **Environ** radio button and then select **Screen** from the **Mapping:** drop-down list. Also, type 1 in the **Blur offset:** spinner.
   By first loading the background image into the **Material Editor**, you can adjust the image.

5. Return to the parent material level in the material tree. Name the material Background Material Map using the drop-down list below the material samples. Close the **Material Editor**.

6. Pick **Environment...** from the **Rendering** pull-down menu.
   The **Environment** dialog box is displayed.

7. Pick the **Environment Map:** button that is currently labeled **None**.
   The **Material/Map Browser** is displayed.

8. Pick the **Mtl Editor** radio button in the **Browse From:** area. Then, double-click on **Diffuse Color: Background Image Map** in the list box. In the dialog box that appears, pick the **Instance** radio button and then the **OK** button.
   Background Image Map replaces the **None** label in the **Environment** dialog box

9. Close the **Environment** dialog box.

Render Scene

10. Pick the **Render Scene** button on the **Main** toolbar. Make sure **Camera01** is selected in the drop-down list at the bottom of the dialog box. Then, pick the **Render** button in the **Render Scene** dialog box that is displayed.

    The rendered view is displayed in the render window, Figure 8-23.

11. Close the render window and the **Render Scene** dialog box. Save the scene.

Figure 8-23. The final rendered scene.

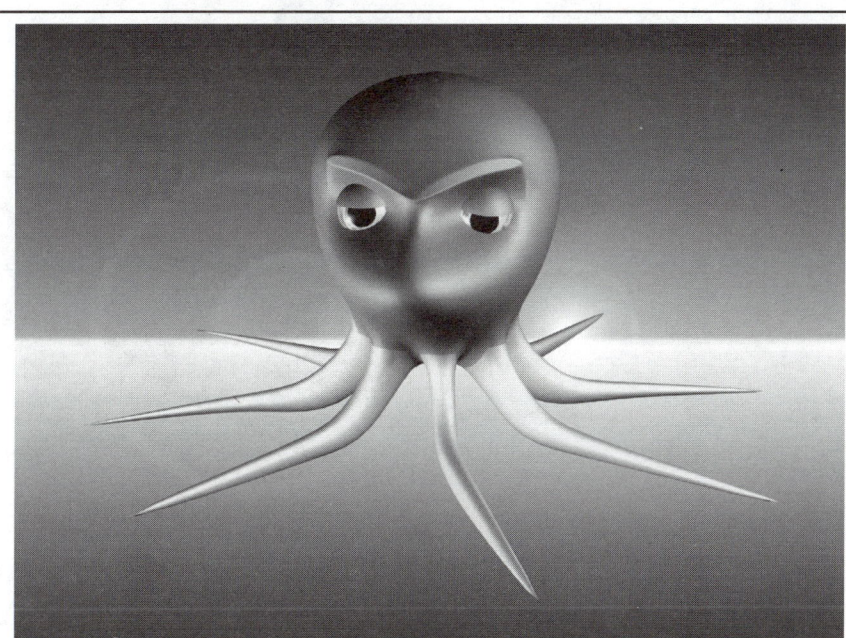

Self-Evaluation Test

Answer the following questions. Then compare your answers with the correct answers given at the end of this chapter.

1. You can convert an object into an editable mesh by selecting **Convert to Editable Mesh** in the cascading menu of the _____ menu.

2. To enter vertex sub-object mode, pick the **Vertex** button in the _____ rollout.

3. You can extrude a polygon of an editable mesh using the **Extrude** button in the _____ rollout.

4. You can select and move, rotate, or scale a vertex, face, edge, or polygon of an editable mesh while in _____ mode.

5. When selecting vertices, faces, edges, or polygons in a mesh, the _____ check box should be checked so only the "front" sub-objects are selected.

6. You can lock a selection set by pressing the _____.

7. When you apply the **MeshSmooth** modifier to an object, the amount of mesh smoothing depends on the value you enter in the _____ spinner.

8. When you apply the _____ modifier to an object, a lattice of control points is attached to the object that, when deformed, deforms the mesh.

9. The _____ modifier is used to change the material ID of an object or sub-object selection.

Exercises

In this exercise, you will create four colored pencils on a box. These are created by drawing standard primitives and applying modifiers to them. Refer to the illustration and use your own dimensions.

1. Create one pencil by drawing a cylinder. Make the height of the cylinder about 10 times the radius. Also, increase the cap segments to two.

2. Convert the cylinder into an editable mesh and then extrude the polygons on top of the cylinder about the same value as the radius. Scale the selection down to about 25%. Then, select the inner circle of polygons on the top of the cylinder. Extrude those about half of the previous amount, then scale the selection down to 0%.

4. Create clones of the pencil and place them on a thin box, similar to those shown.

5. Create a multi/sub-object material with three submaterials for each of the pencils. All three materials should have a black and a light brown color. The third submaterial should be red, green, blue, and purple. Apply the different sub-materials to the different areas of the mesh.

6. Add lights and a camera.

7. Render the scene.

8. Save the scene as Ex08.max in the folder of your choice.

Answers

The following are the correct answers to the questions in the Self-Evaluation Test.

1. quad; 2. **Selection**; 3. **Edit Geometry**; 4. sub-object; 5. **Ignore Backfacing**; 6. [Spacebar]; 7. **Iterations:**; 8. **FFD Box**; 9. **Material**.

Chapter 9

Material Editor: Creating Materials

Learning Objectives

After completing this chapter, you will be able to:

○ Create a new material library.
○ Adjust ambient and diffuse properties.
○ Create a shiny material.
○ Name a new material.
○ Save a material library.
○ Assign materials to objects.
○ Render the scene.

Tutorial Description

In this tutorial, you will create a sign. Then, you will create the materials needed to finish the sign. Six materials will be created from scratch using the **Material Editor**.

Creating the Sign

You will first create a box to be the back of the sign. Then, you will create the logo and text, and place them on the sign.

Create

Geometry

1. Reset the 3ds max. Then, pick **Create** in the **Command Panel**. Pick the **Geometry** button and select **Standard Primitives** from the drop-down list. Then, pick the **Box** button in the **Object Type** rollout. The rollouts for a box are displayed.

2. Activate the Top viewport. Expand the **Keyboard Entry** rollout, then type 155 in the **Length:** spinner, 290 in the **Width:** spinner, and 10 in the **Height:** spinner. Pick the **Create** button. In the **Name and Color** rollout, name the box Sign Back. A box is created in the center of the Top viewport.

Zoom Extents All

3. Pick the **Zoom Extents All** button to zoom to the extents of the object in all viewports.

4. Save the scene as Ch09.max in the folder of your choice.

Drawing the Logo

1. Activate the Top viewport. Then, pick **Create** in the **Command Panel**. Pick the **Geometry** button and select **Standard Primitives** from the drop-down list. Then, pick the **Torus** button in the **Object Type** rollout.
   The rollouts for a torus are displayed.

2. Expand the **Keyboard Entry** rollout, and type 40 in the **Major Radius:** spinner and 5.5 in the **Minor Radius:** spinner. Then, pick the **Create** button. In the **Name and Color** rollout, name the torus Bow01.
   A torus is created at the center of the box.

Select and Rotate

3. In the **Parameters** rollout, pick the **Sides** radio button in the **Smooth:** area. Also, check the **Slice On** check box and type 160 in the **Slice To:** spinner.
   The torus appears segmented around its minor diameter, and is sliced at the angles specified in the "slice" spinners.

Restrict to Z

4. Pick the **Select and Rotate** and **Restrict to Z** buttons on the **Main** toolbar. Rotate the torus 100° about the Z axis, as indicated in the coordinate display, Figure 9-1.

Select and Move

5. Pick the **Select and Move** and **Restrict to Y** buttons on the **Main** toolbar. Move the torus up in the Front viewport so it is on top of the box.

Restrict to Y

6. Pick the **Select and Uniform Scale** and **Restrict to XY Plane** buttons on the **Main** toolbar. Hold down the [Shift] key and scale the torus up in the Top viewport to 137%, as indicated in the coordinate display.
   The **Clone Options** dialog box is displayed.

Select and Uniform Scale

7. In the **Clone Options** dialog box, pick the **Copy** button and name the copy Bow02. Then, pick the **OK** button.

Restrict to XY Plane

8. Select Bow01 in the Top viewport. Scale a copy down to 75%, and name the copy Bow03.

Figure 9-1. The sign back and one of the rainbow "bows" are created.

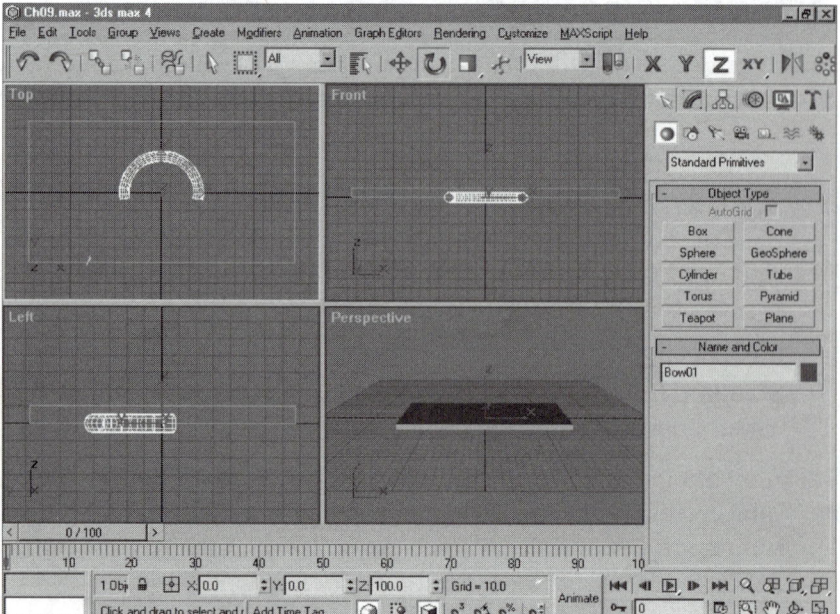

Figure 9-2. All rainbow "bows" are created.

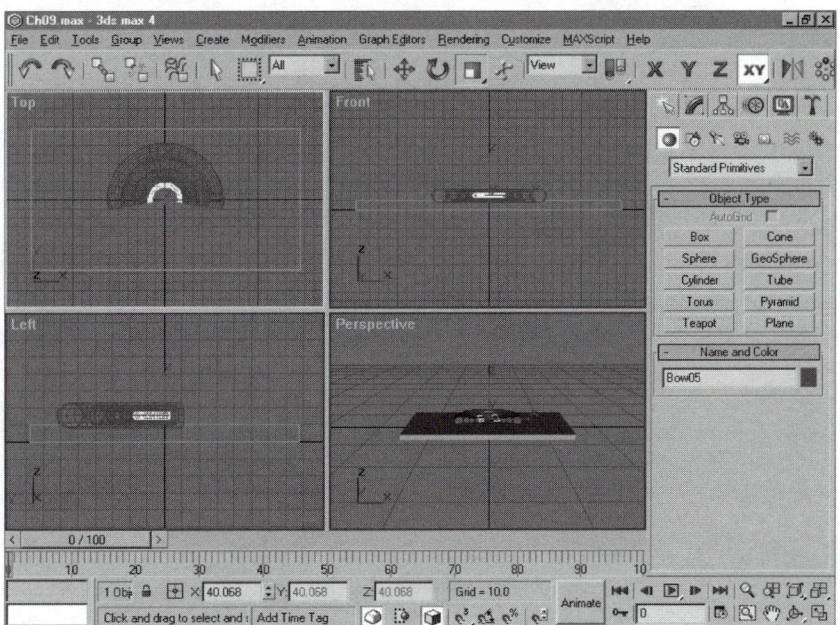

9. With Bow03 selected, scale a copy down to 72%, and name the copy Bow04.

10. With Bow04 selected, scale a copy down to 74%, and name the copy Bow05.
    A set of concentric bows is created, forming a rainbow, Figure 9-2.

11. Activate the Front viewport and maximize it.

12. Pick the **Select and Move** and **Restrict to Y** buttons on the **Main** toolbar. Move each of the bow objects up or down in the Front viewport so all sit on top of the box.

13. Save the scene.

Drawing the Name

1. Display the four-viewport configuration and activate the Top viewport. Pick **Create** in the **Command Panel**. Pick the **Shapes** button and select **Splines** from the drop-down list. Then, pick the **Text** button in the **Object Type** rollout.
   The rollouts for a text spline are displayed.

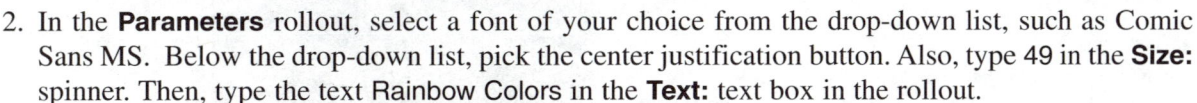
Create

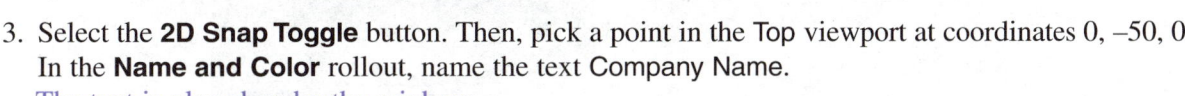
Shapes

2. In the **Parameters** rollout, select a font of your choice from the drop-down list, such as Comic Sans MS. Below the drop-down list, pick the center justification button. Also, type 49 in the **Size:** spinner. Then, type the text Rainbow Colors in the **Text:** text box in the rollout.

3. Select the **2D Snap Toggle** button. Then, pick a point in the Top viewport at coordinates 0, –50, 0. In the **Name and Color** rollout, name the text Company Name.
   The text is placed under the rainbow.

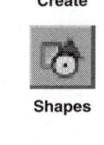
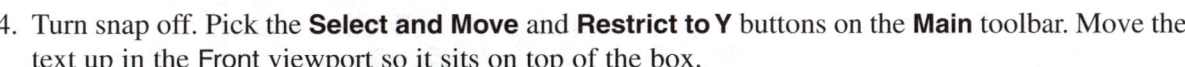
2D Snap Toggle

4. Turn snap off. Pick the **Select and Move** and **Restrict to Y** buttons on the **Main** toolbar. Move the text up in the Front viewport so it sits on top of the box.

5. With the text selected, pick **Mesh Editing** in the **Modifiers** pull-down menu. Then, pick **Extrude** in the cascading menu.
   An extrude modifier is applied to the spline (text), and the **Modify** tab is automatically displayed.

6. In the Parameters rollout, type 10 in the **Amount:** spinner.
   The text is extruded by ten units, Figure 9-3. The sign is now complete and ready for materials.

7. Save the scene.

Figure 9-3. The company name is created.

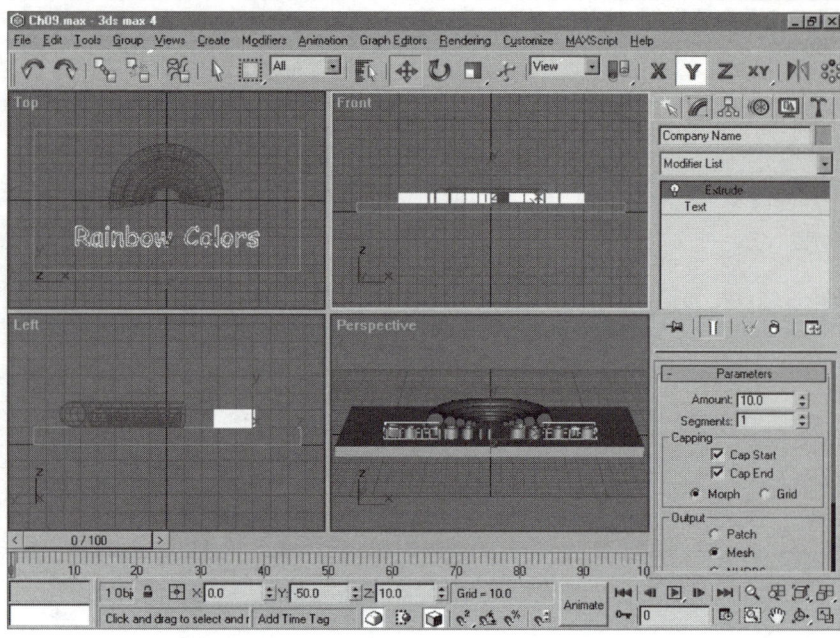

Creating a New Material Library

Now, you will create materials from scratch using the **Material Editor**, and then apply those materials to the objects in the sign. The materials you create in the **Material Editor** will be stored in a material library. To begin, create a new library in which new materials can be placed.

Material Editor

Get Material

1. Pick the **Material Editor** button on the **Main** toolbar, pick **Material Editor...** in the **Rendering** pull-down menu, or press [M] on the keyboard.
   The **Material Editor** is displayed on the screen, Figure 9-4.

2. Pick the **Get Material** button in the **Material Editor**.
   The **Material/Map Browser** is displayed.

Figure 9-4. The **Material Editor** is used to create new materials.

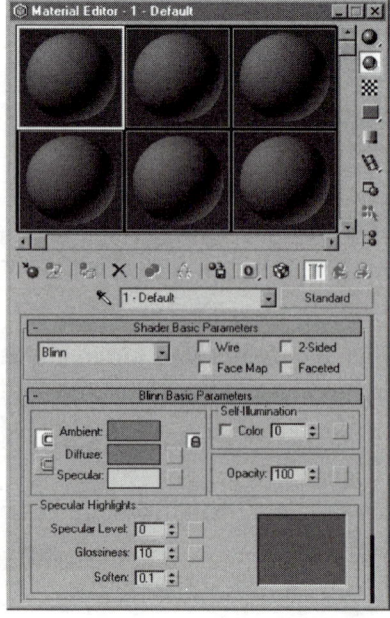

3. In the **Browse From:** area of the dialog box, pick the **Mtl Library** radio button.
   The materials in the current library are displayed in the list box.

4. Pick the **Clear Material Library** button above the list of materials.
   A warning dialog box is displayed asking if you want all the materials in the current library deleted.

Clear Material
Library

5. Pick the **Yes** button.
   The current material library is cleared to allow you to begin with an empty library.

Saving the Material Library

Even though you have not yet created any new materials, it is a good idea to save your "blank" material library. In this way, you do not run the risk of "damaging" the default material library.

1. In the **Material/Map Browser**, select the **Save As...** button in the **File** area of the dialog box.
   The **Save Material Library** dialog box is displayed, Figure 9-5.

2. Type Sign Library in the **File name:** text box of the dialog box. Change to the drive and directory where you want the file stored, and then pick the **Save** button.
   The "blank" material library is saved.

3. Close the **Material/Map Browser**. Leave the **Material Editor** open.

Adjusting Ambient and Diffuse Properties

By adjusting the ambient and diffuse properties of a material, 3ds max knows how to shade an object in the final rendering. The ambient portion of a color describes the part of an object that is not under direct light. The diffuse portion of the color describes the part of the object that is under normal lighting conditions.

1. Open the **Material Editor** and select the first sample slot. Pick in the drop-down list text box below the material samples. Backspace over the default material name 1-Default, type Violet, and press [Enter].
   The material definition in the first sample slot is renamed Violet.

2. In the **Shader Basic Parameters** rollout, select **Blinn** in the drop-down list.
   This sets the shading type for the material. Blinn shading is a basic type of shading, and is the default shading type.

3. In the **Blinn Basic Parameters** rollout, pick the lock button next to the ambient and diffuse color swatches so it is not depressed. Then, pick the ambient color swatch.
   The **Color Selector** dialog box is displayed. The **Red:, Blue:,** and **Green:** color bars control the color. As you increase the value, the color gets lighter. All the three slider bars at a value of 0 produce black, and all the three colors at 255 create white.

Figure 9-5. Saving a material library.

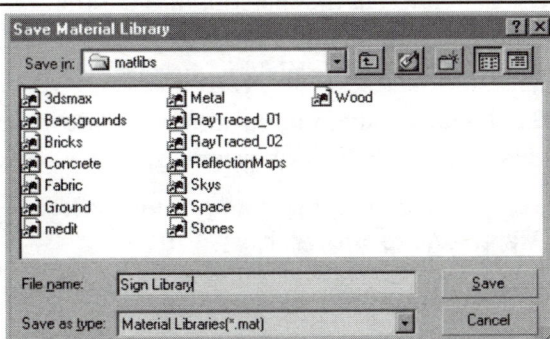

4. Type 15 in the text box next to the **Green:** color bar.
   Most of the green is removed from the color, which becomes a plum color.

5. Type 140 in the text box next to the **Blue:** color bar. The value in the text box next to the **Red:** color bar should be the default 150.
   The color in the ambient color swatch is a dark violet. Close the **Color Selector** dialog box.

6. Pick the diffuse color swatch in the **Blinn Basic Parameters** rollout in the **Material Editor**.

7. In the **Color Selector** dialog box, type 200 in the **Red:** color bar text box, 100 in the **Green:** color bar text box, and 190 in the **Blue:** color bar text box. Then, close the **Color Selector** dialog box.
   The color in the diffuse color swatch is a light violet. Notice the coloring of the material sample.

8. Save the scene.

Making a Material Shiny

Shiny materials have strong specular highlights when rendered. Therefore, materials that are glossy or shiny need to have a high specular value. The specular highlight is controlled by the specular level and glossiness settings. The color of the specular highlight can also be set.

1. With the **Material Editor** open and the Violet material sample current, pick the specular color swatch in the **Blinn Basic Parameters** rollout to display the **Color Selector** dialog box.

2. Set the color to R235, G225, and B235. Then, close the **Color Selector** dialog box.
   The color in the ambient color swatch is a very light violet.

3. In the **Specular Highlights** area of the **Blinn Basic Parameters** rollout, type 60 in the **Specular Level:** spinner.
   This setting determines the intensity of the specular highlight.

4. In the same rollout, type 20 in the **Glossiness:** spinner.
   This setting determines the size of the specular highlight.

5. Save the scene.

Putting a New Material into the Library

Put to Library

Now you have defined the material, it needs to be put into the material library. Once the material is in the library, the library should be saved.

1. Pick the **Put to Library** button in the **Material Editor**.
   The **Put to Library** dialog box is displayed. The current material name is displayed in the **Name:** text box.

2. Pick the **OK** button to put the material into the library with the name Violet.
   You can choose to put the material into the library under a different name by typing a new name in the **Name:** text box before picking the **OK** button.

3. Pick the **Get Material** button in the **Material Editor** to display the **Material/Map Browser**.
   You can see that the Sign Library material library is no longer empty, it contains the Violet material.

4. Pick the **Save...** button in the **File** area of the **Material/Map Browser** to save the library file. Then, close the **Material/Map Browser**.

5. Save the scene.

Creating the Blue Material

1. Select the next unused sample slot in the **Material Editor**. Pick in thc drop-down list text box and name the material Blue.

2. In the **Shader Basic Parameters** rollout, pick **Blinn** from the drop-down list.

3. Pick lock button next to the ambient and diffuse color swatches. Then, pick on the ambient color swatch.
   The **Color Selector** dialog box is displayed.

4. Set the ambient color to R15, G0, and B100. Then, close the **Color Selector** dialog box.
   The color in the ambient color swatch is a dark blue.

5. Now, pick the diffuse color swatch to open the **Color Selector** dialog box. Change the color to R0, G165, and B255. Close the **Color Selector** dialog box.
   The color in the diffuse color swatch is a bright blue.

6. Now, pick the specular color swatch to open the **Color Selector** dialog box. Change the color to R200, G255, and B255. Close the **Color Selector** dialog box.
   The color in the specular color swatch is a very light, almost white blue.

7. In the **Specular Highlights** area of the **Blinn Basic Parameters** rollout, type 60 in the **Specular Level:** spinner.

8. In the **Specular Highlights** area of the **Blinn Basic Parameters** rollout, type 20 in the **Glossiness:** spinner.

9. In the **Material Editor**, pick the **Put to Library** button. In the **Put to Library** dialog box, make sure the name Blue appears in the **Name:** text box. Then, pick the **OK** button to place the material into the library.

10. In the **Material Editor**, pick the **Get Material** button to open the **Material/Map Browser**. Verify that the Blue material is in the Sign Library material library. Then, pick the **Save...** button in the **File** area to save the material library.

11. Close the **Material/Map Browser**. Save the scene.

Creating the Green Material

1. Select the next unused sample slot in the **Material Editor**. Pick in the drop-down list text box and name the material Green.

2. In the **Shader Basic Parameters** rollout, pick **Blinn** from the drop-down list.

3. Pick lock button next to the ambient and diffuse color swatches. Then, pick on the ambient color swatch.
   The **Color Selector** dialog box is displayed.

4. Set the ambient color to R0, G50, and B0. Then, type 60 in the text box next to the **Value:** color bar. Close the **Color Selector** dialog box.
   The value setting controls the brightness of a color. The color in the ambient color swatch is a dark green.

5. Now, pick the diffuse color swatch. Set the diffuse color to R0, G200, and B0. Close the **Color Selector** dialog box.
   The color in the diffuse color swatch is a bright green.

6. Now, pick the specular color swatch. Set the color to R175, G255, and B175. Close the **Color Selector** dialog box.

   The color displayed in the specular color swatch is a very light, almost white green.

7. In the **Specular Highlights** area of the **Blinn Basic Parameters** rollout, type 60 in the **Specular Level:** spinner.

8. In the **Specular Highlights** area of the **Blinn Basic Parameters** rollout, type 20 in the **Glossiness:** spinner.

9. In the **Material Editor**, pick the **Put to Library** button. In the **Put to Library** dialog box, make sure the name Green appears in the **Name:** text box. Then, pick the **OK** button to place the material into the library.

10. In the **Material Editor**, pick the **Get Material** button to open the **Material/Map Browser**. Verify that the Green material is in the Sign Library material library. Then, pick the **Save...** button in the **File** area to save the material library.

11. Close the **Material/Map Browser**. Save the scene.

Creating the Yellow Material

1. Select the next unused sample slot in the **Material Editor**. Pick in the drop-down list text box and name the material Yellow.

2. In the **Shader Basic Parameters** rollout, pick **Blinn** from the drop-down list.

3. Pick lock button next to the ambient and diffuse color swatches. Then, pick on the ambient color swatch.

   *The **Color Selector** dialog box is displayed.*

4. Change the color to R225, G200, and B0. Then, change the value to 200. Close the **Color Selector** dialog box.

   The color displayed in the ambient color swatch is a dark yellow.

5. Now, pick the diffuse color swatch. Change the color to R255, G255, and B55. Close the **Color Selector** dialog box.

   The color displayed in the diffuse color swatch is a bright yellow.

6. Now, pick the specular color swatch. Change the color to R255, G255, and B195. Close the **Color Selector** dialog box.

   The color displayed in the specular color swatch is a light, almost white yellow.

7. In the **Specular Highlights** area of the **Blinn Basic Parameters** rollout, type 60 in the **Specular Level:** spinner.

8. In the **Specular Highlights** area of the **Blinn Basic Parameters** rollout, type 20 in the **Glossiness:** spinner.

9. In the **Material Editor**, pick the **Put to Library** button. In the **Put to Library** dialog box, make sure the name Yellow appears in the **Name:** text box. Then, pick the **OK** button to place the material into the library.

10. In the **Material Editor**, pick the **Get Material** button to open the **Material/Map Browser**. Verify that the Yellow material is in the Sign Library material library. Then, pick the **Save...** button in the **File** area to save the material library.

11. Close the **Material/Map Browser**. Save the scene.

Creating the Red Material

1. Select the next unused sample slot in the **Material Editor**. Pick in the drop-down list text box and name the material Red.

2. In the **Shader Basic Parameters** rollout, pick **Blinn** from the drop-down list.

3. Pick lock button next to the ambient and diffuse color swatches. Then, pick on the ambient color swatch.
   The **Color Selector** dialog box is displayed.

4. Change the color to R125, G0, and B0. Close the **Color Selector** dialog box.
   The color displayed in the ambient color swatch is a dark red.

5. Now, pick the diffuse color swatch. Change the color to R255, G80, and B80. Close the **Color Selector** dialog box.
   The color displayed in the diffuse color swatch is a bright red.

6. Now, pick the specular color swatch. Change color to R255, G235, and B235. Close the **Color Selector** dialog box.
   The color displayed in the specular color swatch is a very light, almost white red.

7. In the **Specular Highlights** area of the **Blinn Basic Parameters** rollout, type 60 in the **Specular Level:** spinner.

8. In the **Specular Highlights** area of the **Blinn Basic Parameters** rollout, type 20 in the **Glossiness:** spinner.

9. In the **Material Editor**, pick the **Put to Library** button. In the **Put to Library** dialog box, make sure the name Red appears in the **Name:** text box. Then, pick the **OK** button to place the material into the library.

10. In the **Material Editor**, pick the **Get Material** button to open the **Material/Map Browser**. Verify that the Red material is in the Sign Library material library. Then, pick the **Save...** button in the **File** area to save the material library.

11. Close the **Material/Map Browser**. Save the scene.

Creating a Second Blue Material

1. Activate the Blue material sample slot.

2. Pick, hold, and drag the material sample to an unused material sample slot.
   A copy of the material definition is placed in the new material sample slot, and has the same name as the original material.

3. Pick in the drop-down list text box below the material samples and rename the copy New Blue.

4. With New Blue active, pick the ambient color swatch. In the **Color Selector** dialog box, change the color to R0, G0, and B75. Close the **Color Selector** dialog box.
   The ambient color is changed to a darker, midnight blue.

5. Now, pick the diffuse color swatch. Change the color to R115, G165, and B200. Close the **Color Selector** dialog box.
   The diffuse color is changed to a "steel" blue. The specular color will remain unchanged.

6. In the **Specular Highlights** area of the **Blinn Basic Parameters** rollout, verify that the value of the **Glossiness:** spinner is 20 and the value of the **Specular Level:** spinner is 60.

7. In the **Material Editor**, pick the **Put to Library** button. In the **Put to Library** dialog box, make sure the name New Blue appears in the **Name:** text box. Then, pick the **OK** button to place the material into the library.

8. In the **Material Editor**, pick the **Get Material** button to open the **Material/Map Browser**. Verify that the New Blue material is in the Sign Library material library. Then, pick the **Save...** button in the **File** area to save the material library.

9. Close the **Material/Map Browser**. Save the scene.

Assigning Materials

All of the materials have been defined. The material library is also saved. Now, the materials need to be assigned to the objects in the scene.

1. Assign the material Violet to Bow02.

2. Assign the material Blue to Bow01.

3. Assign the material Green to Bow03.

4. Assign the material Yellow to Bow04 and Company Name.

5. Assign the material Red to Bow05.

6. Assign the material New Blue to Sign Back.

7. Close the **Material Editor**, if open, and save the scene.

Adding a Spotlight

Create

Lights

1. Activate the Front viewport. Pick the **Zoom** button and zoom out until the objects are displayed about half of their size.

2. Pick the **Pan** button and pan the viewport so the objects are at the bottom of the viewport.

3. Pick **Create** in the **Command Panel**. Pick the **Lights** button and select **Standard** from the drop-down list. Then, pick the **Target Spot** button in the **Object Type** rollout.

4. Pick a point in the upper-right corner to place the light, then drag the target to the center of the sign, Figure 9-6.

5. In the **General Parameters** rollout for the spotlight, check the **Cast Shadows** check box.

6. Open the **Spotlight Parameters** rollout. Then, type 35 in the **Hotspot:** spinner.

7. Save the scene.

Rendering the Scene

Quick Render
(Production)

1. Activate the Perspective viewport.

2. Using the **Arc Rotate**, **Pan**, and **Field-Of-View** buttons, display a view of the sign in the Perspective viewport that is looking straight down on the sign.

3. Pick the **Quick Render (Production)** button on the **Main** toolbar.
   The scene is rendered to the render window, Figure 9-7.

4. Close the render window. Save the scene.
   The material information is saved in the .max file. Make sure the library file is also saved before you reset 3ds max.

Figure 9-6. A spotlight is placed in the scene.

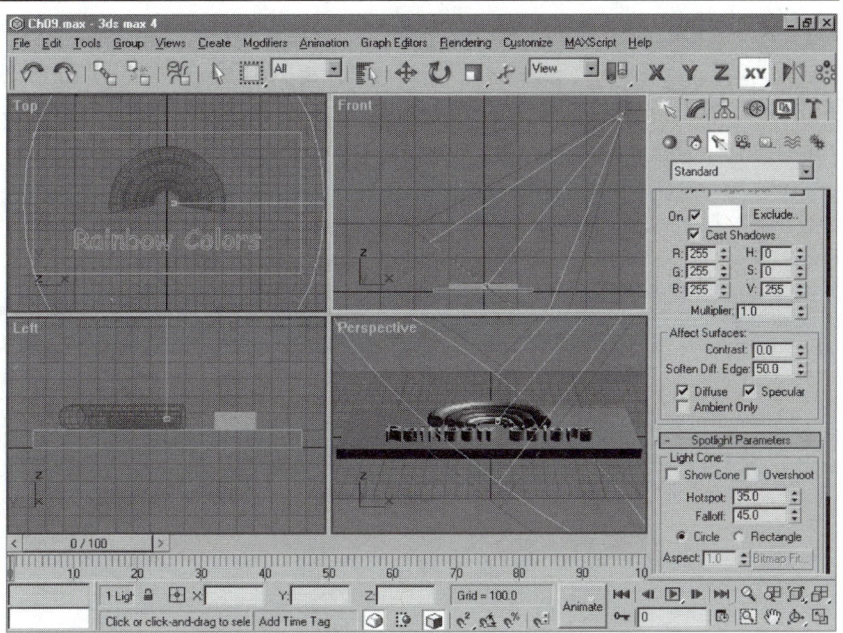

Figure 9-7. The final rendering.

Self-Evaluation Test

Answer the following questions. Then, compare your answers with the correct answers given at the end of this chapter.

1. Materials can be stored in a _____ for future use.

2. The _____ displays all the materials available in the current material library.

3. The _____ color is the portion of an object in shadow.

4. The _____ color describes the portion of an object that is under normal lighting conditions.

5. The _____ controls how strong the highlight is on a material.

6. When a color is set to R0, G0, and B0, the color is _____.

7. _____ is the default shading type in 3ds max.

8. Decreasing the value setting for a material color makes the color _____.

9. How can you copy a material definition from one sample slot to another in the **Material Editor**?

10. Materials defined in the **Material Editor** are saved _____.

Exercises

Create the objects and materials needed to finish the scene shown below. The scene is of three "light buttons" placed on a box. The "lights" are hemispheres. You will need a matte (nonshiny) color for the box and three shiny colors, one for each hemisphere.

1. Create three hemispheres and place them on a box.

2. Create a new material library named Lights.

3. Create the three bright, shiny materials (such as red, green, and blue) to be assigned to the hemispheres.

4. Create a matte (nonshiny) material for the box.

5. Name and put the new materials to the new materials library.

6. Save the new material library and assign the materials to the objects.

7. Render a still image of the Perspective viewport.

Answers

The following are the correct answers to the questions in the Self-Evaluation Test.

1. material library file; 2. **Material/Map Browser**; 3. ambient; 4. diffuse; 5. specular level; 6. black; 7. Blinn; 8. darker; 9. by dragging the sample and dropping it on an unused slot; 10. in the .max file.

Chapter 10

Material Editor: Material Maps I

Learning Objectives

After completing this chapter, you will be able to:

○ Create a new material library.
○ Apply texture maps.
○ View image files.
○ Apply bump maps.

Tutorial Description

In this tutorial, you will create a jewelry box and some coins. These objects will be placed on a carpet. The materials you will create for the objects use maps. Mapped materials are an easy way to quickly add details to an object. A texture map will be used to make the jewelry box look like it is made of marble. A bump map will be used to make the coins look like they have a raised surface.

Creating the Scene

You will first create the carpet, then the jewelry box, and then the coins. These objects are created from standard primitives, and cloned as needed.

1. Reset 3ds max. Make sure you first save the existing scene if you want to keep it.

2. Right-click in the Top viewport to activate it, if it is not already active. Pick **Create** in the **Command Panel**. Pick the **Geometry** button and select **Standard Primitives** from the drop-down list. Then, pick the **Box** button in the **Object Type** rollout.

Create

Geometry

3. Expand the **Keyboard Entry** rollout. Then, type 250 in the **Length:** spinner, 400 in the **Width:** spinner, and 1 in the **Height:** spinner. Pick the **Create** button. In the **Name and Color** rollout, name the box Carpet.
   A box is created at the center of the viewports.

4. Pick the **Zoom Extents All** button to zoom to the extents of the object in the viewport.

Zoom Extents All

5. Pick **Create** in the **Command Panel**. Pick the **Geometry** button and select **Standard Primitives** from the drop-down list. Then, pick the **Box** button in the **Object Type** rollout.

Select and Move

6. In the **Keyboard Entry** rollout, type 80 in the **Length:** spinner, 140 in the **Width:** spinner, and 55 in the **Height:** spinner. Then, pick the **Create** button. In the **Name and Color** rollout, name the box Jewel Box.
Another box is created at the center of the viewports.

Restrict to Y

7. Activate the Front viewport. Pick the **Select and Move** and **Restrict to Y** buttons on the **Main** toolbar. Move Jewel Box up so it sits on top of Carpet.

Select and Rotate

8. Activate the Top viewport. Pick the **Select and Rotate** and **Restrict to Z** buttons on the **Main** toolbar. With Jewel Box selected, rotate the box 30º, as indicated in the coordinate display.

9. Pick **Create** in the **Command Panel**. Pick the **Geometry** button and select **Standard Primitives** from the drop-down list. Then, pick the **Cylinder** button in the **Object Type** rollout.

Restrict to Z

10. With the Top viewport active, expand the **Keyboard Entry** rollout. Type 12 in the **Radius:** spinner and 1.5 in the **Height:** spinner. Pick the **Create** button. In the **Name and Color** rollout, name the cylinder Coin01.
A cylinder is created at the center of the viewport.

Select and Move

11. Pick the **Select and Move** and **Restrict to XY Plane** buttons on the **Main** toolbar. Move Coin01 in the Top viewport to near the lower-right corner of Carpet.

Restrict to XY Plane

12. In the Left viewport, move Coin01 up so it sits on top of Carpet.

13. Activate the Top viewport. Hold down the [Shift] key and move Coin01 up about 30 units. In the **Clone Options** dialog box that is displayed, name the copy Coin01 and pick the **OK** button.
A copy of Coin01 is created.

14. Hold down the [Shift] key and move Coin02 to the left. In the **Clone Options** dialog box that is displayed, name the copy Coin03 and pick the **OK** button.
A copy of Coin02 is created.

15. Hold down the [Shift] key and move Coin03 down. In the **Clone Options** dialog box that is displayed, name the copy Coin04 and pick the **OK** button.
A copy of Coin03 is created, Figure 10-1.

16. Save the scene as Ch10.max in the folder of your choice.

Adding a Lid to the Jewel Box

Select and Move

1. Activate the Front viewport. Pick the **Select and Move** and **Restrict to Y** buttons on the **Main** toolbar. Hold down the [Shift] key and move Jewel Box up so the bottom edge of the clone aligns with the top edge of the original. In the **Clone Options** dialog box that appears, name the copy Lid and pick the **OK** button.
A copy is created on top of the original, which will be the lid of the jewel box.

Restrict to Y

2. Pick the **Select and Non-uniform Scale** button from the **Scale** flyout on the **Main** toolbar. Also, pick the **Restrict to Y** button.
A warning box appears asking you to confirm that you want to continue. Pick the **Yes** button to continue.

Select and
Non-uniform Scale

3. Right-click on the **Select and Non-uniform Scale** button to display the **Scale Transform Type-In** dialog box. In the **Offset: Screen** area on the right side of the dialog box, type 8 in the **Y:** text box and press [Enter]. Close the **Scale Transform Type-In** dialog box.
Lid is scaled down to 8% on the Y axis. The bottom of Lid should still be flush to the top of Jewel Box.

Restrict to Y

Figure 10-1. The objects are created.

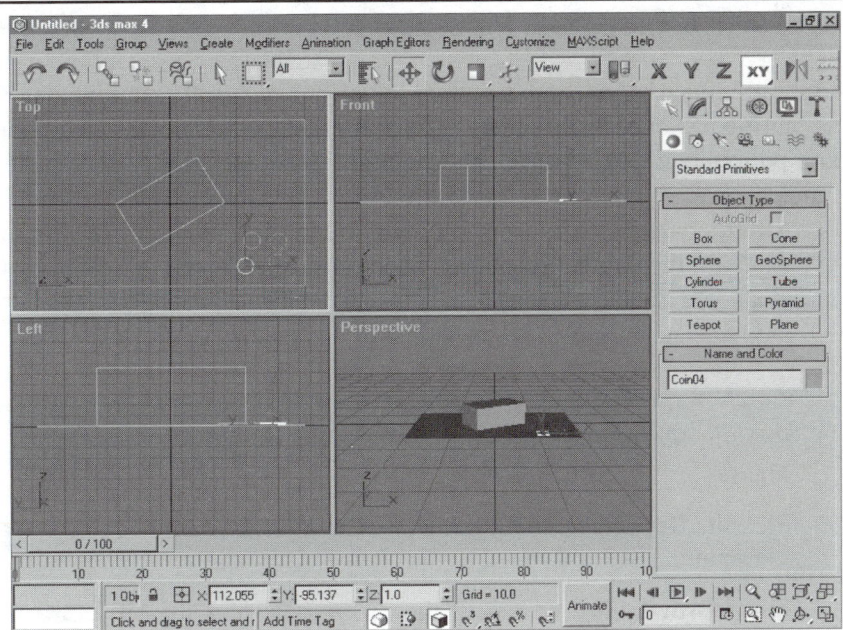

4. Activate the Top viewport. Pick the **Select and Move** and **Restrict to XY Plane** buttons on the **Main** toolbar. Select Coin03 and move it partially over Coin01.

5. Activate the Left viewport. Move Coin03 up so its bottom edge aligns with the top edge of Coin01. Pick the **Select and Rotate** and **Restrict to Z** buttons on the **Main** toolbar. Rotate Coin03 so it touches both Carpet and Coin01. Move Coin03 again as needed so it does not overlap Coin01.

6. Rotate the view in the Perspective viewport to display a better view of the objects. Save the scene. All objects are now created, Figure 10-2.

Figure 10-2. One coin is moved so it rests at an angle on another coin.

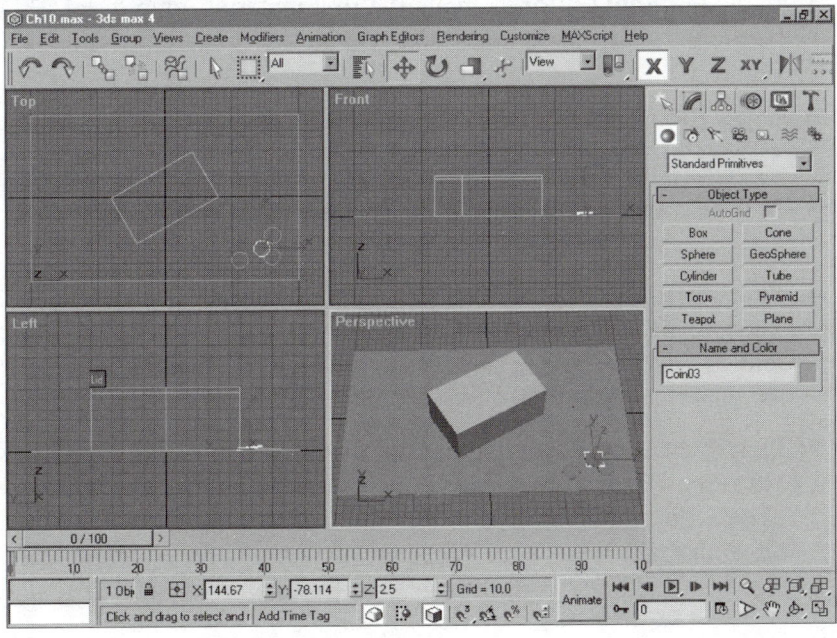

Creating Mapped Materials

Maps are images that can be applied to various material components. You can think of applying a map as putting a sticker on an object. When applied, or "mapped," to a material, the map can control color and pattern, surface texture, opacity, highlights, and many other material components. Maps let you quickly change an ordinary box into a block of wood or piece of marble. Multiple maps can be used in a single material definition to create a complex material. In this tutorial, you will create mapped materials for the carpet, jewel box, and coins. First, create a new library file in which you can save the materials you create.

Creating a New Material Library

1. Pick the **Material Editor** button on the **Main** toolbar.
   The **Material Editor** is displayed.

2. Pick the **Get Material** button below the material samples in the **Material Editor**.
   The **Material/Map Browser** is displayed.

3. In the **Browse From:** area of the dialog box, pick the **Mtl Library** radio button.
   The materials in the current library, 3dsmax.mat, are displayed in the list box.

4. Pick the **Clear Material Library** button in the **Material/Map Browser**.
   A warning box is displayed asking whether or not all the materials in the current library should be deleted. Pick the **Yes** button. The current material library is cleared, allowing you to begin with an empty library.

5. In the **File** area of the **Material/Map Browser**, pick the **Save As...** button. In the **Save Material Library File** dialog box that appears, name the library file Jewels.mat and save it in the folder of your choice.

6. Close the **Material/Map Browser** to return to the **Material Editor**.

Creating the Jewel Box Material

Material Editor

Get Material

Clear Material Library

1. In the **Material Editor**, activate the first material sample slot. Pick in the drop-down list text box below the material samples and rename the material Jewel Box. Then, open the **Maps** rollout, Figure 10-3.

2. In the **Diffuse Color** row, pick the button currently labeled **None** in the **Map** column.
   The **Material/Map Browser** is displayed.

3. In the **Browse From:** area, pick the **New** radio button, if it is not already selected.
   The various types of maps that can be used are displayed.

4. Pick **Mix** in the list, and then pick the **OK** button.
   This sets the map type to a mix of two colors or images, and displays the **Mix Parameters** rollout in the Material Editor at the diffuse map level in the material tree, which is one step "down" from the parent material Jewel Box.

5. Pick in the drop-down list text box below the material samples. Rename the map Jewel Box Mix Map. See Figure 10-4.
   Notice that the default name was not Jewel Box, rather Map #1 (or similar). This is because the name in the drop-down list displays the name of the component at the current level in the material tree. The title bar of the **Material Editor**, however, still displays the parent material name.

Figure 10-3. The **Maps** rollout is displayed for the first material.

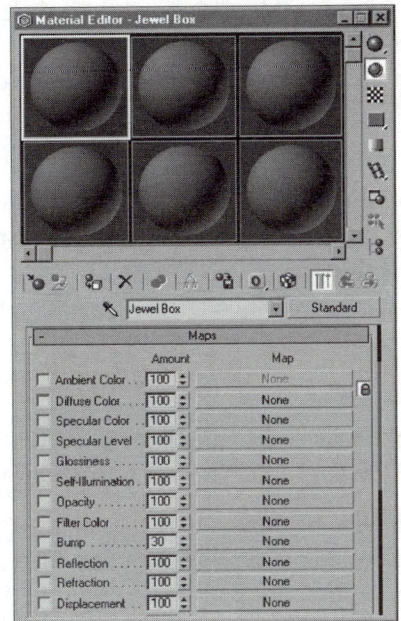

Figure 10-4. The diffuse color level of the material tree for the Jewel Box material.

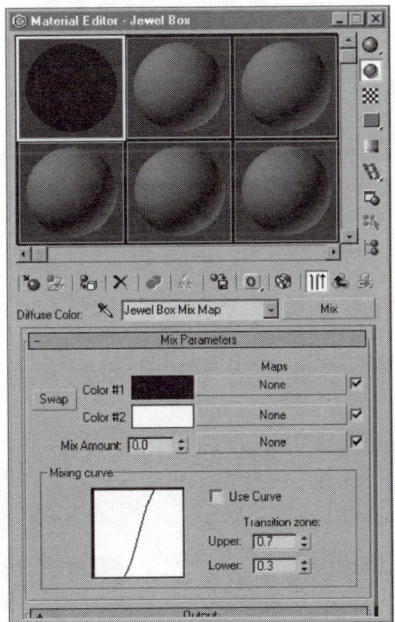

6. Pick the button currently labeled **None** in the **Color #1** row in the **Maps** column. The **Material/Map Browser** is displayed again. In the **Browse From:** area, pick the **New** radio button if it is not already selected.
   The various types of maps that can be used are displayed. This is the same list from which you selected **Mix**.

7. Pick **Bitmap** in the list, and then pick the **OK** button.
   The **Select Bitmap Image File** dialog box is displayed.

8. Navigate to the 3ds max \Maps\Fabric folder. Select the file Pat0007.tga and pick the **Open** button. The **Material/Map Browser** is closed. The **Coordinates**, **Noise**, **Bitmap Parameters**, **Time**, and **Output** rollouts are displayed in the **Material Editor**. These rollouts are at the "color 1" level of the Jewel Box Mix Map diffuse color map of the Jewel Box material. In other words, the current material level is two levels below the parent material.

Box Sample

9. Pick in the drop-down list below the material samples and rename the map Jewel Box Mix Map Color One. Next, pick the **Box** button from the **Sample Type** flyout, located in the top-right corner of the **Material Editor**.
   The material sample is changed from a sphere to a cube.

10. In the drop-down list below the sample slots, select Jewel Box Mix Map.
    This navigates to that level of the material tree, and the **Mix Parameters** rollout is displayed.

11. In the **Color #2** row, pick the button currently labeled **None** in the **Maps** column. In the **Material/Map Browser**, pick the **New** radio button in the **Browse From:** area, if it is not already on.

12. Pick **Bitmap** from the list box, and then pick the **OK** button. In the **Select Bitmap Image File** dialog box, navigate to the 3ds max \Maps\Stones folder. Open the file Travertn.tga from the folder.
    The rollouts for the bitmap are displayed in the **Material Editor**.

13. Pick in the drop-down list below the material samples and rename the map Jewel Box Mix Map Color Two. Then, select Jewel Box Mix Map from the drop-down list to navigate to that level.
    Currently, Color 1 completely covers Color 2. You must set the percentage of Color 2 that will show through Color 1 using the **Mix Amount:** spinner.

14. Type 70 in the **Mix Amount:** spinner.
    The material sample shows 30% of Color 1 and 70% of Color 2.

15. Pick Jewel Box from the drop-down list below the material samples. This navigates you to the top level (parent) of the material tree.

16. Save the scene.

Making the Material Shiny

1. At the parent material level (Jewel Box), expand the **Blinn Basic Parameters** rollout. Then, pick the specular color swatch.

2. In the **Color Selector** dialog box that is displayed, change the color to R255, G255, and B255. Then, close the **Color Selector** dialog box.
   The color displayed in the specular color swatch is pure white.

3. In the **Specular Highlights** area of the **Blinn Parameters** rollout, type 90 in the **Specular Level:** spinner. Also, type 65 in the **Glossiness:** spinner.

4. Save the scene.

Put to Library

Putting the Material into the Library

1. Pick the **Put to Library** button in the **Material Editor**.
   The **Put to Library** dialog box is displayed.

2. In the **Name:** text box, make sure the name Jewel Box is displayed. Then, pick the **OK** button.

3. In the **Material Editor**, pick the **Get Material** button to open the **Material/Map Browser**. Verify that the Jewel Box material is in the Jewels material library. Then, pick the **Save...** button in the **File** area to save the material library.

4. Close the **Material/Map Browser**.

5. Save the scene.

Assigning Bump Maps

A bump map is used to simulate a rough surface on an object. The geometry of the object is not changed, however. Lighter pixels in the map make the surface appear to be raised, while darker pixels in the map make the surface appear to be lowered. You will now create a mapped material, with diffuse color and bump maps, for the carpet to make it look more realistic.

1. Activate the next unused material sample slot in the **Material Editor**. Pick in the drop-down list text box below the material samples and name the material Carpet.

2. Expand the **Maps** rollout. Then, pick the button in the **Diffuse Color** row currently labeled **None** and in the **Map** column. In the **Browse From:** area in the **Material/Map Browser**, pick the **New** radio button if it is not already on.
   The various types of maps that can be used are displayed.

3. Pick **Bitmap** from the list, and then pick the **OK** button. In the **Select Bitmap Image File** dialog box that is displayed, navigate to the 3ds max \Maps\Fabric folder. Then, open the file Tutframe.tga from the folder.
   The diffuse color map level is displayed in the **Material Editor**.

4. Using the drop-down list below the material samples, rename the map to Carpet Border Map. Then, pick the **Box** button in the **Sample Type** flyout.
   The material sample is displayed as a cube, with a patterned border at the edges. To make the material appear three-dimensional and more realistic, you will now apply a bump map.

5. Select Carpet from the drop-down list below the sample slots to return to the parent material level of the material tree.

6. In the **Maps** rollout, pick the button in the **Bump** row currently labeled **None** in the **Map** column. The **Material/Map Browser** is displayed. In the **Browse From:** area, pick the **New** radio button if it is not already on.

7. Select **Bitmap** from the list, and then pick the **OK** button. In the **Select Bitmap Image File** dialog box that appears, navigate to the 3ds max \Maps\Fabric folder. Open the file Carpettan.jpg from the folder.
   The bump map level of the material tree is displayed in the **Material Editor**.

8. Name the map Carpet Bumps. Then, pick Carpet from the drop-down list below the material samples to navigate to the parent material level in the material tree.

9. In the **Maps** rollout, type 30 in the **Amount:** spinner in the **Bump** row.
   This sets the percentage of the bump map that is applied to the material. In other words, this spinner sets how bumpy the surface appears.

10. Now, you need to set the color of the carpet inside the border. In the **Blinn Basic Parameters** rollout, pick the diffuse color swatch. In the **Color Selector** dialog box, set the color to R255, G150, and B0. Then, close the **Color Selector** dialog box.
    The area of the carpet inside the border is now an orange color.

11. Pick the **Put to Library** button.

12. In the **Put to Library** dialog box that is displayed, make sure the name Carpet is displayed in the **Name:** text box. Then, pick the **OK** button.

13. In the **Material Editor**, pick the **Get Material** button to open the **Material/Map Browser**. Verify that the Carpet material is in the Jewels material library. Then, pick the **Save...** button in the **File** area to save the material library.

14. Close the **Material/Map Browser**.

15. Save the scene.

Creating a Material for the Coins

1. Activate the next unused sample slot in the **Material Editor**. Name the material Coin Metal. In the **Shader Basic Parameters** rollout, select **Metal** from the drop-down list.
   The shading type is now set to metal.

2. In the **Maps** rollout, pick the button in the **Diffuse Color** row currently labeled **None** in the **Map** column. In the **Material/Map Browser**, pick the **New** radio button in the **Browse From:** area if it is not already on.

3. Pick **Bitmap** from the list, and pick the **OK** button. In the **Select Bitmap Image File** dialog box that is displayed, navigate to the 3ds max \Maps\Space folder. Open the file Aluminm3.gif from the folder.
   The diffuse color level of the material tree is displayed in the **Material Editor**.

4. Rename the map to Coin Diffuse Color Map. Then, pick Coin Metal from the drop-down list below the material samples to navigate to that level in the material tree.

5. In the **Maps** rollout, type 75 in the **Diffuse Color** spinner.
   This specifies that 75% of the materials diffuse color will come from the map, and 25% will come from the colors defined in the color swatches.

6. In the **Metal Basic Parameters** rollout, pick the diffuse color swatch. In the **Color Selector** dialog box, change the color to R255, G255, and B0. Close the **Color Selector** dialog box.

7. In the **Specular Highlights** area of the **Metal Basic Parameters** rollout, type 150 in the **Specular Level:** spinner. Also, type 55 in the **Glossiness:** spinner.

8. In the **Maps** rollout, pick the button in the **Bump** row currently labeled **None** in the **Map** column. In the **Material/Map Browser**, pick the **New** radio button in the **Browse From:** area if it is not already on.

9. Pick **Bitmap** in the list, and then pick the **OK** button. In the **Select Bitmap Image File** dialog box that is displayed, navigate to the 3ds max \Maps\Metal folder. Open the file GrateStreet.tga from the folder.
   The bump map level is displayed in the material tree.

10. Rename the map to Coin Imprint Map. Then, select Coin Metal from the drop-down list below the material samples to navigate to the parent material level in the material tree.

11. In the **Maps** rollout, type 90 in the **Bump** spinner.

12. Select the **Put to Library** button to display the **Put to Library** dialog box. Make sure the name Coin Metal is displayed in the **Name:** text box. Then, pick the **OK** button.

13. In the **Material Editor**, pick the **Get Material** button to open the **Material/Map Browser**. Verify that the Coin Metal material is in the Jewels material library. Then, pick the **Save...** button in the **File** area to save the material library.

14. Close the **Material/Map Browser**.

15. Save the scene.

Applying Materials and Adding Lights

1. Select Carpet in any viewport. Pick **UV Coordinates** in the **Modifiers** pull-down menu. Then, pick **UVW Map** in the cascading menu.
   A UVW map modifier is applied to Carpet, and the **Modify** tab is automatically displayed.

2. In the **Mapping** area of the **Parameters** rollout, pick the **Planar** radio button, and then pick the **Fit** button in **Alignment** area.

3. Apply the material Carpet to the Carpet object.

4. Now, apply a UVW map modifier to Jewel Box. Set the mapping to **Box**. Then, apply the material Jewel Box to the Jewel Box object.

5. Apply a UVW map modifier to **Lid**. Set the mapping to **Planar**. Then, apply the material **Jewel Box** to the Lid object.

6. One at a time, apply a UVW map modifier to the coins. Set the mapping to **Planar**. Then, apply the material Coin Metal to the coin objects.

7. Close the **Material Editor**.

8. Add two spotlights to the scene. In the Top viewport, place one spotlight in the lower-right corner with its target in the middle of the scene. Place the other in the upper-right corner with its target in the middle of the scene. Set both lights to cast shadows. Move the lights in the Left viewport so they point down onto the carpet.

9. Save the scene.

Rendering the Scene

1. Activate the Perspective viewport. Adjust the viewport until a desired view is displayed.

2. Pick the **Quick Render (Production)** button on the **Main** toolbar. The scene is rendered and displayed in the render window, Figure 10-5.

   The rendered image shows how texture maps save time and effort by adding a great deal of detail to the scene by simply defining and applying a material.

Quick Render
(Production)

3. Close the render window and the **Render Scene** dialog box.

   If you want to see how the bump maps affect the materials, change the value in the **Bump** spinner in the **Maps** rollout to 0 for each material. Then, rerender the scene.

4. Save the scene.

Figure 10-5. The final rendering of the scene.

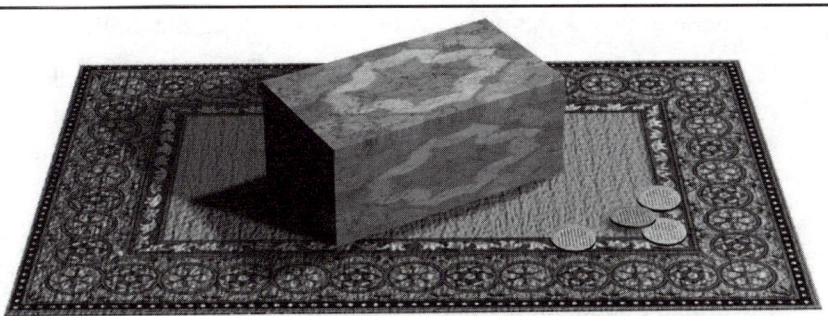

Self-Evaluation Test

Answer the following questions. Then, compare your answers with the correct answers given at the end of this chapter.

1. You can use _____ materials to quickly add details to objects in a scene.

2. Maps are _____ that can be applied to various material components.

3. You can use the _____ type of map to assign a combination of more than one map to a material.

4. The _____ spinner sets the degree to which the two selected maps overlay each other.

5. _____ mapping simulates a rough surface.

6. _____ pixels in a map appear raised and _____ pixels appear to be lower.

7. The spinner in the **Bump** row of the **Maps** rollout sets _____.

8. The _____ shading type is used to create metallic materials.

Exercises

Create the objects, lights, and materials needed to finish the scene shown below. You will need to create a wooden material for the picture frame, a bump-mapped material for the walls, and a diffuse-mapped material for the picture.

1. Create two boxes for walls, a box for the floor, and a box for the ceiling.

2. Create a shape of your own design to be the cross section of the picture frame. Then, draw a rectangle to use as the path. Loft the shape along the path.

3. Draw a box, which will be the picture, that fits inside the frame.

4. Add a target spotlight, an omni light, and a camera to the scene. For the spotlight, in the **Spotlight Parameters** rollout, change the shape of the spotlight to rectangular. Adjust the hotspot and falloff as needed so the light "fits" the frame.

5. Create a new material library named Exhibition.

6. Create a mapped material for the walls named Wall Material. Assign a diffuse color map of Travertn.tga and a bump map Sponge.jpg, which are located in \Maps\Stone and \Maps\Organics respectively. Set the amount of the bump to 90.

7. Create a mapped material named Artwork with a **Mix** type diffuse color map for the picture. Use bitmaps of your own choice for the Color 1 and Color 2 maps. Apply this material to the picture.

8. Create a mapped material named Frame Wood. Apply a diffuse color map and a bump map of a wood bitmap image. Several can be found in the \Maps\Wood folder. Apply this material to the picture frame.

9. Put the new materials into the new material library and save the library.

10. Apply UVW map modifiers as needed.

11. Render a still image of the scene. Save the scene as Ex10.max in the folder of your choice.

Answers

The following are the correct answers to the questions in the Self-Evaluation Test.

1. mapped; 2. images; 3. **Mix**; 4. **Mix Amount:**; 5. Bump; 6. Lighter, darker; 7. amount of bumpiness (surface roughness); 8. metal.

Chapter 11

Material Editor: Material Maps II

Learning Objectives

After completing this chapter, you will be able to:

○ Create transparent materials.

○ Apply opacity maps.

○ Create procedural maps.

Tutorial Description

In this tutorial, you will create a drinking glass containing a liquid, a cherry, and a stirrer. The glass is placed on a wooden block. You will also place a few fern leaves on the wooden block. An opacity map will be used to make a standard box primitive appear like fern leaves. A transparent material will be created for the glass. A procedural map will be used for the piece of wood.

Creating the Scene

You will first create the drinking glass. Then, you will create the piece of wood. Finally, you will create the boxes that will be used for the fern leaves.

1. Reset 3ds max.

2. Maximize the Front viewport.

3. Right-click on the **Snap** flyout to display the **Grid and Snap Settings** dialog box. Then, pick the **Home Grid** tab in the dialog box.

4. Type 5 in the **Grid Spacing** spinner. Also, type 5 in the **Major Lines every Nth** spinner. Then, close the dialog box.

5. Zoom as needed so that each grid square represents 5 units.
   You can see how many units each grid square is by placing the cursor on one grid point, and moving the cursor to the next grid point while watching the coordinate display.

Create

Shapes

2D Snap Toggle

Modify

6. Pick **Create** in the **Command Panel**. Pick the **Shapes** button and select **Splines** from the drop-down list. Then, pick the **Line** button in the **Object Type** rollout.
   The rollouts for a line spline are displayed.

7. Pick the **2D Snap Toggle** button from the **Snap** flyout. Then, draw the shape shown in Figure 11-1 using the coordinates given in the figure. Pick the last point on top of the first point to close the spline.
   A warning box is displayed asking if you want to close the spline. Pick the **Yes** button to close the spline.

8. In the **Name and Color** rollout, name the line Glass. With Glass selected, pick **Modify** in the **Command Panel**. In the **Selection** rollout, pick the **Vertex** button to enter vertex sub-object mode.
   All the vertices in the spline are displayed.

9. Turn snap off. Select all vertices in the spline by dragging a window around the entire shape. Then, right-click on one vertex to display the quad menu. In the upper-left quadrant of the quad menu, pick **Bezier** to change all vertices to that type. Next, pick each vertex individually and adjust the Bézier handles to obtain the shape shown in Figure 11-2.
   You may find it easiest to change the "stem" vertices back to corner type vertices.

10. Pick the **Vertex** button in the **Selection** rollout again to exit sub-object mode. With Glass selected, pick **Patch/Spline Editing** in the **Modifiers** pull-down menu. Then, pick **Lathe** in the cascading menu.
    A lathe modifier is applied to the spline, and the profile is revolved.

11. In the **Direction** area of the **Parameters** rollout, pick the **Z** button. Also, pick the **Max** button in the **Align** area of the rollout.
    The profile is revolved about the Z axis at the shape's right-hand edge.

Zoom Extents All

12. Display the four-viewport configuration and pick the **Zoom Extents All** button.

13. Save the scene as Ch11.max in the folder of your choice.

Figure 11-1. The shape for the drinking glass. The coordinates given in the table are world coordinates. Draw the shape using the cursor in the Front viewport, or using the **Keyboard Entry** rollout in the Top viewport.

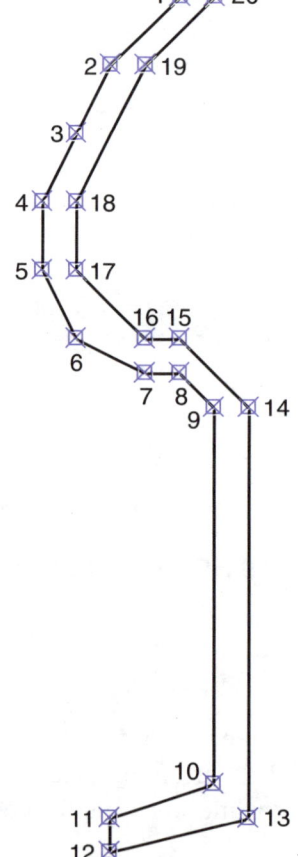

Point	X	Y	Z
1	−15	0	60
2	−25	0	50
3	−30	0	40
4	−35	0	30
5	−35	0	20
6	−30	0	10
7	−20	0	5
8	−15	0	5
9	−10	0	0
10	−10	0	−55
11	−25	0	−60
12	−25	0	−65
13	−5	0	−60
14	−5	0	0
15	−15	0	10
16	−20	0	10
17	−30	0	20
18	−30	0	30
19	−20	0	50
20	−10	0	60

Figure 11-2. The shape is edited at the sub-object level to produce a smooth curve.

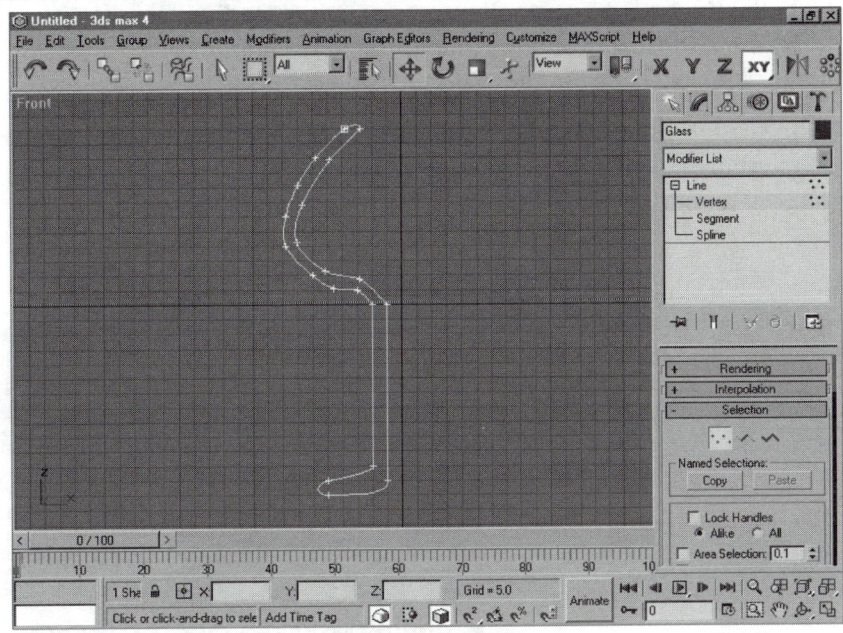

Creating the Wooden Block

1. Activate the Top viewport.

2. Pick **Create** in the **Command Panel**. Pick the **Geometry** button and select **Standard Primitives** from the drop-down list. Then, pick the **Cylinder** button in the **Object Type** rollout.

3. In the **Keyboard Entry** rollout, type 150 in the **Radius:** spinner and –10 in the **Height:** spinner. Then, pick the **Create** button. In the **Name and Color** rollout, name the cylinder Block.
   A cylinder is created in the center of the viewport.

4. Pick the **Zoom Extents All** button.

5. Pick the **Select and Move** and **Restrict to Y** buttons on the **Main** toolbar. Move Glass up in the Front viewport so it sits on top of Block, Figure 11-3.

Select and Move

Restrict to Y

6. Save the scene.

Creating a Stirrer and Cherry

1. Pick **Create** in the **Command Panel**. Pick the **Geometry** button and select **Standard Primitives** from the drop-down list. Then, pick the **Cylinder** button in the **Object Type** rollout.

2. Activate the Top viewport and open the **Keyboard Entry** rollout. Type 1 in the **Radius:** spinner and 75 in the **Height:** spinner. Then, pick the **Create** button. In the **Name and Color** rollout, name the cylinder Stirrer.
   A cylinder is created in the center of the viewport.

3. In the Front viewport, move Stirrer up so its bottom edge touches the inside edge of Glass.

4. Now, pick the **Select and Rotate** and **Restrict to Z** buttons on the **Main** toolbar. Rotate Stirrer about 10° in the Front viewport, as indicated in the coordinate display, or until it touches the rim of the glass.

Select and Rotate

Restrict to Z

5. Activate the Top viewport. Pick **Create** in the **Command Panel**. Pick the **Geometry** button and select **Standard Primitives** from the drop-down list. Then, pick the **Sphere** button in the **Object Type** rollout.

6. In the **Keyboard Entry** rollout, type 5 in the **Radius:** spinner. Then, pick the **Create** button. In the **Name and Color** rollout, name the sphere Cherry.
   A sphere is created at the center of the viewport.

7. In the Front viewport, move Cherry up so it is inside Glass, Figure 11-4. Make sure it does not overlap Stirrer.

8. Save the scene.

Figure 11-3. The glass is placed on top of the cylinder.

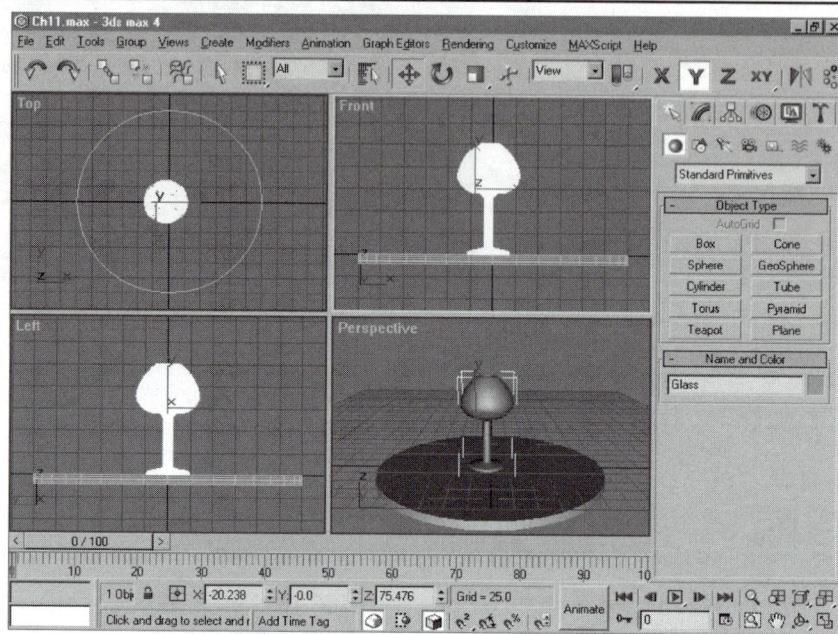

Figure 11-4. A drinking straw and a cherry are added to the scene.

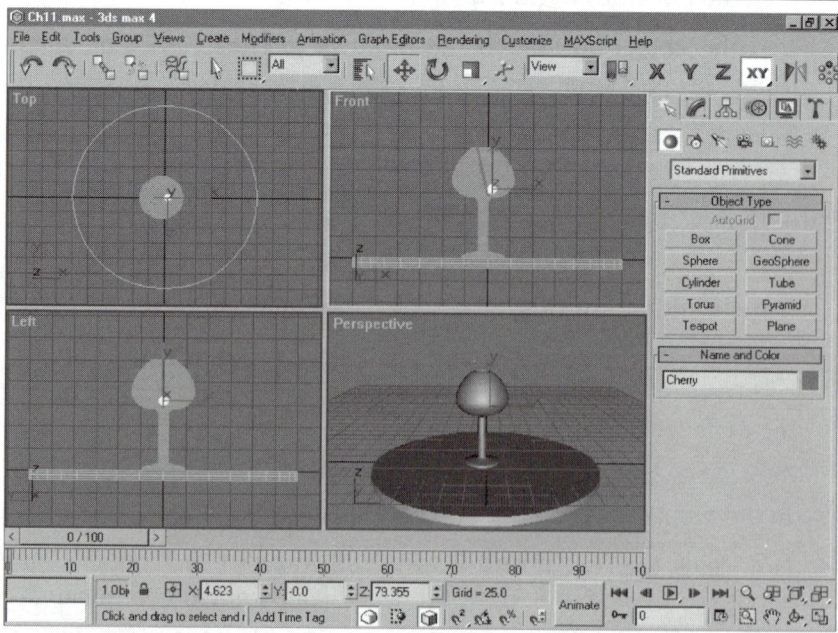

Creating Liquid in the Glass

1. Maximize the Front viewport.

2. Right-click on the **Snap** flyout to display the **Grid and Snap Settings** dialog box. Select the **Home Grid** tab. Change the **Grid Spacing** spinner to 1.0 and close the dialog box.

Region Zoom

3. Pick the **Region Zoom** button and drag a window around the lower-left portion of the glass, not including the stem. Turn snap on.

4. Pick **Create** in the **Command Panel**. Pick the **Shapes** button and select **Splines** from the drop-down list. Then, pick the **Line** button in the **Object Type** rollout. Refer to Figure 11-5 and draw a spline profile for the liquid. The right side of the spline should be straight and on the centerline of the glass. The left side of the spline should match the inside curvature of the glass. Close the spline at the first vertex.
   After the spline is created, you may need to enter vertex sub-object mode and edit the left side of the spline to match the contour of the glass.

5. In the **Name and Color** rollout, name the spline Liquid.

6. With Liquid selected, pick **Patch/Spline Editing** in the **Modifiers** pull-down menu. Then, pick **Lathe** in the cascading menu.
   A lathe modifier is applied to the spline.

7. In the **Direction** area of the **Parameters** rollout, pick the **Y** button. In the **Align** area of the **Parameters** rollout, pick the **Max** button.
   If necessary, pick the **Line** level in the modifier stack, enter vertex sub-object mode, and modify the spline to more closely match the contour of the glass.

8. Display the four-viewport configuration. Pick the **Zoom Extents All** button. Save the scene.

Creating the Fern Leaf Boxes

1. Pick **Create** in the **Command Panel**. Pick the **Geometry** button and select **Standard Primitives** from the drop-down list. Then, pick the **Box** button in the **Object Type** rollout.

Figure 11-5. A profile is drawn, which will be revolved, to create the liquid.

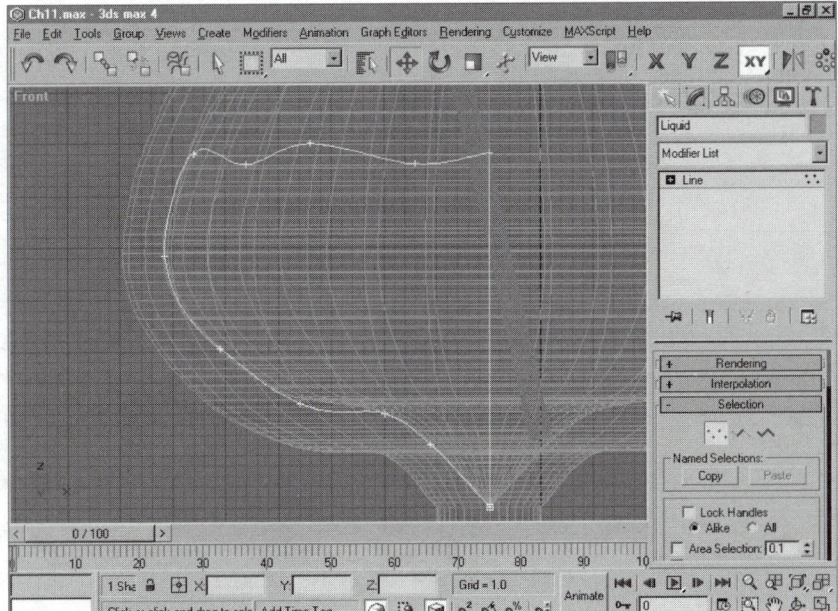

2. Activate the Top viewport. Then, in the **Keyboard Entry** rollout, type 30 in the **Length:** spinner, 70 in the **Width:** spinner, and 1 in the **Height:** spinner. Pick the **Create** button. In the **Name and Color** rollout, name the box Fern01.
   A box is created at the center of the viewport.

3. Turn snap off. Move Fern01 toward the bottom-right edge of Block.

4. Pick the **Select and Rotate** and **Restrict to Z** buttons on the **Main** toolbar. Holding the [Shift] key down, rotate Fern01 60°. In the **Clone Options** dialog box that is displayed, name the copy Fern02.

5. Pick the **Select and Move** and **Restrict to XY Plane** buttons on the **Main** toolbar. Holding down the [Shift] key, move Fern02 up and to the left. In the **Clone Options** dialog box that is displayed, name the copy Fern03.

6. While holding down the [Shift] key, move Fern01 up and to the right. In the **Clone Options** dialog box that is displayed, name the copy Fern04.
   The four boxes that will be the fern leaves are created, Figure 11-6.

7. Save the scene.

Create

Adding Lights

1. Pick **Create** in the **Command Panel**. Pick the **Lights** button and select **Standard** from the drop-down list. Then, pick the **Omni** button in the **Object Type** rollout.

Lights

2. Place an omni light in the upper-left and in the upper-right corner of the Front viewport. In the **General Parameters** rollout, type .65 in the **Multiplier:** spinner for each light.

Zoom All

3. Pick the **Zoom All** button. Zoom out all viewports until the objects are displayed about half of their original sizes.

4. Place a third omni light in the scene on the right of the Left viewport a little above the vertical center of the glass. In the **General Parameters** rollout, type 1.0 in the **Multiplier:** spinner and check the **Cast Shadows** check box.

5. Save the scene.

Figure 11-6. Four boxes are added to the scene, which will become the fern leaves.

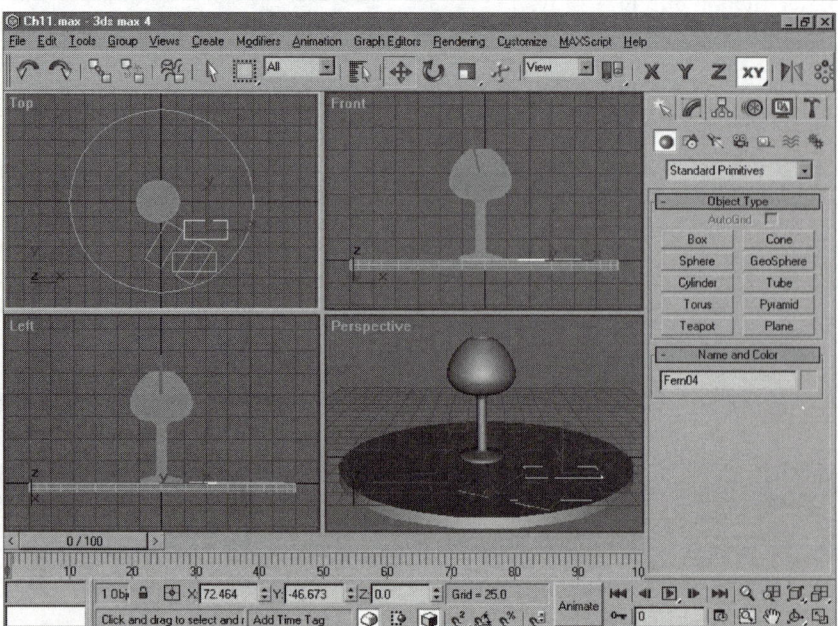

Adding a Camera

1. Pick **Create** in the **Command Panel**. Pick the **Cameras** button and select **Standard** from the drop-down list. Then, pick the **Target** button in the **Object Type** rollout.

Cameras

2. Place the camera in the bottom-right corner of the Top viewport, and drag the target to the center of the objects. Activate the Perspective viewport and press the [C] key to make it the Camera01 viewport.

3. Pick the **Select and Move** and **Restrict to XY Plane** buttons. Move the camera up in the Left viewport to place it near the top-right corner of the viewport.

4. Adjust the camera viewport as needed to display a desired view of the objects. The objects should nearly fill the viewport.

5. Save the scene.

Transparent Materials

You will be creating three transparent materials for the scene. The glass is transparent, and you will be able to see the liquid, cherry, and stirrer through it. The liquid is also transparent. The stirrer is made of a color glass, and is transparent. Start by creating a new, blank material library into which you can put your new materials.

1. Pick the **Material Editor** button on the **Main** toolbar.
   The **Material Editor** is displayed on the screen.

Material Editor

2. Pick the **Get Material** button in the **Material Editor**.
   The **Material/Map Browser** is displayed.

Get Material

3. In the **Browse From:** area, pick the **Mtl Library** radio button.
   The materials in the current library are displayed in the list box.

4. Pick the **Clear Material Library** button.
   A warning dialog box is displayed on screen asking if all the materials in the current library should be deleted. Pick the **Yes** button.

Clear Material Library

5. In the **File** area of the **Material/Map Browser**, pick the **Save As...** button. In the **Save Material Library** dialog box that appears, save the library as Glassware.mat in the folder of your choice.

6. Close the **Material/Map Browser** to return to the **Material Editor**.

Creating the Glass Material

1. Select the first material sample slot in the **Material Editor**. Pick in the drop-down list text box below the material samples. Name the material Glass.

2. In the **Shader Basic Parameters** rollout, select **Blinn** in the drop-down list. Also, check the **2-Sided** check box.
   The **2-Sided** check box forces 3ds max to render both the inside and outside of an object, which takes longer. However, without checking it, you will not be able to see the "back" of a transparent object.

3. In the **Blinn Basic Parameters** rollout, pick the ambient color swatch. In the **Color Selector** dialog box that appears, change the color to R155, G155, and B155. Then, close the **Color Selector** dialog box.
   The ambient color is set to a dark grey.

4. Now, pick the lock button next to the ambient and diffuse color swatches to unlock the colors. Then, pick the diffuse color swatch. In the **Color Selector** dialog box, change the color to R215, G215, and B215. Then, close the **Color Selector** dialog box.
   The diffuse color is set to a light grey.

5. Now, pick the specular color swatch. In the **Color Selector** dialog box, change the color to R255, G255, and B255. Close the **Color Selector** dialog box.
   The specular color is set to pure white.

6. In the **Specular Highlights** area of the **Blinn Basic Parameters** rollout, type 60 in the **Specular Level:** spinner. Also, type 40 in the **Glossiness:** spinner.

7. In the **Blinn Basic Parameters** rollout, type 30 in the **Opacity:** spinner.
   The lower the value in the **Opacity:** spinner, the more transparent the material is that you are creating.

8. Pick the **Background** button at the top right of the **Material Editor**.
   This renders the material sample over a patterned background. This displays the effects of the transparency settings better.

Put to Library

9. Select the **Put to Library** button in the **Material Editor**. In the **Put to Library** dialog box that is displayed, type Glass in the **Name:** field. Then, pick the **OK** button.

10. In the **Material Editor**, pick the **Get Material** button to open the **Material/Map Browser**. Verify that the Glass material is in the Glassware material library. Then, pick the **Save...** button in the **File** area to save the material library.

11. Close the **Material/Map Browser**.

12. Save the scene.

Creating the Liquid Material

1. Select the Glass material sample and drag it to the next unused sample slot. Rename the copy Liquid.

2. In the **Blinn Basic Parameters** rollout, pick the ambient color swatch to open the **Color Selector** dialog box. Change the color to R135, G100, and B130. Close the **Color Selector** dialog box.
   The ambient color is set to a dark purple.

3. Now, pick the diffuse color swatch. In the **Color Selector** dialog box, change the color to R255, G150, and B255. Close the **Color Selector** dialog box.
   The diffuse color is set to a light purple. Leave the specular color set to pure white.

4. In the **Specular Highlights** area of the **Blinn Basic Parameters** rollout, type 50 in the **Specular Level:** spinner and 30 in the **Glossiness:** spinner.

5. In the **Blinn Basic Parameters** rollout, type 50 in the **Opacity:** spinner.

6. Select the **Put to Library** button in the **Material Editor**. In the **Put to Library** dialog box that is displayed, type Liquid in the **Name:** field. Then, pick the **OK** button.

7. In the **Material Editor**, pick the **Get Material** button to open the **Material/Map Browser**. Verify that the Liquid material is in the Glassware material library. Then, pick the **Save...** button in the **File** area to save the material library.

8. Close the **Material/Map Browser**.

9. Save the scene.

Creating the Stirrer Material

1. Select the Glass material sample and drag it to the next unused sample slot. Rename the copy Stirrer.

2. In the **Blinn Basic Parameters** rollout, pick the ambient color swatch to open the **Color Selector** dialog box. Change the color to R100, G60, and B0. Close the **Color Selector** dialog box.
   The ambient color is set to a dark orange, almost brown.

3. Now, pick the diffuse color swatch. In the **Color Selector** dialog box, change the color to R255, G150, and B0. Close the **Color Selector** dialog box.
   The diffuse color is set to a bright orange. Leave the specular color set to pure white.

4. In the **Specular Highlights** area of the **Blinn Basic Parameters** rollout, type 100 in the **Specular Level:** spinner and 75 in the **Glossiness:** spinner.

5. In the **Blinn Basic Parameters** rollout, type 85 in the **Opacity:** spinner.

6. Select the **Put to Library** button in the **Material Editor**. In the **Put to Library** dialog box that is displayed, type Stirrer in the **Name:** field. Then, pick the **OK** button.

7. In the **Material Editor**, pick the **Get Material** button to open the **Material/Map Browser**. Verify that the Stirrer material is in the Glassware material library. Then, pick the **Save...** button in the **File** area to save the material library.

8. Close the **Material/Map Browser**.

9. Save the scene.

Opacity Maps

Opacity maps are another way of controlling the transparency of a material. The image contained on the map controls the transparency. Black pixels in the map are rendered completely transparent, and the white pixels are completely opaque. Pixels in the shades of grey proportionately control the transparency. Simple 3D objects can be used with a scanned image map and a similar opacity map to create the appearance of a complex shape. This is how the box primitives are turned into fern leaves.

1. Activate the next unused material sample slot in the **Material Editor**. Pick in the drop-down list text box below the material samples and rename the material Ferns.

2. Open the **Maps** rollout. Pick the button in the **Diffuse Color** row currently labeled **None** in the **Map** column.
   The **Material/Map Browser** is displayed showing the types of maps that can be added.

3. In the **Browse From:** area, pick the **New** radio button if it is not already on. Then, select **Bitmap** in the list and pick the **OK** button. In the **Select Bitmap Image File** dialog box that is displayed, navigate to the 3ds max \Maps\Organics folder. Open the file Fern.jpg from the folder.
   The image you selected is of a fern leaf on a colored background. However, the background portion of the image should be transparent. This can be accomplished by using an opacity map. The opacity map should be another image of the fern leaf, where the leaf portion is completely white (opaque) and the background portion is completely black (transparent).

4. At the diffuse color map level of the material tree, rename the map Fern Image Map. Then, pick Ferns in the drop-down list to navigate to the parent material level.

5. In the **Maps** rollout, pick the button in the **Opacity** row currently labeled **None** in the **Map** column. In the **Material/Map Browser** that is displayed, pick the **New** radio button in the **Browse From:** area.

6. Select **Bitmap** in the list, and then pick the **OK** button. In the **Select Bitmap Image File** dialog box that is displayed, navigate to the 3ds max \Maps\Organics folder. Open the file Fernopac.jpg from the folder.
   Notice in the preview that the fern area is solid white and the background area is solid black.

7. At the opacity map level of the material tree, rename the map Fern Opacity. Then, return to the parent material level.

8. Select the **Put to Library** button in the **Material Editor**. In the **Put to Library** dialog box that is displayed, type Ferns in the **Name:** field. Then, pick the **OK** button.

9. In the **Material Editor**, pick the **Get Material** button to open the **Material/Map Browser**. Verify that the Ferns material is in the Glassware material library. Then, pick the **Save...** button in the **File** area to save the material library.

10. Close the **Material/Map Browser**.

11. Save the scene.

Using Procedural Maps

A procedural map uses a mathematical algorithm to generate a 3D pattern that goes all the way through the object to which it is assigned. This means that the map will show correctly on exterior edges and interior holes. You will now create a wood procedural map for the block.

1. Activate the next unused sample slot in the **Material Editor**. Pick in the drop-down list text box below the material samples and name the material Wood Block.

2. In the **Maps** rollout, pick the button in the **Diffuse Color** row currently labeled **None** in the **Map** column. In the **Material/Map Browser**, pick the **New** radio button in the **Browse From:** area.

3. Select **Wood** in the list, and then pick the **OK** button.

4. At the diffuse color map level in the material tree, rename the map Wood Map. Then, return to the parent material level in the material tree.

5. Select the **Put to Library** button in the **Material Editor**. In the **Put to Library** dialog box that is displayed, type Wood Block in the **Name:** field. Then, pick the **OK** button.

6. In the **Material Editor**, pick the **Get Material** button to open the **Material/Map Browser**. Verify that the Wood Block material is in the Glassware material library. Then, pick the **Save...** button in the **File** area to save the material library.

7. Close the **Material/Map Browser**.

8. Save the scene.

Creating the Material for the Cherry

1. Select the next unused material sample slot. Pick in the drop-down list text box below the material samples and name the material Cherry Fruit.

2. In the **Maps** rollout, pick the button in the **Diffuse Color** row currently labeled **None** in the **Map** column. In the **Material/Map Browser**, pick the **New** radio button in the **Browse From:** area.

3. Select **Bitmap** in the list, and then pick the **OK** button. In the **Select Bitmap Image File** dialog box that is displayed, navigate to the 3ds max \Maps\Organics folder. Open the file StrawBryTex.jpg from the folder.

4. At the diffuse color map level of the material tree, rename the map Cherry Diffuse Color Map. Then, return to the parent material level.

5. Select the **Put to Library** button in the **Material Editor**. In the **Put to Library** dialog box that is displayed, type Cherry Fruit in the **Name:** field. Then, pick the **OK** button.

6. In the **Material Editor**, pick the **Get Material** button to open the **Material/Map Browser**. Verify that the Cherry Fruit material is in the Glassware material library. Then, pick the **Save...** button in the **File** area to save the material library.

7. Close the **Material/Map Browser**.

8. Save the scene.

Assigning Materials to Objects in the Scene

1. Assign the material Glass to the object Glass.

2. Assign the material Liquid to the object Liquid.

3. Assign the material Stirrer to the object Stirrer.

4. Assign the material Wood Block to the object Block.

5. Assign the material Cherry Fruit to the object Cherry.

6. Assign the material Ferns to the four fern objects. Close the **Material Editor**, if open.

7. Now, select Fern04 in any viewport. Then, pick **Parametric Deformers** in the **Modifiers** pull-down menu. Then, pick **Twist** in the cascading menu.
   A twist modifier is applied to the object, and the **Modify** tab is automatically displayed.

8. In the **Twist Axis:** area of the **Parameters** rollout, pick the **Y** radio button.

9. In the **Twist:** area of the **Parameters** rollout, type 10 in the **Angle:** spinner.

10. Similarly, apply a twist modifier to Fern03.

11. Move the two twisted leaves as needed so they are not "in" the table.

12. One by one, select a fern leaf, pick **UV Coordinates** in the **Modifiers** pull-down menu, and select **UVW Map** in the cascading menu. In the **Parameters** rollout, select the **Planar** radio button and the **Fit** button.
   The planar UVW mapping coordinates are applied to each leaf.

13. Select the object Cherry. Apply a UVW map modifier to the object. In the **Parameters** rollout, pick the **Spherical** radio button and the **Fit** button.

14. Select the object Stirrer. Apply a UVW map modifier to the object. In the **Parameters** rollout, pick the **Cylindrical** radio button and check the **Caps** check box. Select the **Fit** button in the **Alignment** area of the **Parameters** rollout.

15. Save the scene.

Rendering the Scene

Now, when you render the scene, you will be able to see the new materials applied to the objects in the 3D scene.

1. Adjust the view in the camera viewport as needed to get a desired view of the scene. Leave the camera viewport active and proceed to the next step.

Render Scene

2. Pick the **Render Scene** button on the **Main** toolbar. In the **Render Scene** dialog box that appears, pick the **Render** button in the dialog box.
   The scene is rendered and displayed in the render window. The rendered image shows how maps save time and effort by adding a great deal of detail to the scene by only applying a material, Figure 11-7.

3. Close the render window and the **Render Scene** dialog box.

4. Save the scene.

Figure 11-7. The completed, rendered scene.

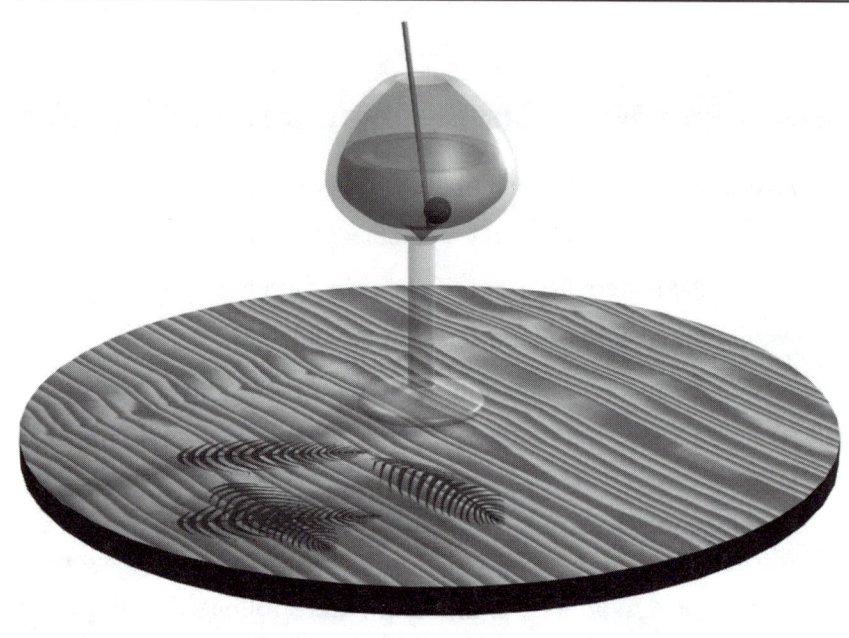

Self-Evaluation Test

Answer the following questions. Then, compare your answers with the correct answers given at the end of this chapter.

1. _____ materials are used to show both the inside and outside of an object.

2. The _____ value of the **Opacity:** spinner, the more transparent the material is that you are creating.

3. When you select the _____ button in the **Material Editor**, the material sample is rendered over a pattern to better show transparency settings.

4. In addition to setting the **Opacity:** spinner, you can also use _____ maps to control the transparency of a material.

5. _____ pixels are rendered transparent and _____ pixels are rendered opaque.

6. _____ maps use mathematical algorithms to generate a 3D pattern.

Exercises

Create the objects and materials needed to finish the scene shown below. The scene is of a glass containing orange juice. A drinking straw is placed in the glass, and the glass sits on top of a piece of marble. Two maple leaves are also placed on top of the marble.

1. Create a box and a cylinder. Subtract the cylinder from the box at one corner.

2. Create a cylinder for the glass. Create a second cylinder centered on the glass, which will be subtracted to hollow it out. Create a copy of the second cylinder for the juice. Then, subtract the second cylinder from the first.

3. Nonuniformly scale the juice cylinder so the glass is about half full.

4. Create a straw from a cylinder. Move and rotate it as needed to align it with the edge of the glass.

5. Create two thin boxes and place them on top of the marble piece. Apply a twist modifier to each.

6. Add lights and a camera to the scene.

7. Create a new, blank material library named Juice.

8. Create a material named Marble. Apply a diffuse color map, and select the marble map type.

9. Create two transparent materials for the glass and the juice using different opacity settings.

10. Create the material for the leaves using a diffuse color map. Select the bitmap map type and apply the bitmap LeafBrown.jpg in the 3ds max \Maps\Organics folder. Apply an opacity map, select the bitmap map type, and apply the bitmap Leafo.gif in the same folder.

11. Put the new materials into the new material library, and save the library.

12. Assign the new materials to the respective objects. Apply UVW map modifiers as needed.

13. Render a still image of the scene.

14. Save the scene as Ex11.max in the folder of your choice.

Answers

The following are the correct answers to the questions in the Self-Evaluation Test.

1. Two-sided; 2. lower; 3. **Background**; 4. opacity; 5. Black, white; 6. Procedural.

Chapter 12

Controlling Texture Maps

Learning Objectives

After completing this chapter, you will be able to:

○ Modify mapping parameters.
○ Apply a material map to simulate a decal or label.
○ Apply reflection maps.
○ Create a material with raytraced material maps.
○ Create and use a multi/sub-object material.
○ Set up an environmental background.

Tutorial Description

In this tutorial, you will create a beach scene. The scene consists of a table placed on the sand, with a bottle and a toy ball on top of the table. A beach umbrella is placed in the scene to shade the table.

Creating the Scene

Start the scene by resetting 3ds max. Save the existing scene before resetting if you do not want to lose it. Then, draw the table first.

Creating the Table

Create

Geometry

1. Activate the Top viewport. Then, pick **Create** in the **Command Panel**. Pick the **Geometry** button and select **Standard Primitives** from the drop-down list. Then, pick the **Box** button in the **Object Type** rollout.

2. Open the **Keyboard Entry** rollout. Type 160 in the **Length:** spinner, 200 in the **Width:** spinner, and 10 in the **Height:** spinner. Then, pick the **Create** button. In the **Name and Color** rollout, name the box Table Top.
   A box is created in the center of the viewport.

Zoom Extents All

3. Pick the **Zoom Extents All** button to zoom to the extents of the object.

4. Pick **Create** in the **Command Panel**. Pick the **Geometry** button and select **Standard Primitives** from the drop-down list. Then, pick the **Cylinder** button in the **Object Type** rollout.

5. In the **Keyboard Entry** rollout, type 10 in the **Radius:** spinner and 100 in the **Height:** spinner. Then, pick the **Create** button. In the **Name and Color** rollout, name the cylinder Leg01. *A cylinder is created in the center of the viewport.*

Select and Move

6. Pick the **Select and Move** and **Restrict to XY Plane** buttons on the **Main** toolbar. Holding down the [Shift] key, move Leg01 up and to the left in the Top viewport to place it near the upper-left corner of Table Top.

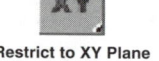

Restrict to XY Plane

7. In the **Clone Options** dialog box that is displayed, name the copy Leg02. Then, pick the **OK** button. *A copy of Leg01 is created and placed near the upper-left corner of Table Top.*

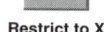

Restrict to X

8. Pick the **Restrict to X** button on the **Main** toolbar. Holding down the [Shift] key, move Leg02 to the right so it is near the upper-right corner of Table Top.

9. In the **Clone Options** dialog box that is displayed, name the copy Leg03. Then, pick the **OK** button. *A copy of Leg02 is created and placed near the upper-right corner of Table Top.*

Restrict to Y

10. Pick the **Restrict to Y** button. Holding down the [Shift] key, move Leg03 down to place it near the lower-right corner of the viewport.

11. In the **Clone Options** dialog box that is displayed, name the copy Leg04. Then, pick the **OK** button. *A copy of Leg03 is created and placed near the lower-right corner of Table Top.*

12. Pick the **Restrict to XY Plane** button. Then, move Leg01 down and to the left to place it near the lower-left corner of Table Top.

13. Activate the Front viewport. Pick the **Zoom Extents All** button. Pick the **Restrict to Y** button on the **Main** toolbar. Move Table Top up and place it on top of the legs. The bottom of Table Top should align with the top of the legs, Figure 12-1.

14. Save the scene as Ch12.max in the folder of your choice.

Figure 12-1. The tabletop and legs are created.

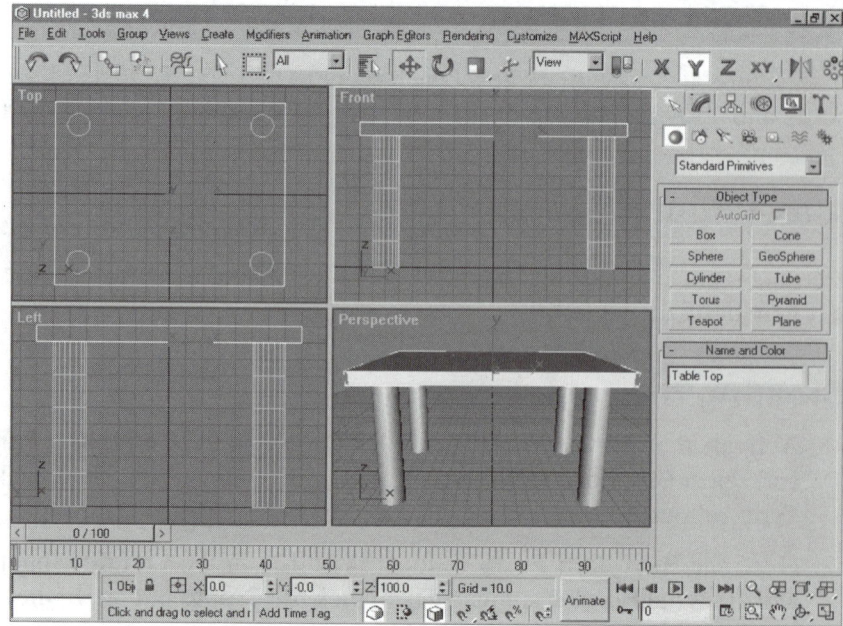

Creating the Bottle

1. Maximize the Front viewport. Then, pan the viewport so only the top edge of Table Top is visible.

2. Right-click on the **Snap** flyout to display the **Grid and Snap Settings** dialog box. Pick the **Home Grid** tab. Type 5 in the **Grid Spacing** spinner and the **Major Lines every Nth** spinner. Close the dialog box.

3. Zoom as needed so each grid square represents five units.
   To see how many units each grid square represents, place your cursor at the intersection of two grid lines. Then, as you look at the coordinate display, move the cursor to the very next grid intersection.

   Create

4. Pick **Create** in the **Command Panel**. Pick the **Shapes** button and select **Splines** from the drop-down list. Then, pick the **Line** button in the **Object Type** rollout.

   Shapes

5. Activate the Front viewport. Also, pick the **2D Snap Toggle** button to turn snap on. Draw the shape shown in Figure 12-2 using the coordinates given in the figure. In the **Name and Color** rollout, name the spline Bottle.
   The profile of the bottle is created above the table.

   2D Snap Toggle

6. With the profile selected, pick **Modify** in the **Command Panel**. In the **Selection** rollout, pick the **Vertex** button to enter sub-object mode.

   Modify

7. Modify the vertices of the profile to produce smooth curves that will form the outside of the bottle. Then, pick the **Vertex** button again to exit sub-object mode.

8. Pick **Patch/Spline Editing** in the **Modifiers** pull-down menu. Then, pick **Lathe** in the cascading menu.
   A lathe modifier is applied to the spline, and the **Modify** tab is automatically displayed.

Figure 12-2. The shape for the bottle. The coordinates given in the table are world coordinates. Draw the shape using the cursor in the Front viewport, or using the **Keyboard Entry** rollout in the Top viewport.

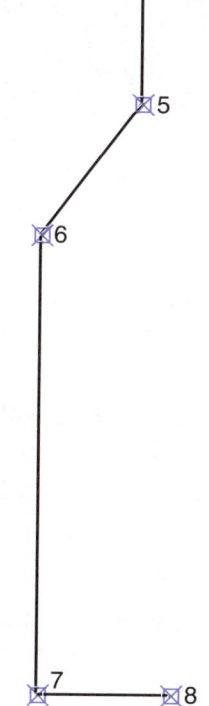

Point	X	Y	Z
1	0	0	250
2	−10	0	250
3	−10	0	245
4	−5	0	245
5	−5	0	220
6	−20	0	200
7	−20	0	130
8	0	0	130

9. In the **Parameters** rollout, pick the **Z** button in the **Direction** area. Also, pick the **Max** button in the **Align** area.

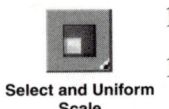
Select and Uniform
Scale

10. Display the four-viewport configuration. Then, pick the **Zoom Extents All** button.

11. Pick the **Select and Uniform Scale** button on the **Main** toolbar. Scale Bottle down in the Front viewport to 75%, as indicated in the coordinate display.
    Bottle is scaled down equally along each of its axes.

12. Pick the **Select and Move** and **Restrict to Y** buttons on the **Main** toolbar. Move Bottle down so it sits on top of Table Top.

13. Activate the Top viewport. Pick the **Restrict to XY Plane** button on the **Main** toolbar. Move Bottle to the right and down so it is near the bottom-right corner of Table Top, Figure 12-3.

14. Save the scene.

Figure 12-3. The bottle is created and placed on top of the table.

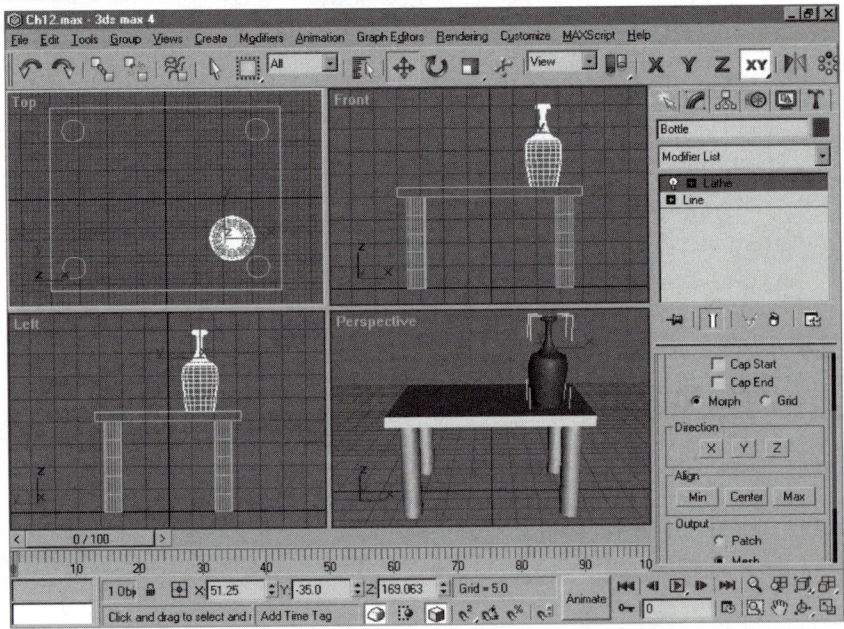

Creating the Toy Ball

1. Pick **Create** in the **Command Panel**. Pick the **Geometry** button and select **Standard Primitives** from the drop-down list. Then, pick the **GeoSphere** button in the **Object Type** rollout. In the **Parameters** rollout, type 2 in the **Segments:** spinner.

2. Activate the Top viewport. Then, expand the **Keyboard Entry** rollout. Type 20 in the **Radius:** spinner and pick the **Create** button. In the **Name and Color** rollout, name the geosphere Toy Ball.
   A geosphere is created in the center of the viewports.

3. Pick the **Select and Move** and **Restrict to XY Plane** buttons on the **Main** toolbar. Move Toy Ball to the left and up in the Top viewport so it is near the upper-left corner of Table Top.

4. In the Front viewport, move Toy Ball up so it sits on top of Table Top.

5. Save the scene.

Creating the Beach Umbrella

1. Pick **Create** in the **Command Panel**. Pick the **Geometry** button and select **Standard Primitives** from the drop-down list. Then, pick the **Cylinder** button in the **Object Type** rollout.

2. Activate the Top viewport. Then, expand the **Keyboard Entry** rollout. Type 5 in the **Radius:** spinner and 350 in the **Height:** spinner. Then, pick the **Create** button. In the **Name and Color** rollout, name the cylinder Rod.
   A cylinder is created at the center of the viewports.

3. Pick the **Zoom Extents All** button. Then, pick the **Select and Move** and **Restrict to Y** buttons on the **Main** toolbar. Move Rod up in the Top viewport so its lower edge aligns with the top edge of Table Top.

Select and Rotate

Restrict to Z

4. Activate the Front viewport. Then, pick the **Select and Rotate** and **Restrict to Z** buttons on the **Main** toolbar. Rotate Rod 15°, as indicated in the coordinate display.

5. Activate the Top viewport. Then, pick **Create** in the **Command Panel**. Pick the **Geometry** button and select **Standard Primitives** from the drop-down list. Then, pick the **Sphere** button in the **Object Type** rollout. In the **Keyboard Entry** rollout, type 175 in the **Radius:** spinner and pick the **Create** button. In the **Name and Color** rollout, name the sphere Umbrella.
   A sphere is created in the viewports.

6. In the **Parameters** rollout, type 8 in the **Segments:** spinner and 0.75 in the **Hemisphere:** spinner. Also, uncheck the **Smooth** check box.

7. Pick the **Select and Move** and **Restrict to XY Plane** buttons on the **Main** toolbar. Move Umbrella up and to the left in the Front viewport so its apex is at the upper end of Rod.

8. Pick the **Select and Rotate** and **Restrict to Z** buttons. Rotate Umbrella 15° in the Front viewport, as indicated in the coordinate display.

9. Pick the **Select and Move** and **Restrict to XY Plane** buttons. Move Umbrella in the Front viewport so its centerline aligns with the centerline of Rod. Align the centerlines in the Left viewport as well, Figure 12-4.

10. Save the scene.

Figure 12-4. The umbrella and toy ball are added to the scene.

Hollowing out the Umbrella

1. Maximize the Front viewport.

2. Pick the **Select and Uniform Scale** button on the **Main** toolbar. Holding down the [Shift] key, scale the umbrella down to 95%, as indicated in the coordinate display. In the **Clone Options** dialog box that is displayed, name the copy Umbrella Drill.

3. Select Umbrella. Then, pick **Create** in the **Command Panel**. Pick the **Geometry** button and select **Compound Objects** from the drop-down list. Pick the **Boolean** button in the **Object Type** rollout.

4. In the **Operation** area of the **Parameters** rollout, pick the **Subtraction (A-B)** radio button. In the **Pick Boolean** rollout, pick the **Move** radio button, then select the **Pick Operand B** button. Select Umbrella Drill. Right-click to complete the operation.

5. Display the four-viewport configuration. Save the scene.

Adding the Ground Plane

1. Activate the Top viewport. Then, pick **Create** in the **Command Panel**. Pick the **Geometry** button and select **Patch Grids** from the drop-down list. Then, pick the **Quad Patch** button in the **Object Type** rollout.

2. Expand the **Keyboard Entry** rollout. Type 500 in the **Length:** spinner and 800 in the **Width:** spinner. Then, pick the **Create** button. In the **Name and Color** rollout, name the quad patch Ground.
   A quad patch is created in the center of the viewports.

3. Pick the **Select and Move** and **Restrict to X** buttons on the **Main** toolbar. Move Ground to the right in the Top viewport so its left edge aligns with the outer edge of the umbrella.

4. With Ground selected, pick **Modify** in the **Command Panel**. In the **Parameters** rollout, type 5 in the **Length Segs:** and **Width Segs:** spinners.

5. Pick **Parametric Deformers** in the **Modifiers** pull-down menu. Then, pick **Noise** in the cascading menu.
   A noise modifier is applied to the quad patch.

6. In the **Noise:** area of the **Parameters** rollout, check the **Fractal** check box. In the **Strength:** area, type 75 in the **Z:** spinner.

7. Save the scene.

Adding Lights and a Camera

Create

Cameras

1. Pick **Create** in the **Command Panel**. Pick the **Lights** button and select **Standard** from the drop-down list. Then, pick the **Omni** button in the **Object Type** rollout. Pick a point in the lower-left corner of the Top viewport to place an omni light. In the **General Parameters** rollout, check the **Cast Shadows** check box. Pick another point at the lower-right corner of the viewport to place another omni light. This light should not cast shadows.
   Two omni lights are created.

2. Activate the Front viewport. Pick the **Select and Move** and **Restrict to XY Plane** buttons. Move both omni lights to the top of the viewport. Select the **Zoom Extents All** button.

Cameras

3. Pick **Create** in the **Command Panel**. Pick the **Cameras** button and select **Standard** from the drop-down list. Then, pick the **Target** button in the **Object Type** rollout. Select a point near the lower-left corner of the Top viewport to place the camera and drag to the center of the table to place the target.

4. Activate the Perspective viewport and press the [C] key to make it the camera viewport.

Figure 12-5. The ground is created, and lights and a camera are added to the scene.

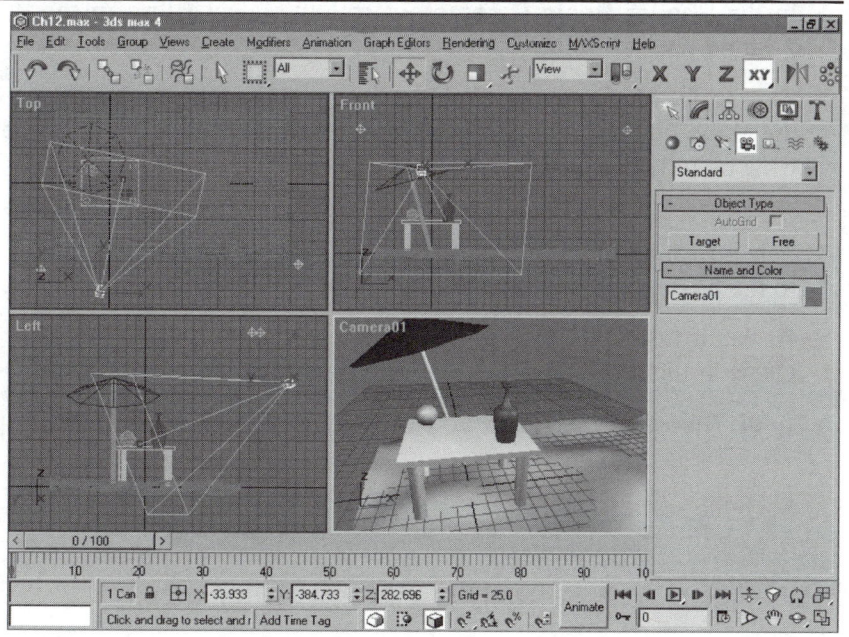

5. Pick the **Select and Move** and **Restrict to XY Plane** buttons. Move the camera up in the Front viewport. Continue moving the camera as needed to get a desired view in the Camera01 viewport, Figure 12-5.

6. Save the scene.

Creating a New Material Library

1. Pick the **Material Editor** button on the **Main** toolbar.
   The **Material Editor** is displayed.

2. Pick the **Get Material** button in the **Material Editor**.
   The **Material/Map Browser** is displayed.

3. In the **Browse From:** area, select the **Mtl Library** radio button.
   The materials in the current library are displayed in the list box.

4. Pick the **Clear Material Library** button.
   A warning dialog box is displayed asking if all materials in the current library should be deleted. Pick the **Yes** button.

5. In the **File** area of the **Material/Map Browser**, pick the **Save...** button. In the **Save Material Library File** dialog box, save the library as Beach.mat in the folder of your choice.

6. Close the **Material/Map Browser** to return to the **Material Editor**.

Material Editor

Get Material

Clear Material Library

Creating the Bottle Material

The bottle has a label on it. This label is placed into the material definition as a map. Most of the bottle shows the base material definition. However, where the label map is, the base material definition cannot be seen.

1. In the **Material Editor**, activate the first unused material sample slot. Pick in the drop-down list text box below the material samples and name the material Bottle Glass.

2. In the **Shader Basic Parameters** rollout, select **Blinn** in the drop-down list. Also, check the **2-Sided** check box.

3. Expand the **Maps** rollout. Pick the button in the **Diffuse Color** row currently labeled **None** and in the **Maps** column. The **Material/Map Browser** is displayed. In the **Browse From:** area, pick the **New** radio button if it is not already selected.
   All the available types of maps are displayed in the list.

4. Select **Bitmap** in the list. In the **Select Bitmap Image File** dialog box that is displayed, navigate to the 3ds max \Maps\Misc folder. Open the file Crossing_Sign.jpg from the folder.

5. At the diffuse color map level of the material tree, name the map Bottle Label. Then, pick Bottle Glass in the drop-down list to return to the parent material level.

Cylinder Sample

6. In the **Sample Type** flyout at the top right of the **Material Editor**, pick the **Cylinder** button.
   The map is displayed on a cylindrical sample.

7. Save the scene.

Modifying the Mapping Parameters

The scale, placement, and rotation angle of the bitmap image can be controlled with the **Coordinates** rollout. You will start by modifying the size of the label.

1. With the Bottle Glass material sample active in the **Material Editor**, expand the **Maps** rollout. Then, pick the button in the **Diffuse Color** in the **Map** column, which is now labeled **Bottle Label**.
   This navigates to the diffuse color map level of the material tree.

2. In the **Coordinates** rollout, type 3.0 in the **U: Tiling** spinner. Also, type 2.0 in the **V: Tiling** spinner.
   A value of 2.0 indicates that the material is scaled down to fit twice in the original space along the vertical axis. In other words, the image is displayed half its original size. A value of 3.0 indicates that the material is scaled down to fit three times in the original space along the horizontal axis.

3. The label is smaller and fits better on the bottle, but the image repeats along the vertical and horizontal axes. You need to place only one image on the bottle. To do this, tiling must be turned off. In the **Coordinates** rollout, uncheck the **U: Tile** and **V: Tile** check boxes.
   The image no longer repeats along either the horizontal or vertical axes.

4. The image is still not quite where it should be. This is done using the **Offset** spinners. Type –0.22 in the **U: Offset** spinner.
   The image moves to the left of its original position. The amount of movement of the image is dependent on the size of the image. For example, a value of 0.5 will move the image halfway of its width to the right and a value of –0.5 will move the image halfway of its width to the left.

5. Type –0.2 in the **V: Offset** spinner.
   The image moves down from its original position. It is also possible to rotate the image, if you want to by entering values in the **U:, V:,** and **W: Angle** spinners, as need be.

6. Return to the parent material level in the material tree. Then, save the scene.

Adjusting the Color of the Bottle

Now that the label is correctly placed on the bottle, the glass portion of the material needs to be defined. The glass is opaque and matches the background color of the label. Therefore, the basic color of the bottle needs to be changed to a light grey.

1. At the parent level of the Bottle Glass material tree, pick the ambient color swatch in the **Blinn Basic Parameters** rollout.

2. In the **Color Selector** dialog box, that is displayed, change the color to R190, G190, and B190. Close the **Color Selector** dialog box.

   The ambient color is set to a dark grey.

3. In the **Blinn Basic Parameters** rollout, pick the lock button next to the ambient and diffuse color swatches to unlock the colors. Then, pick the diffuse color swatch.

4. In the **Color Selector** dialog box that is displayed, change the color to R250, G250, and B250. Close the **Color Selector** dialog box.

   The diffuse color is set to a light grey.

5. Pick the specular color swatch. In the **Color Selector** dialog box, change the color to R255, G255, and B255. Close the **Color Selector** dialog box.

   The specular color is set to pure white.

6. In the **Specular Highlights** area of the **Blinn Basic Parameters** rollout, type 150 in the **Specular Level:** spinner and 50 in the **Glossiness:** spinner.

7. Save the scene.

Adding a Reflection Map

A reflection map is applied to an object to make the scene more realistic by reflecting the surrounding images and elements onto the object. 3ds max provides you with different types of reflective maps. These are reflect/refract, flat mirror, and raytrace. The reflect/refract map can be applied to curved or irregular shaped objects. The flat mirror maps only works on perfectly flat geometry. You can apply a raytrace map as a reflection map to produce raytraced reflections. A reflect/refract map is used for the bottle. Reflection maps are calculated and applied at rendering time. They are not displayed in shaded viewports, but are displayed in ActiveShade viewports.

1. At the parent material level for the Bottle Glass material, expand the **Maps** rollout.

2. Select the button in the **Reflection** row currently labeled **None** in the **Map** column. The **Material/Map Browser** is displayed. In the **Browse From:** area, pick the **New** radio button if not already on.

   All available map types are displayed.

3. Select **Reflect/Refract** in the list, and then pick the **OK** button.

   This map type automatically generates a reflection from the other elements in the scene and places it on the appropriate objects during rendering.

4. At the reflection map level in the material tree, name the map Bottle Reflect. Then, pick Bottle Glass from the drop-down list to return to the parent material level.

5. In the **Maps** rollout, type 20 in the **Reflection** spinner.

   This value controls the amount of reflection in the material.

6. Save the scene.

Saving the Material Library

Put to Library

1. With the Bottle Glass material sample active, pick the **Put to Library** button in the **Material Editor**. In the **Put to Library** dialog box that is displayed, type Bottle Glass in the **Name:** field. Then, pick the **OK** button.

2. In the **Material Editor**, pick the **Get Material** button to open the **Material/Map Browser**. Verify that the Bottle Glass material is in the Beach material library. Then, pick the **Save...** button in the **File** area to save the material library.

3. Close the **Material/Map Browser**.

4. Now, apply the material to the bottle.

5. Save the scene.

Using the Raytrace Map

The table top is a polished wood material. As such, it will reflect the background and other objects. You will add a raytrace map as a reflection map for the table top.

1. Select the next unused material sample slot in the **Material Editor**. Pick in the drop-down list text box below the material samples and name the material Table Wood.

2. Expand the **Maps** rollout. Pick the button in the **Diffuse Color** row that is currently labeled **None** in the **Maps** column. The **Material/Map Browser** is displayed. In the **Browse From:** area, pick the **New** radio button if it is not already on.
   All available map types are displayed.

3. Select **Bitmap** in the list, and then pick the **OK** button.
   The **Select Bitmap Image File** dialog box is displayed.

4. Navigate to the 3ds max \Maps\Wood folder. Open the file Ashen_2.gif from the folder.

5. At the diffuse color map level of the material tree, name the map Table Wood Map. Then, pick Table Wood from the drop-down list to return to the parent material level of the material tree.

6. In the **Maps** rollout, pick the button in the **Reflection** row currently labeled **None** in the **Map** column. The **Material/Map Browser** is displayed. In the **Browse From:** area, pick the **New** radio button if it is not already selected.

7. Select **Raytrace** in the list, and then pick the **OK** button.
   A raytrace map is added as a reflection map.

8. At the reflection map level of the material tree, rename the map Wood Reflection. Then, pick Table Wood from the drop-down list to return to the parent level of the material tree.

9. In the **Maps** rollout, type 20 in the **Reflection** spinner. Also, type 75 in the **Diffuse Color** spinner.

10. In the **Blinn Basic Parameters** rollout, change the ambient color to a dark orange, the diffuse color to a light orange, and the specular color to white.

11. With the Table Wood material sample active, pick the **Put to Library** button in the **Material Editor**. In the **Put to Library** dialog box that is displayed, type Table Wood in the **Name:** field. Then, pick the **OK** button.

12. In the **Material Editor**, pick the **Get Material** button to open the **Material/Map Browser**. Verify that the Table Wood material is in the Beach material library. Then, pick the **Save...** button in the **File** area to save the material library.

13. Close the **Material/Map Browser**.

14. Now, apply the material to Table Top.

15. Save the scene.

Creating the Toy Ball Material

1. Activate the next unused sample slot in the **Material Editor**. Name the material Toy Ball. In the **Shader Basic Parameters** rollout, check the **Wire** and **2-Sided** check boxes.
   Notice that a wireframe sphere is displayed in the sample slot.

2. In the **Blinn Basic Parameters** rollout, change the ambient and diffuse colors to a bright blue. Also, change the specular color to white.

3. In the **Specular Highlights** area of the **Blinn Basic Parameters** rollout, type 60 in the **Specular Level:** spinner.
   The material is now shiny.

4. With the Toy Ball material sample active, pick the **Put to Library** button in the **Material Editor**. In the **Put to Library** dialog box that is displayed, type Toy Ball in the **Name:** field. Then, pick the **OK** button.

5. In the **Material Editor**, pick the **Get Material** button to open the **Material/Map Browser**. Verify that the Toy Ball material is in the Beach material library. Then, pick the **Save...** button in the **File** area to save the material library.

6. Close the **Material/Map Browser**.

7. Now, apply the material to Toy Ball.

8. Save the scene.

Creating a Material for the Rod and Legs

1. Activate the next unused sample slot in the **Material Editor**. Pick in the drop-down list text box below the material samples and name the material Rod Wood.

2. Open the **Maps** rollout. Pick the button in the **Diffuse Color** row currently labeled **None** next in the **Map** column. The **Material/Map Browser** is displayed. In the **Browse From:** area, pick the **New** radio button if not already on.

3. Select **Bitmap** from the list, and then pick the **OK** button. In the **Select Bitmap Image File** dialog box that is displayed, navigate to the 3ds max \Maps\Wood folder. Open the file Drftwd.jpg from the folder.

4. At the diffuse color map level of the material tree, name the map Rod Wood Map. Then, pick Rod Wood from the drop-down list to return to the parent material level of the material tree.

5. With the Rod Wood material sample active, pick the **Put to Library** button in the **Material Editor**. In the **Put to Library** dialog box that is displayed, type Rod Wood in the **Name:** field. Then, pick the **OK** button.

6. In the **Material Editor**, pick the **Get Material** button to open the **Material/Map Browser**. Verify that the Rod Wood material is in the Beach material library. Then, pick the **Save...** button in the **File** area to save the material library.

7. Close the **Material/Map Browser**.

8. Now, apply the material to Rod and the four legs.

9. Save the scene.

Creating the Ground Material

1. Activate the next unused sample slot in the **Material Editor**. Pick in the drop-down list below the material samples and name the material Sandy Beach.

2. Open the **Maps** rollout. Pick the button in the **Diffuse Color** row currently labeled **None** and in the **Map** column. The **Material/Map Browser** is displayed. In the **Browse From:** area, pick the **New** radio button if not already on.

3. Select **Bitmap** from the list, and then pick the **OK** button. In the **Select Bitmap Image File** dialog box that is displayed, navigate to the 3ds max \Maps\Ground folder. Then, open the file Sand3.jpg from the folder.

4. At the diffuse color map level of the material tree, name the map Sand Map. Then, pick Sandy Beach from the drop-down list to return to the parent level of the material tree.

5. With the Sandy Beach material sample active, pick the **Put to Library** button in the **Material Editor**. In the **Put to Library** dialog box that is displayed, type Sandy Beach in the **Name:** field. Then, pick the **OK** button.

6. In the **Material Editor**, pick the **Get Material** button to open the ˙**Material/Map Browser**. Verify that the Sandy Beach material is in the Beach material library. Then, pick the **Save...** button in the **File** area to save the material library.

7. Close the **Material/Map Browser**.

8. Now, apply the material to the ground.

9. Save the scene.

Creating the Material for the Umbrella

You will now create the material for the umbrella. This material is of the multi/sub-object type. Using this material type, in conjunction with the material modifier, you can assign different materials to different portions of the same object.

1. Select the next unused material sample slot in the **Material Editor**. Pick in the drop-down list text box below the material samples and name the material Umbrella Colors. Pick the button next to the material name drop-down list, which is currently labeled **Standard**. The **Material/Map Browser** is displayed. In the **Browse From:** area, pick the **New** radio button if not already on.

2. Select **Multi/Sub-Object** from the list, and then pick the **OK** button.
   The **Replace Material** dialog box is displayed asking if you want to keep the old material as sub-material or discard it.

3. Select the **Discard old material?** radio button, and then pick the **OK** button.
   The **Multi/Sub-Object** rollout is displayed with ten sub-materials. This is the parent material level.

4. Pick the **Set Number** button to display the **Set Number of Materials** dialog box. Type 4 in the **Number of Materials:** spinner, and then pick the **OK** button.
   The Umbrella Colors now consist of four sub-materials instead of ten.

5. In the **Multi/Sub-Object** rollout, pick the top button in the **Sub-Material** column.
   This navigates down one level to the sub-material level in the material tree for the first sub-material. This level is the same as the other standard material parent levels that you have created so far.

6. Name this first sub-material Blue Sub. Then, change the ambient color to a dark blue, the diffuse color to a light blue, and the specular color to white. Also, change the **Specular Level:** spinner to 75, and the **Glossiness:** spinner to 35. Finally, pick Umbrella Colors in the material name drop-down list to return to the multi/sub-object parent material level of the material tree.
   The small sample sphere in the **Multi/Sub-Object** rollout displays a blue material. The material button is now labeled **Blue Sub**. Also, notice that the main material sample is displayed mostly grey with some blue segments.

7. Now, pick the next button in the **Sub-Material** column.
   This navigates down one level to the sub-material level in the material tree for the second sub-material.

8. Name this second sub-material Red Sub. Then, change the ambient color to a dark red, the diffuse color to a light red, and the specular color to white. Also, change the **Specular Level:** spinner to 75, and the **Glossiness:** spinner to 35. Finally, pick Umbrella Colors in the material name drop-down list to return to the multi/sub-object parent material level of the material tree.
The small sample sphere in the **Multi/Sub-Object** rollout displays a red material. The material button is now labeled **Red Sub**. Also, notice that the main material sample is updated with red segments in addition to the blue segments.

9. Now, pick the next button in the **Sub-Material** column.
This navigates down one level to the sub-material level in the material tree for the third sub-material.

10. Name this third sub-material Yellow Sub. Then, change the ambient color to a dark yellow, the diffuse color to a light yellow, and the specular color to white. Also, change the **Specular Level:** spinner to 75, and the **Glossiness:** spinner to 35. Finally, pick Umbrella Colors in the material name drop-down list to return to the multi/sub-object parent material level of the material tree.
The small sample sphere in the **Multi/Sub-Object** rollout displays a red material. The material button is now labeled **Yellow Sub**. Also, notice that the main material sample is updated with yellow segments in addition to the red and blue segments.

11. Now, pick the bottom button in the **Sub-Material** column.
This navigates down one level to the sub-material level in the material tree for the fourth sub-material.

12. Name this fourth sub-material Green Sub. Then, change the ambient color to a dark green, the diffuse color to a light green, and the specular color to white. Also, change the **Specular Level:** spinner to 75, and the **Glossiness:** spinner to 35. Finally, pick Umbrella Colors in the material name drop-down list to return to the multi/sub-object parent material level of the material tree.
The small sample sphere in the **Multi/Sub-Object** rollout displays a red material. The material button is now labeled **Green Sub**. Also, notice that the main material sample is updated with green segments in addition to the red, blue, and yellow segments, and there are no longer any grey areas on the material sample.

13. With the Umbrella Colors material sample active, pick the **Put to Library** button in the **Material Editor**. In the **Put to Library** dialog box that is displayed, type Umbrella Colors in the **Name:** field. Then, pick the **OK** button.

14. In the **Material Editor**, pick the **Get Material** button to open the **Material/Map Browser**. Verify that the Umbrella Colors material is in the Beach material library. Then, pick the **Save...** button in the **File** area to save the material library.

15. Close the **Material/Map Browser**.

16. Now, apply the material to the umbrella.

17. Close the **Material Editor** and save the scene.

Changing Material IDs

Now, the material is applied to the umbrella. However, if you render the scene, the umbrella is completely red. This is because the entire umbrella is assigned the material ID 2, which corresponds to the red sub-material. In order for the different sub-materials to be visible, you must make sub-object selections and apply a material modifier to each select. The material modifier allows you to change the default material ID of a selection.

1. Maximize the Top viewport and zoom in on the umbrella. With the umbrella selected, pick **Selection Modifiers** in the **Modifiers** pull-down menu. Then, pick **Mesh Select** in the cascading menu.
A mesh select modifier is applied to the umbrella, and the **Modify** tab is automatically displayed.

Face

Figure 12-6. Selecting faces to which a material modifier will be applied.

Selected faces

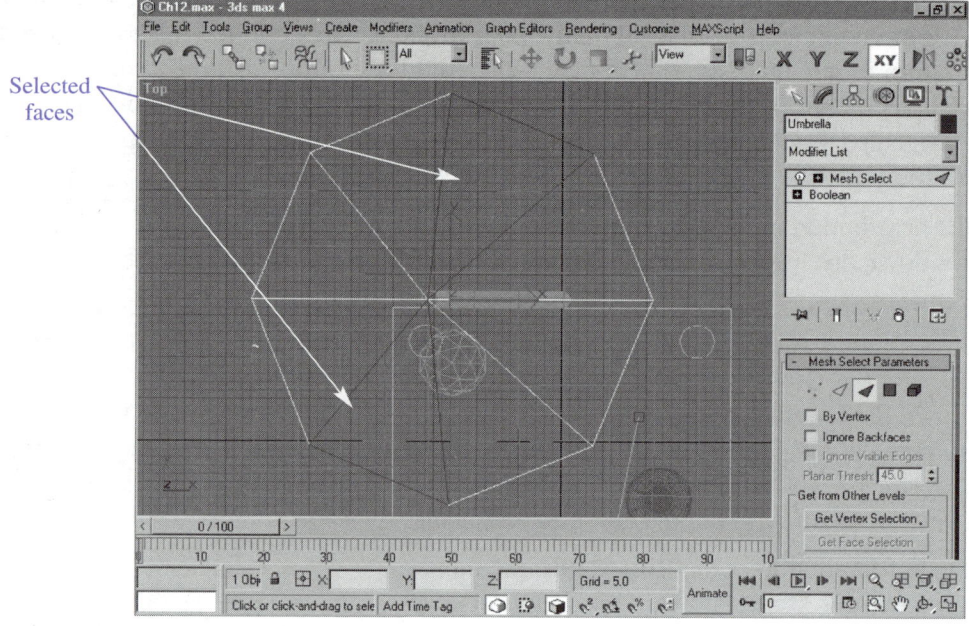

2. In the **Selection** rollout, pick the **Face** button to enter face sub-object mode.

3. Select one of the triangular faces on the umbrella. Drag a small crossing window across a portion of its outer edge. Then, hold down the [Ctrl] key and drag a small crossing window across the outer edge of the face on the other side of the umbrella, Figure 12-6.
   By dragging small crossing windows on the outer edges, you are selecting the face "on the top" and the face "on the bottom."

4. With the faces selected, pick **Surface** in the **Modifiers** pull-down menu. Then, pick **Material** in the cascading menu.
   A material modifier is applied to the selected faces only, not the entire object. The **Modify** tab is automatically displayed.

5. In the **Parameters** rollout, type 1 in the **Material ID:** spinner.
   The first sub-material, Blue Sub, is assigned to the selected faces because that sub-material has a material ID of 1.

6. Now, pick **Selection Modifiers** button in the **Modifiers** pull-down menu. Then, pick **Mesh Select** in the cascading menu.
   Another mesh select modifier is applied to the umbrella. This allows you to make a different sub-object selection.

7. In the **Selection** rollout, pick the **Face** button to enter face sub-object mode. Moving clockwise around the umbrella, select the next set of faces. Then, apply a material modifier to the selection set. Change the material ID to 2.

8. Continue applying mesh select and material modifiers, working your way clockwise around the umbrella. Change the material ID to 3 for the next selection set, and to 4 for the final selection set.
   When done, there should be four mesh select modifiers and four material modifiers applied to the umbrella.

9. Display the four-viewport configuration. Then, pick the **Zoom Extents All** button.

10. Save the scene.

Setting a Background Image

A map can be used as a background for the rendered scene. Since this scene has reflection maps, the background is included in the reflection. You can apply a map directly to the environment background. However, by first applying it to a temporary material in the Material Editor, you have control over the map.

1. Open the **Material Editor** and select the next unused sample. Pick in the drop-down list text box below the material samples and name the material Background.

2. Expand the **Maps** rollout. Pick the button in the **Diffuse Color** row currently labeled **None** in the **Maps** column. The **Material/Map Browser** is displayed. In the **Browse From:** area, pick the **New** radio button if not already on.

3. Select **Bitmap** from the list, and then pick the **OK** button. In the **Select Bitmap Image File** dialog box, navigate to the 3ds max \Maps\Skies folder. Then, open the file Cloud2.jpg from the folder.

4. At the diffuse color map level of the material tree, name the map Background Map. In the **Coordinates** rollout, pick the **Environ** radio button. Then, select **Screen** in the **Mapping** drop-down list.
   The texture map becomes an environment map. Selecting **Screen** scales the bitmap image to fit the screen when rendering takes place.

5. Pick Background in the material name drop-down list to return to the parent material level in the material tree.

6. With the Background material sample active, pick the **Put to Library** button in the **Material Editor**. In the **Put to Library** dialog box that is displayed, type Background in the **Name:** field. Then, pick the **OK** button.

7. In the **Material Editor**, pick the **Get Material** button to open the **Material/Map Browser**. Verify that the Background material is in the Beach material library. Then, pick the **Save...** button in the **File** area to save the material library.

8. Close the **Material/Map Browser**, and then the **Material Editor**.

9. Pick **Environment...** from the **Rendering** pull-down menu to display the **Environment** dialog box.

10. In the **Background:** area of the **Common Parameters** rollout, pick the **Environment Map:** button, which is currently labeled **None**. The **Material/Map Browser** is displayed.

11. In the **Browse From:** area, pick the **Mtl Library** button.
    All valid maps in the **Material Editor** are displayed.

12. Select Background Map from the list, and then pick the **OK** button.
    The map name appears on the button in the **Environment** dialog box. Also, the **Use Map** check box is checked.

13. Close the **Environment** dialog box.
    The cloud image will be placed behind all objects when the scene is rendered.

14. Save the scene.

Rendering the Scene

1. Activate the Camera01 viewport. Make any adjustments to the view needed to display a good view of the scene.

2. Apply UVW map modifiers to the objects and adjust the coordinates as needed.

Render Scene

3. Pick the **Render Scene** button on the **Main** to display the **Render Scene** dialog box. Then, pick the **Render** button in the dialog box.
   The rendered image is displayed on the screen, Figure 12-7. Notice how adding reflections to a scene adds realism.

4. Close the render window and the **Render Scene** dialog box.

5. Save the scene.

Figure 12-7. The final rendered scene.

Self-Evaluation Test

Answer the following questions. Then, compare your answers with the correct answers given at the end of this chapter.

1. The scale, placement, and rotation angle of the bitmap image can be controlled by using the spinners in the _____ rollout.

2. A value of **3.0** in the _____ spinners indicates that the map will be scaled down to one third of its size.

3. To turn off tiling of a bitmap image, you need to uncheck _____ check boxes in the **Coordinates** rollout.

4. To position a mapped image correctly, use the _____ spinners.

5. A _____ map type automatically generates a reflection from the other elements in the scene and places it on the appropriate objects during rendering.

6. Reflection maps are not displayed in _____ viewports, but are in _____ viewports.

7. Checking the _____ check box in the **Shader Basic Parameters** rollout creates a material that is rendered as a wireframe model.

Exercises

Exercise 12-1

Create the object and materials needed to finish the scene shown below. The scene consists of two wheat bread slices and a sunny side up egg, all on a dinner plate. The plate sits on a checker-patterned tablecloth.

1. Create the plate as a loft object. Apply scale deformation to obtain the plate shape. Then, subtract a copy to make a dish.

2. Create and extrude a spline for the egg white and create a sphere hemisphere for the yolk.

3. The bread slices are created as boxes.

4. The tablecloth is created as a quad patch.

5. Apply UVW map modifiers as needed.

6. Add lights and a camera to the scene.

7. Create a new material library named Breakfast. Then, create six new materials of your own design to complete the scene.

8. Put the new materials into the new material library and save the library.

9. Render a still image of the camera viewport.

10. Save the scene as Ex12-01.max in the folder of your choice.

Exercise 12-2

1. Open the file Ch03.max from Chapter 3. Save the scene as Ex12-02.max in the folder of your choice.

2. Apply UVW map modifiers to the objects as needed.

3. Create a new material for the mirror. The mirror should reflect the top of the dresser.

4. Adjust the camera viewport so you are looking slightly down on the dresser.

5. Render a still image of the scene.

6. Save the scene.

Answers

The following are the correct answers to the questions in the Self-Evaluation Test.

1. **Coordinates**; 2. **Tiling**; 3. **Tile**; 4. **Offset**; 5. **Reflect/Refract**; 6. shaded, ActiveShade; 7. **Wire**.

Chapter 13

Animation Basics

Learning Objectives

After completing this chapter, you will be able to:

○ Adjust the number of frames in an animation.
○ Modify object pivot points.
○ Create animation keys.
○ Create a hierarchical link between child and parent objects.
○ Adjust animation keys.
○ Add sound to the animation.
○ Render a final animation.

Tutorial Description

In this tutorial, you will create a merry-go-round and animate its movement. You will set the object pivot points around which the movement will take place. You will then create a hierarchical link between the parent and its children objects. You will also adjust the track and key info of the objects. Finally, you will add a sound file to the animation and render the animation.

Creating the Scene

You will create the merry-go-round by first creating its various components. The components are then assembled to create the final model. Start by resetting 3ds max.

Creating the Base

1. Activate the Top viewport. Pick **Create** in the **Command Panel**. Pick the **Geometry** button and select **Standard Primitives** from the drop-down list. Then, pick the **Box** button in the **Object Type** rollout.

Create

Geometry

2. Expand the **Keyboard Entry** rollout. Type 75 in the **Length:** spinner, 75 in the **Width:** spinner, and 40 in the **Height:** spinner. Then, pick the **Create** button. In the **Name and Color** rollout, name the box Base.
A box is created in the center of the viewports.

3. Pick **Create** in the **Command Panel**. Pick the **Geometry** button and select **Standard Primitives** from the drop-down list. Then, pick the **Cylinder** button in the **Object Type** rollout.

4. Expand the **Keyboard Entry** rollout. Type 30 in the **Radius:** spinner and 75 in the **Height:** spinner. Then, pick the **Create** button. In the **Name and Color** rollout, name the cylinder Pole.
A cylinder is created in the center of the viewports.

Select and Move

5. Pick the **Select and Move** and **Restrict to Y** buttons on the **Main** toolbar. In the Front viewport, move Pole up so it sits on top of Base.

Restrict to Y

6. With Pole selected, pick **Parametric Deformers** in the **Modifiers** pull-down menu. Then, pick **Taper** from the cascading menu.
A taper modifier is applied to the cylinder, and the **Modify** tab is automatically displayed.

7. In the **Parameters** rollout, type –0.45 in the **Amount:** spinner. Also, in the **Taper Axis:** area of the rollout, set the primary axis to Z and the effect to XY. Pick the **Zoom Extents All** button.
The cylinder is tapered at the top, Figure 13-1.

8. Activate the Top viewport. Pick **Create** in the **Command Panel**. Pick the **Geometry** button and select **Standard Primitives** from the drop-down list. Then, pick the **Cylinder** button in the **Object Type** rollout. Expand the **Keyboard Entry** rollout. Type 10 in the **Radius:** spinner and 20 in the **Height:** spinner. Then, pick the **Create** button. In the **Name and Color** rollout, name the cylinder Pole, Top.
A cylinder is created at the center of the viewports.

9. Activate the Front viewport and pick the **Select and Move** and **Restrict to Y** buttons on the **Main** toolbar. Move Pole, Top up so it sits on top of Pole.

10. Pick the **Zoom Extents All** button and activate the Top viewport. Then, pick **Create** in the **Command Panel**. Pick the **Geometry** button and select **Standard Primitives** from the drop-down list. Then, pick the **Tube** button in the **Object Type** rollout.
The rollouts for a tube are displayed.

Figure 13-1. The base and a portion of the center pole are created.

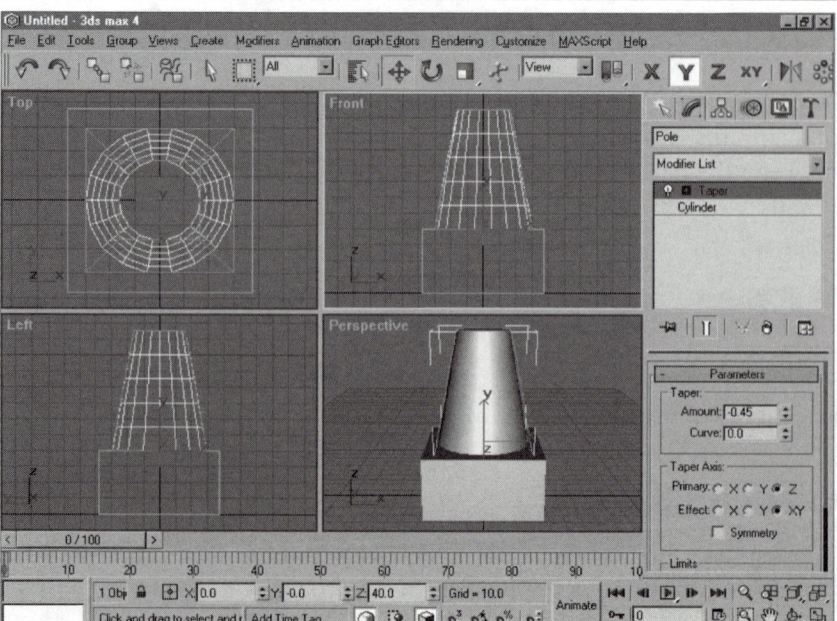

11. Expand the **Keyboard Entry** rollout. Type 15 in the **Outer Radius:** spinner, 10 in the **Inner Radius:** spinner, and 15 in the **Height:** spinner. Then, pick the **Create** button. In the **Name and Color** rollout, name the tube Arm Ring.

12. In the Front viewport, move Arm Ring up so its bottom aligns with the bottom of Pole, Top.

13. With Arm Ring selected, pick **Create** in the **Command Panel**. Pick the **Geometry** button and select **Compound Objects** from the drop-down list. Then, pick the **Boolean** button in the **Object Type** rollout.

14. Select Pole. Then, pick **Create** in the **Command Panel**. Pick the **Geometry** button and select **Compound Objects** from the drop-down list. Then, pick the **Boolean** button in the **Object Type** rollout.

15. In the **Parameters** rollout, pick the **Union** radio button. In the **Pick Boolean** rollout, select the **Move** radio button. Then, select the **Pick Operand B** button and select Pole, Top. Right-click to complete the operation.
    The two cylinders are combined to form a single object, Figure 13-2.

16. Save the scene as Ch13.max in the folder of your choice.

Creating the Arms

1. Activate the Top viewport. Then, pick **Create** in the **Command Panel**. Pick the **Geometry** button and select **Standard Primitives** from the drop-down list. Then, pick the **Box** button in the **Object Type** rollout. Expand the **Keyboard Entry** rollout, and type 10 in the **Length:** spinner, 150 in the **Width:** spinner, and 6 in the **Height:** spinner. Then, pick the **Create** button. In the **Name and Color** rollout, name the box Arm01.

Select and Move

2. Pick the **Select and Move** and **Restrict to X** buttons on the **Main** toolbar. In the Top viewport, move Arm01 to the right until its left edge touches the right edge of Arm Ring. The corners of the box should be inside the cylinder.

Restrict to X

3. Pick the **Restrict to Y** button and then move Arm01 up in the Front viewport to place it at the center of Arm Ring. Pick the **Zoom Extents All** button.

Figure 13-2. The pole is completed, and a ring is created to which the arms will attach.

4. Activate the Top viewport. Then, pick **Create** in the **Command Panel**. Pick the **Geometry** button and select **Standard Primitives** from the drop-down list. Then, pick the **Cylinder** button in the **Object Type** rollout. In the **Keyboard Entry** rollout, type 2 in the **Radius:** spinner and 10 in the **Height:** spinner. Then, pick the **Create** button. In the **Name and Color** rollout, name the cylinder PinA01.
   A small cylinder is created in the center of the viewports.

5. Again, pick **Create** in the **Command Panel**. Pick the **Geometry** button and select **Standard Primitives** from the drop-down list. Then, pick the **Cylinder** button in the **Object Type** rollout. In the **Keyboard Entry** rollout, type 5 in the **Radius:** spinner and 2 in the **Height:** spinner. Then, pick the **Create** button. In the **Name and Color** rollout, name the cylinder PinB01.
   Another cylinder is created in the viewport.

Select and Rotate

6. Select PinA01 and PinB01. Pick the **Restrict to X** button. In the Top viewport, move both cylinders so they are near the right end of Arm01.

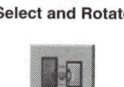

Use Selection
Center

7. Pick the **Select and Rotate** button. Also, pick the **Use Selection Center** button from the **Pivot Point** flyout on the **Main** toolbar. Select PinA01 and PinB01. In the Front viewport, rotate both cylinders 180°, as indicated in the coordinate display.

8. Pick the **Restrict to Y** button. In the Front viewport, move both cylinders so the bottom of PinB01 aligns with the top of Arm01, Figure 13-3.

9. Save the scene.

Creating the Basket

1. Activate the Top viewport. Pick **Create** in the **Command Panel**. Pick the **Geometry** button and select **Standard Primitives** from the drop-down list. Then, pick the **Sphere** button in the **Object Type** rollout.

2. Expand the **Keyboard Entry** rollout. Then, type 40 in the **Radius:** spinner and pick the **Create** button. In the **Name and Color** rollout, name the sphere Basket01.
   A sphere is created in the center of the viewports.

Figure 13-3. An arm is created, and a pin consisting of two cylinders is placed on one end.

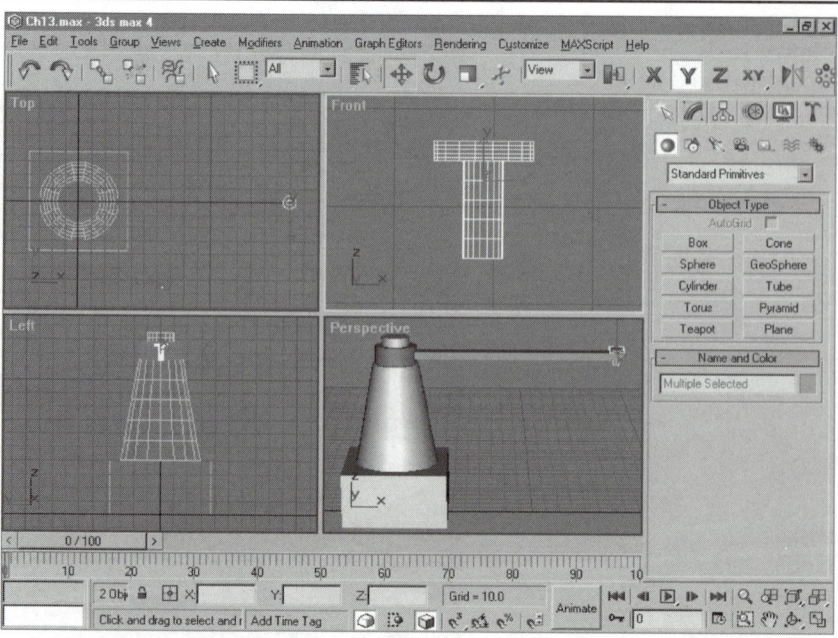

3. In the **Parameters** rollout, type 0.5 in the **Hemisphere:** spinner. Also, type 16 in the **Segments:** spinner.

   A hemisphere is created.

Select and Uniform
Scale

4. Pick the **Select and Uniform Scale** button from the **Scale** flyout. Holding down the [Shift] key, scale Basket01 down to 93%, as indicated in the coordinate display.

5. In the **Clone Options** dialog box that is displayed, name the copy Basket Drill and pick the **OK** button.

   A scaled down copy is created.

6. Pick the **Select and Move** and **Restrict to Y** buttons on the **Main** toolbar. Then, move Basket Drill down about three units in the Front viewport so its bottom edge extends below the bottom edge of Basket01.

7. Select Basket01. Then, pick **Create** in the **Command Panel**. Pick the **Geometry** button and select **Compound Objects** from the drop-down list. Then, pick the **Boolean** button in the **Object Type** rollout.

8. In the **Parameters** rollout, pick the **Subtraction (A-B)** radio button. In the **Pick Boolean** rollout, select the **Move** radio button. Then, select the **Pick Operand B** button and select Basket Drill. Right-click to complete the operation.

   The basket is hollowed out.

9. Pick the **Select and Rotate** and **Restrict to Z** buttons. In the Front viewport, rotate Basket01 180°.

10. Activate the Top viewport. Pick the **Select and Move** and **Restrict to X** buttons. Then, move Basket01 to the right so it is centered on the pins.

11. Pick the **Restrict to Y** button. In the Left viewport, move Basket01 up so its bottom vertically aligns with the top of Base. Pick the **Zoom Extents All** button, Figure 13-4.

12. Save the scene.

Figure 13-4. One basket is created and moved into position.

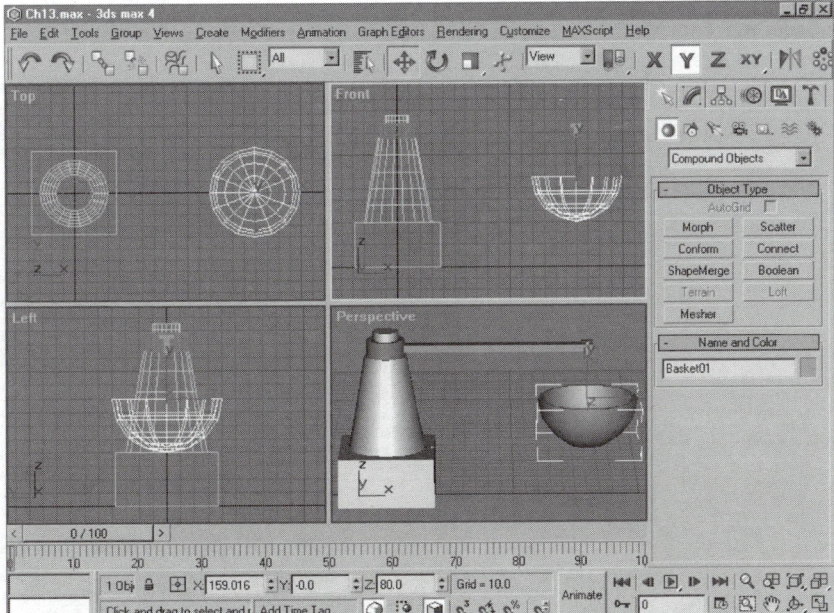

Connecting the Basket to the Arm

1. Activate the Front viewport and maximize it. Zoom in on the top of Basket01 and the part of Arm01 containing the pins.

   You may want to uncheck the **Inhibit Grid Subdivision Below Grid Spacing** check box in the **Grid and Snap Settings** dialog box.

Create

2. Pick **Create** in the **Command Panel**. Pick the **Shapes** button and select **Splines** from the drop-down list. Then, pick the **Line** button in the **Object Type** rollout. Refer to Figure 13-5 as you pick points. Pick the first point at the middle of the top-left edge of the basket, the next point at the bottom of PinA01, and the last point at the middle of the top-right edge of the basket. Right-click to end the command. In the **Name and Color** rollout, name the spline Rope Path.

Shapes

3. Pick **Create** in the **Command Panel**. Pick the **Shapes** button and select **Splines** from the drop-down list. Then, pick the **Circle** button in the **Object Type** rollout. Pick anywhere in the viewport and draw a circle of radius 1.5 units. In the **Name and Color** rollout, name the circle Rope Shape.

4. Select Rope Path. Then, pick **Create** in the **Command Panel**. Pick the **Geometry** button and select **Compound Objects** from the drop-down list. Then, pick the **Loft** button in the **Object Type** rollout. In the **Creation Method** rollout, pick the **Get Shape** button. Select Rope Shape in the viewport. In the **Name and Color** rollout, name the loft object Rope01.

   The circle is lofted along the line.

5. Display the four-viewport configuration.

6. Pick the **Select and Rotate** and **Restrict to Z** buttons on the **Main** toolbar. Activate the Top viewport. Holding down the [Shift] key, rotate Rope01 90°.

7. In the **Clone Options** dialog box that is displayed, name the copy Rope02 and pick the **OK** button.

   A rotated copy is created.

8. Select Basket01. Then, pick **Create** in the **Command Panel**. Pick the **Geometry** button and select **Compound Objects** from the drop-down list. Then, pick the **Boolean** button in the **Object Type** rollout.

Figure 13-5. The path for the rope is created.

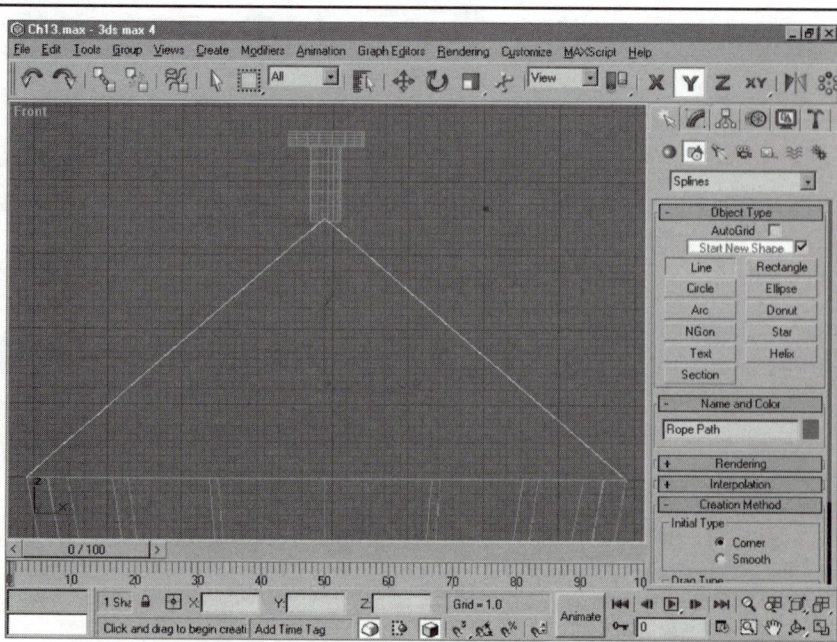

9. In the **Parameters** rollout, pick the **Union** radio button. In the **Pick Boolean** rollout, select the **Move** radio button. Then, select the **Pick Boolean B** button and select Rope01. Right-click to complete the operation.

10. In a similar manner, union Rope02 to Basket01, PinA01 to Basket01, and PinB01 to Basket01.
    The basket, the two ropes, and the two-piece rivet are now a single object, Figure 13-6.

11. Save the scene.

Cloning the Arm and the Basket

1. Select Basket01 and Arm01. Then, pick **Clone** in the **Edit** pull-down menu.

2. Pick the **OK** button in the **Clone Options** dialog box that is displayed.
   Copies of Arm01 and Basket01 are created, and the names Arm02 and Basket02 are assigned.

3. Press the spacebar to lock the selection set, which contains the copies.

4. Pick the **Select and Rotate** button on the **Main** toolbar. Also, pick the **2D Snap Toggle** button from the **Snap** flyout to turn snap on.

5. In the Top viewport, place the cursor at the center of Base (0,0,0) and pick, then rotate the selection set 90°.
   The selection set is rotated about the center of Base, which is where you picked with the cursor.

6. Clone Basket02 and Arm02, lock the selection set, and rotate the selection 90°.

7. Clone Basket03 and Arm03, lock the selection set, and rotate the selection 90°.
   There are now four arms and four baskets, Figure 13-7.

8. Save the scene.

Figure 13-6. One basket is completed.

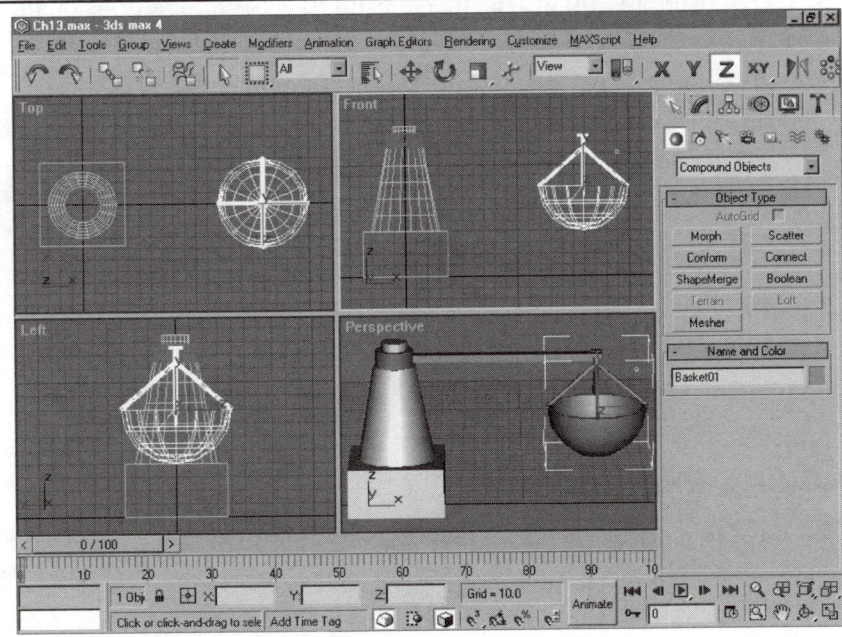

Figure 13-7. All objects are created and properly located. Now, lights and a camera can be added to the scene.

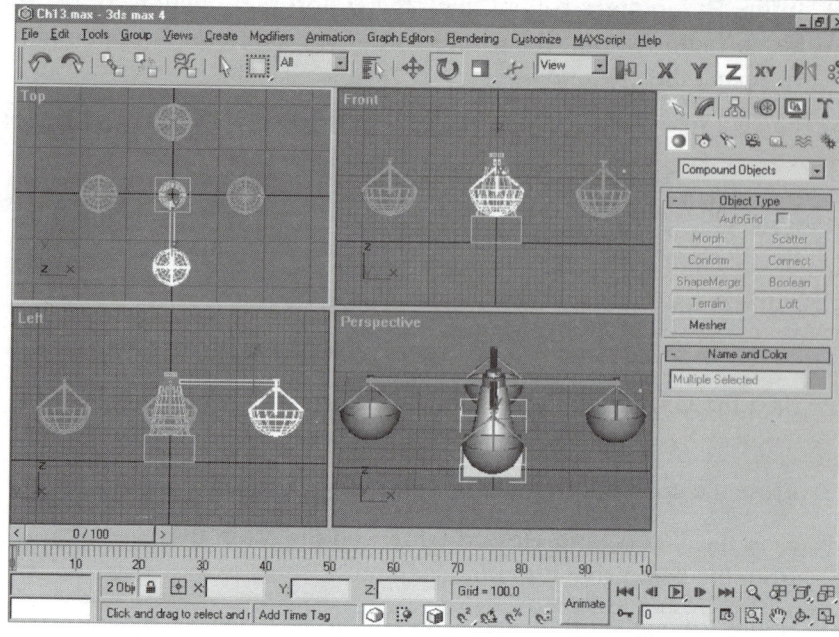

Adding Lights and a Camera to the scene

Create

Lights

Select and Move

Restrict to XY Plane

Cameras

1. Pick **Create** in the **Command Panel**. Pick the **Lights** button and select **Standard** from the drop-down list. Then, pick the **Omni** button in the **Object Type** rollout. Pick a point in the lower-left corner of the Top viewport to place an omni light. In the **General Parameters** rollout, check the **Cast Shadows** check box. Pick another point at the upper-right corner of the viewport to place another omni light. Set this light to cast shadows too. Pick the **Zoom Extents All** button. Two omni lights are placed in the scene.

2. Pick the **Select and Move** and **Restrict to XY Plane** buttons on the **Main** toolbar. In the Left viewport, move both lights up so they are at the top of the viewport.

3. Pick **Create** in the **Command Panel**. Pick the **Cameras** button and select **Standard** from the drop-down list. Then, pick the **Target** button in the **Object Type** rollout. Place the camera near the lower-left corner of the Top viewport and drag the target to the center of the objects.

4. Activate the Perspective viewport and press the [C] key to make it the camera viewport.

5. In the Front viewport, move the camera up.

6. Now, activate the camera viewport and adjust it as needed to get a good view of the scene, Figure 13-8.

7. Save the scene.

Adding the Ground

1. Activate the Top viewport. Pick **Create** in the **Command Panel**. Pick the **Geometry** button and select **Patch Grids** from the drop-down list. Then, pick the **Quad Patch** button in the **Object Type** rollout.

2. Expand the **Keyboard Entry** rollout. Type 1000 in the **Length:** spinner and 1000 in the **Width:** spinner. Then, pick the **Create** button. In the **Parameters** rollout, type 10 in the **Length Segs:** and **Width Segs:** spinners. In the **Name and Color** rollout, name the quad patch Ground. A quad patch is created in the center of the viewports.

Figure 13-8. Lights and a camera are added to the scene, and the camera viewport is adjusted.

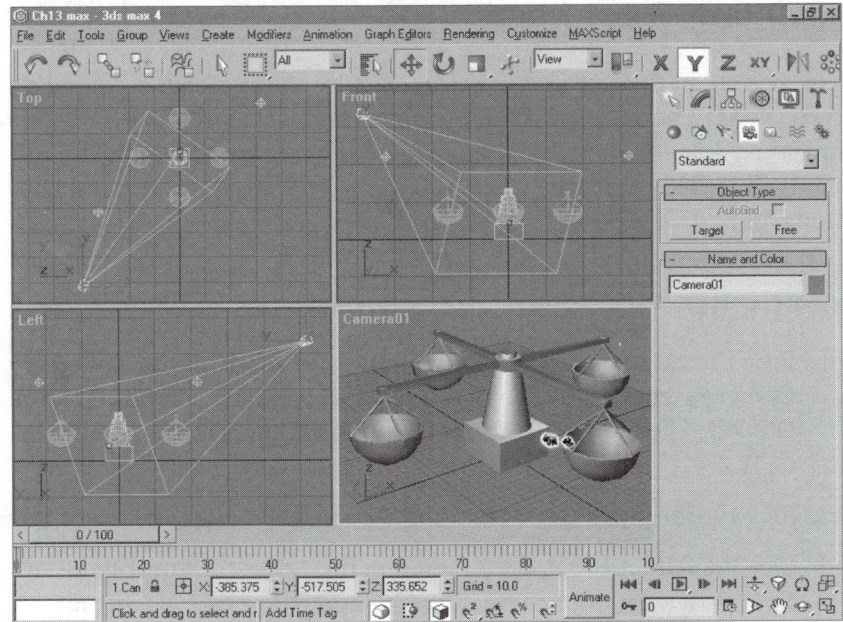

3. With Ground selected, pick **Parametric Deformers** in the **Modifiers** pull-down menu. Then, pick **Noise** in the cascading menu.
   A noise modifier is applied to the quad patch, and the **Modify** tab is automatically displayed.

4. In the **Noise:** area of the **Parameters** rollout, check the **Fractal** check box. In the **Strength:** area of the rollout, type 25 in the **Z:** spinner.

5. Save the scene.
   The basic scene is now complete.

Keyframe Animation

Now that the objects in the scene are created, you will add motion to the scene. Defining the position of the objects in the scene at key points, or *keyframes,* during the animation creates motion in the final rendering. The frames inbetween keyframes are filled in automatically by 3ds max. When the objects are at different positions on different frames, and the series of frames is played together, the objects appear to be in motion. A longer animation needs more frames. A computer typically plays frames at a rate of 30 frames per second. Therefore, an animation that is one minute long needs to be 1800 frames, or 30 frames × 60 seconds = 1800 frames.

1. Pick the **Play Animation** button.
   3ds max cycles through the default 100 frames of animation. Currently, no animation keys are created and hence, there is no movement. Notice that the **Time** slider is labeled 0/100 at frame 0, indicating the current frame and total number of frames in the animation.

Play Animation

2. Pick the **Time Configuration** button to display the **Time Configuration** dialog box.

3. Type 435 in the **Length:** spinner in the **Animation** area of the dialog box. Then, pick the **OK** button.
   The total number of frames in the animation are set to 435, which is 14.5 seconds of playback and matches the length of the sound file that will be assigned to the scene.

Time Configuration

4. Pick the **Go to Start** button to return to frame 0.
   Notice that the **Time** slider now displays 0/435, indicating the current frame and the total number of frames.

Go to Start

5. Save the scene.

Defining Pivot Points

The objects in this scene will be animated rotating about a central point. Some of the objects in the scene need to have their default pivot point relocated in order for the rotation to animate correctly. This has to be done before adding animation keys. If you have incorrectly placed an object's pivot point, you will quickly find out when you animate the object. If this happens, readjust the pivot point on frame 0.

Adjusting the First Pivot Point

Display

1. Pick **Display** in the **Command Panel**. In the **Hide by Category** rollout, check the **Lights** and **Cameras** check boxes. Also, pick the **Hide by Name...** button in the **Hide** rollout and hide Ground. Then, pick the **Zoom Extents All** button to zoom all viewports to their extents.
   Only the objects are displayed in the viewports.

Hierarchy

2. Pick **Hierarchy** in the **Command Panel**. Then, pick the **Pivot** button.

3. Pick the **Affect Pivot Only** button in the **Adjust Pivot** rollout.
   Now, move and rotate transform are applied to the object's pivot point, not the object itself.

4. Select Arm01 in the Front viewport.
   The pivot point for the object is displayed as a small tripod.

Region Zoom

5. Pick the **Region Zoom** button and drag a window around an area containing Arm01 and the center of Pole. Then, maximize the Front viewport, Figure 13-9.

6. Pick the **Select and Move** and **Restrict to X** buttons. Then, move the pivot point to the horizontal center of Pole. Pick the **Restrict to Y** button. Then, move the pivot point to the vertical center of Arm01.

7. Save the scene.

Figure 13-9. Moving the pivot point of Arm01.

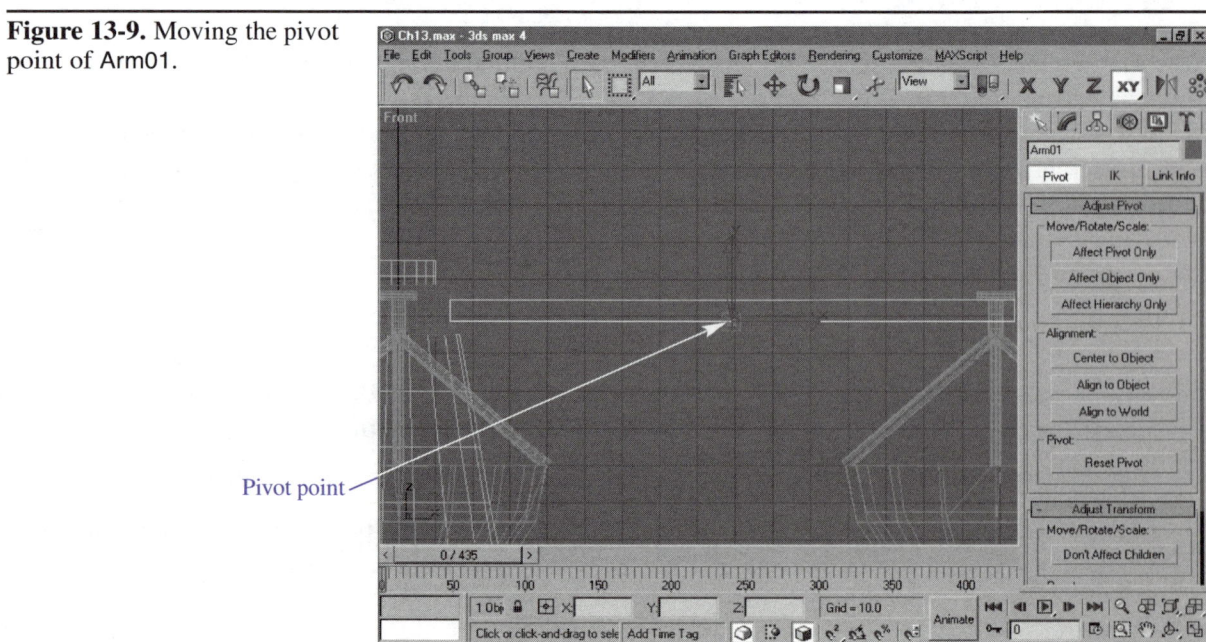

Pivot point

Adjusting the Remaining Pivot Points

1. Pan the Front viewport left so Arm03 and the center of Pole are visible. Move the pivot point of Arm03 to the horizontal center of Pole, and to the vertical center of itself.

2. Display the four-viewport configuration. Activate the Left viewport and maximize it. Zoom in so Arm04 and the center of Pole are visible.

3. Move the pivot point of Arm04 to the horizontal center of Pole, and to the vertical center of itself.

4. Pan the Left viewport left so Arm02 and the center of Pole are visible. Move the pivot point of Arm02 to the horizontal center of Pole, and to the vertical center of itself.

5. Select Basket02. Move its pivot point to the vertical center of Arm02.

6. Pan the Left viewport to the right so Basket04 is visible. Move its pivot point to the vertical center of Arm04.

7. Display the four-viewport configuration. Activate the Front viewport and maximize it. Zoom in so Basket01 and the end of Arm01 are visible. Move the pivot point of Basket01 to the vertical center of Arm01.

8. Pan the viewport left so Basket03 is visible. Move the pivot point of Basket03 to the vertical center of Arm03.

9. Display the four-viewport configuration. Then, select all objects in any viewport. Pick **Hierarchy** in the **Command Panel**. Pick the **Pivot** button in the **Adjust Pivot** rollout, and then the **Affect Pivot Only** button in the **Move/Scale/Rotate:** area of the rollout.
   These buttons should still be active from the previous operations.

10. In the **Alignment:** area of the **Adjust Pivot** rollout, pick the **Align to World** button.
    This aligns the axes of all selected pivot points to the world coordinate system. Notice the pivot points in the viewports. This is an important step when creating advanced linked hierarchies.

11. Pick the **Affect Pivot Only** button to exit pivot adjustment mode.

12. Unselect all objects. Save the scene.

Linking Objects Together

Right now, it is possible to move all objects independently. However, if you link objects to one another, the movement of one object controls the movement of a linked object. Linking creates one way links, where a child object is linked to a parent object and follows its movements. However, the parent does not follow the movement of the child object. Here, you will make the baskets child objects of the arms, and the arms child objects of the ring. This way whenever the arms move up or down, the baskets will follow the motion without having to move them individually. Also, as the ring rotates, so do the arms and baskets.

Select and Link

1. Pick the **Select and Link** button on the **Main** toolbar. Select Basket01 in the Front viewport. Pick and hold on the object, and drag the cursor to Arm01 and release.
   As you drag, a rubber band is attached to the child object and the cursor. When over a valid parent object, the cursor changes to the link cursor. When you release, both objects flash white for a second as the link is established. Basket01 is now a child of the parent Arm01.

2. Select Basket03 and link it to Arm03.
   Basket03 is now a child of Arm03.

3. In the Left viewport, select Basket02 and link it to Arm02.
   Basket02 is now a child of Arm02.

4. Select Basket04 and link it to Arm04.
   Basket04 is now a child of Arm04.

5. In the Top viewport, select Arm01, Arm02, Arm03, and Arm04. Then, pick and hold on one of the objects, and drag to Arm Ring. Release to set the link.
   All arm objects are now children of Arm Ring, and all basket objects are grandchildren of Arm Ring.

6. Pick the **Select object** button to exit link mode.

Select object

7. Save the scene.

Adjusting Link Info

Now, a linked hierarchy exists in the scene with Arm Ring as the top parent object. The arms are children of Arm Ring, and parents of the baskets. The baskets are children of the arms, and grandchildren of Arm Ring. You can fine-tune the relationship between a parent and a child. For example, you can set a child to inherit only rotation about the Y axis, or only movement along the X axis. This is one of the reasons you should always align pivot points to the world when possible.

1. Select Basket01. Then, pick **Hierarchy** in the **Command Panel**. Select the **Link Info** button next to the **Pivot** button.
   The **Locks** and **Inherit** rollouts are displayed. The **Locks** rollout is used to prevent transformation of the child on certain axes. The **Inherit** rollout determines what transforms the child inherits from the parent. These transforms override any locked transforms.

2. Think about the movement of the merry-go-round. The baskets, arms, and ring all rotate about the center of the merry-go-round. In addition, the arms move up and down as they rotate. However, the baskets should continue to "hang" straight down as the arms move. Therefore, the baskets should inherit rotation on the Z axis, and movement on the X, Y, and Z axes.

3. In the **Scale:** area of the **Inherit** rollout, uncheck the **X**, **Y**, and **Z** check boxes.
   Unchecking these check boxes means the child will not inherit any scale transformations from the parent on any axis.

4. In the **Rotate:** area of the **Inherit** rollout, uncheck the **X** and **Y** check boxes. Check the **Z** check box.
   These settings mean the child will not inherit any rotation transformations on the X and Y axes, but will inherit all rotation transformations on the Z axis.

5. In the **Movement:** area of the **Inherit** rollout, check the **X**, **Y**, and **Z** check boxes.
   These settings mean the child will inherit any movement transformation on the X, Y, and Z axes.

6. Repeat Step 3 through Step 5 for the other three basket objects.

7. Save the scene.

Animating the Objects

You will now identify keyframes for the objects. Then, you will create animation keys for the objects on the keyframes. When the animation is rendered, 3ds max fills in the movement between keyframes.

Animating the Ring

Toggle Animation Mode

1. Select Arm Ring in the Top viewport. Pick the **Toggle Animation Mode** button. Drag the **Time** slider to frame 108.

2. Pick the **Select and Rotate** and **Restrict to Z** buttons on the **Main** toolbar. Rotate Arm Ring 360°, as indicated in the coordinate display.
   Notice that two red keys now appear on the track bar, one at frame 0 and one at frame 108.

3. Move to frame 217. Rotate **Arm Ring** another 360°. Move to frame 326, and rotate Arm Ring 360° again. Finally, rotate Arm Ring 360° on frame 435.

Play Animation

4. Pick the **Toggle Animation Mode** button to exit animation mode. Pick the **Play Animation** button with the Camera01 viewport active.
   The ring rotates four complete turns over the entire length of the animation. As the ring rotates, the arms follow the ring, and the baskets follow the arms.

Stop

5. Pick the **Stop** button. Then, pick the **Go to Start** button to return to frame 0.

6. Save the scene.

Go to Start

Animating the Baskets

Currently, the baskets follow the movement of the ring as it rotates. In addition to this rotation, each basket should rotate about itself in the opposite direction. You will now add spinning motion to the baskets.

1. Select Basket01 in the Top viewport. Then, pick the **Toggle Animation Mode** button.

2. Move to frame 108. Pick the **Select and Rotate** and **Restrict to Z** buttons. Then, rotate Basket01 –360°. Select Basket02 and rotate it –360°. Select Basket03 and rotate it –360°. Finally, select Basket04 and rotate it –360°.

3. Move to frame 217. Individually, animate each basket rotating an additional –360°. Move to frame 326. Again, individually animate each basket rotating an additional –360°. Finally, move to frame 435 and rotate each basket –360°.

4. Pick the **Toggle Animation Mode** button to exit animation mode. Pick the **Play Animation** button with the Camera01 viewport active.
   As the baskets follow the rotation of the ring, each one rotates about its own center in the opposite direction.

5. Pick the **Stop** button. Then, pick the **Go to Start** button to return to frame 0.

6. Save the scene.

Animating the Arms

The arms are the last objects that need to be animated. Currently, they follow the rotation of the ring. In addition to this rotation, each arm needs to rotate up and down as it revolves around the center.

Use Pivot Point Center

1. Pick the **Use Pivot Point Center** button from the transform coordinate center flyout on the **Main** toolbar. Also, select **Parent** from the coordinate system drop-down list next to the transform coordinate center flyout.

2. Select Arm01. Press the spacebar to lock the selection set.

3. Activate the Front viewport. Pick the **Select and Rotate** and **Restrict to Y** buttons on the **Main** toolbar.

4. Refer to Figure 13-10. Move to the first keyframe and pick the **Toggle Animation Mode** button to enter animation mode. Rotate Arm01 the number of degrees specified in Figure 13-10. Continue placing animation keys on the keyframes specified in the figure.

5. Press the spacebar to unlock the selection set. Select Arm02 and lock the selection set. Pick the **Restrict to X** button on the **Main** toolbar. Move to the first keyframe for Arm02 and rotate the object the number of degrees specified in Figure 13-10. Continue adding the keys on the keyframes indicated in the figure.

6. Press the spacebar to unlock the selection set. Select Arm03 and lock the selection set. Pick the **Restrict to Y** button on the **Main** toolbar. Add the keys on the keyframes indicated in Figure 13-10 for Arm03.

7. Press the spacebar to unlock the selection set. Select Arm04 and lock the selection set. Pick the **Restrict to X** button on the **Main** toolbar. Add the keys on the keyframes indicated in Figure 13-10 for Arm04. Unlock the selection set.

8. Pick the **Toggle Animation Mode** button to exit animation mode. Move to frame 0.

9. Pick the **Play Animation** button with the Camera01 viewport active.
   The arms opposite each other should move up at the same time and down at the same time. The baskets should remain "attached" to the ends of the arms throughout the animation.

10. Pick the **Stop** button and return to frame 0.

11. Save the scene.

Adjusting Track Info

The **Track View** function of 3ds max stores all animation information for the scene. The animation keys for each object are displayed. These keys can be deleted, copied, or moved. You will use **Track View** to modify the animation.

Currently, the arms rotate up and down in a regular pattern as they rotate about the center. Using **Track View**, you will change the animation so the arms move to their first position (up or down), hold that position for a number of frames, and then continue with the regular pattern of motion.

Figure 13-10. Use this chart to set animation keys for the four arms. Make sure you rotate the arm about the correct parent axis.

Keyframe	Degrees of Rotation (Parent Axis)			
	Arm01 (Y)	Arm02 (X)	Arm03 (Y)	Arm04 (X)
0	0	0	0	0
27	10	10	−10	−10
54	−10	−10	10	10
81	−10	−10	10	10
108	10	10	−10	−10
135	10	10	−10	−10
163	−10	−10	10	10
190	−10	−10	10	10
217	10	10	−10	−10
244	10	10	−10	−10
272	−10	−10	10	10
298	−10	−10	10	10
326	10	10	−10	−10
353	10	10	−10	−10
381	−10	−10	10	10
407	−10	−10	10	10
435	10	10	−10	−10

Removing Keys

1. Pick the **Open Track View** button on the **Main** toolbar.

   Track View is displayed floating on top of the viewports, Figure 13-11. You can maximize the display if needed.

2. Pick the plus sign (+) next to **Objects** to expand that branch.

   The names of all top level objects in the scene are displayed.

3. Pick the plus sign in the box next to **Arm Ring** to expand the parent-child hierarchy.

   The four arm objects are listed below **Arm Ring**.

4. Pick the plus sign in the circle next to **Arm01**, **Arm02**, **Arm03**, and **Arm04**.

   The hierarchy for each arm object, not including its children, is displayed.

5. Pick the plus sign in the circle next to **Transform** for each arm object.

   Tracks for the three transforms (move, rotate, scale) are displayed for each arm object. Notice that the rotation tracks have keys set in the right-hand edit window, Figure 13-12.

6. Pick the **Move Keys** button at the top of **Track View**.

   This button allows you to select and move keys.

7. In the **Rotation** track for Arm01, select the key on frame 27. A selected key is white and an unselected key is dark grey.

   The frame number of the selected key appears in the left-hand text box at the bottom of the edit window. Also, the ruler along the bottom of the edit window indicates the frames of the animation.

8. Press the [Delete] keyboard key to remove the animation key. Select the key on frame 54, and on frames 108 through 190. Use the [Ctrl] key to select multiple animation keys. Delete the selected keys.

   Do not delete the key on frame 81.

9. Repeat Steps 7 and 8 for Arm02, Arm03, and Arm04.

   The regular pattern of movement for the arms is removed at the beginning of the animation. If you minimize **Track View** and play the animation, you can see the effect.

10. Save the scene.

Figure 13-11. Track View is used to adjust animation keys.

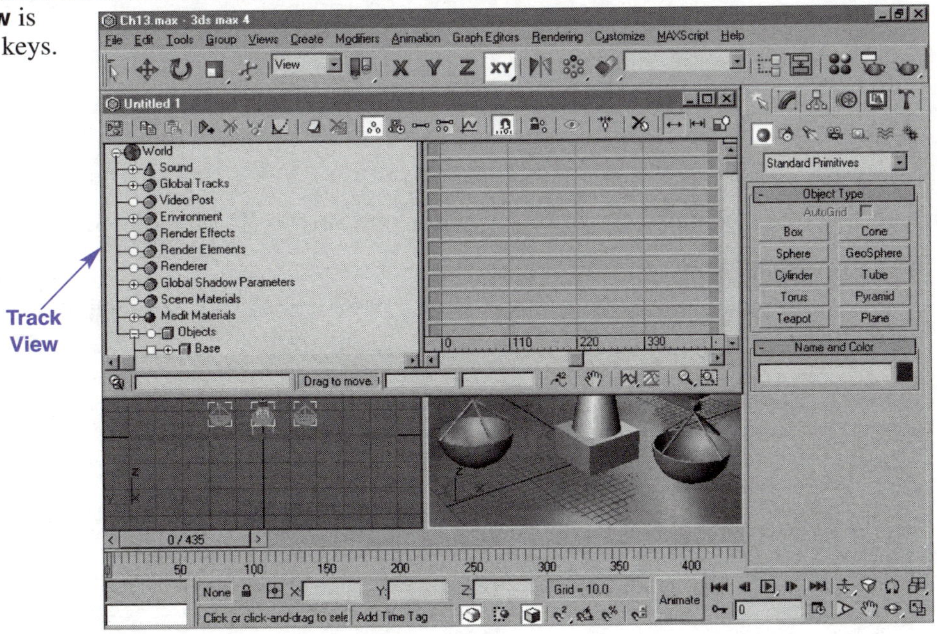

Figure 13-12. Animation keys appear in the rotation tracks for each of the arm objects.

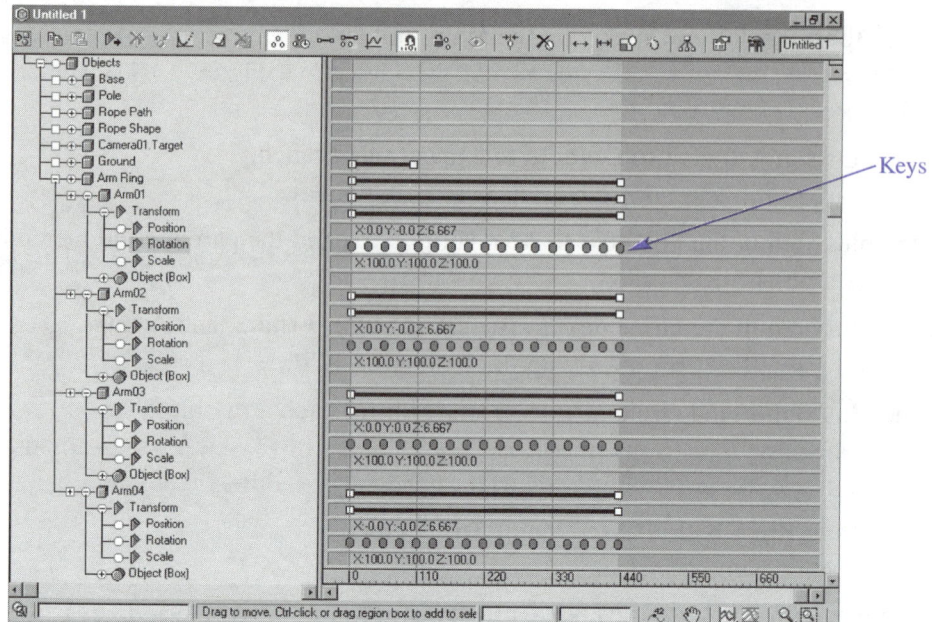

Moving and Copying Keys

Currently, the arms gradually move to their new first position, on frame 81, and gradually move to their new second position, on frame 217. The regular pattern of motion originally defined then continues through the rest of the animation. You will now change the animation so the arms move to their first position sooner, hold that position for a number of frames, and then move to their second position. This is done by moving and copying keys.

1. Open **Track View**, if it is not already open.

2. Expand the hierarchy to show the rotation track for Arm01, Arm02, Arm03, and Arm04.

3. In the rotation track for Arm01, select the key on frame 81. Pick the **Move Keys** button on the **Track View** toolbar. Then, drag the key to the left to reposition it on frame 40.
   The left-hand text box at the bottom of the edit window displays the frame number of the key.

4. Hold down the [Shift] keyboard key and move the animation key, now on frame 40, to frame 180 to place a copy of the animation key on that frame.
   The animation key copied to frame 180 has the same values as the key on frame 40. Since these two keys are the same, the arm will move to its first position on frame 40, hold that position to frame 180, and then move to its second position on frame 217 (the next existing key).

5. Repeat Steps 3 and 4 for Arm02, Arm03, and Arm04, Figure 13-13.

6. Close **Track View** and save the scene.
   If you play the animation in the Camera01 viewport, you can see how the regular motion at the beginning of the animation is replaced with the motion you just defined.

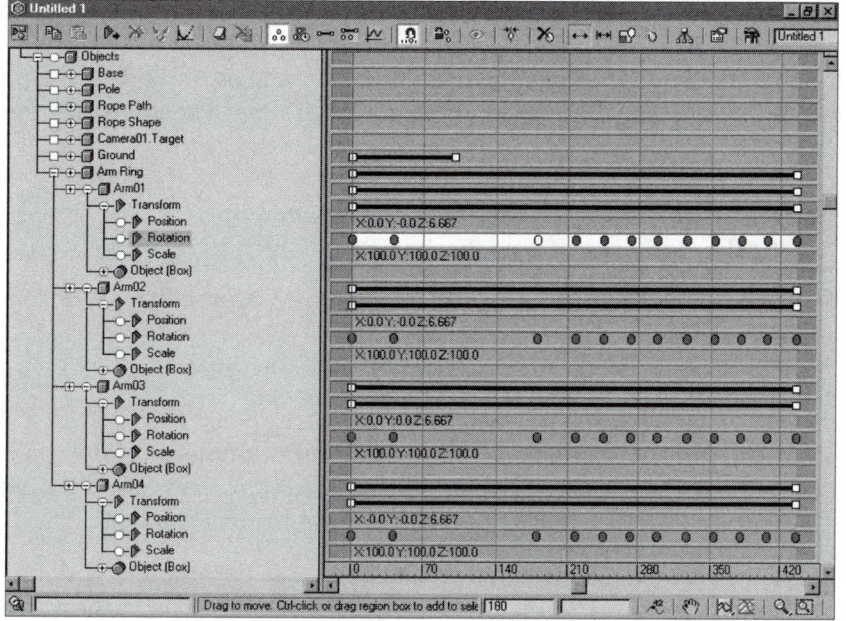

Figure 13-13. Animation keys have been adjusted for the arm objects.

Adding Sound to the Animation

You can also add a sound file to an animation using **Track View**. You will now set up your animation to play one of the sound files that comes with 3ds max. At the beginning of the tutorial, you set the number of frames to 435 so the animation matches the length of the sound file you will use.

1. Pick the **Open Track View** button on the **Main** toolbar.
   Track View is displayed floating on top of the viewports.

Open Track View

2. At the top of the hierarchy, select the **Sound** branch so it is highlighted. Right-click on it to display a shortcut menu, and select **Properties** from the menu.
   The **Sound Options** dialog box is displayed, Figure 13-14.

3. Pick the **Choose Sound** button to display the **Open Sound** dialog box.

4. Navigate to the 3ds max \sounds folder. Then, open the file Tutdrum.wav from the folder.
   The **Audio** area of the **Sound Options** dialog box indicates the sound file you added.

5. Pick the **OK** button in the **Sound Options** dialog box to return to the **Track View**.

6. Expand the **Sound** branch. You can now see the waveform of the sound file in the edit window.

7. Close **Track View** and save the scene.

Figure 13-14. The **Sound Options** dialog box, opened through **Track View**, is used to add sound to the animation.

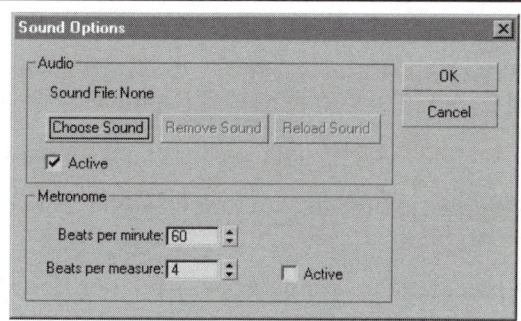

Rendering the Animation

If you want to quickly verify an animation, you can create and view a preview of it. This is a low-color, low-resolution animation and can save a lot of time. Then, create a final rendering of the animation.

Render Scene

1. Make the Camera01 viewport current.

2. Pick the **Render Scene** button on the **Main** toolbar.
   The **Render** dialog box is displayed.

3. In the **Time Output** area of the **Common Parameters** rollout, pick the **Active Time Segment** radio button.
   This specifies that all frames in the current time segment, frame 0 to frame 435, should be rendered in the final animation.

4. In the **Output Size** area of the **Common Parameters** rollout, pick the **320x240** button.
   This sets the size of the final rendering to 320 pixels wide by 240 pixels tall. This smaller size takes less time to render, and the final file is much smaller.

5. In the **Render Output** area of the **Common Parameters** rollout, pick the **Files...** button. In the **Render Output File** dialog box that appears, navigate to the folder of your choice, name the file Ch13.avi, and pick the **Save** button.
   If a "configuration" dialog box appears, pick the **OK** button to accept the default.

6. Pick the **Render** button at the bottom of the **Render Scene** dialog box.
   The render window and **Rendering** dialog box appear. The **Rendering** dialog box shows the progress, and the current frame is rendered in the render window.

7. When the rendering is complete, the **Rendering** dialog box automatically closes. Then, close the render window and the **Render Scene** dialog box.

8. Pick **View Image File...** from the **File** pull-down menu. In the **View File** dialog box that appears, navigate to the folder where Ch13.avi is saved and select the file.
   The animation is played in Windows Media Player. The sound file is incorporated into the animation, and is played during animation playback.

9. Close Media Player and save the scene.

Self-Evaluation Test

Answer the following questions. Then, compare your answers with the correct answers given at the end of this chapter.

1. An animation is created by defining _____ in the scene on certain frames, called _____.

2. To increase the length of the animation, you need to _____ the number of frames.

3. Transforms, such as rotation, can be applied in an animation with respect to an object's _____ point.

4. When you select the _____ button in the **Adjust Pivot** rollout in the **Hierarchy** tab of the **Command Panel**, transformations are applied to the object's pivot point.

5. The _____ function of 3ds max stores all animation information for the scene.

6. You can copy an animation key to a different position in a track by holding the _____ key and moving the key in the track.

7. _____ is a process of creating one-way relationships between children and parent objects.

8. To control the motion of linked objects, you can adjust their _____ using link info.

9. It is possible to associate a sound file with an animation using the _____ dialog box, which is opened through **Track View**.

10. A _____ animation is a low-color, low-resolution rendering.

Exercises

Exercise 13-1

Open Ch06.max *saved in Chapter 6. This scene consists of a fan with three blades. Save the scene as* Ex13-01.max *in the folder of you choice. Animate the fan as follows.*

1. Set the animation length to 80 frames.

2. Move the pivot points of objects as necessary. The fan blades, connecting pieces, and hub should all rotate about the center of the rod.

3. Link the blades to the connectors, and the connectors to the hub. Set inheritance as needed.

4. Animate the hub through 360° of rotation on frame 80.

5. Add a sound file to the animation.

6. Render the animation to a file named Ex13-01.avi in the folder of your choice. Save the scene.

Exercise 13-2

Create the cardboard box shown below. The box should have three flaps that fold to create the lid. Create materials and assign them as needed. You can use a bump map to simulate corrugated cardboard if you like. Save the scene as Ex13-02.max *in the folder of your choice. Then, animate the box as follows.*

1. Set the animation length to 80 frames.

2. Move pivot points as necessary so the flaps rotate correctly. Then, close the box on frame 0.

3. Move to frame 80. Animate all three flaps open (120° of rotation).

4. Using **Track View**, move, copy, and delete keys as needed so the top flap fully opens first, then one side flap opens, and finally the other side flap opens.

5. Render the animation to a file named Ex13-02.avi in the folder of your choice. Save the scene.

Answers

The following are the correct answers to the questions in the Self-Evaluation Test.

1. keys, keyframes; 2. increase; 3. pivot; 4. **Affect Pivot Only**; 5. **Track View**; 6. [Shift]; 7. Linking; 8. inheritance; 9. **Sound Options**; 10. preview.

Chapter 14

Complex Animation

Learning Objectives

After completing this chapter, you will be able to:

○ Create dummy objects.
○ Use dummy objects to create an animation.
○ Create snapshot objects.
○ Hide objects during animations.
○ Animate cameras.

Tutorial Description

In this tutorial, you will create a scene of a dartboard on a wall with a dart-arrow stuck in it. During the animation, the dartboard moves up and is hung on the wall. The arrow then flies out of the board, and back into the board after a period of frames. While the arrow is out of the board, the wall (with dartboard attached) rotates around its vertical axis.

You will create dummy objects to assist in movement during the animation process. You will link objects as children to parent objects. You will also create snapshots of objects. These can be linked to different parent objects. Finally, you will use **Track View** to adjust the visibility of objects during the animation.

Creating the Scene

You will first create the dartboard, then the wall, and finally the arrow stuck in the dartboard. You will also create a floor on which the wall sits.

1. Reset 3ds max.

2. Activate the Front viewport. Pick **Create** in the **Command Panel**. Pick the **Geometry** button and select **Standard Primitives** from the drop-down list. Then, pick the **Cylinder** button in the **Object Type** rollout.

Create

Geometry

3. Expand the **Keyboard Entry** rollout. Type 60 in the **Radius:** spinner and 5 in the **Height:** spinner. Then, pick the **Create** button. In the **Name and Color** rollout, name the cylinder Dartboard.
   A cylinder is created in the center of the viewports.

4. Activate the Top viewport. Pick **Create** in the **Command Panel**. Pick the **Geometry** button and select **Standard Primitives** from the drop-down list. Then, pick the **Box** button in the **Object Type** rollout.

5. Expand the **Keyboard Entry** rollout. Type 15 in the **Length:** spinner, 260 in the **Width:** spinner, and 400 in the **Height:** spinner. Then, pick the **Create** button. In the **Name and Color** rollout, name the box Wall.
   A box is created in the center of the viewports.

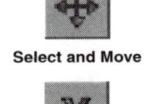

Select and Move

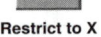

Restrict to X

6. Select Dartboard. Then, pick the **Select and Move** and **Restrict to X** buttons on the **Main**. Move Dartboard to the left in the Front viewport so its right edge is 10 units to the left of the wall's left edge.

7. Pick the **Restrict to Y** button. Move Dartboard down in the Top viewport so its upper edge aligns with the bottom edge of Wall.

8. Move Dartboard up in the Front viewport so its bottom edge is 40 units above the bottom edge of Wall, Figure 14-1.

9. Save the scene as Ch14.max in the folder of your choice.

Drawing the Dart

Zoom Extents All Selected

1. With Dartboard selected, pick the **Zoom Extents All Selected** button to zoom to the extents of the selected object.

2. Activate the Front viewport. Then, pick **Create** in the **Command Panel**. Pick the **Geometry** button and select **Standard Primitives** from the drop-down list. Then, pick the **Cone** button in the **Object Type** rollout.

Figure 14-1. The wall and dartboard are created.

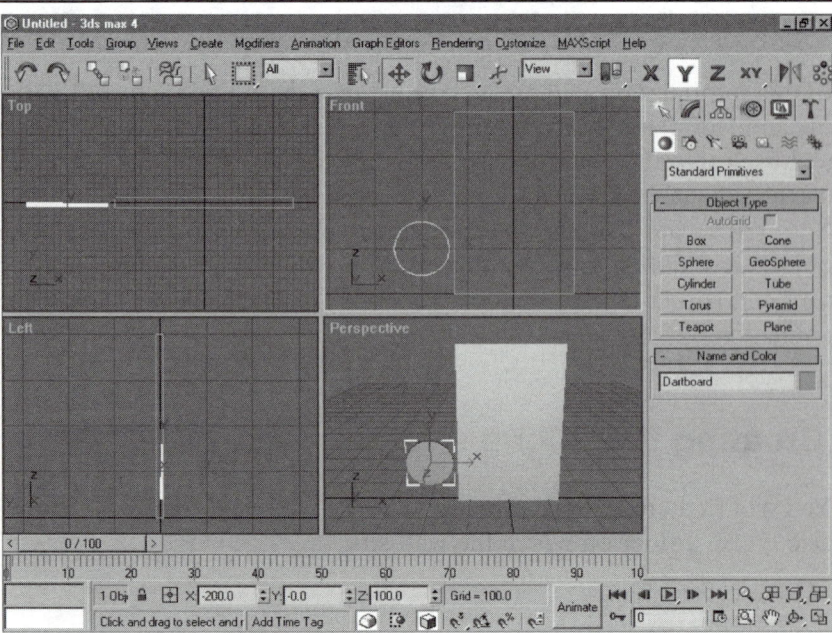

3. Turn on snap. Then, pick a point in the center of Dartboard. Drag to set the first radius and pick. Move the mouse to set the height and pick. Finally, move the mouse and pick to set the second radius. Now, in the **Parameters** rollout, type 4 in the **Radius 1:** spinner, 0 in the **Radius 2:** spinner, and −10 in the **Height:** spinner. In the **Name and Color** rollout, name the cone Dart Head. A cone is created.

4. Pick **Create** in the **Command Panel**. Pick the **Geometry** button and select **Standard Primitives** from the drop-down list. Then, pick the **Cylinder** button in the **Object Type** rollout.

5. Pick at the center of Dartboard, drag, and release to set the radius of the cylinder. Move the mouse and pick to set the height of the cylinder. Then, in the **Parameters** rollout, type 1.2 in the **Radius:** spinner and 50 in the **Height:** spinner. In the **Name and Color** rollout, name the cylinder Dart Shaft. A cylinder is created.

Select and Move

6. Activate the Top viewport and turn snap off. Pick the **Select and Move** and **Restrict to Y** buttons on the **Main** toolbar. Select Dart Head. Hold down the [Shift] key and move Dart Head down so the tip of the cone touches the opposite end of the cylinder. In the **Clone Options** dialog box that appears, name the copy Dart Feathers and pick the **OK** button. A copy is created at the end of the cylinder, Figure 14-2.

Restrict to Y

7. With Dart Feathers selected, pick **Modify** in the **Command Panel**. In the **Parameters** rollout, type 8 in the **Radius 1:** spinner and −15 in the **Height:** spinner. The tip of the cone should now overlap the cylinder.

Modify

8. With Dart Feathers selected, pick **Create** in the **Command Panel**. Pick the **Geometry** button and select **Compound** objects from the drop-down list. Then, pick the **Boolean** button in the **Object Type** rollout.

Create

9. In the **Operation** area of the **Parameters** rollout, pick the **Union** radio button. In the **Pick Boolean** rollout, select the **Move** radio button. Then, select the **Pick Boolean B** button and select Dart Shaft. Right-click to complete the operation. In the **Name and Color** rollout, rename the object Dart.

Geometry

10. With Dart selected, pick **Create** in the **Command Panel**. Pick the **Geometry** button and select **Compound** objects from the drop-down list. Then, pick the **Boolean** button in the **Object Type** rollout.

Figure 14-2. The dart is created. The feathers need to be scaled.

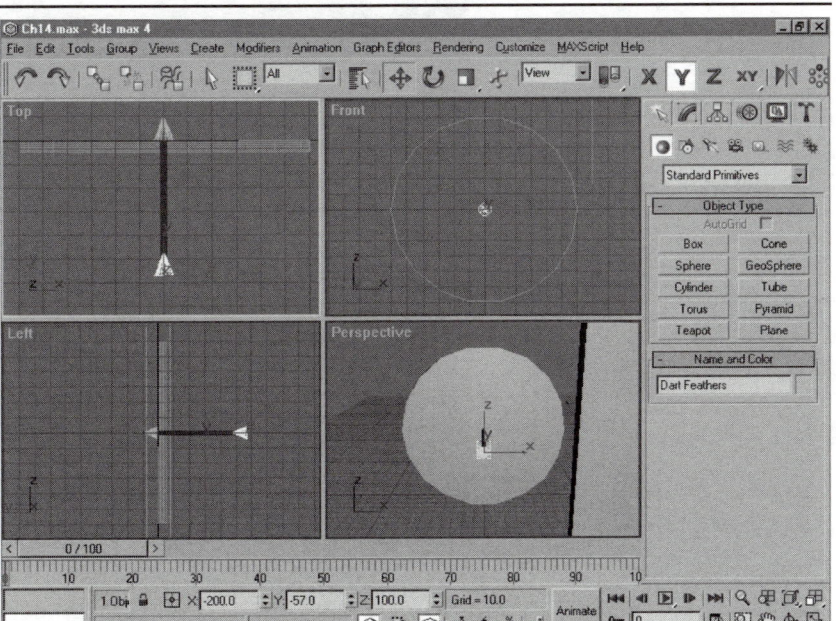

11. In the **Operation** area of the **Parameters** rollout, pick the **Union** radio button. In the **Pick Boolean** rollout, select the **Move** radio button. Then, select the **Pick Boolean B** button and select Dart Head. Right-click to complete the operation.
    The dart is now a single object.

Zoom Extents All

12. In the Top viewport, move Dart straight down so its tip overlaps Dartboard by about two units. Pick the **Zoom Extents All** button, Figure 14-3.

13. Save the scene.

Drawing the Floor

1. Activate the Top viewport.

2. Pick **Create** in the **Command Panel**. Pick the **Geometry** button and select **Patch Grids** from the drop-down list. Then, pick the **Quad Patch** button in the **Object Type** rollout.

3. Expand the **Keyboard Entry** rollout.

4. Type 1000 in the **Length:** and **Width:** spinners. Then, pick the **Create** button.
   A quad patch is created in the center of the viewports, which is the floor.

5. In the **Name and Color** rollout, name the quad patch Floor.

6. Pick the **Zoom Extents All** button. Save the scene.

Creating a New Material Library

Material Editor

1. Pick the **Material Editor** button on the **Main** toolbar.
   The **Material Editor** is displayed.

Get Material

2. Pick the **Get Material** button below the material samples.
   The **Material/Map Browser** is displayed.

Figure 14-3. The objects are created and properly placed. A floor needs to be created.

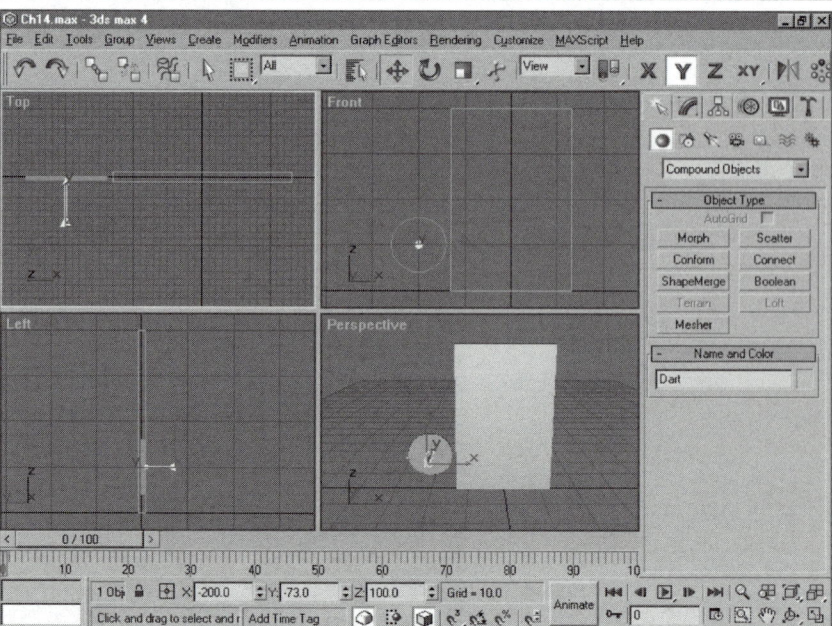

3. In the **Browse From:** area of the **Material/Map Browser**, pick the **Mtl Library** radio button. Then, pick the **Clear Material Library** button to clear the current library.
   In the warning dialog box that appears, pick the **Yes** button.

Clear Material Library

4. In the **File** area of the **Material/Map Browser**, pick the **Save As...** button. In the **Save Material Library** dialog box that appears, name the library Dartboard.mat and save it in the folder of your choice.

5. Close the **Material/Map Browser**.

6. Save the scene.

Defining the Dartboard Material

1. Select the first unused material sample slot in the **Material Editor**. Pick in the drop-down list text box below the material samples and name the material Dartboard Material.

2. Expand the **Maps** rollout. Pick the button in the **Diffuse Color** row currently labeled **None** in the **Map** column.
   The **Material/Map Browser** is displayed.

3. In the **Browse From:** area of the **Material/Map Browser**, pick the **New** radio button. Then, select **Checker** in the list and pick the **OK** button.
   A checkerboard map is applied as a diffuse color map.

4. At the diffuse color map level of the material tree, name the map Dartboard Map. Then, in the **Checker Parameters** rollout, pick the **Color #2:** color swatch, which is currently white. In the color selector dialog box that appears, change the color to R255, G125, and B125. Then, close the color selector. Leave the **Color #1:** color swatch black.

5. Pick Dartboard Material from the drop-down list to return to the parent material level of the material tree.

6. Assign the material to Dartboard.

7. Select Dartboard, then pick **UV Coordinates** in the **Modifiers** pull-down menu. Select **UVW Map** from the cascading menu.
   A UVW map modifier is applied to the dartboard, and the **Modify** tab is automatically displayed.

8. Pick the **Fit** button in the **Alignment:** area of the **Parameters** rollout. In the **Mapping:** area of the rollout, pick the **Spherical** radio button. Also, type 18 in the **U Tile:** spinner and 3 in the **V Tile:** spinner.

9. Save the scene.

Defining the Wall Material

1. Select the next unused sample slot in the **Material Editor**. Pick in the drop-down list text box below the material samples and name the material Wall Material.

2. Expand the **Maps** rollout and pick the button in the **Diffuse Color** row currently labeled **None** in the **Map** column.
   The **Material/Map Browser** is displayed.

3. In the **Browse From:** area of the **Material/Map Browser**, pick the **New** radio button. Then, select **Bitmap** in the list and pick the **OK** button. In the **Select Bitmap Image File** dialog box that appears, navigate to the 3ds max \Maps\Wood folder. Open the file Whtplank.jpg from the folder.

4. At the diffuse color map level of the material tree, name the map Wall Map. Then, pick Wall Material from the drop-down list to return to the parent material level.

5. Assign the material to Wall.

6. Select Wall. Then, pick **UV Coordinates** in the **Modifiers** pull-down menu. Select **UVW Map** from the cascading menu.
   A UVW map modifier is applied to the wall, and the **Modify** tab is automatically displayed.

7. In the **Mapping:** area of the **Parameters** rollout, pick the **Box** radio button. Also, type 2 in the **U Tile:** spinner. Then, in the **Alignment:** area of the rollout, pick the **Fit** button.

8. Save the scene.

Defining the Dart Material

1. Activate the next unused sample slot. Pick in the drop-down list text box below the material samples and name the material Dart Material.

2. Expand the **Maps** rollout. Then, pick the button in the **Diffuse Color** row currently labeled **None** in the **Map** column.
   The **Material/Map Browser** is displayed.

3. In the **Browse From:** area, pick the **New** radio button. The, select **Bitmap** in the list and pick the **OK** button. In the **Select Bitmap Image File** dialog box that appears, navigate to the 3ds max \Maps\Metal folder. Then, open the file Goldfoil.gif from the folder.

4. At the diffuse color map level of the material tree, name the map Dart Map. Then, pick Dart Material from the drop-down list to return to the parent material level.

5. Apply the material to Dart.

6. Select Dart. Then, pick **UV Coordinates** from the **Modifiers** pull-down menu. Select **UVW Map** from the cascading menu.
   A UVW map modifier is applied to the dart, and the **Modify** tab is automatically displayed.

7. In the **Mapping:** area of the **Parameters** rollout, pick the **Cylindrical** radio button and check the **Cap** check box. In the **Alignment:** area of the rollout, pick the **Fit** button.

8. Save the scene.

Defining the Floor Material

1. Activate the next unused sample slot in the **Material Editor**. Pick in the drop-down list text box below the material samples and name the material Floor Material.

2. Expand the **Maps** rollout. Pick the button in the **Diffuse Color** row currently labeled **None** in the **Map** column.
   The **Material/Map Browser** is displayed.

3. In the **Browse From:** area, pick the **New** radio button. Then, select **Bitmap** in the list and pick the **OK** button. In the **Select Bitmap Image File** dialog box that is displayed, navigate to the 3ds max \Maps\Fabric folder. Open the file Carpttan.jpg from the folder.

4. At the diffuse color map level of the material tree, name the map Floor Map. Then, pick Floor Material from the drop-down list to return to the parent material level.

5. Apply the material to Floor.

6. Select Floor. Then, pick **UV Coordinates** in the **Modifiers** pull-down menu. Pick **UVW Map** from the cascading menu.
   A UVW map modifier is applied to the floor, and the **Modify** tab is automatically displayed.

7. In the **Mapping:** area of the **Parameters** rollout, pick the **Planar** radio button. Also, type 3 in the **U Tile:** and **V Tile:** spinners. In the **Alignment:** area, pick the **Fit** button.

8. Save the scene.

Setting the Background

1. Pick **Environment...** from the **Rendering** pull-down menu.
   The **Environment** dialog box is displayed.

2. In the **Background:** area of the **Common Parameters** rollout, pick the **Color:** color swatch.
   The color selector dialog box is displayed.

3. Set the color to R0, G200, B255. Close the color selector dialog box.

4. Close the **Environment** dialog box.

5. Save the scene.

Adding Lights and a Camera

1. Pick **Create** in the **Command Panel**. Pick the **Lights** button and select **Standard** from the drop-down list. Then, pick the **Omni** button in the **Object Type** rollout.

Create

Lights

2. Pick a point at the lower-right corner of the Top viewport to place an omni light. Pick the **Zoom Extents All** button.

3. Pick **Select and Move** and **Restrict to XY Plane** buttons on the **Main** toolbar. Move the omni light up in the Front viewport so it is at the top of the viewport.

4. Pick **Create** in the **Command Panel**. Pick the **Lights** button and select **Standard** from the drop-down list. Then, pick the **Target Spot** button in the **Object Type** rollout.

5. Pick a point in the lower-left corner of the Top viewport to place the light, and drag to the middle of the door to place the target.

6. In the Front viewport, move the spotlight target down so it is in the center of the door. Also, move the spotlight up so it is about level with the omni light.

7. With the spotlight (not target) selected, pick **Modify** in the **Command Panel**. Then, in the **General Parameters** rollout, check the **Cast Shadows** check box.

Create

Cameras

8. Pick **Create** in the **Command Panel**. Pick the **Cameras** button and select **Standard** from the drop-down list. Then, pick the **Target** button in the **Object Type** rollout. Pick a point at the lower-left corner of the Top viewport to place the camera, and drag the target to the center of the objects.

9. Activate the Perspective viewport. Then, press [C] to make it the Camera01 viewport.

10. Adjust the camera viewport as needed to get a good view of the objects, Figure 14-4.

11. Save the scene.

Figure 14-4. The floor is created, and lights and a camera are added to the scene. The camera viewport is adjusted to get a good view of the objects.

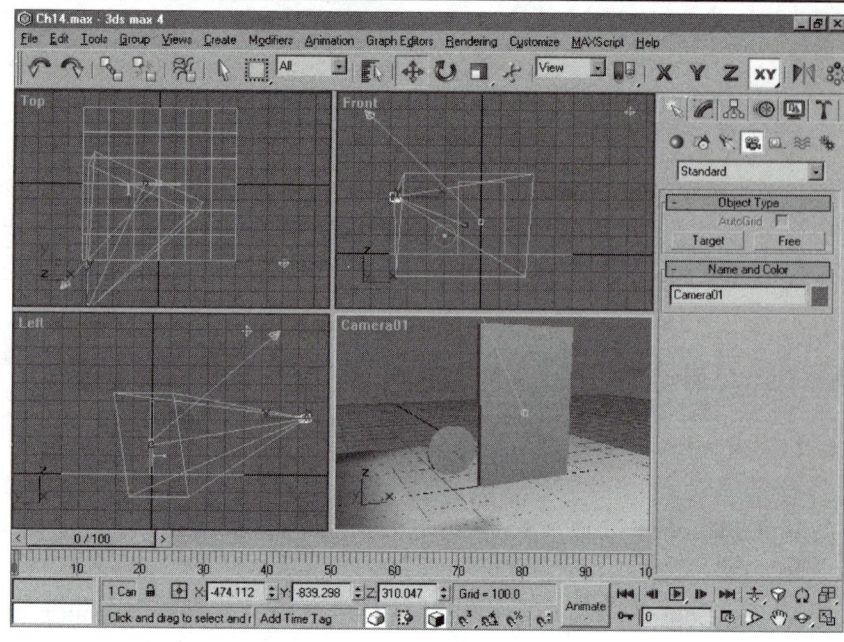

Dummy Objects

Dummy objects are cubes that are not rendered in the final scene. They are typically linked to objects as the parent, and are used to help animate the child objects. When several objects are linked to a single dummy object, the dummy can be used to move all the linked objects simultaneously.

Time Configuration

1. Pick the **Time Configuration** button to display the **Time Configuration** dialog box.

2. In the **Animation** area of the dialog box, type 150 in the **Length:** spinner. Then, pick the **OK** button to close the dialog box.
   The length of the animation is set to 150 frames.

3. Pick **Create** in the **Command Panel**. Pick the **Helpers** button and select **Standard** from the drop-down list. Then, pick the **Dummy** button in the **Object Type** rollout.
   There are no rollouts for a dummy object, other than the **Name and Color** rollout.

Create

Helpers

4. Activate the Front viewport. Pick below Dartboard and drag the cursor to create a small cube.
   The size of the dummy is not important. Make the dummy large enough to select, yet not so large that it interferes with the selection of other objects in the scene.

5. In the **Name and Color** rollout, name the dummy Dart Dummy.

6. Pick below Wall and drag the cursor to create another dummy. In the **Name and Color** rollout, name the dummy Wall Dummy, Figure 14-5.

7. Save the scene.

Linking Objects

Linking more than one object to a dummy can simplify the animation process. You can also individually move the linked objects, if needed.

Select and Link

1. Pick the **Select and Link** button. Then, select Dartboard and link it to **Dart Dummy**.
   Dartboard becomes a child of the dummy object. Dartboard will now follow the movement of Dart Dummy.

Figure 14-5. Two dummy objects are added to the scene.

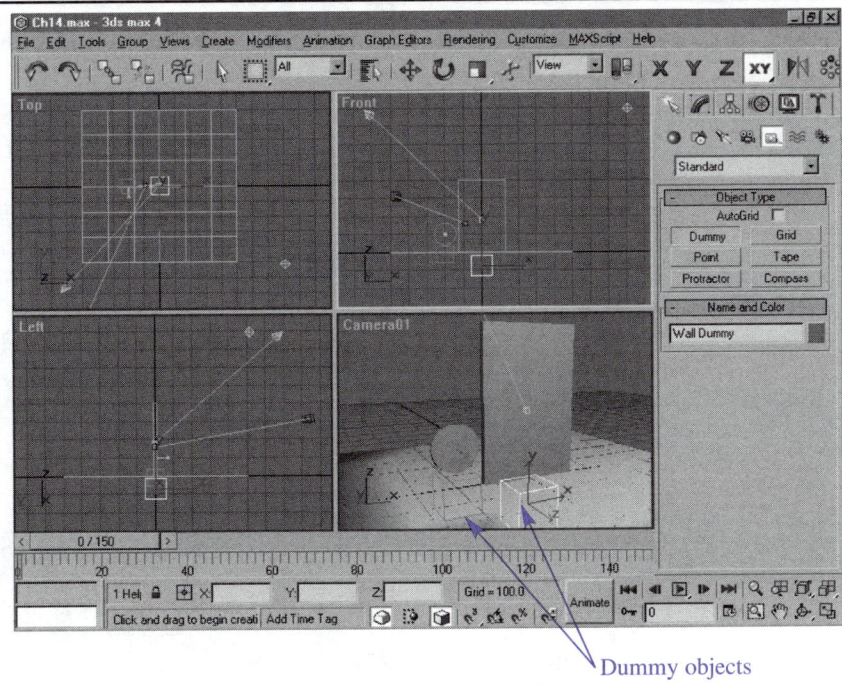

Dummy objects

2. Select Dart. Then, link it to Dart Dummy.
   Dart also becomes a child of the dummy.

3. Select Wall. Then, link it to **Wall Dummy**.
   Wall becomes a child object of the dummy.

4. Pick the **Select object** button, then save the scene.

Setting Animation Defaults

You can control the transition into and out of animation keys. This determines if the motion "floats" and is organic, or is quicker and more mechanical. The transition can be set individually for each key after the keys are created. You can also set default values before creating keys.

1. Select **Preferences...** from the **Customize** pull-down menu to display the **Preference Settings** dialog box. Select the **Animation** tab in the dialog box, Figure 14-6.

2. In the **Controller Defaults** area of the dialog box, select the **Set Defaults...** button to display the **Set Controller Defaults** dialog box, Figure 14-7.

3. Select **Bezier Position** from the list and pick the **Set...** button to display the **Bezier Default Key Values** dialog box.
   This is the default controller applied to movement animations.

4. Pick the left-hand image tile and select the square curve. Also, set the right-hand image tile to the square curve.
   This sets transitions to be more mechanical for all controllers that use Bézier curves.

5. Pick the **OK** button in the **Set Controller Defaults** dialog box to close it. Also, pick the **OK** button in the **Preference Settings** dialog box to close it.

6. Save the scene.

Figure 14-6. The **Animation** tab of the **Preference Settings** dialog box is used to set the default transitions.

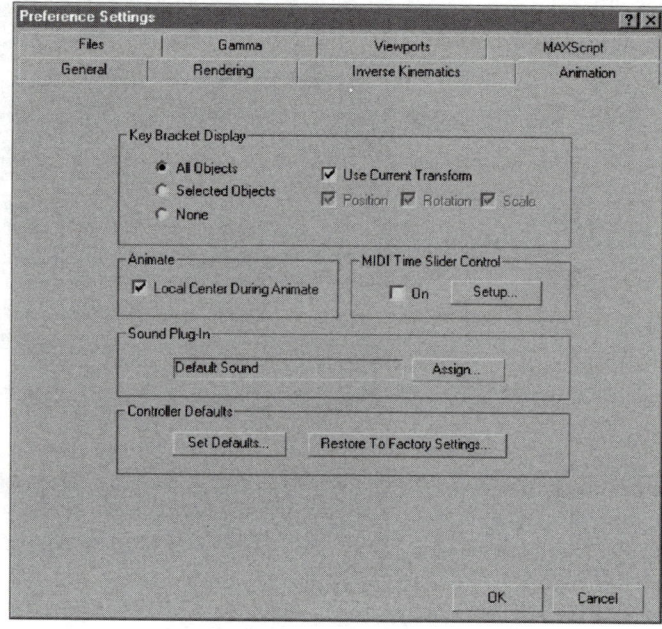

Figure 14-7. Select the controller for which you want to set the default values.

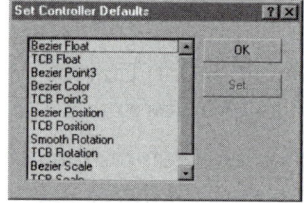

Animating the Dart and Dartboard

You will now create the animation. This is done by creating animation keys on keyframes in the animation. The in-between frames are filled in automatically by 3ds max.

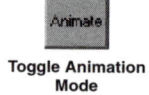

Toggle Animation Mode

1. Activate the Front viewport. Pick the **Toggle Animation Mode** button to turn animation mode on.

2. Move to frame 25. Pick the **Select and Move** and **Restrict to X** buttons on the **Main** toolbar. Then, move Dart Dummy to the right by 200 units.
   Dartboard is centered on Wall.

3. Move to frame 50.

4. Pick the **Restrict to Y** button and move Dart Dummy up by 200 units.

5. Exit animation mode and save the scene.

Starting Movement on Frame 50

Now, if an animation key is created for Dart after frame 50, the movement is applied over all frames, including 0 to 50. The object will then appear as if it is not following its parent object. To prevent this, a position key needs to be added for the dart's position on frame 50 to lock it into place before animating any movement beyond frame 50. **Track View** is used to create this position key.

Open Track View

1. Pick the **Open Track View** button on the **Main** toolbar.
   Track View is displayed.

2. Pick the plus sign (+) next to **Objects** to expand the tree. Pick on the plus sign (+) in the square next to **Dart Dummy**, and then the plus sign (+) next to **Dart**. Pick on the plus sign (+) next to **Transform** to further expand the tree.

3. Select the **Add Keys** button at the top of **Track View**.

Add Keys

4. In the **Position** row of **Dart**, pick a point on frame 50.
   A position key is created on frame 50, Figure 14-8. This key contains the information about the dart's position on frame 50. Now, when movement is added to the dart past frame 50, the movement begins on frame 50 and not frame 0.

5. Close **Track View**.

6. Save the scene.

Continuing to Animate the Dart

1. Move to frame 55 and enter animation mode.

2. Pick **Select and Move** and **Restrict to X** buttons on the **Main** toolbar. In the Left viewport, move Dart to the right by 100 units.
   Arrow detaches from the dartboard and moves away from it.

3. Move to frame 70.

4. Move Dart to the right an additional 100 units. Pick the **Restrict to Y** button and move Dart up by 100.

5. Move to frame 90.

6. Open **Track View**. Pick the **Add Keys** button and add a key in the **Position** row on frame 90 for Dart. Close **Track View**.
   The position of Dart is set in a key on frame 90.

7. Move to frame 105.

8. In the Left viewport, move Dart down by 100 units. Also, move it to the left by 100 units.

9. Move to 110.

Figure 14-8. Using **Track View** to add an animation key.

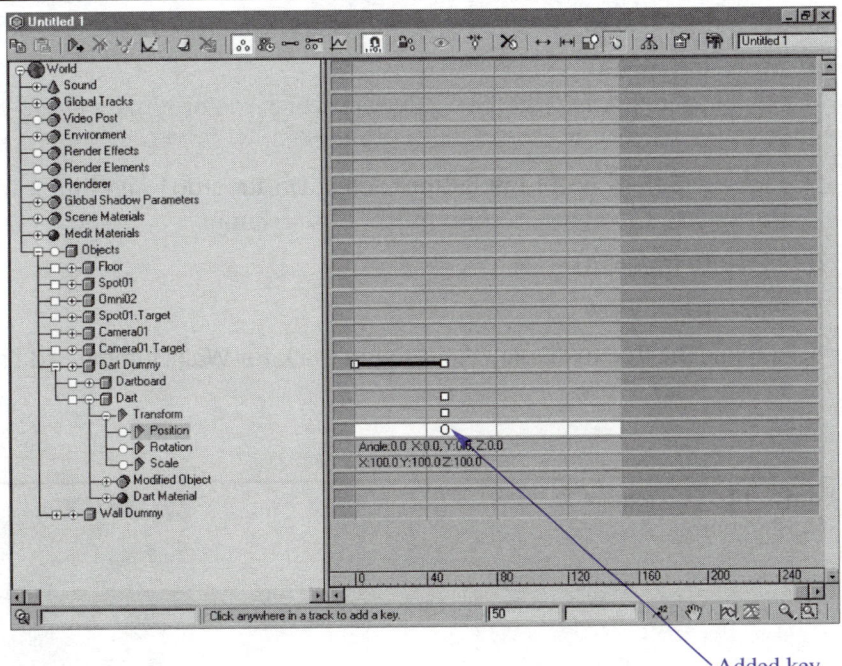

Added key

10. Move Dart to the left by 100 units.
    The dart is again "stuck" in the board.

11. Open **Track View**.

12. Expand the **Dart Dummy** tree to display the **Position** track.

13. Pick the **Add Keys** button and add a key in the **Position** row for Dart Dummy on frame 110. Close **Track View**.

14. Move to frame 130.

15. In the Front viewport, move Dart Dummy down by 200 units.

16. Move to frame 150.

17. Move Dart Dummy to the left by 200 units.

18. Exit animation mode. Play the animation in the Perspective viewport.
    Notice how all the transitions are mechanical, and the objects "jump" from one position to another.

19. Stop the playback and save the scene.

Creating a Snapshot

A snapshot object is a duplicate of an object on a certain frame of an animation. The duplicate is identical to the state of the original object on the frame where the snapshot is created. This copy can be used in complex animation sequences. In this animation, you will be rotating the dartboard 45°. You will create a snapshot object from the dartboard, and then hide the original, to create this effect.

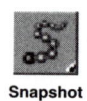
Snapshot

1. Move to frame 50.

2. Select Dartboard. Then, pick the **Snapshot** button from the **Array** flyout on the **Main** toolbar.
   The **Snapshot** dialog box is displayed, Figure 14-9.

3. Pick the **Single** and **Copy** radio buttons. Then, pick the **OK** button in the dialog box.
   A duplicate of Dartboard is created in the current location as the original, and is named Dartboard01. Using this dialog box, you can also create multiple copies of an object over a range of frames. The **Single** radio button creates a single copy of the object.

4. Move to frame 0.
   Notice there are two dartboards in the scene, the original and the copy. The copy is located at the position where it was created on frame 50.

5. Pick the **Select and Link** button. Select Dartboard01 and link it to Wall Dummy.
   Dartboard01 becomes a child object of the dummy.

6. Move to frame 70.

7. Open **Track View**.

8. Expand the tree to display the rotation track for Wall Dummy. Add a key at frame 70 for the object. Close **Track View**.

Figure 14-9. Creating a snapshot object.

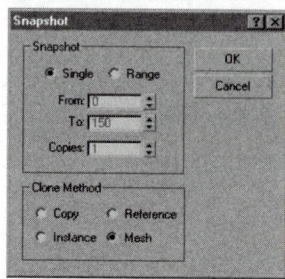

9. Move to frame 80 and enter animation mode.

10. In the Top viewport, rotate Wall Dummy –45° about the Z axis.

11. Move to frame 90.

12. Rotate Wall Dummy 45° about the Z axis in the Top viewport.

13. Exit animation mode. Play the animation in the Perspective viewport.
    Notice how the copy of the dartboard rotates with the wall, but the original does not. The wall rotates "through" the original object.

14. Stop the playback, move to frame 0, and save the scene.

Hide an Object During Animation

To prevent the door from rotating through the original dartboard, you must turn off the visibility, or hide, the dartboards during different segments of the animation. This also prevents two dartboards from being visible at the same time. There are two ways to do this. You can add a visibility track in **Track View** or modify the object's properties.

Adding a Visibility Track

1. Open **Track View**.

2. To see the tree for the objects linked to Dart Dummy, pick the plus sign in the square next to its name in **Track View**.
   The two objects linked to Dart Dummy can now be seen in the hierarchy.

3. Expand the tree for Dartboard. Then, select its name to highlight it. Pick the **Add Visibility Track** button on the **Track View** toolbar. This button is greyed out unless the top level for an object (its name) is selected.

   Add Visibility Track

   A visibility track is added to the tree beneath Dartboard, Figure 14-10. This track is specifically used to control the visibility of the object.

Figure 14-10. Using a visibility track to control the visibility of an object during the animation.

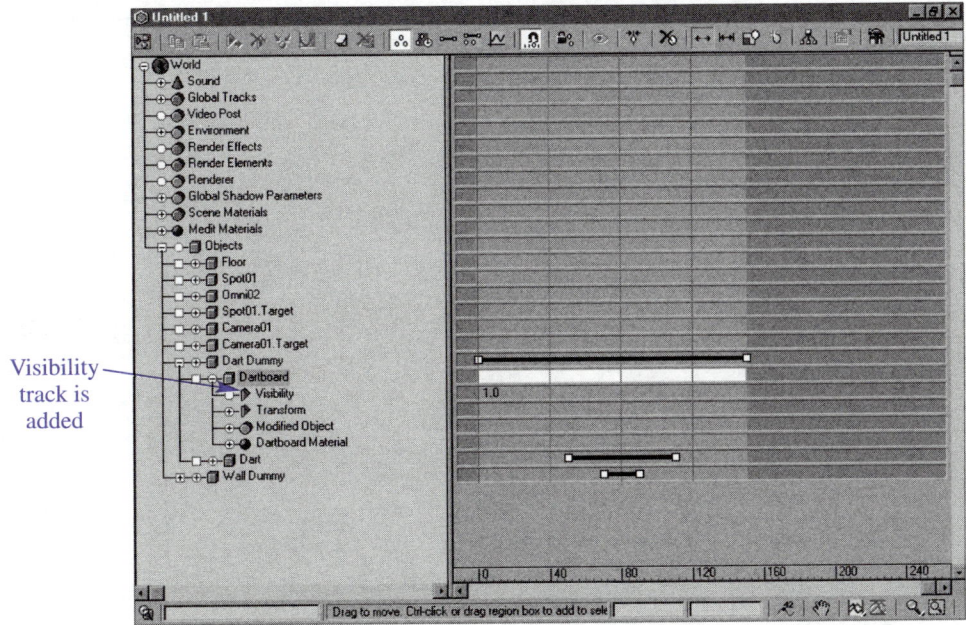

Visibility track is added

4. Now, pick the **Add Keys** button on the **Track View** toolbar. Then, pick in the visibility track for Dartboard on frame 0 to add a key.

5. With the new key selected, right-click on it to display the key info dialog box.

6. Type 1 in the **Value:** spinner, if not already set to 1. Also, set the **In:** and **Out:** image tiles to the mechanical transition. Close the key info dialog box.
   Setting the visibility value to 1 makes the object completely visible on the keyframe. Since you earlier set the default transitions, the image tiles should already be set to the mechanical transition.

7. Add another key in the Dartboard visibility track on frame 50. Then, right-click on the key to display the key info dialog box.

8. Type 0 in the **Value:** spinner. Also, set the **In:** and **Out:** image tiles to the mechanical transition, if not already set. Close the dialog box.
   Setting the visibility value to 0 makes the object completely invisible on the keyframe.

9. Add a third key in the Dartboard visibility track on frame 90. Then, right-click on the key to display the key info dialog box.

10. Type 1 in the **Value:** spinner. Also, set the **In:** and **Out:** image tiles to the mechanical transition, if not already set. Close the dialog box.
    Setting the value to 1 means the object is completely visible again on the keyframe.

11. Close **Track View** and save the scene.

Controlling Visibility with Object Properties

1. Select Dartboard01 in any viewport. Move to frame 0. Then, right-click in the viewport to display the quad menu. Then, select **Properties...** from the lower-right quadrant.
   The **Object Properties** dialog box is displayed, Figure 14-11.

2. Type 0 in the **Visibility:** spinner in the **Rendering Control** area of the dialog box.
   This will make the object invisible on all frames of the animation, until visibility keys are set and edited.

3. Pick the **OK** button in the **Object Properties** dialog box to close it.
   The object is no longer visible in the shaded viewport. However, it is still visible in the wireframe viewports.

Figure 14-11. Controlling object visibility using object properties.

Visibility control

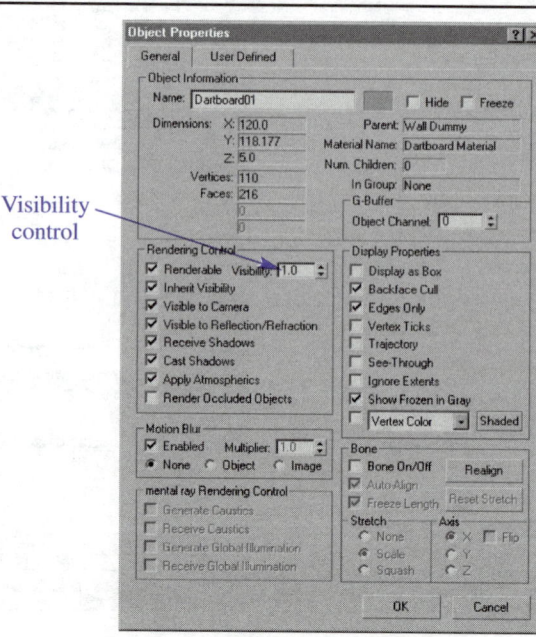

4. Move to frame 50. Pick the **Toggle Animation Mode** button to enter animation mode.

5. With Dartboard01 selected, right-click in the viewport to display the quad menu. Select **Properties...** from the lower-right quadrant.

6. Type 1 in the **Visibility:** spinner in the **Rendering Control** area of the **Object Properties** dialog box. Then, pick the **OK** button to close the dialog box.
This adds a visibility track in **Track View** for the object, with a key on frame 0 and a key on frame 50. The object is now visible on frame 50.

7. Move to frame 90. With Dartboard01 selected, right-click to display the quad menu. Select **Properties...** to display the **Object Properties** dialog box.

8. Type 0 in the **Visibility:** spinner in the **Rendering Control** area of the dialog box. Then, pick the **OK** button to close the dialog box.
A key is added to the visibility track on frame 90. The object is invisible on frame 90.

9. Exit animation mode. Play the animation in the Camera01 viewport. Notice how it appears as though there is only one dartboard in the scene. This is because Dartboard "disappears" on the frame on which Dartboard01 "appears," and vice versa.
Since you changed the default transitions to mechanical, the visibility of an object does not "fade" in and out. However, if you need to change the transitions, use **Track View** and edit the keys in the visibility track.

10. Stop the playback and save the scene.

Adjusting the Movement Transitions

Earlier, you set the default transitions to a mechanical transition. This type of transition works very well for visibility keys to prevent object "fade in" and "fade out." However, as you may have already figured out, the dart and dartboard "jump" from one spot to another. These objects should have smooth transitions between keyframes. Edit the animation keys in **Track View** to fix the problem.

1. Open **Track View**. Make sure you are *not* in animation mode.

2. Expand the tree for Dart Dummy so its position track under **Transform** is displayed. Right-click on the first key in the position track (frame 0) to display the key info dialog box.

3. Change the **In:** and **Out:** image tiles to a smooth curve. Pick the curve second from the bottom.

4. Pick the right-hand arrow next to the key number at the top of the key info dialog box.
This moves the key info dialog box to the next key in sequence, which is on frame 25. The **In:** image tile is already changed, since it is the same as the **Out:** image tile for the previous key.

5. Change the **Out:** image tile to the smooth curve. Repeat this for the remaining keys in the track so all keys have a smooth curve into and out of the key.

6. Expand the tree for Dart (under Dart Dummy) to display its position track under **Transform**. Right-click on the first key in the position track to display the key info dialog box.

7. Change the **In:** and **Out:** image tiles to the same smooth curve used for Dart Dummy. Do this for all keys in the position track.

8. Close **Track View**.

9. Play the animation in the Camera01 viewport.
Notice how the movements of the dartboard and dart are now smooth.

10. Stop the playback and save the scene.

Rendering a Preview Animation

If you want to quickly verify an animation, you can create and view a preview of it. This is a low-color and low-resolution animation, and can save a lot of time. Adjustments can be made to the animation as needed before the final rendering is created.

1. Pick **Make Preview...** from the **Rendering** pull-down menu.
   The **Make Preview** dialog box is displayed, Figure 14-12.

2. In the **Display in Preview** area of the dialog box, check the **Frame Numbers** check box.
   Now, when the preview is played, the number of each frame is displayed.

3. Select Camera01 from the **Render Viewport:** drop-down list. Then, pick the **Create** button to create the preview.
   Each frame is rendered one by one. When the preview is complete, it is played in Windows Media Player. Close Media Player when done viewing the preview.

4. If you want to view the preview of the animation again, pick **View Preview...** from the **Rendering** pull-down menu.
   Close Media Player when done viewing the preview.

5. Save the scene.

Figure 14-12. Creating a preview rendering.

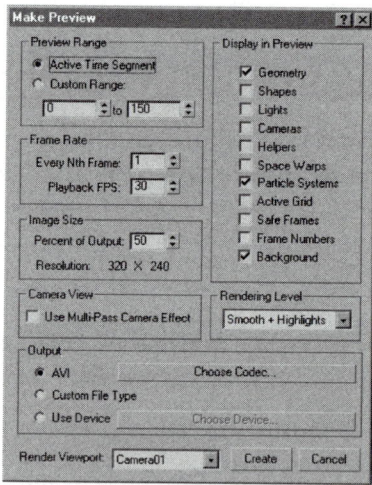

Animating the Camera

A camera can be animated in a scene just like any other object. When a camera is animated, the result in the camera viewport appears as if the entire scene is moving. The target of a target camera can also be animated. You can animate the movement or rotation of a camera or the movement of a target. Since you earlier hid the camera, you will first unhide it. Then, you can select and animate the camera.

1. Pick **Display** in the **Command Panel**.

2. In the **Hide by Category** rollout, uncheck the **Cameras** check box.
   The camera is again displayed in the viewports.

3. Pick the **Zoom Extents All** button to zoom to the extents of the objects in all viewports.

4. Save the scene.

Animating the Camera

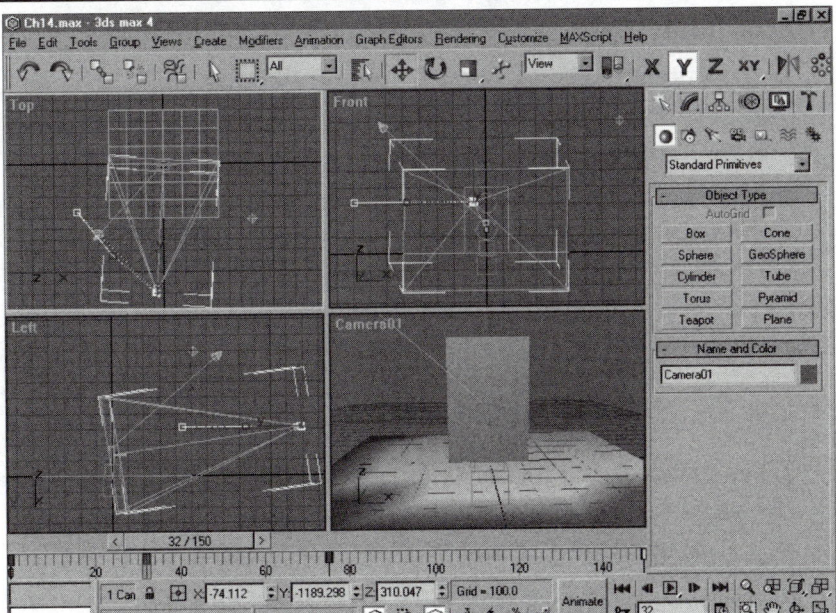

Display

1. Pick the **Toggle Animation Mode** button to enter animation mode.

2. Move to frame 75.

3. Pick the **Select and Move** and **Restrict to Y** buttons on the **Main** toolbar. In the Top viewport, move Camera01 straight up by 400 units.

4. Pick the **Restrict to X** button. Move Camera01 to the left by 320 units.

5. With the camera selected, pick **Display** in the **Command Panel**, if not already selected. Check the **Trajectory** check box in the **Display Properties** rollout.
   The path the camera follows is displayed as a red line. The white boxes represent frames that contain animation keys for the camera.

6. Move to frame 32.

7. Pick the **Select and Move** and **Restrict to X** buttons on the **Main** toolbar. In the Top viewport, move Camera01 to the right by 400 units.

8. Pick the **Restrict to Y** button. Move Camera01 down by 350 units. Also, pick the **Zoom Extents All** button, Figure 14-13. Exit animation mode.
   You must have noticed that the path of the camera bends to fit through the white box keys on the path. More white keys can be added and moved to control the shape of the path.

9. Create another preview of the Camera01 viewport.
   Notice how the camera now moves, as reflected by the scene "moving." Also, notice how the transitions are mechanical, and it appears that different cameras are displaying different views in the same viewport. This is because you earlier set the default transitions to mechanical.

10. Close Media Player.

11. In **Track View**, expand the tree for Camera01 so its position track is displayed below **Transform**.

12. Right-click on the first key in the camera's position track. Then, change the **In:** and **Out:** image tiles to a smooth curve. Repeat this for all of the camera's position keys.

Figure 14-13. The camera is animated.

13. Hold down the [Shift] key and move the first key to frame 150. Close **Track View**.
    A copy of the first key is placed on the last frame of the animation.

14. Make another preview of the Camera01 viewport.
    The camera now moves gently between its keys, and the scene appears to have a fluid motion.

15. Close Media Player and save the scene.

Animating the Target

The camera target can be animated to follow the movement of an object during an animation. You can link a camera target as a child to the object being followed in the animation to simplify the process. If a camera represents a person walking through a scene, you can create a dummy object and link both the camera its target to the dummy. In this way, only the dummy object has to be animated.

1. Pick the **Select and Move** and **Restrict to XY Plane** buttons on the **Main** toolbar.

2. Select the camera target. In the Top, Left, and Front viewports, move the target to the center of Dartboard.

3. Pick **Select and Link** button on the **Main** toolbar. Drag the cursor to Dartboard and release.
   The camera target is now a child of Dartboard and will follow its movements.

4. Pick the **Select object** button to exit link mode.

5. Save the scene.

Render a Final Animation

You will now render a final animation. Before you do so, you may want to render another preview to verify motion in the scene.

1. Activate the Camera01 viewport.

2. Pick **Render...** from the **Rendering...** pull-down menu to display the **Render Scene** dialog box.

3. In the **Time Output** area of the **Common Parameters** rollout, pick the **Active Time Segment** radio button.
   This specifies that all frames in the current time segment, frame 0 to frame 150, should be rendered in the final animation.

4. In the **Output Size** area of the **Common Parameters** rollout, pick the **320x240** button.
   This sets the size of the final rendering to 320 pixels wide by 240 pixels tall. This smaller size takes less time to render, and the final file is much smaller.

5. In the **Render Output** area of the **Common Parameters** rollout, pick the **Files...** button. In the **Render Output File** dialog box that appears, navigate to the folder of your choice, name the file Ch14.avi, and pick the **Save** button.
   If a "configuration" dialog box appears, pick the **OK** button to accept the default.

6. Pick the **Render** button at the bottom of the **Render Scene** dialog box.
   The render window and **Rendering** dialog box appear. The **Rendering** dialog box shows the progress, and the current frame is rendered in the render window.

7. When the rendering is complete, the **Rendering** dialog box automatically closes. Then, close the render window and the **Render Scene** dialog box.

8. Pick **View Image File...** from the **File** pull-down menu. In the **View File** dialog box that appears, navigate to the folder where Ch14.avi is saved and select the file.
   The animation is played in Windows Media Player.

9. Close Media Player and save the scene.

Self-Evaluation Test

Answer the following questions. Then, compare your answers with the correct answers given at the end of this chapter.

1. Objects can be linked to a _____ object to help create complex animations.

2. _____ objects are not rendered but are in shaded viewports.

3. If you link several objects to a single dummy object, what happens when the dummy object is moved?

4. If a box is linked to a sphere, the sphere is the _____ and the box is the _____.

5. You can set the default transitions using the _____ tab in the **Preference Settings** dialog box.

6. _____ is a function that contains all of the keys for the animation, and can be used to adjust and edit keys.

7. A _____ object is a duplicate of an object in the state on a certain frame of an animation.

8. You can adjust the visibility of objects by adding keys to a _____ track in **Track View**.

9. When you animate a camera, the _____ can be moved or rotated, and the _____ can be moved.

10. To represent a person walking through a scene, the _____ and _____ are linked to a dummy object, and the dummy object is animated.

Exercises

Create the scene of a basket and a ball shown below. Use a dummy object to animate the basket and ball moving to the right and down onto the box. Then, move the ball up out of the basket, and, before the ball returns to the basket, the box spins around its axis once. The basket should spin with the box. Then, move the basket and ball back to the original position.

1. Adjust the length of the animation to 150 frames.

2. Create two dummy objects, one below the basket and another below the box. Link the basket and ball to the dummy object below the basket, and link the box to the other dummy object.

3. Create a snapshot of the basket on the frame where the box rotates.

4. Add visibility tracks and adjust keys as needed.

5. Add lights and a camera.

6. Animate the camera and its target. The camera should always look at the ball.

7. Render a final animation named Ex14.avi in the folder of your choice.

8. Save the scene as Ex14.max in the folder of your choice.

Answers

The following are the correct answers to the questions in the Self-Evaluation Test.

1. dummy; 2. Dummy; 3. All linked objects also move.; 4. parent, child; 5. **Animation**; 6. **Track View**; 7. snapshot; 8. visibility; 9. camera, target; 10. camera, target.

Chapter 15

Rendering

Learning Objectives

After completing this chapter, you will be able to:

○ Create a preview animation.
○ Define a current segment of an animation.
○ Render all frames, a single frame, a segment, or a range of an animation.
○ Render a single frame of the animation to a file.
○ Render a final animation containing all frames.

Tutorial Description

Rendering a final animation can take a long time. If there is a mistake in the animation, you will need to rerender the animation after correcting the mistake, and therefore have wasted time. Instead, 3ds max allows you to create a low-resolution rendering called a *preview*. A preview does not include texture maps, shadows, or accurate lighting. A preview animation simply allows you to verify motion. In this tutorial you will render a preview, and then a final animation. You will also render a single frame of the animation to a file.

Preview an Animation

1. Open Ch14.max from the folder where you saved it in the last chapter. Then, save the scene as Ch15.max in the folder of your choice.

2. Pick the **Zoom Extents All** button to zoom to the extents of the viewports.

Zoom Extents All

3. Pick **Create** in the **Command Panel**. Pick the **Cameras** button and select **Standard** from the drop-down list. Then, pick the **Target** button in the **Object Type** rollout.

Create

4. Place the camera at the lower-right corner of the Top viewport and drag the target to the center of Wall.

Cameras

5. Right-click in the Left viewport to activate it. With the second camera selected, press the [C] key to change Left viewport to the Camera02 viewport.

Truck Camera

6. Right-click on the Camera02 viewport label to display a shortcut menu. Select **Smooth + Highlights** from the menu.
The objects in the viewport are shaded.

Field-of-View

7. With the Camera02 viewport active, pick the **Truck Camera** button and pan the viewport so the objects are at the center of the viewport. Pick the **Field-of-View** button and zoom out so the objects fill the viewport. Then, pick the **Orbit Camera** button and rotate the viewing angle to a desirable view, Figure 15-1.

Orbit Camera

8. With Camera02 viewport active, select **Make Preview...** from the **Rendering** pull-down menu.
The **Make Preview** dialog box is displayed, Figure 15-2. The options in this dialog box are used to control the preview.

9. Pick the **Active Time Segment** radio button in the **Preview Range** area of the dialog box.
This tells 3ds max to render the entire active time segment, which is currently frame 0 to frame 150.

10. Pick the **Create** button at the bottom of the dialog box to create the preview.
The viewports are temporarily replaced with a display of the preview being rendered frame by frame. When the preview is completely rendered, it is automatically played in Windows Media Player.

11. Close Media Player after you have viewed the preview animation.

12. To view the preview animation again, select **View Preview...** from the **Rendering** pull-down menu.

13. Save the scene.

Figure 15-1. A second camera is added to the scene, and the Camera02 viewport is adjusted.

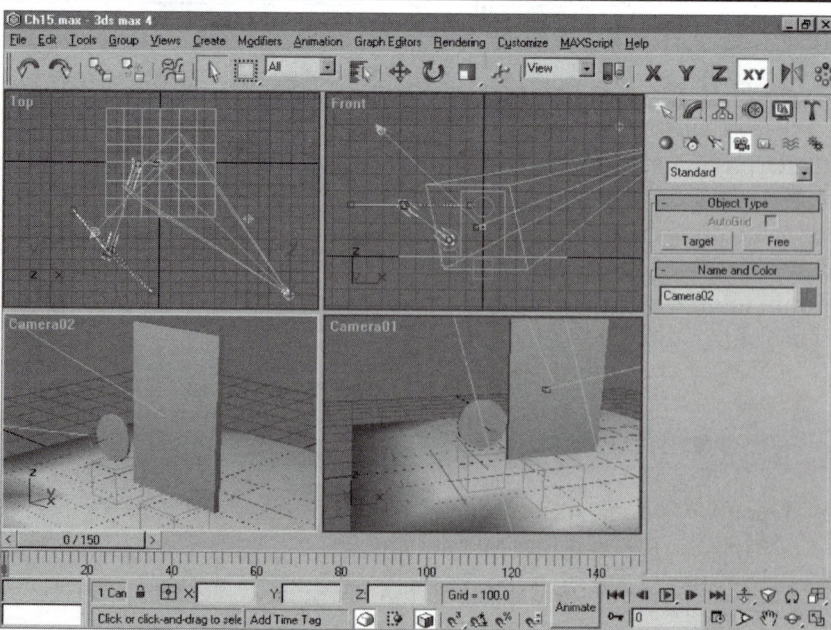

Figure 15-2. The **Make Preview** dialog box contains options for creating a preview animation.

Frames to render

Preview size

Options to include in preview

Shading level

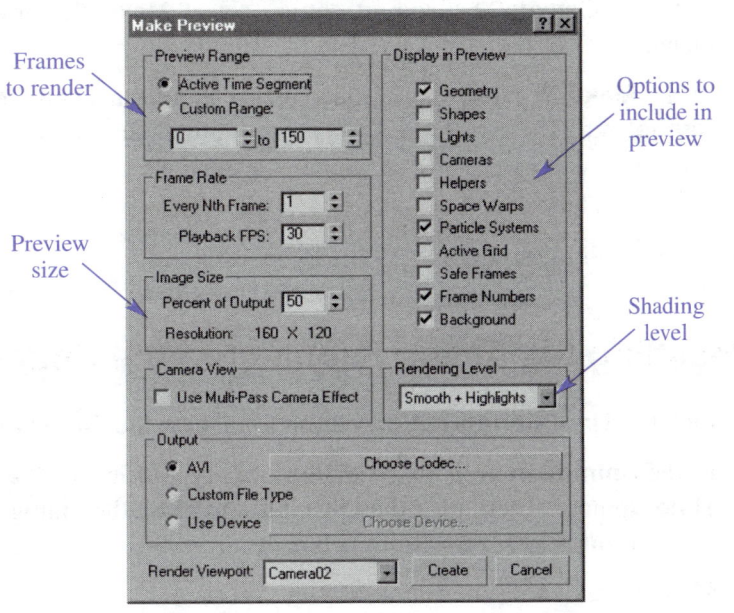

Defining an Active Time Segment

The longer an animation, the more frames it contains. All frames in an animation need to be managed. You can make managing the frames in a long animation easier by defining the active time segment. The *active time segment* is simply a group of sequential frames in the animation. By default, the active time segment is all frames in the animation. Only the frames in the active time segment are displayed on the screen, rendered in a preview, or rendered in a final animation. However, the other frames still exist and can be accessed by redefining the active time segment.

1. Pick the **Time Configuration** button to display the **Time Configuration** dialog box, Figure 15-3.

   Time Configuration

2. In the **Animation** area of the dialog box, type 50 in the **Start Time:** spinner and 100 in the **End Time:** spinner. Then, pick the **OK** button to close the dialog box.
   The active time segment is redefined as frame 50 to frame 100.

Figure 15-3. The **Time Configuration** dialog box is used to define the active time segment.

Starting and ending frames for the active time segment

Length of the time segment active

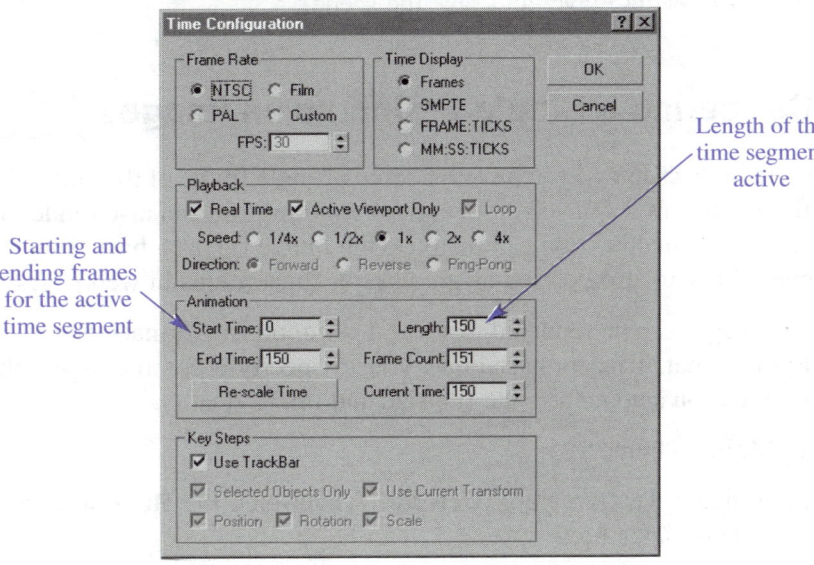

3. With the Camera02 viewport active, select **Make Preview...** from the **Rendering** pull-down menu.

4. In the **Make Preview** dialog box, pick the **Active Time Segment** radio button in the **Preview Range** area. Then, pick the **Create** button to create the preview.
   The preview is rendered, starting at frame 50 and ending at frame 100. The preview is then played in Windows Media Player.

5. Close Media Player and save the scene.

Resetting the Active Segment to the Entire Animation

1. Pick the **Time Configuration** button to display the **Time Configuration** dialog box.

2. In the **Animation** area of the dialog box, type 0 in the **Start Time:** spinner and 150 in the **End Time:** spinner. Then, pick the **OK** button to close the dialog box.
   The current active time segment has been reset to all the frames in the animation.

3. Make a preview of the Camera02 viewport.
   Notice how all frames (0 to 150) are included in the preview.

4. Close Media Player and save the scene.

Rendering a Range of Frames

You can preview a range of frames without redefining the active time segment. This is done using the options in the **Make Preview** dialog box.

1. Make the Camera02 viewport active. Then, select **Make Preview...** from the **Rendering** pull-down menu to display the **Make Preview** dialog box.

2. In the **Preview Range** area of the dialog box, pick the **Custom Range:** radio button.

3. Type 50 in the left-hand spinner below the radio button and 100 in the right-hand spinner. Then, pick the **Create** button.
   The preview is rendered, starting at frame 50 and ending at frame 100. The preview is then played in Windows Media Player. However, notice that the active time segment is still frame 0 to frame 150, as indicated in the track bar at the bottom of the 3ds max drawing screen.

4. Close Media Player and save the scene.

Rendering a Single Frame as an Image

In previous chapters, you have rendered a single frame of the animation (frame 0) as a still image. The still image was displayed in the render window. You can also render a still image to file, in addition to the render window. You can then use the image file as a background or texture map in 3ds max. The image file can also be used as graphics or illustrations in web pages, reports, or slide shows.

Still images can be rendered to several common file formats. Here, you will save the image file in the JPEG format. This format allows you to specify a compression value, which you will set. The file compression amount sets the file size and image quality.

1. Move to frame 125.

Render Scene

2. Activate the Camera02 viewport. Then, pick the **Render Scene** button to display the **Render Scene** dialog box.

3. In the **Time Output** area of the **Common Parameters** rollout, pick the **Single** radio button.
   This specifies that only the current frame in the animation will be rendered, which is why you moved to frame 125 earlier.

4. In the **Output Size** area of the dialog box, pick the **640x480** button.
   This sets the image to be rendered at a resolution of 640 × 480 pixels.

5. In the **Render Output** area of the dialog box, pick the **Files...** button. The **Render Output File** dialog box is displayed.

6. Type Ch15 in the **File name:** text box. Then, select the **JPEG File** from the **Save as type:** drop-down list.

7. Next, pick the **Save** button. The **JPEG Image Control** dialog box is displayed, Figure 15-4.
   This dialog box allows you to adjust the quality, size, and smoothing of the image. You can choose a better image quality if you want to use the picture in a presentation. If you want to use the image on a web page, you can use a smaller file size so that the image downloads faster.

8. Pick the **OK** button to accept the default JPEG settings. The **Render Output File** dialog box is also closed.
   You will notice in the **Render Output** area of the **Render Scene** dialog box that the **Save File** check box is checked and the path and file name are displayed adjacent to the **Files...** button.

9. Make sure Camera02 is selected in the **Viewport:** drop-down list in the **Render Scene** dialog box. Then, pick the **Render** button.
   The render window and the **Rendering** dialog box are displayed. The progress of the rendering is shown in the **Rendering** dialog box, which closes when the rendering is complete. The rendering is displayed in the render window. Notice how all the texture maps are displayed, which they were not in the preview animation.

10. Close the render window and the **Render Scene** dialog box.

11. Make any material adjustments you see fit.

12. Save the scene.

Figure 15-4. The **JPEG Image Control** dialog box is used to adjust the level of compression and image quality in the final file.

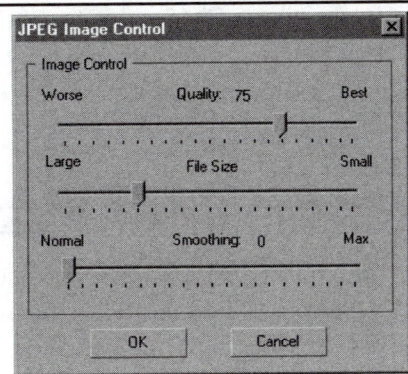

Rendering a Final Animation

Now, you will render a final animation. The final animation contains all movement, just like the preview animation. However, all of the colors, textures, shadows, and highlights are also included. The final animation is like rendering each frame as a still image. Therefore, this can take some time, depending on the speed of your computer and the length, complexity, and resolution of the animation.

1. Make the Camera01 viewport active. Then, pick the **Render Scene** button to display the **Render Scene** dialog box.

2. In the **Time Output** area in the **Common Parameters** rollout, pick the **Active Time Segment** radio button.
   When you select this radio button, all the active frames in the animation are rendered.

3. In the **Output Size** area, select the **320x240** button.
   This sets the animation to be rendered at a resolution of 320 × 240 pixels.

4. In the **Render Output** area, pick the **Files...** button to display the **Render Output File** dialog box.

5. Type Ch15 in the **File name:** text box and select **AVI File (*.avi)** from the **Save as type:** drop-down list. Then, pick the **Save** button.
   The **Video Compression** dialog box is displayed. This allows you to choose a codec for compression, and to set options for the codec you choose.

6. Pick the **OK** button in the **Video Compression** dialog box to accept the defaults.
   Notice that the **Save File** check box is checked and the path of the file is displayed adjacent to the **Files...** button. If the **Save File** check box is not selected, the animation is only rendered on the screen.

7. Make sure Camera01 is selected in the **Viewport:** drop-down list in the **Render Scene** dialog box. Then, pick the **Render** button.
   The **Rendering** dialog box appears showing the status of the rendering. The animation is rendered frame by frame, and each rendered frame is displayed in the render window.

8. Close the render window and the **Render Scene** dialog box.

9. Select **View Image File...** from the **File** pull-down menu to display the **View File** dialog box.

10. Navigate to the folder where Ch15.avi is located and open the file.
    The animation is played in Windows Media Player.

11. Close Media Player and save the scene.

Rendering a Second Camera View

This scene has two cameras. Two viewports are displaying the two different camera views. You just rendered and saved the animation in the first camera view. Now, render the animation in the second camera view and save it to a file as well.

1. Activate the Camera02 viewport. Then, pick the **Render Scene** button to display the **Render Scene** dialog box.

2. Pick the **Active Time Segment** radio button in the **Time Output** area of the dialog box.

3. Pick the **320x240** button in the **Output Size** area of the dialog box.

4. Pick the **Files...** button in the **Render Output** area to display the **Render Output File** dialog box.

5. Type Ch15-2 in the **File name:** text box. Then, select **AVI File (*.avi)** from the **Save as type:** drop-down list. Pick the **Save** button.
The **Video Compression** dialog box is not displayed because you already set compression for this modeling session. If you want to change the compression, pick the **Setup...** button before picking the **Save** button.

6. Make sure Camera02 is selected in the **Viewport:** drop-down list in the **Render Scene** dialog box. Then, pick the **Render** button.
The animation is rendered.

7. Close the render window and the **Render Scene** dialog box.

8. Select **View Image File...** from the **File** menu to display the **View File** dialog box.

9. Navigate to the folder where Ch15-2.avi is located and open the file.
The animation is played in Windows Media Player.

10. Close Media Player and save the scene.

Self-Evaluation Test

Answer the following questions. Then, compare your answers with the correct answers given at the end of this chapter.

1. You can define the active time segment by using the _____ and _____ spinners in the **Time Configuration** dialog box.

2. You can preview a range of frames without redefining the active time segment by picking the _____ radio button in the **Make Preview** dialog box.

3. You can use the options in the _____ dialog box to adjust the quality, size, and smoothing of the image when saving a rendering to a JPEG file.

4. When the rendering is complete, the _____ dialog box automatically closes and the rendered image is displayed in the render window.

5. Only the frames in the _____ are displayed on the screen, rendered in a preview, or rendered in a final animation.

6. The _____ dialog box is used to choose a codec for an animation, and to set options for the codec.

7. If the _____ check box is not checked, the animation is only rendered on the screen.

Exercises

Open the scene Ch13.max *from Chapter 13. Save the scene as* Ex15.max *in the folder of your choice.*

1. Apply materials to the various components of the merry-go-round and add a background to the scene.

2. Open the **Make Preview** dialog box. In the **Display in Preview** area, check the **Geometry, Frame Numbers**, and **Background** check boxes. Uncheck all other check boxes.

3. Create a preview animation.

4. Render a still image of frame 200. Set the output size to 640 × 480. Save the rendering as a JPEG image.

5. Set the active time segment to frame 0 through frame 250.

6. Render the final animation to an AVI file. Set the output size to 320 × 240. Render all frames in the active time segment.

7. Set the active time segment to frame 251 through frame 435.

8. Create a second camera showing a different view. Render this camera view to an AVI file. Set the output size to 320 × 240. Render all frames in the active time segment.

9. View the two final animations.

10. Save the scene.

Answers

The following are the correct answers to the questions in the Self-Evaluation Test.

1. **Start Time:, End Time:**; 2. **Custom Range:**; 3. **JPEG Image Control**; 4. **Rendering**; 5. active time segment; 6. **Video Compression**; 7. **Save File**.

Chapter 16

Walkthrough Animation

Learning Objectives

After completing this chapter, you will be able to:

○ Create a motion path for the camera to follow.
○ Modify a motion path.
○ Assign a path constraint controller to the position track of an object.
○ Adjust camera parameters and animate a camera.
○ Animate objects to create a walkthrough.
○ Render a preview and final walkthrough animation.

Tutorial Description

In this tutorial, you will create a walkthrough animation. A walkthrough can be described as an animation that simulates a person walking through a building. To create this type of animation, you will create a path for and make a camera follow the path. A camera and its target will be linked to a dummy object. A path constraint controller is assigned to the position track of the dummy object so it follows the path. The path will be modified to allow precise control over the animation. In addition, the camera rotation is animated, as is the movement of objects like a door and window. Then, a preview is rendered before the final animation is rendered.

Creating a Motion Path

A walkthrough can be created by first defining a path that the camera will follow precisely representing a person's line of sight. The path needs to have round corners to represent the naturally smooth path a person takes while walking. Also, make sure that the path does not lie too close to any walls, and it must pass through the center of door openings.

1. Open Ch07.max, which is a scene of a cottage saved in Chapter 7. Save the scene as Ch16.max in the folder of your choice.

2. Activate the Top viewport and maximize it.

3. Select Ground. Then, right-click in the viewport to display the quad menu. Pick **Hide Selection** from the upper-right quadrant.
   The object is hidden.

Create

4. Pick the **Zoom Extents All** button.

5. Pick **Create** in the **Command Panel**. Pick the **Shapes** button and select **Splines** from the drop-down list. Then, pick the **Line** button in the **Object Type** rollout.

Shapes

6. In the **Creation Method** rollout, pick the **Smooth** radio button in the **Initial Type** area.
   Now, a smooth curve will be formed when points are picked.

7. Right-click on the current **Snap** button to display the **Grid and Snap Settings** dialog box. Select the **Home Grid** tab. Then, type 5 in the **Grid Spacing** spinner. Close the dialog box.

8. Pick the **2D Snap Toggle** button. Then, draw the spline shown in Figure 16-1 using the coordinates in the figure. Right-click to end the command. In the **Name and Color** rollout, name the spline Walking Path.

9. Display the four-viewport configuration. Make the Left viewport current and maximize it. Pick the **Zoom Extents All** button.

10. Turn snap off. Pick the **Select and Move** and **Restrict to Y** buttons on the **Main** toolbar. Move the path up so it is a little above floor level, Figure 16-2.

11. Save the scene.

Figure 16-1. The coordinates for the motion path. Note: This line is shown with square corners to help locate the vertices. However, your line will have smooth corners.

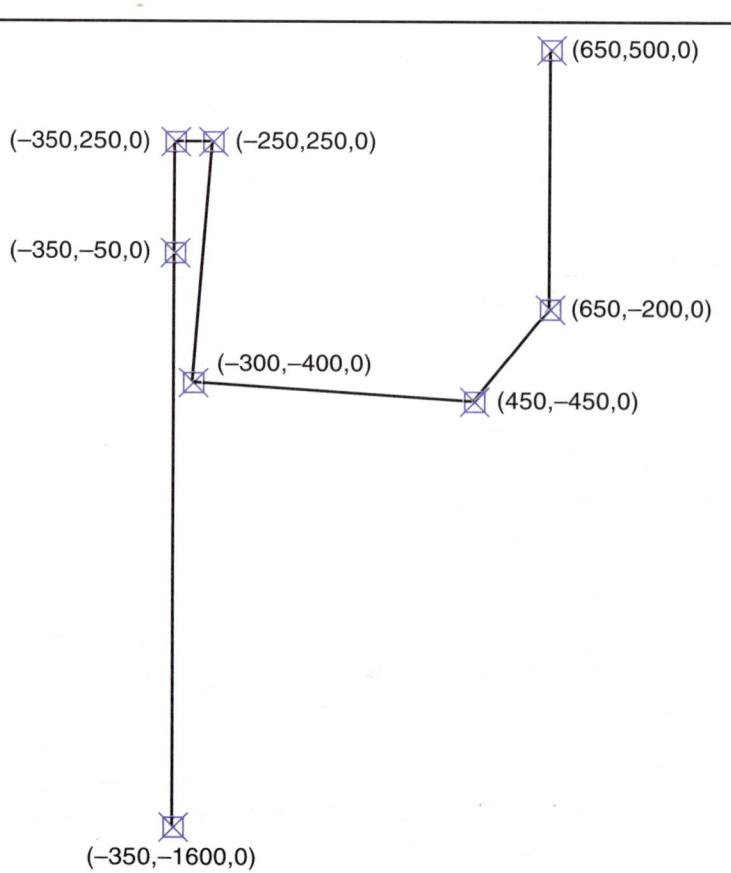

Figure 16-2. The path is moved to the correct vertical position.

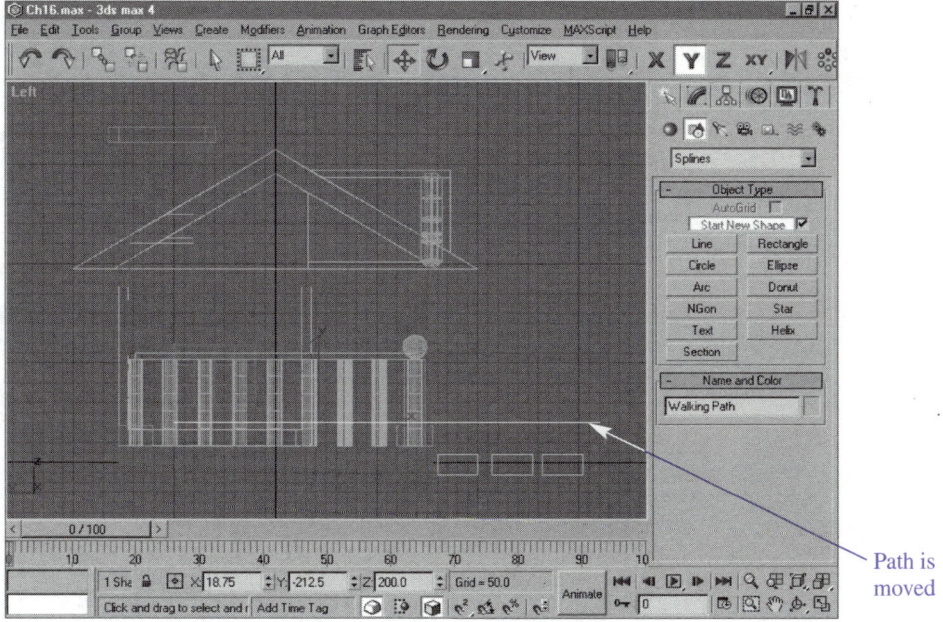

Path is moved

Modifying and Refining the Motion Path

You can now modify the line to create a path exactly as you want. Each of the vertices in the path can be moved and, since the vertices are smooth type, the path will change course through the modified vertex. You can also add new vertices, if there are not enough, by refining the line.

Since the line currently lies on a 2D plane, it does not "go up" the stairs into the cottage. You will now modify the line to follow the elevation levels in the cottage. If the first vertex of the line is moved down to the level of the ground, the motion path bends to fit through the moved vertex. Since the second and third vertices in the path are well inside the cottage, you need to refine the line by adding vertices so the path will not pass through parts of the steps.

1. Display the four-viewport configuration. Activate the Top viewport and maximize it.

2. With the line selected, pick **Modify** in the **Command Panel**.

Modify

3. In the **Selection** rollout, pick the **Vertex** button to enter vertex sub-object mode.
   All the vertices in the path are displayed.

4. Select the **Refine** button in the **Geometry** rollout. Add a new vertex where the path crosses the edge of Step01 closest to the cottage. Add another vertex on the path where it enters the room. Right-click to exit refine mode.
   Two vertices are added to the path.

5. Display the four-viewport configuration. Activate the Left viewport.

6. Pick the **Select and Move** and **Restrict to Y** buttons. Move the first vertex on the path down so it is close to ground level. Move the second vertex on the path (the first one you just added) down so it is close to the floor level of the porch, Figure 16-3.
   The path is modified so the motion will follow the elevation differences in the scene.

Select and Move

Restrict to Y

7. Activate the Top viewport and maximize it. Pick the **Refine** button again in the **Geometry** rollout. Add a vertex on the path where it exits the room. Zoom as needed. Right-click to exit refine mode.

8. Display the four-viewport configuration. Activate the Left viewport.

Figure 16-3. Two vertices are added to the beginning of the path, and moved down.

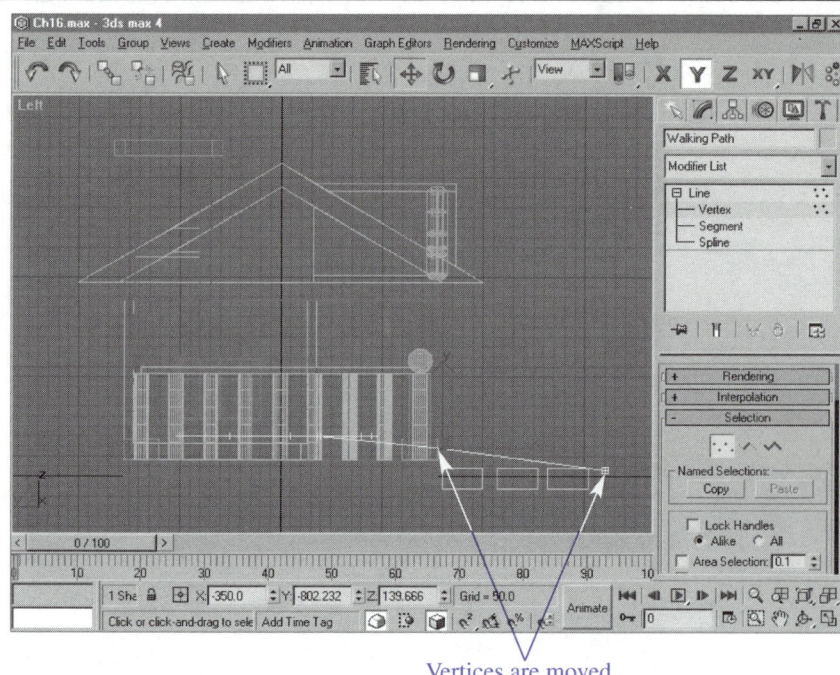

Vertices are moved

9. Pick the **Select and Move** and **Restrict to Y** buttons. Move the last four vertices on the path down to about the level of the porch floor.

10. Pick the **Vertex** button in the **Selection** rollout to exit vertex sub-object mode.

11. Save the scene.

Defining the Length of the Animation

Since a walkthrough animation is simulating a person walking, you will need to have more frames in the animation than those you have created to this point. If a low number of frames is used for the animation, the camera will turn corners very quickly. In addition, it will appear as though the person is running through the scene instead of walking. The more frames in the animation, the smoother the final motion will appear. Generally, you want to set the total number of frames in the animation before adding animation keys.

Time Configuration

1. Select the **Time Configuration** button to display the **Time Configuration** dialog box.

2. Type 1000 in the **Length:** spinner in the **Animation** area of the dialog box.
   The total number of frames in the animation is set to 1000. For a computer playback, this is a little over 30 seconds.

3. Pick the **OK** button to close the dialog box.

4. Save the scene.

Creating and Positioning the Camera

The camera used for a walkthrough animation is usually a free camera. However, a target camera can also be used. If a target camera is used, the camera and its target are linked to a dummy object, and the dummy moves along the motion path. This technique can be used to make other objects follow the path, such as a flashlight held in front of the person walking. You will use a target camera for the walkthrough.

1. Activate the Top viewport.

2. Pick **Create** in the **Command Panel**. Pick the **Cameras** button and select **Standard** from the drop-down list. Then, pick the **Target** button in the **Object Type** rollout.

Create

Cameras

3. Place the camera at the starting point of the path. Drag to place the target a short distance in front of the camera.
   A camera and target are placed in the viewport.

4. Activate the Camera01 viewport. With Camera02 selected, press the [C] key to make the viewport the Camera02 viewport.

5. Activate the Left viewport. Pick the **Select and Move** and **Restrict to Y** buttons. Select both Camera02 and its target by first deselecting the camera, then picking on the light blue line between the camera and target. Move the camera and target up so they are level with the top of the posts, Figure 16-4.
   The view in the Camera02 viewport looks straight at the cottage.

6. Select Camera02 (deselect the target) in the Left viewport. Pick **Modify** in the **Command Panel**. In the **Parameters** rollout, pick the **15mm** button in the **Stock Lenses** area. The **FOV** spinner is automatically set to around 100, which is acceptable.

Create

Helpers

7. Pick **Create** in the **Command Panel**. Pick the **Helpers** button and select **Standard** from the drop-down list. Then, pick the **Dummy** button in the **Object Type** rollout.

8. In the Front viewport, pick near the starting point of the path and drag to create a small cube.

9. Pick the **Select and Move** and **Restrict to Y** buttons. In the Top viewport, move the dummy object so it is under the camera.

10. Pick the **Select and Link** button. Then, select Camera02 and its target. Pick on the camera and drag to Dummy01. Release to link the camera and target to the dummy. Right-click to exit link mode.
    The camera and its target are child objects of Dummy01 and will follow its movements.

11. Save the scene.

Figure 16-4. A camera is added to the scene.

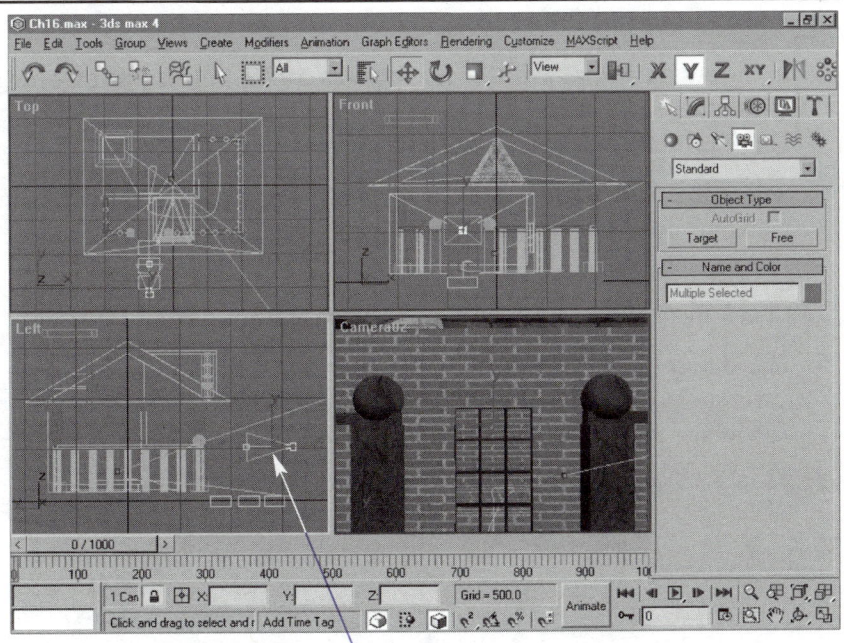

The camera is properly located

Assigning a Path Constraint Controller

A *path constraint* is a controller assigned to an object that makes the object follow a selected path. You will now assign a path constraint controller to the dummy. Then, you will specify the path you created as the motion path for the controller. Since the camera and target are linked to the dummy, they will also move along the same path.

1. Select Dummy01.

Motion

2. Pick **Motion** in the **Command Panel**. Expand the **Assign Controller** rollout.
   A hierarchy tree is displayed in the rollout, which appears similar to **Track View**.

3. Pick the plus sign (+) next to **Transform: Position/Rotation/Scale** to expand the tree, if not already expanded.

Assign Controller

4. Select **Position: Bezier Position** in the hierarchy. Then, pick the **Assign Controller** button at the top of the rollout.
   The **Assign Position Controller** dialog box is displayed, Figure 16-5.

Figure 16-5. The **Assign Position Controller** dialog box.

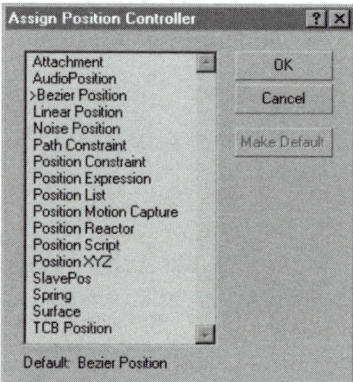

5. In the **Assign Position Controller** dialog box, select **Path Constraint** in the list. Then, pick the **OK** button to close the dialog box.
   The **Path Parameters** rollout now appears in the **Motion** tab of the **Command Panel**.

6. Select the **Add Path** button in the **Path Parameters** rollout. Then, select Walking Path in any viewport. Right-click to exit "add path" mode.
   The dummy object will now move along the path.

7. Check the **Follow** check box in the **Path Parameters** rollout.

8. The dummy, and therefore the camera and target, may rotate on the path. If necessary, pick a different axis radio button in the **Axis:** area of the **Path Parameters** rollout so the camera "looks down" the path.

9. Save the scene.

Turning Off Material Displays

When materials are visible in a viewport, the viewport preview may play very slow. By default, materials are displayed in shaded viewports. In addition, maps that are set to display in a viewport are displayed in shaded viewports. You will now turn off the display of materials in shaded viewports to improve system performance.

1. First, unhide the ground object. Right-click in any viewport to display the quad menu. Then, pick **Unhide All** from the upper-right quadrant.
   Ground is now visible in all viewports.

2. Pick **Display** in the **Command Panel**. In the **Display Color** rollout, pick the **Object Color** radio button next to the **Shaded:** label.
   Materials are no longer visible in any shaded viewport, which includes the Camera02 viewport.

Display

3. Expand the **Hide** rollout, if it is not already expanded.

4. Pick the **Hide by Name...** button to display the **Hide Objects** dialog box.

5. Select Camera01 from the list in the **Hide Objects** dialog box. Then, pick the **Hide** button at the bottom of the dialog box to hide the camera and its target.

6. Activate the Camera02 viewport. Pick the **Play Animation** button to view a playback of the animation.

Play Animation

7. Stop the playback and save the scene.

Adjusting the Camera

As the camera follows the motion of the path up the steps, it tilts up to follow the path. A person walking up the stairs would not do so. Hence, you need to modify the viewing angle of the camera at certain points on the path. In addition, depending on where you placed the camera, it may "pass through" a wall as it follows the path. This needs to be fixed first.

1. On frame 0, move the camera and target as needed. Play the animation in the Camera02 viewport, and further adjust the camera position until it does not pass through any wall during playback.

2. Activate the Left viewport and maximize it. Move to frame 0.

Select and Rotate

3. Pick the **Select and Rotate** and **Restrict to Z** buttons. Select the dummy object and rotate it 10°.
   The dummy, camera, and target tilt down. The "person's" view is slightly below horizontal, which is natural.

Restrict to Z

4. Move to the frame where the camera first moves onto the porch, which should be about frame 100.

5. Pick the **Toggle Animation Mode** button to enter animation mode. Then, rotate the dummy −5°.
   The camera view is more level with the ground.

Toggle Animation Mode

6. Continue animating the rotation of the dummy, and thus the camera view, as needed throughout the animation. The final view in the Camera02 viewport should reproduce the natural motion of a person walking up the steps, into the cottage, around the room, out of the cottage, and around the porch. You may need to add several keys throughout the animation.

7. Play the animation in the Camera02 viewport.

8. Make any further refinements to the camera motion as needed.

9. Save the scene.

Animating Objects in the Scene

Now, you will animate the door and the window of the cottage opening and closing. Currently, the door does not open and the camera walks through it. The door should open before the camera reaches it, and then remain open as the camera passes through it. In order to properly animate the objects, you must first adjust their pivot points.

Adjusting Pivot Points

Hierarchy

1. Move to frame 0 and make sure you are not in animation mode. Select Door in the Front viewport. Maximize the viewport.

2. With Door selected, pick **Hierarchy** in the **Command Panel**. Then, pick the **Affect Pivot Only** button in the **Adjust Pivot** rollout.
   The pivot point is currently displayed at the bottom of Door.

3. Pick the **Select and Move** and **Restrict to X** buttons. Then, zoom in on the door as needed and move the pivot point on the left edge of Door.

4. Display the four-viewport configuration. Select Window in the Left viewport and maximize the viewport.

5. Zoom in on the window as needed and move the pivot point to the left edge of Window.

6. Select both Window and Door. Then, pick the **Align to World** button in the **Alignment:** area of the **Adjust Pivot** rollout. Finally, pick the **Affect Pivot Only** button to deactivate it.

7. Save the scene.

Animating the Door

Open Track View

1. Move to frame 130 and pick the **Open Track View** button on the **Main** toolbar.
   This is the frame where the door should begin to open.

2. Expand the hierarchy until the rotation track for Door is displayed.

3. Pick the **Add Keys** button on the **Track View** toolbar. Then, add an animation key in the rotation track at frame 130.
   This sets a key with the door's original rotation of 0° on frame 130. In other words, the door will remain closed until frame 130.

4. Close **Track View**.

5. Move to frame 170 and enter animation mode. Pick the **Select and Rotate** and **Restrict to Z** buttons.

6. In the Top viewport, select Door and rotate it –90°.

7. Exit animation mode and save the scene.

Animating the Window

1. Move to frame 855. Open **Track View**.
   This is the frame where the window begins to open.

2. Expand the hierarchy so the rotation track for Window is displayed.

3. Pick the **Add Keys** button on the **Track View** toolbar and add an animation key in the rotation track at frame 855. Close the **Track View** dialog box.
   The window remains closed until this frame.

4. Move to frame 875 and enter animation mode.

5. In the Top viewport, rotate Window –75°. Exit animation mode.

6. Open **Track View**. In the rotation track for Window, select the key at frame 855. Holding down the [Shift] key, move a copy to frame 900.

7. Close **Track View**.

8. Activate the Camera02 viewport. Pick the **Play Animation** button to view the animation.

9. Stop the playback and save the scene.

Rendering a Preview Animation

To verify correct motion in the animation you have created, produce a preview rendering. But, before the preview is rendered, hide the motion path so it is not visible in the preview.

1. Select Walking Path in any viewport.

2. Right-click in the viewport to display the quad menu. Pick **Hide Selection** from the upper-right quadrant.
   The path is hidden and will not be visible in the animation now.

3. Activate the Camera02 viewport. Then, select **Make Preview...** in the **Rendering** pull-down menu.
   The **Make Preview** dialog box is displayed.

4. Pick the **Create** button in the **Make Preview** dialog box to accept the default settings and create the preview.
   The preview is generated and then played in Windows Media Player.

5. Close Media Player.

6. Move to frame 0. Save the scene.

Rendering the Final Animation

After you have verified the motion in the animation with a preview, you can render the final animation. The final animation contains all movement and is rendered with colors, textures, and shadows. This process can take some time, depending on the speed of the computer and the length, complexity, and resolution of the animation. With 1000 frames, rendering this animation even at a low resolution may take more than two hours.

1. Make the Camera02 viewport active.

2. Pick the **Render Scene** button on the **Main** toolbar to display the **Render Scene** dialog box, Figure 16-6.

3. Pick the **Active Time Segment:** radio button in the **Time Output** area of the **Common Parameters** rollout.
   All frames in the active time segment are rendered. The active time segment is currently frame 0 to frame 1000.

4. In the **Output Size** area of the rollout, pick the **320 x 240** button.
   This sets the output to a lower resolution.

Figure 16-6. The **Render Scene** dialog box.

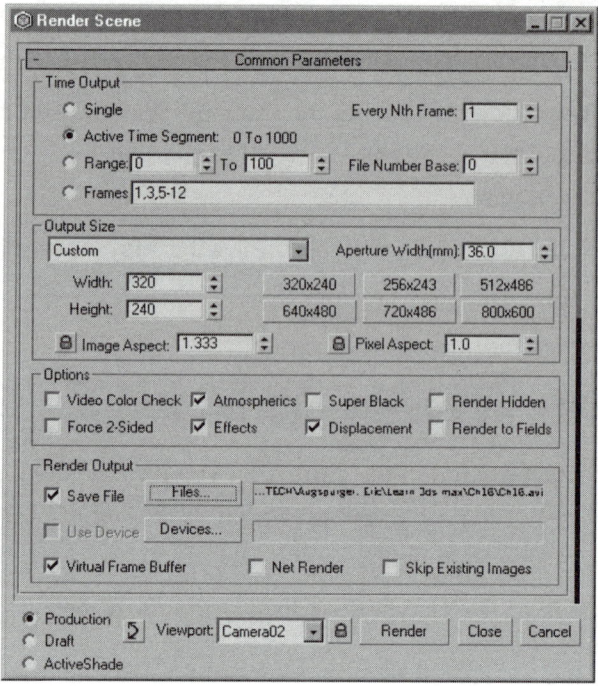

5. Pick the **Files...** button in the **Render Output** area of the rollout.
   The **Render Output File** dialog box is displayed.

6. Type Ch16 in the **File name:** text box. Then, select **AVI File (*.avi)** from the **Save as type:** drop-down list. Finally, pick the **Save** button.
   If the **Video Compression** dialog box is displayed, pick **OK** to accept the default settings.

7. Select Camera02 in the **Viewport:** drop-down list in the **Render Scene** dialog box. Then, pick the **Render** button.

8. When the rendering is complete, close the render window. Also, close the **Render Scene** dialog box. To view the animation, select **View Image File...** from the **File** pull-down menu.
   The **View File** dialog box is displayed.

9. Navigate to the folder where Ch16.avi is located and open the file.
   The animation is played in Windows Media Player.

10. Close Media Player and save the scene.

Self-Evaluation Test

Answer the following questions. Then compare your answers with the correct answers given at the end of this chapter.

1. A walkthrough is an animation that _____.

2. A walkthrough can be created by drawing a _____ for the camera to follow.

3. _____ corners are used to represent the naturally smooth path a person takes while walking.

4. Selecting the _____ radio buttons in the **Initial Type** areas of the **Creation Method** rollout creates a smooth curve when vertices are picked on a line.

5. A walkthrough animation usually requires a _____ number of frames.

6. A _____ allows you to make an object follow a selected path.

7. The final animation contains all movement and is rendered with colors, textures, and shadows. Therefore, the process can take a long time, depending on the speed of the computer and the _____, _____, and _____ of the animation.

8. The _____ the resolution, the longer time it takes to render the animation and the larger the file size will be.

Exercises

Exercise 16-1

Create the scene shown below. Create and apply materials as needed. Add lights and a camera. Then, complete the following steps.

1. Adjust the length of the animation to 500 frames.

2. Create a line to use as a motion path.

3. Create a target camera at the starting point of the motion path behind the ball.

4. Create a dummy object. Assign the camera, camera target, and ball to the dummy as child objects.

5. Using a path constraint controller, make the dummy follow the path.

6. Animate the ball rolling about its axis during the animation. Note: The ball's movement should come from the movement of the dummy.

7. The camera should always look at the ball as it navigates the path.

8. Create a preview animation to verify the speed and movement of the camera. Then, render a final animation.

9. Save the scene as Ex16-01.max in the folder of your choice.

Exercise 16-2

Create the scene shown below. Be sure to include the doors and windows. Create and apply materials as needed. Add lights and a camera. Then, complete the following steps.

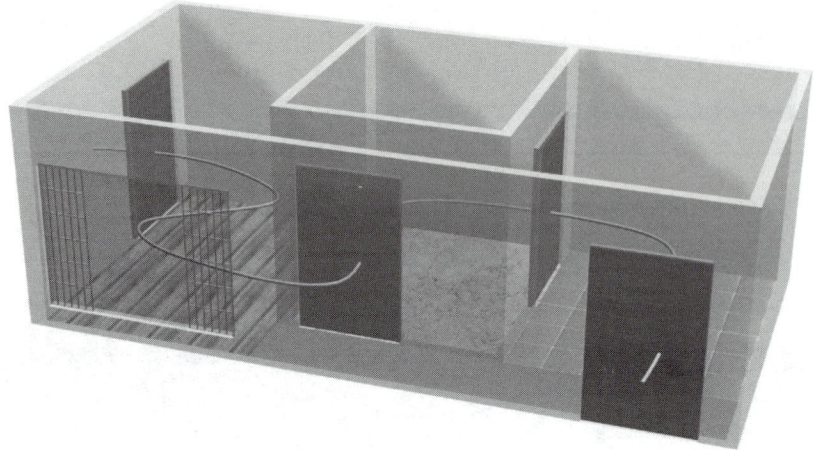

1. Adjust the length of the animation to 1000 frames.

2. Create a line to use as the motion path. The line should enter through the front door, go from room to room, and finally exit through the back door.

3. Create a target camera and a dummy object. Assign a path constraint controller to the dummy. Link the camera and its target to the dummy.

4. Adjust pivot points as needed and animate opening and closing of the doors.

5. Make a preview of the animation to verify motion in the scene.

6. Render a final animation to an AVI file.

7. Save the scene as Ex16-02.max in the folder of your choice.

Answers

The following are the correct answers to the questions in the Self-Evaluation Test.

1. simulates a person walking through a building; 2. path; 3. Smooth; 4. **Smooth**; 5. high; 6. path constraint controller; 7. length, complexity, resolution; 8. higher.

Creating a Clock Tower

Project Description

In this project, you will create the components of a clock tower. You will apply materials to the various objects. Also, you will add lights and a camera to the scene. Finally, you will animate a light and the clock hands. The light will move to simulate the sun with respect to the time on the clock.

Creating the Tower

The tower is drawn in three sections. First, you will create the lower portion. This includes the columns. Next, you will create the middle portion, which is the base for the clock. Finally, you will create the upper portion of the tower.

Creating the Lower Portion

In this section you will create the different parts of the column. Each column consists of a base, shaft, and top. Then, you will assemble the components to create a column. Finally, you will make copies of the original. First, create the overall base for the clock tower.

Create

Geometry

1. Reset 3ds max. Activate the Top viewport.

2. Pick **Create** in the **Command Panel**. Pick the **Geometry** button and select **Standard Primitives** from the drop-down list. Then, pick the **Box** button in the **Object Type** rollout.

3. Expand the **Keyboard Entry** rollout. Type 150 in the **Length:** spinner, 175 in the **Width:** spinner, and 4 in the **Height:** spinner. Then, pick the **Create** button. In the **Name and Color** rollout, name the box Tower Base.
   A box is created at the center of the viewports, which acts as the base of the tower.

4. Pick the **Zoom Extents All** button.

5. Save the scene as Proj01.max in the folder of your choice.

Creating the First Column

1. Activate the Top viewport. Pick **Create** in the **Command Panel**. Pick the **Geometry** button and select **Standard Primitives** from the drop-down list. Then, pick the **Box** button in the **Object Type** rollout.

2. Expand the **Keyboard Entry** rollout. Type 30 in the **Length:** spinner, 30 in the **Width:** spinner, and 40 in the **Height:** spinner. Then, pick the **Create** button. In the **Name and Color** rollout, name the box Base01.
   A box is created at the center of the viewports.

3. In the **Keyboard Entry** rollout, type 35 in the **Length:** spinner, 35 in the **Width:** spinner, and 8 in the **Height:** spinner. Then, pick the **Create** button. In the **Name and Color** rollout, name the box Base01Cap.

4. In the **Keyboard Entry** rollout, type 25 in the **Length:** spinner, 25 in the **Width:** spinner, and 135 in the **Height:** spinner. Then, pick the **Create** button. In the **Name and Color** rollout, name the box Column01Shaft.

Select and Move

Restrict to Y

5. Pick the **Select and Move** and **Restrict to Y** buttons on the **Main** toolbar. In the Front viewport, move Base01 up so its bottom edge aligns with the top edge of Tower Base. Then, move Base01Cap up so its bottom edge aligns with the top edge of Base01.

6. With Base01Cap selected, pick **Parametric Deformers** in the **Modifiers** pull-down menu. Then, pick **Taper** in the cascading menu.
   *A taper modifier is applied to the box, and the **Modify** tab is automatically displayed.*

7. In the **Parameters** rollout, type –.25 in the **Amount:** spinner. Also, set the primary axis as Z and the effect on the XY axes.

8. Pick the **Select and Move** and **Restrict to Y** buttons on the **Main** toolbar. In the Front viewport, move Column01Shaft up so its bottom edge aligns with the top edge of Base01Cap.

9. In the Top viewport, select Base01, Base01Cap, and Column01Shaft. Then, move the objects straight up so the top edge of Base01 aligns with the top edge of Tower Base. The objects should be centered left-to-right on Tower Base as well, Figure P1-1.

10. Save the scene.

Figure P1-1. One column is created.

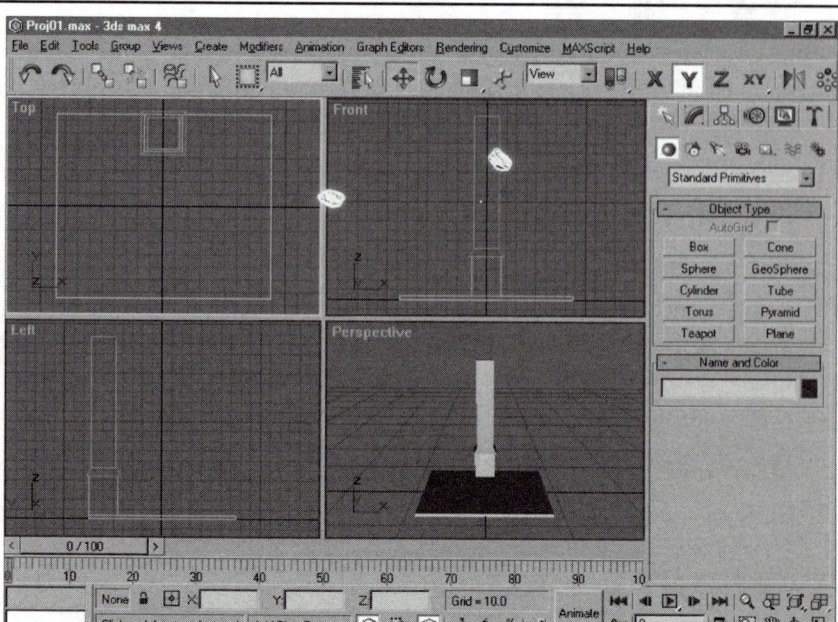

Creating Two More Columns

1. Pick the **Select and Rotate** and **Restrict to Z** buttons on the **Main** toolbar. Select Base01, Base01Cap, and Column01Shaft. In the Top viewport, hold down the [Shift] key and rotate the three objects 30°. In the **Clone Options** dialog box that appears, name the copy Base02Cap.

2. In the Top viewport, move the three objects so the left and right corners of Base02 align with the left and bottom edges of Tower Base. Also, verify that each of the three objects is named "02" and rename as needed.

3. Make sure **View** is selected in the reference coordinate system drop-down list on the **Main** toolbar. With Base02, Base02Cap, and Column02Shaft selected, pick the **Mirror Selected Objects** button on the **Main** toolbar.
   The **Mirror** dialog box is displayed.

4. In the **Clone Selection:** area of the **Mirror** dialog box, pick the **Copy** radio button. Then, in the **Mirror Axis:** area of the dialog box, pick the **X** radio button and type 134 in the **Offset:** spinner. Then, pick the **OK** button to create the mirrored copy, Figure P1-2.

5. Pick the **Zoom Extents All** button. Save the scene.

Figure P1-2. Two copies of the first column are created and correctly located.

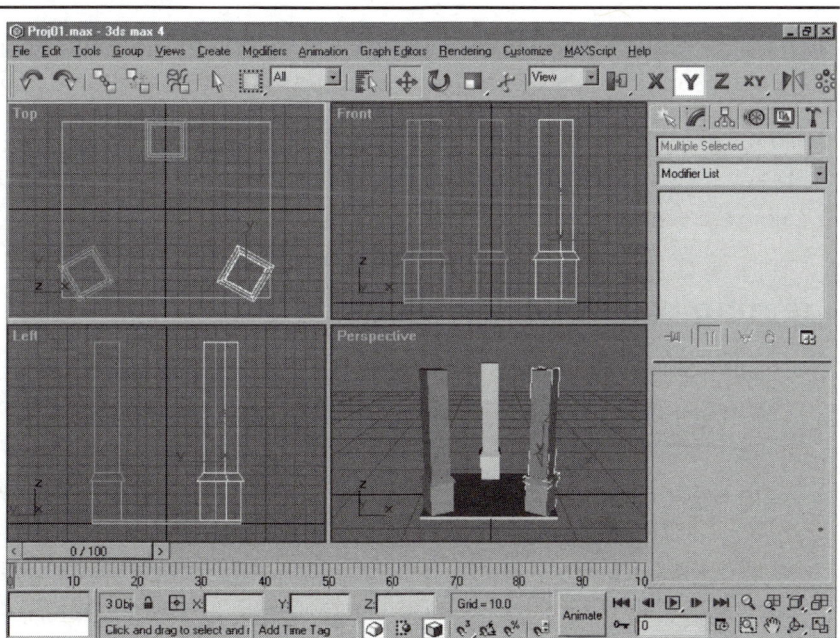

Creating the Middle Portion

1. Pick **Create** in the **Command Panel**. Pick the **Geometry** button and select **Extended Primitives** from the drop-down list. Then, pick the **Gengon** button in the **Object Type** rollout. Draw a gengon of any size anywhere in the Top viewport. In the **Name and Color** rollout, name the gengon Column Top.

2. In the **Parameters** rollout, type 3 in the **Sides:** spinner, 120 in the **Radius:** spinner, 26 in the **Fillet:** spinner, and 4 in the **Height:** spinner.

3. Pick the **Select and Rotate** and **Restrict to Z** buttons on the **Main** toolbar. Then, rotate the gengon –30°.
   The gengon now aligns with the angles of the columns.

Figure P1-3. The column top is created and placed.

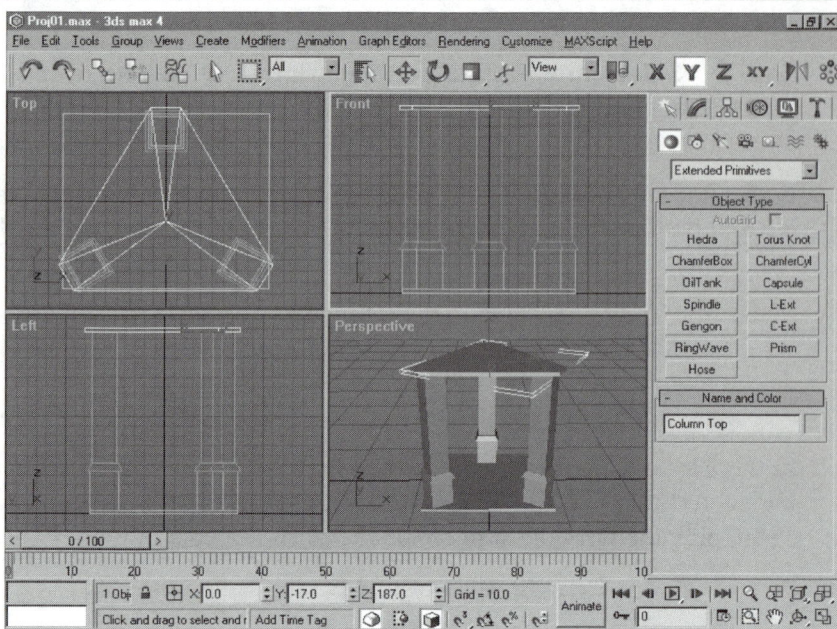

4. Pick the **Select and Move** and **Restrict to XY Plane** buttons on the **Main** toolbar. Move the gengon so it is centered on the three columns. It should extend slightly past all three columns.

5. In the Front viewport, move the gengon up so its bottom edge aligns with the tops of the columns, Figure P1-3.

6. Save the scene.

Creating the Upper Portion

1. Select Column Top. Then, pick **Clone** in the **Edit** pull-down menu. In the **Clone Options** dialog box that appears, name the copy Clock Base and pick the **OK** button.

2. In the Front viewport, move Clock Base up so its bottom edge aligns with the top edge of Column Top.

3. With Clock Base selected, pick **Modify** in the **Command Panel**. In the **Parameters** rollout, type 110 in the **Height:** spinner and 100 in the **Radius:** spinner.

4. Pick the **Restrict to Y** button. Holding down the [Shift] key, move Column Top up so its bottom edge aligns with the top edge of Clock Base. In the **Clone Options** dialog box that appears, name the copy Clock Top.

5. With Clock Top selected, pick **Modify** in the **Command Panel**. In the **Parameters** rollout, type 3 in the **Height Segs:** spinner.

6. Next, pick **Mesh Editing** in the **Modifiers** pull-down menu. Then, pick **Edit Mesh** in the cascading menu.
   An edit mesh modifier is applied to the object, and the **Modify** tab is automatically displayed.

7. In the **Selection** rollout, pick the **Vertex** button to enter vertex sub-object mode.

8. In the Front viewport, select the very top row of vertices. Then, pick the **Select and Move** and **Restrict to Y** buttons and move the selected vertices 50 units straight up.

9. With the top row of vertices selected, pick the **Select and Uniform Scale** button. Scale the vertices down to 1% to form a point. Next, pick the **Select and Move** and **Restrict to X** buttons. In the Left viewport, move the point to the horizontal center of Tower Base, Figure P1-4. Then, pick the **Vertex** button to exit sub-object mode.

10. Save the scene.

Figure P1-4. The clock base and top are created and placed. Notice how the top has been modified.

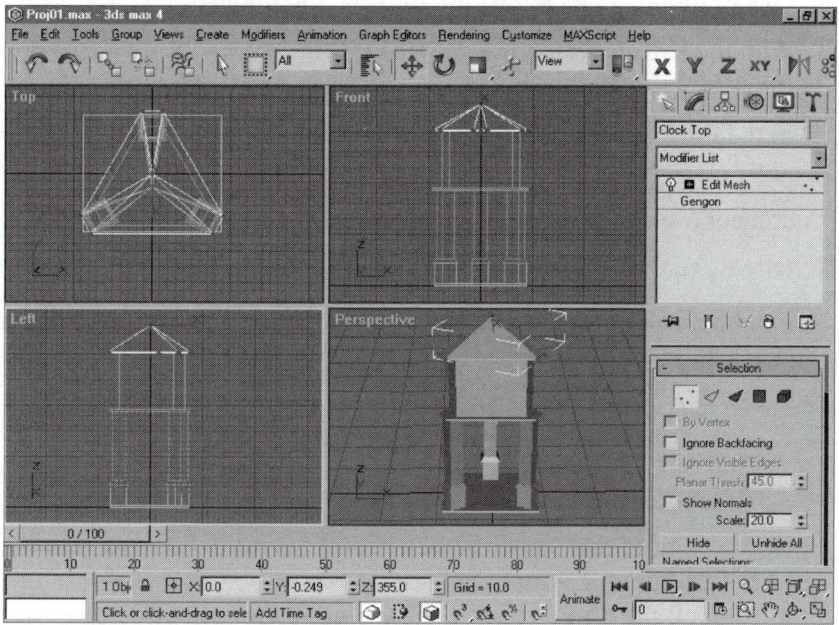

Creating the Clock

There are three clocks in the scene, one on each face of Clock Base. You will create one clock and correctly position in on one face. Then, you will copy the first clock to create the other two.

1. Activate the Front viewport. Pick **Create** in the **Command Panel**. Pick the **Shapes** button and select **Splines** from the drop-down list. Then, pick the **Circle** button in the **Object Type** rollout.

2. Expand the **Keyboard** rollout. Type 35 in the **Radius:** spinner and pick the **Create** button. In the **Name and Color** rollout, name the object Clock Face01.
   A circle is created at the world origin.

3. Pick the **Select and Move** and **Restrict to Y** buttons. Move the circle up so it is vertically centered on Clock Base.

4. With Clock Face01 selected, pick **Mesh Editing** in the **Modifiers** pull-down menu. Then, pick **Extrude** from the cascading menu.
   *An extrude modifier is applied to the circle, and the **Modify** tab is automatically displayed.*

5. In the **Parameters** rollout, type 2 in the **Amount:** spinner.

6. Activate the Top viewport. Pick the **Select and Move** and **Restrict to Y** buttons. Then, move Clock Face01 straight down so its top edge aligns with the bottom edge of Clock Base.

7. Save the scene.

Create

Shapes

Adding Numbers

1. Activate the Front viewport and maximize it.

2. Pick **Create** in the **Command Panel**. Pick the **Shapes** button and select **Splines** from the drop-down list. Then, pick the **Text** button in the **Object Type** rollout.

3. In the **Parameters** rollout, select **Arial Bold** (or other font) from the drop-down list. Type 10 in the **Size:** spinner. Then, type an uppercase letter I in the **Text:** field for a Roman numeral one. In the **Name and Color** rollout, name the text Clock Face01 Text01.

4. Pick at the 12 o'clock position to place the number.

5. With the text selected, pick **Mesh Editing** in the **Modifier** pull-down menu. Then, select **Extrude** from the cascading menu.

6. In the **Parameters** rollout, type 1 in the **Amount:** spinner.

7. Repeat steps 2 through 6 to place II at the 3 o'clock position, III at the 6 o'clock position, and IV at the 9 o'clock position. Rename the text objects as appropriate.

8. Display the four-viewport configuration. Activate the Top viewport and select the four numbers.

9. Pick the **Select and Move** and **Restrict to Y** buttons. Move the four numbers down so their top edges align with the bottom edge of Clock Face01.

10. Save the scene.

Adding Hands

1. Now, you need to create the clock hands. Activate the Front viewport and maximize it. Pick **Create** in the **Command Panel**. Pick the **Shapes** button and select **Splines** from the drop-down list. Then, pick the **Line** button in the **Object Type** rollout.

2. Draw a closed spline similar to the one shown in Figure P1-5. Feel free to use a shape of your own design. However, make sure the spline is closed.

3. When the spline is drawn, center the circular portion on Clock Face01. Also, move the pivot point of the spline so it is centered on Clock Face01. Finally, in the **Name and Color** rollout, name the spline Big Hand01.

Figure P1-5. Sample shapes for creating the hands. The dimensions are approximate. You can use your own shapes and dimensions.

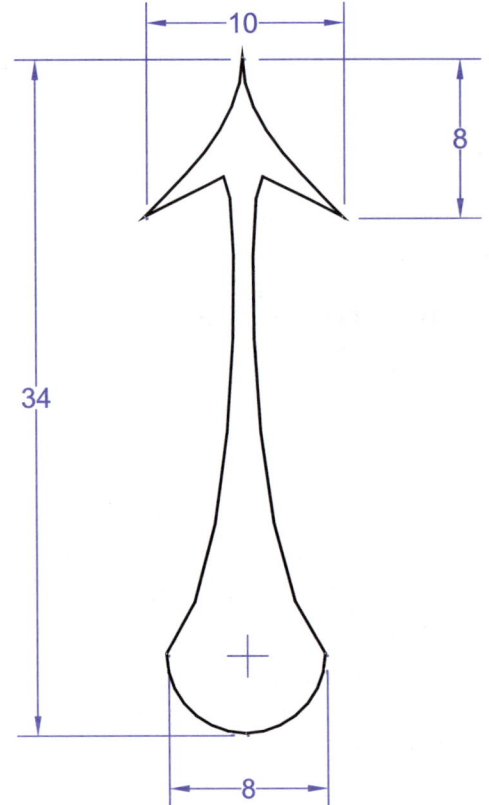
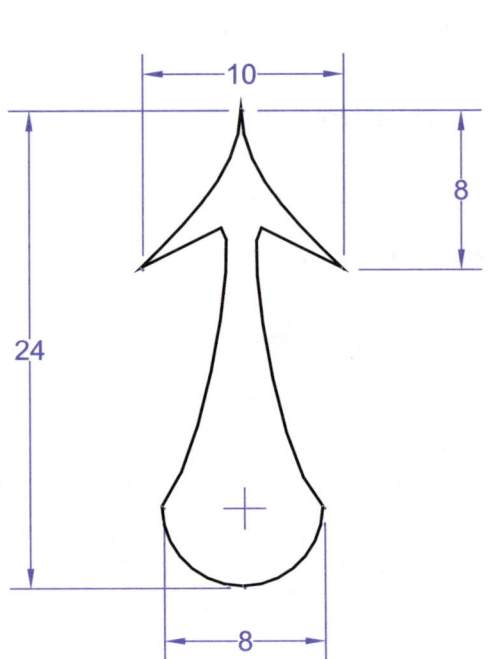

4. Clone a copy of the spline named Little Hand01. At the vertex sub-object level, select the vertices that make up the arrowhead and move them to create a smaller clock hand.

5. Draw a cylinder centered on Clock Face01. The radius of the cylinder should be a little less that the circular portions of the clock hands. Make the height of the cylinder 2 units. In the **Name and Color** rollout, name the cylinder Hands Base01.

6. Select Big Hand01. Pick **Mesh Editing** in the **Modifiers** pull-down menu. Then, pick **Extrude** in the cascading menu. In the **Parameters** rollout, type 4 in the **Amount:** spinner. Also, extrude Little Hand01 four units.

7. Display the four-viewport configuration. Activate the Top viewport and maximize it.

8. Select Hands Base01 and move it down so its top edge aligns with the bottom edge of Clock Face01. Next, select Big Hand01 and move it down so its top edge aligns with the bottom edge of Hands Base01. Finally, select Little Hand01 and move it down so its top edge aligns with the bottom edge of Big Hand01, Figure P1-6.

9. Display the four-viewport configuration and pick the **Zoom Extents All** button.

10. Save the scene.

Creating Two More Clocks

1. Activate the Top viewport and maximize it. Pick the **Select and Rotate** and **Restrict to Z** buttons. Make sure the **Use Selection Center** button is selected in the transform coordinate center flyout.

Use Selection Center

2. Select all components of the first clock. This includes Clock Face01, Clock Face01 Text01, Clock Face01 Text02, Clock Face01 Text03, Clock Face01 Text04, Big Hand01, Little Hand01, and Hands Base01. Press the spacebar to lock the selection.

Figure P1-6. The big hand, little hand, and hand base are correctly located on the clock face.

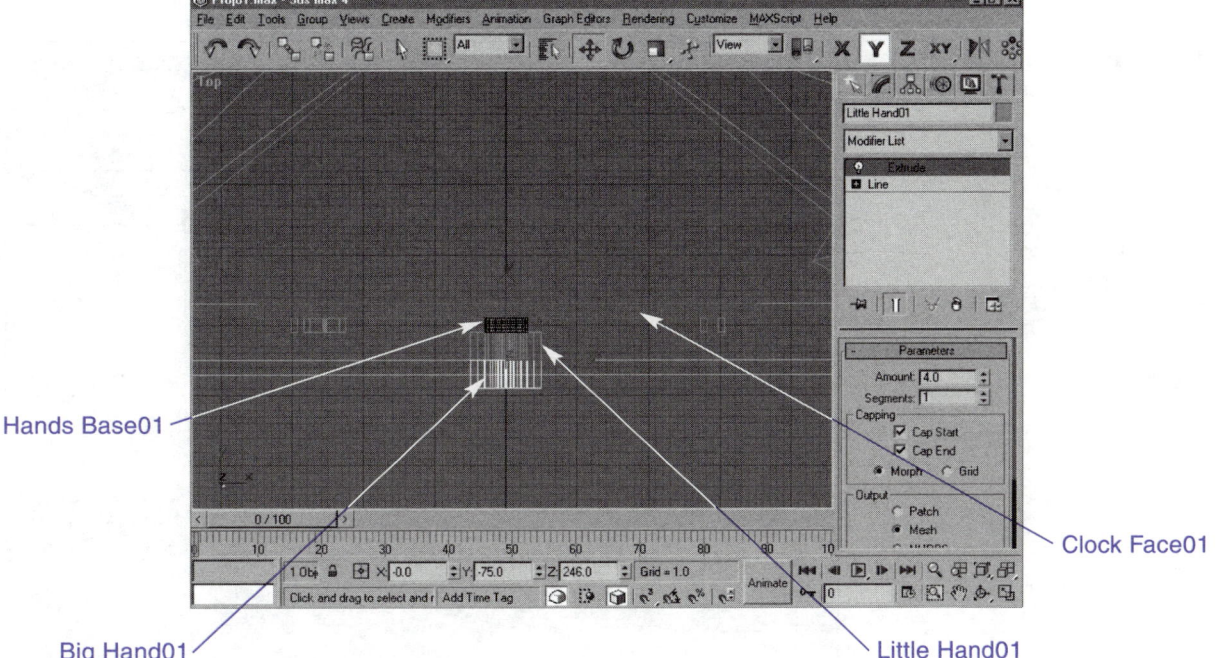

3. Holding down the [Shift] key, rotate all components of the first clock as a group 120°. In the **Clone Options** dialog box that appears, pick the **Copy** radio button and then the **OK** button.
   If you named your objects logically, using the names given in the project, the copies will have proper "sequential" names except for the text objects. Rename these as Clock Face02 Text01, etc., as needed after you move the clock into the correct position.

4. Press the spacebar to lock the selection set of the copied objects. Then, pick the **Select and Move** and **Restrict to XY Plane** buttons. In the Top viewport, move the second clock so it is flush with the right-hand face of Clock Base. Also, center it on the face.

5. Pick the **Select and Rotate** and **Restrict to Z** buttons. Holding down the [Shift] key, rotate the second clock 120º. In the **Clone Options** dialog box that appears, pick the **Copy** radio button and then the **OK** button.
   If you named your objects logically, using the names given in the project, the copies will have proper "sequential" names except for the text objects. Rename these as Clock Face03 Text01, etc., as needed after you move the clock into the correct position.

6. Pick the **Select and Move** and **Restrict to XY Plane** buttons. In the Top viewport, move the third clock so it is flush with the left-hand face of Clock Base. Also, center it on the face.

7. Display the four-viewport configuration and pick the **Zoom Extents All** button, Figure P1-7.

8. Save the scene.

Adding Lights and a Camera

Create

Lights

1. Activate the Front viewport. Then, pick **Create** in the **Command Panel**. Pick the **Lights** button and select **Standard** from the drop-down list. Then, pick the **Omni** button in the **Object Type** rollout.

2. Pick a point at about the vertical center of the columns, and in the center of the tower, to place an omni light. In the **General Parameters** rollout, check the **Cast Shadows** check box and type 0.8 in the **Multiplier:** spinner.

Figure P1-7. Two copies of the clock are created and placed.

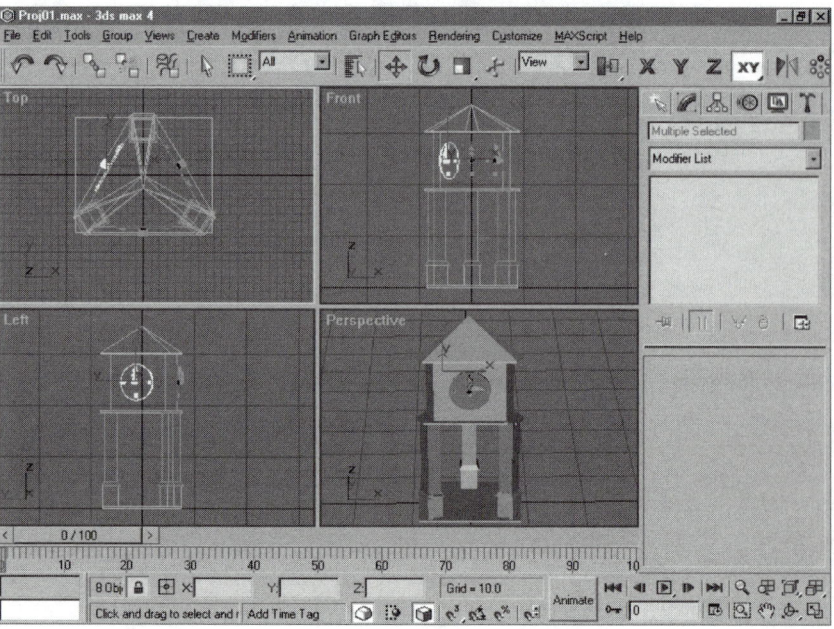

3. Activate the Top viewport and zoom out. Then, pick **Create** in the **Command Panel**. Pick the **Lights** button and select **Standard** from the drop-down list. Then, pick the **Target Direct** button in the **Object Type** rollout.

4. Pick a point on the left side of the viewport and slightly below the centerline of the objects to place the light. Then, drag the target to the center of the objects.

5. Activate the Front viewport. Pick the **Select and Move** and **Restrict to XY Plane** buttons. Move the light to just above the level of the base.

6. With the direct light selected, pick **Modify** in the **Command Panel**. In the **General Parameters** rollout, check the **Cast Shadows** check box. Also, type 1.5 in the **Multiplier:** spinner. In the **Directional Parameters** rollout, type 200 in the **Hotspot:** spinner.

Create

7. Pick **Create** in the **Command Panel**. Pick the **Cameras** button and select **Standard** from the drop-down list. Then, pick the **Target** button in the **Object Type** rollout. In the Top viewport, pick a point at the lower-left corner of the viewport to place the camera. Drag the target to the center of the objects.

Cameras

8. Change the Perspective viewport to the Camera01 viewport. Move the camera and adjust the viewport as needed to get a good view of the objects, Figure P1-8.

9. Save the scene.

Applying Materials

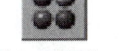

Material Editor

1. Pick the **Material Editor** button on the **Main** toolbar to open the **Material Editor**. Activate the first material sample slot and pick the **Get Material** button.
The **Material/Map Browser** is opened.

Get Material

2. In the **Material/Map Browser**, pick the **Mtl Library** radio button in the **Browse From:** area. Then, double-click on Bricks_Bricks_2 in the list.

3. Similarly, load the material Stones_Limestone into the second material sample slot, Stones_Balmoral into the third material sample slot, Concrete_Stucco into the fourth sample slot, Metal_Brushed into the fifth sample slot, and Metal_Black_Plain into the sixth sample slot.

Figure P1-8. Lights and a camera are added to the scene.

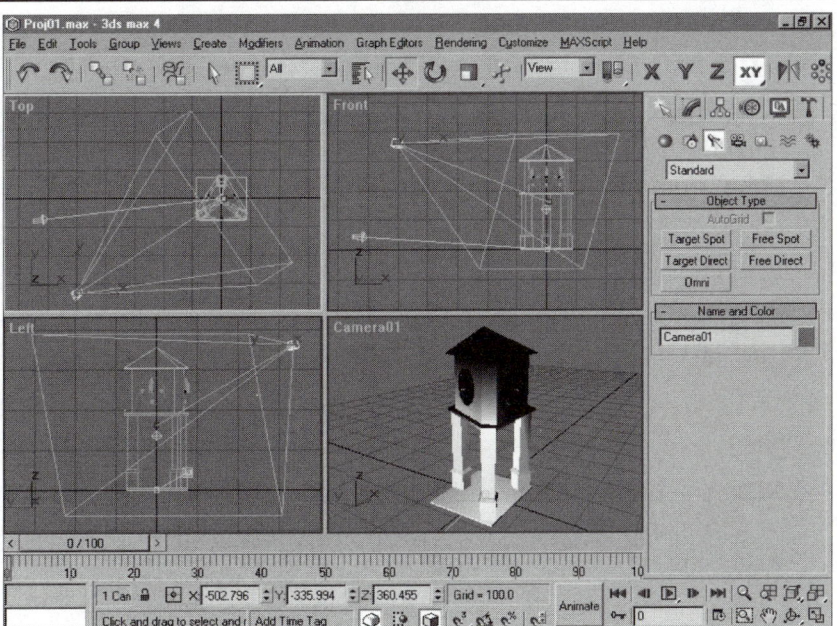

4. Assign the material Bricks_Bricks_2 to the objects Base01, Base02, Base03, Column01Shaft, Column02Shaft, and Column03Shaft. Also, one by one, select each object and pick **UV Coordinates** from the **Modifiers** pull-down menu. Then, pick **UVW Map** from the cascading menu. Adjust the modifier as needed for each object. The scale of the bricks should be the same on the columns as on the bases.

5. Assign the material Concrete_Stucco to the objects Base01Cap, Base02Cap, Base03Cap, Clock Face01, Clock Face02, and Clock Face03. Apply UVW map modifiers to the objects as needed.

6. Assign the material Stones_Limestone to the object Tower Base. Apply a UVW map modifier to the object and adjust as needed.

7. Assign the material Stones_Balmoral to the objects Column Top, Clock Base, and Clock Top. Apply UVW map modifiers to the objects as needed.

8. Assign the material Metal_Brushed to the number objects. Apply UVW map modifiers to the objects as needed.

9. Assign the material Metal_Black_Plain to the hand objects, including the hand bases. Apply UVW map modifiers to the objects as needed.

10. Save the scene.

Animating the Objects

You will now add motion to the scene. The animation will be of the clock tower during 12 hours of the day, from 6 am to 6 pm. The hands of the clocks will move, and the spotlight will move to represent the sun traveling across the sky.

Setting the Animation Length

Time Configuration

1. Pick the **Time Configuration** button to open the **Time Configuration** dialog box.

2. In the **Animation** area of the dialog box, type 1200 in the **Length:** spinner.

3. Pick the **OK** button to close the dialog box.

4. Save the scene.

Animating the Hands and Light

1. Make sure you are on frame 0. The scene starts at 6 am, so the positions of the hands need to reflect this time. Pick the **Select and Rotate** and **Restrict to Z** buttons on the **Main** toolbar. Also, select **Local** from the coordinate system drop-down list.

2. One by one, select the big hand in any viewport and rotate it to point to the 6 o'clock position. Locking the selection set can help.

3. Next, select each little hand and rotate it to point to the 12 o'clock position. The time displayed on each clock should now be 6 o'clock.

4. Move to the last frame in the animation and enter animation mode. One by one, rotate each little hand –360°. Also, rotate each big hand –4320° (360° times 12 hours). Exit animation mode.

5. Now, you need to animate the direct light to simulate the movement of the sun. You will use five positions, including the starting position, to define the motion. Move to frame 0 and verify that the light is just above the Tower Base in the Front viewport.

6. Move to frame 300 and enter animation mode. Also, make sure **View** is selected in the coordinate system drop-down list.

7. In the Front viewport, move the light up and to the right so it is at about a 45° to the world origin, Figure P1-9.
   You should try to move the light so it appears to travel along an invisible arc in the Front viewport.

8. Move to frame 600. Then, move the light up and to the right so it is straight overhead.

9. Move to frame 900. Then, move the light down and to the right so it is at about a 45° to the world origin.

10. Move to frame 1200. Then, move the light down and to the right so it is opposite of its starting position.

11. Move to frame 0 and exit animation mode.

12. Save the scene.

Figure P1-9. The direct light is moved to its proper location on the first keyframe.

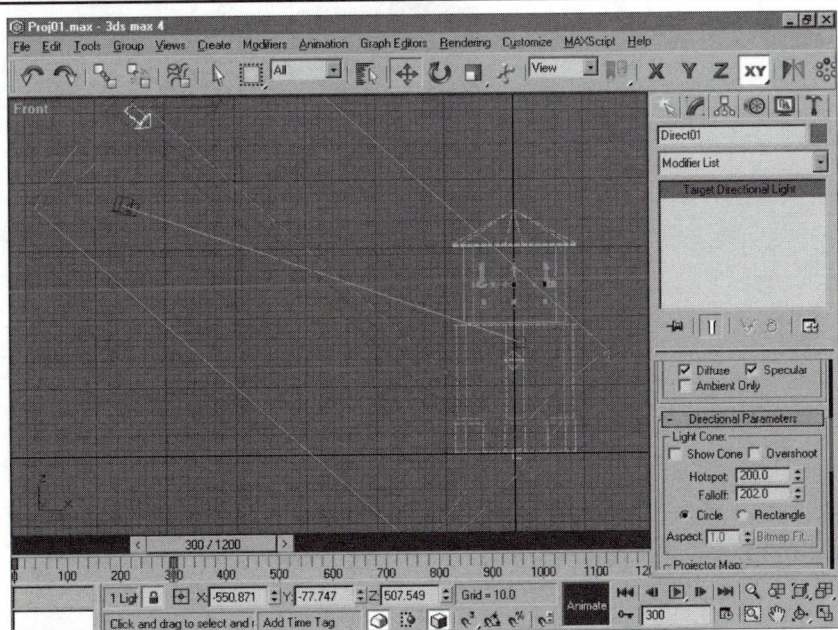

Rendering the Animation

1. To verify motion in the scene, make a preview of the Camera01 viewport.
   Fix any motion problems as needed.

Render Scene

2. Pick the **Render Scene** button on the **Main** toolbar to display the **Render Scene** dialog box. In the **Time Output** area, pick the **Active Time Segment:** radio button.

3. In the **Output Size** area of the dialog box, pick the **320x240** button.

4. In the **Render Output** area of the dialog box, pick the **Files...** button. In the **Render Output File** dialog box that appears, navigate to the folder where you want to store the file. Type Proj01 in the **File name:** text box. Then, pick **AVI File (*.avi)** from the drop-down list and pick the **Save** button.
   If the **Video Compression** dialog box is displayed, pick **OK** to accept the defaults.

5. Make sure the **Save File** check box is checked in the **Render Output** area of the **Render Scene** dialog box.

6. Make sure Camera01 is selected in the **Viewport:** drop-down list. Then, pick the **Render** button.
   It may take an hour or more to render the final animation.

7. When the rendering is complete, close the render window and the **Render Scene** dialog box. Then, pick **View Image File...** from the **File** pull-down menu.
   The **View File** dialog box is displayed.

8. Navigate to the folder where Proj01.avi is located and open the file, Figure P1-10.
   The animation is played in Windows Media Player.

9. Close Media Player and save the scene.

Figure P1-10. A frame from the final rendered animation.

Creating a Pool Room

Project Description

In this project, you will create a pool room that consists of a floor, walls, a ceiling, and a pool table. A lamp with a shade will be suspended from the ceiling. Billiard balls will be added to the pool table and animated. You will also add a painting to the wall. You will then apply materials to the different objects, add lights and a camera to the scene, and render the final animation.

Creating the Scene

First, you will create the floor, walls, and ceiling. Then, you will create the pool table. To complete the scene, you will add details such as a wall poster. Start by resetting 3ds max.

Creating the Floor, Walls, and Ceiling

1. Activate the Top viewport. Then, pick **Create** in the **Command Panel**. Pick the **Geometry** button and select **Standard Primitives** from the drop-down list. Then, pick the **Box** button in the **Object Type** rollout.

Create

Geometry

2. Expand the **Keyboard Entry** rollout. Type 130 in the **Length:** spinner, 130 in the **Width:** spinner, and 1 in the **Height:** text box. Then, pick the **Create** button. In the **Name and Color** rollout, name the box Floor.

   A box is created at the center of the viewports.

3. Activate the Front viewport. Pick the **Zoom Extents All** button.

4. With the **Keyboard Entry** rollout still expanded, type 100 in the **Length:** spinner, 130 in the **Width:** spinner, and 1 in the **Height:** spinner. Then, pick the **Create** button. In the **Name and Color** rollout, name the box Wall01.

   Another box is created at the center of the viewports.

5. Pick the **Select and Move** and **Restrict to Y** buttons on the **Main** toolbar. Move Wall01 up in the Front viewport so its lower edge aligns with the upper edge of Floor.

Select and Move

Restrict to Y

313

Select and Rotate

Restrict to Z

Restrict to XY Plane

Restrict to X

6. Activate the Top viewport. Pick the **Select and Rotate** and **Restrict to Z** buttons on the **Main** toolbar.

7. With Wall01 selected, hold down the [Shift] key and rotate it 90º. In the **Clone Options** dialog box that appears, name the copy Wall02 and pick the **OK** button.

8. Pick the **Select and Move** and **Restrict to XY Plane** buttons. In the Top viewport, move Wall01 so its top edge aligns with the top edge of Floor. Also, move Wall02 to the right so its right edge aligns with the right edge of Floor.

9. Pick the **Select and Move** and **Restrict to X** buttons. Select Wall02, hold down the [Shift] key, and move the object to the left. In the **Clone Options** dialog box that appears, name the copy Wall03 and pick the **OK** button. Then, move Wall03 so its left edge aligns with the left edge of Floor.

10. Activate the Front viewport. Select Floor and pick the **Restrict to Y** button. Holding down the [Shift] key, move Floor up. In the **Clone Options** dialog box that appears, name the copy Ceiling and pick the **OK** button. Then, move Ceiling so its top edge aligns with the top edges of the three walls, Figure P2-1.

11. Save the scene as Proj02.max in the folder of your choice.

Creating the Basic Pool Table

1. Activate the Top viewport. Then, pick **Create** in the **Command Panel**. Pick the **Geometry** button and select **Standard Primitives** from the drop-down list. Then, pick the **Box** button in the **Object Type** rollout.

2. Expand the **Keyboard Entry** rollout. Type 70 in the **Length:** spinner, 45 in the **Width:** spinner, and 10 in the **Height:** spinner. Then, pick the **Create** button. In the **Name and Color** rollout, name the box Table Bottom.

3. Activate the Left viewport. Pick the **Select and Move** and **Restrict to Y** buttons. Move Table Bottom up 26 units.

4. Activate the Top viewport. Pick **Create** in the **Command Panel**. Pick the **Geometry** button and select **Standard Primitives** from the drop-down list. Then, pick the **Box** button.

Figure P2-1. The floor, ceiling, and three walls are created.

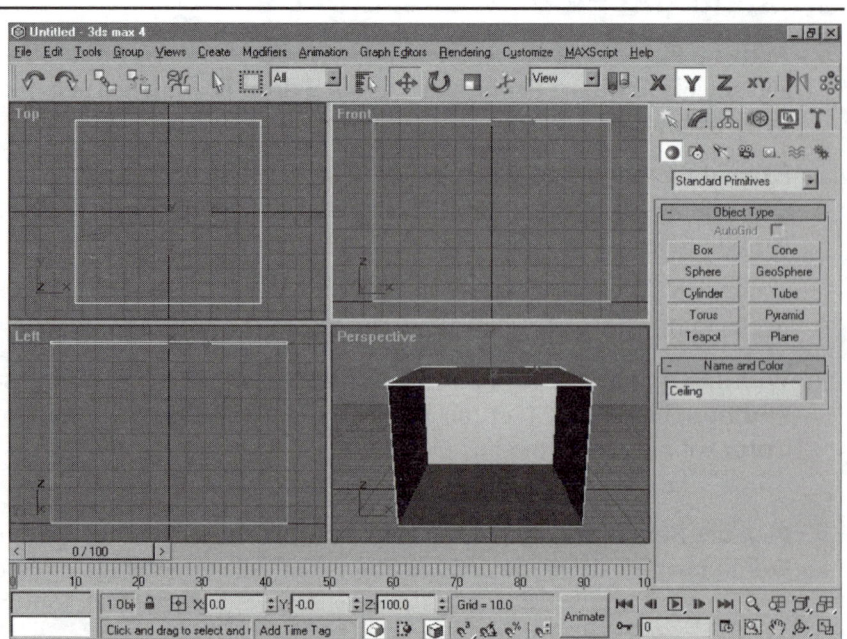

5. Expand the **Keyboard Entry** rollout. Type 62 in the **Length:** spinner, 37 in the **Width:** spinner, and 2.5 in the **Height:** spinner. Then, pick the **Create** button. In the **Name and Color** rollout, name the box Table Drill. In the Left viewport, move Table Drill up so its top edge aligns with the top edge of Table Bottom.

6. Select Table Bottom. Then, pick **Create** in the **Command Panel**. Pick the **Geometry** button and select **Compound Objects** from the drop-down list. Then, pick the **Boolean** button in the **Object Type** rollout.

7. In the **Parameters** rollout, pick the **Subtraction [A-B]** radio button. In the **Pick Boolean** rollout, select the **Move** radio button. Then, select the **Pick Operand B** button and select Table Drill in the viewport. Right-click to complete the operation.

   The drill object is subtracted from the box.

8. Activate the Front viewport. Then, pick **Create** in the **Command Panel**. Pick the **Geometry** button and select **Standard Primitives** from the drop-down list. Then, pick the **Box** button in the **Object Type** rollout. In the **Keyboard Entry** rollout, type 25 in the **Length:** spinner, 10 in the **Width:** spinner, and 12 in the **Height:** spinner. Then, pick the **Create** button. In the **Name and Color** rollout, name the box Leg01.

9. Pick the **Select and Move** and **Restrict to Y** buttons. Move Leg01 up so its lower edge aligns with the top edge of Floor, and its top edge aligns with the bottom edge of Table Top. Activate the Top viewport and pick the **Restrict to XY Plane** button. Move Leg01 so its lower-left corner aligns with the lower-left corner of the inside rails (cutout portion), Figure P1-2.

10. With Leg01 selected, pick the **Mirror Selected Objects** button on the **Main** toolbar. In the **Clone Selection:** area of the **Mirror** dialog box that appears, pick the **Copy** radio button. In the **Mirror Axis:** area of the dialog box, pick the **X** radio button and type 27 in the **Offset:** spinner. Then, pick the **OK** button.

    A mirrored copy of Leg01 is created.

11. Select Leg01 and Leg02. Then, pick the **Mirror Selected Objects** button. In the **Mirror** dialog box, pick the **Copy** radio button. In the **Mirror Axis:** area of the dialog box, pick the **Y** radio button and type 50 in the **Offset:** spinner. Then, pick the **OK** button.

    Mirrored copies of Leg01 and Leg02 are created, Figure P2-3.

12. Save the scene.

Figure P2-2. The table and one leg are created.

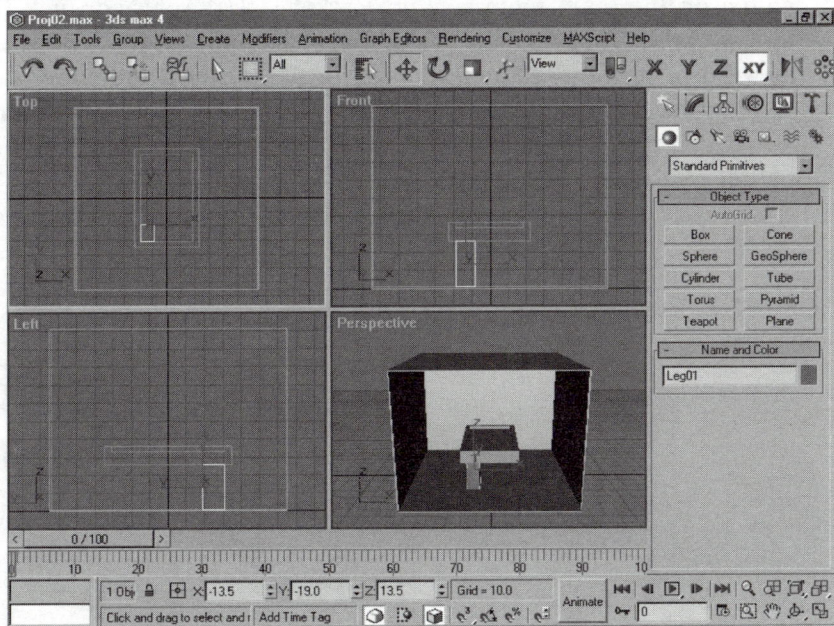

Figure P2-3. Mirrored copies of the first leg are created.

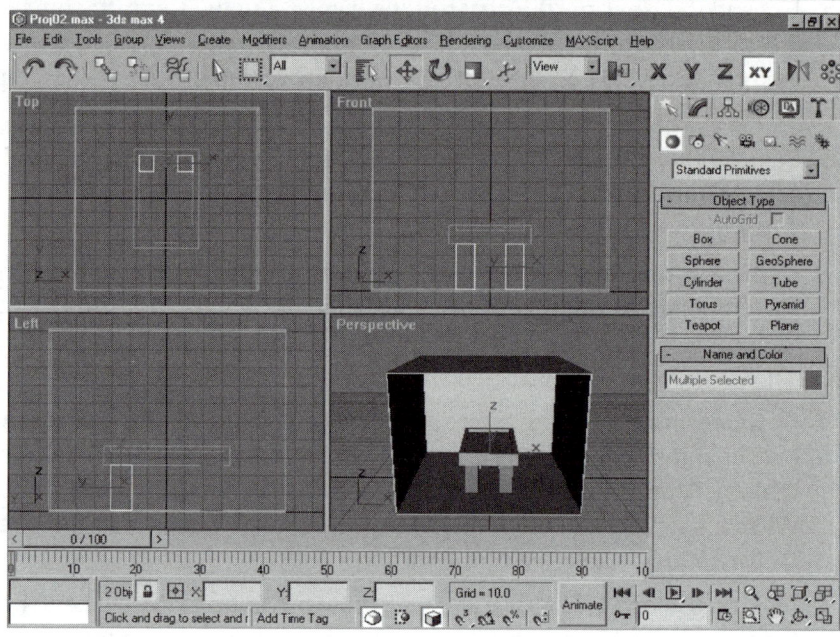

Creating the Pockets

1. Activate the Top viewport. Pick **Create** in the **Command Panel**. Pick the **Geometry** button and select **Standard Primitives** from the drop-down list. Then, pick the **Cylinder** button in the **Object Type** rollout.

2. Expand the **Keyboard Entry** rollout. Type 2.5 in the **Radius:** spinner, and 7 in the **Height:** spinner. Then, pick the **Create** button. In the **Name and Color** rollout, name the cylinder Pocket Drill01.

3. Activate the Front viewport. Pick the **Select and Move** and **Restrict to Y** buttons. Then, move Pocket Drill01 up 30 units.

4. Activate the Top viewport. Move Pocket Drill01 down and to the left so that its center is at the corner of the inside rails.

Use Pivot Point Center

5. In the coordinate system drop-down list, select **View**. Also, pick the **Use Pivot Point Center** button on the **Main** toolbar. With Pocket Drill01 selected, pick the **Array** button on the **Main** toolbar. In the **Array** dialog box that appears, type 37 in the **Move X** spinner in the **Incremental** area. Also, pick the **2D** radio button in the **Array Dimensions** area. Type 2 in the **1D Count** spinner and 3 in the **2D Count** spinner. Also, type 31 in the **Y Incremental Row Offset** spinner. Verify that the total number of objects in the array is listed as 6, Figure P2-4. Then, pick the **OK** button to close the dialog box and create the array.

An array of six cylinders is created in the location for the six pockets.

Figure P2-4. Creating an array for the pockets.

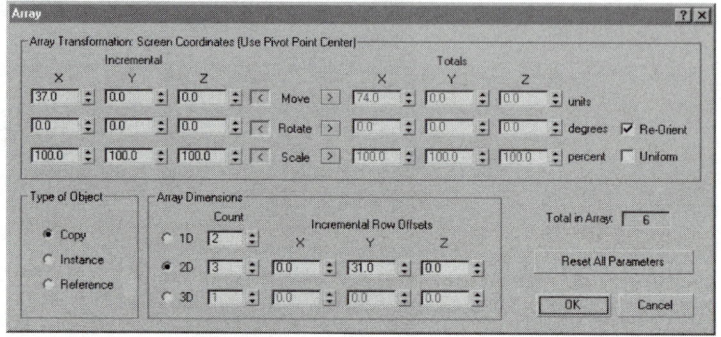

6. Select Table Bottom. Then, pick **Create** in the **Command Panel**. Pick the **Geometry** button and select **Compound Objects** from the drop-down list. Then, pick the **Boolean** button in the **Object Type** rollout.

7. In the **Parameters** rollout, select the **Subtraction [A-B]** radio button. In the **Pick Boolean** rollout, select the **Copy** radio button. Then, select the **Pick Operand B** button and select Pocket Drill01 in the viewport. Right-click to complete the operation.
   One pocket is created, and the cylinder is left for a future operation.

8. Repeat steps 6 and 7 for the remaining five "pocket drill" objects.

9. Save the scene.

Creating the Slate

1. Activate the Top viewport. Then, pick **Create** in the **Command Panel**. Pick the **Geometry** button and select **Standard Primitives** from the drop-down list. Then, pick the **Box** button in the **Object Type** rollout.

2. Expand the **Keyboard Entry** rollout. Type 62 in the **Length:** spinner, 37 in the **Width:** spinner, and .5 in the **Height:** spinner. Then, pick the **Create** button. In the **Name and Color** rollout, name the box Slate.

3. Activate the Front viewport. Pick the **Select and Move** and **Restrict to Y** buttons. Then, move Slate up so its bottom edge aligns with the bottom edge of Table Bottom. Then, move it up an additional 7.5 units to align it in the cutout.

4. With Slate selected, pick **Create** in the **Command Panel**. Pick the **Geometry** button and select **Compound Objects** from the drop-down list. Then, pick the **Boolean** button in the **Object Type** rollout.

5. In the **Parameters** rollout, pick the **Subtraction [A-B]** radio button. In the **Pick Boolean** rollout, select the **Move** radio button. Then, select the **Pick Operand B** and select Pocket Drill01. Right-click to complete the operation.
   The cylinder is subtracted from the slate.

6. Repeat steps 4 and 5 for the remaining five "pocket drill" objects.

7. Save the scene.

Creating a Wall Poster

1. Activate the Front viewport. Then, pick **Create** in the **Command Panel**. Pick the **Geometry** button and select **Standard Primitives** from the drop-down list. Then, pick the **Box** button in the **Object Type** rollout.

2. Expand the **Keyboard Entry** rollout. Type 50 in the **Length:** spinner, 75 in the **Width:** spinner, and .25 in the **Height:** spinner. Then, pick the **Create** button. In the **Name and Color** rollout, name the box Picture.

3. Pick the **Select and Move** and **Restrict to Y** buttons. Then, move the box up 65 units in the Front viewport.

4. Activate the Top viewport. Then, move Picture up so its top edge aligns with the bottom edge of Wall01.

5. Activate the Front viewport. Then, pick **Create** in the **Command Panel**. Pick the **Shapes** button and select **Splines** from the drop-down list. Then, pick the **Rectangle** button in the **Object Type** rollout.

6. Expand the **Keyboard Entry** rollout. Type .65 in the **Length:** spinner, .65 in the **Width:** spinner, and .1 in the **Corner Radius:** spinner. Then, pick the **Create** button. In the **Name and Color** rollout, name the rectangle Frame Shape.
   A small rectangle is created, which will be the shape for a loft object.

7. Type 50.65 in the **Length:** spinner, 75.65 in the **Width:** spinner, and 0 in the **Corner Radius:** spinner. Then, pick the **Create** button. In the **Name and Color** rollout, name the rectangle Frame Path. Another rectangle is created.

8. Pick the **Select and Move** and **Restrict to Y** buttons. Move Frame Path up so it is centered on Picture.

9. With Frame Path selected, pick **Create** in the **Command Panel**. Pick the **Geometry** button and select **Compound Objects** from the drop-down list. Then, pick the **Loft** button in the **Object Type** rollout.

10. In the **Creation Method** rollout, pick the **Get Shape** button. Then, select Frame Shape in any viewport. In the **Name and Color** rollout, name the loft object Frame.

11. Activate the Top viewport. Pick the **Select and Move** and **Restrict to Y** buttons. Then, move Frame up so its top edge aligns with the bottom edge of Wall01.

12. Save the scene.

Creating the Billiard Balls

1. Activate the Top viewport. Pick **Create** in the **Command Panel**. Pick the **Geometry** button and select **Standard Primitives** from the drop-down list. Then, pick the **Sphere** button in the **Object Type** rollout.

2. Expand the **Keyboard Entry** rollout. Type 1 in the **Radius:** spinner and pick the **Create** button. In the **Name and Color** rollout, name the sphere Ball01.

3. Activate the Front viewport. Pick the **Select and Move** and **Restrict to Y** buttons. Move Ball01 up so its bottom is tangent to the top edge of Slate.

4. Activate the Top viewport. Pick the **Restrict to XY Plane** button. Holding down the [Shift] key, move Ball01 up and to the right. In the **Clone Options** dialog box that appears, name the copy Ball02 and pick the **OK** button. Repeat this process to create a total of 15 balls in a pyramid, as shown in Figure P2-5.
   Snap can help when arranging the balls.

5. Make another copy of Ball01 to use as the cue ball.

6. Save the scene.

Figure P2-5. The billiard balls are properly placed.

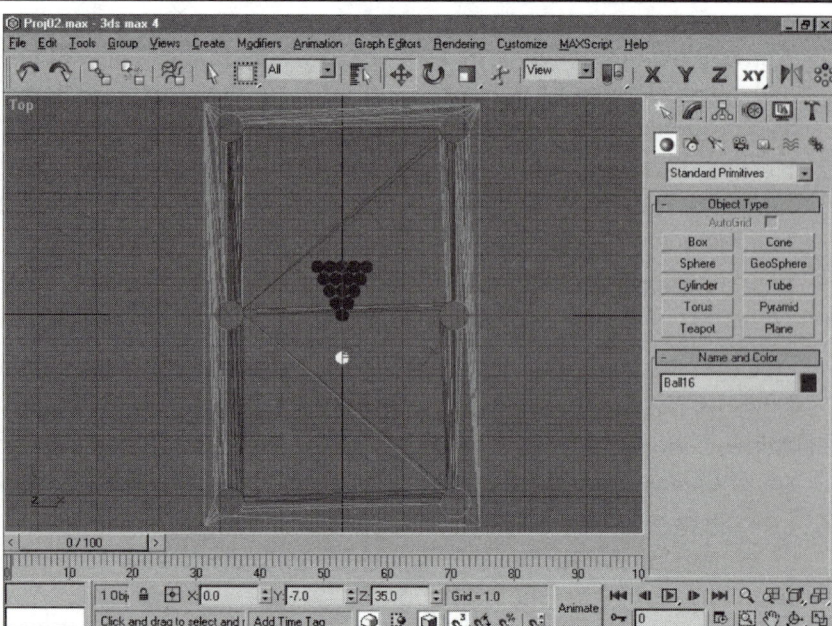

Creating the Lamp and Hanger

1. Activate the Top viewport. Pick **Create** in the **Command Panel**. Pick the **Shapes** button and select **Splines** from the drop-down list. Then, pick the **Star** button in the **Object Type** rollout.

2. In the **Parameters** rollout, type 30 in the **Points:** spinner. Then, expand the **Keyboard Entry** rollout. Type 10 in the **Radius 1:** spinner and 12 in the **Radius 2:** spinner. Pick the **Create** button. In the **Name and Color** rollout, name the star Lamp Shape.
   A star shape is created.

3. Turn snap on. Pick **Create** in the **Command Panel**. Pick the **Shapes** button and select **Splines** from the drop-down list. Then, pick the **Line** button in the **Object Type** rollout. In the Front viewport, draw a vertical line 12 units long. Right-click to end the command. In the **Name and Color** rollout, name the line Lamp Path.
   You may need to zoom in to display the subgrid before drawing the line.

4. With the line selected, pick **Create** in the **Command Panel**. Pick the **Geometry** button and select **Compound Objects** from the drop-down list. Then, pick the **Loft** button in the **Object Type** rollout.

5. In the **Creation Method** rollout, pick the **Get Shape** button. Then, select Lamp Shape in the viewport. In the **Name and Color** rollout, name the loft object Lamp.

6. With the loft object selected, pick **Modify** in the **Command Panel**. In the **Deformations** rollout, pick the **Scale** button.
   The **Scale Deformation** dialog box is displayed.

7. Pick the **Move Control Point** button and move the right-hand control point down to 30%.

8. Pick the **Insert Corner Point** button. Insert a control point at 10 and 90. Now, pick the **Move Control Point** button. Move the control point at 10 to 100%, and the control point at 90 to 30%, Figure P2-6. Close the dialog box.
   The basic shape of the lamp shade is created.

9. With Lamp selected, pick **Clone** from the **Edit** pull-down menu. In the **Clone Options** dialog box that appears, name the copy Lamp Drill and pick the **OK** button.

10. Pick the **Select and Uniform Scale** button on the **Main** toolbar. In the Front viewport, scale Lamp Drill down to 90%. Next, pick the **Select and Move** and **Restrict to Y** buttons. Move Lamp Drill straight down so its lower edge is just below the lower edge of Lamp, about .7 units.

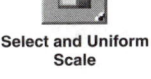

Select and Uniform Scale

11. Select Lamp. Then, pick **Create** in the **Command Panel**. Pick the **Geometry** button and select **Compound Objects** from the drop-down list. Then, pick the **Boolean** button in the **Object Type** rollout.

Figure P2-6. Using a scale deformation to create the shape of the lamp.

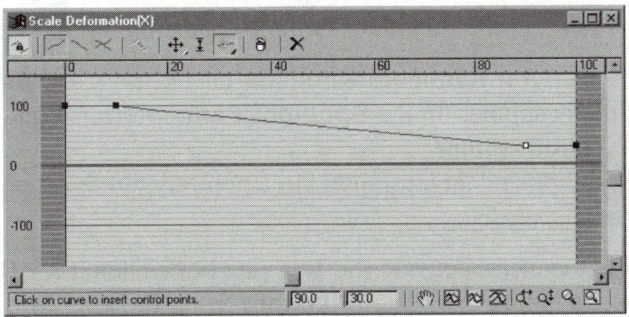

12. In the **Parameters** rollout, pick the **Subtraction [A-B]** radio button. In the **Pick Boolean** rollout, select the **Move** radio button. Then, select the **Pick Operand B** button and select Lamp Drill in the viewport. Right-click to complete the operation.
    The lamp shade is hollowed out.

13. Activate the Top viewport. Pick the **Select and Move** and **Restrict to XY Plane** buttons. Move Lamp to the center of the pool table.

14. Activate the Front viewport. Pick the **Restrict to Y** button. Move Lamp up so its top edge is 30 units from the bottom edge of Ceiling.

15. Pick **Create** in the **Command Panel**. Pick the **Geometry** button and select the **Standard Primitives** from the drop-down list. Then, pick the **Cylinder** button in the **Object Type** rollout.

16. Activate the Top viewport. Expand the **Keyboard Entry** rollout. Type 0.5 in the **Radius:** spinner and 30 in the **Height:** spinner. Then, pick the **Create** button. In the **Name and Color** rollout, name the cylinder Hanger.

17. Activate the Front viewport. Pick the **Select and Move** and **Restrict to Y** buttons. Move Hanger up so its lower edge aligns with the upper edge of Lamp, and its upper edge aligns with the lower edge of Ceiling.
    The cylinder should already be centered on Lamp in the Top viewport. If not, move the cylinder as needed.

18. Save the scene.

Adding Lights and a Camera

Create

Lights

1. Activate the Top viewport. Pick **Create** in the **Command Panel**. Pick the **Lights** button and select **Standard** from the drop-down list. Then, pick the **Omni** button in the **Object Type** rollout. Pick a point near the top-left corner of the pool room to place the light.

2. In the **General Parameters** rollout, type 0.7 in the **Multiplier:** spinner.

3. Pick **Create** in the **Command Panel**. Pick the **Lights** button and select **Standard** from the drop-down list. Then, pick the **Omni** button in the **Object Type** rollout. Pick a point near the bottom-right corner of the pool room to place another light. In the **General Parameters** rollout, type 0.4 in the **Multiplier:** spinner.

4. Activate the Front viewport. Pick the **Select and Move** and **Restrict to Y** buttons. Move both lights up to just below Ceiling.

5. Activate the Front viewport. Then, pick **Create** in the **Command Panel**. Pick the **Lights** button and select **Standard** from the drop-down list. Then, pick the **Target Spot** button in the **Object Type** rollout.

6. Pick a point in the middle of Lamp to place the light, then drag the target to the top of Slate.

7. In the **General Parameters** rollout, check the **Cast Shadows** check box. Also, type 1 in the **Multiplier:** spinner. In the **Spotlight Parameters** rollout, type 60 in the **Hotspot:** spinner and 90 in the **Falloff:** spinner.
   The spotlight and target should already be centered on Lamp in the Top viewport. If not, move both together as needed.

8. To add a camera, activate the Top viewport. Then, pick **Create** in the **Command Panel**. Pick the **Cameras** button and select **Standard** from the drop-down list. Then, pick the **Target** button in the **Object Type** rollout.

9. Pick a point on the right side of the objects inside the wall to place the camera. Then, drag the target to the center of the pool room.

10. Activate the Perspective viewport and make it the Camera01 viewport.

11. Move the camera in various viewports and adjust the Camera01 viewport as needed to display a desired view of the objects, Figure P2-7.
    When properly located, you should not be able to see the edges of the walls.

12. Save your work.

Figure P2-7. Lights and a camera are added to the scene.

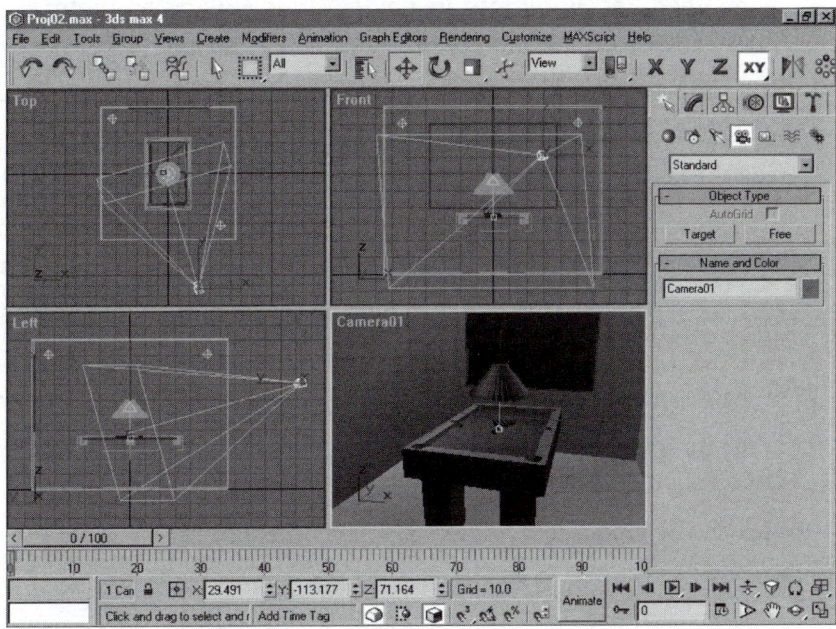

Loading, Defining, and Applying Materials

There are 16 different materials used in this scene. Six of the materials are selected from the default 3ds max material library. The other 10 materials are custom materials you define. Start by loading the predefined materials into the **Material Editor**.

Loading Materials

1. Pick the **Material Editor** button on the **Main** toolbar to open the **Material Editor**.

2. Activate the first material sample slot.

3. Pick the **Get Material** button to open the **Material/Map Browser**.

4. In the **Browse From:** area of the **Material/Map Browser**, pick the **Mtl Library** radio button. Then, double-click on Bricks_Yellow in the list.
   The material is loaded into the first material sample slot in the **Material Editor**.

5. Activate the next unused material sample slot in the **Material Editor**. Then, get the material Concrete_Stucco from the material library.

6. Load the materials Wood_Ashen, Wood_Burloak, Metal_Brushed, and Metal_Dark_Gold into unused material sample slots.

7. Close the **Material/Map Browser**.
   The remaining materials needed for the scene will be defined in the **Material Editor**.

8. Save the scene.

Material Editor

Get Material

Defining Plastic Materials

1. Select the next unused material sample slot in the **Material Editor**. Pick in the drop-down list text box below the material samples and name the material Plastic Red.
   You may need to scroll in the **Material Editor** to display unused material sample slots.

2. Pick the diffuse color swatch to open the color selector. Set the color to R255, G0, and B0. Then, pick the specular color swatch. Set the color to R255, G255, and B255. Close the color selector.

3. In the **Specular Highlights** area of the **Blinn Basic Parameters** rollout, type 150 in the **Specular Level:** spinner. Also, type 75 in the **Glossiness:** spinner.

4. Pick the next unused material sample slot. Name the material Plastic Green.

5. Pick the diffuse color swatch to open the color selector. Set the color to R0, G175, and B0. Then, pick the specular color swatch. Set the color to R255, G255, and B255. Close the color selector.

6. In the **Specular Highlights** area of the **Blinn Basic Parameters** rollout, type 150 in the **Specular Level:** spinner. Also, type 75 in the **Glossiness:** spinner.

7. Pick the next unused material sample slot. Name the material Plastic Blue.

8. Pick the diffuse color swatch to open the color selector. Set the color to R0, G0, and B255. Then, pick the specular color swatch. Set the color to R255, G255, and B255. Close the color selector.

9. In the **Specular Highlights** area of the **Blinn Basic Parameters** rollout, type 150 in the **Specular Level:** spinner. Also, type 75 in the **Glossiness:** spinner.

10. Pick the next unused material sample slot. Name the material Plastic Orange.

11. Pick the diffuse color swatch to open the color selector. Set the color to R255, G150, and B0. Then, pick the specular color swatch. Set the color to R255, G255, and B255. Close the color selector.

12. In the **Specular Highlights** area of the **Blinn Basic Parameters** rollout, type 150 in the **Specular Level:** spinner. Also, type 75 in the **Glossiness:** spinner.

13. Pick the next unused material sample slot. Name the material Plastic Black.

14. Pick the diffuse color swatch to open the color selector. Set the color to R50, G50, and B50. Then, pick the specular color swatch. Set the color to R255, G255, and B255. Close the color selector.

15. In the **Specular Highlights** area of the **Blinn Basic Parameters** rollout, type 150 in the **Specular Level:** spinner. Also, type 75 in the **Glossiness:** spinner.

16. Pick the next unused material sample slot. Name the material Plastic White.

17. Pick the diffuse color swatch to open the color selector. Set the color to R255, G255, and B255. Then, pick the specular color swatch. Set the color to R255, G255, and B255. Close the color selector.

18. In the **Specular Highlights** area of the **Blinn Basic Parameters** rollout, type 150 in the **Specular Level:** spinner. Also, type 75 in the **Glossiness:** spinner.

19. Save the scene.

Defining the Slate, Floor, and Picture Materials

1. Select the next unused material sample slot in the **Material Editor**. Pick in the drop-down list text box below the material samples and name the material Slate.
   You may need to scroll in the **Material Editor** to display unused material sample slots.

2. Pick the diffuse color swatch to open the color selector. Set the color to R0, G125, and B0. Then, pick the specular color swatch. Set the color to R0, G255, and B0. Close the color selector.

3. In the **Specular Highlights** area of the **Blinn Basic Parameters** rollout, type 25 in the **Specular Level:** spinner. Also, type 10 in the **Glossiness:** spinner.

4. Pick the next unused material sample slot. Name the material Floor.

5. Pick the diffuse color swatch to open the color selector. Set the color to R140, G150, and B255. Then, pick the specular color swatch. Set the color to R0, G0, and B255. Close the color selector.

6. In the **Specular Highlights** area of the **Blinn Basic Parameters** rollout, type 15 in the **Specular Level:** spinner. Also, type 10 in the **Glossiness:** spinner.

7. In the **Maps** rollout, pick the button in the **Diffuse Color** row currently labeled **None**. The **Material/Map Browser** is displayed.

8. In the **Browse From:** area of the **Material/Map Browser**, pick the **New** radio button. Then, select Checker in the list and pick the **OK** button. Close the **Material/Map Browser**.

9. At the diffuse color map level of the material tree, name the map Floor Pattern. Then, pick Floor from the drop-down list to return to the parent material level.

10. In the **Maps** rollout, type 30 in the **Diffuse Color** spinner.

11. Pick the next unused material sample slot. Name the material Poster.

12. In the **Maps** rollout, pick the button in the **Diffuse Color** row currently labeled **None**. The **Material/Map Browser** is displayed.

13. In the **Browse From:** area of the **Material/Map Browser**, pick the **New** radio button. Then, select Bitmap in the list and pick the **OK** button. In the Select Bitmap Image File dialog box that appears, navigate to the 3ds max \Images folder and open a bitmap of your choice. Try to select an image that is wider than it is tall, since the poster object is wider than it is tall.

14. At the diffuse color map level of the material tree, name the map Poster Picture. Then, pick Poster from the drop-down list to return to the parent material level.

15. Save the scene.

Applying Materials and UVW Map Modifiers

1. Apply the material Bricks_Yellow to the three wall objects. Then, individually select each wall, pick **UV Coordinates** in the **Modifiers** pull-down menu, and then pick **UVW Map** in the cascading menu. Change the tiling as needed.

2. Apply the material Floor to the Floor object. Also, apply the material Concrete_Stucco to the Ceiling object. Apply a UVW map modifier to each object and adjust tiling as needed.

3. Apply the material Wood_Ashen to Frame and Table Bottom. Apply a UVW map modifier to each object and adjust the tiling as needed.

4. Apply the material Poster to the Picture object. Apply a UVW map modifier and set the tiling to 1.

5. Apply the material Wood_Burloak to the four legs. Apply a UVW map modifier to each object and adjust the tiling as needed.

6. Apply the material Slate to the Slate object.

7. Apply the material Metal_Brushed to the Hanger object. Apply the material Metal_Dark_Gold to the Lamp object. Apply a UVW map modifier to each object and adjust the tiling as needed.

8. Assign the material Plastic White to the cue ball, which is the ball not in the pyramid arrangement.

9. Assign the material Plastic Black to the eight ball, which is the center ball in the third row. Then, starting with the first ball in the pyramid, assign the materials Plastic Red, Plastic Green, Plastic Blue, and Plastic Orange to each row of balls in order.

10. Save the scene.

Animating the Scene

You will now animate the scene. The animation will involve the initial break, sinking one ball, and sinking a second ball. The entire animation will take 10 seconds. Start by setting the length of the animation.

Time Configuration

1. Pick the **Time Configuration** button to open the **Time Configuration** dialog box. In the **Animation Length** area of the dialog box, type 300 in the **Length:** spinner. Then, pick the **OK** button to close the dialog box.

   The number of frames in the animation is set to 300, which at 30 frames per second is 10 seconds.

2. Activate the Top viewport and maximize it. On frame 0, move the cue ball so it is near the bottom rail.

Toggle Animation Mode

3. Move to frame 50. Pick the **Toggle Animation Mode** button to enter animation mode.

4. Move the cue ball to nearly the same location as the first ball in the pyramid. It can overlap the ball. Next, move to frame 51 and randomly scatter the balls in the pyramid.

   As you randomly scatter the balls, make sure each ball will not move "through" other balls.

5. Move to frame 150. Choose a ball to sink in a pocket and move the cue so it touches that ball. Then, move to frame 151 and move the ball you want to sink into the pocket.

   Be sure the cue does not move "through" other balls. If you want, you can choose a combination shot.

6. Move to frame 275. Choose a second ball to sink in a pocket. Move the cue so it touches that ball. Then, move to frame 276 and move the ball you want to sink into the pocket.

7. Display the four-viewport configuration and activate the Camera01 viewport. Play the animation in the viewport.

   You will notice some problems with the motion of the balls.

Open Track View

8. Stop the playback and pick the **Open Track View** button to open **Track View**.

9. Expand the hierarchy so the position track is displayed for each ball. For the cue ball, move the animation key currently on frame 0 to frame 35. Also, copy the key on frame 50 to frame 130, and the key on frame 150 to frame 235.

   If you followed the instructions in this project, the cue ball is named Ball16.

10. Next, for all other 15 balls, move the animation key on frame 0 to frame 50.

11. For the first ball you sunk in a pocket, copy the animation key on frame 51 to frame 150.

12. For the second ball you sunk in a pocket, copy the animation key on frame 51 to frame 275.

13. Now, right-click on the first key in the position track for the cue ball. Change the **In:** and **Out:** image tiles to quicker transitions, as shown in Figure P2-8. Change the transitions for all keys in all tracks to match.

14. Close **Track View** and save the scene.

Figure P2-8. Fine-tuning the motion of the billiard balls.

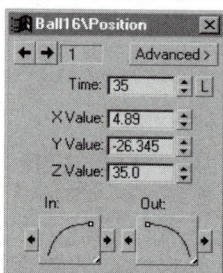

Rendering the Animation

1. With the Camera01 viewport active, play the animation. You can also make a preview animation of the viewport. Identify any remaining motion problems and fix them.

Render Scene

2. Pick the **Render Scene** button on the **Main** toolbar to open the **Render Scene** dialog box.

3. In the **Time Output** area of the dialog box, pick the **Active Time Segment:** radio button. In the **Output Size** area, pick the **320x240** button. In the **Render Output** area, pick the **Files...** button. The **Render Output File** dialog box appears.

4. Navigate to the folder where you want to save the file. In the **File name:** text box, type Proj02 and select **AVI File (*.avi)** in the **Save as type:** drop-down list. Then, pick the **Save** button. If the **Video Compression** dialog box is displayed, pick **OK** to accept the defaults.

5. In the **Render Output** area of the **Render Scene** dialog box, make sure the **Save File** check box is checked. Then, select Camera01 from the **Viewport:** drop-down list. Finally, pick the **Render** button. Each frame of the animation is rendered in the render window. The **Rendering** dialog box displays the progress of the rendering.

6. When the rendering is complete, close the render window and the **Rendering** dialog box.

7. Pick **View Image File...** from the **File** pull-down menu. Navigate to the folder where the AVI file is saved and open the file. See Figure P2-9. The animation is played in Windows Media Player.

8. Close Media Player and save the scene.

Figure P2-9. A frame from the final rendered animation.

Index